John Lennon
Solo Bootleg Discography

John Lennon
Solo Bootleg Discography

Compiled by
John Eustace and Phill Boylett

ATHENA PRESS
LONDON

JOHN LENNON: SOLO BOOTLEG DISCOGRAPHY
Copyright © John Eustace and Phill Boylett 2009

All rights reserved

No part of this book may be reproduced in any form
by photocopying or by any electronic or mechanical means
including information storage or retrieval systems
without permission in writing from both the copyright
owner and the publisher of this book.

ISBN 978 1 84748 567 0

First published 2009
ATHENA PRESS
Queen's House, 2 Holly Road
Twickenham TW1 4EG
United Kingdom

Printed for Athena Press

CONTENTS

Acknowledgements — 7

Introduction — 10

Part One

Vinyl Releases (Entries 001–157) — 14

An alphabetical list of the vinyl bootleg releases with track listings and complete details

Part Two

Compact Discs (Entries 158–388 and 722–914) — 107

An alphabetical list of the compact disc bootleg releases with track listings and complete details

Part Three

The Lost Lennon Tapes (Entries 389–721) — 383

How the American radio series was conceived and full details of the contents of the 218 shows

Part Four

Sources — 469

An examination of the sources of the various recording sessions, live performances and interviews, with a list of the main bootlegs on which they appear

Part Five

Songs Index — 505

Every known unreleased recording is listed showing the bootleg albums where they can be found

Part Six

Discs Index 626

An alphabetical list of all the discs listed in this discography

Part Seven

Ten Lennon Bootlegs You Must Own 650

A selection of the ten important releases which should form the basis of an essential collection of Lennon bootlegs

Part Eight

Stop Press (Additions and Corrections) 654

Details of recent releases and additional information on some of the entries unearthed after completing the manuscript

ACKNOWLEDGEMENTS

Compiling this discography would have been impossible without the help of several sources. The basis has been our own collections of bootleg albums and compact discs. In particular we must express our eternal gratitude to Franco Manaring for the compact discs, artwork discs and track listings. We would also like to mention the *Bootleg Zone* for the wealth of information on their site. We are also especially obliged to the following books, magazines, fanzines, newspapers plus the official release compact disc and DVD which have assisted in checking information and filling in the gaps.

MAGAZINES, FANZINES AND NEWSPAPERS
Beatles Unlimited magazine
Belmo's Beatleg News
Beatles Fan Next Generation
British Beatles Fan Club Magazine
The Beatles Book
Beatlefan
Record Collector
Daily Express
The Sun

BOOKS
Not For Sale by Belmo
You Can't Do That by Charles Reinhart
Unfinished Music No. 1 – An Unauthorized Companion to Year One of The Lost Lennon Tapes by L R E King
Unfinished Music No. 2 – An Unauthorized Companion to Year Two of The Lost Lennon Tapes by L R E King
Do You Want to Know a Secret by L R E King

Fixing a Hole by L R E King

Eight Arms to Hold You – The Solo Beatles Compendium by Chip Madinger and Mark Easter

Compressed Belmo – A Synopsis of Beatles Bootlegs Reviewed in Belmo's Beatleg News *1987–2001* by Charles Iscove

Yellow Dog – The Bootleg Collection Vol. 2 by Azing

The Long and Winding Road (A History of the Beatles on Record) by Neville Stannard

Working Class Heroes (The History of the Beatles Solo Recordings) by Neville Stannard

The Beatles – After the Break-up by Keith Badman

The Making of Imagine by Azing

John Lennon in New York – The Solo Collection Vol. 2 by Azing

The John Lennon Encyclopaedia by Bill Harry

Beatles Undercover by Kristofer Engelhardt

Beatlegmania (Volume Two) by John C. Winn

Hot Wacks Book XIII

All Together Now, The Beatles Again and The End of The Beatles by Harry Castleman and Walter J. Podrazik

The Complete Beatles Chronicle by Mark Lewisohn

Lennon and McCartney – Together Alone by John Blaney

COMPACT DISC

John and Yoko: The Interview (recorded 6 December 1980 with Andy Peebles) BBC CD 6002

DVD

Classic Albums: John Lennon/Plastic Ono Band Eagle Vision EREDV674

SPECIAL THANKS TO:

Franco Manaring for the endless supply of artwork and track listings, and most importantly the sleeves; Jenny for once again patiently tolerating an obsession and for catering, coffee, strawberries and cream and sympathy; Mary and Wayne for being there; Laurie for the CD and the artwork; Big John and Andrew for helping set up the laptop; Rob Batchelor for letting me copy the track listings; the *Bootleg Zone*; and the beautiful pussy cat George despite putting muddy paws on copies of the CD covers!

Note

The manufacture and selling of bootlegs is illegal. The compilation of this discography does not imply that we condone the production and sale of bootleg albums. We cannot tell you where they can be obtained. This is not a catalogue – the object of this work is to provide a record and guide of the unreleased recordings of John Lennon.

INTRODUCTION

The various official releases such as *Lennon Legend*, *Acoustic* and the *John Lennon Anthology* which have been released since his death, containing previously unissued tracks have only really scratched the surface in terms of what is available from the John Lennon archives. In the following pages we examine the unreleased solo recordings of John Lennon including live concerts, demos, rehearsals, outtakes, home recordings, television appearances, unreleased songs, interviews and much more. This meticulously researched book is a goldmine of information about the solo years of one of rock music's greatest talents.

Even though the solo career of John Lennon only lasted just over ten years following the break up of The Beatles until his death in December 1980, a wealth of material can be found on the bootlegs listed in this discography. The radio programme *The Lost Lennon Tapes* which was broadcast in America starting in January 1988 was seized upon with relish by the bootleggers and many discs were issued containing previously unreleased material. The first discs released containing tracks from *The Lost Lennon Tapes* were the vinyl discs from Bag Records which run to thirty-five volumes with the later discs also released on compact discs. The vinyl albums were very well presented with colour sleeves, detailed track listings and good sound. Other labels soon released compact discs titled *The Lost Lennon Tapes*, *The Complete Lost Lennon Tapes* and *The Real Complete Lost Lennon Tapes*. With the amount of material broadcast on *The Lost Lennon Tapes* radio series, bootleggers were able to issue 'alternate' albums such as *The Alternate Imagine*, *The Alternate Mind Games* and so on. Part Three of this discography examines the story behind the radio series and the many releases of *The Lost Lennon Tapes* including details and track listings of all the 218 radio shows. We feel that the radio shows did lose sight of the original intention to include a substantial amount of unreleased Lennon recordings. There were some programmes, for example, which featured Paul McCartney, and another celebrating George Harrison's birthday. There was also a large amount of official Beatles tracks included during the series together with items from other artists. We have included full track listings of two of the sets which include the complete broadcasts.

When we started preparing this volume, we were surprised how many John Lennon vinyl bootlegs had been released although there were the thirty-five *Lost Lennon Tapes* albums from Bag Records. Details of vinyl releases can be found in Part One. These are very difficult to locate now but occasionally a second hand one appears at a record fair, though they can be quite expensive. All the tracks which were originally released on vinyl were subsequently released on compact discs. Bearing in mind that after the break up of The Beatles, Lennon did not undertake a major concert tour and did not release an album between 1975 and 1980 when *Double Fantasy* was issued, there is an amazing amount of bootleg releases. Several of these do contain the same tracks, such as the 'Free John Sinclair Rally' and 'The *Salute To Sir Lew Grade*'. Despite the uninformed stories that Lennon was virtually a recluse during the his so called 'house husband' period between 1975 and 1980, the amount of recordings he made during this time, as can be seen by examining the bootleg listings, should nail this rumour once and for all.

Although the function of this work is to concentrate on John Lennon's solo bootleg recordings, we have included a number of recordings in the Songs Index from his days with The Beatles as these are solo demos and rehearsals. Many of these songs were later developed and included on official Beatles releases.

We would like to claim that the discs listed in Parts One, Two and Three are the complete catalogue of John Lennon bootlegs but despite our intense research we are fully aware that there are almost certainly releases which we have not traced. What we do know is that there are some discs which we know exist but we have been unable to locate further details such as complete track listings. In some cases we have copies of the sleeves in our files. We have included these discs in the listings. However we do believe that the listings include virtually every available track or interview.

The listings in Parts One and Two are in alphabetical order. We have attempted to replicate the details as set out on the album sleeve or compact disc inlay. In some cases, the track listings include details of the song or interview after the title and in these instances we have set this out as it appears. Where details are not included or are shown elsewhere, we have included additional information in the notes for each entry. In Part Three we have listed the discs containing The Lost Lennon Tapes radio shows. These are in the chronological order of the programmes and we have set out the track listings as they are printed on the inlays.

The following pages include demos, outtakes, home recordings, alternate takes, rehearsals, live performances, interviews, radio documentaries and John acting as a DJ. We have tried to identify the take or live performance of each track in the Songs Index but in some cases this is impossible and we have therefore listed these as 'unknown take'. Where we have the disc in our collection, we have been able to compare each track with other discs to ascertain the source of the recording.

We were also surprised how many interviews Lennon gave. Whether these releases can be considered strictly bootlegs is debatable but we have included them in the listings because they are not normally commercially available and because of their historical importance. The Black Cat label in particular have specialised in releasing a number of interesting interview discs.

As the various tracks come from a number of different sources – recording sessions, live performances, television shows and so on – we have listed these in the Sources chapter and the main bootleg albums where they appear.

Preparing the Songs Index (Part Five) did cause us some problems in identifying the sources of some of the tracks. Although we do have a large number of the discs in our collection and copies of most of the sleeves in our files, several of the discs we have traced during our research are virtually impossible to obtain and accordingly we have not heard these in order to ascertain the source or take involved. However, this section will provide a guide as to what tracks are available and the discs they appear on.

Choosing the 'Ten Lennon Bootlegs You Must Own' was an extremely difficult task and caused many sleepless nights. There are many worthy contenders. We chose these in order to give a representation of the solo career of John Lennon also taking into account the historical importance of the release and the sound quality. Some of the choices are controversial.

We have not included any of Lennon's bootleg videos or DVDs which we feel is outside the scope of this discography although the audio soundtrack of television appearances such as '*Salute To Sir Lew Grade*' and the One-to-One concert appear on several of the bootlegs listed. Some of the CD box sets include DVDs which we have mentioned in the listings.

Despite our intense research and carefully checking the manuscript, we are fully aware that there are almost certainly errors and omissions and we would appreciate any corrections, updates, missing items or any additional information which can be incorporated into a possible further edition of this work. If you can help please write to John Eustace at 54 Milford Close, Abbey Wood, London, SE2 0DT, England with, if possible, copies of the sleeves, track listings and any other information or documentary evidence.

John Eustace and Phill Boylett

1. VINYL RELEASES

The vinyl releases listed in this section include the first John Lennon bootlegs issued during the 1970s. Many of these discs are almost impossible to find now but all the tracks have since been reissued on compact discs, usually in better quality. All the thirty-five volumes released on vinyl in *The Lost Lennon Tapes* series (Bag Records) were subsequently released on compact discs, the latter volumes as double albums. The advantage of collecting the vinyl albums is that the larger format sleeves highlight the excellent artwork presented during this series of releases. These vinyl discs are very difficult to obtain now. They were well packaged with colour sleeves and detailed notes and information of the tracks. The early vinyl releases listed in the following pages came in a plain sleeve with a photocopied track listing. The information shown on these first bootlegs was often unreliable.

001. ALL WE NEED IS JOHN

Unknown CX 297

Format: 12-inch vinyl

Source: *Tomorrow Show*, hosted by Tom Snyder, 28 April 1975

Sound quality: very good to excellent mono

Side A
Part One (22.25)

Side B
Part Two (20.12)

Notes: An interesting interview with John and his lawyer. This was also released on a commercial video. This disc was also released as *Doctor Winston O'Boogie on the Tomorrow Show*.

002. ANGEL BABY

Unknown

Format: 12-inch vinyl

Source: various – see notes

Sound quality: varies – good to excellent

Side A

1. Angel Baby, 2. Be My Baby, 3. Attica State, 4. The Luck of the Irish, 5. Imagine

Side B

6. Give Peace a Chance, 7. What's the New Mary Jane, 8. Yer Blues, 9. Peace of Mind, 10. Interview

Notes: Tracks 1 and 2 are from *Roots, John Lennon Sings the Great Rock 'n' Roll Hits*. Tracks 3 and 4 are from the Free John Sinclair Rally on 10 December 1971. Tracks 5 and 6 are from the One-to-One Concert on 30 August 1972. Track 7 was an unreleased Beatles track until it appeared on *Anthology 3* in 1996. Track 8 is from *Rock and Roll Circus* on 11 December 1968. Track 9 is from a tape reportedly found in a dustbin at Apple in 1967. There were rumours that this was a Beatles recording from June 1967 but it is extremely unlikely that there is any Beatles involvement in this recording. Track 10 is an interview from September 1974. Another album was released with the same title but different track running order.

The black-and-white sleeve features the back view of an attractive blond lady wearing a short skirt. The caption at the top reads 'John Winston Lennon – ex MBE Angel Baby'. The track listing is shown at the bottom, both sides of the legs of the young lady!

003. ANGEL BABY

WRMB 326

Format: 12-inch vinyl

Source: various – see notes

Sound quality: varies – good to excellent

Side A

1. Angel Baby, 2. Yer Blues, 3. Interview (September 1974), 4. What's the New Mary Jane, 5. Attica State

Side B

1. Be My Baby, 2. Peace of Mind, 3. Luck of the Irish, 4. Imagine, 5. Give Peace a Chance

Notes: See entry above for sources of these tracks.

004. ANGEL BABY

ABBY 80 L 739

Format: 7-inch vinyl 45 rpm

Source: *Rock 'n' Roll* session

Sound quality: very good mono

Side A

Angel Baby

Side B

Be My Baby

Notes: Black-and-white sleeve – similar to *Rock 'n' Roll* album.

005. ANGEL BABY/ONE-TO-ONE CONCERT AND MORE

WRMB 362/301

Format: 12-inch vinyl (double)

Source: various

Sound quality: unknown

Notes: This is a Japanese double album copy of *Angel Baby* (WRMB 362) and *One-to-One and More* (WRMB 301).

Deluxe purple cover.

006. ANN ARBOR: NOW HEAR THIS

CBM WEC R1 3665

Format: 12-inch vinyl

Source: Free John Sinclair Rally, 18 December 1971

Sound quality: unknown

Side A

1. John Sinclair, 2. Attica State, 3. Sisters Oh Sisters

Side B

1. The Luck of the Irish, 2. Now Hear This Song of Mine (Paul McCartney)

Notes: The final track is by Paul McCartney and from the *Ram* promo disc. This release was reissued several times – see *John and Paul in Michigan* (unknown), *Lennon/McCartney* (CBM), *Lennon/McCartney* (King Kong), *John Lennon/Paul McCartney – Ann Arbor: Now Hear This* (unknown), *Now Hear This* (unknown).

007. ANOTHER FANTASY

Winston O'Boogie Record Works DR 001

Format: 12-inch vinyl

Released: 1991

Source: *Double Fantasy* sessions, August 1980

Sound quality: excellent

Side A

1. (Just Like) Starting Over, 2. (Just Like) Starting Over, 3. Clean-up Time, 4. Clean-up Time, 5. Beautiful Boy, 6. Beautiful Boy, 7. Beautiful Boy

Side B

8. Watching the Wheels, 9. Watching the Wheels, 10. Woman, 11. Woman, 12. Dear Yoko, 13. Dear Yoko, 14. I'm Losing You, 15. Only the Lonely, 16. Mystery Train

Notes: The tracks on this release are virtually unedited.

Sleeve features a black-and-white cover with an alternate *Double Fantasy* picture. The back has track listing below a photo of John and Yoko at the New York Hit Factory studios. A fold out sleeve shows all the people cooperating on the album.

008. ARCHIVES VOL. 1

Paper Plane Music BRCH 111

Format: 12-inch vinyl

Source: various

Sound quality: very good to excellent mono/stereo

Side A

1. Strawberry Fields Forever, Parts 1–4 (home demo, 1970) (4.05), 2. Peggy Sue (late 70s) (0.54), 3. Watching the Wheels, Parts 1–2 (Dakota and Hit Factory, 1980) (3.03), 4. Be-Bop-A-Lula (Hit Factory) (1.00), 5. God (1970) (1.25), 6. (I Know) I'm Losing You, Parts 1–2 (Dakota, 1979 and Hit Factory, 1980) (1.22), 7. Beautiful Boy, Parts 1–2 (Bermuda, 1979) (3.00), 8. Life Begins at Forty (Dakota, 1980) (2.02), 9. Power to the People (Record Plant, 1971) (2.43), 10. Clean-up Time, Parts 1–2 (2.59)

Side B

1. Mucho Mungo, Parts 1–3 (demo, 1973) (7.15), 2. Girls and Boys (Dakota) (2.17), 3. Woman (Bermuda) (3.07), 4. Happy Rishikesh (Dakota) (1.45), 5. Rock Island Line (Dakota) (2.32), 6. John Henry (Dakota) (1.37), 7. Tennessee, Oh Tennessee, Parts 1–2 (Dakota) (1.54), 8. Surprise Surprise (Sweet Bird of Paradox) (demo, 1974) (1.19), 9. Child of Nature (EMI studios) (2.34)

Notes: This eight disc set were issued as separate volumes. All tracks were taken from *The Lost Lennon Tapes* radio series. The set was also released on eight compact discs (see entries in Part Two – Compact Discs).

Label says 'test pressing'.

009. ARCHIVES VOL. 2

Paper Plane Music BRCH 222

Format: 12-inch vinyl

Source: various

Sound quality: very good to excellent mono/stereo

Side A

1. The Luck of the Irish, Parts 1–2 (studio demos, 1971), 2. Everyman Has a Woman (Hit Factory, 1980), 3. He Said She Said, Parts 1–2 (home demo, Weybridge and EMI studios 1966), 4. Grow Old with Me (first demo from Dakota), 5. Little Sunshine Boy (John and Ringo, London, 1967), 6. I'm the Greatest, Parts 1–2 (home demo, Ascot, 1970 and Regents Park, 1971), 7. Make Love Not War (home demo, Ascot, 1970), 8. I Promise (home demo, Ascot, 1970), 9. Good Night, Vienna (Record Plant West, 1974)

Side B

1. Help (Dakota), 2. You Know My Name (Look Up the Number) (home demo, Weybridge, June 1967), 3. How Do You Sleep? (home studio outtake, Ascot, 1971), 4. (Just Like) Starting Over (Dakota, take 3, 1980), 5. Sea Ditty Melody (Dakota, 1979), 6. Borrowed Time (Bermuda, 1979), 7. I Don't Want to Face It (outtake, Hit Factory, 1980)

Notes: Volumes 1 and 2 were reissued as a double album under the title *Memories*. Deluxe black-and-white sleeve with blue text. Excellent sleeve notes.

010. ARCHIVES VOL. 3

Paper Plane Music BRCH 333

Format: 12-inch vinyl

Source: various

Sound quality: very good to excellent mono/stereo

Side A

1. Whatever Gets You Through the Night, Parts 1–2 (home demo, 1974) (5.27), 2. Dear John (demo, 1980) (4.18), 3. Across the Universe

(unused mix, 1968) (3.45), 4. What's the New Mary Jane (original demo with George) (2.35), 5. Cooking in the Kitchen of Love (demo for Ringo's *Rotogravure* album, 1976) (2.48), 6. Knocking on Dylan's Door: Talking Roget's Thesaurus Headline Blues (acoustic satire, 1979) (2.18)

Side B

1. Revolution (Paul's house 1968) (see notes) (3.50), 2. Serve Yourself (piano demo, 1979) (5.25), 3. Getting Better (home demo, 1967) (1.03), 4. Everyone Had a Hard Year (home demo, 1968) (1.34), 5. Everybody's Got Something to Hide Except Me and My Monkey (rehearsal, 1968) (2.56), 6. I'm a Man (Dakota) (1.54), 7. Brown Eyed Handsome Man/Get Back (Dakota) (2.14), 8. 'Twas a Night Like Ethel Merman (poem) (1.02), 9. Medley: Beyond the Sea/Blue Moon/Young Love (Dakota) (4.03)

Notes: Deluxe black-and-white sleeve with orange text. Side B, Track 1, the sleeve is incorrect; this was recorded at George's house in Esher.

011. ARCHIVES VOL. 4

Paper Plane Music BRCH 444

Format: 12-inch vinyl

Source: various

Sound quality: very good to excellent mono/stereo

Side A

1. Power to the People (alternate take), 2. Attica State/The Luck of the Irish/John Sinclair (John Sinclair Rally, 10 December 1971), 3. Rock 'n' Roll People (demo), 4. Rock 'n' Roll People (take 5)

Side B

1. Real Life (piano demo), 2. Stepping Out (Bermuda, demo), 3. Tight A$ (demo), 4. Rock Island Line (early take), 5. Love (remix for UK 45 single, 1982)

Notes: Deluxe colour cover.

012. ARCHIVES VOL. 5

Paper Plane Music BRCH 555

Format: 12-inch vinyl

Source: various

Sound quality: very good to excellent mono/stereo

Side A

1. God Save Us, versions 1–2 (home demo and Morgan studios, 1971), 2. Jealous Guy (studio outtake, summer 1971), 3. Mirror Mirror on the Wall parts 1–5 (Dakota, 1977), 4. Maurice DuPont Agent Provocateur (Dakota, 1978), 5. Dear Prudence (outtake, 1968), 6. Watching the Wheels, versions 1–2 (home demos, Dakota, 1979)

Side B

1. Dear Yoko (Bermuda, 1979), 2. My Life, Parts 1–2 (home demos Dakota, 1979), 3. Don't Be Crazy (home demo, Dakota, 1979), 4. (Just Like) Starting Over (studio warm up track, 1980)

013. ARCHIVES VOL. 6

Paper Plane Music BRCH 666

Format: 12-inch vinyl

Source: various

Sound quality: very good to excellent mono/stereo

Side A

1. Maybe Baby (St. Regis Hotel, New York, 1971), 2. Rave On (St. Regis Hotel, New York, 1971), 3. Not Fade Away, versions 1–2 (St. Regis Hotel, New York, 1971 and the Record Plant, New York 1973), 4. That'll Be the Day (The Record Plant, New York 1973), 5. Woman, versions 1–5 (first home demo and outtakes), 6. Maggie Mae (Record Plant, New York 1973), 7. Maurice DuPont Agent Provocateur (Dakota mid-1970s), 8. Clean-up Time (piano demo, Dakota, 1979)

Side B

1. Honey, Don't (London, 1969), 2. Don't Be Cruel (London, 1969), 3. Matchbox (London, 1969), 4. Here We Go Again (studio demo, 1973),

5. Cold Turkey, versions 1–2 (home demos, 1969), 6. Sweet Little Sixteen (outtake from *Rock 'n' Roll* session, extended), 7. You Can't Catch Me (outtake from *Rock 'n' Roll* session, extended)

014. ARCHIVES VOL. 7

Paper Plane Music BRCH 777

Format: 12-inch vinyl

Source: various

Sound quality: very good to excellent mono/stereo

Side A

1. One of the Boys (home demo, Dakota, 1979), 2. Mind Games (unreleased version), 3. I Don't Want to Face It (Bermuda demo, 1980), 4. Medley: Heartbeat/Peggy Sue Got Married/Peggy Sue (*Clock* soundtrack), 5. Roll Over Beethoven (Studio rehearsal for One-to-One concert), 6. Whole Lotta Shaking Going On/I'll Be Looking For You (studio rehearsal for One-to-One concert)

Side B

1. Corrina Corrina (Dakota, 1979), 2. Serve Yourself (piano demo, Dakota), 3. Circus Jam (*Rock and Roll Circus* rehearsal, 18 December 1968), 4. Yer Blues (*Rock and Roll Circus*), 5. Yer Blues (*Rock and Roll Circus* rehearsal, 18 December 1968), 6. Yer Blues (*Rock and Roll Circus* outtake)

015. ARCHIVES VOL. 8

Paper Plane Music BRCH 888

Format: 12-inch vinyl

Source: various

Sound quality: very good to excellent mono/stereo

Side A

1. Watching the Wheels (acoustic demo, Bermuda, 1980), 2. Down In Cuba with Julio Juanita LeNono (tongue in cheek calypso send up), 3. Maurice DuPont Agent Provocateur Dejour part 3, 4. Crippled Inside (outtake, summer 1971), 5. Imagine (outtake with Ringo and Klaus

Voorman), 6. Sally and Billy (demo, Ascot, 1970), 7. A Case of the Blues (demo)

Side B

1. It's So Hard (outtake, Ascot, summer 1971), 2. Send Me Some Loving (New York 1971 or 1972), 3. Nobody Loves You (When You're Down and Out) (acoustic demo, 1974), 4. Stranger's Room (early piano demo, Dakota, late 1979), 5. I'm Losing You (acoustic guitar version, Bermuda, 1980), 6. New York City, versions 1–2 (St. Regis Hotel, September 1971), 7. Woman Is the Nigger of the World (acoustic guitar demo), 8. Borrowed Time (long acoustic guitar version, Bermuda, 1980)

Notes: All tracks on this eight disc set are from the American radio show series *The Lost Lennon Tapes*.

016. ASPEN 7 – THE BRITISH BOX – SPRING AND SUMMER

Section 11 *Aspen* No. 7

Format: 7-inch vinyl EP

Source: extracts from the official release *Life with the Lions*

Sound quality: excellent mono

Side A

Yoko sings songs for John: Let's Go Flying, Snow Is Falling all the Time, Mummy's only Looking for Her Hand in the Snow, No Bed for Beatle John (9.40)

Side B

Radio Play (7.57)

Notes: This release was issued by *Aspen* magazine as a two-sided 33-rpm 8-inch square mono flexi disc as part of a special box set that also included a Lennon diary plus other related items. This is a very rare and hard to find release. This was pirated as *Life with The Lennons* (Tobe Milo 4Q 13/14).

017. BEFORE PLAY – AUGUST 1980

Gnat Records, Paper Plane Music DFV 880-1

Format: 12-inch vinyl

Released: 1984

Source: probably from soundtrack of footage shot as basis for promo video, August 1980

Sound quality: very good mono – John's voice is clear with the backing muted

Side A

1. She's a Woman (1.28), 2. C'mon Everybody (0.34), 3. She's a Woman (0.03), 4. Starting Over (1.22), 5. She's a Woman (0.55), 6. Rip It Up (1.05), 7. I'm a Man (1.31), 8. Be-Bop-A-Lula (0.59), 9. I'm Losing You (0.36), 10. Blues in the Night (0.05), 11. Starting Over (2.24), 12. I'm Losing You (0.48), 13. Blues Improvisation (2.24)

Side B

1. I'm Losing You (4.14), 2. Dream Lover/Stay (3.57), 3. She's a Woman (0.16), 4. Mystery Train (3.00)

Notes: The majority of the tracks are excerpts, with 'I'm Losing You' on Side B: the only real complete performance. Most of the items on this disc are also available on *Winston O'Boogie*.

Front cover features a 1980 colour picture of John and Yoko with a black-and-white photo on the back of John and Yoko with the backing musicians from the *Double Fantasy* album.

018. BODY STRIPPING OFF THE WALLS

JFK 71374

Format: 12-inch vinyl

Source: *Walls and Bridges* sessions, Sunset Sound Studio, New York, 13 July 1974

Sound quality: excellent

Side A

1. Steel and Glass, 2. Going Down on Love, 3. Move Over Ms L, 4. Surprise Surprise (Sweet Bird of Paradox), 5. Beef Jerky

Side B

1. Scared, 2. Old Dirt Road, 3. Bless You, 4. Whatever Gets You Through the Night, 5. Nobody Loves You (When You're Down and Out)

Notes: See also *Off The Walls* and *Something Precious and Rare*.

019. BOTH SIDES

MIW 8

Format: 12-inch vinyl

Source: various Beatles and ex-Beatles tracks – John's contributions as below

Sound quality: excellent mono/stereo

Side A

The Luck of the Irish (John and Yoko, *Mike Douglas Show* 1972)

Side B

Christmas Song (John and Yoko, press conference, Denmark 1970), Child of Nature, Too Many Cooks (Mick Jagger with John on mixing desk)

Notes: This disc includes items from The Beatles, plus all four solo Beatles. 'Christmas Song', also called 'O'Kristəlighed' (O Christianity), and was recorded during a press conference in Denmark on 5 January 1970.

020. BRITISH BLUES JAM

CBM 3426

Format: 12-inch vinyl

Source: *Rock and Roll Circus*, 11 December 1968

Sound quality: unknown

Notes: Track 1 only has a Lennon involvement, that being 'Yer Blues' from the *Rock and Roll Circus* on 11 December 1968. The remaining tracks are by The Rolling Stones.

021. CHRONICLE, PART 1 (THE BEATLE YEARS)

Toasted Record Works TRW 1940
Format: 12-inch vinyl (double)
Source: various
Sound quality: excellent

Side A
1. Some Other Guy (Cavern Club), 2. Soldier of Love (BBC Radio), 3. Bad to Me (demo), 4. Help (instrumental), 5. He Said She Said (demo), 6. Strawberry Fields Forever (demo), 7. Strawberry Fields Forever (electric), 8. Strawberry Fields Forever (take 1), 9. Getting Better (demo), 10. I Am the Walrus (basic track)

Side B
1. Across the Universe (alternate mix), 2. Revolution (demo), 3. Revolution (alternate mix), 4. Child of Nature (demo), 5. What's the New Mary Jane (demo), 6. Everybody's Got Something to Hide (demo), 7. Julia (demo)

Side C
1. Dear Prudence (demo), 2. Dear Prudence (alternate mix), 3. Everybody Had a Hard Year (demo), 4. Yer Blues (*Rock and Roll Circus* 1968), 5. Mean Mr Mustard (*Get Back* sessions), 6. Watching Rainbows (*Get Back* sessions)

Side D
1. Mailman, Bring Me No More Blues (complete), 2. Maybe Baby, 3. Dig It (complete), 4. Because, 5. What's the New Mary Jane (remix)

Notes: Toasted Records is an Australian producer. This set includes a lot of John's Beatles songs including the demos recorded for the *White Album* at George's house in Esher, tracks from the *Get Back* sessions plus a few solo items.

022. CLASSIFIED DOCUMENT

Instant Analysis BBR 014
Format: 12-inch vinyl

Source: a compilation of solo tracks from the four Beatles plus group items

Sound quality: varies

John's contributions are as follows:

Side 2

Borrowed Time (demo), Woman (outtake), I Don't Wanna Face It (outtake), Beautiful Boy (demo)

Notes: Also released as *Confidential Document*.

023. A COLLECTION OF 'ROCK 'N' ROLL' REHEARSALS
Unknown WI-86

Format: 12-inch vinyl sepia tone picture disc

Source: *Rock 'n' Roll* session

Sound quality: good to very good mono

Side A

1. Ain't That a Shame (1.01), 2. Bring It on Home to Me/Send Me Some Loving (3.33), 3. Ya Ya (2.33), 4. That'll Be the Day (2.25), 5. Do You Want to Dance (3.15), 6. Stand By Me (3.28), 7. Ain't That a Shame (2.32)

Side B

1. Do You Want to Dance (3.33), 2. Medley: Rip It Up/Ready Teddy (1.26), 3. Peggy Sue (2.06), 4. Be-Bop-A-Lula (excerpt) (1.48), 5. Slippin' and Slidin' (excerpt) (1.54), 6. Guitar Jam including Rumble (0.44) and Whole Lotta Love (0.09) (1.58), 7. Thirty Days (0.59), Slippin' and Slidin' (2.07)

Notes: This is a picture disc version of *The May Pang Tapes* although the artwork is different. The sound quality is sharper on this disc. This was first issued in America and was limited to two hundred copies and is almost impossible to find.

024. COME BACK JOHNNY
Melvin Records MM09

Format: 12-inch vinyl

Source: various – see notes

Sound quality: unknown

Side A

1. John and Bob Dylan 1965, 2. New York City, 3. It's So Hard, 4. Woman Is the Nigger of the World, 5. Station break: *Walls and Bridges*, 6. Well, Well, Well, 7. Instant Karma, 8. Station break: *Goodnight, Vienna*

Side B

1. With Howard Cosell, 2. Mother, 3. Come Together, 4. Cold Turkey, 5. Hound Dog, 6. Medley: Baby Please Don't Go/Rock Island Line/Maybe Baby/Peggy Sue, 7. Johnny B. Goode, 8. Imagine, 9. Lennon/McCartney feud

Notes: 'John and Bob Dylan' is from the film *Eat the Document*. 'New York City', 'It's So Hard', 'Woman Is the Nigger of the World', 'Instant Karma', 'Mother', 'Come Together', 'Cold Turkey' and 'Hound Dog' are from the One-to-One concert at Madison Square Garden on 30 August 1972. The two station breaks and 'Well, Well, Well' are from John's appearance on WNEW radio as a guest DJ. The interview with Howard Cosell is from *Monday Night Football*. The medley is from an interview with ABC News prior to the One-to-One concert. 'Johnny B. Goode' and 'Imagine' are from the *Mike Douglas Show* 14–18 February 1972. 'Johnny B Goode' is with Chuck Berry. The last track is an unknown source.

025. CONFIDENTIAL DOCUMENT

Instant Analysis BBR 014

Format: 12-inch vinyl

Source: a compilation of solo tracks from the four Beatles, plus group items

Sound quality: varies

John's contributions are as follows:

Side 2

Borrowed Time (demo), Woman (outtake), I Don't Wanna Face It (outtake), Beautiful Boy (demo)

Notes: Also released as *Classified Document*.

026. DAY TRIPPER JAM

CBN 4242

Format: 12-inch vinyl

Source: various

Sound quality: All tracks mono – varies (see notes)

Side A

1. Give Peace a Chance (Holland), 2. What's the New Mary Jane, 3. Day Tripper Jam, 4. God Save Us

Side B

1. The Luck of the Irish, 2. Attica State, 3. Imagine, 4. Give Peace a Chance

Notes: Side A: All tracks excellent mono except 'Day Tripper Jam' – poor mono.

Side B: 'Luck of the Irish' and 'Attica State' – good mono, 'Imagine' – very good. 'Give Peace a Chance' – excellent. This disc was reissued on Instant Analysis 1056. This was later released on compact disc.

027. DAY TRIPPER JAM

Instant Analysis 1056

Format: 12-inch vinyl

Source: various

Sound quality: All tracks mono – varies (see notes)

Notes: A reissue of CBM 4242. This was later reissued on compact disc.

028. DOCTOR WINSTON O'BOOGIE ON THE *TOMORROW SHOW*

Unknown CX 297

Format: 12-inch vinyl

Source: *Tomorrow Show*, hosted by Tom Snyder, 28 April 1975

Sound quality: very good to excellent mono

Side A

Part One (22.35)

Side B

Part Two (20.12)

Notes: An interesting interview with John and his lawyer. This was also released on a commercial video. This disc was also released as *All We Need Is John*.

029. DOLL'S HOUSE

Maidenhead Records MHR JET 909-1

Format: 12-inch vinyl (double)

Source: various Beatles and solo tracks. Lennon's tracks as listed below. Side A only.

Sound quality: varies

Side A

1. A message from John and Yoko (0.29), 2. Give Peace a Chance (0.36), 3. Instant Karma (1.58), 4. A message from Yoko (Part 1) (4.01), 5. A message from Yoko (Part 2) (4.30)

Notes: 1. Probably October 1969 – in Japanese, excellent mono. 2. Source unknown – John and Yoko – acoustic, excellent mono. 3. Excerpt from *Top of the Pops*, February 1970 – very good mono. 4. and 5. In Japanese. Yoko talks while John plays acoustic guitar, including brief versions of 'Sun King' and 'Dear Prudence'. Yoko talks about 'Give Peace a Chance' and their time in Toronto.

Trivia note: *Doll's House* was the working title of The Beatles album that became the *White Album*.

030. DREAM LOVER

NN-01

Format: 12-inch vinyl

Source: various

Sound quality: unknown

Side A

1. Intro: Make Love to the End (Bed-In outtake), 2. God Save Us (demo), 3. Instant Karma (studio demo), 4. Radio Peace Jingle (1970), 5. Imagine (acoustic), 6. I'm the Greatest (demo), 7. As Time Goes By, 8. Let's Twist Again (Lennon and Bowie outtake)

Side B

1. Goodnight, Vienna (demo), 2. Goodnight, Vienna (radio spot), 3. Mucho Mungo (demo), 4. I Saw Her Standing There (rehearsal with Elton John), 5. *Walls and Bridges* (radio spot), 6. Old Dirt Road (demo), 7. Starting Over/Dream Lover/Stay (studio demos 1980), 8. As Time Goes By, 9. Starting Over (longer fade version – withdrawn)

031. FLOWER

TKRWN 1803/8018/JL 517

Format: 12-inch vinyl (triple)

Source: as below

Sound quality: Disc One – excellent mono. Disc Two – as original. Disc Three – excellent stereo

Notes: Disc one is a copy of *Joshua Tree Tapes*. Disc two is a copy of *Telecasts*. Disc three is a copy of *Roots*.

032. FULFILLING THE FANTASIES

TAKRL FTP 1000

Format: 12-inch vinyl

Source: various

Sound quality: good to very good

Side A

1. Clean-up Time (take 7) (4.48), 2. I'm Losing You (alternate take) (4.41), 3. Beautiful Boy (Darling Boy) (unedited rough mix) (4.17), 4. I'm Moving On (alternate take) (2.37), 5. I'm Your Angel (rough mix) (2.51), 6. Dear Yoko (rehearsal – mono) (3.46)

Side B

1. I'm Stepping Out (rehearsal August 1980) (4.01), 2. Nobody Told Me (take 1 – mono) (3.57), 3. Borrowed Time (acoustic guitar, overdub) (1.43), 4. I Don't Wanna Face It (rough mix – mono) (3.12), 5. Walking on Thin Ice (rough mix – mono) (3.21)

Notes: 'I'm Losing You' on Side A: runs too fast. Two tracks – 'I'm Losing You' and 'I'm Moving On' – are possibly with Cheap Trick.

The sleeve is black and white with a picture of John and Yoko on the front, and track listing and photo of John and Yoko with backing musicians on the back. This set was later released on compact disc with a slightly different track listing and a different sleeve.

033. GOD SAVE US DEMO

NW + 1

Format: 7-inch vinyl 45 rpm

Source: Side One – demo. Side Two – probably from sessions for *Fame*

Sound quality: very good

Side One

God Save Us (demo version)

Side Two

Let's Twist Again (Bowie and Lennon)

Notes: Black-and-white paper sleeve.

034. GOODNIGHT, VIENNA

Dakota Records DR 6975

Format: 12-inch vinyl

Released: 1985

Source: various – see notes

Sound quality: varies – see notes

Side A

1. Goodnight, Vienna (2.54), 2. Thirty Days (1.29), 3. C'mon Everybody (2.10), 4. A Salute to Lew Grade: Slippin' and Slidin'. Stand By Me, Imagine (9.04)

Side B

1. Israel interview excerpt (1.15), 2. Amsterdam Hilton 1969, includes Hava Nagila (0.09), 3. I Want You (0.52), 4. Jerusalaim (0.25), 5. Tequila (3.57), 6. Bunny Hop (4.42), 7. A Fool Was I (1.44)

Notes: Side A: Track 1 demo for Ringo Starr, summer 1984 (very good mono). Tracks 2 and 3 *Rock 'n' Roll* session (good to very good mono). Track 4 live – '*Salute To Sir Lew Grade*' 13 June 1975 (good audience tape).

Side B: Tracks 2 and 3 Amsterdam Hilton, March 1969 (good mono). Tracks 4 and 5, Willowbrook (One-to-One concert) rehearsals. Track 7, sleeve says 'probably John Lennon' – it almost certainly is not.

The front cover shows a black-and-white drawing of John from the 'Bed-In' period with details of the tracks on the back.

035. THE GREAT ROCK AND ROLL CIRCUS

Mushroom Records GRC 1383

Format: 12-inch vinyl

Source: *The Rolling Stones Rock and Roll Circus*

Sound quality: unknown

Notes: Lennon appears on one track as follows: Track 1 – 'Yer Blues', jam with John and Yoko, Eric Clapton, Keith Richard, Mitch Mitchell and Ivry Gitlis.

036. GREAT TO HAVE YOU WITH US

MHR-JET-909-3

Format: 12-inch vinyl (double)

Source: various tracks from ex-Beatles. John's contribution shown below.

Sound quality: very good

Side D

Too Many Cooks (Mick Jagger with John on mixing desk)

037. A GUITAR'S ALL RIGHT JOHN, BUT YOU'LL NEVER EARN YOUR LIVING BY IT

Audifon R.6015

Format: 10 inch vinyl

Released: 1975

Source: various – see notes

Sound quality: good to very good

Side A: (14.34)

1. Whatever Gets You Through the Night, 2. Lucy in the Sky with Diamonds, 3. I Saw Her Standing There

Side B: (15.54)

1. Slippin' and Slidin', 2. Stand By Me, 3. Oh, My Love, 4. Lady Marmalade, 5. Working Class Hero, 6. Day Tripper

Notes: Side A: features John's appearance with Elton John at Madison Square Garden on the 28 November 1974.

Side B: tracks 1 and 2 are from *The Old Grey Whistle Test* broadcast on 18 April 1975. Track 3 is probably from the *Imagine* session. Track 4 is from a March 1975 interview with an ad-lib performance. Track 5, according to *You Can't Do That* by Charles Reinhart, was recorded at a party in New York in the spring of 1972. The exact source remains unclear. Track 6 is from BBC Radio One programme *Top Gear* featuring Jimi Hendrix. Rumours persist that John is also on this track but the evidence is inconclusive. This release was pressed on several different shades of vinyl, including clear, blue, red and orange. It was re-released by Ruthless Rhymes (see entry number 038).

The cover features a teenage John in a 'teddy boy' pose with Stuart Sutcliffe holding his bass guitar in the background. The title of this release was taken from a comment made to a teenage John Lennon by his

Aunt Mimi who felt that John was paying more attention to his guitar than his education.

038. A GUITAR'S ALL RIGHT JOHN, BUT YOU'LL NEVER EARN YOUR LIVING BY IT

Ruthless Rhymes

Format: 10 inch vinyl

Released: 1975

Source: various – see notes

Sound quality: good to very good

Side A: (14.34)

1. Whatever Gets You Through the Night, 2. Lucy in the Sky with Diamonds, 3. I Saw Her Standing There

Side B: (15.54)

1. Slippin' and Slidin', 2. Stand By Me, 3. Oh, My Love, 4. Lady Marmalade, 5. Working Class Hero, 6. Day Tripper

Notes: This is a re-release of the Audifon disc with the same track listing. There are some minor differences. The photo on the front cover is reversed. On the original release John was on the right with Stuart Sutcliffe, on the left. On the cover of this release those positions are reversed. This also came in several colours of vinyl including black, green, red and orange.

039. GULP

RL007

Format: 12-inch vinyl

Source: *Rock and Roll Circus*, 11 December 1968

Sound quality: unknown

Notes: This release includes tracks from The Who, Buffalo Springfield and Captain Beefheart. The one contribution from John is 'Yer Blues' – Side A: Track 1.

040. A Hard Road

Morriphon L72808

Format: 12-inch vinyl

Source: various

Sound quality: excellent mono

Side A

1. 1970 Christmas Message, 2. Mother, 3. Come Together, 4. Give Peace a Chance, 5. Imagine

Side B

1. December 1980 interview (BBC), 2. Press conference (1966), 3. A Day in the Life (edit 0.31)

Notes: Side A: Tracks 2–5 One-to-One concert (evening show). Side B: Track 1 with Andy Peebles.

041. Hound Dog

Instant Analysis CMB 5040

Format: 12-inch vinyl

Source: Willowbrook, One-to-One concert, Madison Square Garden, New York, 30 August 1972 (Evening Show)

Sound quality: very poor

Side A

1. Come Together, 2. Instant Karma, 3. Cold Turkey, 4. Hound Dog, 5. Give Peace a Chance

Side B

1. It's So Hard, 2. Move On Fast, 3. Woman Is the Nigger of the World

Notes: These recordings from the One-to-One concert appear in far better quality on other bootlegs.

The black-and-white cover features a cartoon drawing of a dog with the track listing at the bottom.

042. HOUND DOG/LONG TALL SALLY
Heavy 101

Format: 7-inch vinyl 45 rpm

Source: One-to-One concert, Madison Square Garden, New York, 30 August 1972

Sound quality: unknown

Side A

Hound Dog (John with Elephant's Memory)

Notes: Side B: is 'Long Tall Sally' by Paul McCartney and Wings recorded on 18 March 1973.

The disc was issued in a black-and-white picture sleeve with a picture of John holding a pig.

043. IMAGINE – THE ALTERNATE ALBUM
Apple Records (bogus) SW-A-3379

Format: 12-inch vinyl

Released: 1990

Source: *Imagine* album alternate versions and outtakes

Sound quality: excellent

Side A

1. Imagine, 2. Crippled Inside, 3. Jealous Guy, 4. It's So Hard, 5. How Do You Sleep? 6. Give Me Some Truth, 7. Oh, My Love

Side B

1. How Do You Sleep? No. 2, 2. How? 3. Oh, Yoko, 4. San Francisco Bay Blues

Notes: A limited number of this disc were later released on white vinyl. Later released on compact disc (Sidewalk Music SM 89009).

044. 'JE SUIS LE PLUS MIEUX'
Jazz Series SD 6757

12-inch vinyl 45 rpm

Source: demos for the Ringo album

Sound quality: excellent stereo

Side A
I'm the Greatest (3.38)

Side B
I'm the Greatest (3.49)

Notes: Two demos of the song John gave to Ringo for his album called simply *Ringo*. The label says *Jazzercise* and calls the track 'Boogaloo At Thirty-two'. Full colour jacket.

045. JOE POPE'S STRAWBERRY FIELDS CHRISTMAS RECORDINGS

Strawberry Fields Forever

Format: 7-inch flexi disc

Source: various

Sound quality: unknown

Notes: These discs were only given to the members of the fan club and were given away with issues 18, 24, 27, 32, 36 and 40 of *Strawberry Fields Forever* magazine. They included rare interviews, outtakes and demos.

046. JOHN AND PAUL IN MICHIGAN

Unknown

Format: 12-inch vinyl

Source: Free John Sinclair Rally, 18 December 1971

Sound quality: unknown

Notes: Reissue of *Ann Arbor: Now Hear This*.

047. JOHN LENNON INTERVIEW/DAVID PEEL AND THE APPLE BAND

OR 70078 PD

Format: 7-inch picture disc

Source: as below
Sound quality: unknown

Side A
John Lennon about David Peel

Side B
In My Life by David Peel

048. JOHN LENNON/PAUL MCCARTNEY – ANN ARBOR 'NOW HEAR THIS'

Unknown
Format: 12-inch vinyl
Source: Free John Sinclair Rally
Sound quality: unknown

Notes: Reissue of *Ann Arbor: Now Hear This*.

049. JOHN LENNON WITH JIMI HENDRIX, CHUCK BERRY

LSD Records JCJ 37037
Format: 12-inch vinyl
Released: 1986
Source: various live performances – see notes
Sound quality: good/very good

Side A
1. Imagine, 2. Memphis, 3. Johnny B. Goode, 4. It's So Hard, 5. Midsummer New York, 6. We're All Water (see notes)

Side B
1. Day Tripper, 2. Come Together, 3. Instant Karma, 4. Cold Turkey, 5. Hound Dog

Notes: Side A: is from the *Mike Douglas Show*, 1972. Side B: track 1 is from *Top Gear*, BBC Radio October 1967. Tracks 2–5, One-to-One concert.

Black-and-white cover with photos of John, Jimi Hendrix and Chuck Berry. The last track on Side A: is 'The Luck of the Irish' and not 'We're All Water' as stated on the sleeve.

050. JOHN PAUL GEORGE AND RINGO IN THE 1970S

Melvin Records MR-12

Format: 12-inch vinyl

Source: various from all Beatles – John's contributions are shown below

Sound quality: unknown

Side A

Track 5 – Angel Baby

Side B

Track 4 – Move Over Ms L, Track 12 – Be My Baby

Notes: This release contains tracks from all four ex-Beatles, with three contributions from Lennon. 'Angel Baby' and 'Be My Baby' are from the *Roots* album.

051. JOHNNY MOONDOG

Boxtop Records KOK-1-5832

Format: 12-inch vinyl

Released: 1986

Source: various – see notes

Sound quality: varies – see notes

Side A

1. Goodnight, Vienna (2.45), 2. Imagine (2.51), 3. Serve Yourself (3.48), 4. Mucho Mungo (7.06), 5. Ya Ya (2.34), 6. Poems: I Sat Belonely/Frank Cummings (1.06)

Side B

1. God Save Us (2.54), 2. Theme from *Rape* (0.57), 3. Hava Nagila (0.09), 4. Jerusalaim (0.27), 5. Yer Blues (8.25), 6. That'll Be the Day (2.23), 7. Do the Oz (3.06)

Notes: Side A: track 1, demo for Ringo Starr (very good mono). Track 2, live Apollo Theatre 17 December 1971 (excellent mono). Track 3, Bermuda July 1980. Track 4, sessions for *Pussycats* album (Harry Nilsson) – excellent mono. Track 5, *Rock 'n' Roll* session. Track 6, John reading poetry from his books.

Side B: track 1, demo June 1971. Track 2, from the film *Rape* (very good mono). Tracks 3 and 4, Amsterdam Hilton March 1969. Track 5, from *Rock and Roll Circus*, 11 December 1968. Track 6, from *Rock 'n' Roll* session. Track 7, June 1971 from Apple 1835 (excellent stereo).

Cover features colour photo on front with track listing on sticker.

052. JOHN'S LAST SONGS

Shaved Fish Records SF 80001
Format: 7-inch vinyl 33 rpm
Released: 1989
Source: various
Sound quality: excellent

Side A
1. (Just Like) Starting Over (home demo with acoustic guitar and drum machine), 2. Lennon and Starr radio spots for *Walls and Bridges* and *Goodnight, Vienna*

Side B
1. Make Love Not War (home demo), 2. I'm the Greatest (studio demo)

Notes: Tracks taken from *The Lost Lennon Tapes* radio series.

053. JOHN LENNON

In Step Records JL 101
Format: 7-inch vinyl 45 rpm
Source: unknown but probably from One-to-One concert
Sound quality: unknown

Side A

Mother

Side B

Come Together

054. JOSHUA TREE TAPES

TKBWM 1803

Format: 12-inch vinyl

Source: various – see notes

Sound quality: unknown

Side A

1. Imagine, 2. Mother, 3. Come Together, 4. Give Peace a Chance

Side B

1. Yer Blues, 2. John Sinclair, 3. It's So Hard, 4. The Luck of the Irish, 5. Woman Is the Nigger of the World, 6. Johnny B. Goode

Notes: Side A: One-to-One concert, 30 August 1972. Side B: track 1, *Rock and Roll Circus*, 11 December 1968. Tracks 2–6, *Mike Douglas Show*, 14–18 February 1972.

The photocopied sepia sleeve has a picture of John from the *Imagine* period with the track listing down the side.

055. JUST TALKING

BFR 003/M-008-1

Format: 7-inch one sided flexi disc 33 rpm

Source: various – see notes

Sound quality: good

Jewellery remark from Royal Variety Show 1963, Ronnie Hawkins Rap, Radio spot: 'Whatever Gets You Through the Night', weather forecast.

056. THE KYA 1969 PEACE TALK

KYA 1969

Format: 7-inch blue vinyl 45 rpm

Source: KYA 1260 San Francisco interview with Tom Campbell and Bill Holley

Sound quality: excellent mono

Notes: This 7-inch release comprises an interview John gave to hosts Tom Campbell and Bill Holley.

057. LENNON/MCCARTNEY

CBM WEC R1 3665

Format: 12-inch vinyl

Source: Free John Sinclair Rally, 10 December 1971

Sound quality: unknown

Notes: Reissue of *Ann Arbor: Now Hear This*. This disc was also issued with the same title on an unknown label (see below). For full track listing see original release.

058. LENNON/MCCARTNEY

Unknown

Format: 12-inch vinyl

Source: Free John Sinclair Rally, 18 December 1971

Sound quality: unknown

Notes: Reissue of *Ann Arbor: Now Hear This* containing the same tracks. This was also reissued under the title *Lennon/McCartney* (CBM WEC R1 3665). For full track listing see the original release.

059. LENNON/ONO BOX SET

Various

Format: 12-inch vinyl box set of nine albums. Released: 1987

Source: various

Sound quality: varies

Notes: A box set containing *Something Precious and Rare, Before Play, You Should've Been There, The Willowbrook Rehearsals, Off the Walls, Johnny Moondog* and *Telecasts*.

060. LENNON ROOTS

RTS

Format: 12-inch vinyl

Source: *Rock 'n' Roll* album sessions

Sound quality: very good

Side A

1. Be-Bop-A-Lula, 2. Ain't That a Shame, 3. Stand By Me, 4. Sweet Little Sixteen, 5. Medley: Rip It Up/Ready Teddy/Angel Baby/Do You Want to Dance/You Can't Catch Me

Side B

1. Bony Moronie, 2. Peggy Sue, 3. Medley: Bring It on Home to Me/Send Me Some Loving, 4. Slippin' and Slidin', 5. Be My Baby, 6. Ya Ya, 7. Just Because

Notes: Same track listing as *Rock 'n' Roll album* with two numbers added – 'Angel Baby' and 'Be My Baby'. 'Angel Baby' is shown on the sleeve as 'My Angel Baby'.

061. LENNON VS THE WORLD VOL. 1

Original Rock 1009

Format: 12-inch vinyl

Source: Lennon official release version followed by original artist version

Sound quality: unknown

Side A

1. Be-Bop-A-Lula (Lennon), 2. Be-Bop-A-Lula (Gene Vincent), 3. Ain't That a Shame (Lennon), 4. Ain't That a Shame (Fats Domino), 5. Bring It on Home to Me (Lennon), 6. Bring It on Home to Me (Sam Cooke)

Side B

1. Do You Want to Dance (Lennon), 2. Do You Want to Dance (Bobby Freeman), 3. Just Because (Lennon), 4. Just Because (Lloyd Freeman), 5. Peggy Sue (Lennon), 6. Peggy Sue (Buddy Holly)

Notes: An interesting concept where John's version is followed by the original artist recording. Lennon's versions are the commercial releases from the *Rock 'n' Roll* album. Two further volumes followed.

062. LENNON VS THE WORLD VOL. 2

Original Rock 1010

Format: 12-inch vinyl

Source: Lennon official release version followed by original artist version

Sound quality: unknown

Side A

1. Ready Teddy (Lennon), 2. Ready Teddy (Little Richard), 3. Rip It Up (Lennon), 4. Rip It Up (Little Richard), 5. Send Me Some Loving (Lennon), 6. Send Me Some Loving (Little Richard)

Side B

1. Slippin' and Slidin' (Lennon), 2. Slippin' and Slidin' (Little Richard), 3. Stand By Me (Lennon), 4. Stand By Me (Ben E King), 5. Well (Baby Please Don't Go) (Lennon), 6. Well (Baby Please Don't Go) (The Olympics)

063. LENNON VS THE WORLD VOL. 3

Original Rock 1011

Format: 12-inch vinyl

Source: Lennon official release version followed by original artist version

Sound quality: unknown

Side A

1. Sweet Little Sixteen (Lennon), 2. Sweet Little Sixteen (Chuck Berry), 3. You Can't Catch Me (Lennon), 4. You Can't Catch Me (Chuck Berry), 5. Ya Ya (Lennon), 6. Ya Ya (Lee Dorsey)

Side B

1. Angel Baby (Lennon), 2. Angel Baby (Rosie and The Originals), 3. Be My Baby (Lennon), 4. Be My Baby (The Ronnettes), 5. Bony Moronie (Lennon), 6. Bony Moronie (Larry Williams)

064. LIFE WITH THE LENNONS

TOBE MILO 4Q 13/14

Format: 7-inch vinyl EP 33⅓ rpm

Source: extracts from the official release *Life with the Lions*

Sound quality: excellent mono

Side A

Yoko sings song for John: Let's Go Flying, Snow Is Falling all the Time, Mummy's Only Looking for Her Hand in the Snow, No Bed For Beatle John (9.40)

Side B

Radio Play (7.57)

Notes: Deluxe black-and-white sleeve. 1,000 numbered copies. This release is a pirate of the disc issued by *Aspen Magazine*: 'Aspen 7 – The British Box – Spring and Summer' (Section 11 Aspen No. 7). Back of sleeve includes lyrics.

065. LIFTING MATERIAL FROM THE WORLD

Apple Records SAPCOR 43

Format: 12-inch vinyl (double)

Source: various, each of the four sides features tracks from the ex-Beatles. Lennon's tracks are on Side D

Sound quality: generally excellent stereo

Side D

1. Imagine (*Salute To Sir Lew Grade*, 13 June 1975) (3.17), 2. John Sinclair Benefit Concert introduction/Attica State/The Luck of the Irish/John Sinclair (12.49), 3. Give Peace a Chance (rehearsal, Montreal, 1969) (2.26), 4. *Eat the Document* (outtake with Bob Dylan) (0.16), 5. John

interviewed by Howard Cosell (Monday Night Football, 9 December 1974) (1.27), 6. John talks about meeting Chuck Berry (WNEW, 28 September 1974) (0.23), 7. John sings and talks about Paul's *Ram* lyrics (probably 1971) (0.15), 7. Listen To This radio spot: Ringo does *Walls and Bridges* prom, John does Goodnight, Vienna promo (WNEW-FM, 28 September 1974) (2.45), 8. Acoustic Medley: Well (Baby Please Don't Go)/Rock Island Line/Maybe Baby/Peggy Sue (from *Eyewitness News* television broadcast, summer 1972)

Notes: 'John Sinclair Benefit Concert' is good to very good mono. Rest of the tracks are very good to excellent mono.

066. LIMITED EDITION

Bag Records 5069

Format; 12-inch vinyl

Source: various – see notes

Sound quality: varies – see notes

Side A

1. As Time Goes By (0.08), 2. I Saw Her Standing There (3.00), 3. Whatever Gets You Through the Night (1.44), 4. Move Over Ms L (2.54), 5. Angel Baby (3.08), 6. I Found Out (3.42), 7. Happy Xmas (War Is Over) (3.32), 8. Nutopian National Anthem (long version) (0.05), 9. Give Peace a Chance (4.49)

Side B

1. I'm the Greatest (3.55), 2. Be My Baby (4.34), 3. Yer Blues (3.57), 4. Do the Oz (3.06), 5. What's the New Mary Jane (0.14), 6. What's the New Mary Jane (6.39), 7. Unknown (0.03), 8. As Time Goes By (0.10), 9. (Just Like) Starting Over (0.52), 10. Good Night (0.32)

Notes: Side A: track 1, Earth News Radio, January 1976 (excellent stereo). Track 2, probably a rehearsal with Elton John prior to live performance on 28 November 1974. Track 3, *Walls and Bridges* session 13 November 1974. Track 4, Apple 1881 (excellent stereo). Track 5, *Rock 'n' Roll* session. Track 6, album version with longer fade (Australian pressing) – excellent stereo. Track 7, from Apple 1842 (excellent stereo). Track 8, silent track. Track 9, Montreal 1 June 1969 from Apple 1809 (excellent stereo).

Side B: track 1, demo (see 'Je Suis Le Plus Mieux'). Track 2, *Rock 'n' Roll* session. Track 3, from *Rock and Roll Circus*, 11 December 1968 (excerpt). Track 4, from Apple 1835. Track 5, probably from Earth News Radio. Track 6, excellent stereo. Track 8, from Earth News Radio. Track 9, extended ending from 12-inch (excellent stereo). Track 10, from *Wedding Album*.

Album comes with twelve page booklet containing song lyrics, photos and drawing. See also *Toy Boy*. Later released on CD with bonus tracks.

067. LISTEN TO THIS PICTURE RECORD

Unknown

Format: 12 inch colour picture disc

Source WNEW-FM Radio 28 September 1974

Sound quality: excellent mono

Side A

Interview and acting as DJ to promote *Walls and Bridges* album (17.26)

Side B

Interview and acting as DJ to promote *Walls and Bridges* album (continued) (14.53)

Notes: The original show runs for two hours. This disc includes most of John's material. He deals with a variety of topics including commercials and the weather.

068. LIVE FROM THE LIVE

Black Disc Inc 7PP 1082

Format: 12-inch vinyl

Source: One-to-One concert and live with Elton John, Madison Square Garden, New York, 28 November 1974

Sound quality: unknown

Side A

1. Mother, 2. Imagine, 3. Come Together, 4. Give Peace a Chance

Side B

1. Cold Turkey, 2. Hound Dog, 3. Whatever Gets You Through the Night, 4. Lucy in the Sky with Diamonds, 5. I Saw Her Standing There

Notes: Side A: and Side B: tracks 1–2: One-to-One concert. Side B:, tracks 3–5 live with Elton John. Japanese picture disc – limited to 1,000 copies.

THE LOST LENNON TAPES (BAG RECORDS)

The first album in this series from Bag Records was the vinyl album which was released in 1988. There were thirty-five vinyl albums released in this series. From volume twenty-four they also were released on compact disc – most as single albums but some as double-disc sets containing three of the original vinyl releases. Details of these can be found in Part 2 – Compact Discs. However, the first twenty-three vinyl albums are available on compact discs as they were reissued by the Dutch label Walrus Records with extra tracks. The story behind the radio series *The Lost Lennon Tapes* is featured in Part Three.

069. THE LOST LENNON TAPES – VOLUME 1

Bag Records 5073

Format: 12-inch vinyl

Released: 1988

Source: various – see notes

Sound quality: excellent

Side A

1. Strawberry Fields Forever (3.03), 2. The Happy Rishikesh Song (1.52), 3. Rock Island Line (2.31), 4. John Henry (1.38), 5. Surprise Surprise (Sweet Bird of Paradox (1.21), 6. Keep Right on to the End of the Road (0.40), 7. Goodnight, Vienna (2.52), 8. Tennessee (takes 1 and 4) (1.56), 9. God Save Us (3.07), 10. With a Little Help from My Friends (0.38)

Side B

1. Power to the People (2.28), 2. Here We Go Again (1.22), 3. Mucho Mungo (2.11), 4. God (1.25), 5. Life Begins at Forty (2.04), 6. Woman (3.06), 7. Girls and Boys (2.20), 8. Clean-up Time (3.08), 9. Beautiful Boy (2.46)

Notes: Side A: tracks 1 and 2, demos. Tracks 3–5, acoustic demos, Dakota. Track 6, from flexi single given with *Oz* magazine 1971. Track 7, John's demo for Ringo Starr. Track 8, piano demo. Track 9, demo. Track 10, John with Sean.

Side B: track 1, rough mix. Tracks 2 and 3, outtakes. Track 4, acoustic. Track 5, demo for Ringo Starr. Track 6, acoustic, Bermuda. Tracks 7 and 8, outtakes, track 9, outtake Bermuda.

The black-and-white sleeve features a picture of John from the 1966 film *How I Won the War*.

070. THE LOST LENNON TAPES – VOLUME 2

Bag Records 5074

Format: 12-inch vinyl

Released: 1988

Source: various – see notes

Sound quality: excellent

Side A

1. Revolution (3.52), 2. Child of Nature (2.33), 3. He Said He Said/She Said She Said (1.07), 4. I'm the Greatest (early demo) (1.21), 5. Make Love Not War (3.13), 6. How Do You Sleep? (8.07), 7. Daddy's Little Sunshine Boy (0.28)

Side B

1. I'm the Greatest (2.50), 2. The Luck of the Irish (3.11), 3. Every Man Has a Woman Who Loves Him (3.17), 4. Starting Over (4.53), 5. I Promise (1.56), 6. Sea Ditty/Leaning on a Lamp Post (2.35), 7. Grow Old with Me (3.20)

Notes: 'Revolution' and 'Child of Nature' are demos by The Beatles recorded at George's house in 1968 (the sleeve says Paul's house which is incorrect). 'I'm the Greatest' (early demo), 'Make Love Not War', 'I Promise' and 'Sea Ditty' are demos featuring John at the piano. 'He Said He Said, She Said She Said' and 'The Luck of the Irish' are acoustic demos. 'Starting Over' is guitar and drum machine. 'Grow Old with Me' is piano and drum machine. 'I'm the Greatest' and 'How Do You Sleep?' are full ensemble productions. 'Every Man Has a Woman Who Loves Him' is a duet with Yoko. 'Daddy's Little Sunshine Boy' features Ringo on vocal with impatient encouragement from John.

The sleeve features a black-and-white photograph of John with the colour drawing from the cover of John's book *Skywriting by Word of Mouth* on the reverse with the track listing and notes.

071. THE LOST LENNON TAPES – VOLUME 3

Bag Records 5075

Format: 12-inch vinyl

Released: 1988

Source: various – see notes

Sound quality: excellent

Side A

1. Strawberry Fields Forever (2.41), 2. What's the New Mary Jane (2.35), 3. Julia (3.40), 4. Across the Universe (3.45), 5. You Know My Name (Look Up the Number) (1.00), 6. Help! (0.42), 7. Whatever Gets You Through the Night (5.27), 8. We Must Not Forget The General Erection (0.34), 9. The Wumberlog (or Magic Dog) (0.34)

Side B

1. Dear John (4.14), 2. Whatever Happened To (4.55), 3. Cookin' (In The Kitchen of Love) (2.28), 4. Peggy Sue (0.54), 5. Watching the Wheels 1 (0.38), 6. Watching the Wheels 2 (1.46), 7. I'm Losing You (0.45), 8. Beautiful Boy (1.40), 9. Clean-up Time (2.23), 10. One-To-One radio spot outtakes (1.27)

Notes: 'Strawberry Fields Forever' is a demo (electric guitar) from 1966. 'What's the New Mary Jane' and 'Julia' are *White Album* demos performed by The Beatles. 'Across the Universe' (Beatles) is a different mix. Piano backed demos: 'Cookin'', 'Watching the Wheels 1' and 'You Know My Name'. Guitar based demos: 'Whatever Gets You Through the Night', 'Watching the Wheels 2' and 'Beautiful Boy'. John at home: 'Help!' (piano), 'Peggy Sue' (guitar) and two unreleased songs, 'Dear John' and 'Whatever Happened To' (from the proposed Broadway play The Ballad of John and Yoko').

Record Plant recordings: 'I'm Losing You', 'Clean-up Time' and 'Beautiful Boy'. 'The General Erection' and 'The Magic Dog' feature John reading from *A Spaniard In The Works*.

The front cover has a colour photo of John with one of his colour sketches on the back.

072. THE LOST LENNON TAPES – VOLUME 4

Bag Records 5076

Format: 12-inch vinyl

Released: 1988

Source: various – see notes

Sound quality: excellent

Side A

1. Revolution (3.22), 2. Power to the People (2.47), 3. Attica State (3.22), 4. The Luck of the Irish (3.22), 5. John Sinclair (3.31), 6. I'm a Man (1.54), 7. 'Twas a Night like Ethel Merman (1.05), 8. Medley: Beyond the Sea/Blue Moon/Young Love (4.08)

Side B

1. Clean-up Time (3.22), 2. Good Morning, Good Morning (1.01), 3. Everybody's Got Something to Hide Except Me and My Monkey (2.55), 4. Everyone Had a Hard Year (1.33), 5. Brown Eyed Handsome Man (2.14), 6. Serve Yourself (5.25), 7. Lord Take This Make-up Off Me (2.20), 8. The News of the Day (from Reuters) (4.25)

Notes: 'Revolution' is a remixed version of The Beatles single. 'Good Morning, Good Morning' is John's original demo from early 1967. 'Everybody's Got Something to Hide Except Me and My Monkey' (called 'Come On Come On' at the time of this recording) is The Beatles demo version. 'Everyone Had a Hard Year' is John's demo from 1968 – this was eventually incorporated into 'I've Got a Feeling'. 'Attica State', 'The Luck of the Irish' and 'John Sinclair' are live stereo recordings from the Free John Sinclair Rally in Ann Arbor, Michigan on 10 December 1971. 'Clean-up Time' is a different mix from *Double Fantasy*. 'Power to the People' – early alternate take. 'I'm a Man', 'Brown Eyed Handsome Man', the recitation 'Twas a Night like Ethel Merman' and the medley are all Dakota cassette recordings.

The final three tracks are some of John's Bob Dylan parodies. The version of 'Serve Yourself' features a piano accompaniment with 'clean' lyrics. The guitar version with raunchier lyrics can be found on the vinyl releases 'Serve Yourself' (Love and Peace Records) and 'Yin Yan' (Bag Records).

The sleeve shows a colour photo of John (probably from 1966) with a black-and-white photo of John and Yoko on the back with notes on the tracks.

073. THE LOST LENNON TAPES – VOLUME 5

Bag Records 5077

Format: 12-inch vinyl

Released: 1988

Source: various – see notes

Sound quality: excellent

Side A

1. Dear Prudence (4.42), 2. Jealous Guy (4.06), 3. God Save Us (1.55), 4. Rock 'n' Roll People (2.10), 5. Rock Island Line (2.48), 6. Real Life (4.51)

Side B

1. My Life (take 1) (0.55) 2. My Life (take 3) (2.38) 3. Don't Be Crazy (1.38), 4. The Worst is Over (3.29). 5. In the Studio (2.30), 6. Starting Over (vocal booth) (4.23), 7. Starting Over (4.17)

Notes: 'Dear Prudence' is a 1969 demo. 'Jealous Guy' is a studio outtake from the *Imagine* session. 'God Save Us' and 'Rock 'n' Roll People' – acoustic demos. 'Rock Island Line' is the electric guitar version recorded at the Dakota. 'My Life', 'Don't Be Crazy' and 'The Worst is Over' are demos recorded at the Dakota. 'Starting Over' features two versions. Firstly a rough take is presented as it would be heard from inside John's vocal booth. The final track is an early outtake of the number with a rough vocal.

The colour sleeve has a picture of John and Yoko on the front.

074. THE LOST LENNON TAPES – VOLUME 6

Bag Records 5078

Format: 12-inch vinyl

Released: 1988

Source: various – see notes

Sound quality: excellent

Side A

1. Maggie Mae (0.23), 2. Honey Don't (1.35), 3. Don't Be Cruel (1.29), 4. Matchbox (1.53), 5. Dear Prudence (3.55), 6. Cold Turkey (3.36), 7. Here We Go Again (take 2) (3.00), 8. Woman (3.29), 9. The Neville Club

Side B

1. Rock 'n' Roll People (6.00), 2. Not Fade Away (0.56), 3. Sweet Little Sixteen (4.18), 4. You Can't Catch Me (3.26), 5. Mirror Mirror (take 1) (2.38), 6. Mirror Mirror (take 5) (2.39)

Notes: 'Maggie Mae' was recorded at The Hit Factory in 1980. 'Honey Don't', 'Matchbox' and 'Don't Be Cruel' featuring John's Elvis impression were recorded during the making of the *Plastic Ono Band* album with Ringo drums, Klaus Voorman bass and Yoko wind. 'Dear Prudence' is The Beatles – different mix. 'Cold Turkey' – original demo. 'Here We Go Again', 'Woman' and 'Mirror Mirror' are also demos. 'The Neville Club' is John reading from his book *In His Own Write*. 'Not Fade Away' is an out of control jam with the Elephant's Memory Band. The rest of the tracks are John working with Phil Spector including alternate versions of 'Rock 'n' Roll People', 'Sweet Little Sixteen' and 'You Can't Catch Me'.

The sleeve has a colour photo of John from 1980 with a sketch drawing on the back with the track listing and notes on the tracks.

075. THE LOST LENNON TAPES – VOLUME 7
Bag Records 5079
Format: 12-inch vinyl
Released: 1988
Source: various – see notes
Sound quality: excellent

Side A

1. Mind Games (4.03), 2. Cold Turkey (4.58) 3. One of the Boys (3.12), 4. Tight A$ (3.32), 5. Studio Banter (2.09), 6. Woman (vocal booth)

Side B

1. Dear Yoko (3.44), 2. I Don't Wanna Face It (2.33), 3. Watching the Wheels (3.32), 4. I'm Stepping Out (4.34), 5. Clean-up Time (2.59), 6. Woman (3.16)

Notes: Side A: track 1, alternate take with rough vocal. Track 2, taken from the only known acetate and some clicks and pops are audible. Track 3, Dakota recording. Track 4, original demo. The remainder of the album covers the *Double Fantasy/Milk and Honey* era with outtakes and demos.

The cover features a head only photo of John with dark glasses and a black cap. The reverse has track listing and notes.

076. THE LOST LENNON TAPES – VOLUME 8
Bag Records 5080
Format: 12-inch vinyl
Released: 1988

Source: various – see notes

Sound quality: excellent

Side A

1. Roll Over Beethoven (2.29), 2. Whole Lotta Shakin' Goin' On (2.41), 3. It'll Be Me (2.37), 4. One-To-One radio spot outtakes (2.51), 5. New York City (0.53), 6. God Save Oz (3.08), 7. Introduction (Lennon and Jagger) (0.52), 8. Dirty Mac Jam (3.41), 9. Maurice DuPont Agent Provocateur (3.10)

Side B

1. That'll Be the Day (1.05), 2. Rave On (1.13), 3. Not Fade Away (0.54), 4. Maybe Baby (1.54), 5. Heartbeat (1.11), 6. Peggy Sue Got Married (1.13), 7. Peggy Sue (2.15), 8. Corrina Corrina (1.15), 9. Serve Yourself (M.O.T.H.E.R.) (2.37), 10. The Best Things In Life Are Free (0.17), 11. *Eat the Document* (7.52), 12. A Nice Noise (1.54)

Notes: This release has a *Rock 'n' Roll* theme. Side A: tracks 1–3 and 5 are One-To-One rehearsals with Elephant's Memory. Track 6, complete demo. Tracks 7 and 8, from *Rock and Roll Circus*.

Side B: Track 1, The Quarrymen. Tracks 2–7 were recorded at St. Regis Hotel, New York for the film *Clock*.

The sleeve cover has an early photo of John at The Cavern with Pete Best on drums in the background. A black-and-white photo of a teenage John is shown on the back with the track listing and notes.

077. THE LOST LENNON TAPES – VOLUME 9

Bag Records 5081

Format: 12-inch vinyl

Released: 1988

Source: various – see notes

Sound quality: excellent

Side A

1. Tomorrow Never Knows (3.10), 2. Strawberry Fields Backwards Talk Test (0.38), 3. Aerial Tour Instrumental (Flying) (2.04), 4. Cry Baby Cry (2.33), 5. Dear Prudence (4.36), 6. Sexy Sadie (2.24), 7. Julia (3.41)

Side B

1. Child of Nature (2.38), 2. The Continuing Story of Bungalo Bill (2.38), 3. I'm So Tired (2.44), 4. Yer Blues (3.31), 5. Everybody's Got Something to Hide Except Me and My Monkey (3.01), 6. What's the New Mary Jane (2.39), 7. Revolution (3.12)

Notes: This edition in the series features recordings made by John with The Beatles. 'Tomorrow Never Knows' is a rough mix. 'Strawberry Fields' is John making some 'backwards speech' intended to be incorporated into 'Strawberry Fields Forever' (this concept was abandoned). The rest of the tracks are demos prior to the making of the *White Album*.

The front cover shows a psychedelic picture of John against a bright yellow background.

078. THE LOST LENNON TAPES – VOLUME 10

Bag Records 5082

Format: 12-inch vinyl

Released: 1988

Source: various – see notes

Sound quality: excellent

Side A

1. Imagine (3.06), 2. Crippled Inside (3.49), 3. It's So Hard (2.25), 4. A Case of the Blues (2.54), 5. Billy and Sally (0.31), 6. Billy and Sally (take 3) (3.25), 7. Send Me Some Loving (3.10), 6. Woman Is the Nigger of the World (2.13), 7. New York City (1.17)

Side B

1. Only You (3.13), 2. Down In Cuba (2.06), 3. Surprise Surprise (Sweet Bird of Paradox) (3.14), 4. Whatever Gets You Through the Night (3.53),

5. Watching the Wheels (3.03), 6. I'm Losing You (1.32), 7. Borrowed Time (4.42), 8. Tobias Casuals (1.04)

Notes: Side A: 'Imagine', 'Crippled Inside' and 'It's So Hard' are studio outtakes from the *Imagine* session. 'A Case of the Blues', 'Sally and Billy' and 'Down In Cuba' (on Side B:) are unreleased songs. 'Send Me Some Loving' has acoustic guitar accompaniment. 'Woman Is the Nigger of the World' and 'New York City' are demos.

Side B: 'Only You' is John's completed studio version – Ringo later recorded his own vocals over the backing track. 'Whatever Gets You Through the Night' is an early studio run through. 'Surprise Surprise (Sweet Bird of Paradox)', 'Watching the Wheels' and 'Borrowed Time' are guitar based unedited demos. 'I'm Losing You' is an early piano-backed demo.

The back of the sleeve shows a cartoon strip of John.

079. THE LOST LENNON TAPES – VOLUME 11

Bag Records 5083
Format: 12-inch vinyl
Released: 1988
Source: various – see notes
Sound quality: excellent

Side A
1. Happy Birthday John (1.07), 2. Julia (3.02), 3. Mother (3.22), 4. I Found Out (3.57), 5. What'd I Say (0.36), 6. How? (3.37), 7. Yellow Submarine (0.35), 8. Chi-Chi's Cafe (3.27), 9. New York City (1.17)

Side B
1. Beautiful Boy (2.44), 2. Howling at the Moon (1.58), 3. Memories (2.32), 4. I'm Losing You (3.15), 5. Everybody's Talking Nobody's Talking (2.23), 6. Nobody Told Me (3.18), 7. Beautiful Boy (3.22)

Notes: Side A: tracks 1, 5 and 7 were recorded at John's thirty-first birthday party. Track 2, demo from 1968. Tracks 3 and 6 are outtakes.

Track 4, an alternate and longer mix. Track 8 features a bit of impromptu lunacy from the Sixties with John and Ringo. Track 9 is a demo.

Side B: outtakes and demos from the *Double Fantasy/Milk and Honey* period.

The sleeve has a colour picture of John on the front from the film *How I Won the War* with a black-and-white photo of John and Ringo from the *Sgt. Pepper* era on the back.

080. THE LOST LENNON TAPES – VOLUME 12

Bag Records 5084

Format: 12-inch vinyl

Released: 1989

Source: various – see notes

Sound quality: excellent

Side A

1. New York City (2.10), 2. Don't Be Cruel (1.33), 3. Hound Dog (2.52), 4. Send Me Some Loving (2.33), 5. I Found Out (2.57), 6. Happy Xmas (War Is Over) (3.18), 7. John and Yoko's Happy Xmas Ditty (1.24), 8. Tobias Casuals No. 2 (1.15)

Side B

1. Borrowed Time (3.01), 2. God (2.43), 3. Serve Yourself (4.46), 4. Imagine (2.44), 5. Mucho Mungo (2.15), 6. Mt. Elga (1.13), 7. Gone from This Place (3.16)

Notes: Side A: track 1, demo – later version than on Volume 10. Tracks 2–4 are jamming in the studio with Elephant's Memory. Track 5, original demo on acoustic guitar. Tracks 6 and 7, original demo for 'Happy Xmas (War Is Over)' plus an additional ditty recorded at home.

Side B: track 1, alternate studio take. Track 2, early demo. Track 3, slow and bluesy version at the piano. Track 4, studio outtake. Tracks 5 and 6 were recorded with Harry Nilsson on acoustic guitar and electric piano. Track 7 is an unreleased Dakota recording.

The front of the sleeve shows John wearing his New York City tee shirt with the War Is Over poster on the back.

081. THE LOST LENNON TAPES – VOLUME 13

Bag Records 5085

Format: 12-inch vinyl

Released: 1989

Source: various – see notes

Sound quality: excellent

Side A

1. The Great Wok (2.02), 2. Yer Blues (1.29), 3. I Found Out (3.20), 4. Oh, Yoko (0.58), 5. How? (2.57), 6. Pill (1.40), 7. Out the Blue (4.15), 8. No. 9 Dream (1.23)

Side B

1. Tobias Casuals (1.03), 2. John Henry (1.00), 3. She is a Friend of Dorothy (3.27), 4. Real Love (3.43), 5. Dear Yoko (3.07), 6. (Just Like) Starting Over (4.17), 7. The Return of Maurice DuPont (2.41)

Notes: Side A: track 1, taped at the Dakota in 1979 and is spoken word with John taking on the role of an Eastern mystic where he predicts the karmic trend for the coming year. Track 2, *Rock and Roll Circus* rehearsal. Tracks 3–5 are demos. Track 6 is a demo of an unreleased song from the *Sometime in New York City* sessions. Track 7, basic track with rough vocals. Track 8, demo.

Side B: tracks 2–7 are Dakota recordings. Tracks 5 and 6 are studio recordings from the *Double Fantasy* sessions.

The picture on the front of the sleeve features a teenage John Lennon with the image from the *With the Beatles* album on the back.

082. THE LOST LENNON TAPES – VOLUME 14

Bag Records 5086

Format: 12-inch vinyl

Released: 1989

Source: various – see notes

Sound quality: excellent

Side A

1. Wedding Album commercial (0.10), 2. Stay In Bed (Grow Your Hair) (0.50), 3. Because (2.10), 4. Oh, Yoko (5.49), 5. Grapefruit excerpts (6.20), 6. Imagine (3.00)

Side B

1. Give Me Some Truth (3.34), 2. How? (3.34), 3. San Francisco Bay Blues (1.12), 4. Oh, My Love (2.24), 5. How Do You Sleep (5.52), 6. Tobias Casuals (1.12)

Notes: Side A: track 2, from the official album. Track 3, Beatles outtake – vocals only. Track 4, outtake from the *Imagine* session at Ascot featuring extended ending. Track 5, John and Yoko read excerpts from her book. Track 6, the second outtake taped at Ascot in 1971.

Side B: tracks 1 and 2 are *Imagine* outtakes. Track 3 is an ad lib version taped during the *Imagine* session. Track 4, another *Imagine* session outtake with mistakes in John's vocals and Klaus Voorman's bass lines. Track 5, the second time this song has appeared in *The Lost Lennon Tapes* series and this is a lot nearer to completion than the version on Volume 2.

The front of the sleeve shows a thoughtful Lennon sitting at a typewriter.

083. THE LOST LENNON TAPES – VOLUME 15

Bag Records 5087

Format: 12-inch vinyl

Released: 1989

Source: various – see notes

Sound quality: excellent

Side A

1. I'm Stepping Out (5.40), 2. I'm the Greatest (2.13), 3. Move Over Ms L (1.31), 4. Bring on the Lucie (Freeda People) (0.57), 5. Bring On The Lucy (Freeda People) (3.54), 6. No. 9 Dream (2.07), 7. People (1.51), 8. The Luck of the Irish (0.45), 9. The Luck of the Irish (1.33), 10. Only People (2.39)

Side B

1. Rock 'n' Roll People (2.36), 2. Mind Games promo (0.54), 3. Forgive Me (My Little Flower Princess) (3.21), 4. Tower Records spot (0.57), 5. I Don't Want to Be a Soldier, Mama (I Don't Wanna Die) (5.45), 6. How Do You Sleep? (4.33), 7. Well Baby Please Don't Go (5.59)

Notes: 'I'm Stepping Out' is an alternate version recorded on the first day of the *Double Fantasy* sessions. The demo of 'I'm the Greatest' is from the *Imagine* session and is the second take. 'Move Over Ms L' is the earliest demo with May Pang providing the telephone background. The two versions of 'Bring on the Lucie' are firstly a riff fragment followed by a complete rough mix of the nearly completed track. 'No. 9 Dream' is an early demo. 'People' is a demo of a tune that evolved into 'Angela'. The two versions of 'The Luck of the Irish' are firstly an early attempt with unfinished lyrics and secondly a more polished version. 'Only People' is a rough mix. 'Rock 'n' Roll People' from *Mind Games* is an alternate take. 'Forgive Me (My Little Flower Princess)' is a Dakota demo (take 3).

The final three tracks are from the 1971 *Imagine* session. The album cover shows a colour photograph of John playing his guitar from around 1965.

084. THE LOST LENNON TAPES – VOLUME 16

Bag Records 5088

Format: 12-inch vinyl

Released: 1989

Source: various – see notes

Sound quality: excellent

Side A: (22.34)

1. Move Over Ms L (1.54), 2. Tobias Casuals No 5 (1.15), 3. Clean-up Time (3.32), 4. Forgive Me (My Little Flower Princess) (3.38), 5. Mother (5.34), 6. I'm Stepping Out (4.28), 7. Only the Lonely (2.55)

Side B: (24.00)

1. Radio Free London/Oz Magazine Message (3.22), 2. Rip It Up/Ready Teddy (1.31), 3. I'm Crazy (4.07), 4. Beautiful Boy (3.55), 5. *Walls and Bridges* promo (1.00), 6. Stranger's Room (6.02), 7. Woman (3.44)

Notes: 'Move Over Ms L' is the second demo (see Volume 15 for the first demo). 'Clean-up Time' is a piano demo from the *Double Fantasy* sessions. 'Forgive Me (My Little Flower Princess)' is an alternate take. 'Mother' is an electric guitar demo. 'I'm Stepping Out', 'Beautiful Boy' and 'Woman' are double-tracked guitar demos from the *Double Fantasy* album sessions. 'Only the Lonely' features John using this as an example of an overdub he wants. 'Rip It Up/Ready Teddy' is a rough mix from *Rock 'n' Roll*. 'I'm Crazy' evolved into 'Watching the Wheels'. 'Stranger's Room' is a piano demo of a song that became 'I'm Losing You'.

The album cover shows a front view of John at the keyboards during the 'Instant Karma' promo. The back has a picture of John with Cynthia and a very young Julian plus the track listing and notes on the tracks.

085. THE LOST LENNON TAPES – VOLUME 17

Bag Records 5089

Format: 12-inch vinyl

Released: 1989

Source: various – see notes

Sound quality: excellent

Side A: (22.07)

1. I'm Losing You (3.54), 2. Mailman Bring Me No More Blues (2.35), 3. Peggy Sue (2.06), 4. Cold Turkey (3.58), 5. Dear Yoko (5.54), 6. Bless You (3.50)

Side B: (23.40)

1. Move Over Ms L (2.39), 2. Living on Borrowed Time (4.57), 3. Don't Let Me Down (2.53), 4. Oh, My Love (2.37), 5. Jealous Guy (4.06), 6. Surprise Surprise (2.54), 7. Gone from This Place (3.17)

Notes: 'I'm Losing You' is a rough mix from the *Double Fantasy* sessions. 'Mailman Bring Me No More Blues' is from the film *Clock*. 'Peggy Sue' is a rough mix. 'Cold Turkey' is an acoustic demo, take 1. 'Dear Yoko' is an acoustic demo, takes 2 and 3 are featured on this disc. 'Bless You' is from the *Walls and Bridges* sessions. 'Move Over Ms L' is a hard rocking rough mix. 'Living on Borrowed Time' is a demo from Bermuda. 'Don't Let Me Down' is a 1968 home demo. 'Oh, My Love' and 'Jealous Guy' are rough mixes from *Imagine* session. 'Surprise Surprise' is an acoustic demo. 'Gone from This Place' is take 4 of an unreleased song.

The black-and-white picture on the front of the sleeve shows John in the early days of The Beatles with a colour photo of John and Yoko from their 'Bed Peace' campaign.

086. THE LOST LENNON TAPES – VOLUME 18

Bag Records 5090

Format: 12-inch vinyl

Released: 1991

Source: various – see notes

Sound quality: excellent

Side A: (23.18)

1. Living on Borrowed Time (6.04), 2. Michael Lindsey Hogg talks with John Lennon (0.35), 3. Yer Blues (0.42), 4. Yer Blues (3.59), 5. Don't Let Me Down (2.07), 6. Just Gotta Give Me Some Rock 'n' Roll/Shoeshine (3.37), 9. How Do You Sleep? (5.57)

Side B: (21.30)

1. I Know (3.40), 2. Power to the People (1.18), 3. Love (2.20), 4. Out the Blue (4.04), 5. Bony Moronie (3.51), 6. Be My Baby (5.49)

Notes: 'Living on Borrowed Time' is an early alternate take from the *Double Fantasy* sessions complete with studio talk. The next three tracks are from the shooting of the *Rock and Roll Circus* film on 11 December 1968. Firstly director Michael Lindsey Hogg asks John about his group, The Dirty Macs. Next Lennon and Jagger with an impromptu version of 'Yer Blues' followed by a full rehearsal with the band. This is virtually an instrumental as John's vocal is a long way back in the mix. 'Don't Let Me Down' is a home demo. 'Just Gotta Give Me Some Rock 'n' Roll' and 'Shoeshine' is a medley that later turned into 'Meat City' on the *Mind Games* album. 'How Do You Sleep?' is another alternate take which differs from previous versions. 'I Know' is a rough version and 'Power To the People' is a ragged take with John attempting a reggae vocal. 'Love' is a guitar demo. 'Out the Blue' is a *Mind Games* rough mix. The final two tracks are rough mixes from the *Rock 'n' Roll* session.

A colour picture of John from 1967 is featured on the front of the sleeve with the track listing and notes on the back.

087. THE LOST LENNON TAPES – VOLUME 19

Bag Records 5091

Format: 12-inch vinyl

Released: 1991

Source: various – see notes

Sound quality: excellent

Side A: (21.40)

1. Power to the People (3.45), 2. Oh, Yoko (4.09), 3. What You Got (3.25), 4. Real Love (4.05), 5. Woman (3.22), 6. Cookin' (In The Kitchen of Love) (2.54)

Side B: (22.52)

1. Free as a Bird (3.25), 2. Intuition (2.21), 3. Intuition (2.47), 4. Call My Name (1.25), 5. Call My Name (5.07), 6. Aisumasen (I'm Sorry) (4.42), 7. One of the Boys (3.02)

Notes: 'Power to the People' is an alternate take which is closer to the released take and is not as rough as the version on Volume 18 in this series. 'Oh, Yoko' is another alternate take and was recorded at Tittenhurst Park. 'What You Got' was one of the last songs written for *Walls and Bridges* and is presented on this disc as an acoustic demo. 'Real Love' is an acoustic demo, take 4. 'Woman' is an alternate take from the *Double Fantasy* sessions of summer 1980. 'Cookin'' is a piano demo and was written for Ringo's *Rotogravure* album. 'Free as a Bird' is a piano demo. Two versions of 'Intuition' follow. Firstly a composing demo followed by a rough mix. 'Aisumasen' evolved from the demos of 'Call My Name' and we have two versions here. The first one dates from mid-1971 and is incomplete. This is followed by a full version and a rough mix. The last track is a song from the late 1970s.

The sleeve shows a bearded John Lennon from the early seventies.

088. THE LOST LENNON TAPES – VOLUME 20

Bag Records 5092

Format: 12-inch vinyl

Released: 1991

Source: various – see notes

Sound quality: excellent

Side A: (22.30)

1. Honey Don't (1.52), 2. Glad All Over (0.50), 3. Lend Me Your Comb (1.24), 4. Duane Eddy Jam (0.51), 5. No. 9 Dream (3.11), 6. 12 Bar Original (6.37), 7. Well, Well, Well (1.09), 8. Well, Well, Well (3.33), 9. He Got the Blues (2.33)

Side B: (21.14)

1. Look at Me (3.05), 2. My Mummy's Dead (1.11), 3. Real Life (3.23), 4. Woman Is the Nigger of the World (2.08), 5. Cold Turkey (3.21), 6. I'm Stepping Out (4.47), 7. Watching the Wheels (2.50)

Notes: Tracks 1–4 on Side A: are from the film *Clock*. 'No. 9 Dream' is a more polished version. 'Twelve-Bar Original' is a Beatles recording from the *Rubber Soul* era. This is the full length version. 'Well, Well, Well' is presented on this disc in two versions. Firstly a demo followed by an alternate take from an acetate. 'He Got the Blues' is an acoustic Lennon original from the late 1970s. 'Look at Me' and 'My Mummy's Dead' are *Plastic Ono Band* album outtakes. 'Real Life' is a piano demo. 'Woman Is the Nigger of the World' is an acoustic demo. 'Cold Turkey' is an acoustic demo, take 3. 'I'm Stepping Out' is take 1 from the *Double Fantasy* sessions. Finally, 'Watching the Wheels' is an electric blues style demo.

The sleeve features a colour picture from the film *How I Won the War*.

089. THE LOST LENNON TAPES – VOLUME 21

Bag Records 5093

Format: 12-inch vinyl

Released: 1991

Source: various – see notes

Sound quality: excellent

Side A: (24.01)

1. Run for Your Life (1.16), 2. The Maharishi Song (3.03), 3. Julia (2.54), 4. When a Boy Meets a Girl (2.06), 5. God (2.12), 6. Look at Me (2.49), 7. Oh, Yoko (4.35), 8. How? (4.30)

Side B

1. Imagine (2.55), 2. Jam (0.38), 3. How Do You Sleep? (4.29), 4. Oh, My Love (2.08), 5. Imagine (3.06), 6. J.J. (1.09), 7. Attica State (3.33), 8. Woman Is the Nigger of the World (5.33)

Notes: This edition of *The Lost Lennon Tapes* covers the period 1965 to 1972. 'Run for Your Life' is from The Beatles *Rubber Soul* sessions. 'The Maharishi Song' is a home recording from 1968. 'Julia' is the second tape of a home recording. 'When a Boy Meets a Girl' and 'God' are demos from the *Plastic Ono Band* album – 'Look at Me' is an alternate take. 'Oh, Yoko' is an acoustic demo with Yoko contributing some vocals on the chorus. 'How?' Is a piano demo. 'Jam' is from the *Imagine* session. 'How Do You Sleep?' is an interesting version with John singing an octave lower. 'Oh, My Love' and 'Imagine' are alternate mixes. 'J.J.' was recorded at St. Regis Hotel in 1972 and is an early version of 'Angela'. 'Attica State' has two attempts at an acoustic demo. Finally, 'Woman Is the Nigger of the World' is an alternate version.

A photo of John wearing a white shirt with black dots from the early Beatles days is shown on the front of the sleeve.

090. THE LOST LENNON TAPES – VOLUME 22

Bag Records 5094

Format: 12-inch vinyl

Released: 1991

Source: various – see notes

Sound quality: excellent

Side A: (21.10)
1. Sweet Little Sixteen (4.02), 2. Bless You (5.57), 3. Many Rivers to Cross (3.00), 4. Cookin' (In The Kitchen of Love) (2.33), 5. In My Life (3.12), 6. I Watch Your Face (2.12)

Side B: (22.55)
1. Serve Yourself (6.10), 2. The Worst is Over (2.18), 3. Watching the Wheels (2.50), 4. Beautiful Boy (11.33)

Notes: 'Sweet Little Sixteen' is an alternate take. 'Bless You' is an early rehearsal. From his early days as a 'house husband' comes a home recording of 'Many Rivers to Cross'. 'Cookin'' is a demo of a song given to Ringo for his *Rotogravure* album. 'My Life' and 'I Watch Your Face' are both demos – songs which became 'Starting Over'. 'Serve Yourself' is a piano demo. 'The Worst is Over' is another home demo which also evolved into 'Starting Over'. 'Watching the Wheels' is a blues demo. This set closes with an extended composing tape of 'Beautiful Boy' with the lyrics as they appear on the finished version taking shape.

The front of the sleeve has a colour picture of John from 1967 with a colour picture from the *Salute To Sir Lew Grade* show on the back.

091. THE LOST LENNON TAPES – VOLUME 23

Bag Records 5095

Format: 12-inch vinyl

Released: 1991

Source: various – see notes

Sound quality: excellent

Side A: (21.54)

1. I Don't Want to Face It (1.38), 2. Medley: Beautiful Boy/Howling at the Moon/Dakota Rap/Across the River (5.06), 3. Real Love (2.45), 4. Beautiful Boy (4.02), 5. Clean-up Time (7.56)

Side B: (24.45)

1. Stepping Out (4.42), 2. Beautiful Boy (3.56), 3. Watching the Wheels (3.31), 4. Dear Yoko (2.27), 5. Clean-up Time (4.24), 6. You Saved My Soul (2.37), 7. Illusions (2.43)

Notes: This release contains demos, rehearsals and rough mixes from the *Double Fantasy* era. 'I Don't Want to Face It' is take 1 of an acoustic demo. The medley is set to the beat of John's drum machine. 'Real Love' is take 5 of the acoustic demo. 'Beautiful Boy' is a demo. 'Clean-up Time' on Side A: is a rehearsal. 'Stepping Out' is an alternate take. 'Beautiful Boy', 'Watching the Wheels', 'Dear Yoko' and 'Clean-up Time' are alternate mixes of the album versions. 'You Saved My Soul' evolved into 'Serve Yourself'. 'Illusions' is an unreleased song which made its first appearance on this disc.

The sleeve shows a colour picture of John wearing dark glasses and white cap from 1975.

092. THE LOST LENNON TAPES – VOLUME 24

Bag Records 5096

Format: 12-inch vinyl

Released: 1992

Source: various – see notes

Sound quality: excellent

Side A: (22.22)

1. He Said He Said (2.01), 2. She Said She Said (0.55), 3. Yer Blues (4.31), 4. Oh, My Love (1.24), 5. Oh, My Love (1.19), 6. Because (0.37), 7. Happiness Is a Warm Gun (0.41), 8. Give Peace a Chance (0.38), 9. Give Peace a Chance (2.12), 10. Give Peace a Chance (1.28), 11. Give Peace a Chance (5.22), 12. Give Peace a Chance (0.25)

Side B: (24.43)

1. God (3.41), 2. My Mummy's Dead (0.46), 3. It's So Hard (4.24), 4. Come Together (3.52), 5. Honky Tonk Blues (2.49), 6. I Know (3.14), 7. Rock 'n' Roll People (2.50), 8. Only People (2.44)

Notes: Side A: tracks 1–3 are John's composing tapes from 1966. 'Yer Blues' is take 1 from the *Rock and Roll Circus* film. The two takes of 'Oh, My Love' dates from December 1968. 'Because', 'Happiness Is a Warm Gun' and the first 'Give Peace a Chance' originate from the King Edward Hotel in Toronto on 25 May 1969. Four further outtakes follow. 'God' is an acoustic demo. 'My Mummy's Dead' is a rough mix. 'It's So Hard' is the sax overdub. 'Come Together' and 'Honky Tonk Blues' are One-to-One rehearsals with Elephant's Memory Band. 'I Know' is an acoustic demo (take 3). 'Rock 'n' Roll People' is a rough mix of take 7. 'Only People' is an alternate mix.

The front of the sleeve has a photo of John's Aunt Mimi at home in *Menlove Avenue* sitting reading a newspaper with a framed photograph of John on top of the television.

093. THE LOST LENNON TAPES – VOLUME 25

Bag Records 5097

Format: 12-inch vinyl

Released: 1992

Source: various – see notes

Sound quality: excellent

Side A: (21.26)

1. Whatever Gets You Through the Night (2.52), 2. Steel and Glass (5.11), 3. Beef Jerky (3.18), 4. You Saved My Soul (1.29), 5. Serve Yourself (8.25)

Side B: (20.50)

1. Memories (3.30), 2. Real Life (3.18), 3. Watching the Wheels (3.15), 4. Don't Be Crazy (3.07), 5. Woman (2.43), 6. (Just Like) Starting Over (4.14), 7. I Don't Want to Face It (0.43)

Notes: 'Whatever Gets You Through the Night' is an acoustic demo from June 1974. 'Steel and Glass' and 'Beef Jerky' are from the *Walls and Bridges* 8-track. 'You Saved My Soul' is an electric guitar demo from November 1980. 'Serve Yourself' is a piano demo. Other takes of this song feature on other volumes of *The Lost Lennon Tapes* series. 'Memories' is take 1 of a piano demo. 'Real Life' is a piano demo from 1977. 'Watching the Wheels' and 'Don't Be Crazy' are piano versions from the mid-1980s. 'Don't Be Crazy' later evolved into 'Starting Over'. 'Woman' is a Bermuda demo from June 1980. 'Starting Over' is an acoustic demo from the Dakota. 'I Don't Want to Face It' is an early guitar demo recorded at the Dakota in late 1977.

The front of the sleeves features an early photograph of John and Cynthia with a reproduction of the film poster from *How I Won the War* on the back plus the track listing and notes.

094. THE LOST LENNON TAPES – VOLUME 26

Bag Records 5098

Format: 12-inch vinyl

Released: 1992

Source: various – see notes

Sound quality: excellent

Side A: (22.13)

1. Nobody Told Me (3.13), 2. Real Love (3.09), 3. I'm Losing You (4.20), 4. Beautiful Boy (7.23), 5. Nobody Told Me (3.59)

Side B: (22.19)

1. Clean-up Time (4.35), 2. Starting Over (3.58), 3. Lennon's Lost Diary Tape (13.36)

Notes: 'Nobody Told Me' is a double-tracked demo, probably dating from summer 1980. 'Real Love' is a piano demo. 'I'm Losing You' is the abandoned early studio version featuring Rick Nielson and Bun E. Carlos of Cheap Trick from late July or early August 1980. 'Beautiful Boy' is John teaching the session musicians. This is take 1 from the vocal booth recorded at The Hit Factory in New York in August 1980. 'Nobody Told Me' is from the vocal booth. 'Clean-up Time' is a rough mix of the backing track. 'Lennon's Lost Diary Tape' is John's personal diary tape from September 1979. This tape was thought to be too revealing to be included in the original radio broadcast series of *The Lost Lennon Tapes*.

The colour sleeve shows a bearded John on the front wearing his glasses and a trilby hat. The track listing and notes are shown on the back cover.

095. THE LOST LENNON TAPES – VOLUME 27

Bag Records 5099

Format: 12-inch vinyl

Released: 1992

Source: various – see notes

Sound quality: excellent

Side A

1. If I Fell, 2. I Sat Belonely, 3. The National Health, Foyle Speech, 4. Strawberry Fields Forever, 5. Get It Together, 6. Happy Christmas, 7. Power to the People, 8. Don't Be Cruel, 9. Hound Dog, 10. I'm the Greatest

Side B

1. I Know, 2. Rock 'n' Roll People, 3. Meat City, 4. Meat City, 5. Meat City, 6. One Day at a Time, 7. Only People

Notes: A collection of items from various sources. Side B: features outtakes from the *Mind Games* album. 'Get It Together' is an acoustic guitar rendition from the Montreal Bed-In.

096. THE LOST LENNON TAPES – VOLUME 28

Bag Records 5100

Format: 12-inch vinyl

Released: 1992

Source: various – see notes

Sound quality: excellent

Side A

1. Tight A$, 2. You Are Here, 3. Going Down on Love, 4. No. 9 Dream, 5. Whatever Gets You Through the Night, 6. Surprise Surprise (Sweet Bird of Paradox)

Side B

1. John on KHJ-AM LA, 2. Do You Wanna Dance, 3. You Can't Catch Me, 4. Free as a Bird, 5. Serve Yourself, 6. She'll Be Coming Round the Mountain, 7. She Runs Them Round In Circles, 8. Beautiful Boy

Notes: A collection of items from various sources. Side A: features outtakes from the *Walls and Bridges* album.

097. THE LOST LENNON TAPES – VOLUME 29

Bag Records 5101

Format: 12-inch vinyl

Released: 1992

Source: various – see notes

Sound quality: excellent

Side A

1. Memories, 2. Watching the Wheels, 3. Stranger's Room, 4. Woman, 5. Woman, 6. I'm Stepping Out, 7. (Just Like) Starting Over

Side B

1. Dream Lover, 2. Stay, 3. Clean-up Time, 4. Beautiful Boy, 5. Watching the Wheels, 6. Borrowed Time, 7. I'm Stepping Out, 8. Woman

Notes: This volume concentrated on outtakes and demos from the *Double Fantasy* sessions.

098. THE LOST LENNON TAPES – VOLUME 30

Bag Records 5102

Format: 12-inch vinyl

Released: 1992

Source: various – see notes

Sound quality: excellent

Side A: (22.40)

1. It's Not Too Bad (3.29), 2. She Can Talk to Me (0.46), 3. Cry Baby Cry (3.23), 4. *Two Virgins* outtake (1.47), 5. Plastic Ono Band Jam (1.39), 6. Look at Me (2.52), 7. I'm the Greatest (0.37), 8. How?/Child of Nature/Oh, Yoko (4.25), 9. Oh, Yoko (3.23)

Side B: (22.17)

1. Sally and Billy (2.03), 2. Come Together (1.47), 3. Happy Girl (1.10), 4. I'll Make You Happy (3.56), 5. How Do You Sleep? (3.45), 6. It's So Hard (4.44), 7. I Don't Want to Be a Soldier Mama (I Don't Want to Die) (4.34)

Notes: This volume starts with three demo tracks recorded in Spain in late 1966. 'It's Not Too Bad' became 'Strawberry Fields Forever'. The early piano demo of 'She Can Talk to Me' became 'Hey Bulldog'. 'Cry Baby Cry' is comprised of early piano and electric demo fragments. The 'Two Virgins' outtake is John and Yoko playing around in his home studio. 'Plastic Ono Band Jam' is a send up of Fifties rockabilly. 'Look at Me' is an outtake from *Plastic Ono Band* album sessions with alternate vocals. 'I'm the Greatest' and the medley of 'How?'/'Child of Nature'/'Oh, Yoko' and 'Oh, Yoko' and 'Sally and Billy' are all piano demos recorded in December 1970. 'Come Together' is from the One-To-One rehearsals in August 1972. From just prior to the *Mind Games* era we have Yoko's

'Happy Girl' and John's 'I'll Make You Happy' (which includes some lyrics from 'Cold Turkey').

This set concludes with some music from the *Imagine* session. Firstly, rehearsals of 'How Do You Sleep?' followed by more run-throughs from the King Curtis sax overdub sessions in New York for 'It's So Hard' and 'I Don't Wanna Be A Soldier'.

The front of the sleeve has a colour photo of John probably from 1965 with two black-and-white photos on the back – John as a young boy with his mother and his Aunt Mimi holding a car.

099. THE LOST LENNON TAPES – VOLUME 31
Bag Records 5103
Format: 12-inch vinyl
Released: 1992
Source: various – see notes
Sound quality: excellent

Side A: (22.58)
1. Intuition (3.04), 2. I Know (3.00), 3. I Know (3.43), 4. Aisumasen (I'm Sorry) (3.43), 5. Steel and Glass (1.44), 6. *Walls and Bridges* Rundown (1.56), 7. Mirror Mirror (On the Wall) (4.34)

Side B: (22.50)
1. Tennessee (2.26), 2. Memories (6.03), 3. Sally and Billy (3.28), 4. She is a Friend of Dorothy (3.55), 5. The Boat Song (2.08), 6. Pedro the Fisherman (1.04), 7. Many Rivers to Cross part 2/My Girl (2.24), 8. Instrumental 1979 (1.02)

Notes: 'Intuition' is take 4 of a series of piano demos. 'I Know' is take 2 of a series of guitar demos. 'Aisumasen' is a near final mix. 'Steel and Glass' is a dark piano version featuring extra lyrics. To promote the *Walls and Bridges* album John called a Canadian radio station and gave a run down of the album's contents. 'Mirror Mirror (On the Wall)' is take 2 of the piano demos. 'Tennessee', 'Memories' and 'Sally and Billy' are home demos from 1976. 'She is a Friend of Dorothy' is from 1977. Lennon explores a nautical theme in the piano demos 'The Boat Song' and 'Pedro the Fisherman'. 'Many Rivers to Cross' is part of a demo and has John doodling on the old Motown song 'My Girl'.

The front of the sleeve shows Tittenhurst Park, John's home in the late Sixties and early Seventies. The back has the track listing and notes.

100. THE LOST LENNON TAPES – VOLUME 32

Bag Records 5104

Format: 12-inch vinyl

Released: 1992

Source: various – see notes

Sound quality: excellent

Side A: (22.03)
1. I'm Stepping Out (1.29), 2. Dear Yoko (5.04), 3. Woman (4.26), 4. Woman (1.54), 5. Woman (2.13), 6. Clean-up Time (6.01)

Side B: (22.48)
1. Nobody Told Me (3.51), 2. I Am the Walrus/Watching the Wheels (4.01), 3. Woman (2.26), 4. Woman (3.39), 5. Living on Borrowed Time (4.20), 6. I'm Losing You (3.54)

Notes: The focus of this album is the *Double Fantasy* sessions which began on 6 August 1980. 'I'm Stepping Out' is an incomplete take. 'Dear Yoko' is interrupted when John breaks a string on his guitar. 'Woman' is presented in three stages. 'Clean-up Time' is a rehearsal. 'Nobody Told Me' is a run through of a song which would be released on the *Milk and Honey* album. 'Watching the Wheels' is preceded by a brief parody of 'I Am the Walrus'.

The first version of 'Woman' on Side B: is an instrumental which is followed by an alternate take. 'Borrowed Time', also destined for *Milk and Honey*, is an early take. 'I'm Losing You' is an alternate take followed by some studio chat.

The front cover has a picture of John with a small picture of John and Sean on the back with the track listing and notes on the tracks.

101. THE LOST LENNON TAPES – VOLUME 33

Bag Records 5105

Format: 12-inch vinyl

Released: 1992

Source: various – see notes

Sound quality: excellent

Side A: (23.28)

1. Imagine (2.57), 2. How Do You Sleep? (2.53), 3. J.J. (1.11), 4. Rock Island Line/Maybe Baby/Peggy Sue (3.50), 5. Out the Blue (3.15), 6. Old Dirt Road (4.52), 7. Steel and Glass (4.15)

Side B: (21.58)

1. Whatever Gets You Through the Night (3.30), 2. Rock 'n' Roll radio spot (1.02), 3. Stand By Me (4.09), 4. Serve Yourself (3.17), 5. Everybody (2.48), 6. Everybody/Nobody Told Me (3.11), 7. Nobody Told Me (3.49)

Notes: This set opens with two songs from the *Imagine* session in June 1971. 'Imagine' has an alternate vocal track. 'How Do You Sleep?' is a run through which breaks down. 'J.J.' is the second demo in this series. The medley of 'Rock Island Line'/'Maybe Baby'/'Peggy Sue' is from footage shot by an ABC news crew prior to the One-To-One Concert. 'Out the Blue' is the third rough mix. 'Old Dirt Road' and 'Steel and Glass' are off line monitor mixes from the July 1974 Record Plant sessions. 'Whatever Gets You Through the Night' is a rough mix minus Elton John. 'Stand By Me' is from *The Old Grey Whistle Test*. 'Serve Yourself' is a gospel style piano demo. This disc concludes with a series of demos for 'Nobody Told Me'. 'Everybody' dates from 1975–76 and is performed on piano with drum machine. The last track is take 2.

A colour photo of John from his Beatles days is shown on the front of the sleeve with the track listing and detailed notes on the back.

102. THE LOST LENNON TAPES – VOLUME 34

Bag Records 5106

Format: 12-inch vinyl

Released: 1992

Source: various – see notes

Sound quality: excellent

Side A: (24.15)

1. Falling In Love Again, 2. Cathy's Clown, 3. You Send You, 4. Real Love, 5. My Life, 6. My Life, 7. Dear Yoko, 8. I'm Stepping Out

Side B: (20.50)

I'm Stepping Out

Notes: This disc comprises outtakes and demos from the *Double Fantasy* sessions. 'Falling In Love Again' is an acoustic demo. 'Cathy's Clown' and 'You Send Me' are early takes. 'Real Love' is a demo. There are two versions of 'My Life' – firstly on piano and then a guitar version. 'Dear Yoko' is a composing run through. 'I'm Stepping Out' on Side A: is an overdub for take 1. Side B: comprises twenty minutes of control room tape sessions from 6 August 1980.

The front of the sleeve shows a black-and-white photo of John from the *Imagine* period.

103. THE LOST LENNON TAPES – VOLUME 35

Bag Records 5107

Format: 12-inch vinyl

Released: 1992

Source: various – see notes

Sound quality: excellent

Side A: (22.20)

1. I'm Stepping Out, 2. Borrowed Time

Side B: (22.20)

1. I Don't Wanna Face it, 2. Watching the Wheels, 3. Beautiful Boy, 4. (Just Like) Starting Over, 5. (Just Like) Starting Over

Notes: 'I'm Stepping Out' on Side A: is a studio run through. 'Borrowed Time' is a session tape. 'I Don't Wanna Face It' is a rough mix. 'Watching the Wheels' is a session tape. 'Beautiful Boy' is an alternate take. This set concludes with two versions of 'Starting Over'. Firstly a monitor mix is followed by a rough mix of the basic track.

104. MAKE LOVE TO THE END

SST

Format: European numbered silver 45 rpm flexi

Source: unknown – possibly Montreal Bed-In

Sound quality: excellent mono

Make Love to the End

Notes: It is claimed that this disc includes Yoko Ono, Ringo Starr and Mal Evans. There seems no evidence to support this. See also disc below. There are rumours that this odd 'tune' was recorded during the Montreal Bed-In.

105. MAKE LOVE TO THE END

SHOL 2481

Format: 7-inch one sided flexi 45 rpm

Source: unknown – possibly Montreal Bed-In

Sound quality: excellent mono

Make Love to the End

Notes: It is claimed that this disc includes Yoko Ono, Ringo Starr and Mal Evans. There seems no evidence to support this. See also disc above. There are rumours that this odd 'tune' was recorded during the Montreal Bed-In.

106. Man of the Decade

MOTD 1269

Format: Single sided 12-inch vinyl

Source: all songs are official releases

Sound quality: excellent mono

1. Give Peace a Chance (1.03), 2. Reporter (1.27), 3. If I Fell (1.06), 4. Lennon (0.07), 5. Reporter (0.41), 6. *A Hard Day's Night* Train Scene (1.42), 7. Reporter (0.22), 8. Live At The Shea: I'm Down, 9. Lennon On Acid (0.36), 10. All You Need Is Love (0.52), 11. Lennon (1.00), 12. Give Peace a Chance (0.11), 13. Lennon (1.00), 14. Lennon from Bed-Interview (1.54), 15, Reporter (1.00), 16. Lennon (1.25), 17. Reporter (0.45), 18. Lennon (2.00), 19. All You Need Is Love (0.12), 20. Reported (1.10), 21. Studio Toga (4.10)

Notes: Black-and-white deluxe cover made to look like an Italian promo.

107. The Master Showman

168 High A21250

Format: 12-inch vinyl

Released: 1986

Source: various

Sound quality: excellent mono and stereo

Side A

1. Slippin' and Slidin', 2. Imagine, 3. Mucho Mungo (take 1), 4. Mucho Mungo (take 2), 5. Mucho Mungo (take 3), 6. Do the Oz, 7. Will You Touch Me, 8. Feeling, 9. Yellow Girl

Side B

1. Yer Blues, 2. John Sinclair, 3. Dog Town (guitar version), 4. Dog Town (piano version), 5. Stand By Me, 6. Love

108. The May Pang Tapes

Beetle Records LEN 4080

Format: 12-inch vinyl

Released: 1985
Source: *Rock 'n' Roll* album sessions
Sound quality: good to very good mono

Side A

1. Ain't That a Shame (1.01), 2. Bring It on Home to Me/Send Me Some Lovin' (3.33), 3. Ya Ya (2.33), 4. That'll Be the Day (2.25), 5. Do You Want to Dance (3.15), 6. Stand By Me (3.28), 7. Ain't That a Shame (2.32)

Side B

1. Do You Want to Dance (3,33), 2. Medley: Rip It Up/Ready Teddy (1.26), 3. Peggy Sue (2.06), 4. Be-Bop-A-Lula (1.48), 5. Slippin' and Slidin' (excerpt) (1.54), 6. Guitar Jam including Rumble (0.44) and Whole Lotta Love (0.09) (1.58), 7. Thirty Days (0.59), 8. Slippin' and Slidin' (2.07)

Notes: These recordings were known as *The May Pang Tapes* because they were recorded during the period John was with her. The rehearsals for the *Rock 'n' Roll album* took place on 21–24 October 1974 with Phil Spector.

Laminated colour sleeve. Many tracks have count-ins and false starts. See also *A Collection of Rock 'n' Roll Rehearsals*.

109. THE MAY PANG TAPES

May

Format: 12-inch vinyl

Released: 1965

Source: *Rock 'n' Roll* album sessions

Sound quality: fair – inferior to original

Notes: Reissue in a plain white sleeve with rubber stamped title. The track list included is a photocopy of the original sleeve.

110. THE MAY PANG TAPES

QS 85022

Format: 12-inch vinyl

Released: 1965

Source: *Rock 'n' Roll* album sessions

Sound quality fair – inferior to original

Notes: Another reissue but this time with the same full colour sleeve as the original. Disc is pressed on green vinyl.

111. MEMORIES

MacLen-Hawk Records 8RCH-11-22

Format: 12-inch vinyl (double)

Source: various

Sound quality: very good

Notes: This two-disc set in a black-and-white sleeve is a reissue of *Archives* (Volumes 1 and 2)

112. MYSTERY BOX (FRANK ZAPPA)

Nifty Tuff and Bitchen 8611

See *Randomonium*.

113. NOW HEAR THIS

Unknown

Format: 12-inch vinyl

Source: Free John Sinclair Rally, 18 December 1971

Sound quality: unknown

Notes: Reissue of *Ann Arbor: Now Hear This*.

114. OFF THE WALLS

Trade Mark of Quality JFK 72174-2

Format: 12-inch vinyl

Released: 1987

Source: rehearsals for *Walls and Bridges* album. Recorded at the Record Plant, Sunday afternoon, 21 July 1974

Sound quality: very good

Side A

1. Bless You (5.20), 2. Move Over Ms L (2.45), 3. Scared (4.47), 4. Surprise Surprise (Sweet Bird of Paradox) (3.00), 5. Whatever Gets You Through the Night (3.11), 6. Going Down on Love (3.51)

Side B

1. Nobody Loves You (When You're Down and Out) (5.00), 2. What You Got (7.31), 3. Old Dirt Road (5.00), 4. Steel and Glass (5.56)

Notes: Sleeve says, 'Produced by John Lennon'. Cover features one of John's sketch drawings. The back has four photographs and track listing. 'What You Got' (Side B:, track 2) comprised three outtakes. Re-released on white vinyl. A further album was released featuring outtakes from the *Walls and Bridges* rehearsals titled *Something Precious and Rare*.

115. ONCE UPON A TIME

Unknown JOL-40-801

Format: 12-inch vinyl

Source: various – see notes

Sound quality: varies – see notes

Side A

1. Mother (chimes only) (0.22), 2. Blue Suede Shoes (2.07), 3. Take This Hammer (2.53), 4. I Sat Belonely (0.45), 5. Oh, My Love (2.49), 6. Gimme Some Truth (0.54), 7. Jealous Guy (Child of Nature version) (1.51), 8. Yer Blues (0.30), 9. Yer Blues (8.45), 10. What's the New Mary Jane (6.35)

Side B

1. (Just Like) Starting Over (chimes only) (0.05), 2. Love (3.09), 3. I Found Out (3.44), 4. I'm the Greatest (3.38), 5. I Saw Her Standing There (3.20), 6. Whatever Gets You Through the Night (1.47), 7. Mucho Mungo (3.39), 8. Lady Marmalade (1.25), 9. Walking on Thin Ice (5.56)

Notes: Side A: tracks 2, 3, 6 and 7 from The Beatles *Get Back* sessions (very good to excellent mono/stereo). Track 4, John reading poetry. Track 5, *Imagine* session (good mono). Track 8, ad-lib version with Mick

Jagger from *Rock and Roll Circus* sessions. Track 9 from *Rock and Roll Circus*, 11 December 1968 (excellent stereo). Track 10, different version. Side B: track 2, remix from 1982 with piano brought forward (excellent stereo). Track 3, album version with longer fade out (Australian pressing). Track 4, demo with Ringo. Track 5, probably a rehearsal with Elton John for the live performance on 28 November 1974 (excellent stereo). Track 6, *Walls and Bridges* sessions 13 July 1974 (excellent stereo). Track 7, from *Pussycats* sessions. Track 8, from interview. Track 9, from US 45 release (GEF 49683) (excellent stereo).

116. ONCE UPON A TIME

JOL 40-80
Format: 12-inch vinyl
Released: 1985
Source: various
Sound quality: fair to very good

Side A

1. Mother (chimes only), 2. Blue Suede Shoes, 3. Take This Hammer, 4. I Sat Belonely, 5. Oh, My Love, 6. Gimme Some Truth, 7. Jealous Guy, 8. Yer Blues Intro, 9. What's the New Mary Jane

Side B

1. Love, 2. I Found Out, 3. Happy Xmas, 4. I'm the Greatest, 5. I Saw Her Standing There, 6. Whatever Gets You Through the Night, 6. Mucho Mungo, 7. Voulez Vous Coucher Avec Moi, 8. Walking on Thin Ice

Notes: 'Yer Blues' is from *Rock and Roll Circus*. Tracks include recordings from the *Get Back* sessions. Almost the same track listing as the disc above.

117. ONE AND ONE AND ONE IS THREE – PART ONE

John Lennon, Yoko Ono and The Elephant's Memory Band
Benefit Records 001
Format: 12-inch vinyl
Released: 1985

Source: rehearsals for the two One-to-One concerts, Madison Square Garden, New York on 23 August 1972

Sound quality: very good

Side A

1. Instrumental, 2. New York City, 3. It's So Hard, 4. Move On Fast, 5. Woman Is the Nigger of the World

Side B

1. Sisters Oh Sisters, 2. Give Peace a Chance, 3. Instrumental

118. ONE AND ONE AND ONE IS THREE – PART TWO

John Lennon, Yoko Ono and The Elephant's Memory Band

Benefit Records 002

Format: 12-inch vinyl

Released: 1985

Source: rehearsals for the two One-to-One concerts, Madison Square Garden, New York on 23 August 1972

Sound quality: very good

Side A

1. Unchained Melody, 2. Well, Well, Well, 3. Born in a Prison, 4. Instant Karma

Side B

1. Mother, 2. We're All Water, 3. Come Together, 4. Open Your Box

119. ONE AND ONE AND ONE IS THREE – PART THREE

John Lennon, Yoko Ono and The Elephant's Memory Band

Benefit Records 003

Format: 12-inch vinyl

Released: 1985

Source: rehearsals for the two One-to-One concerts, Madison Square Garden, New York on 23 August 1972

Sound quality: very good

Side A

1. Cold Turkey, 2. Don't Worry Kyoko, 3. Instrumental, 4. Instrumental

Side B

1. We're All Water, 2. Roll Over Beethoven, 3. Give Peace a Chance

Notes: These three albums were all available separately. The sleeve describes the band as 'also known as Plastic Ono Elephant's Memory Band. 'Don't Worry, Kyoko' is not listed on the sleeve. The musicians were: John Lennon – guitar and vocals, Yoko Ono – vocals, Stan Bronstein – sax, Gary Van Scyox – bass, Adam Ippolito – keyboards, Rick Frank – drums, Wayne Tex Gabriel – guitar.

All three albums feature the same photo on the sleeve of John and Yoko from the 'Bed-In' period both giving the peace sign.

120. ONE AND ONE AND ONE IS THREE

John Lennon, Yoko Ono and The Elephant's Memory Band

Benefit Records 001/002/003

Format: 12-inch vinyl (three discs)

Released: 1985

Source: rehearsals for the two One-to-One concerts, Madison Square Garden, New York on 23 August 1972

Sound quality: very good

Notes: A reissue in the same sleeves as the original release but this time on coloured vinyl. *Volume One – Red, Volume Two – Blue, Volume Three – Orange.*

121. ONE + ONE CONCERT + MORE

Wizardo Records WRMB 301

Format; 12-inch vinyl

Source: One-to-One concert, Free John Sinclair

Rally and original recordings

Sound quality: unknown

Side A

1. Imagine, 2. Come Together, 3. Instant Karma, 4. Cold Turkey, 5. Mother, 6. Give Peace a Chance

Side B

1. Attica State, 2. The Luck of the Irish, 3. John Sinclair, 4. God Save Us, 5. Power to the People

Notes: Side A: One-to-One concert. Side B: tracks 1–3, John Sinclair Benefit Concert. Tracks 4 and 5 are original recordings. The photocopied sleeve includes the track listing

122. ONE/ONE

Cumbat R1-3665/WE 3949 AX

Format: 12-inch vinyl

Source: John Sinclair Rally and One-to-One concert

Sound quality: unknown

Side A

1. John Sinclair, 2. Attica State, 3. Oh Sisters, 4. The Luck of the Irish

Side B

1. Mother, 2. We're All Water, 3. Imagine, 4. Come Together, 5. Give Peace a Chance

123. ONE-TO-ONE CONCERT

CBM 3665

Format: 12-inch vinyl

Source: One-to-One concert and Free John Sinclair Rally

Sound quality: unknown

Side A

1. Mother, 2. Yoko Sings, 3. Come Together, 4. Give Peace a Chance, 5. Imagine

Side B

1. Attica State, 2. The Luck of the Irish, 3. Oh Sisters

Notes: Side A: One-to-One concert at Madison Square Garden on 30 August 1972. Side B: John Sinclair Rally held in Attica State, Ann Arbor, Michigan on 10 December 1971. Track 2 on Side A: described as 'Yoko Sings' is probably 'We're All Water'.

124. ONE-TO-ONE CONCERT

RT 34

Format: 12-inch vinyl

Source: One-to-One concert, Madison Square Garden, New York, 30 August 1972 (Evening Show)

Sound quality: poor–fair

Side A

1. Imagine, 2. Mother, 3. Come Together, 4. Instant Karma, 5. Cold Turkey, 6. Hound Dog

Side B

1. New York City, 2. It's So Hard, 3. Woman Is the Nigger of the World, 4. Well, Well, Well, 5. Give Peace a Chance

Notes: Plain white sleeve with glued on insert. German bootleg with limited run of 300 copies.

125. ONLY YOU/SEND ME SOME LOVIN'

Love Devotion Records LS)!

Format: 7-inch vinyl 45 rpm

Source: as below

Sound quality: very good stereo

Side A

Only You (Roots outtake)

Side B

Send Me Some Lovin' (*Rock 'n' Roll* outtake)

126. PLOP PLOP... FIZZ FIZZ

Sean Mark HAR 170

Format: 12-inch vinyl – issued on multi colour blue vinyl

Source: various – see notes

Sound quality: unknown

Side A

1. Mother, 2. Imagine, 3. Come Together, 4. Give Peace a Chance

Side B

1. Cold Turkey, 2. Hound Dog, 3. Slippin' and Slidin', 4. Imagine, 5. Whatever Gets You Through the Night, 6. Move Over Ms L

Notes: Side A: One-to-One concert, 30 August 1972 (Afternoon Show). Side B: tracks 1 and 2, One-to-One concert, 30 August 1972 (Evening Show). Tracks 3 and 4, *Salute To Sir Lew Grade* 13 June 1975. Track 5, with Elton John at Madison Square Garden, New York on 25 November 1974.

127. RANDOMONIUM (FRANK ZAPPA)

Nifty Tuff and Bitchen 8611

Format: 12-inch vinyl (ten disc box set)

Released: 1988

Source: see notes

Sound quality: fair audience tape

Well (Baby Please Don't Go)

Notes: This album was included as part of a Frank Zappa ten-disc boxset titled *Mystery Box* which is the only place it can be found. Included on this record is the full length version of 'Well (Baby Please Don't Go)' which was performed by John and Yoko with Frank Zappa and The Mothers on 6 June 1971. An edited version can be found on the official release *Sometime In New York City* (Apple Records) which runs 4 minutes 50 seconds. This version is the full 7 minutes 47 seconds. In 1992 Frank Zappa released his *Psychotic Playground* album which contained a longer version of 'Baby (Please Don't Go)' plus remixes of 'Scumbag, Jamrag and Au'. Also included were two previously unreleased songs, 'Say Please' and 'Aaak'. Three different mixes of the Lennon and Zappa live items can be found on the two CD set *The Fillmore Tapes* (Masters of Orange) – the no editing version direct from mixing board, the Frank Zappa mix and the original Lennon mix.

128. RAVE ON

Toasted Records Works TRW 1941

Format: 12-inch vinyl (double)

Source: various

Sound quality: very good to excellent

Side A

1. Cold Turkey (demo), 2. Cold Turkey (alternate take), 3. I'm the Greatest (demo), 4. Make Love Not War (demo), 5. I Promise (demo), 6. Help (piano run through), 7. Love (alternate take), 8. God (demo fragment)

Side B

1. Sally and Billy (demo), 2. Power to the People (outtake), 3. Power to the People (alternate take), 4. God Save Us (demo), 5. God Save Us (studio demo from acetates), 6. I'm the Greatest (studio demo), 7. Imagine (take 1), 8. Crippled Inside (alternate take)

Side C

1. Jealous Guy (alternate take), 2. It's So Hard (raw version), 3. How Do You Sleep? (extended alternate take), 4. Send Me Some Loving, 5. Maybe Baby, 6. Rave On

Side D

1. Not Fade Away, 2. Heartbeat/Peggy Sue Got Married, 3. Peggy Sue, 4. New York City, 5. The Luck of the Irish (demo), 6. Attica State, 7. The Luck of the Irish, 8. John Sinclair

Notes: Side C: tracks 4–6 and Side D tracks 1–4 were recorded at St. Regis Hotel, New York. Side D: tracks 6–8 are the John Sinclair Benefit Concert. Later issued on compact disc.

129. RECOVERED TRACKS

Barnoby Records FF-9

Format: 12-inch vinyl (double)

Source: various – Lennon's contributions as listed below

Sound quality: very good to excellent

Side A

John talks about 'How Do You Do It' (source unknown) (0.43), John talks about 'I Wanna Be Your Man' (WNEW-FM, 28 September 1974) (0.33)

Side D

Kenny Everett interview 1968 (includes 'Cottonfields', 'Goodbye Jingle', 'Tiny Tim For President') (6.36)

Notes: A compilation of items from several sources including Beatles tracks. The Kenny Everett interview appears in a more complete form than most previous releases.

130. ROCK AND ROLL CIRCUS

RRE 101

Format: 12-inch vinyl

Source: *Rock and Roll Circus*, 11 December 1968

Sound quality: unknown

Side A

Track 1 – Yer Blues

Notes: John's only contribution is 'Yer Blues'.

131. ROLLING STONES ROCK AND ROLL CIRCUS

Unknown

Format: 12-inch vinyl

Source: *Rock and Roll Circus*, 11 December 1968
Sound quality: unknown

Side B
4. Yer Blues

Notes: All tracks are by The Rolling Stones except 'Yer Blues' which is Lennon.

132. ROOTS JOHN LENNON SINGS THE GREAT ROCK AND ROLL HITS

Adam VIII A8018
Format: 12-inch vinyl
Released: 1975
Source: *Rock 'n' Roll* session
Sound quality: excellent

Side A
1. Be-Bop-A-Lula, 2. Ain't That a Shame, 3. Stand By Me, 4. Sweet Little Sixteen, 5. Rip It Up, 6. Angel Baby, 7. Do You Want to Dance, 8. You Can't Catch Me

Side B
1. Bony Moronie, 2. Peggy Sue, 3. Bring It on Home to Me, 4. Slippin' and Slidin', 5. Be My Baby, 6. Ya Ya, 7. Just Because

Notes: In early 1975, Adam VIII Records of New York started to advertise a new John Lennon album. This was only available through TV mail order. Morris Levy, who was the owner of Adam VIII, claimed he had made a deal with John Lennon who authorised the release of the *Roots* album which had been produced by Levy from an early mixed tape of the *Rock 'n' Roll* session. John then sued Levy claiming that the release was illegal. When it got to court, Lennon admitted he had given Levy a tape being 'a rough mix' but no deal had been finalised. A court order banned Adam VIII from advertising or selling any more copies of *Roots*. The original album is quite rare as apparently only 2,500 copies were produced plus 500 copies of an 8-track cartridge. Apple/Capital soon rush released their own *Rock 'n' Roll album*. The *Roots* album contained different mixes and longer fade outs together with two songs, 'Angel Baby' and 'Be My Baby', which were not on the Apple release. Counterfeit copies of the album became available.

These can be detected as the spine says 'John Lennon Sings Greatest Rock 'n' Roll Hits' instead of as on the original 'John Lennon Sings the Great Rock 'n' Roll Hits'. However recent counterfeit have corrected the spine to read 'Great' which obviously makes it more difficult to detect the original from a counterfeit. The front cover shows a picture of John against a yellow background with the track listing down the right hand side.

133. ROOTS

King Kong

Format: 12-inch vinyl

Source: *Rock 'n' Roll* session

Sound quality: excellent stereo

Side A

1. Be-Bop-A-Lula, 2. Ain't That a Shame, 3. Stand By Me, 4. Sweet Little Sixteen, 5. Gonna Shake It Up Tonight, 6. Angel Baby, 7. Do You Want to Dance, 8. Don't Catch Me

Side B

1. Bony Marony, 2. Peggy Sue, 3. Bring Your Sweet Loving Home To Me, 4. Slippin' and Slidin', 5. Be My Baby Tonight, 6. Sitting In My La La Waiting For My Ya Ya, 7. Darling I Would Rather Let You Go

Notes: This release is a pirate of the *Adam VIII* album. A number of the titles shown on the album sleeve as listed above are incorrect as follows: 'Gonna Shake it up Tonight' is 'Rip It Up'. 'Don't Catch Me' is 'You Can't Catch Me'. 'Bony Marony' is 'Bony Moronie', 'Bring Your Sweet Loving Home To Me' is 'Bring It on Home to Me'. 'Be My Baby Tonight' is 'Be My Baby'. 'Sitting In My La La Waiting For My Ya Ya' is 'Ya Ya'. 'Darling I Would Rather Let You Go' is just 'Because'.

134. SERVE YOURSELF

Love and Peace Records Bag 009

Format: 12-inch vinyl

Released: 1984

Source: various as below

Sound quality: very good

Side A

1. I'm the Greatest (complete rehearsal from 1973 with George Harrison, Ringo Starr and Klaus Voorman).

Side B

1. Yer Blues (*Rock and Roll Circus*, 11 December 1968), 2. Serve Yourself (1980 acoustic version)

Notes: Front cover features colour picture of John probably from 1980. This disc included a version of 'Serve Yourself' for the first time. There was some discussion whether this was, in fact, by John Lennon but further releases with different versions of this song have confirmed that this is a Lennon outtake.

135. SERVE YOURSELF

Karma Records DD1 D183

Format: 7-inch vinyl 45 rpm

Released: 1983

Source: see blow

Sound quality: very good stereo

Side A

Serve Yourself (3.51)

Side B

John and Yoko interview (Everson Museum, 6 October 1971) (35.59)

Notes: Limited edition 1,400 copies. Black-and-white sleeve.

136. SNAP SHOTS

Gnat Records/Paper Plane Music GN70083-1

Format: 12-inch vinyl (double)

Released: 1984

Source: various

Sound quality: excellent mono and stereo

Disc One

Side A

1. Some Other Guy, 2. Keep Your Hands off My Baby, 3. Honey Don't, 4. Twist and Shout, 5. Voulez Vous, 6. Be My Baby, 7. Angel Baby

Side B

1. All I Want Is You, 2. Blue Suede Shoes, 3. Bad Boy, 4. Almost Grown, 5. Child of Nature/Ob-La-Di-Ob-La-Da, 6. Help, 7. Madman, 8. Mean Mr Mustard

Disc Two

Side C

1. Mother, 2. Cold Turkey, 3. Slippin' and Slidin', 4. Stand By Me, 5. Imagine

Side D

1. Whatever Gets You Through the Night, 2. I'm the Greatest

Notes: A collection of items from various sources, including Beatles tracks, which had all been previously released. Side A: track 1, 'Cavern Club'. Tracks 2–4, BBC Radio. Track 5, rehearsal. Tracks 6 and 7, from *Roots* album. Side B: Tracks 1–8, *Get Back* sessions. Side C: tracks 1 and 2, One-to-One concert. Tracks 3–6, '*Salute To Sir Lew Grade*'. 'Voulez Vous', 'Help' and 'Mean Mr Mustard' are not listed on the sleeve.

Laminated full colour cover with snapshots of John.

137. SOMETHING PRECIOUS AND RARE

Trade Mark of Quality JFK 72174-1

Format: 12-inch vinyl

Released: 1986

Source: rehearsals for *Walls and Bridges* album. Recorded at the Sunset Sound, Saturday morning, 13 July 1974

Sound quality: very good

Side A

1. Steel and Glass (5.19), 2. Going Down on Love (4.04), 3. Move Over Ms L (2.52), 4. Surprise Surprise (Sweet Bird of Paradox), 5. Beef Jerky (3.18)

Side B

1. Scared (4.56), 2. Old Dirt Road (4.45), 3. Bless You (6.35), 4. Whatever Gets You Through The Night (1.44), 5. Nobody Loves You (When You're Down and Out) (5.18)

Notes: Sleeve says, 'Produced by John Lennon'. Cover features one of John's sketch drawings. The back has five photographs and track listing. Re-released on white vinyl. A further album was released featuring further outtakes from the *Walls and Bridges* rehearsals titled *Off the Walls*.

138. SOUNDCHECK (THE BEATLES)

Rock Solid RSR 256

Format: 12-inch vinyl (double)

Source: 'I'm the Greatest' demos

Sound quality: excellent stereo

Side B

I'm the Greatest (17.39)

Notes: The double-disc set contains outtakes from The Beatles *Get Back* sessions with the exception of the full rehearsals for 'I Am the Greatest' (see also 'Je Suis Le Plus Mieux' and 'Serve Yourself'). Disc two in this set is a reissue of The Beatles vinyl release *The Real Case Has Just Begun*.

139. SPICY BEATLES SONGS

TMOQ 71076

Format: 12-inch vinyl

Source: various

Sound quality: excellent

Lennon's contributions to this album are as follows: 'What's the New Mary Jane' (outtake), 'Cottonfields' (ad libbed from *Kenny Everett Show*)

Notes: This disc was also released as *Mary Jane* (CBM).

140. STAND BY ME

Toasted Record Works TRW 1942

Format: 12-inch vinyl (double)

Source: various

Sound quality: very good to excellent

Side A

1. Imagine (live at The Apollo), 2. New York City (final demo), 3. Memphis, 4. Johnny B Goode, 5. Roll Over Beethoven, 6. Whole Lotta Shakin' Goin' On/I'll Be Looking For You (*Sometime in New York City* rehearsal)

Side B

1. Rock 'n' Roll People (composing demo), 2. Tight A$ (composing demo), 3. Rock 'n' Roll People (take 5), 4. Mind Games (early mix, scratch vocal), 5. Here We Go Again (demo), 6. Sweet Little Sixteen (alternate take)

Side C

1. You Can't Catch Me (alternate take), 2. Mucho Mungo (demo for Jesse Ed Davis), 3. Goodnight (studio demo), 4. Surprise Surprise (Sweet Bird of Paradox) (home demo), 5. Whatever Gets You Through the Night (John composing the song), 6. Whatever Get You Through The Night (studio demo), 7. Beef Jerky (alternate take)

Side D

1. Going Down on Love (alternate take), 2. Move Over Ms L (alternate take), 3. Surprise Surprise (Sweet Bird of Paradox), 4. I Saw Her Standing There (studio rehearsal with Elton John), 5. Slippin' and Slidin' (*The Old Grey Whistle Test*)

Notes: Side A: tracks 3–5 with Chuck Berry on the *Mike Douglas Show*.

141. STUDIO OUTTAKES

Tobe Milo TMLP 4Q 11/12

Format: 7-inch vinyl EP

Sound quality: unknown

Side A

Track 3 – Oh, My Love

Side B

Track 1 – Day Tripper (with Jimi Hendrix), Track 3 – Voulez Vous Coucher Avec Moi

Notes: This release is also available as a twelve-inch LP. Opinions are split as to whether John appeared on the Jimi Hendrix track.

142. TEDDY BOY

Melvin Records MM 09

Format: 12-inch vinyl

Notes: A re-release of *Come Back Johnny*.

143. TEDDY BOY

Melvin Records MM 09

Format: 12-inch vinyl

Notes: A colour picture disc copy of *Teddy Boy*.

144. TELECASTS (JOHN LENNON AND YOKO ONO)

TMOQ 71046

Format: 12-inch vinyl

Released: 1976
Source: various – see notes
Sound quality: fair mono

Side A

1. John Sinclair (2.26), 2. It's So Hard (2.04), 3. The Luck of the Irish (2.52), 4. Sisters Oh Sisters (2.48), 5. We're All Water, 6. Woman Is the Nigger of the World (tracks 5 and 6, 10.23)

Side B

1. Attica State (2.52), 2. Midsummer New York (2.51), 3. Sakura (1.34), 4. Theme and greetings (0.16), Chuck Berry's guest shot (7.22), 5. Memphis, 6. Johnny B. Goode. 7. Imagine (3.31)

Notes: 'Sakura' is a traditional song. Side A:, tracks 1–4 live on *The David Frost Show*, 13 January 1972. Tracks 5 and 6, live on *The Dick Cavett Show*, 11 May 1972. Side B: live on *The Mike Douglas Show*, 14–18 February 1972.

145. TELECASTS (JOHN LENNON AND YOKO ONO)

Unknown JL 517

Format: 12-inch vinyl

Source: various

Sound quality: fair mono

Notes: Re-released in 1980 of TMOQ 71046

146. TELECASTS (JOHN LENNON AND YOKO ONO)

Unknown JL 517

Format: 12-inch vinyl

Source: various

Sound quality: fair mono

Notes: Colour picture disc copy.

147. TELECASTS (JOHN LENNON AND YOKO ONO)

LXXXIV Series No. 28
Format: 12-inch vinyl
Source: various
Sound quality: fair mono

Notes: Re-release of TMOQ 71046 on magenta vinyl. Limited to approximately 100 numbered copies.

148. THIS IS NOT HERE (YOKO ONO)

Bag Records 5070
Format: 12-inch vinyl
Source: various
Sound quality: very good

Side A

1. Joseijoi Banzai (part 1), 2. Who Has Seen The Wind? 3. Listen The Snow Is Falling, 4. Midsummer New York, 5. Sakura (Cherry Blossoms), 6. Sisters Oh Sisters (acoustic), 7. Remember Love

Side B

1. Walking on Thin Ice, 2. Sisters Oh Sisters (electric), 3. It Happened, 4. Joseijoi Banzai (part 2)

Notes: This was the first Yoko Ono bootleg. The sleeve cover is blue, similar to *Live Peace in Toronto*. The back features a black-and-white image of Yoko as a child with her parents.

149. TOY BOY

LXXXIV Series No. 38
Format: 12-inch vinyl
Source: various
Sound quality: unknown

Notes: A re-release of *Limited Edition* (Bag Records 5069) with paper insert cover. Limited to approximately 100 numbered copies.

150. THE TOY BOY
Bag Records 5069

Format: 12-inch vinyl

Source: various

Sound quality: unknown

Notes: see *Limited Edition*.

151. WHAT A SHAME MARY JANE HAD A PAIN AT THE PARTY
R. 8028

Format: 12-inch vinyl 45 rpm

Released: 1983

Source: studio outtake

Sound quality: excellent

Side A

What a Shame Mary Jane Had a Pain at the Party (version 1) (6.35)

Side B

What a Shame Mary Jane Had a Pain at the Party (version 2) (7.04)

152. WILLOWBROOK REHEARSALS
John Lennon and Yoko Ono with Elephant's Memory Band

Unknown L.27229

Format: 12-inch vinyl (double)

Source: rehearsals for the One-to-One concert held at Madison Square Garden, New York on 30 August 1972. The probable date for these rehearsals is 18 August 1972

Sound quality: very good to excellent mono

Disc One

Side A

1. Recording the commercial for added matinee (excerpt) (10.31), 2. New York City (0.49), 3. New York City (0.23), 4. New York City (1.06),

5. Unchained Melody/It's Only Make Believe (2.58), 6. Come Together (instrumental) (0.26), 7. Chat and tuning and piano lessons, Tequila (2.10), 8. New York City (4.37)

Side B

1. It's So Hard (2.47), 2. Back off Boogaloo (0.08), 3. Woman Is the Nigger of the World (5.19), 4. Instrumental (improvisation)

Disc Two

Side C

1. Unchained Melody/It's Only Make Believe (3.45), 2. Well, Well, Well (5.05), 3. Instant Karma (3.06), 4. Instant Karma (0.23), 5. Mother (4.08), 6. Mother (0.14), 7. Come Together (3.39)

Side D

1. Cold Turkey (4.09), 2. Instrumental (4.15), 3. Instrumental (4.12), 4. Roll Over Beethoven (3.16), 5. Give Peace a Chance (7.30)

Notes: Some studio chat is included. Yoko's songs have been edited out. The band comprised: John – guitar and vocals, Yoko – vocals, Stan Bronstein – sax, Gary Von Scyox – bass, Adam Ippolito – keyboards, Richard Frank Jr – drums, Wayne Tex Gabriel – guitar. Apart from the commercial on Side A: this material with Yoko's songs is available on the three-disc set *One and One and One Is Three*. See also the CD release *The Lost Lennon Rehearsal* (John Records 004).

153. WINSTON O'BOOGIE

Bag Records 5072

Format: 12-inch vinyl

Released: 1987

Source: various – see below

Sound quality: Side A: excellent stereo (track 6 excellent mono). Side B: very good mono with John's vocal coming through well

Side A

1. Move Over Ms L (2.45), 2. Going Down on Love (3.52), 3. Surprise Surprise (Sweet Bird of Paradox) (3.26), 4. Beef Jerky (3.08), 5. Whatever Gets You Through the Night (1.36), 6. Just Because (5.59)

Side B

1. Starting Over (2.22), 2. I'm Losing You (4.12), 3. Dream Lover/Stay (3.56), 4. Mystery Train (2.59), 5. She's a Woman No 1 (0.33), 6. Rip It Up (0.55), 7. I'm a Man (1.30), 8. Be-Bop-A-Lula (0.57), 9. She's a Woman No. 2 (1.17), 10. C'mon Everybody (0.34)

Notes: The tracks 1–5 on Side A: are from the *Walls and Bridges* sessions, 13 July 1974. These also appear on *Something Precious and Rare*. Track 6 is from the *Rock 'n' Roll* session. Side B: was recorded probably in August 1980 for the *Double Fantasy* sessions. These also appear on *Before Play*.

The sleeve is designed to look like a packet of Winston cigarettes and unusually opens at the top.

154. WORKING CLASS HERO

Chet Mar Records CMR-75

Format: 12-inch vinyl (double)

Source: various

Sound quality: excellent mono

Disc One

Side A

1. Be My Baby (4.33), 2. Angel Baby (4.32), 3. Yer Blues (8.31)

Side B

1. Imagine (3.22), 2. Mother (5.15), 3. Come Together (4.35), 4. Give Peace a Chance (7.47)

Disc Two

Side C

1. Slippin' and Slidin' (2.20), 2. Stand By Me (3.50), 3. Whatever Gets You Through the Night, Lucy in the Sky with Diamonds, I Saw Her Standing There (14.30)

Side D

1. Lady Marmalade (1.22), 2. Memphis, Johnny B. Goode (7.45), 3. Oh, My Love (2.47), 4. Working Class Hero (2.20), 5. Day Tripper (3.10), 6. Do the Oz (3.09)

Notes: Side A: 'Be My Baby' and 'Angel Baby' are *Rock 'n' Roll outtakes*. 'Yer Blues' is from *The Rolling Stones Rock and Roll Circus*. Side B: 'Imagine' is from *The Mike Douglas Show* 1972. 'Mother', 'Come Together' and 'Give Peace a Chance' are from the One-to-One concert. Side C: 'Slippin' and Slidin'' and 'Stand By Me' are *The Old Grey Whistle Test* outtakes. 'Whatever Gets You Through the Night', 'Lucy in the Sky with Diamonds' and 'I Saw Her Standing There' are with Elton John at Madison Square Garden in 1974. Side D: 'Lady Marmalade' is a Dakota recording. 'Memphis' and 'Johnny B. 'Goode' are from *Mike Douglas Show* in 1972. 'Oh, My Love' is an outtake. 'Working Class Hero' is from John's thirty-first birthday party. 'Day Tripper' is from *Top Gear* in 1967 with Jimi Hendrix. 'Do the Oz' is an Elastic Oz Band single from 1974. This set was later reissued on vinyl and compact disc.

155. YER BLUES

NEMS Records NR 103

Format: 7-inch vinyl picture disc 45 rpm

Source: *Rock and Roll Circus*

Sound quality: very good

Side One

Yer Blues

Side Two

Lucille (Paul McCartney and Wings, 1979 tour)

Notes: Japanese picture disc. Transparent sleeve. Side two features a track by Paul McCartney from his 1979 tour.

156. YIN YANG

Bag Records 5071

Format; 12-inch vinyl

Released: 1984

Source: various

Sound quality: excellent stereo

Side A

1. Serve Yourself (3.53), 2. Mucho Mungo (take 1) (0.45), 3. Mucho Mungo (take 2) (2.56), 4. Stand By Me (4.03), 5. Slippin' and Slidin' (2.20), 6. Yer Blues (8.39)

Side B

1. Mucho Mungo (take 3) (3.38), 2. Imagine (2.54), 3. Radio Peace (0.15), 4. Love (3.13), 5. Walking on Thin Ice (7.45), 6. Give Peace a Chance (4.52)

Notes: 'Serve Yourself' is a Bermuda demo. The three *Mucho Mungo* outtakes are from the *Pussycats* sessions March–May 1974. 'Stand By Me' and 'Slippin' and Slidin'' are from *The Old Grey Whistle Test*. 'Yer Blues' is from *The Rolling Stones Rock and Roll Circus*. 'Imagine' is live at the Apollo Theatre, 13 June 1975. 'Radio Peace' was recorded in Amsterdam on 26 March 1969. 'Love' is a remix with more prominent piano. 'Walking on Thin Ice' is a 1980 recording featuring Yoko. 'Give Peace a Chance' is a One-to-One rehearsal.

Deluxe laminated sleeve with a picture of John as a boy on his bike. The back shows a colour picture of Yoko as a young girl with details of the tracks.

157. YOU SHOULD'A BEEN THERE

Unknown YSB 7374-1

Format: 12-inch vinyl (double), coloured vinyl with full colour jacket

Source: *Rock 'n' Roll* album sessions

Sound quality: Sides A–C good to very mono. Side D very good to excellent stereo

Disc One

Side A

1. Ain't That a Shame (excerpt including one false start) (1.31), 2. Be-Bop-A-Lula (2.39), 3. Ya Ya (2.30), 4. Do You Want to Dance (including one false start) (3.58), 5. Stand By Me (3.58), 6. Slippin' and Slidin' (2.21), 7. Rip It Up/Ready Teddy (1.33)

Side B

1. Bring It on Home to Me/Send Me Some Loving (2.08), 2. Bring It on Home to Me/Send Me Some Loving (3.43), 3. Peggy Sue (2.06), 4. Ain't That a Shame (2.46), 5. Stand By Me (excerpt) (0.48), 6. Bring It on Home to Me/Send Me Some Loving (3.51), 7. Ya Ya (including one false start) (2.46), 8. That' I Be the Day (including one false start) (2.36)

Disc Two

Side C

1. Do You Want to Dance (3.34), 2. Stand By Me (3.34), 3. Peggy Sue (2.14), 4. Be-Bop-A-Lula (excerpt) (1.59), 5. Slippin' and Slidin' (excerpt) (2.03), 6. Guitar Jam including Rumble (0.44) and Whole Lotta Love (0.09), 7. Thirty Days (1.34), 8. C'mon Everybody (2.20), 9. Ain't That a Shame (excerpt) (2.30)

Side D

1. Be My Baby (4.34), 2. Angel Baby (3.09), 3. Just Because (5.57), 4. Be My Baby (long version) (6.17)

Notes: Sides A–C are rehearsals. Side D are fully produced takes. Side D: tracks 1 and 2 are from *Roots*. (Adam VIII A8018).

2. Compact Discs

The discs listed in this section are in alphabetical order. We have ignored the prefixes 'A' and 'The'. Where necessary, we have cross referenced the title of the disc. For example *Walls and Bridges Rockspeak '74* is cross referenced with *Rockspeak '74*. A number of titles start with a number such as 1970 *Plastic Ono Band – Home and Studio* and *1974 Walls and Bridges* Sessions. These are shown at the end of this section – again cross referenced where necessary. As far as rating the sound quality, unless we have actually heard the disc or have seen a reliable review, we have shown this in the listings as 'unknown'. However we have come a long way since the first vinyl bootleg releases where many discs were barely audible. Very few bootleg releases now can be considered very poor quality.

We have shown, where known, the track times (although these are sometimes unreliable) and release dates. In some instances, where we do not have the disc in our collection, we have obtained a copy of the sleeve but quite often the details shown are sketchy and we have been unable to ascertain the sources of the tracks – are they studio outtakes, demos, rehearsals or live performances? When details are shown on these sleeves this is sometimes incorrect. Quite often the title of the track is slightly incorrect – for instance 'Give Me Some Truth' is listed on some discs as 'Gimme Some Truth' and 'I Don't Want to Be a Soldier' as 'I Don't Wanna Be A Soldier'. We have in these cases referred to the official release. The CD release of *Imagine* lists these tracks as 'I Don't Want to Be a Soldier' and 'Give Me Some Truth'. There are some anomalies. On the original CD release of the *Rock 'n' Roll album*, track 6 is shown as 'Do You Want to Dance' but on the reissue in 2004 this is shown as 'Do You Wanna Dance'. Which is correct? 'Out the Blue' (from the *Mind Games* album) is often shown on bootleg sleeves as 'Out of the Blue'. We have attempted to correct for the purposes uniformity, where necessary, the song titles in the listings.

As mentioned in the Introduction, there are a vast amount of releases from *The Lost Lennon Tapes* radio series. We have included the track listings for the CD releases of *The Complete Lost Lennon Tapes* (Walrus Records), *The Lost Lennon Tapes* (Bag Records) and *The Lost Lennon Tapes* (Living Legend) in this section together with the information we have located on the Angry Dog releases – *The Real Complete Lost Lennon Tapes*. We believe that there are without doubt further releases in the Angry Dog series apart from the ten volumes we know exist – track listings for the first four volumes. Details of the set of thirty five vinyl releases (Bag Records) can be found in Part One. The latter volumes in this series were reissued on compact discs. As far as the two sets of containing the complete 218 radio broadcasts, we have listed these in Part Three together with track listings. In Part Three we also investigate the story behind *The Lost Lennon Tapes*.

We have included a number of items which are complete radio shows such as the Andy Peebles interview for BBC Radio on 6 December 1980 and some documentaries and interviews for various radio stations. The Andy Peebles interview was issued as an official release on a double CD set by the BBC but this is very difficult to find. Many of the interview discs were released by the Black Cat label who seem to specialise in interview and documentary albums. We were surprised how many interviews John Lennon gave. There are several promoting the *Walls and Bridges* album and the *Double Fantasy* album. Whether these can be strictly considered bootlegs is debatable but we have included them here for their historical importance and because you will not normally find them in your local record store. We have listed the various interviews in the Songs Index section and the discs where they can be located.

We have shown in the listings some items where we know the disc exists (we have copies of the sleeves in our files) but despite our research have been unable to ascertain full track details. These are included for the record.

158. ABC Radio Today Lennon Anthology Special

Unknown

Format: CD (double)

Source: see notes

Sound quality: unknown

Notes: Sleeve states: 'Originally aired Monday, 2 November through Sunday, 8 November 1998 on radio stations along the Radio Today network'. Track details unknown.

159. Absolute Elsewhere

Vigotone VT-158/VT-159/VT-160

Format: CD (three-disc boxed set)

Time: Disc One 63.20, Disc Two 76.31, Disc Three 71.15

Source: *Mind Games* album sessions – outtakes, demos

Sound quality: excellent

Disc One

The Alternate Album

1. Mind Games (4.11), 2. Tight A$ (4.24), 3. Aisumasen (I'm Sorry) (4.43), 4. One Day at a Time (3.21), 5. Bring on the Lucie (Freda People) (4.22), 6. Nutopian National Anthem (0.04), 7. Intuition (2.51), 8. Out the Blue (4.13), 9. Only People (3.05), 10. I Know (I Know) (3.46), 11. You Are Here (4.40), 12. Meat City (2.34), 13. Radio spot 1 (0.58), 14. Radio spot 2 (0.47)

The Sessions

15. Rock 'n' Roll People (take 6, 1 August 1973) (4.22), 16. Rock 'n' Roll People (take 7, 1 August 1973) (3.10), 17. Rock 'n' Roll People (take 5, 4 August 1973) (6.03), 18. Rock 'n' Roll People (take 6, 4 August 1973) (2.45), 19. Rock 'n' Roll People (take 7, 4 August 1973) (2.57)

Disc Two

The Alternates

1. Tight A$ (4.43), 2. Tight A$ (4.15), 3. Aisumasen (I'm Sorry) (4.44), 4. One Day at a Time (3.15), 5. Out the Blue (4.11), 6. Out the Blue

(3.21), 7. Only People (2.53), 8. I Know (I Know) (3.43), 9. I Know (I Know) (3.48), 10. I Know (I Know) (1.58), 11. I Know (I Know) (3.40), 12. Meat City (US 45 mix) (2.54)

The Demos

13. I Promise (piano, late 1970s) (1.57), 14. Make Love Not War (piano, late 1970s) (3.31), 15. Rock 'n' Roll People (piano, late 1970s) (3.29), 16. Call My Name (electric guitar) (5.18), 17. Call My Name (acoustic guitar version, from *Clock* film) (4.33), 18. Call My Name (acoustic guitar) (5.16)

Disc Three

The Demos (continued)

1. Shoeshine (acoustic, October 1971) (3.45), 2. Free The People (acoustic slide guitar) (1.04), 3. Meat City (electric guitar version No. 1) (4.07), 4. Meat City (electric guitar version No. 2) (2.45), 5. Rock 'n' Roll People (electric guitar) (2.50), 6. Tight A$ (electric guitar) (3.39), 7. Intuition (piano, take 3) (2.24), 8. Intuition (piano, take 4) (3.07), 9. Here We Go Again (acoustic guitar, take 2) (3.17), 10. I Know (I Know) (acoustic guitar, take 2) (3.03), 11. I Know (I Know) (acoustic guitar, take 3) 3.15), 12. I Know (I Know) (acoustic guitar, take 4) (3.16), 13. I Know (I Know) (double-tracked acoustic guitar, take 1) (3.11), 14. I Know (I Know) (double-tracked acoustic guitar, take 2) (3.11), 15. I Know (I Know) (double-tracked acoustic guitar, take 3) (3.10), 16. I Know (I Know) (double-tracked acoustic guitar, take 4) (3.20), 17. I Know (I Know) (double-tracked acoustic guitar, take 5) (3.30), 18. I Know (I Know) (double-tracked acoustic guitar, take 6) (2.36), 19. Just Because (acoustic guitar, part 1) (2.50), 20. Just Because (acoustic guitar, part 2) (1.34), 21. Just Because (acoustic guitar, Part 3), (6.42), 22. Steel and Glass (acoustic guitar) (4.25)

Notes: The sleeve says this is 'the ultimate *Mind Games* anthology'. The set comes with a thirty two page booklet with details of backing musicians, evolution of the tracks and photographs. This is another quality release from the Vigotone label and is worthy of a place on the shelves of all Lennon collectors.

160. ACETATES AND ALTERNATE MIXES

Unicorn Records UC-083

Format: CD

Released: 2001

Source: tracks 1-9 and 13 from acetates. Tracks 11-12 alternate multi-track mixes

Sound quality: very good

1. Cold Turkey (7" Apple acetate), 2. Don't Worry Kyoko (7" Apple acetate), 3. Look at Me (7" Apple acetate – different mix), 4. Mother (7" Apple acetate), 5. Remember (7" Apple acetate), 6. Oh, My Love (2 Sided Bell acetate), 7. I Don't Want to Be a Soldier (2 Sided Bell acetate), 8. Everglade Woman (Elephant's Memory Band 10" Metformedia acetate), 9. Woman (10" stereo acetate), 10. Starting Over (12" home version), 11. Borrowed Time (alternate mix 1), 12. Borrowed Time (alternate mix 2), 13. Amazing Talking Guitar (7" Apple acetate)

161. ACOUSTIC MASTERPIECES

Birthday Records BR.019

Format: CD (digipack)

Released: 1998 (reissued 2002)

Time: 68.20

Source: various – see notes

Sound quality: excellent

1. Imagine, 2. Watching the Wheels, 3. Woman Is the Nigger of the World, 4. Girls and Boys, 5. The Luck of the Irish, 6. Maggie Mae, 7. Corrina Corrina, 8. Look at Me, 9. J.J./People, 10. Beautiful Boy, 11. God, 12. Maybe Baby, 13. Love, 14. The Happy Rishikesh Song, 15. I Know (I Know), 16. Woman, 17. What You Got, 18. I'm a Man, 19. Dear Yoko, 20. (Just Like) Starting Over, 21. Mucho Mungo, 22. Howling at the Moon, 23. I'm Losing You, 24. Mother, 25. My Mummy's Dead

Notes: Track 1, live Apollo Theatre in New York 17 December 1971. Tracks 2, 4, 7, 14, 18, 20 and 22 home demos – Dakota, 1980. Track 3, blues rendition, Greenwich Village 1971. Track 5, demo November 1971. Tracks 6 and 10, *Double Fantasy* sessions August 1980. Track 8, Weybridge, 1968. Track 9, demo for 'Angela'. Tracks 11, 13, 24 and 25, home demo, Tittenhurst Park. Track 12, *Clock* sessions. Track 15, *Mind Games* sessions 1973. Tracks 16, 19 and 23, early demo, Bermuda June 1980. Track 17, home demo, Los Angeles, June 1974. Track 21, demo for Harry Nilsson. This is a reissue of *Unplugged*.

The front sleeve shows a colour photo of John wearing a hat and playing a guitar.

162. AFTER THE REMEMBER

Masterfraction MFCD 008/009

Format: CD (double)

Source: outtakes, alternate mixes, acetates of early tracks

Sound quality: very good

Disc One

1. Cold Turkey (acetate), 2. Well, Well, Well (studio outtake), 3. I Found Out (studio outtake), 4. Look at Me (studio outtake), 5. Remember (acetate), 6. Power to the People (studio outtake), 7. Power to the People (studio outtake), 8. Power to the People (studio outtake), 9. God Save Us (acetate), 10. I'm the Greatest (studio outtake), 11. I'm the Greatest (studio outtake), 12. I Don't Want to Be a Soldier, Mama (I Don't Want To Die) (studio outtake), 13. Well (studio outtake), 14. Give Me Some Truth (studio outtake), 15. How Do You Sleep? (studio outtake), 16. How Do You Sleep? (studio outtake), 17. How Do You Sleep? (acetate)

Disc Two

1. Crippled Inside (studio outtake), 2. Oh, Yoko (studio outtake), 3. It's So Hard (studio outtake), 4. Imagine (studio outtake), 5. Happy Xmas (War Is Over) (studio outtake), 6. Woman Is the Nigger of the World (studio outtake), 7. Mind Games (studio outtake), 8. Bring on the Lucie (Freeda People) (studio outtake), 9. Tight A$ (studio outtake), 10. Intuition (studio outtake), 11. Only People (studio outtake), 12. Out the Blue (studio outtake), 13. Meat

City (studio outtake), 14. Rock 'n' Roll People (studio outtake), 15. Sweet Little Sixteen (studio outtake), 16. You Can't Catch Me (studio outtake), 17. Goodnight, Vienna (studio outtake), 18. Laugh (acetate)

Notes: Black-and-white sleeve front and back.

163. AFTERNOON READING
Unknown
Format: CD
Source: BBC Radio 4
Sound quality: unknown

Notes: Four short stories inspired by John Lennon, broadcast on BBC Radio 4.

164. ALEX BENNETT SHOW
Unknown
Format: CD
Source: radio show phone in from 1971
Sound quality: unknown

Notes: We have been unable to trace further details but the content is probably the same as *Have You Had Your Breakfast Yet*.

165. THE ALTERNATE *DOUBLE FANTASY*
Pear Records PDP 038
Format: CD (double)
Released: 2005
Source: *Double Fantasy* album outtakes and home demos
Sound quality: excellent

Disc One

The Alternate Album – Studio Sessions

1. (Just Like) Starting Over (early take, no backing vocals), 2. Clean-up Time (rehearsal, more guitar, no backing vocals), 3. I'm Losing You

(rehearsal, more guitar, no backing vocals), 4. Beautiful Boy (Darling Boy) (different mix), 5. Watching the Wheels (rough mix, different vocals), 6. Woman (rough mix with additional keyboards), 7. Dear Yoko (rough mix with more overdubs), 8. I'm Stepping Out (take 2, more guitar, extra lyrics – 'in my pants'), 9. I Don't Wanna Face It (rough mix), 10. Nobody Told Me (rough mix, more guitar, no overdubs), 11. Borrowed Time (rough mix), 12. Forgive Me (My Little Flower Princess) (early take), 13. Grow Old with Me (original piano demo)

The Alternates – Studio Sessions

14. Maggie Mae (studio alternate), 15. (Just Like) Starting Over (different mix, longer fadeout), 16. Clean-up Time (unedited mix with alternate sound effects – not used on the released version), 17. I'm Losing You (rough mix with Cheap Trick), 18. Beautiful Boy (Darling Boy) (early acoustic take), 19. I Am the Walrus/Watching the Wheels (take 3, basic backing track, different vocals), 20. Woman (unedited mix, alternate backing vocals), 21. Woman (vocal booth), 22. Dear Yoko (vocal booth), 23. Nobody Told Me (early take with studio chat), 24. It's Now Or Never ('come hold my penis' version)

Disc Two

The Alternate Album – Home Demos

1. (Just Like) Starting Over (complete home demo), 2. Clean-up Time (piano demo), 3. Stranger's Room (early version of 'I'm Losing You', piano demo), 4. Beautiful Boy (Darling Boy) (take 2, acoustic demo with drum machine), 5. Watching the Wheels (acoustic demo in blues style), 6. Woman (acoustic demo with drum machine), 7. Dear Yoko (acoustic take plus false start), 8. I'm Stepping Out (take 3, acoustic demo), 9. I Don't Want to Face It (acoustic demo), 10. Nobody Told Me (acoustic demo with drum machine), 11. Borrowed Time (acoustic demo, incomplete lyrics)

The Alternates – Home Demos

The Evolution of Starting Over (tracks 12 – 15), 12. I Watch Your Face (acoustic demo), 13. My Life (acoustic demo), 14. Don't Be Crazy (piano demo), 15. The Worst is Over (acoustic demo with drum machine), 16. I'm

Losing You (acoustic demo with drum machine), 17. Beautiful Boy (Darling Boy) (take 1, acoustic demo recorded in Bermuda), 18. I'm Crazy (early version of 'Watching the Wheels', piano demo). 19. Emotional Wreck (early version of 'Watching the Wheels')/Howling at the Moon (piano demo), 20. Watching the Wheels (acoustic take, John as folk singer), 21. I'm Stepping Out (take 1, acoustic demo), 22. I Don't Wanna Face It (take 2, acoustic demo), 23. Borrowed Time (acoustic version with overdubs)

Notes: Black-and-white sleeve with full track listing details on back – digipack.

166. THE ALTERNATE IMAGINE

Pear Records PDP 032

Format: CD

Released: 2005

Source: *Imagine* album outtakes and home demos

Sound quality: excellent

The Alternate Imagine

1. Imagine (take 7, alternate vocal), 2. Crippled Inside (take 2), 3. Jealous Guy (take 1, no overdubs or strings), 4. It's So Hard (take 2, no overdubs sax piano or strings), 5. I Don't Want to Be a Soldier Mama (I Don't Want to Die) (take 1 with sax), 6. Give Me Some Truth (alternate vocal), 7. Oh, My Love (alternate take 1b), 8. How Do You Sleep? (take 2, early version – hit it George), 9. How? (take 12, no overdubs, no editing), 10. Oh, Yoko (take 9, runs one-and-half minutes longer)

The Alternates

11. I'm the Greatest (early version, incomplete lyrics), 12. San Francisco Bay Blues (outtake, acoustic version), 13. Well (Baby Please Don't Go) (outtake), 14. Imagine (rehearsal), 15. Crippled Inside (take 17, rough version of the released track, 'message to Northern Songs shareholders')

The Home Demos

16. How?/Child of Nature/Oh, Yoko (early piano demo, late 1970 – early 1971), 17. Oh, My Love (acoustic home demo, late 1968), 18. Oh, Yoko (acoustic guitar demo, mid-1969)

The Beatles Versions

19. Jealous Guy (Child of Nature) (Esher session 1968), 20. Give Me Some Truth (*Get Back* sessions 1969)

The Live Versions

21. Imagine (live, One-to-One concert, King Biscuit mix 1972), 22. It's So Hard (live, *The Mike Douglas TV Show* 1972)

Notes: Colour front similar to official release with track listing including take numbers and other details on the back – digipack.

167. THE ALTERNATE JOHN LENNON/PLASTIC ONO BAND

Ghost Records CD 53-40

Format: CD

Released: 1991

Source: *Plastic Ono Band* album outtakes plus other outtakes and interviews

Sound quality: very good to excellent mono/stereo except 'Everson Museum Press Conference' – good mono

1. Mother (demo), 2. I Found Out (alternate mix – full length), 3. Love (guitar demo), 4. Well, Well, Well (acoustic demo), 5. Look at Me (1968 acoustic demo), 6. God (acoustic demo), 7. My Mummy's Dead (take 2), 8. Honey Don't (jam session), 9. Don't Be Cruel (jam session), 10. Matchbox (jam session), 11. Mother No. 2 (guitar demo), 12. I Found Out No. 2 (guitar demo), 13. Well, Well, Well No. 2 (alternate mix), 14. Look at Me No. 2 (alternate mix), 15. I Found Out (guitar demo, take 2)

Bonus Tracks

16. One-to-One concert radio ad outtakes – complete and unedited, 17. New York City (part of radio ad for One-to-One concerts), 18. Come Together (One-to-One concert – matinee), 19. John interviewed about David Peel, 20. Serve Yourself (obscene lyrics version), 21. Everson Museum Press Conference (John and Yoko 8 October 1971), 22. How I Won the War (from 45 rpm release – Musketeer Gripweed and the Third Troop)

Notes: Sleeve is original *Plastic Ono Band* cover on front with detailed track listing on back.

168. THE ALTERNATE MIND GAMES

Pear Records PDP 034

Format: CD (double)

Released: 2005

Source: *Mind Games* album outtakes and home demos

Sound quality: excellent

The Alternate Album

1. Mind Games (rough mix), 2. Tight A$ (rough mix with guitar overdub), 3. Aisumasen (I'm Sorry) (rough mix with steel guitar overdub), 4. One Day at a Time (rough mix with overdubs), 5. Bring on the Lucie (Freeda People) (rough mix less overdubs and reference vocal), 6. Nutopian International Anthem (rough mix without overdubs), 7. Intuition (rough mix), 8. Out the Blue (rough mix, no edit at 3.11 but a second instrumental part, longest known version), 9. Only People (rough mix), 10. I Know (I Know) (rough mix), 11. You Are Here (rough mix with additional verse 1.04 – 1.55), 12. Meat City (rough mix with harmony guide vocal which is mixed out of the commercial release), 13. Rock 'n' Roll People (take 7, rough mix)

The Home Demos

14. I Promise (Mind Games) (early version), 15. Make Love Not War (Mind Games) (early version), 16. Tight A$ (electric guitar demo), 17. Call My Name (Aisumasen) (electric guitar demo), 18. Free The People (Bring on the Lucie) (acoustic guitar demo), 19. Intuition/How?/God (piano demo), 20. I Know (I Know) (acoustic guitar demo), 21. Shoeshine (Meat City) (acoustic guitar demo), 22. Meat City (electric guitar demo), 23. Rock 'n' Roll People (piano demo), 24. Here We Go Again (acoustic guitar demo), 25. Just Because (acoustic guitar demo), 26. Nutopian International Anthem (rough mix with backwards message and reversed backward message)

Notes: Tracks 6 and 26 are silent tracks. Front cover of sleeve has colour picture similar to the official release with track listing showing details of the sources of the tracks on the back – digipack.

169. THE ALTERNATE MIND GAMES AND SHAVED FISH

Ghost Records CD 53-39

Format: CD

Released: 1991

Source: outtakes from *Mind Games* and *Shaved Fish* albums

Sound quality: very good to excellent mono stereo

1. Mind Games (rough vocal – early mix), 2. Tight A$ (guitar demo), 3. Aisumasen (I'm Sorry) (rough mix), 4. Bring on the Lucie (Freeda People) (alternate mix), 5. Out the Blue (rough mix – alternate vocal), 6. Only People (rough mix), 7. Give Peace a Chance (acoustic demo), 8. Cold Turkey (alternate vocals – early mix for acetate), 9. Instant Karma (film clip version – double-tracked vocals), 10. Power to the People (alternate version), 11. Mother (One-to-One concert – matinee), 12. Woman Is the Nigger of the World (acoustic demo), 13. Imagine (One-to-One concert – matinee), 14. Whatever Gets You Through the Night (alternate version), 15. Mind Games (Make Love Not War prototype version), 16. No. 9 Dream (acoustic demo), 17. Happy Xmas (War Is Over), 18. Give Peace a Chance (One-to-One concert)

Notes: Tracks 1–6 are *Mind Games* and tracks 7–18 are *Shaved Fish*. The front cover features the official *Music For Pleasure* release with the single picture cover on the back with detailed track listing. Not included on this disc are alternate versions of 'One Day at a Time', 'Intuition', 'I Know (I Know)', 'You Are Here' and 'Meat City'.

170. THE ALTERNATE PLASTIC ONO BAND

Pear Records PDP 031

Format: CD (double)

Released: 2005

Source: *Plastic Ono Band* album outtakes and home demos

Sound quality: excellent

The Alternate Album

1. Mother (alternate take, different beginning), 2. I Found Out (rough mix), 3. Working Class Hero (Australian album version, censored), 4. Remember (different mix from acetate – see notes for further details), 5. Love (remix with clear piano), 6. Well, Well, Well (rough mix), 7. Look at Me (rough mix), 8. God (electrified acoustic guitar demo), 9. My Mummy's Dead (electrified acoustic guitar demo), 10. When a Boy Meets a Girl (take 2, electrified acoustic guitar demo)

The Alternates

11. Mother (different mix from acetate, different vocal, longer fade), 12. Mother (One-to-One rehearsal), 13. I Found Out (Australian version, censored and longer), 14. Look at Me (electrified acoustic guitar demo)

The Home Demos

15. Mother (electrified acoustic guitar demo), 16. I Found Out (electrified acoustic guitar demo), 17. Love (electrified acoustic guitar demo), 18. Well, Well, Well (acoustic), 19. Look at Me (acoustic), 20. God (acoustic with false start), 21. My Mummy's Dead (acoustic), 22. When a Boy Meets a Girl (acoustic)

The Live Versions

23. Mother (One-to-One concert)

Notes: Track 4, This version runs 3.45 longer, after the closing of '5 of November' at 4.30. Instrumental part with unique jew's harp. Front cover of sleeve similar to official release with close up picture of John and Yoko leaning against a tree. Back shows track listing with take numbers and other details.

171. THE ALTERNATE ROCK 'N' ROLL

Pear Records PDP 036

Format: CD

Released: 2005

Source: *Rock 'n' Roll* album outtakes and home demos

Sound quality: excellent

The Alternate Album

1. Be-Bop-A-Lula (Roots mix), 2. Stand By Me ('Hello Julian', rehearsal, different lead vocal), 3. Medley: Rip It Up/Ready Teddy (rough mix), 4. You Can't Catch Me (rough mix, very different), 5. Ain't That a Shame (rough mix, longer fade out), 6. Do You Want to Dance (Roots mix, lasts 10 seconds longer), 7. Sweet Little Sixteen (rough mix, different lead vocal, lasts 1.30 longer), 8. Slippin' and Slidin' (Roots mix, longer fade. The Rock 'n' Roll mix has a boost in the volume at 1.05), 9. Peggy Sue (rough mix, the acoustic guitar is mixed more up front), 10. Medley: Bring It on Home to Me/Send Me Some Loving (rehearsal), 11. Bony Moronie (rough mix, superior to the *Rock 'n' Roll* mix, longer fade), 12. Ya Ya (rehearsal), 13. Just Because (Roots mix, longer fade)

The Alternates

14. Angel Baby (*Roots* mix, the *Menlove Avenue* mix lasts 35 seconds longer, at 1 59 the section from 0.52 to 1.26 is reinserted), 15. Be My Baby (rough mix), 16. That'll Be the Day (rehearsal), 17. Thirty Days (rehearsal) 18. C'mon Everybody (rehearsal), 19. Here We Go Again (acoustic demo), 20. Lady Marmalade (rehearsal), 21. Be-Bop-A-Lula (rehearsal), 22. Stand By Me (rehearsal), 23. Be My Baby (rough mix, different vocal and longer fade)

The Live Versions

24. Slippin' and Slidin' (live on The *Old Grey Whistle Test*), 25. Stand By Me (live on The *Old Grey Whistle Test*), 26. *Rock 'n' Roll* Promo spot

Notes: Black-and-white front cover with photograph similar to official release. Track listing and other details on the back.

172. THE ALTERNATE SHAVED FISH

Pear Records PDP 037

Format: CD (double)

Released: 2005

Source: *Shaved Fish* album outtakes and home demos

Sound quality: excellent

The Alternate Album

1. Give Peace a Chance (rehearsal), 2. Cold Turkey (One-to-One rehearsal), 3. Instant Karma (different mix), 4. Power to the People (rough mix with longer intro and ending), 5. Mother (alternate take), 6. Woman Is the Nigger of the World (alternate take), 7. Imagine (take 1), 8. Whatever Gets You Through the Night (rough mix), 9. Mind Games (rough mix), 10. No. 9 Dream (monitor mix), 11. Happy Xmas (War Is Over) (rough mix)

The Alternates

12. Give Peace a Chance (rehearsal, complete, 5.20), 13. Cold Turkey (rough mix), 14. Instant Karma (US single mix), 15. Power to the People (alternate take), 16. Power to the People (alternate take – no backing vocals)

Home Demos

17. Give Peace a Chance (acoustic guitar), 18. Cold Turkey (acoustic guitar demo), 19. Whatever Gets You Through the Night (acoustic guitar demo), 20. No. 9 Dream (acoustic guitar demo), 21. Happy Xmas (War Is Over) (acoustic guitar demo – only John on vocals)

Live Versions

22. Imagine (*Jerry Lewis TV Show*), 23. Whatever Gets You Through the Night (live with Elton John)

173. THE ALTERNATE SOMETIME IN NEW YORK CITY

John Records John 003

Format: CD

Time: 71.38

Source: *Sometime in New York City* album, outtakes, demos, rehearsals and live performances

Sound quality: varies from good to excellent

1. Woman Is the Nigger of the World (acoustic demo), 2. Sisters Oh Sisters (Yoko, live rehearsal, One-to-One concert), 3. Attica State (*David Frost Show*, 1972), 4. Born in a Prison (Yoko, live rehearsal, One-to-One concert),

5. New York City (acoustic demo), 6. The Luck of the Irish (studio outtake, take 2), 7. John Sinclair (*David Frost Show* 1972), 8. Angela (early prototype originally called 'People'), 9. We're All Water (Yoko, live rehearsal, One-to-One concert), 10. Cold Turkey (live rehearsal, One-to-One concert), 11. Don't Worry Kyoko (Yoko, live rehearsal, One-to-One concert), 12. Well Baby Please Don't Go (studio rehearsal for Zappa gig), 13. Woman Is the Nigger of the World (*Dick Cavett Show*, 11 May 1972), 14. Sisters Oh Sisters (*David Frost Show* 1972), 15. Attica State (Free John Sinclair Rally, 10 December 1971), 16. New York City (acoustic demo as 'Que Pasa'), 17. The Luck of the Irish (Free John Sinclair Rally, 10 December 1971), 18. John Sinclair (Free John Sinclair Rally, 10 December 1971), 19. Angela (early prototype called J.J.), 20. We're All Water (*Dick Cavett Show*, 11 May 1972), 21. The Luck of the Irish (*David Frost Show*, 1972), 22. Attica State (*David Frost Show*, 1972), 23. John speaks Japanese, 24. Give Peace a Chance (John and Yoko impromptu version)

Notes: A collection of tracks from several sources. Sleeve is black and white using the original artwork from the single release 'Happy Xmas'.

174. THE ALTERNATE SOME TIME IN N. Y.

Pear Records PDP 033

Format: CD (double)

Released: 2005

Source: *Some Time in New York City* album outtakes and home demos

Sound quality: excellent

The Alternate Album

1. Woman Is the Nigger of the World, 2. Attica State, 3. New York City, 4. The Luck of the Irish, 5. John Sinclair, 6. J.J.

The Alternates

7. Woman Is the Nigger of the World (One-to-One rehearsal), 8. New York City (One-to-One rehearsal), 9. New York City (One-to-One rehearsal), 10. The Luck of the Irish (take 1, acoustic), 11. Woman Is the Nigger of the World (acoustic), 12. New York City (acoustic), 13. The Luck of the Irish (early acoustic), 14. People

Oldies Jam

15. Roll Over Beethoven, 16. Honey Don't, 17. Ain't That a Shame, 18. My Baby/Not Fade Away, 19. Send Me Some Loving, 20. Whole Lotta Shakin'/It'll Be Me, 21. Honey Hush, 22. Don't Be Cruel/Hound Dog, 23. Caribbean, 24. Honky Tonk

Live Versions

25. Attica State, 26. The Luck of the Irish, 27. John Sinclair

Notes: Tracks 25–27, John Sinclair Rally.

175. ALTERNATE TORONTO MIX AND MORE

Goblin Records CD 3009

Format: CD

Released: 1991

Source: tracks 1–9, live Toronto 13 September 1969. The rest, bonus tracks

Sound quality: excellent

1. Introduction, 2. Blue Suede Shoes, 3. Money, 4. Dizzy Miss Lizzy, 5. Yer Blues, 6. Cold Turkey, 7. C'mon Wake Up (preamble), 8. Give Peace a Chance, 9. Don't Worry Kyoko, 10. John John (Let's Hope For Peace), 11. Why Not, 12. Greenfield Morning, 13. Pushed An Empty Baby Carriage All Over Town, 14. Papers Shoes, 15. Touch Me, 16. Midsummer New York, 17. Mind Train (edit)

Notes: Track 8 is with Eric Clapton (vocals).

176. THE ALTERNATE WALLS AND BRIDGES

Pear Records

Format: CD

Released: 2005

Source: *Walls and Bridges* album outtakes and home demos

Sound quality: excellent

The Alternate Album

1. Going Down on Love (studio rehearsal, no horns), 2. Whatever Gets You Through the Night (rough mix, no horns), 3. Old Dirt Road (rehearsal, no strings), 4. What You Got (alternate take, incomplete lyrics), 5. Bless You (rehearsal, same version as used on *Menlove Avenue* album, unedited and longer), 6. Scared (rehearsal, same version as used on *Menlove Avenue* album, unedited and 35 seconds longer), 7. No. 9 Dream (acoustic guitar demo), 8. Surprise Surprise (Sweet Bird of Paradox) (rehearsal missing the vocal overdub), 9. Steel and Glass (same version as used on *Menlove Avenue* album, unedited and runs a minute longer), 10. Beef Jerky (alternate take), 11. Nobody Loves You (When You're Down and Out) (rehearsal, no strings), 12. Move Over Ms L (rehearsal), 13. Goodnight, Vienna (rough mix)

The Alternates

14. Whatever Gets You Through the Night (rehearsal), 15. Move Over Ms L (take 3 with piano intro)

The Home Demos

16. Whatever Gets You Through the Night (acoustic guitar demo), 17. What You Got (acoustic guitar demo), 18. Surprise Surprise (Sweet Bird of Paradox) (acoustic guitar demo), 19. Surprise Surprise (Sweet Bird of Paradox) (electric guitar demo), 20. Move Over Ms L (acoustic guitar demo), 21. Mucho Mungo (acoustic guitar demo)

The radio spots

22. *Walls and Bridges* Rundown (Canadian radio station promo spot. John Lennon runs down all the songs), 23. Listen To This (with a little help from Ringo), 24. John On KHJ-AM Los Angeles (John appears as a DJ)

Notes: Colour front cover of sleeve is picture of John wearing three pairs of glasses. Back cover has track listing and details of the tracks – digipack.

177. ALTERNATES OF FREE AS A BIRD AND 14 OTHER SONGS

Unknown

Format: CD

Source: various

Sound quality: unknown

Tracks Include: Free As Bird (take 1), Free as a Bird (take 2), Real Love (take 1), Real Love (Girls and Boys), Real Love (take 5)

Notes: Complete track listing unknown. Sleeve says, 'Famous Da-Ko-Ta Tapes and Heart Play Sessions at NT Hit Factory Studio 1980 August'.

178. ANOTHER FLAMING PIE

No Label Records NLR 9714

Format: CD

Source: tracks by The Beatles and John, Paul, George and Ringo

Sound quality: unknown

John Lennon's tracks on this release are as follows: Track 6: Remember A Fly Is Just A Fly (1.42) (John and Yoko), from 'The Making of Fly' 1971, mono. Track 7: The Luck of the Irish (4.03) (John and Yoko), from *The Luck of the Irish – A Videotape By John Relly*, recorded in New York City, Greenwich Village, 105 Bank Street, 12 November 1971, mono. New York City riff + The Luck of the Irish (rehearsal). Track 8: The Luck of the Irish (rehearsal) (1.43). Track 9: The Luck of the Irish – false start + take 1 (5.00). Track 10: The Luck of the Irish – take 1 breakdown (0.51). Track 11: The Luck of the Irish – take 2 (2.42). Track 12: The Luck of the Irish – take 3 (1.38). Track 14: Attica State, from *Sometime in New York City* sessions, March 1972 (rehearsal) (2.53)

179. ANTHOLOGY

Invasion Unlimited IU 9749

Format: CD (double)

Released: 1997

Source: various – unreleased studio outtakes, home demos, live recordings

Sound quality: very good

Disc One

1. Imagine (piano version), 2. Yer Blues (rehearsal), 3. Cold Turkey (demo), 4. Cold Turkey (studio), 5. Love, 6. God, 7. Honey Don't/Matchbox, 8. God, 9. I'm the Greatest, 10. Oh, My Love, 11. I Don't Want to Be a Soldier, 12. Happy Xmas (War Is Over), 13. Woman Is the Nigger of the World, 14. It's So Hard, 15. Mother, 16. Come Together, 17. Out the Blue, 18. You Are Here, 19. Aisumasen (I'm Sorry), 20. Bless You

Disc Two

1. Scared, 2. Steel and Glass, 3. Goodnight, Vienna, 4. That'll Be the Day, 5. Whatever Happened To, 6. Free as a Bird, 7. Everybody's Talking Nobody's Talking, 8. Nobody Told Me, 9. Real Love, 10. Corrina Corrina, 11. Watching the Wheels, 12. I'm Stepping Out, 13. (Just Like) Starting Over (home demo), 14. (Just Like) Starting Over (studio take), 15. I'm Losing You, 16. Beautiful Boy, 17. Woman, 18. Dream Lover/Stay, 19. Dear John, 20. Imagine (guitar version)

Notes: The front cover is a black-and-white picture of John sitting at his white piano. The track listing on the back is in a similar style to the official Beatles *Anthology* releases.

180. ANTHOLOGY RADIO SPECIAL

Unknown

Format: CD (double)

Source: see notes

Sound quality: unknown

Notes: See *ABC Radio Today Lennon Anthology Special*.

181. ANTHOLOGY: WEYBRIDGE

Fire Power FP. 9040

Notes: See *John Lennon Anthology: Weybridge*.

182. APPLE ACETATE (JOHN LENNON AND YOKO ONO)
Sweet Zapple SZ-202

Format: CD

Source: various

Sound quality: unknown

1. Bad To Me (1.31), 2. Laugh (December 1969) (4.07), 3. Cold Turkey (4.54), 4. Mother (5.01), 5. Remember (8.06), 6. Well, Well, Well (3.39), 7. Power to the People (single version, longer than CD), 8. Open Your Box (single version), 9. God Save Us (3.12), 10. Imagine (3.02), 11. How Do You Sleep (3.34), 12. Happy Xmas (3.32), 13. Attica State (acoustic version take 1 with Yoko) (2.53), 14. The Luck of the Irish (acoustic version) (2.31), 15. Cold Turkey (US single version, missing edit) (5.01), 16. I Found Out (long uncensored, longer than CD) (3.44), 17. Stand By Me (single version, longer than CD) (3.30)

183. APPLE 2 x 1 SIDED ROUGH ACETATE
Unicorn Records UC-081

Format: CD

Source: *Imagine* album acetates

Sound quality: unknown

Notes: For track listing see *Imagine: Apple 2 x 1 Sided Rough Acetate*.

184. ARCHIVES VOL. 1
JLBUT-0301

Format: CD

Source: various

Sound quality: very good to excellent mono/stereo

1. Strawberry Fields Forever parts 1–4 (home demo, 1970) (4.05), 2. Peggy Sue (late 70s) (0.54), 3. Watching the Wheels part 1–2 (Dakota and Hit Factory, 1980) (3.03), 4. Be-Bop-A-Lula (Hit Factory) (1.00), 5. God (1970 (1.25), 6. (I Know) I'm Losing You, Parts 1–2 (Dakota 79 and Hit Factory, 1980) (1.22), 7. Beautiful Boy, Parts 1–2 (Bermuda, 1979)

(3.00), 8. Life Begins at Forty (Dakota, 1980) (2.02), 9. Power to the People (Record Plant 1971) (2.43), 10. Clean-up Time, Parts 1–2 (2.59), 11. Mucho Mungo parts 1–3 (demo, 1973) (7.15), 12. Girls and Boys (Dakota) (2.17), 13. Woman (Bermuda) (3.07), 14. Happy Rishikesh (Dakota) (1.45), 15. Rock Island Line (Dakota) (2.32), 16. John Henry (Dakota) (1.37), 17. Tennessee Oh Tennessee, Parts 1–2 (Dakota) (1.54), 18. Surprise Surprise (Sweet Bird of Paradox) (demo, 1974) (1.19), 19. Child of Nature (EMI studios) (2.34)

185. ARCHIVES VOL. 2

JLBUT-0302

Format: CD

Source: various

Sound quality: very good to excellent mono/stereo

1. The Luck of the Irish, Parts 1–2 (studio demos 1971), 2. Every Man Has a Woman (Hit Factory, 1980), 3. He Said She Said, Parts 1–2 (home demo, Weybridge and EMI studios 1966), 4. Grow Old with Me (first demo from Dakota), 5. Little Sunshine Boy (John and Ringo, London, 1967), 6. I'm the Greatest, Parts 1–2 (home demo, Ascot, 1970 and Regents Park, 1971), 7. Make Love Not War (home demo Ascot, 1970), 8. I Promise (home demo Ascot, 1970), 9. Good Night Vienna (Record Plant West, 1974), 10. Help (Dakota), 11. You Know My Name (Look Up the Number) (home demo, Weybridge, June 1967), 12. How Do You Sleep? (home studio outtake, Ascot, 1971), 13. (Just Like) Starting Over (Dakota, take 3, 1980), 14. Sea Ditty Melody (Dakota, 1979), 15. Borrowed Time (Bermuda, 1980), 16. I Don't Want to Face It (outtake, Hit Factory, 1980)

Notes: The vinyl releases Volumes 1 and 2 were reissued as a double vinyl album under the title *Memories*.

186. ARCHIVES VOL. 3

JLBUT-0303

Format: CD

Source: various

Sound quality: very good to excellent mono/stereo

1. Whatever Gets You Through the Night, Parts 1-2 (home demo, 1974) (5.27), 2. Dear John (demo, 1980) (4.18), 3. Across the Universe (unused mix 1968) (3.45), 4. What's the New Mary Jane (original demo with George) (2.35), 5. Cooking in the Kitchen of Love (demo for Ringo's *Rotogravure* album, 1976) (2.48), 6. Knocking On Dylan's Door: Talking Roget's Thesaurus Headline Blues (acoustic satire, 1979) (2.18), 7. Revolution (Paul's house, 1968) (3.50), 8. Serve Yourself (piano demo, 1979) (5.25), 9. Getting Better (home demo, 1967) (1.03), 10. Everyone Had a Hard Year (home demo, 1968) (1.34), 11. Everybody's Got Something to Hide Except Me and My Monkey (rehearsal, 1968) (2.56), 12. I'm a Man (Dakota) (1.54), 13. Brown Eyed Handsome Man/Get Back (Dakota) (2.14), 14. 'Twas a Night like Ethel Merman (poem) (1.02), 15. Medley: Beyond the Sea/Blue Moon/Young Love (Dakota) (4.03)

Notes: Track 7: The sleeve is incorrect; this was recorded at George's house in Esher.

187. ARCHIVES VOL. 4
JLBUT-0304

Format: CD

Source: various

Sound quality: very good to excellent mono/stereo

1. Power to the People (alternate take), 2. Attica State/Luck of the Irish/John Sinclair (John Sinclair Rally, 10 December 1971), 3. Rock 'n' Roll People (demo), 4. Rock 'n' Roll People (take 5), 5. Real Life (piano demo), 6. Stepping Out (Bermuda demo), 7. Tight A$ (demo), 8. Rock Island Line (early take), 9. Love (1982 remix for UK 45 single)

188. ARCHIVES VOL. 5
JLBUT-0305

Format: CD

Source: various

Sound quality: very good to excellent mono/stereo

1. God Save Us, versions 1–2 (home demo and Morgan studios, 1971), 2. Jealous Guy (studio outtake, summer 1971), 3. Mirror Mirror (On the Wall) parts 1–5 (Dakota, 1977), 4. Maurice DuPont Agent Provocateur (Dakota, 1978), 5. Dear Prudence (outtake, 1968), 6. Watching the Wheels, versions 1–2 (home demos, Dakota, 1979), 7. Dear Yoko (Bermuda, 1979), 8. My Life, Parts 1–2 (home demos, Dakota, 1979), 9. Don't Be Crazy (home demo, Dakota, 1979), 10. (Just Like) Starting Over (studio warm up track, 1980)

189. ARCHIVES VOL. 6

JLBUT-0306

Format: CD

Source: various

Sound quality: very good to excellent mono/stereo

1. Maybe Baby (St. Regis Hotel, New York, 1971), 2. Rave On (St. Regis Hotel, New York, 1971), 3. Not Fade Away, versions 1–2 (St. Regis Hotel, New York, 1971 and the Record Plant, New York 1973), 4. That'll Be the Day (The Record Plant, New York 1973), 5. Woman, versions 1–5 (first home demo and outtakes), 6. Maggie Mae (Record Plant, New York 1973), 7. Maurice DuPont Agent Provocateur (Dakota, mid-1970s), 8. Clean-up Time (piano demo, Dakota, 1979), 9. Honey Don't (London, 1969), 10. Don't Be Cruel (London, 1969), 11. Matchbox (London, 1969), 12. Here We Go Again (studio demo, 1973), 13. Cold Turkey, versions 1–2 (home demos, 1969), 14. Sweet Little Sixteen (outtake from *Rock 'n' Roll* session, extended), 15. You Can't Catch Me (outtake from *Rock 'n' Roll* session, extended)

190. ARCHIVES VOL. 7

JLBUT-0307

Format: CD

Source: various

Sound quality: very good to excellent mono/stereo

1. One of the Boys (home demo, Dakota, 1979), 2. Mind Games (unreleased version), 3. I Don't Want to Face It (Bermuda demo,

1980), 4. Medley: Heartbeat/Peggy Sue Got Married/Peggy Sue (*Clock* soundtrack), 5. Roll Over Beethoven (Studio rehearsal for One-to-One concert 1972), 6. Whole Lotta Shaking Going On/I'll Be Looking For You (studio rehearsal for One-to-One concert), 7. Corrina Corrina (Dakota, 1979), 8. Serve Yourself (piano demo, Dakota), 9. Circus Jam (*Rock and Roll Circus* rehearsal 18 December 1968), 10. Yer Blues (*Rock and Roll Circus*), 11. Yer Blues (*Rock and Roll Circus* rehearsal 18 December 1968), 12. Yer Blues (*Rock and Roll Circus* outtake)

191. ARCHIVES VOL. 8

JLBUT-0308

Format: CD

Source: various

Sound quality: very good to excellent mono/stereo

1. Watching the Wheels (acoustic demo, Bermuda, 1980), 2. Down In Cuba with Julio Juanita LeNono (tongue in cheek calypso send up), 3. Maurice DuPont Agent Provocateur Dejour part 3, 4. Crippled Inside (outtake, summer 1971), 5. Imagine (outtake with Ringo and Klaus Voorman), 6. Sally and Billy (demo, Ascot, 1970), 7. A Case of the Blues (demo), 8. It's So Hard (outtake, Ascot, summer 1971), 9. Send Me Some Loving (New York 1971 or 1972), 10. Nobody Loves You (When You're Down and Out) (acoustic demo, 1974), 11. Stranger's Room (early piano demo, Dakota, late 1979), 12. I'm Losing You (acoustic guitar version, Bermuda, 1980), 13. New York City, versions 1–2 (St. Regis Hotel, September 1971), 14. Woman Is the Nigger of the World (acoustic guitar demo), 15. Borrowed Time (long acoustic guitar version, Bermuda, 1980)

Notes: This set of eight compact discs was first released on vinyl (Paper Plane Music). All tracks are from the radio show *The Lost Lennon Tapes*. The artwork on all the discs in this series is similar. The fronts are black with a different picture in the centre. The backs are black with the track listings printed in white.

192. Artefacts III (The Definite Collection of Beatles Rarities 1969–1974)

Big Music Big BX 009

Format: CD (four-disc set)

Released: 1996

Source: various, a collection of items from all four ex-Beatles, John's contributions (first three-discs only) are listed below

Sound quality: very good to excellent mono/stereo

Disc One

1. Cold Turkey (demo), 2. Give Peace a Chance (demo) (0.28), 3. Instant Karma (BBC Television 11 February 1970), 4. God (demo) (2.12), 5. Well, Well, Well (demo) (1.10), 6. My Mummy's Dead (1.14), 7. Happy Birthday John (1.13), 8. I'm the Greatest (demo) (1.19), 9. God Save Us (demo) (1.56), 10 Imagine (3.06), 11. I Don't Want to Be a Soldier (5.47), 12. How Do You Sleep? (5.46), 13. John's 31 Birthday (2.47), 14. Happy Xmas (War Is Over) (alternate mix) (2.47), 15. Luck of the Irish (demo) (3.13), 16. Two Face Man (3.49), 17. Attica State (Free John Sinclair Rally)

Disc Two

1. Johnny B. Goode (3.10), 2. Don't Be Cruel (rehearsal March 1972), 3. Hound Dog (rehearsal March 1972), 4. Mother (4.55), 5. Make Love Not War (3.17), 6. Move Over Ms L (outtake) (2.55), 7. I Saw Her Standing There (rehearsal with Elton John) (2.54)

Disc Three

1. As Time Goes By (0.14), 2. Mucho Mungo (0.47), 3. News of the Day (4.32), 4. With a Little Help from My Friends (0.38), 5. Beautiful Boy (2.46), 6. Watching the Wheels (3.00), 7. I'm Losing You (4.21), 8. Serve Yourself (3.38), 9. Dear John (4.17)

Notes: Virtually all the items on this set had been released previously on vinyl bootlegs and difficult to locate CDs. Comes with twenty-four-page colour booklet.

193. Artist – The Beatle Years
DIY GB No. 28
Format: CD
Released: 2001
Source: various
Sound quality: unknown

Notes: see *John Lennon Artist – The Beatle Years*.

194. Ascot Sound Studios: 21 May 1971
Stoneage Music SAM 011
Format: CD
Source: tracks 1–10 Ascot Sound Studios, Tittenhurst Park. Tracks 11–13 *Salute To Sir Lew Grade*. Tracks 14–15 *The Old Grey Whistle Test*

Tracks 1–10: Oh, My Love, 1. 1.52, 2. 3.37, 3. 3.40, 4. 0.43, 5. 4.28, 6. 2.31, 7. 2.55, 8. 7.07, 9. 3.00, 10. 3.39, 11. Slippin' and Slidin', 12. Stand By Me, 13. Imagine, 14. Slippin' and Slidin', 15. Stand By Me

Notes: Sleeve says, 'Filmed and Recorded 21th May 1971, Ascot Sound Studios, Tittenhurst Park, Ascot'. Title on side says '21th' and not '21st'.

195. Avant Garde Happening
Unknown
Format: CD
Source: WPLJ-FM, New York City, 6 June 1971
Sound quality: unknown
All tracks are untitled. Times are as follows:

1. 4.54, 2. 2.55, 3. 4.54, 4. 2.24, 5. 3.59, 6. 4.36, 7. 5.37, 8. 4.39, 9. 3.45, 10. 3.25, 11. 4.53, 12. 5.23, 13. 3.16, 14. 4.31, 15. 3.56, 16. 3.32

196. Bakhall Bonus CDs
Phantom Recording PH1002CD
Format: CD

Source: various
Sound quality: unknown

1. John sings 'My Life'. Recorded at the Dakota in late 1979, later combined with 'Don't Be Crazy' and reworked into 'Starting Over' (2.30), 2. John talks about how he met Yoko and their relationship (1.44), 3. John sings 'Dear John', home recording from the Dakota in November 1980 (4.10), 4. John talks about the 'Cosmic Joke Number 9'; the paradox of responsibility and the idea of leadership as a false God (1.30), 5. John sings his Bob Dylan parody 'Lord, Take this Make-up off Me' (2.18), 6. John talks about how important it is for everyone to produce their own dreams and go their own ways. Don't follow headers (1.13), 7. John sings 'Make Love Not War'. Recorded at Tittenhurst Park in late 1970, this song later developed into 'Mind Games' (3.13), 8. John talks about the rock star life. He is not interested in all that any longer, he is now interested in the family and in making music (1.45), 9. John sings 'Here We Go Again,' Demo recording made before the *Rock 'n' Roll* sessions in October 1973. The finished version was released on the *Menlove Avenue* album (2.57), 10. John talks about the pacifists that got shot, Ghandi, Martin Luther King. Yoko talks about the beauty of life (0.57), 11. Yoko talks about her feeling that John's spirit is still here (0.46), 12. John Lennon gave this interview to RKO General Radio of New York on the same day as he was killed. These excerpts were chosen from a more than hour long tape (3.18)

Notes: The spoken word tracks derive from the interview which John and Yoko gave to the reporter David Sheff in the autumn of 1980, except for track 11 which derives from an interview that Yoko gave to Elliot Mintz in 1981. Sleeve says, track 1–11 from *A Spaniard in the Works* bonus CD. Track 12 from the *Skywriting by Word of Mouth* bonus CD.

197. BBC Tribute to John Lennon (Long Version) (Volume One)

Unknown
Format: CD (double)
Source: BBC interview with Andy Peebles, 6 December 1980
Sound quality: excellent

Disc One: Part One

1. Give Peace a Chance/Hit Factory in New York/*Saturday Club*/Three Cool Cats/Ticket to Ride/Avant Garde/Bagism/Bed-In/Give Peace a Chance, 2. Toronto/Blue Suede Shoes/Money/Dizzy Miss Lizzie/Yer Blues/Goodbye Amsterdam Goodbye/No. 9 Dream/Mother

Disc Two: Part Two

1. Power to the People/Cold Turkey/Drug Bust/Plastic Ono Band/Mother/No. 9 Dream, 2. Instant Karma/Two Virgins/Hard Times are Over/Power to the People/Every Man Has a Woman Who Loves Him/Creative Rivalry/How Do You Sleep?/Beautiful Boy

198. BBC Tribute to John Lennon (Long Version) (Volume Two)

Unknown

Format: CD (double)

Source: BBC interview with Andy Peebles, 6 December 1980

Sound quality: excellent

Disc Three: Part Three 1972–1974

1. Ready Teddy/Just Because/Lost Weekend/Whatever Gets You Through the Night/I Saw Her Standing There (with Elton John)/Stand By Me

Part Four: 1975–1979

2. No. 9 Dream/Fame (David Bowie)/Across the Universe (David Bowie)/Phil Spector/Stand By Me/Just Because/Be Bop A Lula/*Shaved Fish*, 3. You've Got to Hide Your Love Away/Cooking/Writing/Watching the Wheels

Disc Four: Part Five

1. Woman/Geffen Records/*Double Fantasy*/Just Like Starting Over/Walking on Thin Ice/Kiss Kiss Kiss/Oh, Yoko/Beautiful Boy, 2. I'm Losing You/Woman/Reggae/B 52s/Give Peace a Chance

199. BBC Tribute to John Lennon (Short Version)

Unknown
Format: CD (double)
Source: BBC interview with Andy Peebles, 6 December 1980
Sound quality: excellent

Disc One: Parts 1, 2 and 3

Part 1

1. intro/We Come Along On Saturday Morning/Three Cool Cats/Ticket to Ride, 2. John Meets Yoko, 3. *Rape* and Bag/Ballad of John and Yoko, 4. Life with the Lions/Miscarriage, 5. Bed-In/Give Peace a Chance, 6. Toronto Concert/Wedding Album/Goodbye Amsterdam Goodbye

Part 2

7. Intro/Imagine, Power to the People/Drug Bust, 8. Plastic Ono Band/Mother, 9. 1970 *Top of the Pops*/Instant Karma/Artistic Control, 10. March 1971, 11. November 1971/Rivalry

Part 3 1972–1974

12. Deportation Case/Frank Zappa, 13. Reggae, 14. Plastic Ono Band

Disc Two: Part 3

1. Feminists/Lost Weekend/*Walls and Bridges*, 2. Elton John/Madison Square Garden/John and Yoko Reunion

Disc Two: Parts 4 and 5

Part 4 1975–1979

3. 1975–1979, 4. Phil Spector, 5. *Shaved Fish*, 6. Writing

Part 5

7. Intro/Woman/David Geffen/*Double Fantasy*/Starting Over, 8. Lyrics/Kiss Kiss Kiss, 9. Beautiful Boy/Woman, 10. New Wave Music/Sex Pistols/Reggae/B 52s, 11. Private Life/Security/Thank You/Give Peace a Chance

200. BEATLE LENNON: STEPPIN' OUT 1964–1969

Unknown

Format: CD

Source: various items from 1964–1969 (see track listing)

Sound quality: unknown

Not Only… But Also (29 November 1964, Skits from John's book) (7.50):

1. Introduction by Dudley Moore (0.26), 2. Deaf Ted, Danoota (and me) (2.23), 3. About The Awful (0.46), 4. All Aboard Speeching (1.14), 5. Good Dog Nigel (0.35), 6. Unhappy Frank (1.35), 7. The Wrestling Dog (0.53)

8. Interview on The Set of How I Won the War, November 1966 (13.50); Rolling Stones Rock and Roll Circus 10–11 December 1968:

9. Mick's introduction (0.20), 10. Blues Jam (with commentary) (4.08), 11. Yer Blues (alternate version, rehearsal) (3.55), 12. Interview with John, Julian and Mick (0.41), 13. Yer Blues (alternate version, take 1) (4.27), 14. John and Mick's 'battle of the minds' (1.04), 15. Yer Blues (alternate version, bass mix) (4.02), 16. Yer Blues (4.34)

Bed-In For Peace: Acoustic Beatle Song Performances:

17. Radio Peace (with Yoko March 1969) (0.15), 18. Don't Let Me Down/Those Were The Days (March 1969) (1.50), 19. I Want You (She's So Heavy) (March 1969) (0.54), 20. Because (late May 1969) (0.40), 21. Happiness Is a Warm Gun (late May 1969) (0.46)

John: Pop Goes The Bulldog (early December 1969) (see notes):

22. Part One (9.08), 23. Part Two (11.31), 24. Part Three (3.21)

Notes: 'John: Pop Goes the Bulldog'. The following is taken from the sleeve:

> 'Straight on the heels of his Toronto Peace Festival performance on September 13th, John's exclusive interview is the featured narrative for this history of rock music programme broadcast in December 1969. Surprisingly, John gives very technical (sic) explanation of the Beatles sound through the years, as well as rock's influences from Elvis to John Cage, and Little Richard to Stauckhausen. These references are all given great musical examples.'

201. BEATLES UNDERCOVER
C G Publishing Inc CGPINT 8008

Format: CD

Source: see below

Sound quality: excellent

1. Incantation (Dog Soldier with Patrick Jude) (3.20), 2. Let's Spend the Night Together (vocals by Lori Burton and Patrick Jude) (3.08), 3. Answer Me My Love (vocals by Lori Burton) (2.47)

Notes: This release is a pirate of the bonus CD supplied with the book *Beatles Undercover* by Kristofer Engelhardt. Track 1 – Produced by Roy Cicala and John Lennon. Lyrics by Roy Cicala and John Lennon. Track 2 – Produced and Arranged by John Lennon. Track 3 – Produced by Roy Cicala and John Lennon.

202. BEDISM
Dress To Kill 155

Format: CD

Source: conversations with John and Yoko during their Bed-In period, 1969

Sound quality: very good

1. Quebec, 2. Toronto

Notes: Disc distributed by BMG. Includes various items including the famous sparring with Al Capp as seen on the DVD release. Set comes with an eight page booklet and a postcard.

203. BEFORE PLAY – AUGUST 1980
Gnat Records, Paper Plane Music DFV 880-1

Format: CD

Source: probably from soundtrack of footage shot as basis for promo video, 18 August 1980

Sound quality: very good mono – John's voice is clear with the backing muted

1. She's a Woman (1.28), 2. C'mon Everybody (0.34), 3. She's a Woman (0.03), 4. Starting Over (1.22), 5. She's a Woman (0.55), 6. Rip It Up (1.05), 7. I'm a Man (1.31), 8. Be-Bop-A-Lula (0.59), 9. I'm Losing You (0.36), 10. Blues In The Night (0.05), 11. Starting Over (2.24), 12. I'm Losing You (0.48), 13. Blues Improvisation (2.24), 14. I'm Losing You (4.14), 15. Dream Lover/Stay (3.57), 16. She's a Woman (0.16), 17. Mystery Train (3.00)

Notes: The majority of the tracks are excerpts with 'I'm Losing You' on Side B: the only real complete performance. Most of the items on this disc are also available on the vinyl release *Winston O'Boogie*. This is a reissue of the vinyl release. The cover shows a colour picture of John and Yoko from 1980.

204. BERMUDA SHORTS
Grand High Exalted UMRK-0003

Format: CD

Source: unedited demos recorded in Bermuda in 1980

Sound quality: unknown

1. Borrowed Time, 2. Watching the Wheels, 3. Girls and Boys, 4. Beautiful Boy, 5. Serve Yourself, 6. I Don't Want to Face It, 7. I Don't Want to Face It, 8. I'm Losing You, 9. I'm Stepping Out, 10. Watching the Wheels, 11. Watching the Wheels, 12. Watching the Wheels, 13. Emotional Wreck, 14. Watching the Wheels, 15. Watching the Wheels, 16. Watching the Wheels, 17. Watching the Wheels, 18. Watching the Wheels, 19. Watching the Wheels, 20. Don't Be Afraid, 21. Woman, 22. ...For Richie

Notes: Sleeve says, 'For the first time the complete unedited demos John Lennon recorded in Bermuda, 1980. This is the way John's tape ran from start to finish.' Black-and-white cover.

205. BETWEEN THE LINES – VOL. 1
Pine Apple PNA 001

Format: CD

Source: outtakes 1975–1977

Sound quality: very good

1–3. Tennessee (takes 1, unknown and 4), 4. Everybody, 5–6. Sally and Billy (takes 2 and 3), 7. Mucho Mungo, 8–10. Cookin' (In The Kitchen of Love) (takes 1, unknown and 8), 11–12. She is a Friend of Dorothy (takes 2 and 7), 13. I Don't Want To Lose You, 14–15. Free as a Bird (takes 1 and 3), 16. 'Turned out nice again', 17–18. Whatever Happened To (takes 1 and 2)

206. BETWEEN THE LINES – VOL. 2

Pine Apple PNA 002

Format: CD

Source: outtakes late 1977–1979

Sound quality: very good

1–2. One of the Boys (takes 1 and 2), 3–5. Mirror Mirror (On the Wall) (takes 1, 2, 4 and 5), 6. Sea Ditties, 7–9. Maurice DuPont (Act 1/Act 11/Act 111), 10. Too Much Monkey Business/Subterranean Homesick Blues, 11. Rock Island Line, 12. Brown Eyed Handsome Man/Get Back, 13. Beyond the Sea/Blue Moon/Young Love, 14. Satire 1, 15. Satire 2, 16. Satire 3/Maggie Mae, 17. Falling In Love Again, 18. I'm a Man, 19. 'Twas A Night Like Ethel Merman, 20. Dialogue for a silent TV, 21. The Great Wok, 22–23. I Don't Want to Face It (take 2 and unknown take), 24. I Watch Your Face, 25. It's Real

207. BETWEEN THE LINES – VOL. 3

Pine Apple PNA 003

Format: CD

Source: outtakes

Sound quality: very good

Notes: Track details unknown.

208. BETWEEN THE LINES – VOL. 4

Pine Apple PNA 004

Format: CD

Source: outtakes

Sound quality: very good

Notes: Track details unknown.

209. BETWEEN THE LINES – VOL. 5
Pine Apple PNA 005

Format: CD

Source: outtakes

Sound quality: very good

Notes: Track details unknown.

210. BETWEEN THE LINES – VOL. 6
Pine Apple PNA 006

Format: CD

Source: outtakes, early – April 1980

Sound quality: very good

1. Watching the Wheels, 2. Stranger's Room, 3–5. John Henry, 6. Watching the Wheels, 7. Corrina Corrina, 8–9. Stranger's Room, 10–13. My Life (takes 1, 2, 3 and unknown take), 14–15. Serve Yourself, 16. Memories (take 1), 17. Cathy's Clown, 18. You Send Me, 19. Memories (take 2), 20. Welcome To Cold Spring Harbour, 21. Dear Yoko (takes 1 and 2), 22. Dialogue of Cannon Hill, 23. Blues instrumental

211. BETWEEN THE LINES – VOL. 7
Pine Apple PNA 007

Format: CD

Source: outtakes, Bermuda June 1980

Sound quality: very good

1–2. Dear Yoko (takes 1, 2 and 3), 3. Borrowed Time, 4–6. I'm Stepping Out (takes 1, 2 and unknown take), 7–9. Beautiful Boy (takes 1, 2 and overdubbed take 2), 10. Borrowed Time, 11. Dear Yoko, 12. I Don't Want to Face It, 13. Girls and Boys (overdubbed take 6), 14. Watching the

Wheels, 15. Serve Yourself, 16. Nobody Told Me (overdubbed Everybody), 17. Memories

Notes: Track 16: The sleeve states that 'Nobody Told Me' is 'overdubbed Everybody'. We have listened to all known versions of 'Nobody Told Me' but cannot trace what this refers to.

212. BETWEEN THE LINES – VOL. 8
Pine Apple PNA 008
Format: CD
Source: outtakes, Bermuda July 1980
Sound quality: very good

1–3. I'm Losing You (unknown take, overdubbed unknown take and another overdubbed version), 4. I'm Stepping Out, 5. I Don't Want to Face It, 6. I'm Stepping Out, 7. Mr Hyde's Gone (Don't Be Afraid), 8. The Happy Rishikesh Song/Something Is Wrong, 9–10. Real Love (takes 1 and 4), 11. Grow Old with Me, 12. Real Love (overdubbed take 5), 13–16. Woman (takes 1, 4, 7 and 8), 17–18. Nobody Told Me (overdubbed takes 1 and 2), 19–20. Woman (overdubbed take 8), 21. Forgive Me (My Little Flower Princess) (take 3)

213. BETWEEN THE LINES – VOL. 9
Pine Apple PNA 009
Format: CD
Source: outtakes, July–November 1980
Sound quality: very good

1–2. The Worst is Over (takes 1 and 2), 3. Help Me to Help Myself (takes 2 and 3), 4–6. My Life (takes 1, 2 and 4), 7. Serve Yourself, 8–9. Clean-up Time, 10–12. Starting Over (takes 1, 2 and 3), 13–15. Gone from This Place (takes 1, 4 and fragment), 16. Dear John, 17. You Saved My Soul

214. BIGGER THAN JESUS
Unknown
Format: CD

Source: BBC Radio documentary

Sound quality: unknown

Notes: This documentary, which was broadcast on BBC radio, examines the circumstances surrounding John's 'bigger than Jesus' remark which sparked an enormous protest in America.

215. THE BIRTHDAY TAPE

Unknown

Format: CD

Source: John's thirty-first birthday, Syracuse, New York, 9 October 1971.

Sound quality: good

1. What'd I Say (3.22), 2. Yellow Submarine (2.51), 3. On Top of Old Smokey (2.03), 4. Goodnight Irene (2.56), 5. Jesse James Was a Man/Take This Hammer ((0.15), 6. He's Got the Whole World in His Hands (2.44), 7. Like a Rolling Stone/Twist and Shout/Louie Louie/La Bamba (3.20), 8. Bring It on Home to Me (2.47), 9. Yesterday (1.44), 10. Tandoori Chicken (2.25), 11. Power to the People (0.48), 12. Maybe Baby (2.52), 13. Peggy Sue (2.28), 14. Bring out the Joints (0.27), 15. My Baby Left Me (2.05), 16. Blue Suede Shoes (3.05), 17. Crippled Inside (1.09). 18. Give Peace a Chance (3.07), 19. Crippled Inside (reprise) (0.37), 20. Uncle Albert (1.49), 21. Happy Birthday (1.02), 22. Uncle Albert (reprise) (0.18). 23. My Sweet Lord (0.25), 24. Imagine (0.48), 25. Oh, Yoko

Notes: Cover shows a black-and-white cartoon of John and Yoko surrounded by other characters.

216. BORROWED TIME

Toasted, Condor 1967

Format: CD

Released: 1989

Source: various

Sound quality: very good to excellent

1. I Found Out, 2. Rock 'n' Roll People, 3. Corrina Corrina, 4. Steel and Glass, 5. Borrowed Time, 6. How? 7. Tight A$, 8. (Just Like) Starting Over, 9. Make Love Not War, 10. How Do You Sleep? 11. Whatever Happened To, 12. Rockabilly Rave Up, 13. Dear John, 14. Crippled Inside, 15. The Happy Rishikesh Song, 16. John Henry, 17. My Life, 18. Mother

Notes: 'I Found Out', 'Borrowed Time', 'Tight A$', 'Whatever Happened To', 'Dear John', 'The Happy Rishikesh Song' and 'My Life' are demos. 'Rock and' Roll People', 'Crippled Inside' and 'Mother' are alternate versions. 'Corrina Corrina' and 'John Henry' (piano run through) are home recordings. 'Steel and Glass' is a run through. 'Starting Over' is an early mix. 'Make Love Not War' is a demo of 'Mind Games'.

217. BRANDY ALEXANDERS AND THE WALL OF SOUND – VOL. 1

Vigotone VT 235

Format: CD

Released: 2001

Time: 69.32

Source: *Rock 'n' Roll album* outtakes plus Lennon with Elton John

Sound quality: excellent

1. Be-Bop-A-Lula (2.38), 2. Ain't That a Shame (2.39), 3. Stand By Me (3.28), 4. Sweet Little Sixteen (3.01), 5. Rip It Up/Ready Teddy (1.32), 6. Angel Baby (3.07), 7. Do You Wanna Dance (3.06), 8. You Can't Catch Me (4.06), 9. Bony Moronie (3.50), 10. Peggy Sue (2.02), 11. Medley: Bring It on Home to Me/Send Me Some Loving (3.39), 12. Slippin' and Slidin' (2.21), 13. Be My Baby (4.32), 14. Ya Ya (2.16), 15. Just Because (4.24), 16. I Saw Her Standing There (3.19), 17. Whatever Gets You Through the Night (4.50), 18. Lucy in the Sky with Diamonds (6.14), 19. I Saw Her Standing There, 20. I Saw Her Standing There (3.49)

Notes: Tracks 1–15, the original *Roots* album including 'Angel Baby' and 'Be My Baby' which were omitted from the EMI release. Tracks 16–20, with Elton John. Track 16 is a rehearsal taped on 24 November 1974.

Tracks 17–19, live at Madison Square Garden, New York on 28 November 1974. Track 20, the officially B-side to Elton John's single 'Philadelphia Freedom'. This is the first of a set of CDs in clear cases enclosed in a folded carton box.

It comes with a thirty-two page booklet with photographs including John at the *Salute To Sir Lew Grade* show, detailed track listing, credits, the story behind the *Roots/Rock 'n' Roll* album, with memories of May Pang, a reproduction of the original *Roots* album vinyl disc. This sleeve on this first volume reproduces the original *Roots* album as released by Adam VIII Records.

218. BRANDY ALEXANDERS AND THE WALL OF SOUND – VOL. 2

Vigotone VT 236

Format: CD

Released: 2001

Time: 70.35

Source: *Rock 'n' Roll* album outtakes plus Lennon with Elton John

Sound quality: excellent

1. Be My Baby (6.14), 2. Just Because (6.07), 3. You Can't Catch Me (4.00), 4. Sweet Little Sixteen (4.35), 5. Bony Morony (3.55), 6. Medley: Rip It Up/Ready Teddy (1.32), 7. Ain't That a Shame (2.31), 8. Peggy Sue (2.03), 9. Be My Baby (5.45), 10. Stand By Me/Be-Bop-A-Lula (2.42), 11. Ya Ya (2.30), 12. Do You Want to Dance (0.20), 13. Do You Want to Dance (3.34), 14. Stand By Me (3.57), 15. Slippin' and Slidin' (2.24), 16. Medley: Rip It Up/Ready Teddy (1.38), 17. Medley: Bring It on Home to Me/Send Me Some Loving (2.06), 18. Medley: Bring It on Home to Me/Send Me Some Loving (3.42), 19. Peggy Sue (2.07), 20. radio spot (1.03)

Notes: Tracks 1 and 2, rough mixes from Phil Spector sessions. Tracks 3–9, rough mixes from the Lennon sessions. Tracks 10–19, offline rough mixes from the Lennon sessions. Track 20, a radio spot promoting the recently released *Rock 'n' Roll* album.

219. BRANDY ALEXANDERS AND THE WALL OF SOUND – VOL. 3

Vigotone VT 237
Format: CD
Released: 2001
Time: 71.25
Source: various – see notes
Sound quality: excellent

1. Medley: Bring It on Home to Me/Send Me Some Loving (3.45), 2. Ya Ya (1.09), 3. Ya Ya (2.25), 4. That'll Be the Day (0.09), 5. That'll Be the Day (2.22), 6. Do You Want to Dance (3.29), 7. Stand By Me (3.40), 8. Peggy Sue (2.13), 9. Be-Bop-A-Lula (1.57), 10. Slippin' and Slidin' (1.57), 11. Instrumental (2.00), 12. Thirty Days (1.29), 13. C'mon Everybody (2.15), 14. Ain't That a Shame (0.28), 15. Ain't That a Shame (1.54), 16. Ain't That a Shame (0.17), 17. Ain't That a Shame (1.16), 18. Instrumental (0.10), 19. Instrumental (0.35), 20. Slippin' and Slidin' (2.34), 21. Stand By Me (3.39), 22. Imagine (3.00), 23. Slippin' and Slidin' (2.22), 24. Imagine (3.07), 25. Imagine (3.14), 26. Stand By Me (4.09), 27. Slippin' and Slidin' (1.34), 28. Stand By Me (4.26), 29. Slippin' and Slidin' (2.25), 30. Stand By Me (3.54), 31. Slippin' and Slidin' (2.25), 32. Lady Marmalade (1.27)

Notes: Tracks 1–19, rehearsal taped in Ghent, New York in October 1974. Tracks 20–25, from the television special *Salute To Sir Lew Grade*. Taped at Waldorf Hotel, New York on 18 April 1975. Tracks 20–22, audience recording. Tracks 23 and 24, broadcast version. Track 25 is the commercial version. Tracks 26–31, recorded at Record Plant East Studios, New York in March 1975 for the BBC television programme *The Old Grey Whistle Test*. Track 26, stereo mix. Track 27, instrumental backing. Track 28, take 2. Track 29, raw version including count-in. Tracks 30 and 31, broadcast versions. Track 32, interview by Jean Francois Vallee for French television.

220. BRING ON THE LUCIE

Luna Records LU 9423
Format: CD

Time: 77.27

Source: various including *Mind Games* and *Walls and Bridges* sessions

Sound quality: unknown

1. Mind Games (4.06), 2. Tight A$ (4.15), 3. Aisumasen (I'm Sorry) (4.39), 4. One Day at a Time (3.19), 5. Bring on the Lucie (Freeda People) (4.02), 6. Intuition (2.53), 7. Out the Blue (4.11), 8. Only People (2.42), 9. I Know (I Know) (3.46), 10. Meat City (2.33), 11. Make Love Not War (3.16), 12. I Promise (1.59), 13. Tight A$ No. 2 (3.20), 14. Call My Name (5.14), 15. Call My Name No. 2 (1.27), 16. Bring on the Lucie (Freeda People) No. 2 (1.00), 17. Intuition No. 2 (2.24), 18. I Know (I Know) No. 2 (3.15), 19. Just Gotta Give Me Some Rock 'n' Roll/Shoeshine (3.41), 20. Meat City No. 2 (2.36), 21. Borrowed Time (4.57), 22. Surprise Surprise (Sweet Bird of Paradox) (2.58), 23. Watching the Wheels (2.53), 24. Move Over Ms L (1.50)

Notes: Sleeve says, all tracks recorded between 1973 and 1974 although tracks 21 and 23 are from the *Double Fantasy* sessions 1979/1980.

221. CHANNELING THE CENTER FROM WITHIN

Two Boys Limited Labs TDL-004

Format: CD

Time: 65.58

Source: all tracks taken from 5.1 centre channel mixes of *Lennon Legend* DVD (released 2003)

Sound quality: excellent

1. Imagine (3.02), 2. Instant Karma (3.30), 3. Jealous Guy (4.14), 4. Power to the People (bass and drums) (3.43), 5. Cold Turkey (5.02), 6. Love (backing track) (2.14), 7. Mind Games (4.10), 8. Whatever Gets You Through the Night (3.34), 9. No. 9 Dream (4.43), 10. Stand By Me (4.03), 11. Woman (instrumental) (3.32), 12. Beautiful Boy (Darling Boy) (3.45), 13. Watching the Wheels (3.31), 14. Nobody Told Me (3.58), 15. Borrowed Time (4.39), 16. Happy Xmas (War Is Over) (3.22), 17. Give Peace a Chance (4.56)

222. CHRISTMAS PRESENT

White Fly WF 001/3
Format: CD (triple box set with booklet)
Source: various
Sound quality: varies

Disc One
1. Mother (5.04), 2. Imagine (3.31), 3. Come Together (4.15), 4. Give Peace a Chance (7.37), 5. Cold Turkey (acoustic demo) (3.31), 6. Too Much Monkey Business (acoustic demo) (1.58), 7. Brown Eyed Handsome Man (acoustic demo) (2.44), 8. Rock Island Line (acoustic demo) (2.35), 9. Chords of Fame (John with Phil Ochs) (4.08), 10. Rock Island Line (electric version) (2.53), 11. Jealous Guy (4.18), 12. Mirror Mirror (On the Wall) (take 1) (2.28), 13. Mirror Mirror (On the Wall) (take 5) (2.38), 14. Dear Prudence (*White Album* demo, 1968) (2.28), 15. Cold Turkey (electric rehearsal) (4.14), 16. New York City (live) (3.00), 17. Watching the Wheels (demo) (3.54), 18. Dear Yoko (3.46), 19. My Life (version 1) (2.21), 20. (Just Like) Starting Over (rough mix) (4.56)

Disc Two
1. I Found Out (acoustic) (4.05), 2. God (2.47), 3. The Worst is Over (take 1) (2.26), 4. Beautiful Boy (composing sequence) (5.53), 5. When a Boy Meets a Girl (take 1) (2.11), 6. I'm So Tired (with Mike Love) (3.02), 7. Sexy Sadie (2.20), 8. The Maharishi Song (with Yoko) (3.16), 9. Revolution (1968) (3.56), 10. God (2.20), 11. How? (4.32), 12. Beautiful Boy/Memories/Howling at the Moon (1.59), 13. The Dakota Rap/Across the River (3.33), 14. I'm the Greatest (take 4 with Ringo, 1973), 15. How Do You Sleep? (7.39), 16. Oh, My Love (2.10), 17. Untitled Jam (1.51), 18. Imagine (piano solo) (2.58), 19. Woman Is the Nigger of the World (John and Yoko 1972) (1.56), 20. Real Life (piano solo) (4.16), 21. I'm Stepping Out (take 1) (5.04), 22. I Don't Want to Face It (1.54), 23. I Watch Your Face (2.07), 24. My Life (take 1) (3.12)

Disc Three
1. Woman Is the Nigger of the World (5.53), 2. Well, Well, Well (rehearsal 22 August 1972) (5.53), 3. Come Together (rehearsal 18 August 1972)

(5.33), 4. Hound Dog/Long Tall Sally (jam 21 August 1972) (5.21), 5. Don't Let Me Down (2.03), 6. Yer Blues (with Keith Richards, Eric Clapton and Mitch Mitchell) (4.04), 7. Rock 'n' Roll People (3.02), 8. Mind Games (2.14), 9. Jealous Guy (4.17), 10. Imagine (*Mike Douglas Show*) (3.36), 11. Give Me Some Truth (3.36), 12. Power to the People (4.16), 13. John Sinclair (2.50), 14. Instant Karma (3.00), 15. Ain't That a Shame (2.25), 16. On The Caribbean (3.06), 17. Intuition (3.51), 18. Stand By Me (partial mix) (1.52), 19. Oh, Yoko (4.00), 20. I Saw Her Standing There (with Elton John), 21. I'm Losing You (3.51)

Notes: Each of the three volumes features a different front cover showing a close up of John's face, Disc 1 mouth, Disc 2 eye, Disc 3 nose. Detailed track listing on the back of each volume.

223. CLOCK

Sky 101

Format: CD

Released: 1997

Time: 28.29

Source: St Regis Hotel, New York, September 1971

Sound quality: good mono

1. Aisumasen (three takes), 2. Shazam (instrumental), 3. Honey Don't, 4. Instrumental, 5. Glad All Over, 6. Lend Me Your Comb, 7. New York City (instrumental), 8. Wake Up Little Susie, 9. Baby I Don't Care, 10. Vacation Has Just Began, 11. Heartbeat/Peggy Sue Got Married, 12. Peggy Sue 1 and 2, 13. Maybe Baby, 14. Mailman Bring Me No More Blues, 15. Rave On/Instrumental

Notes: These tracks were recorded in John's hotel room at the St Regis Hotel, New York City in September 1971. They were intended for the soundtrack of the film *Clock* which was subsequently screened at Yoko's art exhibition on 9 October in Syracuse, New York. The songs on this recording are in the main John accompanying himself on guitar with Yoko joining in now and then. We also hear telephone calls that interrupt the session. These songs have been previously bootlegged, for example on *The Lost*

Lennon Tapes but some of the versions on this disc are more complete. These songs were also recorded but were omitted from this disc: 'Not Fade Away', 'Send Me Some Loving' and, possibly, 'J.J. (Angela)'.

The track listing on the back does not include 'Mailman Bring Me No More Blues', 'Rave On', 'Heartbeat', 'Maybe Baby'. This release appears to be from unedited tape and no edits are evident although we do know that other songs were recorded. The recording is quite good quality but it does sound as though the taping equipment used was not the best available.

224. COME BACK JOHNNY

Melvin Records MM.09

Format: CD

Source: various

Sound quality: unknown

1. Comment to a bleary eyed Bob Dylan (from *Eat the Document*) (0.17), 2. New York City (5.02), 3. It's So Hard (3.14), 4. Woman Is the Nigger of the World (5.15), 5. *Walls and Bridges* radio spot (with Ringo) (0.28), 6. WNEW radio guest DJ (1.04), 7. Well, Well, Well (5.24), 8. Instant Karma (3.15), 9. Goodnight, Vienna – radio spot (0.30), 10. WNEW radio guest DJ (1.23), 11. With Howard Cosell (1.23), 12. Mother (4.43), 13. Come Together (4.05), 14. Cold Turkey (5.18), 15. Hound Dog (2.50), 16. Medley: Well/Rock Island Line/Maybe Baby/Peggy Sue (1.56), 17. About Chuck Berry (0.46), 18. Johnny B. Goode (with Chuck Berry) (2.55), 19. Imagine (3.24), 20. Lennon/McCartney feud (0.16)

Notes: Tracks 2, 3, 7, 8, 12, 13, 14 and 15 are from the One-to-One concert.

225. COME ON, LISTEN TO ME

His Masters Choice HMC 004

Format: CD (double) with hardback book Released: 2007

Source: *Walls and Bridges* outtakes, demos and rehearsals

Sound quality: excellent

Disc One

Come On, Listen To Me

1. Going Down on Love (rehearsal) (4.01), 2. Whatever Gets You Through the Night (overdub on take 7) (3.35), 3. Old Dirt Road (rehearsal) (4.41), 4. What You Got (alternate take) (4.08), 5. Bless You (rehearsal with false start) (6.32), 6. Scared (rehearsal) (4.53), 7. No. 9 Dream (promo edit) (2.52), 8. Surprise Surprise (Sweet Bird of Paradox) (3.36), 9. Steel and Glass (rehearsal) (5.16), 10. Beef Jerky (rehearsal) (3.17), 11. Nobody Loves You (When You're Down and Out) (5.14)

Whatever Gets You Through the Night sessions (part 1)

12. Whatever Gets You Through the Night (take unknown) (3.15), 13. Whatever Gets You Through the Night (take unknown) (2.50), 14. Whatever Gets You Through the Night (take unknown) (3.18), 15. Whatever Gets You Through the Night (take unknown) (3.05), 16. Whatever Gets You Through the Night (take unknown) (3.34), 17. Whatever Gets You Through the Night (take unknown) (2.13), 18. Whatever Gets You Through the Night (take unknown) (4.14), 19. Whatever Gets You Through the Night (take unknown) (3.34), 20. Whatever Gets You Through the Night (take unknown) (4.17)

Disc Two

Whatever Gets You Through the Night sessions (part 2)

1. Ain't She Sweet (improvisation) (0.27), 2. Whatever Gets You Through the Night (take unknown) (2.43), 3. Whatever Gets You Through the Night (take unknown) (3.34), 4. Whatever Gets You Through the Night (take unknown) (2.35), 5. Whatever Gets You Through the Night (take unknown) (0.47), 6. Whatever Gets You Through the Night (take unknown) (3.23), 7. Whatever Gets You Through the Night (take unknown) (1.46), 8. Whatever Gets You Through the Night (take unknown) (2.50), 9. Whatever Gets You Through the Night (take unknown) (2.57), 10. Whatever Gets You Through the Night (take unknown) (4.02), 11. Whatever Gets You Through the Night (take unknown) (1.23), 12. Whatever Gets You Through the Night (take unknown) (2.02), 13. Whatever Gets You Through the Night (take 10) (4.02), 14. Whatever

Gets You Through the Night (take 11) (4.02), 15. Whatever Gets You Through the Night (takes 12 and 13) (0.56), 16. Whatever Gets You Through the Night (take 14) (4.01), 17. Whatever Gets You Through the Night (take 15) (2.28), 18. Whatever Gets You Through the Night (takes 16 and 17) (0.32), 19. Whatever Gets You Through the Night (take 18) (3.49), 20. Whatever Gets You Through the Night (take unknown) (2.19), 21. Whatever Gets You Through the Night (take unknown) (2.44)

Walls and Bridges outtakes

22. Whatever Gets You Through the Night (alternate take) (3.48), 23. Move Over Ms L (rehearsal with false start) (2.55), 24. Bless You (alternate take) (3.51), 25. Whatever Gets You Through The Night (rehearsal) (1.44), 26. Beef Jerky (alternate take) (3.27), 27. Move Over Ms L (alternate take) (2.40), 28. Whatever Gets You Through The Night (rough mix) (3.30)

Notes: This was the third release by a new label, His Masters Choice, the first being *The Beatles and The Great Concert At Shea!* (details of this will be shown in *The Beatles Bootleg Discography*). This set concentrates on the *Walls and Bridges* album and comes packaged as a hardback book with twenty pages of text and includes colour photographs.

Copies of the set have since become available in a slimline DVD case but without the book. Two other John Lennon releases in a similar format were issued: It's Gonna Be Alright (John Lennon/Plastic Ono Band) (HMC 002) and Remember New York City (John Lennon/Yoko Ono) (HMC 003).

226. COME TOGETHER

Oil Well RSC 025 CD

Format: CD

Source: various

Sound quality: unknown

1. Mother, 2. Imagine, 3. Come Together, 4. Give Peace a Chance, 5. Cold Turkey No. 1, 6. Too Much Monkey Business, 7. Brown Eyed Handsome Man, 8. Rock Island Line No. 1, 9. Chords of Fame, 10. Rock Island Line No. 2, 11. Jealous Guy, 12. Dear Prudence, 13. Cold Turkey

No. 2, 14. New York City, 15. Watching the Wheels, 16. Dear Yoko, 17. My Life, 18. (Just Like) Starting Over

Notes: Sleeve says, 'Live in Providence, Rhode Island, December 30, 1973'.

227. COME TOGETHER

Undercover UC-006

Format: CD

Source: tracks 1–4 One-to-One concert rehearsals, August 1972. Tracks 5–11 One-to-One concert, Madison Square Garden, New York, 30 August 1972 (evening show)

Sound quality: unknown

1. Honky Tonk, 2. Mind Train, 3. Come Together, 4. We're All Water, 5. Mother, 6. Imagine, 7. Interview, 8. Come Together, 9. Interview, 10. Give Peace a Chance, 11. Interview

228. COME TOGETHER

Alegra CD 9004

Format: CD

Released: 1995

Time: 50.14

Source: various live performances (see notes)

Sound quality: unknown

1. Come Together (4.02), 2. Attica State (2.55), 3. John Sinclair (2.50), 4. Instant Karma (3.13), 5. Imagine (2.57), 6. Yer Blues (3.33), 7. Woman Is the Nigger of the World (5.35), 8. Mother (4.40), 9. Blue Suede Shoes (2.12), 10. Money (3.00), 11. The Luck of the Irish (3.13), 12. Cold Turkey (2.56), 13. Imagine (acoustic version) (2.56), 14. Give Peace a Chance (3.06), 15. Dizzy Miss Lizzie (3.05)

Notes: Live performances: Track 13 Apollo Theatre, New York, November 1971. Tracks 1, 8, 4, 5 Madison Square Garden, New York, 30 August 1972. Tracks 6, 9, 10, 12, 14, 15 Toronto, September 1969. Tracks 2, 3, 11 Ann Arbor, Michigan, 10 December 1971. Track 7 February 1972.

229. COME TOGETHER: A JOHN LENNON CHRISTMAS

Black Cat BC 026
Format: CD
Source: various
Sound quality: unknown

Segment One
1. Introduction, 2. Nobody Told Me, 3. Julian Lennon Message, 4. I Want to Hold Your Hand, 5. Twist and Shout, 6. Mike Love Message

Segment Two
7. Whatever Gets You Through the Night, 8. Elton John Interview, 9. I Saw Her Standing There

Segment Three
10. Ron Wood Message, 11. John Lennon Interview, 12. Ain't That a Shame, 13. Yoko Ono Interview, 14. In My Life, 15. Tom Petty Message

Segment Four
16. 1969 Fan Club Message, 17. Happy Xmas (War Is Over), 18. Yoko Ono Interview, 19. Imagine

Notes: Front cover features John dressed as Father Christmas with Yoko, also dressed as Father Christmas but with a black beard, and Mary Hopkin in front of a Christmas tree.

230. COME TOGETHER (BEATLES IN THE 90S)

Fab 3 FAB 3
Format: CD
Released: 1996
Time: 63.39
Source: various
Sound quality: good to excellent mono/stereo

1. Free as a Bird (5.11), 2. Real Love (3.05), 3. Real Love (4.12), 4. Strawberry Fields Forever (0.23), 5. I Will (0.34), 6. Derradune (0.39), 7. Free as a Bird (3.27), 8. Free as a Bird (2.42), 9. Real Love (3.47), 10. Real Love (3.57), 11. Real Love (2.47), 12. Real Love (2.21), 13. Real Love (3.09), 14. Real Love (1.30), 15. It Don't Come Easy (1.41), 16. The Long and Winding Road (3.32), 17. Let It Be (4.00), 18. Come Together (3.33), 19. While My Guitar Gently Weeps (8.07), 20. Studio mistakes (1.25)

Notes: Track 1, full length video version with 'wings' intro and backwards message reversed. Track 2, alternate Beatles mix. Track 3, Beatles video mix. Track 4, from *Anthology*. Track 5, Paul, George and Ringo on *Anthology*. Track 6, George on *Anthology*. Track 7, Lennon demo 1. Track 8, Lennon demo 3. Track 9, Lennon demo 1. Track 10, Lennon demo 4. Track 11, Lennon demo 5. Track 12, Lennon demo 6. Track 13, Lennon demo, take unknown. Track 14, from *Imagine*. Track 15, George demo for Ringo. Tracks 16 and 17, *Let It Be* outtakes. Track 18, 'Smokin' Mojo Filters' alternate mix with Paul on vocals. Track 19, George at the Natural Law Party concert, Royal Albert Hall, 6 April 1992. Track 20, collage of outtakes from *Anthology* video. A collection of items from various sources. This release was followed by a similar disc *When I Get Older (Beatles in the 90s)*.

231. COMPLETED RARITIES VOL. 1

Polyphone PH 1313

Format: CD

Released: 1990

Source: various

Sound quality: unknown

1. Every Man Has a Woman Who Loves Him (John solo), 2. (Just Like) Starting Over, 3. Do the Oz, 4. Yer Blues (*Rock and Roll Circus*), 5. Jam (*Rock and Roll Circus*), 6. Attica State (*David Frost Show*), 7. Attica State (reprise to emphasise lyrics), 8. Dogtown (John and Yoko), 9. Will You Touch Me (John and Yoko), 10. Mucho Mungo (take 1), 11. Mucho Mungo (take 2), 12. Mucho Mungo (take 3), 13. Slippin' and Slidin'

(*Salute To Sir Lew Grade*), 14. Imagine (*Salute To Sir Lew Grade*), 15. Serve Yourself (acoustic, obscene lyrics), 16. Imagine (acoustic, Apollo, New York, 1971), 17. Radio Peace (promo, 1969), 18. Angel Baby (from Roots), 19. I Saw Her Standing There (rehearsal with Elton John), 20. *Walls and Bridges* Ad (with Ringo), 21. As Time Goes By (John and Yoko), 22. Peace Message/Make Love to the End, 23. As Time Goes By (John solo), 24. Oh, My Love (outtake), 25. Lady Marmalade (during interview), 26. Give Peace a Chance (1969 rehearsal), 27. Let's Twist Again (outtake, Lennon and Bowie, 1974)

Notes: This release from Polyphone is titled *Volume 1*. We have not been able to trace any further volumes in this series.

232. COMPLETED RARITIES – VOL. 1
B and B Communications CDB 007
Format: CD
Released: 2000
Source: various
Sound quality: unknown

1. Cold Turkey (demo, 1969), 2. Give Peace a Chance (demo, 1969), 3, Instant Karma (BBC TV 11 February 1970), 4. God (demo, summer 1970), 5. Well, Well, Well (demo, summer 1970), 6. My Mummy's Dead (demo, summer 1970), 7. I'm the Greatest (piano demo, 1970), 8. God Save Oz (demo June 1971), 9. Imagine (early take), 10. I Don't Want to Be a Soldier (early take), 11. How Do You Sleep? (early take), 12. Rave On/Not Fade Away (from *Clock*), 13. Yellow Submarine (John's thirty-first birthday), 14. Happy Xmas (alternate take), 15. The Luck of the Irish, 16. Attica State (Ann Arbor), 17. Johnny B. Goode (*Mike Douglas Show* with Chuck Berry), 18. Don't Be Cruel (*Sometime in New York City* rehearsal)

233. COMPLETED RARITIES – VOL. 2
B and B Communications CDB 008
Format: CD
Released: 2000

Source: various

Sound quality: unknown

1. Hound Dog (*Sometime in New York City* rehearsals), 2. Mother (One-to-One rehearsal), 3. Make Love Not War (demo), 4. Lucille (John and Paul, Los Angeles 1974), 5. Only You (John demo for *Ringo*), 6. Move Over Ms L (outtake), 7. I Saw Her Standing There (John with Elton John, rehearsal), 8. As Time Goes By (John and Yoko during Elliot Mintz interview), 9. Mucho Mungo (demo), 10. News of the Day (parody of Dylan), 11. My Life (demo), 12. With a Little Help from My Friends (John and Sean), 13. Beautiful Boy (demo), 14. Watching the Wheels (demo), 15. I'm Losing You (outtake with Cheap Trick), 16. Serve Yourself, 17. Dear John (demo), 18. Free as a Bird (original piano demo)

THE COMPLETE LOST LENNON TAPES (WALRUS RECORDS)

This set of twenty-two volumes was issued as eleven double CD sets. The track listing is the same as the thirty five vinyl release set issued by Bag Records (the later volumes also issued on compact disc). Details of the Bag Records vinyl releases can be found in Part One – Vinyl Releases. Each of the double CD sets issued by Walrus Records came in a standard double jewel case with a colour front sleeve and full track listing on the back. The sound quality during this series is an upgrade of the Bag Records set.

234. THE COMPLETE LOST LENNON TAPES – VOLS 1 AND 2

Walrus Records 002/003

Format: CD (double)

Released: 1997

Time: Disc One 62.08, Disc Two 65.04

Source: various

Sound quality: very good to excellent

Disc One – Volume 1

1. Strawberry Fields Forever (3.05), 2. The Happy Rishikesh Song (1.54), 3. Rock Island Line (2.34), 4. John Henry (1.39), 5. Surprise Surprise (Sweet Bird of Paradox) (1.21), 6. Keep Right on to the End of the Road (0.41),

7. Goodnight Vienna (2.54), 8. Tennessee (takes 1 and 4) (1.56), 9. God Save Us (3.09), 10. With a Little Help from My Friends (3.08), 11. Power to the People (2.31), 12. Here We Go Again (2.31), 13. Mucho Mungo (2.13), 14. God (1.27), 15. Life Begins at Forty (2.04), 16. Woman (3.08), 17. Girls and Boys (2.22), 18. Clean-up Time (3.11), 19. Beautiful Boy (2.48), 20. Revolution (3.54), 21. Child of Nature (2.34), 22. He Said He Said/She Said She Said (1.08), 23. I'm the Greatest (early demo) (1.23), 24. Make Love Not War (3.15), 25. How Do You Sleep? (8.10), 26. Daddy's Little Sunshine Boy (0.30)

Disc Two – Volume 2

1. I'm the Greatest (2.53), 2. The Luck of the Irish (3.13), 3. Every Man Has a Woman Who Loves Him (3.19), 4. Starting Over (4.55), 5. I Promise (1.58), 6. Sea Ditty/Leaning on a Lamp Post (2.36), 7. Grow Old Along With Me (3.21), 8. Strawberry Fields Forever (2.44), 9. What's the New Mary Jane (2.37), 10. Julia (3.41), 11. Across the Universe (3.48), 12. You Know My Name (Look Up the Number) (1.02), 13. Help (0.44), 14. Whatever Gets You Through the Night (5.30), 15. We Must Not Forget The General Erection (0.34), 16. The Wumberlog or the Magic Dog (0.32), 17. Dear John (4.17), 18. Whatever Happened To (4.17), 19. Cookin' (In The Kitchen of Love) (2.30), 20. Peggy Sue (0.56), 21. Watching the Wheels (0.39), 22. Watching the Wheels (1.47), 23. I'm Losing You (0.48), 24. Beautiful Boy (1.42), 25. Clean-up Time (2.25), 26. One-to-One radio spot outtakes (1.25)

Notes: This set comprises Volumes 1–3 of the vinyl releases *The Lost Lennon Tapes* (Bag Records). Disc One is Volume One (tracks 1–19) plus seven tracks of Volume Two. Disc Two contains the rest of Volume Two plus Volume Three.

These discs have been declicked and upgraded from the original releases and are superb sound quality.

235. THE COMPLETE LOST LENNON TAPES – VOLS 3 AND 4

Walrus Records 010/11

Format: CD (double)

Released: 1997

Source: various

Sound quality: very good to excellent

Disc One – Volume 3

1. Revolution (3.22), 2. Power to the People (2.47), 3. Attica State (3.22), 4. The Luck of the Irish (3.27), 5. John Sinclair (3.31), 6. I'm a Man (1.54), 7. 'Twas a Night like Ethel Merman (1.05), 8. Medley: Beyond the Sea/Blue Moon/Young Love (4.08), 9. Clean-up Time (3.22), 10. Good Morning, Good Morning (1.01), 11. Everybody's Got Something to Hide Except Me and My Monkey (2.55), 12. Everyone Had a Hard Year (1.33), 13. Brown Eyed Handsome Man (2.14), 14. Serve Yourself (5.25), 15. Lord, Take This Make Up off Me (2.20), 16. The News of the Day (from Reuters) (4.25), 17. Dear Prudence (4.42), 18. Jealous Guy (4.06), 19. God Save Us (1.55), 20. Rock 'n' Roll People (2.10), 21. Rock Island Line (2.48), 22. Real Life (4.51), 23. My Life (take 1) (0.55), 24. My Life (take 3) (2.38), 25. Don't Be Crazy (1.38), 26. The Worst is Over (3.29)

Disc Two – Volume 4

1. In The Studio (2.30), 2. Starting Over (vocal booth) (4.23), 3. Starting Over (4.17), 4. Maggie Mae (0.23), 5. Honey Don't (1.35), 6. Don't Be Cruel (1.29), 7. Matchbox (1.53), 8. Dear Prudence (3.55), 9. Cold Turkey (3.36), 10. Here We Go Again (take 2) (3.00), 11. Woman (3.29), 12. The Neville Club (0.42), 13. Rock 'n' Roll People (6.00), 14. Not Fade Away (0.56), 15. Sweet Little Sixteen (4.18), 16. You Can't Catch Me (3.26), 17. Mirror Mirror (take 1) (2.38), 18. Mirror Mirror (take 5), 19. Mind Games (alternate take), 20. Cold Turkey (from acetcte), 21. One of the Boys (Dakota tape), 22. Tight A$ (original demo), 23. Studio Banter, 24. Woman (vocal booth), 25. Dear Yoko (demo), 26. I Don't Want to Face It (demo)

Notes: Disc One: 'Revolution' is a significantly remixed version of The Beatles single (Nicky Hopkins piano and John's guitar are not audible on this version). 'Good Morning, Good Morning', original demo from 1967. 'Everybody's Got Something To Hide' (called 'Come On, Come on' at the time of this recording) is The Beatles demo version. 'Everyone Had a Hard Year', demo from 1968 – this song wcs eventually incorporated into 'I've Got a Feeling'. 'Attica State', 'The Luck of the Irish' and 'John Sinclair' are from the Free John Sinclair Rally. 'Clean-up Time', unreleased mix. 'Power to the People', alternate take. 'I'm a Man', 'Brown Eyed Handsome Man', 'Twas A Night Like Ether Merman' and the oldies medley are Dakota cassette recordings. Tracks 14–16 are Bob Dylan parodies ('Serve Yourself' is the piano version with 'clean' lyrics). 'Dear Prudence' is the 1968 demo. 'Jealous Guy', studio outtake. 'God Save Us' and 'Rock 'n' Roll People', original acoustic demos. 'Rock Island Line', electric guitar version, Dakota. 'Real Life', piano demo, Dakota.

Disc Two: Tracks 1–3 chronicle the evolution of 'Starting Over' from the *Double Fantasy* album. 'Maggie Mae' was recorded at the Hit Factory in 1980. 'Honey Don't', 'Matchbox' and 'Don't Be Cruel' were recorded during the *Plastic Ono Band* album sessions. 'Dear Prudence' is a different mix of The Beatles track. 'Cold Turkey', original demo. 'Here We Go Again', 'Woman' and the unreleased song 'Mirror Mirror' are demos. 'The Neville Club' is John reading from his book *In His Own Write*. Most of the remaining tracks feature recordings from John's working relationship with Phil Spector as well as an out of control jam of 'Not Fade Away' with the Elephant's Memory Band.

236. THE COMPLETE LOST LENNON TAPES – VOLS 5 AND 6
Walrus Records 014/015
Format: CD (double)
Released: 1997
Time: Disc One 76.53, Disc Two 75.35
Source: various
Sound quality: very good to excellent

Disc One – Volume 5

1. Watching the Wheels (demo), 2. I'm Stepping Out (demo), 3. Clean-up Time (demo), 4. Woman (outtake), 5. Roll Over Beethoven, 6. Whole Lotta Shakin', 7. It'll Be Me, 8. One-to-One Radio outtakes, 9. New York City (rehearsals with Elephant's Memory), 10. God Save Us (demo), 11. Introduction (by John and Mick Jagger), 12. Dirty Mac Jam (*Rock and Roll Circus* outtake), 13. Maurice DuPont (Dakota demo), 14. That'll

Be the Day (Quarrymen), 15. Rave On, 16. Not Fade Away, 17. Maybe Baby, 18. Heartbeat, 19. Peggy Sue Got Married, 20. Peggy Sue, 21. Corrina Corrina, 22. Serve Yourself (demo), 23. The Best Things In Life Are Free, 24. *Eat the Document* (with Bob Dylan), 25. A Nice Noise (with Sean), 26. Tomorrow Never Knows (rough mix), 27. Strawberry Fields Backwards Test (abandoned test), 28. Aerial Tour Instrumental (unreleased version of 'Flying'), 29. Cry Baby Cry, 30. Dear Prudence, 31. Sexy Sadie

Disc Two – Volume 6
1. Julia, 2. Child of Nature, 3. The Continuing Story of Bungalo Bill, 4. I'm So Tired, 5. Yer Blues, 6. Everybody's Got Something to Hide Except Me and My Monkey, 7. What's the New Mary Jane, 8. Revolution. 9. Imagine, 10. Crippled Inside. 11. It's So Hard, 12. A Case of the Blues, 13. Sally and Billy, 14. Sally and Billy (take 3), 15. Send Me Some Loving (acoustic outtake), 16. Woman Is the Nigger of the World (demo), 17. New York City (demo Que Pasa New York), 18. Only You (John's guide version for Ringo Starr), 19. Down In Cuba (unreleased track), 20. Surprise Surprise (unedited demo), 21. Whatever Gets You Through the Night (early studio run through), 22. Watching the Wheels (guitar demo), 23. I'm Losing You (early piano demo), 24. Borrowed Time (guitar demo), 25. Tobias Casuals (words from the sponsor), 26. Happy Birthday John (from John's 30 birthday party), 27. Julia (demo)

Notes: Tracks have been de-noised and de-clicked. Disc One: tracks 15–20 are acoustic demos. Disc Two: Tracks 1–8 are *White Album* demos. Tracks 9–11 are *Imagine* album outtakes.

237. THE COMPLETE LOST LENNON TAPES – VOLS 7 AND 8
Walrus Records 017/018
Format: CD (double)
Released: 1997
Source: various
Sound quality: very good to excellent

Disc One – Volume 7

1. Mother (3.24) (outtake), 2. I Found Out (longer alternate mix) (3.57), 3. What'd I Say (0.37), 4. How (outtake) (3.36), 5. Yellow Submarine (0.36), 6. Chi-Chi's Cafe (3.28), 7. Beautiful Boy (demo) (2.46), 8. Howling at the Moon (unreleased) (1.57), 9. Memories (unreleased) (2.33), 10. Stranger's Room (guitar and drum machine demo), 11. Everybody's Talking Nobody's Talking (1.37), 12. Nobody Told Me (3.20), 13. Beautiful Boy (3.24), 14. New York City (demo), 15. Don't Be Cruel (jamming with Elephant's Memory), 16. Hound Dog (jamming with Elephant's Memory), 17. Send Me Some Loving (jam), 18. I Found Out (acoustic demo), 19. Happy Xmas (War Is Over) (original demo) (3.15), 20. John and Yoko's Happy Xmas Ditty (home recording) (1.32), 21. Tobias Casuals No. 2 (1.11), 22. Borrowed Time (alternate studio take) (3.03), 23. God (early demo) (2.41), 24. Serve Yourself (slow and bluesy outtake) (4.48), 25. Imagine (studio outtake) (2.55), 26. Mucho Mungo (acoustic guitar and electric piano version) (2.17), 27. Mount Elga (acoustic guitar and electric piano version) (1.12), 28. Gone from This Place (Dakota recording) (3.18), 29. Stand By Me (2.32)

Disc Two – Volume 8

1. The Great Wok (2.01), 2. Yer Blues (*Rock and Roll Circus* rehearsal) (1.30), 3. I Found Out (demo, take 2) (3.23), 4. Oh, Yoko (demo) (0.55), 5. People Get Ready/How? (demo) (3.01), 6. Pill (1.40), 7. Out the Blue (basic track with no overdubs, no instrumental overdubs, longer than released take) (4.16), 8. No. 9 Dream (demo), 9. Tobias Casuals No. 3 (1.04), 10. John Henry (Dakota demo) (1.02), 11. She is a Friend of Dorothy (Dakota demo, piano) (2.37), 12. Real Love (Dakota piano demo, take 1) (3.56), 13. Dear Yoko (rough take, unfinished version) (3.09), 14. (Just Like) Starting Over (longer fade out) (4.19), 15. The Return of Maurice DuPont (2.45), 16. *Wedding Album* Commercial (0.16), 17. Stay In Bed (Grow Your Hair (0.47), 18. Because (vocals only) (2.15), 19. Oh, Yoko (outtake) (5.52), 20. *Grapefruit* excerpts (reading from Yoko's book), 21. Imagine (alternate take) (2.48), 22. Give Me Some Truth (Tittenhurst outtake) (3.41), 23. How? (alternate Take) (3.43), 24. San Francisco Bay Blues (acoustic) (1.18), 25. Oh, My Love (Tittenhurst outtake) (2.26), 26. How Do You Sleep? (outtake) (5.54), 27. Tobias Casuals No. 4 (1.13), 28. Stand By Me (3.48)

238. THE COMPLETE LOST LENNON TAPES – VOLS 9 AND 10

Walrus Records 019/020

Format: CD (double)

Released: 1997

Source: various

Sound quality: very good to excellent

Disc One – Volume 9

1. I'm Stepping Out (*Double Fantasy* sessions, 1 day) (5.35), 2. I'm the Greatest (take 2) (2.15), 3. Move Over Ms L (early *May Pang* demo) (1.34), 4. Bring on the Lucie (Freeda People) (riff fragment) (1.02), 5. Bring on the Lucie (Freeda People) (rough mix of nearly completed take) (4.02), 6. No. 9 Dream (earliest demo) (2.10), 7. People (demo for Angela), 8. The Luck of the Irish (early attempt, unfinished lyrics) (0.54), 9. The Luck of the Irish (more polished version) (1.42), 10. Only People (rough mix) (2.39), 11. Rock 'n' Roll People (alternate take) (2.41), 12. Mind Games Promo (Ringo giving John help for a radio spot) (0.59), 13. Forgive Me (My Little Flower Princess) (Dakota demo, take 3) (3.25), 14. Tower Records Spot (KHJ-AM guest appearance), 15. I Don't Want to Be a Soldier, Mama (I Don't Want To Die) (outtake) (5.49), 16. How Do You Sleep? (rehearsal) (4.24), 17. Well (Baby Please Don't Go) (6.03), 18. Move Over Ms L (second demo) (1.56), 19. Tobias Casuals No. 5 (1.16), 20. Clean-up Time (Dakota piano version) (3.30), 21. Forgive Me (My Little Flower Princess) (alternate with studio talk) (3.43), 22. Mother (electric guitar demo, heavy tremolo sound 1970) (4.39), 23. I'm Steppin' Out (double-tracked guitar demo, overdubbed) (4.36), 24. Only the Lonely (overdub version) (4.39), 25. Radio Free London/*Oz* Magazine Message (3.29), 26. Rip It Up/Ready Teddy (rough mix) (1.41)

Disc Two – Volume 10

1. I'm Crazy (take 1) (4.10), 2. Beautiful Boy (double-tracked guitar demo, overdubbed) (4.04), 3. *Walls and Bridges* Promo (Ringo promotes John's album) (1.02), 4. Stranger's Room (piano demo for 'I'm Losing You') (6.07), 5. Woman (double-tracked guitar demo) (4.48), 6. I'm Losing You (rough mix) (3.57), 7. Mailman Bring Me No More Blues (acoustic) (2.35), 8. Peggy

Sue (unreleased rough mix) (2.06), 9. Cold Turkey (acoustic demo, take 1) (3.56), 10. Dear Yoko (acoustic demo, takes 2 and 3) (5.19), 11. Bless You (rehearsal, different from *Menlove Avenue*) (3.53), 12. Move Over (Ms L (hard rocking rough mix, take 3) (2.47), 13. Living on Borrowed Time (Bermuda demo) (5.00), 14. Don't Let Me Down (home demo, late 1968) (2.58), 15. Oh, My Love (rough mix) (2.53), 16. Jealous Guy (rough mix) (4.14), 17. Surprise Surprise (acoustic demo) (3.02), 18. Gone from This Place (take 4) (3.20), 19. Living on Borrowed Time (talk version 1980) (6.00), 20. Michael Lindsey Hogg talks with John Lennon (*Rock and Roll Circus*, 11 December 1968) (0.37), 21. Yer Blues (Mick Jagger and John Lennon) (0.41), 22. Yer Blues (almost instrumental version) (4.03), 23. Don't Let Me Down (second home demo)

239. THE COMPLETE LOST LENNON TAPES – VOLS 11 AND 12

Walrus Records 022/023

Format: CD (double)

Released: 1997

Source: various

Sound quality: very good to excellent

Disc One – Volume 11

1. Just Gotta Give Me Some Rock 'n' Roll/Shoeshine (early version of Meat City) (3.37), 2. How Do You Sleep? (alternate take) (5.57), 3. I Know (rough mix, different vocals) (3.40), 4. Power to the People (ragged take, reggae version) (1.18), 5. Love (guitar demo, heavy tremolo effect) (2.20), 6. Out the Blue (rough mix, early guide vocal) (4.04), 7. Bony Moronie (*Rock 'n' Roll* album sessions) (3.51), 8. Be My Baby (*Rock 'n' Roll* album sessions) (5.49), 9. Power to the People (alternate take, almost finished version) (3.45), 10. Oh, Yoko (outtake, Tittenhurst Park) (4.09), 11. What You Got (acoustic demo) (3.25), 12. Real Love (acoustic demo, take 4) (4.05), 13. Woman (outtake), 14. Cookin' (In The Kitchen of Love) (piano demo for *Ringo*) (2.54), 15. Free as a Bird (piano demo) (3.25), 16. Intuition (composing demo) (2.21), 17. Intuition (rough mix) (2.47), 18. Call My Name (incomplete demo) (1.25), 19. Call My Name (complete demo) (5.07), 20. Aisumasen (I'm Sorry) (4.32), 21. One of the Boys (demo) (3.02), 22. Love (remix)

Disc Two – Volume 12

1. Honey Don't (*Clock* soundtrack) (1.52), 2. Glad All Over (*Clock* soundtrack) (0.50), 3. Lend Me Your Comb (*Clock* soundtrack) (1.24), 4. Duane Eddy Jam (acoustic lick version) (0.51), 5. No. 9 Dream (second more polished demo) (3.11), 6. 12 Bar Original (*Rubber Soul* sessions, acetate version) (6.37), 7. Well, Well, Well (demo) (1.09), 8. Well, Well, Well (take 4 acetate version) (3.33), 9. He Got the Blues (acoustic Lennon original) (2.33), 10. Look at Me (*White Album* sessions, acoustic demo) (3.05), 11. My Mummy's Dead (take 2) (1.11), 12. Real Life (piano demo, take 2) (3.23), 13. Woman Is the Nigger of the World (acoustic demo) (2.08), 14. Cold Turkey (acoustic demo, take 3) (3.21), 15. I'm Stepping Out (take 1) (4.57), 16. Watching the Wheels (electric blues style demo) (2.50), 17. Run for Your Life (abbreviated mix) (1.16), 18. The Maharishi Song (home recording 1968) (3.03), 19. Julia (home demo, take 2) (2.54), 20. When a Boy Meets a Girl (acoustic demo) (2.06), 21. God (early demo) (2.12), 22. Look at Me (alternate mix) (2.49), 23. Oh, Yoko (acoustic demo) (4.35), 24. How? (piano demo) (4.30), 25. Imagine (complete solo piano, take) (3.06), 26. Jam (*Imagine* session) (0.38), 27. How Do You Sleep? (early run through, John sings octave lower) (4.29), 28. Oh, My Love (alternate mix) (2.08)

240. THE COMPLETE LOST LENNON TAPES – VOLS 13 AND 14

Walrus Records 024/025

Format: CD (double)

Released: 1997

Source: various

Sound quality: very good to excellent

Disc One – Volume 13

1. Imagine (alternate mix) (3.06), 2. J.J. (St Regis Hotel 1972, early version of 'Angela') (1.09), 3. Attica State (acoustic demo) (3.33), 4. Woman Is the Nigger of the World (alternate version) (5.33), 5. Sweet Little Sixteen (alternate take) (4.02), 6. Bless You (early rehearsal) (5.57), 7. Many Rivers to Cross (home recording) (3.00), 8. Cookin' (In The Kitchen of Love) (demo of song given to Ringo) (2.33), 9. My Life (demo, evolved into 'Starting Over') (3.12), 10. I Watch Your Face (demo,

evolved into 'Starting Over') (2.12), 11. Serve Yourself (piano demo) (6.10), 12. The Worst is Over (home demo) (2.18), 13. Watching the Wheels (blues demo version) (2.50), 14. Beautiful Boy (extended composing tape) (11.33), 15. I Don't Want to Face It (1.38), 16. Medley: Beautiful Boy/Howling at the Moon/Dakota Rap/Across the River (medley set to beat of drum machine) (5.06), 17. Real Love (take 5 acoustic demo) (2.45), 18. Beautiful Boy (take 2) (4.02), 19. Stepping Out (alternate take) (4.42)

Disc Two – Volume 14

1. Clean-up Time (rehearsal with John directing studio musicians) (7.56), 2. Beautiful Boy (alternate mix) (3.56), 3. Watching the Wheels (alternate mix) (3.31), 4. Dear Yoko (alternate mix) (2.27), 5. Clean-up Time (alternate mix) (4.24), 6. You Saved My Soul (demo) (2.37), 7. Illusions (unreleased track) (2.43), 8. He Said He Said (composing tape 1966) (2.01), 9. She Said She Said (demo with finished lyrics) (0,55), 10. Yer Blues (*Rock and Roll Circus*, take 1) (4.31), 11. Oh, My Love (1.24), 12. Oh, My Love (early demo) (1.19), 13. Because (0.37), 14. Happiness Is a Warm Gun (0.41), 15. Give Peace a Chance (Bed-In, King Edward Hotel, Toronto, 25 May 1969) (0.38), 16. Give Peace a Chance (Queen Elizabeth Hotel, Montreal, 1 June 1969, early rehearsal) (2.12), 17. Give Peace a Chance (later rehearsal) (1.28), 18. Give Peace a Chance (soundtrack of documentary film) (5.22), 19. Give Peace a Chance (unknown) (0.25), 20. God (acoustic demo) (3.41), 21. My Mummy's Dead (rough mix) (0.46), 22. It's So Hard (King Curtis joins John on sax), 23. Come Together (One-to-One rehearsal) (3.52), 24. Honky Tonk Blues (One-to-One rehearsal) (2.49), 25. I Know (acoustic demo, take 3), 26. Rock 'n' Roll People (rough mix of take 7) (2.50), 27. Only People (second alternate mix) (2.44), 28. Whatever Gets You Through the Night (acoustic demo) (2.52)

241. THE COMPLETE LOST LENNON TAPES – VOLS 15 AND 16

Walrus Records 026/027

Format: CD (double)

Released: 1997

Source: various

Sound quality: very good to excellent

Disc One – Volume 15

1. Steel and Glass (*Walls and Bridges*, 8-track version, extended fade out) (5.11), 2. Beef Jerky (*Walls and Bridges*, 8-track version) (3.18), 3. You Saved My Soul (electric guitar demo, November 1980) (1.29), 4. Serve Yourself (piano demo) (8.25), 5. Memories (take 1, evolved into Tennessee), 6. Real Life (piano demo) (3.18), 7. Watching the Wheels (piano version) (3.15), 8. Don't Be Crazy (piano version, later evolved into 'Starting Over') (3.09), 9. Woman (Bermuda demo) (2.43), 10. (Just Like) Starting Over (acoustic demo) (4.14), 11. I Don't Want to Face It (early guitar demo, Dakota, 1977) (0.43), 12. Nobody Told Me (double-tracked demo) (3.13), 13. Real Love (piano demo) (3.09), 14. I'm Losing You (with Cheap Trick) (4.20), 15. Beautiful Boy (vocal booth, take 1, Hit Factory August 1980) (7.23), 16. Nobody Told Me (vocal booth, take 1) (3.59), 17. Clean-up Time (rough mix of backing track, take 7) (4.25), 18. (Just Like) Starting Over (rough mix minus overdubs) (3.58), 19. If I Fell (John's 1963 composing tape) (3.59), 20. I Sat Belonely (0.43), 21. Foyle's Speech (0.04)

Disc Two – Volume 16

1. National Health Cow (speech held honouring John for his first book *In His Own Write*) (0.32), 2. Strawberry Fields Forever (home demo) (2.36), 3. Get It Together (Peace message from John and Yoko, acoustic guitar rendition, probably Montreal Bed-In) (1.57), 4. Happy Xmas (War Is Over) (different mix) (3.20), 5. Power to the People (early reggae version) (1.22), 6. Don't Be Cruel/Hound Dog (One-to-One rehearsal with Elephant's Memory) (4.17), 7. I'm the Greatest (rough mix) (3.11), 8. I Know (acoustic demo) (3.16), 9. Rock 'n' Roll People (piano demo) (3.26), 10. Meat City (take 1, electric guitar demo) (2.34), 11. Meat City (take 2, electric guitar demo) (3.28), 12. Meat City (alternate mix) (2.29), 13. One Day at a Time (alternate mix) (3.17), 14. Only People (alternate mix) (2.54), 15. Tight A$ (alternate mix) (4.16), 16. You Are Here (alternate mix) (4.37), 17. Going Down on Love (acoustic demo) (4.08), 18. No. 9 Dream (monitor mix of early version) (4.40), 19. Whatever Gets You Through the Night (quadraphonic 8-track mix) (3.20), 20. Surprise Surprise (Sweet Bird of Paradox) (quadraphonic 8-track mix) (2.35), 21. John on KHJ-AM Los Angeles (promoting *Walls and Bridges* album), 22. Do You

Want to Dance (monitor mix of alternate take) (3.05), 23. You Can't Catch Me (alternate take), 24. Free as a Bird (take 3)

242. THE COMPLETE LOST LENNON TAPES – VOLS 17 AND 18

Walrus Records 028/029

Format: CD (double)

Released: 1997

Source: various

Sound quality: very good to excellent

Disc One – Volume 17

1. Serve Yourself (5.15), 2. She'll Be Coming Round the Mountain (1.01), 3. She Run Them Round In Circles/Beautiful Boy (5.38), 4. Memories/Watching the Wheels (4.18), 5. Stranger's Room (demo 1, early version of 'I'm Losing You') 3.51), 6. Woman (acoustic demo, false start, take 4) (0.30), 7. Woman (complete acoustic demo, take 9) 3.53), 8. I'm Stepping Out (demo, take 1) (1.42), 9. I'm Stepping Out (demo, take 3) (6.14), 10. (Just Like) Starting Over (demo) (3.43), 11. Dream Lover/Stay (3.41), 12. Clean-up Time (vocal overdubs) (0.55), 13. Beautiful Boy (Darling Boy) (vocal overdubs) (2.03), 14. Watching the Wheels (vocal overdubs) (4.41), 15. Borrowed Time (rough mix) (4.08), 16. I'm Stepping Out (take 8) (5.01), 17. Woman (rough mix) (3.08), 18. Lennon's Lost Diary Tape (5 September 1979) (13.36)

Disc Two – Volume 18

1. It's Not Too Bad (early version of 'Strawberry Fields Forever', Spain' 1966) (3.29), 2. She Can Talk to Me (early piano demo of 'Hey Bulldog') (0.46), 3. Cry Baby Cry (early piano and electric guitar demo fragments) (3.23), 4. Two Virgins outtake (May 1968, John and Yoko) (1.47), 5. Plastic Ono Band Jam (send-up Fifties rockabilly) (1.39), 6. Look at Me (alternate vocals) (2.52), 7. I'm the Greatest (piano demo) (0.37), 8. How?/Child of Nature/Oh, Yoko (Medley: piano demo) (4.25), 9. Oh, Yoko (piano demo) (3.23), 10. Sally and Billy (from 1970) (2.03), 11. Come Together (One-to-One rehearsals) (1.47), 12. Happy Girl (Yoko's call and response song) (1.10), 13. I'll Make You Happy (John's call and response song,

lyrics from 'Cold Turkey') (3.56), 14. How Do You Sleep? (session rehearsal) (3.45), 15. It's So Hard (run through from King Curtis sax overdub sessions) (4.44), 16. I Don't Want to Be a Soldier Mama (I Don't Want To Die) (run through from King Curtis sax overdub sessions) (4.34), 17. Intuition (piano demo, take 4) (3.04), 18. I Know (guitar demo, take 2) (3.00), 19. I Know (alternate mix) (3.43), 20. Aisumasen (I'm Sorry) (near final mix) (4.00), 21. Steel and Glass (dark piano version, extra lyrics) (1.44), 22. *Walls and Bridges* rundown (radio promo spot) (1.56), 23. Mirror Mirror (On the Wall) (piano demo, take 2) (4.34), 24. Memories (home demo, 1976 guitar over earlier piano demo)

243. THE COMPLETE LOST LENNON TAPES – VOLS 19 AND 20

Walrus Records 030/031

Format: CD (double)

Released: 1997

Source: various

Sound quality: very good to excellent

Disc One – Volume 19

1. Tennessee (home demo, 1974) (3.04), 2. Sally and Billy (home demo, 1974) (3.28), 3. She is a Friend of Dorothy (3.55), 4. The Boat Song (demo) (2.08), 5. Pedro the Fisherman (demo) (1.04), 6. Many Rivers to Cross, Part 2/My Girl (2.24), 7. Instrumental (1979) (1.02), 8. I'm Stepping Out (incomplete take) (1.29), 9. Dear Yoko (incomplete take, John breaks guitar string) (5.04), 10. Woman (rehearsal) (4.26), 11. Woman (John recording his vocals) (1.54), 12. Woman (John adding the whispered intro) (2.13), 13. Clean-up Time (rehearsal followed by studio doodle 'Let's Get Peculiar') (6.01), 14. Nobody Told Me (different take) (3.51), 15. I Am the Walrus/Watching the Wheels (rehearsal) (4.01), 16. Woman (instrumental, guitar overdub) (2.26), 17. Woman (alternate take) (3.39), 18. Living on Borrowed Time (early take) (4.20), 19. I'm Losing You (alternate take followed by studio talk) (3.54), 20. Imagine (2.57), 21. How Do You Sleep? (2.53), 22. J.J. (1.14), 23. Rock Island Line/Maybe Baby/Peggy Sue (3.50), 24. I'm Ready To Sing For The World (0.26)

Disc Two – Volume 20

1. Out the Blue (3.15), 2. Old Dirt Road (4.52), 3. Steel and Glass (4.52), 4. Whatever Gets You Through the Night)3.30), 5. Rock 'n' Roll radio spot (1.02), 6. Stand By Me (4.09), 7. Serve Yourself (3.17), 8. Everybody (2.48), 9. Everybody/Nobody Told Me (3.11), 10. Nobody Told Me (3.49), 11. Falling In Love Again (1.24), 12. Cathy's Clown (1.12), 13. You Send Me (2.08), 14. Real Life (4.20), 15. My Life (1.35), 16. My Life (2.44), 17. Dear Yoko (5.16), 18. I'm Stepping Out (4.50), 19. I Don't Want to Face It (2.33). 20. Watching the Wheels (6.08), 21. Beautiful Boy (3.58), 22. Interview: More popular than Jesus, 23. Interview: John's book

244. THE COMPLETE LOST LENNON TAPES – VOLS 21 AND 22

Walrus Records 035/036

Format: CD (double)

Released: 1997

Source: various

Sound quality: very good to excellent

Disc One – Volume 21

1. I'm Stepping Out (first day of *Double Fantasy* sessions, breakdowns and complete take) (10.35), 2. I'm Stepping Out (first day of *Double Fantasy* sessions, dinner orders and complete take) (7.55), 3. I'm Stepping Out (first day of *Double Fantasy* sessions, breakdowns and complete take) (8.46), 4. Borrowed Time (*Double Fantasy* sessions, John working out the arrangement following a brief run through) (8.37), 5. Borrowed Time (aborted take) (5.33), 6. Borrowed Time (breakdowns with acoustic guitar overdub) (1.40), 7. (Just Like) Starting Over (offline monitor mix) (4.16), 8. (Just Like) Starting Over (rough mix of the basic track) (3.40), 9. John Sinclair (*David Frost Show*) (2.35), 10. It's So Hard (*Mike Douglas Show*) (2.10), 11. The Luck of the Irish (*Mike Douglas Show*) (3.01), 12. Sisters Oh Sisters (*Mike Douglas Show*) (2.55), 13. We're All Water (*Dick Cavett Show*) (5.03), 14. Woman Is the Nigger of the World (*Dick Cavett Show*) (5.45)

Disc Two – Volume 22

1. Aisumasen (I'm Sorry) (5.33), 2. Honey Don't (2.08), 3. Glad All Over (1.07), 4. Lend Me Your Comb (1.43), 5. Wake Up Little Suzie (1.41),

6. Baby I Don't Care (1.42), 7. Vacation Has Just Began (2.01), 8. Heartbeat (1.31), 9. Peggy Sue Got Married (1.13), 10. Peggy Sue (2.33), 11. Maybe Baby (2.25), 12. Mailman Bring Me No More Blues (2.43), 13. Rave On (2.03), 14. Tell Me What I Say (3.19), 15. Yellow Submarine (2.51), 16. Old Smokey Mountain (2.04), 17. Goodnight Irene (3.10), 18. He's Got the Whole World (2.44), 19. Like a Rolling Stone/Twist and Shout/Louie Louie/La Bamba (Medley) (3.19), 20. Bring It on Home to Me (2.46), 21. Yesterday (1.46), 22. Dance For The Chicken (2.23), 23. Power to the People (0.49), 24. Maybe Baby (2.52), 25. Peggy Sue (2.55), 26. My Baby Left Me (2.08), 27. Blue Suede Shoes (3.01), 28. Crippled Inside (1.09), 29. Give Peace a Chance (3.09), 30. Crippled Inside (0.32), 31. Uncle Albert (1.52), 32. Happy Birthday (1.02), 33. Uncle Albert (0.16), 34. My Sweet Lord (0.19)

Notes: Volume 22: Tracks 1–13, Recorded at the St Regis Hotel, New York City, June 1971. Tracks 14–34, Recorded at a house party in the early 1970s.

245. THE COMPLETE MAY PANG TAPES
Orange Fifteen

Format: CD

Released: 1995

Source: rehearsals for the *Rock 'n' Roll album* at Morris Levy's Farm, New York

Sound quality: very good to excellent

1. Slippin' and Slidin' (2.19), 2. Rip It Up/Ready Teddy (1.35), 3. Bring It on Home to Me/Send Me Some Loving (2.05), 4. Bring It on Home to Me/Send Me Some Loving (3.35), 5. Peggy Sue (2.04), 6. Ain't That a Shame (2.42), 7. Ain't That a Shame (excerpt) (1.16), 8. Be-Bop-A-Lula (2.41), 9. Ya Ya (2.24), 10. Do You Want to Dance (3.35), 11. Stand By Me (4.22), 12. Bring It on Home to Me/Send Me Some Loving (3.48), 13. Ya Ya (2.46), 14. That'll Be the Day (2.35), 15. Do You Want to Dance (3.27), 16. Stand By Me (3.39), 17. Peggy Sue (2.11), 18. Be-Bop-A-Lula (1.56), 19. Slippin' and Slidin' (1.59), 20. Whole Lotta Lovin'/Rumble (2.04), 21. Thirty Days (excerpt) (1.03)

Notes: This release is a compilation of the double vinyl album *You Should-a Been There* and the compact disc *Rock 'n' Roll Sessions (Vol. 1)* in better quality. However this is not the complete *May Pang Tapes*.

The sleeve, which has an orange border, features the same black-and-white photo as the official *Rock 'n' Roll album* with the track listing on the back.

246. COMPOSITIONS

Vigotone VT-191

Format: CD

Released: 2000

Time: 61.43

Source: home demos, recorded at Tittenhurst Park in 1970

Sound quality: excellent

1. Make Love Not War (4.14), 2. I'm the Greatest (1.36), 3. I'm the Greatest (0.40), 4. How? (1.49), 5. Child of Nature (0.56), 6. Child of Nature (1.15), 7. Oh, Yoko (0.49), 8. Sally and Billy (1.16), 9. Sally and Billy (1.17), 10. Rock 'n' Roll People (4.21), 11. Oh, Yoko (2.50), 12. Oh, Yoko (0.48), 13. Help! (2.24), 14. Instrumental (4.12), 15. Happy Christmas (3.18), 16. Happy Christmas (2.26), 17. People Get Ready/How? (5.26), 18. How? (5.06), 19. How? (2.31), 20. My Heart Is In Your Hands (1.34), 21. Mailman Bring Me No More Blues (2.06), 22. I Promise (2.47), 23. You Know How Hard It Is (1.59), 24. I'll Make You Happy (1.56), 25. I'll Make You Happy (3.42)

Notes: Track 1, one of the earliest versions of the song that would evolve into 'Mind Games'. Tracks 2 and 3, early attempts at the song given to Ringo. Track 4, first attempt at the song later released on the *Imagine* album. Tracks 5 and 6, a song written in India and already rehearsed with The Beatles. Track 7, brief run through – slower version. Tracks 8 and 9, John would again return to this song at the Dakota in 1976. Track 10, this is possibly the earliest version of this song. Tracks 11 and 12, further early versions – performed in a low voice. Track 13, a slower version of a Beatles classic. This is followed by some improvisation leading into two takes (tracks 15 and 16) of a Christmas message. Tracks 17–19, three run takes of the song 'How?' On the first version John sang 'How can we go forward...' This was changed to 'How can I go forward...'. Track 20, unknown 1950s-style rocker. Track 21, a song previously recorded with The Beatles. Track 22, this song would later be incorporated into 'Mind Games'. Track 23, unknown song. Tracks 24 and 25, unfinished and unreleased song.

This tape of home demos was recorded at John's Tittenhurst Park estate in late autumn 1970. Some of the recordings had appeared on *The Lost Lennon Tapes* but this was the first time the entire tape had been bootlegged. In 1971 the Lennons would leave Tittenhurst Park and therefore this recording is one of the last recordings made by John Lennon in England. This is an essential disc but difficult to locate.

The disc is contained in a carton folded jacket with a twenty-eight page booklet with many excellent black-and-white photos and track listing with extensive notes about the recording sessions. The booklet contains several photos taken at Tittenhurst Park including a long range view of the house on the cover. The CD inlay contains more photos.

247. A CONSPIRACY OF SILENCE

Black Cat BC 045/046

Format: CD (double)

Source: see below

Sound quality: unknown

Disc One

Earth News Radio

1. The Early Beatles (26 January 1976), 2. Picking A Career (26 January 1976), 3. The 1 Album/Live Shows (27 January 1976), 4. What's the New Mary Jane (27 January 1976), 5. The Breakup of The Beatles (28 January 1976), 6. Wayward Fathers (28 January 1976), 7. The Invisible Beatle Empire (29 January 1976), 8. Beatle Reunions (29 January 1976), 9. Meeting John (30 January 1976), 10. Mrs Lennon (30 January 1976), 11. A Blessed Event (31 January 1976), 12. Naming The Baby (31

January 1976), 13. The List of Lists (1 February 1976), 14. A Turbulent Year (1 February 1976).

Earth News Radio outtakes

15. Interview with John (1 January 1976)

Disc Two

Earth News Radio outtakes

1. Interview with John and Yoko (1 January 1976)

Sean's First Interview

2. December 1975

Mucho Mungo

3. Acoustic guitar rendition

Cookin' (In The Kitchen of Love)

4. Piano demo, take 1, 5. Piano demo, unknown take, 6. Piano demo, take 8

She is a Friend of Dorothy

7. Piano demo, take 2, 8. Piano demo, take 7

Sally and Billy

9. Piano/drum machine demo, take 2, 10. Piano/drum Machine demo, take 3

Everybody

11. Piano/drum machine demo

Tennessee

12. Piano demo, take 1, 13. Piano/drum machine demo, unknown take, 14. Piano/drum machine demo, take 4

Notes: Front insert has five pictures (only one in colour) of John with Yoko and with Sean.

248. A Conspiracy of Silence Speaks Louder than Words

Darthouse DD 014-015

Format: CD (double)

Source: interview for RKO on 8 December 1980

Sound quality: good

Notes: See Unedited RKO Interview

249. The Dakota and Bermuda Demos 1977–1980, Vol. 1

Poor Muffin Records

Format: CD

Released: 1999 Total

Time: 148 mins

Source: demos

Sound quality: unknown

Disc One

1. Free as a Bird (3.27), 2. Real Love (4.07), 3. Now and Then (5.02), 4. Real Love No. 2 (4.02), 5. I Don't Want to Face It (2.04), 6. Sally and Billy (0.28), 7. Mucho Mungo (1.24), 8. Stranger's Room (3.16), 9. Free as a Bird No. 3 (2.40), 10. Dear John (4.32), 11. Serve Yourself (3.47), 12. Mirror Mirror (2.35), 13. The Dakota Rap (5.00), 14. India (3.05), 15. Gone from This Place (3.24), 16. My Life (2.34), 17. Real Love No. 4 (4.12), 18. One of the Boys (3.10), 19. I'm Losing You (3.16), 20. Sally and Billy No. 2 (3.28), 21. Life Begins at 40 (2.36), 22. Woman (4.01)

Disc Two

1. Watching the Wheels (2.56), 2. Mucho Mungo No. 2 (2.46), 3. Across the River (2.38), 4. That's the Way the World It (3.04), 5. Sally and Billy No. 3 (3.24), 6. The Rishikesh Song (2.25), 7. Don't Be Crazy (3.12), 8. Mirror Mirror (On the Wall) (2.35), 9. Illusions (2.42), 10. Baby Make Love To You (2.16), 11. Real Love No. 7 (3.05), 12. Woman No. 2 (1.07), 13. She is a Friend of Dorothy (4.07), 14. You Saved My Soul (1.34), 15. Mr Hyde Is Gone (2.40), 16. Whatever Happened To (4.40), 17. Help Me to Help Myself (2.08),

18. Borrowed Time (3.58), 19. Grow Old with Me (3.04), 20. It's Real Life (0.57), 21. Maurice DuPont Act No. 1 (1.58), 22. Maurice DuPont Act No. 2 (1.06), 23. Maurice DuPont Act No. 3 (2.41), 24. Screaming Lord McNasty (0.53), 25. Chi Chi's Bar Act No. 1 (0.55), 26. Chi Chi's Bar Act No. 2 (2.04), 27. Chi Chi's Bar Act No. 3 (0.43), Bonus Tracks: 28. Dear Prudence (1968 demo) (4.45), 29. Child of Nature (1968 demo) (2.27)

Notes: The front cover of the sleeve is coloured brown with a black-and-white picture of John in the centre sitting on a bed playing an acoustic guitar.

250. A Day On the Radio
Unknown
Format: CD (double)
Source: unknown
Sound quality: unknown

Disc One

1. Scott Muni intro, 2. Be-Bop-A-Lula, 3. A Hard Day's Night, 4. Stand By Me, 5. Mind Games, 6. Sweet Little Sixteen, 7. Rock 'n' Roll Music, 8. Ain't That a Shame, 9. Whatever Gets You Through the Night, 10. Instant Karma, 11. Do You Want to Dance

Disc Two

1. Slippin' and Slidin', 2. Starting Over, 3. Peggy Sue, 4. Bring It On Home, 5. Revolution, 6. Imagine, 7. No. 9 Dream, 8. You've Got to Hide Your Love Away, 9. I'm a Loser, 10. I Saw Her Standing There (live with Elton John), 11. Just Because, 12. Happy Christmas

Notes: Front cover has a colour picture of John from the mid seventies. The back has a black-and-white picture of John from circa 1964 wearing horn-rimmed glasses.

251. Day Tripper Jam
Instant Analysis/King Kong 4242
Format: CD

Source: various outtakes

Sound quality: varies between excellent mono and poor mono

1. Give Peace a Chance (Holland), 2. Medley: Interview/What's the New Mary Jane, 3. Day Tripper (BBC Radio, *Top Gear*, 15 December 1967), 4. God Save Us, 5. The Luck of the Irish, 6. Attica State, 7. Imagine (from *Jerry Lewis Telethon*, 6 September 1972), 8. Give Peace a Chance

Notes: It was rumoured that John Lennon appeared with Jimi Hendrix on the 'Day Tripper' track. It is now believed that the backing vocals were provided by Noel Redding and not John Lennon. The track is available on the BBC official CD release *Jimi Hendrix, BBC Sessions* in much better sound quality.

252. DEDICATED TO JOHN LENNON (PART 1)

Unknown

Format: CD

Source: tracks taken from *The Lost Lennon Tapes* radio series

Sound quality: very good

Notes: This release is a copy of *The Lost Lennon Tapes* – Vol. 1 (Bag Records 5073)

253. DEDICATED TO JOHN LENNON (PART 2)

Unknown

Format: CD

Source: tracks taken from *The Lost Lennon Tapes* radio series

Sound quality: very good

Notes: This release is a copy of *The Lost Lennon Tapes* – Vol. 5 (Bag Records 5077)

254. DEDICATED TO JOHN LENNON (PART 3)

Unknown

Format: CD

Source: tracks taken from *The Lost Lennon Tapes* radio series

Sound quality: very good

Notes: Track details unknown

255. Dedicated to John Lennon (Part 4)

Unknown

Format: CD

Source: tracks taken from *The Lost Lennon Tapes* radio series

Sound quality: very good

1. Power to the People (outtake), 2. Attica State (live, Ann Arbor, Michigan, 10 December 1971), 3. The Luck of the Irish (live, Ann Arbor, Michigan, 10 December 1971), 4. John Sinclair (live, Ann Arbor, Michigan, 10 December 1971), 5. Rock 'n' Roll People (demo, Sunset Sound, 15 May 1973)/Rock 'n' Roll People (outtake, Sunset Sound, 4 August 1973), 6. Real Life (Dakota, 1974), 7. I'm Stepping Out (Bermuda, summer 1979), 8. Tight A$ (demo, Sunset Sound, May 1973), 9. Rock Island Line (electric version, Dakota), 10. Love (studio outtake, London, 1970)

256. Dedicated to John Lennon (Part 5)

Unknown

Format: CD

Source: tracks taken from *The Lost Lennon Tapes* radio series

Sound quality: very good

Notes: This release is a copy of *The Lost Lennon Tapes* – Vol. 13 (Bag Records 5085)

257. Dirty Mac Sessions

Unicorn Records UC-091

Format: CD

Released: 2002

Source: various – see notes

Sound quality: unknown

1. Yer Blues (rehearsal), 2. Blues Jam, 3. John and Mick's Intro of 'The Dirty Macs', 4. Yer Blues (film soundtrack), 5. Whole Lotta Yoko, 6. John and Mick, Yer Blues a cappella, 7. Yer Blues (take 1), 8. Yer Blues (take 2),

9. Yer Blues (IBC mono acetate), 10. Jam (IBC mono acetate), 11. Mini Opera (IBC mono acetate), 12. Purple Haze (IBC mono acetate), 13. Wild Thing (IBC mono acetate)

Notes: Tracks 1–11 from *Rock and Roll Circus*, filmed on 11 December 1968, side 2 of mono acetate. Tracks 12 and 3 recorded at San Francisco Winterland Arena 10 December 1968. Tracks 1 and 2 unused rehearsal versions. Tracks 3–5 from film soundtrack. Track 6 studio dialogue. Tracks 7 and 8 early versions with no vocals. Tracks 9–13 taken from IBC mono acetate.

The set comes with a colour front and back sleeve with full track listing and a reproduction of the IPC Sound Studios demo disc with a hand written track listing on the label.

258. DJ WINSTON O'BOOGIE

Unicorn Records UC-079/80

Format: CD (double)

Source: radio WNEW-FM 102.7 New York. Hosted by Dennis Elsas 28 September 1974. With DJ Winston O'Boogie

Sound quality: unknown

Disc One

1. Intro, 2. Whatever Gets You Through the Night/chat about *Walls and Bridges*, 3. No. 9 Dream/John on George Martin, 4. Watch Your Step (Bobby Parker), 5. Day Tripper (The Beatles)/chat about the Butcher Cover, 6. I Call Your Name (The Beatles)/Ads With John, 7. Show Down (ELO), 8. I Heard It Through The Grapevine (Marvin Gaye)/producing Harry Nilsson's album, 9. Save The Last Dance With Me/Weather Forecast with John/George's Dark Horse, 10. Gravy Train (Splinter), 11. I'm the Greatest (Ringo Starr), 12. What You Got/Weather and ads with John, 13. Some Other Guy (Richie Barrett)

Disc Two

1. What'd I Say (Ray Charles)/John on The Rolling Stones, 2. I Wanna Be Your Man (Rolling Stones), 3. I Wanna Be Your Man (The Beatles)/John on

The Rolling Stones, 4. Daddy Rolling Stone (Derek Martin)/Station Break/Immigrants, 5. Scared, 6. Commercials/ads with John, 7. I Am the Walrus (The Beatles), 8. John talks about Revolution 9/Beef Jerky

Notes: Black-and-white cover with full track listings on the back.

259. DOUBLE FANTASY/MILK AND HONEY

CDM 1199-367
Format: CD (double)
Source: official released albums
Sound quality: excellent

Disc One: Double Fantasy
1. Starting Over, 2. Kiss Kiss Kiss, 3. Clean-up Time, 4. Give Me Something, 5. I'm Losing You, 6. I'm Moving On, 7. Beautiful Boy (Darling Boy), 8. Watching the Wheels, 9. Yes I'm Your Angel, 10. Beautiful Boys, 11. Dear Yoko, 12. Every Man Has a Woman Who Loves Him, 13. Hard Times Are Over

Disc Two: Milk and Honey
1. I'm Stepping Out, 2. Sleepless Night, 3. I Don't Wanna Face It, 4. Don't Be Scared, 5. Nobody Told Me, 6. O' Sanity, 7. Borrowed Time, 8. Your Hands, 9. My Little Flower Princess, 10. Let Me Count The Ways, 11. Grow Old with Me, 12. You're the One

260. DOUBLE FANTASY – DEMOS AND OUTTAKES

Hen 015
Format: CD
Source: *Double Fantasy* and *Milk and Honey* album sessions
Sound quality: unknown

Notes: This is a copy of *Double Fantasy Working Version.*

261. DOUBLE FANTASY WORKING VERSION (JOHN LENNON AND YOKO ONO)

Master of Beatles Essentials MBEJ 001
Format: CD

Released: 2002

Source: *Double Fantasy* and *Milk and Honey* album sessions

Sound quality: unknown

1. Starting Over (intro session), 2. Starting Over, 3. I'm Your Angel, 4. Beautiful Boy (with Sean's goodnight), 5. Don't Be Scared, 6. Watching the Wheels, 7. Every Man Has a Woman, 8. I'm Losing You (Cheap Trick version), 9. Walking on Thin Ice, 10. Dear Yoko, 11. Woman, 12. I'm Moving On (Cheap Trick version), 13. Clean-up Time, 14. Hard Times Are Over

Bonus Tracks

15. I'm Stepping Out, 16. I Don't Want to Face It, 17. Nobody Told Me, 18. Borrowed Time, 19. Forgive Me (My Little Flower Princess), 20. Nobody Sees Me Like You Do

Notes: Front cover has colour picture of John and Yoko similar to the one on the official *Double Fantasy* album. The front insert is in the form of a four-page booklet with some notes about the recordings and a couple of colour pictures. The back has a further colour picture and track listing.

262. THE DREAM IS OVER

Pegboy 1006

Format: CD

Released: 1997

Source: home demos and studio recordings from *Plastic Ono Band* album sessions

Sound quality: excellent

Demos

1. Love, 2. Mother, 3. When a Boy Meets a Girl, 4. When a Boy Meets a Girl, 5. God, 6. God, 7. God, 8. God, 9. Well, Well, Well, 10. I Found Out, 11. I Found Out, 12. My Mummy's Dead, 13. My Mummy's Dead, 14. Look at Me

Alternates

15. Mother, 16. I Found Out, 17. I Found Out, 18. Well, Well, Well, 19. Look at Me, 20. Look at Me

Session outtake

21. P.O.B. Medley: That's All Right Mama/Glad All Over/Honey Don't/Don't Be Cruel/Hound Dog/Unknown/Matchbox/Jam Remix, 22. Love

Notes: Re-released on unknown labels: JL 03 and XS 007. This set comes with a colour sleeve and a booklet containing detailed notes about the recording sessions and John's comments on each of the tracks.

263. DREAM IS OVER (DISC ONE)

Dill Archives JLTD101

Format: CD

Source: news items

Sound quality: unknown

Notes: A private collection of news items following the death of John Lennon on 8 December 1980.

264. DREAMING OF THE PAST

Vigotone VT-CD-09

Format: CD

Released: 1996

Time: 66.30

Source: various

Sound quality: very good to excellent

1. Clean-up Time (backing track), 2. Here We Go Again (acoustic demo), 3. Tight A$ (early rough mix), 4. Tennessee (piano demo), 5. Move Over Ms L (piano demo), 6. Maybe Baby (home tape), 7. Rave On (home tape), 8. Only People (early rough mix), 9. Whatever Gets You Through the Night (acoustic demo), 10. Woman (acoustic demo), 11. God Save Us (acoustic demo), 12. I Know (I Know) (take 3 – acoustic demo), 13. You Saved My Soul (electric guitar demo), 14. Look at Me

(early rough mix), 15. (Just Like) Starting Over (acoustic demo), 16. Imagine (alternate mix), 17. Beautiful Boy (acoustic demo), 18. Meat City (electric guitar demo), 19. Send Me Some Loving (home demo), 20. Peggy Sue (alternate mix), 21. Lord Take This Make-up Off Me (home tape), 22. Dear Yoko (early rough mix), 23. Happy Xmas (War Is Over) (rough mix), 24. Give Peace a Chance (acoustic demo)

Notes: Tracks taken from *The Lost Lennon Tapes* radio series. Sleeve says, 'Part nine of a collection of rare and unreleased demos and outtakes'.

265. DREAMING OF THE PAST
Howdy CD 555-01
Format: CD
Source: various
Sound quality: very good to excellent

Notes: Re-release of Vigotone VT-CD-09.

266. DREAMING OF THE PAST
PEG/Westwood One 05-41
Format: CD (triple)
Source: radio special, 9 October 1975
Sound quality: unknown

Notes: This three hour radio special was broadcast on 9 October 1975.

267. FAMILY TREE
Unknown
Format: CD
Source: various – tracks by members of Lennon family
Sound quality: unknown

1. That's My Life (My Heart and My Home) (Freddie Lennon), 2. Charlie Lennon's Song (Charlie Lennon), 3. Master Cowley's The Jug of Punch (Charlie Lennon and Joe Burke), 4. Whatever Happened To (John Lennon), 5. 1969 Christmas Mess (edit) (John, Yoko and Julian Lennon),

6. Radio Peace (outtake) (John and Yoko), 7. Mildred Mildred (unreleased) (Yoko Ono), 8. Yang Yang (Yoko), 9. Hiroshima Sky Is Always Blue (Yoko with Sean and Paul), 10. Those Were The Days (Cynthia Lennon), 11. Walking In The Rain (Cynthia Lennon), 12. Ya Ya (from *Walls and Bridges* album) (John and Julian), 13. The Vanishing (edit from *Hunting of the Snark*) (Julian Lennon), 14. Saltwater (on KBCO radio show) (Julian Lennon), 15. Should Have Known (on KBCO radio show) (Julian Lennon), 16. I Don't Wanna Know (on KBCO radio show) (Julian Lennon), 17. Ruby Tuesday (Rolling Stones cover) (Julian Lennon), 18. Sean's Little Help (Sean Lennon with John and Yoko), 19. Sean's Loud (Sean Lennon with John and Yoko), 20. Sean's in the Sky (Sean Lennon with John and Yoko), 21. Dear Prudence (unreleased Beatles cover) (Sean Lennon), 22. Heart and Lung (from Japanese single) (Sean Lennon), 23. Winged Elephants (at home with groove machine) (Sean Lennon), 24. Give Peace a Chance (Peace Choir with Yoko Sean and others)

Bonus Track

25. Rare Interview (Julia Baird and Paul McCartney)

Notes: Album is subtitled *The Lennon Family Register*.

268. FBI FILES

Democracy Now DNFBI 001

Format: CD

Released: 2005

Time: 49.03

Source: see notes

Sound quality: very good

Notes: Amy Goodman of Pacifica Radio Network hosts a talk with Jon Wiener, history professor at the University of California Irvine and the author of two books on Lennon – *Gimme Some Truth: The John Lennon Files* and *Come Together: John Lennon and His Times*. The sleeve features the same picture as *A Guitar's All Right John, But You'll Never Earn Your Living By It*. American release.

269. THE FILLMORE TAPES (JOHN LENNON WITH FRANK ZAPPA)

Master of Orange MOO-00002

Format: CD (double)

Source: Fillmore East, New York

Sound quality: excellent

Disc One

Alternate Mix – Unedited Version Direct From The Mixing Board

1. Well, 2. Say Please, 3. Aaak, 4. Scumbag, 5. A Small Eternity (with Yoko Ono)

Frank Zappa Mix

6. Well, 7. Say Please, 8. Aaak, 9. Scumbag, 10. A Small Eternity (with Yoko Ono)

Disc Two

The Original John Lennon Mix

1. Well (Baby Please Don't Go), 2. Jamrag, 3. Scumbag, 4. Au

Notes: The artwork for the sleeve is based on the official release *Sometime in New York City* with the mocked up newspaper and the handwritten inserts complete with parts scribbled out.

270. FILMING THE FANTASIES

(The *Double Fantasy* Filming Sessions + Infamous Diary Tape)

VOXX Records Voxx 0009-01

Format: CD

Source: various – see notes

Sound quality: Tracks 1–18, very good stereo. Track 19, good mono. Track 20, good

1. She's a Woman/chat/C'mon Everybody (2.15), 2. She's a Woman (0.58), 3. Rip It Up/chat (1.28), 4. I'm a Man/chat (1.23), 5. Be-Bop-A-

Lula/chat (1.55), 6. I'm Losing You/chat (1.48), 7. Starting Over/chat (3.43), 8. I'm Losing You/chat (1.30), 9. Chat/riffs/tuning/camera set up (4.31), 10. I'm Losing You/chat/riffs (0.38), 11. I'm Losing You/more riffs/tuning (3.47), 12. I'm Losing You (complete) (4.31), 13. Film chat/riffs (1.13), 14. Dream Lover (3.14), 15. Stay (0.49), 16. chat/riffs (1.27), 17. Mystery Train (3.05), 18. Chat/riffs (1.57), 19. John's last filmed interview – October 1980 (23.09), 20. John's diary tape – 5 September 1979 (13.40)

Notes: Tracks 1–18, John's last film session on 18 October 1980. Filmed by photographer Bob Gruen at New York's Hit Factory Studios. This was first released on the vinyl bootleg *Before Play* (Gnat Records) in 1987 but is superior sound quality on this disc. Track 19, John is interviewed by Robert Hilburn and talks about the recently completed *Double Fantasy* album and the television debut of *Magical Mystery Tour* (shown in black and white). John talks about *Yellow Submarine*, *Imagine*, *Some Time in New York City* and *Walls and Bridges*, Hilburn also asks John what it was like taking a five year break from recording and how much he sees of Paul. Track 20, a revealing diary tape. Front cover has a colour picture of John and Yoko with the track listing and a small colour picture of John and Yoko on the back. The insert includes a transcription of some studio chat from John during the recording session.

271. FOR THE OTHER HALF OF THE SKY
Barrier BAR 010/011
Format: CD (double)
Source: *Double Fantasy* and *Milk and Honey* sessions
Sound quality: excellent

Disc One
1. I Watch Your Face (demo), 2. My Life (demos 1, 2 and 3), 3. Don't Be Crazy (demo), 4. Don't Be Crazy/The Worst is Over (demo), 5. Starting Over (demo), 6. Starting Over (demo, take 3), 7. (Just Like) Starting Over (8 versions, vocal overdubs, playbacks and mix downs), 8. Nobody Told Me comment, 9. Everybody's Talking Nobody's Talking (demo, take 1), 10. Everybody's Talking Nobody's Talking (demo with overdubs),

11. Nobody Told Me (demo, take 2), 12. Nobody Told Me (rehearsal, take 1), 13. Nobody Told Me (rehearsal), 14. Nobody Told Me (rough mix)

Disc Two

1. Woman (audio verite), 2. Woman (demo, take 1), 3. Woman (demo remake, take 1), 4. Woman (demo, take 9), 5. Woman (four demos), 6. Woman (acoustic backing track), 7. Woman (four vocal booth recordings), 8. Woman (two audio verite), 9. Woman (three alternate mixes), 10. Walking on Thin Ice (vocal booth recording), 11. Walking on Thin Ice (three alternate mixes)

Notes: This release is a follow up to *It's Hard to Be Butterflies* (Barrier Records). The front cover of the sleeve has the same picture of John as the official vinyl release from 1982 *The John Lennon Collection*.

The set comes with an eight page booklet with extensive notes on the recording sessions and the songs.

272. FREE AS A BIRD

No Label FAB 1

Format: CD

Released: 1996

Time: 73.40

Source: various

Sound quality: good to very good

1. Free as a Bird (take 1 – John's demo) (3.25), 2. Free as a Bird (take 3 – John's demo) (2.41), 3. Real Love (take 1) (3.45), 4. Real Love (take 4) (3.56), 5. Real Love (take 5) (2.46), 6. Real Love (take 6) (2.19), 7. Real Love (unknown take) (3.08), 8. Real Love (unknown take) (1.28), 9. Oh, My Love (rehearsals) (32.05), 10. Starting Over (12 inch promo long version) (4.17), 11. I Need Your Loving (from *Ready Steady Go* live 16 April 1965) (2.13), 12. Open Your Box (acetate) (3.32), 13. Greenfield Morning (acetate) (5.30), 14. Don't Let Me Down (home demo) (2.09)

Notes: Sleeve features colour picture of John and Yoko with a black-and-white picture of a topless Yoko on the back.

273. FREE AS A BIRD: THE DAKOTA BEATLE DEMOS

Pegboy 1001

Format: CD

Source: various demos

Sound quality: very good

1. Free as a Bird (take 1) (3.27), 2. Real Love (take 1) (4.08), 3. Now and Then (take 1) (5.03), 4. Grow Old with Me (demo) (3.04), 5. Free as a Bird (take 3) (3.40), 6. Dear John (demo) (4.33), 7. That's the Way the World It (demo) (3.04), 8. India (demo) (3.04), 9. Mirror Mirror (On the Wall) (take 1) (2.36), 10. Gone from This Place (demo) (3.24), 11. Across the River (unknown take) (2.42), 12. Don't Be Crazy (demo) (3.12), 13. Illusions (demo) (2.42), 14. Baby Make Love To You (unknown take) (2.16), 15. Life Begins at Forty (demo) (2.36), 16. She is a Friend of Dorothy (take 7) (4.07), 17. You Saved My Soul (demo) (1.34), 18. Sally and Billy (demo) (3.28), 19. Whatever Happened To (demo) (4.39), 20. One of the Boys (take 2) (3.10), 21. Help Me to Help Myself (demo) (2.06), 22. Real Love (take 4) (4.00)

Notes: This is an excellent set. The material is outstanding including the original demos used for the *Anthology* album. The packaging and notes are also very well done with details of the songs and other information. The front cover has a cartoon of John playing the piano. 'Now and Then' was considered for *Anthology 3* but rejected. However, a report in February 2007 suggested that Paul and Ringo were working on this track for possible release. A number of the tracks were issued on *When I Get Older* (Fab 4).

274. FREE AS A BIRD: THE DAKOTA BEATLE DEMOS

Odeon 1001

Format: CD

Source: various demos

Sound quality: very good

Notes: This release is a European issue of the American release on the Pegboy label.

275. FULFILLING THE FANTASIES

Salamander SCD 1019

Format: CD

Source: *Double Fantasy* and *Milk and Honey* album sessions

Sound quality: very good

1. Clean-up Time, 2. I'm Losing You, 3. Beautiful Boy (Darling Boy), 4. Dear Yoko, 5. I'm Steppin' Out, 6. I'm Steppin' Out, 7. Nobody Told Me, 8. Borrowed Time, 9. Borrowed Time, 10. Jam/Borrowed Time, 11. I Don't Want to Face It, 12. I'm Losing You, 13. I'm Losing You, 14. Beautiful Boy (Darling Boy), 15. I Don't Want to Face It, 16. I'm Steppin' Out (vocal booth session)

Notes: An album was released on vinyl with the same title but a slightly different track listing. The front cover of the compact disc has a black-and-white 1980 picture of John against a pastel blue and white background with the titles in red. The back has track listing with another black-and-white picture of John.

276. GIVE PEACE A CHANCE

The Easy Rider Years 930132

Format: CD

Released: 1993

Source: various live performances (see notes)

Sound quality: very good

1. Imagine (acoustic version) (2.56), 2. Come Together (4.02), 3. Cold Turkey (3.00), 4. The Luck of the Irish (3.13), 5. Attica State (2.56), 6. Mother (4.40), 7. Money (3.05), 8. Yer Blues (3.35), 9. John Sinclair (2.50), 10. Woman Is the Nigger of the World (5.36), 11. Instant Karma (3.13), 12. Blue Suede Shoes (2.12), 13. Give Peace a Chance (3.06), 14. Imagine (2.58), 15. Dizzy Miss Lizzie (3.05)

Notes: Track 1, Apollo Theatre, New York, December 1971. Tracks 2, 6, 11 and 14, Madison Square Garden, New York, 30 August 1972. Tracks 3, 7, 8, 12, 13 and 15 Toronto September 1969. Tracks 4, 5 and 9 Ann

Arbour, Michigan, 10 December 1971. Track 10, February 1972. Sleeve has picture of John and Yoko on the front with full track listing and details of the sources of the tracks on the back.

277. GONE FROM THIS PLACE

Vigotone VT-CD-01

Format: CD

Source: various – see notes

Sound quality: very good–excellent

1. God (2.39), 2. I'm Stepping Out (5.33), 3. Real Love (3.52), 4. Going Down on Love (3.56), 5. Pill (1.38), 6. Gone from This Place (1.34), 7. Dear Yoko (2.41), 8. Memories (2.31), 9. I'm Losing You (3.14), 10. God Save Us (3.08), 11. I Found Out (3.18), 12. Borrowed Time (3.00), 13. Rock Island Line (2.31), 14. I'm the Greatest (2.33), 15. (Just Like) Starting Over (4.52), 16. Serve Yourself (5.32), 17. Well (Baby Please Don't Go) (5.49), 18. Cold Turkey (3.25), 19. Clean-up Time (3.12), 20. Beef Jerky (3.10), 21. Gone from This Place

Notes: Track 1, acoustic. Track 2, rough mix. Track 3, Dakota piano, take. Track 4, *Walls and Bridges* rehearsal. Track 5, acoustic – early 1972. Track 6, acoustic. Track 7, rough mix with chat and riffs. Track 8, Dakota piano, take, late 1970s. Track 9, acoustic with rhythm box, Bermuda mid-1980. Track 10, rough mix, Tittenhurst, June 1971. Track 11, acoustic, summer 1970. Track 12, rough mix. Track 13, acoustic, mid – late 1970s. Track 14, June 1971. Track 15, acoustic, take 3 with rhythm box. Track 16, piano version. Track 17, June 1971. Track 18, acoustic, summer 1969. Track 19, alternate mix. Track 20, guitar version. Track 21, acoustic.

The front cover of the sleeve has a close up colour picture of John's face. The back has full track listing with details of the sources and a colour picture of John with a ponytail.

278. GOODNIGHT, VIENNA

Dakota Records DR 6975

Format: CD

Source: various
Sound quality: unknown

1. Goodnight, Vienna, 2. Thirty Days/Come On Everybody, 3. Come On Everybody/Slippin' and Slidin', 4. Stand By Me, 5. Imagine, 6. I Want You, 7. Jerusalaim, 8. Tequila, 9. Instrumental, 10. A Fool Was I

Bonus Tracks

11. Lennon on Jesus quote, 12. Twist and Shout (The Beatles), 13. Lennon on Jesus quote, 14. Money (The Beatles), 15. Lennon on Jesus quote (Hula Hoop), 16. Mr Moonlight (The Beatles), 17. Lennon on Butcher cover, 18. Ask Me Why (The Beatles), 19. Lennon on song writing, 20. To Know Her Is to Love Her (The Beatles), 21. Lennon on *How I Won the War*, 22. I'm Gonna Sit Right Down and Cry (The Beatles), 23. Cottonfields, 24. Memphis Tennessee (The Beatles), 25. Matchbox (The Beatles), 26. Lennon on Yoko and life, 27. Talking About You (The Beatles), 28. Lennon on musicians, 29. Lennon – Goodbye Goodbye, 30. Sweet Little Sixteen (The Beatles), 31. Goodbye to Kenny Everett/Jingle Bells

Notes: The black-and-white cover has a drawing of John from around the 'Bed-In' period. The back has the track listing.

279. GREATEST HITS LIVE

Chartbusters CHER-072-A
Format: CD
Time: 74.20
Source: various
Sound quality: unknown

1. Imagine (3.32), 2. Come Together (4.08), 3. Mother (4.29), 4. Give Peace a Chance (6.49), 5. (Just Like) Starting Over (4.11), 6. Woman (3.28), 7. Watching the Wheels (3.02), 8. Nobody Told Me (3.10), 9. Happy Xmas (War Is Over) (3.14), 10. Mind Games (3.27), 11. Love (2.24), 12. Cold Turkey (3.28), 13. No. 9 Dream (3.10), 14. Whatever Gets You Through the Night (3.46), 15. Beautiful Boy (3.28), 16. Oh, Yoko (4.37), 17. I'm Stepping Out (4.32), 18. Borrowed Time (4.55), 19. I'm Losing You (3.16), 20. I Don't Want to Face It (2.03)

Notes: The front cover has a colour picture of John from the One-to-One concert with the track listing on the back.

280. A GUITAR'S ALL RIGHT JOHN, BUT YOU'LL NEVER EARN YOUR LIVING BY IT

Audifon Records R.6015

Format: CD

Source: various

Sound quality: good

1. Whatever Gets You Through the Night, 2. Lucy in the Sky with Diamonds, 3. I Saw Her Standing There, 4. Slippin' and Slidin', 5. Stand By Me, 6. Oh, My Love, 7. Voulez Vous Coucher Avec Moi, Ce Soir (Lady Marmalade), 8. Working Class Hero, 9. Day Tripper

Notes: Tracks 1–3, with Elton John Madison Square Garden, New York, 28 November 1974. Tracks 4 and 5, *The Old Grey Whistle Test*, 18 April 1975. Track 6, outtake. Track 7, recorded 18 March 1975. Track 8, alternate. Track 9, rumoured to be with Jimi Hendrix, BBC radio.

281. HARD TIMES ARE OVER (YOKO AND JOHN)

Sweet Zapple SZ-203

Format: CD

Source: various

Sound quality: unknown

1. Every Man Has a Woman Who Loves Him (John and Yoko discussion and play back – Yoko vocals on overdub rough vocals), 2. Every Man Has a Woman Who Loves Him (*Double Fantasy*. John and Yoko vocals), 3. Forgive Me (My Little Flower Princess) (studio chat and take 3 – Go Home version), 4. Hard Times Are Over (alternate mix with John's backing vocals), 5. Hard Times Are Over (backing vocals version and John's chat, handclaps), 6. I'm Your Angel (rough mix), 7. Walking on Thin Ice (vocal booth, alternate take), 8. I'm Having A Baby My Love (Yoko vocal and piano, 1975), 9. I'm Not as Strong as You Think (Yoko vocal), 10. No One Sees Me Like You Do (outtake, 1973), 11. Oh, My Love (Yoko vocal, John backing guitar), 12. Somewhere

in the Sky (Yoko vocal), 13. Yoko a cappella (with intro John's chat, July 1970), 14. Dear Yoko (Bermuda acoustic take 1 – breakdown, take 2 – breakdown, take 3 – with chat), 15. You Can't Catch Me (alternate take), 16. Sweet Little Sixteen (alternate take)

Notes: The front cover has a cartoon of a naked John and Yoko eating bananas with a photographer taking a picture of them. The back cover is sky blue with the complete track listing.

282. HAVE YOU HAD YOUR BREAKFAST YET? (JOHN AND YOKO)

Black Cat BC 038

Format: CD

Source: John and Yoko with Alex Bennet, WPLJ FM 95.5, New York City, 8 June 1971

Sound quality: unknown

1. Meeting Celebrities, 2. We've Got Until Tuesday, 3. A Lot of Chopped Heads, 4. I Wouldn't Have Missed Any of It, 5. Let's Play A Record, 6. Caller One, 7. Shut Up You Bitch, 8. My Mummy's Dead/Don't Worry, 9. There's Two Books, 10. That Apple Jazz, 11. That Was One In Ten, 12. Mother/Why, 13. Any Sound Is Interesting, 14. A Very Healthy Thing, 15. A Typical Couple, 16. Caller Two, 17. A Summons In The Morning, 18. Caller Three, 19. Donating To The Wildlife Fund, 20. Caller Four, 21. Caller Five, 22. Expectations, 23. Caller Six, 24. Grapefruit Readings, 25. Caller Seven, 26. Caller Eight, 27. Caller Nine, 28. Caller Ten, 29. The Other Solo Albums, 30. Caller Eleven, 31. Caller Twelve, 32. Caller Thirteen, 33. Unreleased Beatle Material, 34. The Village Scene

Notes: The colour front cover has a picture of John, wearing a *Grapefruit* tee shirt, together with Yoko. *Grapefruit* was the title of Yoko's book of poems which was first published in 1970. The back has a colour picture of John and Yoko with the track listing printed on top.

283. A HEART PLAY

No Manufacturer Listed

Format: CD (double)

Released: 1999

Time: Disc One 70.17, Disc Two 66.48

Source: Disc One, studio sessions for *Double Fantasy*. Disc Two, home demos.

Sound quality: very good to excellent

Discs One: Studio sessions, Hit Factory, New York, August–September 1980

1. I'm Stepping Out (take 1) (5.01), 2. I'm Losing You (with Cheap Trick) (4.19), 3. Clean-up Time (rehearsal) (2.25), 4. Clean-up Time (early take) (4.26), 5. Clean-up Time (sound mix) (3.24), 6. (Just Like) Starting Over (studio talk) (2.31), 7. (Just Like) Starting Over (dry mix) (4.10), 8. Beautiful Boy (sweet mix) (4.07), 9. Dear Yoko (additional overdubs) (4.11), 10. Watching the Wheels (early mix) (3.35), 11. I'm Am The Walrus (0.16), 12. Woman (studio talk) (2.07). 13. Woman (mix 1) (3.20), 14. Dream Lover/Stay (3.42), 15. Forgive Me (My Little Flower Princess) (early take) (3.39), 16. Nobody Told Me (early take) (3.52), 17. I Don't Want to Face It (rock mix) (2.34), 18. Borrowed Time (rough mix) (4.07), 19. Woman (mix 2) (3.40), 20. I'm Stepping Out (4.40), 21. Maggie Mae (0.25)

Disc Two: Demos and home recordings, 1979–1980

1. The Great Wok (2.03), 2. Watching the Wheels (1.57), 3. Watching the Wheels (2.50), 4. Corrina Corrina (1.16), 5. Watching the Wheels (3.02), 6. I Don't Want to Face It (0.44), 7. Welcome To The Bermudas (0.10), 8. I Don't Want to Face It (2.04), 9. Woman (3.08), 10. Stepping Out (4.33), 11. Everybody's Talking/Nobody Told Me (2.21), 12. Nobody Told Me (3.12), 13. Beautiful Boy (2.37), 14. Borrowed Time (3.45), 15. Dear Yoko (3.37), 16. Too Much Monkey Business/Subterranean Homesick Blues (1.18), 17. Clean-up Time (2.41), 18. Stranger's Room (3.18), 19. I'm Losing You (1.30), 20. I'm Losing You (1.36), 21. Howling at the Moon (1.55), 22. I'm a Man (1.53), 23. I Watch Your Face (1.10), 24. My Life (2.33), 25. Don't Be Crazy (1.37), 26. The Worst is Over (2.12), 27. (Just Like) Starting Over (4.45), 28. The Best Things In Life Are Free (2.25)

Notes: All tracks taken from *The Lost Lennon Tapes* radio series. Sleeve comprises four-page booklet with photos from the summer of 1980 with a reproduction of John and Yoko's Christmas card on the front and a Hit Factory studio picture on the back. Inside is a complete and detailed track listing. The song 'My Life', which is an early version of '(Just Like) Starting Over', was officially released in 1997 on the five-track CD with the Swedish reprint of *A Spaniard in the Works*.

284. HEART PLAY DIALOG (JOHN AND YOKO)
Unknown
Format: CD
Source: see below (taken from sleeve notes)
Sound quality: very good

1. Ear play... what the album is, 2. Working with Yoko. She's trained as a musician. Would talk to engineers, 3. Yoko: making dreams and prayers stronger, 4. Fantasy vs. Reality: Wish fulfilment, 5. John as artist. Didn't want to continue as R and R star and go to Vegas, 6. Being an artist who's life doesn't reflect work. Dying in public. Bed-Ins. Other music to do together, 7. Why work together? Just another couple, 8. Walking away is harder than carrying on, 9. Unfilled space. YO: What does John do now? Caring for baby, 10. John: no need to be a teen idol, sex symbol. Proud to be house husband, 11. Fulfilling dreams. Being a trapped artist. Having a companion who tells the truth, 12. John at 40. Feels fine. Sean and 5 songs inspired by life experiences, 13. Looking to break away from Beatles since '65. How I Won War... Straw F, 14. A guy she liked, 15. Teacher/pupil relationship. Hard lessons when they separated in '74, 16. Y: Love will never die. Fighting to keep relationship going. Instant Karma, 17. Arguments, 18. Beautiful days, 19. No one controls John, 20. Cosmic, 21. Leadership false god, 22. Listen to message, 23. Make your own dreams, 24. Y: Day dreams. 25. Pacifists getting shot. Yoko reflects circa 1984

285. HIDDEN ARCHIVES
Fire Power FP-038A/B
Format: CD (double)
Source: various
Sound quality: very good

Disc One

1. Stranger's Room (chat and piano demo), 2. Brown Eyed Handsome Man/Get Back (acoustic), 3. Memories (piano demo), 4. Dear Yoko (rehearsal), 5. Starting Over (playback tape), 6. I'm Losing You (horn section overdub), 7. I'm Losing You (alternate take), 8. Brown Eyed Handsome Man/Blue Moon/Young Love (acoustic), 9. Help Me to Help Myself (piano, take 2 and 3), 10. 99 Annual Dakota Mind Movie Delta Blues Festival (live version), 11. Sea Ditties (piano demo), 12. The Great Wok (Dakota, 1978), 13. J.J. (acoustic demo), 14. I'm the Greatest (piano demo, 1970), 15. Many Rivers to Cross/My Girl (guitar and rhythm), 16. Sally and Billy (piano and rhythm, take 2, summer 1976), 17. She is a Friend of Dorothy (early piano version, summer 1976), 18. Attica State (acoustic demo with count-in with Yoko)

Disc Two

1. Going Down on Love (acoustic demo), 2. Clean-up Time (vocal overdub), 3. Attica State (rehearsal with Yoko and Elephant's Memory), 4. No One Sees Me Like You Do (*Double Fantasy* rehearsal), 5. I Don't Wanna Face It (demo with rhythm box), 6. Borrowed Time (discussion and riff), 7. Help Me to Help Myself (guitar demo), 8. Baby Make Love To You (piano demo), 9. Boys and Girls (piano demo), 10. Boys and Girls (piano demo), 11. Real Love (piano demo), 12. The Worst is Over (guitar with rhythm box), 13. Dear Yoko (acoustic demo, take 1, Cold Spring Harbor 1980), 14. Dear Yoko (acoustic demo, take 2, Cold Spring Harbor 1980), 15. Attica State (1971), 16. Attica State (Apollo Theater 17 December 1972), 17. Attica State (Radio Hilversum March 1972), 18. The Luck of the Irish (Radio Hilversum March 1972)

286. HUSHED BELLS OVER

Masterfraction MFCD 017

Format: CD

Released: 2001

Source: *Plastic Ono Band* album outtakes and demos

Sound quality: excellent

1.Mother (acetate version), 2. Remember (acetate version), 3. I Found Out (rough mix), 4. Mother (alternate version), 5. Look at Me (rough mix), 6. Well, Well, Well (studio outtake), 7. Rock 'n' Roll Jam: That's All Right Mama/Glad All Over/Honey Don't/Don't Be Cruel/Hound Dog/Matchbox. 8. God (demo version 1), 9. God (demo version 2), 10. God (demo version 3), 11. God (demo version 4), 12. Love (demo version), 13. Mother (demo version), 14. Well, Well, Well (demo version), 15. When a Boy Meets a Girl (unreleased track), 16. When a Boy Meets a Girl (unreleased track), 17. I Found Out (demo version 1), 18. I Found Out (demo version 2), 19. Look at Me (demo version), 20. My Mummy's Dead (complete version)

Notes: This disc includes the extended version of 'Remember' which develops into a jam and runs for 8 minutes and 29 seconds. Most of the tracks on this disc appeared on the 1997 bootleg *The Dream is Over* but are better quality on this disc.

The cover features a picture similar to the official release *John Lennon/Plastic Ono Band* but only John is sitting under the tree. The back has the track listing with a colour picture of John and Yoko.

287. I FOUND OUT

Luna Records LU 9424

Format: CD

Time: 73.10

Source: various

Sound quality: very good

1. Mother (3.51), 2. I Found Out (3.57), 3. Love (2.25), 4. Well, Well, Well (1.11), 5. Look at Me (2.58), 6. God (2.43), 7. My Mummy's Dead (1.17), 8. Mother No. 2 (4.36), 9. I Found Out No. 2 (4.01), 10. Well, Well, Well No. 2 (3.37), 11. Look at Me No. 2 2.51), 12. I Found Out No. 3 (3.22), 13. Honey Don't (1.33), 14. Don't Be Cruel (1.28), 15. Matchbox (1.54), 16. Yer Blues (instrumental rehearsal) (3.58), 17. Yer Blues (3.44), 18. No. 9 Dream (3.11), 19. Pill (1.41), 20. Mucho Mungo (2.52), 21. When A Boy Needs A Girl (2.07), 22. Child of Nature (2.34), 23. Julia (2.56), 24. Don't

Let Me Down (2.55), 25. Don't Let Me Down No. 2 (2.10), 26. Everyone Had a Hard Year (1.42), 27. Oh, My Love (1.22)

Notes: Tracks 1–15, 1970. Tracks 16 and 17, 1968. Tracks 18–21, 1972. Tracks 22–27, 1968.

Colour cover with track listing on the back.

288. IMAGINE

Images IM 02

Format: CD

Source: *Imagine* album sessions

Sound quality: unknown

1. Imagine, 2. Crippled Inside, 3. Jealous Guy, 4. It's So Hard, 5. How Do You Sleep? 6. Give Me Some Truth, 7. Oh, My Love, 8. How Do You Sleep? 9. How? 10. Oh, Yoko, 11. San Francisco Bay Blues

289. IMAGINE ACETATE

Unknown

Format: CD

Source: *Imagine* album acetate

Sound quality: unknown

1. Imagine, 2. Crippled Inside, 3. Jealous Guy, 4. It's So Hard, 5. I Don't Want to Be a Soldier, 6. Give Me Some Truth, 7. Oh, My Love, 8. How Do You Sleep? 9. How? 10. Oh, Yoko

290. IMAGINE… ALL THE OUTTAKES, VOLS. 1–3

Vigotone VT-118/119/120

Format: CD (triple box set with 34 page booklet)

Released: 1994

Source: *Imagine* album outtakes

Sound quality: excellent stereo

Disc One: The Outtakes (48.41)

1. Imagine (version 2, take 1), 2. Crippled Inside (take 17), 3. Jealous Guy (take 2), 4. It's So Hard (take 2), 5. I Don't Want to Be a Soldier, Mama (I Don't Want To Die) (take 2), 6. Give Me Some Truth (alternate vocal), 7. Oh, My Love (take 2), 8. How Do You Sleep? (alternate vocal), 9. How? (alternate vocal), 10. Oh, Yoko (take 9), 11. 'Just A Little Story…' (studio monologue). 12. Well (Baby Please Don't Go)

Disc Two: The Outtakes (62.21)

1. Imagine (take 1), 2. Imagine (take 2), 3. Imagine (take 3), 4. Imagine (alternate vocal), 5. Crippled Inside (take 2), 6. Jealous Guy (take 1), 7. Jealous Guy (take 7), 8. Jealous Guy (vocal, take 20), 9. I Don't Want to Be a Soldier, Mama (I Don't Want To Die) (take 1), 10. I Don't Want to Be a Soldier, Mama (I Don't Want To Die) (alternate mix), 11. Oh, My Love (alternate take 1a), 12. Oh, My Love (alternate take 1b), 13. How? (take 12), 14. How? (alternate vocal), 15. How? (alternate vocal), 16. Oh, Yoko (take 7), 17. I'm the Greatest (piano demo), 18. Imagine (rehearsal), 19. San Francisco Bay Blues (impromptu studio solo)

Disc Three: The Sessions and The Demos (73.20)

1. How Do You Sleep? (rehearsal), 2. Oh, My Love (acoustic demo), 3. How? (piano demo), 4. People Get Ready/How? (piano demo), 5. Medley: How?/Child of Nature/Oh, Yoko (piano demo), 6. Oh, Yoko (acoustic and piano demo), 7. It's So Hard (sax overdub), 8. I Don't Want to Be a Soldier, Mama (I Don't Want To Die) (sax overdub), 9. How Do You Sleep? (reprise)

Notes: Disc One is an upgrade of *Imagine – The Alternate Album*. It was copied by Birthday Records – see *The Imagine Outtakes Vols 1-3*. Vigotone released two further CDs in this series as a double set titled *Imagine… More Session Tapes*. This was also copied by Birthday Records and released as two separate albums (see *The Imagine Outtakes Vols 4 and 5*). This set is the definitive collection of outtakes, rehearsals, alternate versions, home demos and studio overdubs. Some of the tracks had been previously released on *The Lost Lennon Tapes* but not in the superb sound quality on this three-disc CD set.

This comes in a box with a thirty-six-page booklet with excellent notes and includes an interview with John (probably from *Rolling Stone*), detailed track listing, the story of the *Imagine* album and some nice black-and-white pictures. The box is blue with a picture of John on the front playing a psychedelic guitar. The picture looks like a painting. The back of the box has the track listing with a small picture of George playing a guitar. The sources date back to 1968 with early home demos through to the final overdub sessions. This set is highly recommended.

291. IMAGINE – THE ALTERNATE

Unknown

Format: CD

Source: Imagine album alternate versions and outtakes

Sound quality excellent

1. Imagine (different version with different drum pattern), 2. Crippled Inside (rough mix with different vocals), 3. Jealous Guy (different version with acoustic guitar), 4. It's So Hard (rough mix – no sax overdub), 5. I Don't Want to Be a Soldier (I Don't Want to Die), 6. Give Me Some Truth (rough mix with different vocal), 7. Oh, My Love (very early rough mix), 8. How Do You Sleep? (very different version), 9. How? (rough mix with acoustic guitar), 10. Oh, Yoko (rough mix with different vocals and different harmonica solo), 11. I'm the Greatest (early version), 12. Power to the People (early rehearsal version), 13. God Save Us (see notes), 14. Do the Oz (the B-side of track 13), 15. Well (Baby Please Don't Go), 16. Jealous Guy (rough mix), 17. How Do You Sleep? (very early rehearsal), 18. Imagine (rough mix – great Lennon vocal)

Notes: Track 13: The A-side of a very rare single issued in July 1971 by the Elastic Oz Band in support of the underground magazine *Oz* and sung by Bill Elliot. This is the same version but has John Lennon on lead vocal.

292. IMAGINE – THE ALTERNATE ALBUM

Sidewalk Music SD 89009

Format: CD

Released: 1989
Time: 44.23
Source: *Imagine* album alternate versions and outtakes
Sound quality: excellent

1. Imagine, 2. Crippled Inside, 3. Jealous Guy, 4. It's So Hard, 5. How Do You Sleep?, 6. Give Me Some Truth, 7. Oh, My Love, 8. How do You Sleep? No.1, 9. How? 10. Oh, Yoko, 11. San Francisco Bay Blues

Notes: A vinyl edition of this disc was available in 1990 on Apple Records (bogus) – SW-A-3379. A limited amount were later released on white vinyl. All tracks are taken from *The Lost Lennon Tapes* series with the only missing song from the original LP being 'I Don't Want to Be a Soldier, Mama' which had not been included on *The Lost Lennon Tapes* albums.

Sleeve features the poster which had been given with the original official album. The front cover has a picture of John playing the white piano. There is an error on the label on the disc where 'Imagine' is spelt 'Imagne' both on the disc title and the track listing.

293. IMAGINE: APPLE 2 X 1 SIDED ROUGH ACETATE
Unicorn Records UC-081
Format: CD
Released: 2001
Source: *Imagine* album acetates
Sound quality: unknown

1. Imagine, 2. Crippled Inside, 3. Jealous Guy, 4. It's So Hard, 5. I Don't Want to Be a Soldier, 6. Give Me Some Truth, 7. Oh, My Love, 8. How Do You Sleep? 9. How? 10. Oh, Yoko, 11. Imagine, 12. Crippled Inside, 13. Jealous Guy, 14. It's So Hard, 15. I Don't Want to Be a Soldier Mama (I Don't Want to Die), 16. Give Me Some Truth, 17. Oh, My Love, 18. How Do You Sleep?

Notes: Tracks 1–10 taken from A*n Apple Custom Label Rough Acetate*. Tracks 11–18 Edit – taken from *An Apple Custom Label Rough Acetate*. See *Apple 2 x 1 Sided Rough Acetate*.

294. IMAGINE COLLECTORS EDITION

Unknown

Format: CD (double)

Source: *Imagine* album outtakes, demos, rehearsals

Sound quality: excellent

Disc One: Quadraphonic

1. Imagine (3.03), 2. Crippled Inside (3.48), 3. Jealous Guy (4.12), 4. It's so Hard, 5. I Don't Want to Be a Soldier Mama (I Don't Want to Die) (5.58), 6. Give Me Some Truth (3.10), 7. Oh, My Love (2.44), 8. How Do You Sleep? (5.19), 9. How? (3.40), 10. Oh, Yoko (4.17)

Disc Two: Making The Album

1. Imagine (rehearsal) (1.49), 2. Imagine (take 1) (3.10), 3. Crippled Inside (take 2) (3.51), 4. Jealous Guy (vocal overdub) (2.39), 5. It's So Hard (take 2) (2.29), 6. I Don't Want to Be a Soldier Mama (I Don't Want to Die) (take 1) (5.56), 7. Give Me Some Truth (from *Get Back* sessions) (1.06), 8. Give Me Some Truth (rough mix) (3.39), 9. Oh, My Love (alternate take) (2.52), 10. How Do You Sleep? (rehearsal) (4.31), 11. Jam (0.39), 12. How Do You Sleep? (vocal overdub) (1.24), 13. People Get Ready/How? (piano demo) (2.59), 14. How? (vocal overdub) (1.38), 15. Oh, Yoko (take 9) (5.47), 16. Oh, Yoko (vocal overdub) (1.42), 17. Well (Baby Please Don't Go) (5.54), 18. Imagine (alternate take) (3.25), 19. I'm the Greatest (studio demo), 20. San Francisco Bay Blues (1.16), 21. Imagine (soundtrack from movie) (2.30)

295. IMAGINE COMPLETE SESSIONS

BMI

Format: CD (triple)

Released: 1999

Source: *Imagine* album outtakes, demos, rehearsals

Sound quality: excellent

Disc One

Imagine

1. original demo version (3.32), 2. take 1 (3.30), 3. take 2 (2.57), 4. take 3 (3.13), 5. alternate take 1 (3.23), 6. alternate take 2 (3.13), 7. version 2 (3.18)

Crippled Inside

8. take 2 (3.52), 9. take 17 (3.49)

Jealous Guy

10. take 1 (4.15), 11. take 2 (4.27), 12. take 7 (4.11), 13. vocal overdub session (2.41), 14. take 20 (4.17)

It's So Hard

15. take 2 (2.30), 16. sax overdub session (8.28)

I Don't Want to Be a Soldier Mama (I Don't Want to Die)

17. take 1 (5.54), 18. take 2 (5.41), 19. sax overdub session (4.37), 20. New York studio chat (0.12)

Disc Two

I Don't Want to Be a Soldier Mama (I Don't Want to Die)

1. alternate version (5.54)

Give Me Some Truth

2. alternate take (3.37)

Oh, My Love

3. rehearsal, take 1 (5.24), 4. rehearsal, take 2 (3.43), 5. rehearsal, take 3 (0.52), 6. rehearsal, take 4 (4.26), 7. rehearsal, take 5 (1.32), 8. rehearsal, take 6 (4.03), 9. rehearsal – Mind Games (2.10), 10. rehearsal, take 7 (4.17), 11. rehearsal, take 8 (0.30), 12. rehearsal, take 9 (1.42), 13. rehearsal, take 10 (1.03), 14. rehearsal, take 11 (1.16), 15. rehearsal, take 12 (0.33), 16. rehearsal, take 13 (1.49), 17. take 1 mix A (2.53), 18. take 1 mix B (2.51), 19. take 2 (2.58)

How Do You Sleep?

20. rehearsal, take 1 (2.09), 21. rehearsal, take 2 (4.27), 22. rehearsal, take 3 (5.57), 23. rehearsal, take 4 (1.44), 24. Instrumental Jam (0.40), 25. take 2 (8.03), 26. take unknown (2.57)

Disc Three

How Do You Sleep?

1. version 2 (5.48), 2. vocal overdub session (1.29), 3. version 3 (6.36), 4. alternate take 1 (6.46), 5. alternate take 2 (4.15), 6. no string acetate version (3.33)

How?

7. take 2 (3.44), 8. take unknown (3.44), 9. alternate take 1 (3.42), 10. alternate take 2 (3.45), 11. take 12 (2.51), 12. vocal overdub session (1.39)

Oh, Yoko

13. take 7 (4.12), 14. Vocal overdub session (1.42), 15. take 9 (5.49)

I'm the Greatest

16. version 1 (2.45), 17. version 2 (1.56), 18. Well Baby Please Don't Go (5.54), 19. Just A Little Story (1.07), 20. San Francisco Bay Blues (1.16)

296. IMAGINE 5.1

Unknown CDP 7 46641 2

Format: CD

Time: 39.43

Source: *Imagine* album, 5.1 mixes

Sound quality: excellent

1. Imagine, 2. Crippled Inside, 3. Jealous Guy, 4. It's So Hard, 5. I Don't Want to Be a Soldier Mama (I Don't Want to Die), 6. Give Me Some Truth, 7. Oh, My Love, 8. How Do You Sleep? 9, How? 10. Oh, Yoko

Notes: This release is a copy of the quad mix album.

297. IMAGINE... MORE SESSION TAPES

Vigotone VT 185/VT 186
Format: CD (double)
Released: 1999
Time: Disc One 57.44, Disc Two 61.56
Source: *Imagine* album outtakes
Sound quality: excellent

Disc One

How Do You Sleep? (Tracks 1–16): 1. first rehearsal, 2. riffing, 3. another pass, 4. tuning jam, 5. slow rehearsal, 6. a bit of reggae, 7. low vocal false start, 8. low vocal false start 2, 9. low vocal rehearsal, 10. piano solo false start, 11. piano solo, 12. piano solo rehearsal, 13. eight track, take 1, 14. Phil's rhythm instructions, 15. Eight track take 2, 16. ...From George's solo, 17. Imagine, 18. How? 19. I'm the Greatest

Disc Two

It's So Hard (Tracks 1–13): 1. John starts tape, 2. King Curtis arrives, 3. intro playback, 4. John demonstrates on acoustic, 5. King Curtis riffs, 6. first pass and more filling, 7. second pass, 8. King Curtis asks John a question, 9. third pass, 10. John gives King Curtis feedback, 11. another pass at the intro, 12. another pass at the intro 2, 13. last pass

I Don't Want to Be a Soldier Mama (I Don't Want to Die) (Tracks 14–23): 14. John discusses the 1966 tour, 15. first playback, 16. playback continued – the first hit. 17. playback continued – the second hit, 18. John and Curtis talk, 19. first pass, 20. John instructs King Curtis, 21. second pass, 22. third pass, 23. last pass

Notes: This double-disc set contains the King Curtis sax overdubs. It was copied by Birthday Records and released in 2000 as two separate albums *The Imagines Outtakes: Vols 4 and 5*. This was the last release by Vigotone in the *Imagine* series as they were subsequently 'busted'. However Birthday Records released four further albums in the series (see below for details).

The two-discs in this set are housed in a slipcase.

298. THE IMAGINE OUTTAKES, VOLS 1–3

Birthday Records BRO 015/BRO 016/BRO 017

Format: CD (triple box set)

Released: 1998

Source: *Imagine* album outtakes

Sound quality: excellent stereo

Disc One: All the Outtakes (48.41)

1. Imagine (version 2, take 1), 2. Crippled Inside (take 17), 3. Jealous Guy (take 2), 4. It's So Hard (take 2), 5. I Don't Want to Be a Soldier, Mama (I Don't Want To Die) (take 2), 6. Give Me Some Truth (alternate vocal), 7. Oh, My Love (take 2), 8. How Do You Sleep? (alternate vocal), 9. How? (alternate vocal), 10. Oh, Yoko (take 9), 11. 'Just A Little Story…' (studio monologue). 12. Well (Baby Please Don't Go)

Disc Two: The Outtakes (62.21)

1. Imagine (take 1), 2. Imagine (take 2), 3. Imagine (take 3), 4. Imagine (alternate vocal), 5. Crippled Inside (take 2), 6. Jealous Guy (take 1), 7. Jealous Guy (take 7), 8. Jealous Guy (vocal, take 20), 9. I Don't Want to Be a Soldier, Mama (I Don't Want To Die) (take 1), 10. I Don't Want to Be a Soldier, Mama (I Don't Want To Die) (alternate mix), 11. Oh, My Love (alternate take 1a), 12. Oh, My Love (alternate take 1b), 13. How? (take 12), 14. How? (alternate vocal), 15. How? (alternate vocal), 16. Oh, Yoko (take 7), 17. I'm the Greatest (piano demo), 18. Imagine (rehearsal), 19. San Francisco Bay Blues (impromptu studio solo)

Disc Three: The Sessions and The Demos (73.20)

1. How Do You Sleep? (rehearsal), 2. Oh, My Love (acoustic demo), 3. How? (piano demo), 4. People Get Ready/How? (piano demo), 5. Medley: How?/Child of Nature/Oh, Yoko (piano demo), 6. Oh, Yoko (acoustic and piano demo), 7. It's So Hard (sax overdub), 8. I Don't Want to Be a Soldier, Mama (I Don't Want To Die) (sax overdub), 9. How Do You Sleep? (reprise)

Notes: This set is a copy of the Vigotone release *Imagine… All the Outtakes, Vols 1–3*.

299. THE IMAGINE OUTTAKES, VOL. 4

Birthday Records BR 070
Format: CD
Released: 2000
Source: *Imagine* album outtakes
Sound quality: excellent stereo

How Do You Sleep? (Tracks 1–16): 1. First rehearsal, 2. Riffing, 3. Another pass, 4. Tuning jam, 5. Slow rehearsal, 6. A bit of reggae, 7. Low vocal false start, 8. Low vocal false start 2, 9. Low vocal rehearsal, 10. Piano solo false start, 11. Piano solo, 12. Piano solo rehearsal, 13. Eight track 1, 14. Phil's rhythm instructions, 15. Eight track take 2, 16. …From George's solo, 17. Imagine, 18. How? 19. I'm the Greatest

Notes: This disc is a copy of CD 1 of the Vigotone Records release *Imagine… More Session Tapes*.

300. THE IMAGINE OUTTAKES, VOL. 5

Birthday Records BR 071
Format: CD
Released: 2000
Time: 61.56
Source: *Imagine* album outtakes
Sound quality: excellent

It's So Hard (Tracks 1–13): 1. John starts tape, 2. King Curtis arrives, 3. Intro playback, 4. John demonstrates on acoustic, 5. King Curtis riffs, 6. first pass and more filling, 7. second pass, 8. King Curtis asks John a question, 9. third pass, 10. John gives King Curtis feedback, 11. Another pass at the intro, 12. Another pass at the intro 2, 13. last pass

I Don't Want to Be a Soldier Mama (I Don't Want to Die) (Tracks 14–23): 14. John discusses the 1966 tour, 15. First playback, 16. Playback continued – the first hit. 17. Playback continued – the second hit, 18. John and Curtis talk, 19. first pass, 20. John instructs King Curtis, 21. second pass, 22. third pass, 23. last pass

Notes: This disc is a copy of CD 2 of the Vigotone Records release *Imagine... More Session Tapes*.

301. THE IMAGINE OUTTAKES, VOL. 6

Birthday Records BR 087

Format: CD

Released: 2001

Time: 72.31

Source: *Imagine* album outtakes

Sound quality: excellent stereo

Imagine – The Film, 1972

1. Imagine (slower version), 2. Crippled Inside, 3. Jealous Guy, 4. It's So Hard (plus extra guitar part), 5. I Don't Want to Be a Soldier (with John's religious introduction), 6. Give Me Some Truth (with Power to the People intro), 7. Oh, My Love, 8. How Do You Sleep? 9. How? 10. Oh, Yoko

Imagine Live

11. Imagine (Apollo Theatre 13 June 1975), 12. It's So Hard (One-to-One concert). 13. Imagine (One-to-One concert), 14. It's So Hard (One-to-One concert), 15. Imagine (One-to-One concert), 16. Imagine (King Biscuit mix), 17. It's So Hard (*Mike Douglas TV Show*), 18. Imagine (*Mike Douglas TV Show*), 19. Imagine (*Jerry Lewis TV Show*), 20. Imagine (*Salute To Sir Lew Grade*)

Notes: This disc is divided into two parts. 1. The *Imagine* film outtakes. 2. Live recordings of songs from the Imagine album.

302. THE IMAGINE OUTTAKES, VOL. 7

Birthday Records BR 088

Format: CD

Released: 2001

Time: 71.02

Source: *Imagine* album quad two channel mix, plus 'Oh, My Love' sessions

Sound quality: excellent stereo

Imagine Quad 2 Channel Stereo Mix

1. Imagine, 2. Crippled Inside, 3. Jealous Guy, 4. It's So Hard, 5. I Don't Want to Be a Soldier, Mama (I Don't Want To Die), 6. Give Me Some Truth, 7. Oh, My Love, 8. How Do You Sleep? 9. How? 10. Oh, Yoko

'Oh, My Love' Sessions

11. early run through/studio talk, 12. rehearsal, complete version, 13. rehearsal, run through, piano part, 14. George Harrison tuning his guitar, instrumental run through, 15. tuning, 16. rehearsal, 17. early version with complete intro, 18. John playing piano, 19. Make Love – Not War (very early version of 'Mind Games'), 20. run through/practising the intro, 21. instrumental version with intro/practising the intro, 22. instrumental version with intro/john says 'f***ing hell'

Notes: This disc has two themes. 1. The quad mixes which are different from the standard release. 2. Outtakes from the sessions for 'Oh, My Love'.

303. THE IMAGINE OUTTAKES, VOL. 8

Birthday Records BR 089

Format: CD

Released: 2001

Time: 72.31

Source: *Imagine* album outtakes

Sound quality: excellent stereo

The Making of *Imagine*

1. Instrumental, 2. Imagine – piano rehearsal, 3. Imagine – John discussing with Phil Spector, 4. Imagine – different mix used for the making of Imagine film (two different parts), 5. Crippled Inside – a cappella intro/studio talk, 6. Jealous Guy/studio talk, 7. It's So Hard – short version/studio talk, 8. I Don't Want to Be a Soldier – short version/talk, 9. Give Me Some Truth – recording session, 10. Oh, My Love – recording session/studio talk, 11. How Do You Sleep? – recording session, 12. How? 13. Oh, Yoko – session plus studio talk, 14. Look At me

5.1 Surround Mixes – Look at Me

15. Centre channel vocals up front, 16. Front channel, 17. Rear channel backing track

5.1 Surround Mixes – Oh, Yoko

18. Centre channel, 19. Front channels, 20. Rear channels

The Beatles Versions

21. Child of Nature ('Jealous Guy') (Esher demo), 22. On The Road To Marrakesh ('Jealous Guy'), 23. Give Me Some Truth (acoustic rehearsal), 24. Give Me Some Truth (rehearsal), 25. Give Me Some Truth (McCartney on vocals), 26. Give Me Some Truth (rehearsal)

All The Rest

27. Crippled Inside, 28. Crippled Inside (live at a house party early 1970), 29. Imagine (early version from the *Imagine* movie)

Notes: Tracks 1–14 are from the video/DVD release Give Me Some Truth. The disc includes 5.1 surround mixes of two songs. The remaining 5.1 mixes are on Volume 9.

304. THE IMAGINE OUTTAKES, VOL. 9

Birthday Records BR 090

Format: CD

Released: 2001

Time: 65.58

Source: *Imagine* album 5.1 surround mixes

Sound quality: excellent stereo

Imagine

1. Centre channel, 2. Front channels, 3. Rear channels

Crippled Inside

4. Centre channel, 5. Front channels, 6. Rear channels

Jealous Guy
7. Centre channel, 8. Front channels, 9. Rear channels

It's So Hard
10. Centre channel, 11. Front channels, 12. Rear channels

I Don't Want to Be a Soldier Mama (I Don't Want to Die)
13. Centre channel, 14. Front channels, 15. Rear channels

Give Me Some Truth
16. Centre channel, 17. Front channels, 18. Rear channels

Oh, My Love
19. Centre channel, 20. Front channels, 21. Rear channels

How?
22. Centre channel, 23. Front channels, 24. Rear channels

Notes: This set of nine CDs from Vigotone and Birthday Records consisting of outtakes and live performances from the *Imagine* album really is the ultimate from these sessions and is highly recommended.

305. IMAGINE – QUADRASONICS

Quadrapple 004

Format: CD

Released: 1999

Time: 39.43

Source: *Imagine* album, quadraphonic recordings

Sound quality: excellent

1. Imagine, 2. Crippled Inside, 3. Jealous Guy, 4. It's So Hard, 5. I Don't Want to Be a Soldier Mama (I Don't Want to Die), 6. Give Me Some Truth, 7. Oh, My Love, 8. How Do You Sleep? 9. How? 10. Oh, Yoko

Notes: The Imagine album was also released as a quadraphonic vinyl album during the seventies. This disc is virtually impossible to obtain now. This CD bootleg was reissued by Birthday Records.

306. IMAGINE – THE SESSIONS

Vigotone VT-CD-08

Format: CD

Source: *Imagine* album alternate takes, demos and rehearsals – Tittenhurst Park June 1971

Sound quality excellent stereo and mono

1. Imagine (3.06), 2. Crippled Inside (3.46), 3. Jealous Guy (4.03), 4. It's So Hard (2.20), 5. I Don't Want to Be a Soldier, Mama (I Don't Want To Die (5.45), 6. Give Me Some Truth (3.35), 7. Oh, My Love (2.23), 8. How Do You Sleep? (8.06), 9. Oh, Yoko (5.45), 10. Jam (0.38), 11. How Do You Sleep? (4.29), 12. Oh, My Love (2.38), 13. I'm the Greatest (2.33), 14. Well Baby Please Don't Go (5.49), 15. How Do You Sleep? (7.34), 16. Imagine (2.55), 17. San Francisco Bay Blues (0.46)

Notes: All tracks taken from *The Lost Lennon Tapes* radio series. Tracks 1–9 are alternate takes. Track 11, 'How Do You Sleep?' is a rehearsal. 'Oh, My Love' is the second version. 'I'm the Greatest' is a demo. 'Well Baby Please Don't Go' is a session outtake. Track 15, 'How Do You Sleep?', features a low octave vocal from John. Track 16, 'Imagine', features a solo piano. 'San Francisco Bay Blues' is a solo acoustic version. Although *The Lost Lennon Tapes* radio broadcast stated that the take of 'Give Me Some Truth' featured on this disc was the second to last, based on Phil Spector stating they need one more take, with John replying 'Oh, wasn't that it?'; this was the one used for the commercial release.

The front cover has a picture of John and Yoko sitting on the grass outside Tittenhurst Park with the track listing on the back.

307. IMAGINE WORLD

Unknown

Format: CD

Source: *Imagine* album outtakes

Sound quality: very good

1. Imagine, 2. Crippled Inside, 3. Jealous Guy, 4. It's So Hard, 5. I Don't Want to Be a Soldier Mama (I Don't Want to Die). 6. Give Me Some Truth, 7. Oh, My Love, 8. How Do You Sleep, 9. How?, 10. Oh, Yoko, 11. Imagine, 12. Crippled Inside, 13. Jealous Guy, 14. Give Me Some Truth, 15. Oh, My Love, 16. How?, 17. Oh, Yoko

308. I'M JUST SITTIN' HERE, REMINISCING

Black Owl Records BO-CD 079/080

Format: CD (double)

Source: BBC interview, John and Yoko talking with Andy Peebles, 6 December 1980

Sound quality: excellent

Disc One

1. Prestart, 2. We Come Along On Saturday Morning, 3. *Saturday Club*, 4. The Ballad of John and Yoko, 5. State of Mind In '66, 6. John and Yoko Collaborations, 7. Two Virgins, 8. In between Yoko and The Beatles, 9. The Beatles – Job, 10. Yoko and Paul, George and Ringo, 11. Back to Britain, 12. Life with the Lions, 13. Give Peace a Chance, 14. Live Peace in Toronto, 15. The Wedding Album, 16. Cold Turkey, 17. Changing Attitudes Towards Drugs, 18. Peace For Christmas (UNICEF Concert 1969), 19. Instant Karma (We All Shine On), 20. The Plastic Ono Band album, 21. Pressure In 1971, 22. Power to the People, 23. Imagine, 24. The 1972 Deportation Order, 25. Struggling For Peace With Humour, 26. *Some Time in New York City*, 27. Woman Is the Nigger of the World, 28. Happy Xmas (War Is Over), 29. The Story of The Plastic Ono Band, 30. Toilet break

Disc Two

1. Mind Games, 2. Listening To The Radio, 3. Feminism, 4. The Lost Weekend, 5. *Walls and Bridges*, 6. The Kitchen Years, 7. Elton John, 8. No. 9 Dream, 9. David Bowie, 10. The *Rock 'n' Roll album*, 11. Going Underground, 12. Reversing Roles, 13. *Double Fantasy*, 14. Fawlty Towers and other British TV series, 15. (Just Like) Starting Over, 16. Interpreting lyrics, 17. Walking on Thin Ice, 18. John and Yoko On and off The Media, 19. Beautiful Boy (Darling Boy), 20. I'm Losing You, 21. Woman – The

Beatle track, 22. New Wave Music, 23. Reggae and Yoko's Old New Wave, 24. Private Life, Security and Coming To The End

309. I'M THE GREATEST/SOMETHING PRECIOUS AND RARE
Vigotone VT-CD-07

Format: CD

Notes: See *Something Precious and Rare*.

310. IN HIS LIFE
Mastertone Multimedia 8048

Format: CD

Released: 1996

Source: interviews – see below

Sound quality: unknown

1. John and Yoko, highlights from the Montreal Bed-In, 1 June 1969 (9.29), 2. American radio broadcast, 18 September 1974, John plays DJ (38.52)

Notes: Sleeve says, 'John Lennon – In His Life contains 20 rare photographs of John and Yoko at their Tittenhurst Park home in 1969 and a compact disc featuring interviews from 1969 and 1974'.

311. IN MY LIFE
Dressed To Kill DTKBOX 92

Format: CD (triple disc box set)

Released: 1998

Source: see below

Sound quality: unknown

Lennon In His Own Words interspersed by Early Beatle Recordings which include:

Disc One

Lennon on old tunes, Sweet Georgia Brown, Darwin Airport, 1964, Sydney Airport 1964, Liking All Genres/Gigging, Ya Ya, Hong Kong 1964, Lennon on writing partners, Let's Dance, Adelaide Balcony 1964, Wellington 1964, Melbourne 1964, Sydney 1964

Disc Two

Education and Rock Influence, Cry for a Shadow, Seattle 1966, Lennon on machismo, Press Conference 1965, Why Can't You Love Me Again, Melbourne 1964, Lennon on borders/religion

Disc Three

Bernice Lamb Re dedication to music, What'd I Say, Madrid 1965, Lennon cutting, Miami 1964, Lennon cutting, Lennon on mellowing, Take Out Some Insurance, Lennon on avant garde music, Ruby Baby, Lennon on future and surviving, Lennon on positive projection, Lennon on artists role and women, Lennon on mother and life's work

Notes: The front cover has a close up picture of John smoking a cigarette with a bright red background. Details of the tracks are itemised on the back.

312. THE INSIDE TRACK: JOHN LENNON

DIR Broadcasting DIR-09-1982

Format: CD

Time: 46.00

Source: interview, 24 September 1980

Sound quality: unknown

Notes: Lisa Robinson Interview, 24 September 1980, at the Record Plant, New York City.

313. IN THE MIDDLE OF A CLOUD

Unicorn Records UC-071

Format: CD

Released: 2000

Source: various

Sound quality: unknown

1. Dear Yoko (demo, take 1), 2. Dear Yoko (demo, take 2), 3. John and Yoko Home Video, 4. Stand By Me, 5. Bob Harris Interview, 6. Slippin' and Slidin', 7. BBC Interview, 8. John and Yoko, 9. Elliot Mintz Interview, 10. Oh, Yoko (demo 1), 11. Oh, Yoko (demo 2), 12. Oh, Yoko (demo 3)

Notes: Tracks 1–3: Long Island, Cold Spring Harbour 1980, Tracks 4–6: *The Old Grey Whistle Test*, BBC TV, 18 April 1974. Tracks 7 and 8: Unedited BBC TV footage. Track 9: Channel 7. 1973. Tracks 10–12: Composing demos 1970.

314. INTERVIEWS: NOV–DEC 1969
Fan Collection JLINTV1969VOL1

Format: CD

Time: 35.51

Source: various interviews

Sound quality: Track 1 poor. Track 2 very good. Track 3 poor

1. Everett Is Here – Lennon interview, 8 November 1969. Various matters discussed. (3.23), 2. Ken Zelig interview, This interview is on the subject of John returning his MBE. This was broadcast on *The Lost Lennon Tapes* radio series (4.20), 3. Radio Luxembourg interview. This rare interview is about the *Live Peace in Toronto* album. John is asked about the concert, the Plastic Ono Band and the album. Tracks from the album are played during the broadcast but have been edited from this recording.

Notes: This item is from a fan collection and does not come with any booklet or packaging.

315. INTERVIEWS: 1969–1970 (VOL. 1)
Fan Collection JLGHINTV196970VOL1

Format: CD

Time: 41.13

Source: various interviews

Sound quality: varies

1. Radio South Africa, interview 12 December 1969, This interview is mainly a promotion for the LP Live Peace in Toronto 1969 but John also discusses forthcoming plans. Some sources believe that the date of this recording was 10 December but during the interview the host mentioned that the record came out today which confirms the date as 12 December. (7.15), 2. Midday Spin, 15 February 1970. Radio interview with Emperor Rosko as host. John and Yoko discuss the nature of the Plastic Ono Band, 'Instant Karma', a Beatles live show and peace. (8.15), 3. Fact Or Fantasy? Prayer and Meditation. This television interview was recorded at Apple Studios, London on 10 April 1970 and broadcast on BBC1 on 26 April 1970. It features George Harrison who talks about meditation and his spiritual goals. Film of this television appearance probably exists. (7.20), 4. Toronto Press Conference, 17 December 1969. (9.53), 5. Toronto Press Conference, 17 December 1969. (8.29)

316. INTERVIEWS: 1971 – THE DON SINGLETON INTERVIEW

Fan Collection NYDN 1971

Format: CD

Time: 71.31

Source: John and Yoko are interviewed by Don Singleton of *New York Daily News*, November 1971

Sound quality: good

Notes: This rare interview with John and Yoko was conducted by Don Singleton of the *New York Daily News*. Lennon is outspoken about a wide variety of topics. Yoko is in attendance but does not have much to say.

This item is from a fan collection and does not come with any booklet or packaging.

317. INTERVIEWS: 1974 (DISC 1)

Fan Collection JLINTV1947D1

Format: CD

Time: 51.51

Source: various interviews, late 1974, promoting *Walls and Bridges* album

Sound quality: varies

1. EMI promo tape, September 1974. Lennon replies to questions and encourages record sellers to support the new album (3.44), 2. RKO Radio, 25 September 1974. This is possibly the longest versions of this interview in existence (14.59), 3. CHUM FM Radio, Toronto station interview. John talks about *Walls and Bridges*, Yoko, the UFO story, Beatles reunion and other topics, 26 September 1974 (18.48), 4. WAXB FM, Mark Parenteau interviews John on the Detroit radio station. This is a better interview than CHUM with a wider range of questions (14.19)

Notes: This item is from a fan collection and does not come with any booklet or packaging.

318. INTERVIEWS: 1974 (DISC 2)
Fan Collection JLINTV1947D2

Format: CD

Time: 66.35

Source: various interviews, late 1974, promoting *Walls and Bridges* album

Sound quality: varies

1. KQRS Minneapolis interview, by Alan Stone (11.32), 2. 2SM 1269 AM Sydney, Australia, October 1974. John answers questions about the album and other matters, and the new album is played track by track although these are edited. This disc contains the full interview in good sound (29.47), 3. Unknown interview (0.30), 4. RKO Radio interview, 25 September 1974

Notes: This item is from a fan collection and does not come with any booklet or packaging.

319. INTERVIEWS: 1974 (DISC 3)
Fan Collection WRKO 1974

Format: CD

Time: 39.58

Source: WRKO interview, 29 September 1974

Sound quality: good

Notes: The host, commercials and music have been edited out. This item is from a fan collection and does not come with any booklet or packaging.

320. INTERVIEWS: 1974/1975
Unknown

Format: CD

Source: various – see below

Sound quality: unknown

1. The entire fifty-minute programme was allocated to John and his lawyer Leon Wildes, who appeared during the final part of the show (*Tomorrow Show*, 8 April 1975), 2. As part of his fight against deportation in 1974, John and his lawyer also appeared on this morning TV programme (*Today*, 16 December 1974), 3. 'The *Old Grey Whistle Test*: 'Stand By Me' and 'Slippin' and Slidin", 4. As part of their preparations for a new series of the BBC2 show, *The Old Grey Whistle Test*, Bob Harris and his producer Michael Appleton went to America for an interview with John at the Dakota (Bob Harris interview, March 1975), 5. Also recorded at the Dakota, this interview with the journalist Jean-Francois Vallee was for inclusion in the French television programme *Un Jour Futur*. John sings and plays Labelle's hit, 'Lady Marmalade', with the famous question 'voulez-vous coucher avec moi, ce soir?' (Jean-Francois Vallee interview, 7 April 1975), 6. Imagine, *Salute To Sir Lew Grade*, 18 April 1975

321. IT'S GONNA BE ALRIGHT (JOHN LENNON/PLASTIC ONO BAND)
His Masters Choice HMC 002

Format: CD (double) with hardback book Released: 2007

Source: *Plastic Ono Band* album outtakes, demos and rehearsals

Sound quality: excellent

Disc One

1. Mother (alternate mix with alternate vocal and longer fade) (5.02), 2. Hold On (take 1) (3.13), 3. Hold On (take 2) (2.52), 4. I Found Out

(rough 'Carl Wolf' mix) (3.57), 5. Working Class Hero (censored version) (3.47), 6. Remember (take unknown) (0.50), 7. Remember (take unknown) (3.21), 8. It'll Be Me (improvisation) (1.17), 9. Love (acoustic guitar rehearsal) (1.19), 10. (You're So Square) Baby I Don't Care (improvisation) (0.24), 11. Love (acoustic guitar/piano rehearsal) (0.40), 12. Well, Well, Well (rough mix) (5.54), 13. Look at Me (rough mix) (2.51), 14. God (acoustic guitar demo) (3.42), 15. God (acoustic home demo) (2.11), 16. My Mummy's Dead (complete acoustic guitar demo) (1.15), 17. Hold On (unknown up tempo take), 18. Hold On (take 30) (1.00), 19. Hold On (instrumental take unknown) (2.15), 20. Hold On (take unknown), 21. Love (acoustic guitar rehearsal) (2.40), 22. Love (acoustic guitar rehearsal) (2.03), 23. Love (acoustic guitar rehearsal) (2.29), 24. Love (acoustic guitar rehearsal) (1.29)

Disc Two
1. Love (piano rehearsal) (1.09), 2. Love (acoustic guitar/piano, take 1) (4.02), 3. Love (acoustic guitar/piano, take 2) (3.02), 4. Love (improvisation) (0.41), 5. Love (acoustic guitar/piano, take 14) (1.33), 6. Love (acoustic guitar/piano, take 15) (3.18), 7. Love (acoustic guitar/piano, take 16) (3.58), 8. Love (acoustic guitar/piano, take 17 and 18) (1.26), 9. Love (acoustic guitar/piano, take 19) (3.09), 10. Love (acoustic guitar/piano, take 20) (1.09), 11. Love (acoustic guitar/piano, take 21) (3.12), 12. Love (acoustic guitar/piano, take 21 and 22) (0.40), 13. Love (acoustic guitar/piano, take 23 (3.13), 14. Hold On (take 3) (1.52), 15. Hold On (take 4) (2.17), 16. Hold On (take 5) (1.52), 17. Hold On (take 6) (2.48), 18. Hold On (take unknown) (3.33), 19. Hold On (take unknown), 20. Hold On (take unknown) (1.54), 21. Hold On (take unknown) (1.52), 22. Hold On (take unknown) (2.04), 23. Look at Me (take unknown) (0.48), 24. Hold On (take unknown) (1.52), 25. Hold On (take unknown) (1.53), 26. Hold On (take unknown) (2.05), 27. Hold On (take unknown) (2.27)

Notes: This was the second release by a new label, His Masters Choice – the first being *The Beatles and The Great Concert At Shea!* (details of this will be shown in *The Beatles Bootleg Discography*). This set concentrates on the Plastic Ono Band album and comes packaged as a hardback book with twenty pages of text and photographs.

Copies of the set have since become available in a slimline DVD case but without the book. Two further John Lennon releases in a similar format soon followed: *Remember New York City – John Lennon/Yoko Ono* (HMC 003) and *Come On Listen To Me* (HMC 004).

322. IT'S HARD TO BE BUTTERFLIES

Barrier BAR 007/8

Format: CD (double)

Source: *Double Fantasy* and *Milk and Honey* demos and outtakes

Sound quality: excellent

Disc One

1. I'm Stepping Out (demo), 2. I'm Stepping Out (demo), 3. I'm Stepping Out (demo), 4. Sean visits the studio (vocal booth recording), 5. I'm Stepping Out (take 1 – multi-track mix down), 6. I'm Stepping Out (take 2 – multi-track mix down), 7. I'm Stepping Out (take 1 – vocal booth recording), 8. I'm Stepping Out (discussions and rehearsal – vocal booth recording), 9. I'm Stepping Out (take 2 – vocal booth recording), 10. I'm Stepping Out (discussions and rehearsals – vocal booth recording), 11. I'm Stepping Out (discussions and rehearsals – vocal booth recording), 12. I'm Stepping Out (discussions and rehearsals – vocal booth recording), 13. I'm Stepping Out (discussions and rehearsals – vocal booth recording), 14. I'm Stepping Out (take 3 – vocal booth recording), 15. I'm Stepping Out (take 4 – vocal booth recording), 16. I'm Stepping Out (take 5 – vocal booth recording), 17. I'm Stepping Out (take 6 – vocal booth recording), 18. Hard Times Are Over (choir overdub – multi-track mix down), 19. Hard Times Are Over (choir overdub – multi-track mix down), 20. Hard Times Are Over (choir overdub – multi-track mix down)

Disc Two

1. Ordering Dinner (vocal booth recording), 2. I'm Stepping Out (take 7 – vocal booth recording), 3. I'm Stepping Out (discussions and rehearsals – vocal booth recording), 4. I'm Stepping Out (take 8 – vocal booth recording), 5. I'm Stepping Out (playback – vocal booth recording), 6. I'm Stepping Out (take 6 – vocal booth recording), 7. I'm Stepping Out

(take 9 – multi-track mix down), 8. I'm Stepping Out (take 1 multi-track mix down), 9. I'm Stepping Out (take 1 multi-track mix down), 10. I'm Stepping Out (take 2 multi-track mix down), 11. Every Man Has a Woman Who Loves Him (vocal booth recording), 12. Every Man Has a Woman Who Loves Him (vocal booth recording), 13. Every Man Has a Woman Who Loves Him (vocal booth recording), 14. Every Man Has a Woman Who Loves Him (multi-track mix down), 15. Every Man Has a Woman Who Loves Him (multi-track mix down), 16., Every Man Has a Woman Who Loves Him (multi-track mix down), 17. Every Man Has a Woman Who Loves Him (multi-track mix down)

Notes: The set comes with a four-page booklet. The front has two pictures of John at a mixing desk.

323. IT'S NOT TOO BAD (JOHN LENNON/THE BEATLES)

Pegboy 1008

Format: CD

Released: 1998

Time: 59.16

Source: 'Strawberry Fields Forever' demos (see notes)

Sound quality: excellent mono and stereo

Santa Isabel Demos
1. warm up (0.27), 2. take 1 (0.47), 3. take 2 (1.19), 4. take 3 (1.29), 5. take 4 (1.47), 6. takes 5 and 6 (2.13), 7. rehearsal (0.14)

Strawberry Fields Forever – Kenwood Demos
8. electric guitar overdub, 9. electric guitar overdubs into instrumental demo (2.09), 10. demo playback/chat (0.16), 11. vocal overdub (double tracking lead vocal) on to demo (2.15), 12. demo playback (0.31), 13. electric guitar demo (take 1) (0.37), 14. electric guitar composing sequence (take 2–7) (4.03), 15. electric guitar demo (take 8) (1.57), 16. Mellotron/vocal overdubs on to composing sequence (4.10)

Strawberry Fields Forever – The EMI Sessions
17. take 1 (3.16), 18. take 2 (3.11), 19. take 3 and 4 (3.37), 20. takes 5 and 6 (4.42), 21. take 7 (tape reduction take 6) (3.32), 22. take 7 (3.08),

23. take 25 with inserts (3.49), 24. take 26 with inserts (3.47), 25. stereo remix 5/backwards speech (4.54)

Notes: This disc examines the evolution of 'Strawberry Fields Forever'. A wonderful looking box set with a slipcase and a booklet. This disc contains the complete collection of John's holiday demos from Santa Isabel which were made during the filming of *How I Won the War* and his home demos made at Kenwood plus the EMI 'Strawberry Fields Forever' sessions. The recording quality is excellent. Some of the items had previously appeared on bootlegs but these have a better sound quality.

Many of the photos from the 'Strawberry Fields Forever' time in the outstanding booklet are quite rare. The disc contents include John's first experiments to creating a masterpiece up to the last remix. Originals of this disc are almost impossible to find.

324. JAPAN INTERVIEW
Unknown
Format: CD
Source: interviews, 1971
Sound quality: unknown

1. Yoko Speaks in Japanese, 2. John and Yoko talk about *Imagine* LP, Japanese

325. JEALOUS GUY – THE IMAGINE SESSIONS
Luna Records LU 9308
Format: CD
Released: 1990
Source: *Imagine* album alternate versions and outtakes
Sound quality: excellent

1. Imagine, 2. Crippled Inside, 3. Jealous Guy, 4. It's So Hard, 5. I Don't Want to Be a Soldier Mama (I Don't Want to Die), 6. Give Me Some Truth, 7. Oh, My Love, 8. How Do You Sleep? 9. How? 10. Oh, Yoko, 11. Deep Water, 12. How Do You Sleep? 13. Oh, My Love, 14. I'm the Greatest,

15. Well Baby (Please Don't Go), 16. How Do You Sleep? 17. Imagine, 18. I Found Out, 19. Well, Well, Well, 20. San Francisco Bay Blues, 21. Corrina Corrina, 22. J.J.

Notes: Front cover has the same picture as *In My Life* with a different background.

326. THE JERRY LEVITAN INTERVIEW
Air-Check Levitan 1969
Format: CD
Released: 2005
Time: 33.53
Source: interview, May 1969, during the Toronto Bed-In
Sound quality: good but some hiss is evident

Notes Adopted From *Bootleg Zone*: This interview by Jerry Levitan was originally recorded in May 1969 during the Toronto Bed-In, as heard on KMYL Star 94.1 FM San Diego, where Jerry played and annotated on air. This is the Levitan/Lennon personal interview and includes previously unheard portions played for the first time on this radio appearance.

'As a 14-year-old from Dufferin Heights Junior High in Toronto, using the guise of a reporter from the non-existent Canadian News, Jerry managed to visit John and Yoko during their peace mission visit at the King Edward Hotel in May 1969. John gave him an autographed copy of *Two Virgins*, along with original sketches, and a further personal interview later the same day.'

Many thanks to Jerry Levitan for allowing his unique interview to be enjoyed by collectors.

327. JIM LADD INTERVIEW 1974 – UPGRADED
Unknown
Format: CD
Time: 77.51
Source: *Walls and Bridges* promo interview, October 1974
Sound quality: good

1. Jim Ladd intro/A Typical Day In The Life of John Lennon/I Know (I Know)/What Is It Like To Be John Lennon?/Baby You're a Rich Man (10.21), 2. Looking For Exactly What I Wanna Hear/Hidden Messages and Jokes/Discussing Steel and Glass/Steel and Glass/Musician Or Philosopher/A Day In The Life/Still Getting My Rocks off (Writing Those Songs) (14.34), 3. Ringo Anti Hard Drugs Message (0.29), 4. The Immigration Struggle/Help/John's Vision of The Future/The 60s Generation/I'm Scared/Drugs (Uppers and Downers)/Cold Turkey (One-to-One concert) (20.02), 5. John's 'trips'/Do You Think It's Ever Going To Get Together Collectively/Discussing The New Album, Pt 1: Whatever Gets You Through the Night/Whatever Gets You Through the Night/Discussing The New Album, Pt 2: Bless You/Bless You/Discussing The Relationship With Yoko/How Are Paul, Ringo and George Doing? (16.54), 6. Isolation/Jim Ladd Narration/Performing Live, Performing For Free/Old Dirt Road/The Biggest Mother Show On Earth For Peace/All You Need Is Love/Closing Remarks By Jim Ladd/Imagine (15.30)

328. JOHN LENNON AND FRIENDS LIVE: 1968–1971

KTKK Fun Boots DIY GB No. 25

Format: CD

Source: various – see notes

Sound quality: unknown

1. Yer Blues a cappella, 2. Dirty Mac Jam, 3. Yer Blues. 4. A Whole Lotta Yoko (Her Blues), 5. Blue Suede Shoes, 6. Money, 7. Dizzy Miss Lizzie, 8. Yer Blues, 9. Cold Turkey, 10. Give Peace a Chance, 11. Don't Worry Kyoko, 12. John John. 13. Instant Karma, 14. Well (Baby Please Don't Go), 15. Say Please – Jamrag, 16. Aaak, 17. (Gonna Put My Ono Records In A...) – Scumbag, 18. A Small Eternity with Yoko Ono

Notes: Tracks 1–4, *Rock and Roll Circus*. Tracks 5–12, *Live Peace in Toronto*. Track 13, from BBC Television, *Top of the Pops*. Tracks 14–18, Fillmore East 6 June 1971 with Frank Zappa.

The front and back covers feature a superb collection of black and white cartoons of the various musicians on this album including John and Yoko, Mick Jagger (this one has to be seen to be believed!), Keith

Richard, Eric Clapton and many others. Keith Richards name is spelt Kieth on the sleeve. The back of the sleeve has full track listing and details of the sources and the musicians involved

329. JOHN LENNON ANTHOLOGY: WEYBRIDGE

Fire Power FP-9040
Format: CD
Released: 1999
Source: various
Sound quality: unknown

1. He Said He Said, No. 1, 2. He Said He Said, No. 2, 3. She Said She Said, 4. Good Morning, Good Morning, 5. Across the Universe No. 1, 6. She's Walking Past My Door/You Know My Name, 7. She Can Talk to Me No. 1/She Can Talk to Me No. 2, 8. Cry Baby Cry No. 1/Cry Baby Cry No. 2/Across the Universe No. 2/Cry Baby Cry No. 3/Across the Universe No. 3/Cry Baby Cry No. 4, 9. Julia No. 1, 10. Julia No. 2, 11. Julia No. 3, 12. Oh, My Love No. 1, 13. Oh, My Love No. 2, 14. The Maharishi Song, 15. I Want You, 16. A Case of the Blues, 17. Don't Let Me Down No. 1, 18. Don't Let Me Down No. 2, 19. Everyone Had a Hard Year, 20. Mellotron Improvisation, 21. Mellotron Improvisation, 22. Mellotron Improvisation, 23. Mellotron Improvisation, 24. Mellotron Improvisation, 25. Stranger in My Arms, 26. Pedro the Fisherman, 27. Down In Cuba, 28. Chi Chi's Cafe, 29. Daddy's Little Sunshine Boy, 30. Yer Blues

Notes: The front cover has one of John's cartoons with a message from John underneath in block printing which reads 'Thanks you fab gear wackers from the boys the men… The Beatls (sic)'. The back has the track listing and a colour photograph of John from *Top of the Pops* performing 'Instant Karma'.

330. JOHN LENNON ARTIST THE BEATLE YEARS

DIY GB No. 28
Format: CD
Released: 2001
Source: various
Sound quality: unknown

1. Look at Me, 2. The Neville Club, 3. I'll Cry Instead, 4. Alec Speaking, 5. I Call Your Name, 6. Foyles Literary Luncheon Acceptance Speech, 7. A Hard Day's Night, 8. I Sat Belonely, 9. I Feel Fine, 10. Good Dog Nigel, 11. Help, 12. About The Awful, 13. You've Got to Hide Your Love Away, 14. The Wrestling Dog, 15. In My Life, 16. The National Health Cow, 17. I'm Only Sleeping, 18. Automatic Pier/The Fat Budgie, 19. Norwegian Wood, 20. We Must Not Forget The General Erection/The Wumberlog (or The Magic Dog), 21. Tomorrow Never Knows, 22. Liberation, 23. Strawberry Fields Forever, 24. This Week's Golden Dress/Lucy of The Little Town, 25. A Day In The Life, 26. Four of Five Musicians, 27. I Am the Walrus, 28. Jock and Yono/Once Upon a Pool Table, 29. Across the Universe, 30. Sitting In My Broken Car, 31. Revolution, 32. Who Could Tell What He Was Saying, 33. Julia, 34. Once Upon A Tarmac/Behind Two Virgins/Invite A Home/A Bunch of Flowers/Help

Bonus Track

35. Help

Notes: The front insert has the same cartoon as used on John Lennon Anthology: Weybridge (see above). The back has a collage of black-and-white photos of John through the years together with the track listing.

331. JOHN LENNON: A CELEBRATION

Dill Archives JLAC 1

Format: CD

Source: radio Broadcast, NBC, 8 December 1981

Sound quality: very good

Disc One

46.45

Disc Two

41.49

Notes: These comments were taken from the *Bootleg Zone*:

> 'John Lennon – A Celebration aired on 8 December 1981 on NBC affiliated stations, produced by the 'source', NBC Radio, and hosted by Ben Chandler. This is a radio show focusing on Lennon's life with The Beatles and Yoko. Full of interviews and generally well produced. It contains occasional news reporting about the crowds gathered in various places around the world mourning the loss of Lennon and marking the one year anniversary of his death. This version has scoped music and ads but the sound is very good quality. The full show (with music) also exists as a vinyl set released in 1982.'

There is no booklet or packing – the release is from fan archives but a cue sheet exists for the LP collection.

332. JOHN LENNON FOREVER
Laserlight 12 593
Format: CD
Released: 1995
Source: various interviews
Sound quality: very good

This release consists of various interviews including Julia Baird, Paddy Delaney (Cavern Club doorman), Alistair Taylor and Bob Wooler. Written and read by Geoffrey Giuliano.

333. JOHN LENNON: THE HALL OF FAME (CAPITAL RADIO INTERVIEW 1975)
G Cap Media OSS JLCR 11975
Format: CD
Released: 2005
Time: 26.00
Source: Capital Radio, originally broadcast in 1975
Sound quality: good

Notes: This release was taken from a transmission in 2005. The following comments are from the *Bootleg Zone*: 'This interview, from the Capital

Radio archives, was recorded in 1975 when John returned to New York after his lost weekend. It was eventually found in the Capital Radio archive where it had been resting for 30 years. The source tape was a deteriorating 8 inch reel, the original interviewer has been edited out and replaced by the host of the Hall of Fame interview series. John's part of the interview is intact despite the alteration. John talks about life in the United States, the demise of Apple, getting back with Yoko, his relationship with Paul and the rest of the former Beatles, his musical legacy, and going on *The Dick Cavett Show* to justify his paranoia.'

334. JOHN LENNON LIVE

CDDV 5516

Format: CD

Time: 29.53

Source: live performances

Sound quality: unknown

1. Imagine, 2. Give Peace a Chance, 3. Cold Turkey, 4. John Sinclair, 5. Yer Blues, 6. Dizzy Miss Lizzie, 7. Blue Suede Shoes, 8. The Luck of the Irish, 9. Attica State, 10. Money

Notes: Track 1, New York, November 1971. Track 2, 3, 5–7 and 10, Toronto September 1969. Tracks 4, 8 and 9, Ann Arbor 10 December 1971.

335. JOHN LENNON LIVE (SL. 15)

Apple House Music BAN-020-A

Format: CD

Released: 1993

Time: 44.51

Source: various

Sound quality: unknown

1. Watching the Wheels (3.01), 2. Corrina Corrina (1.14), 3. Beautiful Boy (2.43), 4. Dear Yoko No. 1 (1.00), 5. Dear Yoko No. 2 (4.23), 6. Living on Borrowed Time (5.01), 7. Move Over Ms L (1.34), 8. Move

Over Ms L (1.54), 9. Here We Go Again (3.01), 10. Maybe Baby (1.55), 11. Rave On (1.16), 12. Whatever Gets You Through the Night (5.30), 13. Woman (2.47), 14. God Save Us (1.58), 15. I Know (3.16), 16. Starting Over (4.18)

336. JOHN LENNON LIVE (SL. 16)

Apple House Music BAN-020-B

Format: CD

Released: 1993

Time: 45.46

Source: various

Sound quality: unknown

1. Meat City (2.30), 2. Send Me Some Loving (3.11), 3. Give Peace a Chance (0.31), 4. God (2.41), 5. Real Love (3.56), 6. I'm Losing You (3.16), 7. I Found Out (3.20), 8. Rock Island Line (2.34), 9. Starting Over (4.54), 10. Cold Turkey (3.27), 11. Tight A$ (3.21), 12. Julia (2.55), 13. Happy Xmas (3.16), 14. Watching the Wheels (2.51), 15. Many Rivers to Cross (3.03)

337. JOHN LENNON LIVE (SL. 17)

Apple House Music BAN-020-C

Format: CD

Released: 1993

Time: 47.51

Source: various

Sound quality: unknown

1. Cookin' (2.31), 2. Nobody Told Me (2.22), 3. Woman Is the Nigger of the World (2.13), 4. I'm Stepping Out (4.34), 5. New York City (2.12), 6. Woman No. 1 (3.32), 7. Beautiful Boy (4.03), 8. Mind Games (3.31), 9. I Found Out (4.06), 10. Watchingced the Wheels (3.21), 11. Woman No. 2 (3.59), 12. Nobody Told Me (3.19), 13. Rock 'n' Roll People (3.28), 14. Oh, Yoko (4.40)

338. JOHN LENNON LIVE (SL. 18)
Apple House Music BAN-020-D

Format: CD

Released: 1993

Time: 44.46

Source: various

Sound quality: unknown

1. People Get Ready (3.02), 2. God (3.45), 3. Borrowed Time (3.45), 4. She Said She Said No. 1 (1.06), 5. She Said She Said No. 2 (0.59), 6. She Said She Said No. 3 (1.00), 7. Starting Over (2.18), 8. Cooking (2.42), 9. Only the Lonely (1.02), 10. Mucho Mungo (3.03), 11. No. 9 Dream (3.11), 12. I'm Stepping Out (3.30), 13. Well, Well, Well (1.15), 14. Watching the Wheels (3.02), 15. San Francisco Bay Blues (0.45), 16. Look at Me (3.06), 17. Cold Turkey (3.44), 18. Maggie Mae (0.28), 19. Julia (2.54)

Notes: All the discs in this set from Apple House Music have full colour sleeves with full track listings on the back.

339. JOHN LENNON: THE MAN, THE MEMORY (WMJQ)
Air-Check WMJQ

Format: CD (triple)

Time: 60.08

Source: broadcast 14 December 1980

Sound quality: excellent

Notes: This radio programme was broadcast on 14 December 1980. It includes part of the interview with John and Yoko on 8 December 1980 for the RKO Radio Networks. This radio special contains a large amount of the interview plus Lennon's music and comments from the host Dave Sholin who together with Ron Hummel, Laurie Kaye and Bert Keane participated in the interview on 8 December.

340. JOHN LENNON/PLASTIC ONO BAND

Dr. Ebbetts SW 3372

Format: CD

Source: *Plastic Ono Band* album

Sound quality: unknown

Notes: This release is a copy of the album.

341. JOHN LENNON/PLASTIC ONO BAND 5.1

Unknown

Format: CD

Source: *Plastic Ono Band* album, 5.1 mixes

Sound quality: unknown

Notes: This release is a copy of the album.

342. JOHN LENNON PRESENTS... ABBEY ROAD ON RADIO LUXEMBOURG

Blackbird Records 013

Format: CD

Source: John plays tracks from The Beatles' new album

Sound quality: unknown

1. Jingle and introduction, 2. John Lennon Interview, 3. Come Together, 4. John Lennon Interview, 5. Something, 6. John Lennon Interview, 7. Maxwell's Silver Hammer, 8. John Lennon Interview, 9. Oh Darling, 10. John Lennon Interview, 11. Octopus's Garden, 12. John Lennon Interview, 13. I Want You (She's So Heavy), 14. John Lennon Interview, 15. Here Comes the Sun, 16. John Lennon Interview, 17. Because, 18. John Lennon Interview, 19. You Never Give Me Your Money, 20. John Lennon Interview, 21. Sun King, 22. John Lennon Interview, 23. Mean Mr Mustard, 24. John Lennon Interview, 25. Polythene Pam, 26. John Lennon Interview, 27. She Came in Through the Bathroom Window, 28. John Lennon Interview, 29. Golden Slumbers, 30. John Lennon Interview, 31. Carry That Weight, 32. John Lennon Interview, 33. The End, 34. Her Majesty, 35. John Lennon Interview

Notes: Sleeve states: 'For your listening pleasure the music tracks have been replaced by Stereo versions'. Programme broadcast on Radio Luxembourg 27 September 1969.

The front cover has a reproduction of the *Abbey Road* album sleeve in the centre with a faded image of the album cover in the background. The back has track listing with a small picture of the *Abbey Road* sleeve.

343. THE JOHN LENNON STORY: VOLS ONE AND TWO
Black Cat BC 001/002

Format: CD (double)

Source: WNEW-FM, broadcast 6–10 April 1981 (Andy Peebles interview 6 December 1980)

Sound quality: unknown

Disc One – Volume One: 1966–1969

1. WNEW-FM Introduction, 2. Introduction, 3. Remembering the BBC, 4. Three Cool Cats, 5. Ticket to Ride, 6. John meets Yoko, 7. Bored with The Beatles, 8. *Rape* and Bagism, 9. On the Ballad of John and Yoko, 10. The Ballad of John and Yoko, 11. The Beatles and Yoko, 12. Englishmen, 13. England, 14. Having a baby, 15. The Bed-Ins, 16. Give Peace a Chance, 17. Mastication, 18. Live Peace in Toronto, 19. Blue Suede Shoes, 20. Dizzy Miss Lizzie, 21. A Beatle record, 22. The *Rock and Roll Circus*, 23. Yer Blues, 24. Performing without The Beatles, 25. The Wedding Album, 26. Amsterdam, 27. Gibraltar, 28. The Ballad of John and Yoko, 29. Closing

Disc Two – Volume Two: 1969–1971

1. Introduction, 2. On Cold Turkey, 3. Cold Turkey, 4. Drug Use, 5. The Lyceum Concert, 6. Don't Worry Kyoko, 7. Plastic Ono Band, 8. Mother, 9. Wishing Bells, 10. Self Indulgence, 11. Phil Spector, 12. Remembering criticism, 13. God, 14. Interacting with fans, 15. Instant Karma, 16. Artistic control, 17. Supporting each other, 18. On 'Power to the People', 19. Power to the People, 20. Releasing 'Imagine' as a single, 21. Imagine, 22. Resenting Paul, 23. How Do You Sleep?, 24. Closing

344. THE JOHN LENNON STORY: VOLS THREE AND FOUR

Black Cat BC 003/004

Format: CD (double)

Source: WNEW-FM, broadcast 6–10 April 1981 (Andy Peebles interview 6 December 1980)

Sound quality: unknown

Disc One – Volume Three: 1972–1974

1. Introduction, 2. The deportation case, 3. Playing with Frank Zappa, 4, Well, 5. *Sometime in New York City*, 6. On 'Woman Is the Nigger of the World', 7. Woman Is the Nigger of the World, 8. On 'Sisters Oh Sisters', 9. Sisters Oh Sisters, 10. Dick Cavett, 11. Children's Rights, 12. On 'Happy Christmas War Is Over', 13. Happy Christmas War Is Over, 14. The real Plastic Ono Band, 15. The BBC World Service, 16. On 'Mind Games', 17. Mind Games, 18. Music radio, 19. Feeling The Space, 20. Men Men Men, 21. Feminists, 22. The Lost Weekend begins, 23. Elton John, 24. Whatever Gets You Through the Night, 25. Playing Madison Square Garden, 26. Saw Her Standing There, 27. Closing

Disc Two – Volume Four: 1975–1980

1. Introduction, 2. On 'No. 9 Dream', 3. No. 9 Dream, 4. Working with Bowie, 5. Across the Universe, 6. John Lennon: King of Rock, 7. The *Rock 'n' Roll* LP, 8. Stand By Me, 9. Saying farewells to the business, 10. Be Bop A Lula, 11. *Shaved Fish*, 12. Reissuing Beatles records, 13. You've Got to Hide Your Love Away, 14. Going underground, 15. Cooking, 16. Raising Sean, 17. No writing songs, 18. Peer pressures, 19. Watching the Wheels, 20. Closing

345. THE JOHN LENNON STORY: VOL. FIVE

Black Cat BC 005

Format: CD

Source: WNEW-FM, broadcast 6–10 April 1981 (Andy Peebles interview, 6 December 1980)

Sound quality: unknown

Volume Five: 1980

1. Introduction, 2. Selecting a record company, 3. Selecting the musicians, 4. Fawlty Towers, 5. On 'Starting Over', 6. Starting Over, 7. Poetic lyrics, 8. On 'Walking on Thin Ice', 9. Walking on Thin Ice, 10. On 'Kiss Kiss Kiss', 11. Kiss Kiss Kiss, 12. Interpreting visions, 13. Being prolific again, 14. Dear Yoko, 15. Writing about Sean, 16. Sean's interest in music, 17. Beautiful Boy, 18. LP packaging, 19. On 'I'm Losing You', 20. I'm Losing You, 21. The Beatles track, 22. Woman, 23. New Wave, 24. Reggae, 25. American radio, 26. Going to discos, 27. Yoko's new audience, 28. Feeling safe in New York City, 29. Farewell and thank you, 30. Closing, Bonus Track: 31. Radio One Christmas Message, 8 December 1980.

Notes: Andy Peebles interviewed John and Yoko in New York on 6 December 1980 for BBC Radio and this set of five discs is the complete interview. This programme was originally broadcast on BBC Radio. A book of the transcript of the interview was issued by the BBC plus a double CD minus the music.

Each of the three releases has a different colour picture on the front taken at the time of the interview with full track listing on the back.

346. JOHN LENNON'S THIRTY-FIRST BIRTHDAY PARTY

Rockin' Records JLBP-01

Format: CD

Source: live, hotel room in Syracuse, New York, 9 October 1971 (John's thirty-first birthday)

Notes: This is a re-release of *Let's Have A Party* (Quality Compact Prod) with the following extra tracks: 'Happy Birthday To John', 'My Sweet Lord' (short), 'Imagine' (short), 'Oh, Yoko'.

347. JOHN LENNON WITH TOM SNYDER

Unknown

Format: CD

Source: interview, The Tom Snyder Show, 28 April 1975

Sound quality: unknown

From Sleeve Notes:

1. Parents wanted to stamp out Rock 'n' Roll because it was Black music/Beatles made music a little more White/Screaming got boring/Are we that good?/Broke up out of boredom; 2. Beatles were sending subliminal messages/Working class singers/Groupies/Sexual aspect of singing/Early days of groupies; 3. Not boring now – different musicians – Beatles, long time together – got stale/Likes disco and reggae/Music moves in cycles – inventing new; 4. Bed-In, a theatrical event/Two Virgins cover/Can walk down the street now/Glad it happened but don't miss it; 5. Happy for other Beatles success/Drugs in music business/Make advertisement about drugs – can't fool kids/Discusses drugs bust in England – crooked cop/Decided to live in New York; 6. Leon Wiles (lawyer) explains John's deportation case; 7. Wants to live in the land of the free/Lots of people in charge of his case/Reputation of being ego maniac/Believe in what I do

348. JOHN LOST IN THE STUDIO
Mongoose Records Mong CD028
Format: CD
Released: 1991
Source: various
Sound quality: unknown

1. In The Studio No. 1 (John chastises Hugh 'I played on *Ram* McCracken), 2. Starting Over (vocal booth), 3. Starting Over (playback – different vocals), 4. Clean-up Time (early mix), 5. Beautiful Boy (John gets impatient), 6. Clean-up Time (John leading Earl Slick – vocal booth), 7. Dear Yoko (vocal booth – joke version), 8. In The Studio No. 2 (John discusses double tracking and The Beatles), 9. Woman (vocal booth), 10. Not Fade Away (with Elephant's Memory), 11. Sweet Little Sixteen (alternate vocal), 12. The Luck of the Irish (take 1, guitar, John and Yoko), 13. The Luck of the Irish (take 2, guitar, John and Yoko), 14. Imagine (alternate take), 15. San Francisco Bay Blues (John and guitar only), 16. San Francisco Bay Blues (reprise – John gets impatient), 17. Imagine (very early take with drums missing from middle part), 18. Power to the

People (different take), 19. Yer Blues (instrumental mix of *Rock and Roll Circus* version with Keith Richards, Eric Clapton and Mitch Mitchell), 20. Daddy's Little Sunshine Boy (John prompting Ringo), 21. Dear Prudence (different mix and full ending), 22. Revolution (different mix, no organ or backing vocals)

Bonus Tracks

23. Starting Over, 24. I'm Losing You, 25. In The Studio No. 3, 26. Dream Lover, 27. Stay, 28. She's a Woman No. 1), 29. Mystery Train, 30. She's a Woman No. 2, 31. Rip It Up, 32. I'm a Man, 33. Be-Bop-A-Lula, 34. She's a Woman No. 3, 35. C'mon Everybody, 36. She's a Woman No. 3

Notes: The sleeve has colour pictures of John on the front and the back with the track listing on the back cover.

349. JOHN'S LOST HOME DEMOS, VOL. 1
John Records John 001
Format: CD
Released: 1991
Source: various
Sound quality: unknown

1. The Worst is Over (guitar and rhythm box), 2. Good Morning, Good Morning (demo, 1968), 3. Brown Eyed Handsome Man (guitar), 4. Serve Yourself (piano), 5. You Know My Name (Look Up the Number) (piano), 6. Help! (piano), 7. Cooking (in the Kitchen of Love) (piano), 8. Watching the Wheels (piano), 9. I'm Losing You (piano, guitar and rhythm box), 10. I'm the Greatest (early version), 11. Grow Old with Me (original before album additions), 12. John Henry (piano, no applause), 13. Surprise Surprise (Sweet Bird of Paradox), 14. Tennessee (take 1), 15. Mucho Mungo (guitar), 16. I'm a Man (guitar), 17. Medley: Beyond the Sea/Blue Moon/Young Love (guitar), 18. Sea Ditty/My Old Man's A Dustman/I Do Like To Be Beside The Seaside/Leaning on a Lamp Post (guitar), 19. Keep Right on to the End of the Road (with Yoko), 20. Life Begins at Forty (guitar and rhythm box)

Bonus Tracks

21. 'Twas a Night like Ethel Merman (with backing tapes), 22. We Must Not Forget The General Erection (poetry), 23. The Wumberlog (The Magic Dog), 24. With a Little Help from My Friends (Sean sings), 25. Saturday Morning, 26–29. Tobias Casuals Radio Adverts 1–4, 30. Maurice DuPont, 31. Attica State, 32. The Luck of the Irish, 33. John Sinclair

Notes: Tracks 31–33, John Sinclair Benefit Concert.

350. JOHN'S LOST HOME DEMOS, VOL. 2
John Records John 002

Format: CD

Released: 1991

Source: various

Sound quality: unknown

1. Oh, Yoko, 2. John Henry (guitar, no applause), 3. She is a Friend of Dorothy, 4. Serve Yourself (early version with mistakes), 5. Mucho Mungo (with Harry Nilsson), 6. Mt. Elga (with Harry Nilsson), 7. Happy Birthday John (Ringo's greeting), 8. Sally and Billy (take 1), 9. New York City (Que Pasa New York, early guitar demo), 10. Surprise Surprise (Sweet Bird of Paradox), 11. Serve Yourself (M.O.T.H.E.R), 12. Dear Yoko, 13. Watching the Wheels (very early attempt), 14. Clean-up Time (long intro), 15. Maggie Mae, 15. Maggie Mae, 16. Mirror Mirror (take 1), 17. Mirror Mirror (take 5), 18. Rock 'n' Roll People (electric guitar), 19. Real Life, 20. My Life (take 3, early section of Starting Over), 21. Don't Be Crazy (early section of 'Starting Over')

Bonus Tracks

22. We're Alive (quote), 23. *Wedding Album* radio ad, 24. *Grapefruit* excerpts, 25. The Great Wok, 26. The Return of Maurice DuPont, 27. John and Yoko's Xmas Ditty, 28. Chi-Chi's Cafe (with Ringo and backing tapes), 29. Down In Cuba (with backing tapes), 30. *Rock and Roll Circus* Intro (John and Mick Jagger), 31. The Best Things In Life Are Free, 32. *Eat the Document* (excerpts, John and Bob Dylan), 33. Radio request for Tight A$, 34. Strawberry Fields Forever (backwards talk test tape), 35. The Neville Club

Notes: Tracks 1, 3, 4, 8, 11, 13, 14, 16, 17, 19, 21, 27 with piano. Tracks 5, 6, 10, 12, 15, 20, 21, 31 with guitar. The two volumes both have colour front inserts with pictures of John including one with Sean and full track listing on the back.

351. JOHNNY 'L' (FOR GENE AND EDDIE AND ELVIS… AND BUDDY!)
Star Records CD 099
Format: CD
Released: 1990
Source: alternate takes
Sound quality: excellent

1. Starting Over (studio run through), 2. Starting Over, 3. Mind Games, 4. Medley: Honey Don't/Don't Be Cruel/Matchbox, 5. Maggie Mae, 6. Woman, 7. Cold Turkey, 8. Jealous Guy, 9. God Save Us (Lennon vocal, different lyrics), 10. The Luck of the Irish (takes 1 and 2), 11. How Do You Sleep? 12. Strawberry Fields Forever (run through and alternate take), 13. Lennon Civil Rights Movement demonstration report, 14. Power to the People, 15. What's the New Mary Jane, 16. It's So Hard, 17. Crippled Inside

Notes: It was claimed that these alternate takes were uncensored *Lost Lennon* outtakes. They are presented here in better sound quality than previous releases and more complete.

The front insert has colour pictures of John. The back is black with the track listing printed in white.

352. JOHNNY MOONDOG
Box Top Records
Format: CD (double)
Released: 1989
Source: various
Sound quality: unknown

Disc One

1. Goodnight, Vienna, 2. Imagine, 3. Serve Yourself, 4. Mucho Mungo, 5. Ya Ya, 6. I Sat Belonely /Frank Cummings, 7. God Save Us, 8. Theme from *Rape*, 9. Radio Israel, 10. Yer Blues, 11.That'll Be the Day, 12. Do the Oz

Disc Two

1. John Sinclair, 2. It's So Hard, 3. The Luck of the Irish, 4. Sisters Oh Sisters, 5. We All Woke Up, 6. Woman Is the Nigger of the World, 7. Attica State, 8. Sakura, 9. Memphis, 10. Johnny B. Goode, 11. Imagine

Notes: The front cover has a colour picture of John on a bed playing a guitar.

353. JOURNALS (PARTS 1 AND 2)

CEDRAM CD-121/125 and 126/130

Format: CD (ten disc set)

Released: 1994 (rereleased in 2008 – see notes)

Source: various

Sound quality: varies but generally very good to excellent

Notes: This set of ten discs consists of previously released material. When it was released in America in 1994 it sold for $250. The tracks on the discs were in chronological order:

(Part 1) Vol. 1: Plastic Ono Band (1968–72)

CEDRAM CD. 121 Time 74.11

1. Intro (0.17), 2. Yer Blues (4.04), 3. Give Peace a Chance (2.41), 4. Goodbye Amsterdam (0.18), 5. Hair Peace/Bed Peace/Grow Your Hair (0.16), 6. Good Night (0.29), 7. Cold Turkey (4.58), 8. Instant Karma (3.25), 9. Mother (3.46), 10. I Found Out (3.57), 11. Well, Well, Well (3.37), 12. Look at Me (2.55), 13. My Mummy's Dead (1.14), 14. Honey Don't (0.52), 15. Don't Be Cruel (0.38), 16. Jam (Matchbox) (1.41), 17. All Over You Jam (2.54), 18. Matchbox (1.20), 19. Power to the People No. 1 (2.48), 20. Power to the People No. 2 (3.50), 21. Power to the People No. 3 (2.46), 22. Power to the People No. 4 (3.09), 23. Well Baby Please Don't

Go (5.50), 24. God Save Us (3.09), 25. Do the Oz (2.42), 26. San Francisco Bay Blues (0.45), 27. San Fran (reprise) (2.27), 28. Happy Xmas (War Is Over) (3.21), 29. The Luck of the Irish No. 1 (0.49), 30. The Luck of the Irish No. 2 (2.33), 31. Woman Is the Nigger of the World (5.37)

(Part 1) Vol. 2: Jealous Guy (1972)

CEDRAM CD. 122

Time: 71.53

1. Imagine No. 1 (3.08), 2. Imagine No. 2 (2.53), 3. Imagine No. 3 (3.11), 4. Imagine No. 4 (3.10), 5. Imagine No. 5 (3.14), 6. Crippled Inside No. 1 (3.48), 7. Crippled Inside No. 2 (3.47), 8. Jealous Guy No. 1 (4.11), 9. Jealous Guy No. 2 (4.27), 10. Jealous Guy No. 3 (4.07), 11. Jealous Guy No. 4 (4.12), 12. It's So Hard (2.28), 13. I Don't Want to Be a Soldier No. 1 (5.48), 14. I Don't Want to Be a Soldier No. 2 (5.39), 15. Give Me Some Truth (3.36), 16. Oh, My Love No. 1 (2.54), 17. Oh, My Love No. 2 (2.49), 18. Oh, My Love No. 3 (2.49), 19. How Do You Sleep? (5.19)

Notes: Track 2, electric piano version. Track 3, acoustic piano version. Track 4, final arrangement. Track 5, alternate mix. Track 6, take 2. Track 7, take 17, false start. Track 8, take 1. Track 9, take 2. Track 10, take 17. Track 11, Final backing tracks. Track 12, without sax. Track 13, take 1. Track 14, take 2, without sax. Track 15, backing track, Track 16, take 1. Track 17, take 2. Track 18, take 3. Track 19, stereo.

(Part 1) Vol. 3: How Do You Sleep (1971)

CEDRAM CD. 123

Time: 73.29

1. How Do You Sleep No. 1 (1.54), 2. How Do You Sleep No. 2 (0.57), 3. How Do You Sleep No. 3 (4.25), 4. How Do You Sleep No. 4 (7.33), 5. How Do You Sleep No. 5 (5.48), 6. How Do You Sleep No. 6 (8.10), 7. How Do You Sleep No. 7 (6.35), 8. How Do You Sleep No. 8 (6.14), 9. How Do You Sleep No. 9 (6.47), 10. How? No. 1 (3.45), 11. How? No. 2 (3.47), 12. How? No. 3 (3.44), 13. How? No. 4 (3.47), 14. Oh, Yoko No. 1 (4.14), 15. How No. 2 (5.49)

(Part 1) Vol. 4: I'm the Greatest (1973)

CEDRAM CD. 124

Time: 73.22

1. I'm the Greatest No. 1 (2.41), 2. I'm the Greatest No. 2 (0.50), 3. I'm the Greatest No. 3 (0.30), 4. I'm the Greatest No. 4 (0.24), 5. I'm the Greatest No. 5 (3.38), 6. I'm the Greatest No. 6 (0.50), 7. I'm the Greatest No. 7 (0.19), 8. I'm the Greatest No. 8 (4.26), 9. I'm the Greatest No. 9 (0.48), 10. I'm the Greatest No. 10 (2.19), 11. I'm the Greatest No. 11 (3.55), 12. Mind Games (3.05), 13. Tight A$ (4.15), 14. Aisumasen (I'm Sorry) No. 1 (4.38), 15. Aisumasen (I'm Sorry) No. 2 (4.44), 16. One Day (at a Time) (3.19), 17. Bring on the Lucie (Freeda People) (4.03), 18. Intuition (2.53), 19. Out of Blue No. 1 (4.10), 20. Out the Blue No. 2 (4.13), 21. Only People No. 1 (2.44), 22. Only People No. 2 (2.43), 23.I Know (I Know) (3.46), 24. You Are Here (4.43), 25. Meat City (2.30)

(Part 1) Vol. 5: In Concert (1969–74)

CEDRAM CD. 125

Time: 74.39

1. Into (0.54), 2. Blue Suede Shoes (2.10), 3. Money (3.05), 4. Dizzy Miss Lizzie (3.17), 5. Yer Blues (3.42), 6. Into (0.12), 7. Cold Turkey No. 1 (2.56), 8. Intro (0.26), 9. Give Peace a Chance No. 1 (3.15), 10. Intro (0.23), 11. Cold Turkey No. 2 (3.46), 12. Intro (1.06), 13. Well Baby Please Don't Go (4.46), 14. Say Please (aka Jamrag) (1.24), 15. King Kong (aka Jamrag) (1.10), 16. Aaak (aka Jamrag) (3.11), 17. Scumbag (6.11), 18. A Small Eternity With Yoko (4.53), 19. Finale (Get off Her Jeers) (1.30), 20. Imagine No. 1 (2.59), 21. Intro (0.25), 22. Mother (4.33), 23. Imagine No. 2 (3.17), 24. Intro (0.17), 25. Come Together (4.14), 26. Give Peace a Chance No. 2 (7.40), 27. I Saw Her Standing There (3.01)

(Part 2) Vol. 6: Roots (1973–75)

CEDRAM CD. 126

Time: 66.35

1. Sweet Little Sixteen (4.20), 2. You Can't Catch Me (3.39), 3. Bony Moronie (3.58), 4. Be My Baby No. 1 (8.34), 5. Be My Baby No. 2 (5.54), 6. Be My Baby No. 3 (6.47), 7. Just Because/Yes Sir That's My Baby (6.02),

8. Studio Talk (0.37), 9. Little Bitty Pretty One (0.29), 10. Lucille (3.48), 11. Studio Talk (0.34), 12. Stand By Me No. 1 (5.12), 13. Only You (3.17), 14. Goodnight, Vienna (2.55), 15. Peggy Sue (2.08), 16. Slippin' and Slidin' No. 1 (2.21), 17. I Saw Her Standing There ((3.21), 18. Stand By Me No. 2 (3.57), 19. Studio Talk (0.20), 20. Slippin' and Slidin' No. 2 (2.20)

(Part 2) Vol. 7: Move Over Ms L (1974)

CEDRAM CD. 127 Time 74.05

1. Going Down on Love (4.01), 2. Whatever Gets You Through the Night No. 1 (1.48), 3. Whatever Gets You Through the Night No. 2 (3.51), 4. Whatever Gets You Through the Night (3.20), 5. Old Dirt Road (4.45), 6. Bless You No. 1 (4.49), 7. Bless You No. 2 (0.28), 8. Bless You No. 3 (0.35), 9. Bless You No. 4 (5.33), 10. Scared (5.00), 11. Surprise Surprise (Sweet Bird of Paradox) (3.40), 12. Steel and Glass No. 1 (5.15), 13. Steel and Glass No. 2 (5.07), 14. Beef Jerky (3.23), 15. Nobody Loves You (When You're Down and Out) (5.18), 16. Rock 'n' Roll People No. 1 (2.39), 17. Rock 'n' Roll People No. 2 (3.00), 18. Rock 'n' Roll People/Hound Dog (6.00), 19. Move Over Ms L No. 1 (0.20), 20. Move Over Ms L No. 2 (2.40), 21. Move Over Ms L No. 3 (2.43)

(Part 2) Vol. 8: Starting Over (1980)

CEDRAM CD. 128

Time: 74.38

1. Only the Lonely No. 1 (0.29), 2. In The Studio No. 1 (0.40), 3. Only the Lonely No. 2 (0.40), 4. Gone from This Place (0.27), 5. (Just Like) Starting Over No. 1 (0.35), 6. In The Studio No. 2 (0.13), 7. In The Studio No. 3 (1.27), 8. In The Studio No. 4 (0.32), 9. In The Studio No. 5 (0.22), 10. (Just Like) Starting Over No. 2 (4.30), 11. (Just Like) Starting Over No. 3 (4.14), 12. (Just Like) Starting Over No. 4 (4.18), 13. In The Studio No. 6 (0.29), 14. Clean-up Time No. 1 (1.33), 15. In The Studio No. 7 (0.31), 16. In The Studio No. 8 (0.26), 17. Cleanup No. 2 (4.58), 18. In The Studio No. 9 (0.14), 19. Clean-up Time No. 3 (5.52), 20. In The Studio No. 10 (0.17), 21. Clean-up Time No. 4 (4.38), 22. Clean-up Time No. 5 (4.36), 23. In The Studio No. 11 (0.52), 24. Clean-up Time No. 6 (3.26), 25. I'm Losing You No. 1 (4.17), 26. I'm Losing You No. 2 (3.54), 27. In The Studio No. 12 (1.35), 28. Beautiful Boy No. 1 (0.11), 29. In The Studio No. 13 (0.34),

30. In The Studio No. 14 (1.12), 31. Beautiful Boy No. 2 (3.54), 32. In The Studio No. 15 (0.13), 33. In The Studio No. 16 (1.12), 34. Beautiful Boy No. 3 (3.55), 35. In The Studio No. 17 (0.54), 36. Watching the Wheels No. 1 (3.32), 37. I Am the Walrus (0.15), 38. Watching the Wheels No. 2 (3.31), 39. In The Studio No. 18 (3.35)

(Part 2) Vol. 9: Stepping Out (1980)

CEDRAM CD. 129

Time: 74.37

1. In The Studio No. 1 (0.46), 2. Woman No. 1 (3.35), 3. In The Studio No. 2 (0.19), 4. Woman No. 2 (0.34), 5. In The Studio No. 3 (1.12), 6. In The Studio No. 4 (0.27), 7. Woman No. 3 (1.36), 8. In The Studio No. 5 (0.11), 9. In The Studio No. 6 (0.19), 10. In The Studio No. 7 (0.18), 11. Woman No. 4 (0.49), 12. In The Studio No. 8 (0.25), 13. In The Studio No. 9 (0.31), 14. Woman No. 5 (2.49), 15. Woman No. 6 (3.21), 16. Woman No. 7 (2.29), 17. Woman No. 8 (3.42), 18. In The Studio No. 10 (0.12), 19. Dear Yoko No. 1 (0.39), 20. Dear Yoko No. 2 (1.47), 21. In The Studio No. 11 (1.06), 22. Dear Yoko No. 3 (1.26), 23. Dear Yoko No. 4 (0.25), 24. In The Studio No. 12 (0.22), 25. Dear Yoko No. 5 (2.23), 26. Dear Yoko No. 6 (2.29), 27. I'm Stepping Out No. 1 (5.02), 28. I'm Stepping Out No. 2 (4.42), 29. I'm Stepping Out No. 3 (5.16), 30. I'm Stepping Out No. 4 (1.16), 31. I'm Stepping Out No. 5 (5.38), 32. In The Studio No. 13 (0.23), 33. In The Studio No. 14 (0.29), 34. Nobody Told Me No. 1 (3.53), 35. Nobody Me No. 2 (3.21), 36. In The Studio No. 15 (0.28), 37. Borrowed Time (3.22), 38.Forgive Me (My Little Flower Princess) (3.27), 39. In The Studio No. 16 (0.14), 40. Walking on Thin Ice (3.15)

(Part 2) Vol. 10: Rehearsals (1972–1980)

CEDRAM CD. 130

Time: 74.10

1. Come Together No. 1 (3.53), 2. Paul McCartney discussion (0.55), 3. Come Together No. 2 (3.46), 4. Cold Turkey (4.10), 5. Well, Well, Well (5.22), 6. It's So Hard (2.55), 7. Back off Boogaloo (0.14), 8. New York City (4.42), 9. Don't Be Cruel (1.16), 10. Hound Dog No. 1 (3.06), 11. On The Caribbean (2.59), 12. Whole Lotta Shakin' Goin' On (2.56), 13. It'll Be Me (2.20), 14. Ain't That a Shame (2.21), 15. Who Put The Bomp (1.00),

16. Roll Over Beethoven (2.26), 17. Send Me Some Loving (2.30), 18. Hound Dog No. 2 (2.11), 19. Long Tall Sally (3.03), 20. (Just Like) Starting Over (2.32), 21. I'm Losing You (4.47), 22. Dream Lover (3.05), 23. Stay (0.51), 24. She's a Woman No. 1 (0.36), 25. Mystery Train (3.06), 26. She's a Woman No. 2 (0.56), 27. Rip It Up (1.12), 28. I'm a Man (1.28), 29. Be-Bop-A-Lula (1.19), 30. She's a Woman No. 3 (1.28), 31. C'mon Everybody (0.36), 32. She's a Woman No. 4 (0.05)

Notes: This set of ten compact discs covers the entire period of Lennon's solo career with outtakes, rehearsals, demos and live performances from all his major albums. The originals releases came in ten separate jewel cases with a different colour picture on John on the front. The backs were black with the full track listings printed in white. This set was reissued in 2008 as a CD sized box set containing the original track listings, each disc contained in a plastic sleeve.

The box included a twenty-eight-page booklet with detailed track listings, extensive notes and colour photographs. The set also included three DVDs which feature rare films such as John and Yoko's avant garde films *Bottoms*, *Two Virgins* and *Rape*.

354. KALEIDOSCOPE EYES

Delta 46076

Format: CD

Source: interview from 1969

Sound quality: unknown

1. Intro, 2. Image and Friends, 3. Brian Epstein and leaders, 4. Andy Warhol, 5. Avant Garde, 6. Earnings, 7. Living diary, 8. Movements, 9. Beatles in '69, 10. Bed-In, 11. Mutual Attraction, 12. Yoko's effect, 13. Lennon comments on Yoko, 14. What new, 15. Public Reunion, 16. Let It Be project, 17. Beatles style, 18. Sgt. Pepper, 19. Second Bed-In, 20. Billy Preston, 21. What's A Building, 22. Ballad of John and Yoko, 23. What's It Like Being A Beatle, 24. Mantic writing, 25. Phyloso Rock

Notes: Front cover has black-and-white picture of John with his glasses in colour with a psychedelic image. This picture was also used on the compact disc release *The Village Tapes*.

355. KENNY EVERETT TALKS TO JOHN LENNON
(Radio Monte Carlo International)
Blackbird Records BBR 025
Format: CD
Released: 2000
Time: 54.56
Source: interview, broadcast 27 March 1971
Sound quality: unknown

1. Introduction, 2. Interview includes guitar noodling, 3. The Man Who Broke The Bank In Monte Carlo (ad lib)/Interview includes guitar noodling, 4. Rule Britannia (ad lib)/Interview continued), 5. Interview includes guitar noodling, 6. The Laughing Policeman (ad lib)/Interview continued, 7. Mother, 8. Interview continued, 9. Hold On John (ad lib)/Interview continued, 10. Hold On John, 11. Interview includes guitar noodling, 12. I Found Out, 13. Interview includes guitar noodling, 14. Working Class Hero, 15. Interview includes guitar noodling, 16. Isolation, 17. Interview includes guitar noodling, 18. Shake Hands With Your Uncle Dick, 19. Remember, 20. Interview continued, 21. Love, 22. Interview continued, 23. Station break, 24. Interview continued, 25. Look at Me, 26. Interview continued, 27. Well, Well, Well, 28. Interview continued, 29. God, 30. Outroduction

Notes: Kenny Everett's association with The Beatles goes back to the sixties. He was the first disc jockey to play tracks from the *Sgt. Pepper* album on the radio and interview them several times on his radio show.

Front cover has colour pictures of John and Kenny Everett with the track listing on the back.

356. KFRC AM: FOCUS '71 (THE JANN WENNER INTERVIEW)
Air-Check KFRC71
Format: CD
Time: 62.01
Source: radio show with excerpts of Wenner interviews
Sound quality: poor

1. Jann Wenner Interview (31.00), 2. Jann Wenner Interview (31.01)

Notes: The following notes regarding this release are taken from the *Bootleg Zone*: 'As indicated by the host's introduction, one month after the Jann Wenner interviews, KRFC AM 610 (San Francisco, CA) aired excerpts of the interview and added various edited and unedited Beatles and Lennon solo songs on a radio show called Focus '71. The show may be incomplete as it does cut off at 60+ minutes. There are drop outs, radio distortions and hiss on the recording; for completists and radio show enthusiasts.

357. KSAN T OM D ONAHUE I NTERVIEW

Unknown
Format: CD (double)
Time: Disc One 43.41, Disc Two 67.35
Source: interview
Sound quality: very good

John interviewed by Tom Donahue about the *Walls and Bridges* album.

358. KYA-FM 1969 AND M AN OF THE D ECADE

Unknown
Format: CD Time:36.24
Source: see below
Sound quality: unknown

1. KYA-FM San Francisco, Tom Campbell and Bill Holley's interview of Lennon from his Montreal Bed-In (29 May 1969), 2–13. Man of The Decade Special, hosted by Dr. Desmond Morris, 14. Get Back medley (taped 2 December 1969, aired 30 December 1969)

359. T HE L AST W ORD

Baktabak CBAK 4014
Format: CD
Source: interview, 8 December 1980
Sound quality: unknown

Notes: This was John's last interview.

360. LENNON LEGACY – PART 1 (BEATLES FOR SALE)

Unknown

Format: CD

Source: BBC Radio 2 documentary, broadcast December 1999

Sound quality: unknown

1. Just A Band, 2. Oh, My Love, 3. Yoko On Writers, 4. That'll Be the Day, 5. Paul talks, 6. Hamburg, 7. John talks, 8. Paul talks, 9. Albums, 10. John talks, 11. American breakthrough, 12. Next Big Thing/I Want to Hold Your Hand, 13. A Hard Day's Night, 14. Class, 15. Lovable Moptops, 16. If I Fell, 17. British Invaders, 18. David Crosby, 19. You Can't Do That, 20. John's Book, 21. Nowhere Man, 22. Songwriters, 23. Expanded Horizons, 24. Individual Characteristics, 25. George Martin talks/In My Life, 26. Help, 27. Fans, 28. Bahamas, 29. Hospital, 30. Humiliation, 31. Help, 32. John's Fat Elvis Period, 33. Jesus Comments, 34. No More Touring/Strawberry Fields Forever, 35. EMI Studios, 36. John talks, 37. John on George Martin, 38. 1967 Sessions/I Am the Walrus, 39. Curiosity, 40. Sign off

361. LENNON LEGACY – PART 2 (BALLAD OF JOHN AND YOKO)

Unknown

Format: CD

Source: BBC Radio 2 documentary, broadcast December 1999

Sound quality: unknown

1. intro, 2. Insane Government/All You Need Is Love, 3. Yoko's Arrival, 4. Revolution, 5. Live With Image, 6. Free Spirit, 7. Yoko talks, 8. George Martin/Avant Garde, 9. John, 10. Unapproved, 11. Yer Blues, 12. Mick Jagger, 13. Don't Let Me Down, 14. Pose Nude/Heroin, 15. 1969 rehearsal/I Want You, 16. Humour/Ballad of John and Yoko, 17. Stay In Bed, 18. Bed-In/Give Peace a Chance, 19. Headlines/America, 20. Instant Karma, 21. Imagine, 22. Utopia, 23. Yoko, 24. Songs/John Sinclair, 25. Nixon/I'm Scared, 26. John surveillance, 27. Freedom of Information/Working Class Hero, 28. Love and Peace, 29. Organize, 30. Happy Xmas (War Is Over), 31. Sign off

362. LENNON LEGACY – PART 3 (GIVE ME SOME TRUTH)

Unknown

Format: CD

Source: BBC Radio 2 documentary, broadcast December 1999

Sound quality: unknown

1. Robert Lindsay/Yoko/Give Me Some Truth, 2. Experiment, 3. Arts and Music/There's a Place, 4. Only Child, 5. Paul talks, 6. Julia, 7. Paul talks, 8. Stu Sutcliffe, 9. Baby's In Black, 10. Drugs, 11. Survive, 12. LSD/Cynthia, 13. Open Minded John/I'm Only Sleeping, 14. Tripping/She Said She Said, 15. 1969/Meditation, 16. Mike Love/India/Dear Prudence, 17. Maharishi, 18. Keith Richards/Heroin/Cold Turkey, 19. Banned, 20. Fans, 21. Primal Therapy/Mother, 22. Yoko/I Found Out, 23. Spiritual Decline, 24. Users, 25. Lost Weekend, 26. Brandy Alexanders/Nobody Loves You (When You're Down and Out), 27. May Pang/Fighting, 28. *Rock 'n' Roll* LP/Stand By Me/Beautiful Boy, 29. Making Bread/Woman/Dear John, 30. Legacy of Peace/Hold On John, 31. Sign off

Notes: The three-discs all have the same cover – a picture of John and Yoko in front of the American Flag. The full track listing is on the back of each volume.

363. *LENNON LEGEND* DVD 5.1 MIXES

Unknown

Format: CD (triple)

Source: 5.1 mixes from *Lennon Legend* DVD

Sound quality: excellent

Disc One – Centre Channel

1. Imagine, 2. Instant Karma, 3. Mother, 4. Jealous Guy, 5. Power to the People, 6. Cold Turkey, 7. Love, 8. Mind Games, 9. Whatever Gets You Through the Night, 10. No. 9 Dream, 11. Stand By Me, 12. (Just Like) Starting Over, 13. Woman, 14. Beautiful Boy (Darling Boy), 15. Watching the Wheels, 16. Nobody Told Me, 17. Borrowed Time, 18. Working Class Hero, 19. Happy Xmas (War Is Over), 20. Give Peace a Chance

Disc Two – Front Left + Front Right

1. Imagine, 2. Instant Karma, 3. Mother, 4. Jealous Guy, 5. Power to the People, 6. Cold Turkey, 7. Love, 8. Mind Games, 9. Whatever Gets You Through the Night, 10. No. 9 Dream, 11. Stand By Me, 12. (Just Like) Starting Over, 13. Woman, 14. Beautiful Boy (Darling Boy), 15. Watching the Wheels, 16. Nobody Told Me, 17. Borrowed Time, 18. Working Class Hero, 19. Happy Xmas (War Is Over), 20. Give Peace a Chance

Disc Three – Surround Left + Right

1. Imagine, 2. Instant Karma, 3. Mother, 4. Jealous Guy, 5. Power to the People, 6. Cold Turkey, 7. Love, 8. Mind Games, 9. Whatever Gets You Through the Night, 10. No. 9 Dream, 11. Stand By Me, 12. (Just Like) Starting Over, 13. Woman, 14. Beautiful Boy (Darling Boy), 15. Watching the Wheels, 16. Nobody Told Me, 17. Borrowed Time, 18. Working Class Hero, 19. Happy Xmas (War Is Over), 20. Give Peace a Chance

364. *LENNON LEGEND* 5.1 CHANNELS MIXES (A COMPILATION)

Unknown

Format: CD (double)

Source: *Lennon Legend* CD

Sound quality: excellent

Disc One

1. (Just Like) Starting Over (mix 1), 2. (Just Like) Starting Over (mix 2), 3. (Just Like) Starting Over (mix 3), 4. Woman (mix 1), 5. Woman (mix 2), 6. Beautiful Boy (mix 1), 7. Beautiful Boy (mix 2), 8. Watching the Wheels (mix 1), 9. Watching the Wheels (mix 2), 10. Nobody Told Me (mix 1), 11. Borrowed Time (mix 1), 12. Borrowed Time (mix 2), 13.Borrowed Time (mix 3), 14. Working Class Hero (mix 1), 15. (Happy Christmas) War Is Over (mix 1), 16. (Happy Christmas) War Is Over (mix 2), 17. (Happy Christmas) War Is Over (mix 3), 18. Give Peace a Chance (mix 1)

Disc Two

1. Imagine (mix 1), 2. Imagine (mix 2), 3. Instant Karma (mix 1), 4. Instant Karma (mix 2), 5. Mother (mix 1), 6. Jealous Guy (mix 1), 7. Jealous Guy (mix 2), 8. Power to the People (mix 1), 9. Cold Turkey (mix 1), 10. Love

(mix 1), 11. Love (mix 2), 12. Mind Games (mix 1), 13. Mind Games (mix 2), 14. Mind Games (mix 3), 15. Whatever Gets You Through the Night (mix 1), 16. Whatever Gets You Through the Night (mix 2), 17. No. 9 Dream (mix 1), 18. Stand By Me (mix 1), 19. Stand By Me (mix 2)

365. LENNON PICTURES

Unknown YB001-2

Format: CD (double)

Source: first solo Beatles sampler featuring officially released tracks

Sound quality: excellent

Disc One

1. Give Peace a Chance, 2. Cold Turkey, 3. Instant Karma, 4. Mother, 5. Working Class Hero, 6. Love, 7. Well, Well, Well, 8. God, 9. Power to the People, 10. Imagine, 11. Jealous Guy, 12. Oh, My Love, 13. How? 14. It's So Hard, 15. Happy Xmas (War Is Over), 16. Woman Is the Nigger of the World, 17. New York City, 18. Mind Games, 19. Whatever Gets You Through the Night, 20. I Saw Her Standing There (live)

Disc Two

1. No. 9 Dream, 2. Nobody Loves You (When You're Down and Out), 3. Stand By Me, 4. Ya Ya, 5. Be-Bop-A-Lula, 6. Sweet Little Sixteen, 7. To Know Her Is to Love Her, 8. Angel Baby, 9. Be My Baby, 10. Move Over Ms L, 11. (Just Like) Starting Over, 12. Woman, 13. Beautiful Boy (Darling Boy), 14. Watching the Wheels, 15. I'm Losing You, 16. Nobody Told Me, 17. I'm Stepping Out, 18. Borrowed Time, 19. Grow Old with Me, 20. Every Man Has a Woman Who Loves Him, 21. Real Love

366. LENNON REMEMBERS – PART ONE (THE WORKING CLASS HERO)

Darthouse DD 003/4

Format: CD (double)

Source: *Rolling Stone* interview

Sound quality: excellent

Disc One

1. Tape set up and testing, 2. The *POB* album (part one), 3. Primal, 4. His singing, 5. 'Working Class Hero', 'Remember', 6. *POB* as personal, 7. God and pain, 8. George Martin and Phil Spector, 9. 'Let's start again' – the POB album, 10. 'God', 11. 'All those songs just came out of me', 12. Yer Blues, parody, 13, Yoko and John on each other's music, 14. Heroin, 15. Back to *POB*, Pepper, 16. Toronto Rock 'n' Roll revival, 17. On George, Paul and Dylan – JL's tastes, 18. The Beatles as a band, 19. Lennon as a guitarist, 20. Ringo's solo records, 21. Paul, *Let It Be* and the break up, 22. Brian's death, the Maharishi, 23. Paul takes over, *Magical Mystery Tour*, 24. Lennon-McCartney song writing, 25. Maharishi, 26. Apple, events, MBE, etc. 27. The break up announced, 28. Northern songs, 29. Manoeuvring

Disc Two

1. Genius is pain, 2. Living in the past, 3. Beatle vs. Yoko, 4. 'They imitate us', 5. More on the break up, The Beatles, Yoko, 6. Bigger than Elvis, Wm Mann, messages, 7. LSD, 8. *A Hard Day's Night*, 9. 'Day Tripper', drugs and alcohol, 10. *Rubber Soul*, 11. Derek and Brian, 12. Satyricon on tour, 13. Holiday with Brian, Brian vs. Klein, 14. 'We were the biggest bastards', 15. The Rolling Stones vs. The Beatles, 16. The press vs. The Beatles, 17. The Beatles protected, 18. Not being without Yoko, 19. Working or not working, avant-garde stuff, 20. Magic Alex, Manson, balmy fans, 21. Giving up their private lives, 22. Strange doings in Denmark

367. LENNON REMEMBERS – PART TWO (LIFE WITH THE LIONS)

Darthouse DD 005/6

Format: CD (double)

Source: *Rolling Stone* interview

Sound quality: excellent

Disc One

1. Directness of rock, 'Blues is a chair', 2. The Beatles music – early studio work, 3. Live recordings, concerts, 4. 'Ticket to Ride', 'Walrus', 5. Song dedications, 6, 'Abbey Road', plagiarism, suit, 7. 'Instant Karma',

Spector, Wenner's instamatic, 8. Stereo, taking control of production, 9. 'Give Peace a Chance', 'Working Class Hero', 10. *POB* album – picking the single, 11. Guitar vs. piano, 12. JL's favourite JL songs, 13. *Let It Be* in more depth, 14. More on McCartney, 15. Cripples and humiliation, 16. 'If I could be a fisherman I would', 17. The Beatles effect – 'Nothing has changed', 18. The Beatles in America – 1940s horses, 19. 'Revolution', 20. More on *POB*, 'Working Class Hero'

Disc Two

1. 'Happiness Is a Warm Gun', 2. *Pepper*, *White Album*, *POB* simplicity, 3. Allan Klein, 4. Eastman and Klein, 5. Straightening the finances, Epstein, 6. Paul vs. Ringo, 7. Beatle roles, Beatles myth, 8. George, 9. 'Not interested in other music', 10. 'I've always been a genius', 11. Yoko, Zappa, Warhol and Welles, 12. 'Will you retire?', 13. Prejudice against Yoko, 14. NYC, Liverpool, SF and London, 15. Dylan, 16. 'Magical Misery Tour' (from National Lampoon Radio Dinner)

Notes: The complete interview John did for Rolling Stone magazine which was published in two parts, 21 January and 4 February 1971.

The front covers feature a reproduction of the issues of *Rolling Stone* magazine which carried the original interviews with full details of the track listing on the back.

368. LENNON RENUMBERS

Bell Bottom 022

Format: CD

Released: 1998

Source: various – see below

Sound quality: unknown

1. Well Baby Please Don't Go (7.57), 2. Jamrag (5.37), 3. Scumbag (6.06), 4. Au (3.24), 5. Woman Is the Nigger of the World (0.56), 6. Woman Is the Nigger of the World (5.37), 7. Chords of Fame (4.09), 8. Well, Well, Well (5.32), 9. Hound Dog/Long Tall Sally, 10. Too Much Monkey Business/Subterranean Homesick Blues (1.16), 11. Brown Eyed

Handsome Man (1.37), 12. Tequila/Instrumental (5.35), 13. Hava Nagila/I Want You (1.20), 14. Jerusalaim (0.39)

Notes: Tracks 1–4: Fillmore East, New York, 6 June 1971 with Frank Zappa and the Mothers. Track 5: slide guitar demo with Yoko 1969). Track 6: No strings, unedited, different vocal. Track 7: Hotel room session with Phil Ochs after the John Sinclair Rally. Tracks 9 and 12: One-to-One concert rehearsals. Tracks 10 and 11: Home demos. Tracks 13 and 14: Amsterdam Bed-In. Black-and-white front cover with John at the mixing desk.

369. THE LENNON WIVES ON 'FRESH AIR'
NPR NPR0003
Format: CD
Time: 58.41
Source: various – see below
Sound quality: excellent

1. Interview, Fresh Air, Cynthia Powell Lennon, Yoko Ono Lennon and Jon Wiener (39.58), 2. Yoko Philanthropic NPR Spot (7.32), 3. 2003 NPR Spot on the *Lennon Legend* (11.10)

370. LET'S HAVE A PARTY
Quality Compact Prod. QCP 72003
Format: CD Released: 1989
Time: 38.12
Source: live, hotel room in Syracuse, New York, 9 October 1971 (John thirty-first birthday)
Sound quality: good mono

1. What I Say, 2. Yellow Submarine (Ringo), 3. On Top of Old Smokey, 4. Goodnight Irene, 5. He's Got the Whole World in His Hands, 6. Like a Rolling Stone, 7. Twist and Shout/Louie Louie/La Bamba, 8. Bring It on Home to Me, 9. Yesterday, 10. Tandoori Chicken, 11. Power to the People, 12. Maybe Baby, 13. Peggy Sue, 14. Since My Baby Left Me, 15. Blue Suede Shoes, 16. Crippled Inside, 17. Give Peace a Chance, 18. Crippled Inside (reprise), 19. Uncle Albert

Notes: This was recorded live in a hotel room in New York on 9 October 1971 to celebrate John Lennon's thirty-first birthday. In attendance with John were Yoko, Ringo, Klaus Voorman, Phil Spector and Allen Ginsberg. A varied collection of songs were sung by John and friends – they had clearly had a glass or two! This tape has been edited so presumably there are further recordings not yet released. Apparently US Customs seized most of the copies of this disc prior to distribution so this is a difficult to find item. This album was re-released as *John Lennon's 31 Birthday Party* (Rockin' Records) with extra tracks.

The front cover has a cartoon of a naked John and Yoko with John playing his guitar surrounded by other cartoon characters.

371. LIFE IS WHAT HAPPENS
Barrier Records
Format: CD (double)
Source: *Double Fantasy* sessions, studio, Bermuda, Dakota
Sound quality: very good

Disc One

1. Beautiful Boy (1980, electric guitar demo with rhythm box), 2. Beautiful Boy (1980, electric guitar demo with rhythm box), 3. Beautiful Boy (1980, electric guitar demo with rhythm box – take 1), 4. Beautiful Boy (1980 Bermuda, electric guitar demo with hand claps), 5. Beautiful Boy (1980 Bermuda, electric guitar demo with rhythm box take 2), 6. Beautiful Boy (1980 studio rehearsal), 7. Beautiful Boy (1980 studio take 1), 8. Beautiful Boy (1980 studio, take ending overdub), 9. Audio verite (1980 studio – rehearsal discussions during recording of Beautiful Boy, 10. Beautiful Boy (1980 studio – alternate vocal, take from vocal booth), 11. Beautiful Boy (1980 studio – unedited rough mix), 12. Serve Yourself (1979, piano demo version 1), 13. Serve Yourself (1979, piano demo version 2), 14. Serve Yourself (1979, piano demo version 3), 15. Serve Yourself (1979, piano demo version 4), 16. Serve Yourself (1979, piano demo version 5), 17. Serve Yourself (1979, piano demo version 6), 18. Serve Yourself (1979, piano demo version 7)

Disc Two

1. Untitled instrumental (1976, acoustic guitar demo), 2. Illusion (1980, acoustic guitar demo), 3. Knocking On Heaven's Door (1978, acoustic guitar demo), 4. News of the Day (1980, electric guitar demo, take 3), 5. Maggie Mae (1980, acoustic guitar studio jam), 6. Be-Bop-A-Lula (1980, electric guitar studio jam), 7. You Saved My Soul (1980, last Dakota demos electric guitar, take 1), 8. You Saved My Soul (1980, last Dakota demos electric guitar, take 2), 9. Life Begins at 40 (1980, last Dakota demos acoustic guitar with rhythm box), 10. Grow Old with Me (1980, last Dakota demos piano with rhythm box), 11. Grow Old with Me (1980, from the movie *Imagine* soundtrack), 12. Audio verite (1980, last Dakota demos, John and Sean), 13. Dear John (1980, last Dakota demos acoustic guitar with rhythm box), 14. She is a Friend of Dorothy (1980, last Dakota demos piano, take 1), 15. She is a Friend of Dorothy (1980, last Dakota demos piano, take 2), 16. She is a Friend of Dorothy (1980, last Dakota demos piano, take 7), 17. Audio verite (1979, John and Sean), 18. Audio verite (1979, Thanksgiving John, Yoko and Sean), 19. Audio verite (1980, interview with Japanese radio)

372. LIFE WITH THE LIONS

Goblin Records CD 3010

Format: CD

Source: copy of official album plus additional items

Sound quality: unknown

Notes: A copy of the official release of *Life with the Lions* plus some *Get Back* sessions

373. LIMITED EDITION

Bag Records

Format: CD

Released: 1997

Source: various

Sound quality: unknown

1. As Time Goes By/I Saw Her Standing There, 2. Whatever Gets You Through the Night, 3. Move Over Ms L, 4. Angel Baby, 5. I Found Out, 6. Happy Xmas (War Is Over)/Nutopian International Anthem (long version), 7. Give Peace a Chance, 8. I'm the Greatest, 9. Be My Baby, 10. Yer Blues, 11. Do the Oz, 12. What a Shame Mary Jane Had a Pain at the Party, 13. As Time Goes By No. 2/Starting Over (post script)/Good Night

Bonus Tracks

14. Only the Lonely, 15. Move Over Ms L. 16. Be My Baby (short version), 17. No. 9 Dream, 18. Every Man Has a Woman Who Loves Him, 19. Walking on Thin Ice (remix), 20. It Happened (long version)

Notes: Sleeve notes say:

> 'In the early 80s a special record was released worldwide as a tribute to our beloved John Lennon. The record was called *Limited Edition* and soon became a special collector's item. Since then the history has changed so much and it was never released again in any format. Now to show that the love you take is equal to the love you make, we decided to make a new release, this time on CD with seven bonus tracks included here for the first time. Congratulations, you have in your hand a real teasure.'

The white front cover with gold lettering simply says *Limited Edition* with John's signature underneath.

374. LISTEN TO THIS

Vigotone VT-175/VT-176/VT-177

Format: CD (three-disc box set)

Time: Disc One 72.29, Disc Two 65.06, Disc Three 73.01

Source: *Walls and Bridges* rehearsals, alternate takes and rough mixes

Sound quality: Discs one and two, excellent. Disc three, very good

Disc One

Record Plant Rehearsals, 13 July 1974

1. Steel and Glass (5.19), 2. Going Down on Love (4.03), 3. Move Over Ms L (2.58), 4. Surprise Surprise (Sweet Bird of Paradox) (3.40), 5. Beef

Jerky (3.22), 6. Scared (4.55), 7. Old Dirt Road (4.43), 8. Bless You (6.34), 9. Whatever Gets You Through the Night (1.48), 10. Nobody Loves You (When You're Down and Out) (5.17)

Alternate Takes and Rough Mixes, July 1974

11. Move Over Ms L (2.45), 12. Bless You (3.53), 13. Beef Jerky (3.35), 14. Whatever Gets You Through the Night (3.54), 15. What You Got (4.12), 16. Move Over Ms L (2.41), 17. Whatever Gets You Through the Night (3.32), 18. (It's All Da-Da-Da Down To) Goodnight, Vienna/Under The Influence (5.18)

Disc Two

Record Plant Remix Session – 21 July 1974

1. Bless You (5.28), 2. Move Over Ms L (2.49), 3. Scared (4.52), 4. Surprise Surprise (Sweet Bird of Paradox) (3.09), 5. Whatever Gets You Through the Night (3.15), 6. Going Down on Love (3.02), 7. Nobody Loves You (When You're Down and Out) (5.02), 8. Whatever Gets You Through the Night/Executive Privilege (3.02), 9. What You Got (3.21), 10. What You Got (3.31), 11. What You Got (0.51), 12. Old Dirt Road (5.07), 13. Steel and Glass (6.09)

Record Plant Monitor Mixes – July 1974

14. No. 9 Dream (4.49), 15. Old Dirt Road (5.02), 16. Steel and Glass (4.38)

Disc Three

Walls and Bridges Home Recordings 1973–1974

1. No. 9 Dream (3.10), 2. No. 9 Dream (2.47), 3. Move Over Ms L (4.52), 4. Move Over Ms L (2.07), 5. Whatever Gets You Through the Night (4.21), 6. Whatever Gets You Through the Night (2.13), 7. Whatever Gets You Through the Night (2.54), 8. What You Got (3.22), 9. What You Got (6.34), 10. Surprise Surprise (Sweet Bird of Paradox) (3.08), 11. Surprise Surprise (Sweet Bird of Paradox) (3.22), 12. Nobody Loves You (When You're Down and Out) (3.21), 13. Going Down on Love (2.02), 14. Going Down on Love (4.51), 15. Going Down on Love (3.54), 16. Going Down on Love (6.43), 17. Steel and Glass (4.31), 18. Improvisation/The Boat Song

Notes: This is the ultimate *Walls and Bridges* Anthology. Vigotone warns us on the back of the box: 'These ought to get you through the night'. All tracks have been digitally upgraded, de-clicked and de-noised.

The three discs come in a black box with a thirty-four-page book which includes reproductions from *The Daily Howl*, John's 'newspaper' he produced as a schoolboy.

375. LISTEN TO THIS RADIO SHOW

Mad Scott Records MS 01/02

Format: CD (double)

Released: 2001

Source: John as guest DJ on WNEW, New York City, The Dennis Elsa Show, 28 September 1974

Sound quality: unknown

Disc One

1. Intro Dr Winston O'Boogie (1.21), 2. Whatever Gets You Through the Night (3.29), 3. About The New Album (4.56), 4. No. 9 Dream (4.26), 5. More About The Album (1.38), 6. George Martin (1.07), 7. Oldies But Goldies (1.02), 8. Watch Your Step – B. Parker (2.41), 9. Day Tripper (The Beatles) (2.48), 10. Butcher Cover/US Albums (4.48), 11. I Call Your Name (The Beatles) (2.03), 12. Commercial/ELO (1.30), 13. Showdown – ELO (4.11), 14. I Heard It Through The Grapevine (Marvin Gaye) (3.18), 15. Producing Pussy Cats/LA (3.28), 16. Save The Last Dance – Nilsson (3.31), 17. Weather/Solo Beatles (3.27), 18. Gravy Train – Splinter (2.12), 19. I'm the Greatest – Ringo (3.19), 20. What You Got (3.06), 21. Playlist/Station Identification/Commercials (4.11)

Disc Two

1. More About Playing Oldies (1.07), 2. Some Other Guy – Richie Barratt (2.17), 3. What'd I Say – Ray Charles (4.17), 4. Piano – guitar licks/Rolling Stones (3.03), 5. I Want To Be Your Man – Rolling Stones (1.47), 6. I Want To Be Your Man – The Beatles (1.59), 7. The Rolling Stones (2.12), 8. Daddy Rolling Stone – Derek Martin (2.26), 9. Station ID/Immigration (5.48), 10. Scared (4.44), 11. Commercial (0.25), 12. Heroes (3.39),

13. Doing Radio (3.23), 14. About 'I Am the Walrus' (0.22), 15. I Am the Walrus – The Beatles (4.40), 16. More About 'Walrus'/'Revolution'/'No. 9' (2.05), 17. Beef Jerky/Outro (0.49)

Bonus Tracks

Howard Cosell

18. Immigration Case (9.01), 19. The Beatles (5.21), 20. The Beatles Today (3.07), 21. Lennon Today (9.32), 22. Monday Night Football 1/2 Time Guest (1.52), 23. Track List of *Walls and Bridges* (2.00), 24. radio spot (1.06), 25. Television Spot (0.32)

Notes: Sleeve notes say:

> This is the most famous of John Lennon's radio appearances to promote *Walls and Bridges*. On September 28, 1974, he dropped into WNEW studios and joined Dennis Elsas on his afternoon program. John talked about his new album, The Beatles, their solo careers and his immigration problems. He played new tracks as well as some favourite oldies. You can tell John was having fun as he talked with Dennis, spun records, did commercials and news. Enjoy a moment is history.

376. LIVE – VOL. 1

Joker JOK-042-A

Format: CD

Source: various

Sound quality: unknown

1. Don't Let Me Down No. 1, 2. Don't Let Me Down No. 2, 3. Rock 'n' Roll People, 4. Clean-up Time, 5. Watching the Wheels, 6. Dear Yoko, 7. Surprise Surprise, 8. New York City, 9. Mucho Mungo, 10. Oh, Yoko, 11. I Don't Want to Face It, 12. I'm Losing You, 13. Rock Island Line, 14. I'm Stepping Out/Real Love, 15. Forgive Me (My Little Flower Princess), 16. No. 9 Dream, 17. Mother

377. LIVE – VOL. 2

Joker JOK-042-B

Format: CD

Source: various

Sound quality: unknown

1. Clean-up Time, 2. Love, 3. What You Got, 4. Aisumasen (I'm Sorry), 5. Aisumasen (I'm Sorry), 6. Bring on the Lucie (Freeda People), 7. Intuition/God, 8. Mucho Mungo (take 1), 9. Mucho Mungo (take 3), 10. As Time Goes By (take 1), 11. As Time Goes By (take 2), 12. Lady Marmalade, 13. Give Peace a Chance, 14. Mt. Elga, 15. (Just Like) Starting Over, 16. Brown Eyed Handsome Man, 17. Cooking (In The Kitchen of Love), 18. Watching the Wheels, 19. I'm Losing You, 20. I'm the Greatest, 21. Surprise Surprise (Sweet Bird of Paradox), 22. I'm a Man

Notes: The tracks on Volumes 1 and 2 are demos from *The Lost Lennon Tapes* series.

378. LIVE AND RARE

Unknown

Format: CD

Source: various

Sound quality: unknown

1. Mother, 2. Imagine, 3. Come Together, 4. Give Peace a Chance, 5. New York City, 6. Yer Blues, 7. Imagine, 8. John Sinclair, 9. Instant Karma, 10. Ain't That a Shame, 11. On The Caribbean

Notes: There are no details on the sleeve on the sources but tracks 1–5 are possibly from the One-to-One concert.

379. LIVE IN ANN ARBOR/APOLLO THEATRE

Unknown

Format: CD

Source: various

Sound quality: unknown

1. *Abbey Road* LP – George – Interview At KQV Pasadena, 1969, 2. Attica State – Luck of the Irish, 3. Attica State – Imagine

Notes: Track 2, live in Ann Arbor 10/11 December, 1971. Track 3, live at the Apollo Theatre, December 17, 1971.

380. LIVE IN L.A. AND 31 BIRTHDAY PARTY 1974
INP 060

Format: CD

Source: see notes

Sound quality: unknown

1. Bluesy Jam Session (5.36), 2. Lucille (5.53), 3. Nightmare (2.27), 4. Stand By Me/Cupid/Take This Hammer (15.24), 5. Tell Me What'd I Say (3.19), 6. Yellow Submarine (2.50), 7. Old Smokey Mountain/Goodnight Irene/He's Got the Whole World/Like a Rolling Stone/Twist and Shout/Louie Louie/La Bamba/Bring It on Home to Me (14.06), 8. Yesterday (1.44), 9. Dance For The Chicken/Power to the People/Maybe Baby (6.06), 10. Peggy Sue (2.55), 11. My Baby Left Me (2.05), 12. Blue Suede Shoes (2.53), 13. Crippled Inside/Give Peace a Chance/Crippled Inside/Uncle Albert (8.07)

Notes: Tracks 1–4, studio live rehearsal, Los Angeles, California with Paul McCartney, Stevie Wonder and Harry Nilsson. Tracks 5–13, John's thirty-first birthday party.

381. LIVE JAM (LIVE '72) (JOHN LENNON AND YOKO ONO)
Beatles Fan Peace BFP 004

Format: CD

Source: unknown

Sound quality: unknown

Notes: Track details unknown.

382. LIVE LENNON TAPES
The Early Years 02-CD-3329

Format: CD

Released: 1990

Source: live performances

Sound quality: good to very good

1. Imagine (2.56), 2. Attica State (3.22), 3.The Luck of the Irish (3.27), 4. John Sinclair (3.31), 5. John Sinclair (2.52), 6. It's So Hard (2.10), 7. The Luck of the Irish (3.36), 8. Sisters Oh Sisters (2.46), 9. We're All Water (4.27), 10. Woman Is the Nigger of the World (5.45), 11. Attica State (2.45), 12. Midsummer New York (2.45), 13. Sakura (2.40), 14. Memphis (3.12), 15. Johnny B. Goode (3.00), 16. Imagine (3,20), 17. Come Together (4.35), 18. Give Peace a Chance (7.47)

Notes: Track 1, Apollo Theatre, New York November 1971. Tracks 2–4, John Sinclair Benefit Concert. Tracks 5–16, various US television shows February 1972. Tracks 17 and 18, One-to-One concert (evening show).

Colour front with picture of John. Back has full track listing against a pink background.

383. LIVE PEACE IN TORONTO 1969 AUDIENCE

Misterclaudel MCCD-029

Format: CD

Released: 2005

Time: 38.22

Source: Toronto Rock 'n' Roll Festival, 13 September 1969

Sound quality: good audience tape

1. Introduction (1.34), 2. Blue Suede Shoes (2.22), 3. Money (That's What I Want) (3.26), 4. Dizzy Miss Lizzie (3.19), 5. Yer Blues (3.57), 6. Cold Turkey (3.37), 7. Give Peace a Chance (3.47), 8. Don't Worry Kyoko (Mummy's Only Looking for Her Hand in the Snow) (4.58), 9. John John (Let's Hope For Peace) (11.19)

Notes: Sleeve consists of four-page booklet with same blue background as official album with black-and-white photo of Plastic Ono Band on the front. This recording was originally available on a vinyl bootleg for a short time before t was announced that an official album would be released. The sound quality on this disc is good considering this is an audience recording and taken from the vinyl release. The concert presented here is unmixed and shows what it probably sounded like on the day. Some of Yoko's performance was edited out of the official release but appears here in full. This source was used previously for a very rare CDR recording JL-YO-EC 91369.

384. LOOK AT ME

Vigotone VT-CD-06

Format: CD

Source: varicus – see notes

Sound quality: very good – excellent

1. How Do You Sleep? (5.52), 2. Look at Me (2.49), 3. 'Club Dakota' Medley: Beautiful Boy (Darling Boy)/Howling at the Moon/Club Dakota Rap/Across the River (5.09), 4. I'm the Greatest (3.53), 5. Clean-up Time (4.25), 6. Honey Don't (1.49), 7. Glad All Over (0.48), 8. Lend Me Your Comb (1.22), 9. Duane Eddy Jam (Shazam!) (0.48), 10. Mucho Mungo (2.52), 11. So Long (3.08), 12. I Found Out (3.41), 13. Watching the Wheels (3.25), 14. Julia (2.53), 15. When a Boy Meets a Girl (2.05), 16. Real Life (3.26), 17. I'm Stepping Out (4.49), 18. Well, Well, Well (1.09), 19. Well, Well, Well (3.35), 20. Power to the People (2.46), 21. She Was A Friend of Dorothy (4.07), 22. Look at Me (3.07), 23. My Mummy's Dead (1.13)

Notes: Track 1, alternate take. Track 2, alternate mix. Track 3, electric with rhythm box, Dakota Spring 1980. Track 4, take 4 vocal John. Track 5, rough mix with reference vocal. Tracks 6–9, acoustic performances from *Clock*, St Regis Hotel, New York. Track 10, acoustic take, Spring 1974. Track 11, unknown. Track 12, rough mix, October 1970. Track 13, rough mix with count-in. Track 14, acoustic, Kenwood mid-1968. Track 15, acoustic 1970. Track 16, piano, take 2, Track 17, take 1. Track 18, acoustic. Track 19, take 4 from acetate. Track 20, rough mix with reference vocal. Track 21, piano, take 7 with chat, Dakota. Track 22, acoustic 1968. Track 23, acoustic – take 2. Colour front cover with picture of John.

385. LOST AND FOUND TAPES

PR Records IMM 41.95000

Format: CD

Source: various

Sound quality: unknown

1. Be My Baby (5.50), 2. Dear Yoko (2.26), 3. I Found Out (3.16)

Notes: Oddly, this release has only three tracks and runs for under twelve minutes.

386. LOST IN WEYBRIDGE

Tea Bag One STAB 10

Format: CD (digipack)

Released: 2003

Time: 78.55

Source: home recording, Weybridge

Sound quality: very good

1, The General Erection, 2. He Said He Said No. 1, 3. He Said He Said No. 2, 4. She Said She Said No. 1, 5. Good Morning, Good Morning, 6. Across the Universe, 7. She's Walking Past My Door, 8. You Know My Name, 9. Cry Baby Cry (four takes), 10. Julia No. 1, 11. Julia No. 2, 12. Julia No. 3, 13. On *Two Virgins* album (interview on underground radio), 14. *Two Virgins* outtake (rehearsal with Yoko), 15. She's Not A Girl Who Misses Much, 16. On Weybridge Tapes and inviting Yoko, 17. Look at Me, 18.The Maharishi Song (with Yoko), 19. I Love You My Love (with Yoko), 20. Oh, My Love (Nos. 1 and 2), 21. A Case of the Blues, 22. Don't Let Me Down No. 1, 23. Don't Let Me Down No. 2, 24. Everyone Had a Hard Year, 25. On freaky muse at home and inviting Yoko, 26–30. Mellotron Improvisations, 31. Stranger in My Arms

Bonus Tracks

32. A Nice Sound aka Sean's Loud, 33. Don't Let Me Down (by Julian), 34. Magical Mystery Tour Parody

Notes: A varied collection of home demos, taped at John's home called Kenwood, in Weybridge between 1966 and 1968. Some tracks were released previously with others new to bootleg. 'She's Not A Girl Who Misses Much' is an early version of 'Happiness Is a Warm Gun'. The four-minute version of 'Don't Let Me Down' is sung by Julian. 'She's Walking Past My Door' grew into 'You Know My Name'. 'I Love You My Love' is an obscene duet with Yoko.

Full colour sleeve with a bearded John wearing a hat and a flower in his mouth. Inside are black-and-white photos of Kenwood and John and Yoko naked holding a copy of *The Times* newspaper.

387. LOST LENNON ARCHIVES – VOL. 1

Bell Edge Records BE-001

Format: CD

Released: 2001

Source: various

Sound quality: unknown

1. Life Is Something/My Life, 2. The Sadness of Your Soul/Memories, 3. God, 4. She'll Be Coming Round the Mountain, 5. Mama You're So Beautiful This Morning, 6. Stay In Bed/Grow Your Hair, 7. Get It Together, 8. Goodnight Irene, 9. Old Smokey Mountain, 10. You Are A Stranger in My Arms, 11. Chi Chi's Cafe Down In Cuba, 12. The Calypso Song, 13. The Boat Song/Pedro the Fisherman, 14. People Get Ready, 15. I'll Make You Happy, 16. You Know How Hard It Is, 17. My Heart Is In Your Hands, 18. Saturday Morning Song/Sweater, 19. Keep Right On To The End of The Road, 20. Many Rivers to Cross, 21. She Runs Them Round In Circles, 22. Across the River/Howling at the Moon, 23. Mt. Elga, 24. Illusions, 25. I Watch Your Face, 26. Face it, 27. Emotional Wreck (take 1), 28. Everybody, 29. You Send Me/Kathy's Clown, 30. Falling In Love Again, 31. Chords of Fame, 32. Amazing Walk, 33. I'm Ready To Sing For The World

Notes: Some of the titles as listed on the sleeve are a bit dubious. For example, 'The Sadness of Your Soul' is 'You Saved My Soul'. This release is titled *Volume 1* but we have been unable to trace further releases in this series. Track 7: acoustic guitar rendition probably from Montreal Bed-In. Also released as *The Tropical Lennon Trax* (Bell Edge Records).

388. THE LOST LENNON REHEARSAL

John Records John 004

Format: CD

Released: 1993

Source: rehearsals for the One-to-One concert

Sound quality: very good mono

1. Introduction, 2. Come Together (John advises on keyboards), 3. Jam No. 1, 4. New York City (reprise), 5. Move On Fast, 6. Back off Boogaloo, 7. Woman Is the Nigger of the World (false start), 8. Give Peace a Chance (reggae version and jam), 9. Jam No. 2, 10. Unchained Melody, 11. It's Only Make Believe, 12. Stage chat re feedback and stage problems, 13. Instant Karma, 14. Mother, 15. We're All Water, 16. Jam No. 3, 17. Discussion (re ending of 'Come Together'), 18. Come Together (reprise of end to help band), 19. Open Your Box, 20. Roll Over Beethoven, 21. Give Peace a Chance (reggae version and jam)

Notes: John and Yoko with the Elephant's Memory Band in rehearsal for the One-to-One concert to be held at Madison Square Garden, New York on 22 August 1972. This release is a compilation of the 1985 three-disc vinyl set One and One and One is Three (Benefit Records). Some of this session was also previously available as the double vinyl set Willowbrook Rehearsals.

Full colour sleeve.

THE LOST LENNON TAPES

Following the broadcast in America of *The Lost Lennon Tapes* series which began in January 1988, the bootleggers had this wealth of material which started with the vinyl releases by Bag Records. Details of all thirty-five vinyl albums can be found in Part One. Although the first twenty-three albums from Bag Records were only available on vinyl, volumes twenty-four to thirty-five were also released on compact disc.

Further compact disc releases followed on different labels such as Living Legend Records who issued their own series, also titled *The Lost Lennon Tapes*, with a different track listing but the same front covers. Walrus Records also released a series of double CDs titled *The Complete Lost Lennon Tapes*. To add to the confusion Angry Dog Records issued a series titled *The Real Complete Lost Lennon Tapes* containing the complete shows. If they were not enough to keep collectors busy a further set of CDs is available containing the complete show, minus the advert breaks, starting with the Premiere show which was broadcast on 18 January 1988. Details of track listings of these releases are in Part Three – *The Lost Lennon Tapes*.

389–500. THE LOST LENNON TAPES (TREE)

501–721. THE LOST LENNON TAPES (WESTWOOD ONE)

See Part Three – *The Lost Lennon Tapes*, for track listings.

The first set (Tree) comprises mainly double albums. The second set (Westwood One) is all single albums. Each side consists of one radio show. The track listings are identical.

722. THE LOST LENNON TAPES – VOL. 1

Living Legend Records LLRCD 045

Format: CD

Source: various – see notes

Sound quality: excellent stereo except as noted

1. Roll Over Beethoven (2.29), 2. Whole Lotta Shakin' Goin' On (2.41), 3. It'll Be Me (2.37), 4. One-to-One radio spot (1.50), 5. Introduction by Lennon and Jagger (0.52), 6. Dirty Mac Jam (3.41), 7. That'll Be the Day (poor mono) (1.05), 8. Rave On (1.13), 9. Not Fade Away (0.54), 10. Maybe Baby (1.54), 11. Heartbeat (1.11), 12. Peggy Sue Got Married (1.13), 13. Peggy Sue (2.15), 14. *Eat the Document* (good mono) (7.52), 15. Lord Take This Make-up Off Me (4.25), 16. The News of the Day (4.25)

Notes: Tracks 1–3, with Elephant's Memory. Track 7, The Quarrymen, Tracks 8–13, acoustic at St Regis Hotel, New York. Track 14, outtake from the film. Tracks 15 and 16, Dylan parodies. This series of compact discs has a different track listing to the vinyl releases from Bag Records.

723. THE LOST LENNON TAPES – VOL. 2

Living Legend Records LLRCD 046

Format: CD

Source: various – see notes

Sound quality: excellent stereo except as noted

1. I Found Out (4.05), 2. Corrina Corrina (1.19), 3. A Case of the Blues (2.53), 4. Everyone Had a Hard Year (1.26), 5. Revolution (3.26), 6. Good Morning, Good Morning (1.01), 7. Everybody's Got Something to Hide Except Me and My Monkey (2.55), 8. Julia (2.58), 9. Strawberry Fields Forever (2.12), 10. What's the New Mary Jane (2.35), 11. Across the Universe (3.45), 12. Look Up the Number (1.00), 13. Help! (0.42, 14. The General Erection (0.34), 15. The Magic Dog (0.34), 16. Dear Prudence (4.42)

Notes: 'I Found Out' is a demo from 1969. A case of the blues and 'Everyone Had a Hard Year' are demos from 1968. 'Revolution' is a remix. 'Good Morning, Good Morning' is a demo from 1967. 'Everybody's Got Something to Hide', 'Julia', 'Strawberry Fields Forever', 'What's the New Mary Jane', 'Across the Universe' and 'Dear Prudence' are all demos. 'Look Up the Number' and 'Help!' are home recordings. 'The General Erection' and 'The Magic Dog' are John reading poetry. All tracks are excellent stereo except 13–15 which are very good mono.

724. THE LOST LENNON TAPES – VOL. 3

Living Legend Records LLRCD 047

Format: CD

Source: various – see notes

Sound quality: excellent stereo except as noted

1. Tomorrow Never Knows (3.10), 2. Strawberry Fields Backwards (0.38), 3. Aerial Tour Instrumental (2.04), 4. Cry Baby Cry (2.33), 5. Dear Prudence (4.36), 6. Sexy Sadie (2.24), 7. Child of Nature (2.38), 8. The

Continuing Story of Bungalow Bill (2.38), 9. I'm So Tired (2.24), 10. Yer Blues (3.31), 11. What's the New Mary Jane (2.39), 12. Revolution (3.12), 13. He Said He Said/She Said She Said (1.07), 14. Daddy's Little Sunshine Boy (0.38), 15. With a Little Help from My Friends (0.38)

Notes: 'Tomorrow Never Knows' is a rough mix. 'Strawberry Fields Backwards' is a talk test. 'Aerial Tour Instrumental' is 'Flying'. 'Daddy's Little Sunshine Boy' features Ringo on vocal. 'With a Little Help from My Friends' is John and Sean. Tracks 6–12 are acoustic demos recorded at Paul's house in 1968. All tracks are excellent stereo except 6–12 which are excellent mono. Track 15 is very good mono.

725. THE LOST LENNON TAPES – VOL. 4
Living Legend Records LLRCD 054
Format: CD
Source: various – see notes
Sound quality: very good to excellent stereo except as noted

1. I'm the Greatest (2.50), 2. The Luck of the Irish (3.11), 3. Tell Me What I Say (3.16), 4. Yellow Submarine (2.50), 5. Old Smokey (2.05), 6. Come Together (4.33), 7. Dear Prudence (4.40), 8. Imagine (3.02), 9. Love (3.09), 10. Yer Blues (8.33)

Notes: 'I'm the Greatest' is an early version. 'The Luck of the Irish' is an acoustic demo. Tracks 3–5 are from John's thirty-first birthday party. 'Come Together' is from the One-to-One concert. 'Imagine' and 'Love' are early live versions. 'Yer Blues' is from the *Rolling Stones Rock and Roll Circus*. Tracks 3–5 are very good mono.

726. THE LOST LENNON TAPES – VOL. 5
Living Legend Records LLRCD 055
Format: CD
Source: various – see notes
Sound quality: excellent stereo except as noted

1. Mother (5.10), 2. Give Peace a Chance (7.51), 3. Attica State (3.24), 4. The Luck of the Irish (3.23), 5. John Sinclair (3.29), 6. Yesterday (1.50),

7. Memphis Tennessee (3.33), 8. God (1.49), 9. God Save Us (2.00), 10. Johnny B. Goode (3.08), 11. Peggy Sue (2.40)

Notes: 'Mother' and 'Give Peace a Chance' are from the One-to-One concert. 'Attica State', 'The Luck of the Irish' and 'John Sinclair' are from the Free John Sinclair Rally. 'Yesterday' and 'Peggy Sue' are from John's thirty-first birthday party. 'Memphis Tennessee' and 'Johnny B. Goode' are live with Chuck Berry. Tracks 6, 7, 10 and 11 are very good mono.

727. THE LOST LENNON TAPES – VOL. 6

Living Legend Records LLRCD 056

Format: CD

Source: various – see notes

Sound quality: excellent stereo except as noted

1. Cold Turkey (4.58), 2. Send Me Some Loving (3.10), 3. Down To Cuba (2.06), 4. Instant Karma (3.21), 5. Blue Suede Shoes (3.03), 6. Give Peace a Chance (3.07), 7. Chi Chi's Cafe (3.27), 8. Give Peace a Chance (4.56), 9. Dear John (4.14), 10. Corrina Corrina (1.15), 11. Serve Yourself (2.37), 12. The Best Things In Life Are Free (0.17), 13. A Nice Noise (1.54)

Notes: 'Cold Turkey' is an early demo. 'Send Me Some Loving' – acoustic version. 'Instant Karma' is live from the One-to-One concert. 'Blue Suede Shoes' and 'Give Peace a Chance' (tracks 5 and 6) are from John's thirty-first birthday party. 'Chi Chi's Café' is Ringo and John. 'Give Peace a Chance' is a rehearsal. 'A Nice Noise' is John and Sean. Sound is excellent except tracks from John's thirty-first birthday party and 'Chi Chi's Café' which are excellent mono.

728. THE LOST LENNON TAPES – VOL. 7

Living Legend Records LLRCD 066

Format: CD

Source: various – see notes

Sound quality: very good to excellent mono

1. How Do You Sleep? (8.18), 2. Sally and Billy (3.21), 3. Make Love Not War (3.29), 4. Girls and Boys (2.17), 5. Woman (3.07), 6. Happy Rishikesh (1.45), 7. Rock Island Line (2.32), 8. John Henry (1.37), 9. Tennessee Oh Tennessee (Pts 1 and 2) (1.54), 10. God (1.10), 11. I'm the Greatest (Pts 1 and 2) (3.54), 12. Make Love Not War/I Promise (5.14)

Notes: The insert says: 'live in front of a small audience between 1968 and 1970'. It sounds more like various outtakes!

729. THE LOST LENNON TAPES – VOL. 8
Living Legend Records LLRCD 068

Format: CD

Source: various – see notes

Sound quality: very good to excellent stereo/mono

1. Woman Is the Nigger of the World (2.25), 2. Whatever Happened To (4.42), 3. New York City (2.16), 4. The News of the Day (4.20), 5. Well (5.55), 6. Honey Don't (1.50), 7. Glad All Over (0.55), 8. Lend Me Your Comb (1.27), 9. Duane Eddy Jam (0.54), 10. When a Boy Meets a Girl (2.11), 11. Look at Me (2.58), 12. My Mummy's Dead (1.19), 13. Mother (4.41)

Notes: 'Woman Is the Nigger of the World' is an early acoustic demo. 'Whatever Happened To', 'New York City', 'When a Boy Meets a Girl', 'Look at Me' and 'My Mummy's Dead' are acoustic versions. 'The News of the Day' is a Bob Dylan parody. 'Well, Well, Well' is a live jam. 'Honey Don't', 'Glad All Over', 'Lend Me Your Comb' and 'Duane Eddy Jam' are from *Clock*. 'Mother' is the tremolo guitar version.

730. THE LOST LENNON TAPES – VOL. 9
Living Legend Records LLRCD 069

Format: CD

Source: various – see notes

Sound quality: excellent stereo except as noted

1. Yer Blues (4.20), 2. Warm Up Jam (3.38), 3. Yer Blues (3.59), 4. John Henry (2.15), 5. Love (2.27), 6. Well Alright (0.44), 7. Imagine (3.00), 8. San Francisco Bay Blues (0.50), 9. Happy Xmas (War Is Over) (3.16), 10. Serve Yourself (6.15), 11. Pill (1.37), 12. Gone from This Place (1.40), 13. Cold Turkey (3.35)

Notes: 'Yer Blues' (instrumental) and 'Warm Up Jam' are from *Rock and Roll Circus* sessions. 'Yer Blues' (track 3) is the vocal version from *Rock and Roll Circus*. 'John Henry' is the electric live version. 'Love' is the tremolo guitar version. 'Well Alright' is an electric jam. 'Imagine' is a piano solo. 'San Francisco Bay Jues', 'Happy Xmas', 'Gone from This Place' and 'Cold Turkey' are acoustic versions. 'Serve Yourself' is the piano version. 'Pill' is an unreleased song.

731. THE LOST LENNON TAPES – VOL. 10
Living Legend Records LLRCD 096
Format: CD
Released: 1991
Source: various – see below
Sound quality: excellent

1. Attica State (*David Frost Show*) (3.06), 2. Attica State (reprise) (0.59), 3. Slippin' and Slidin' (*Salute To Sir Lew Grade*) (2.20), 4. Imagine (*Salute To Sir Lew Grade*) (3.00), 5. Imagine (acoustic, Apollo Theatre, New York) (2.51), 6. Radio Peace (1969) (0.15), 7. I Saw Her Standing There (3.12), 8. As Time Goes By (John and Yoko) (0.10), 9. Peace Message/Make Love to the End (1.10), 10. As Time Goes By (John solo) (0.09), 11. Let's Twist Again (with David Bowie) (3.04), 12. Instant Karma (One-to-One concert) (3.25), 13. Mother (One-to-One concert) (4.28), 14. Come Together (One-to-One concert) (4.04), 15. The Inner Light (instrument backing track) (2.32)

732. THE LOST LENNON TAPES – VOL. 11
Living Legend Records LLRCD 147
Format: CD
Released: 1991

Source: various – see below

Sound quality: excellent

1. Intro, 2. Blue Suede Shoes, 3. Money, 4. Dizzy Miss Lizzie, 5. Yer Blues, 6. Cold Turkey, 7. C'mon Everybody, 8. Give Peace a Chance, 9. Don't Worry Kyoko, 10. John John

Bonus Tracks
11. Touch Me, 12. Mid Summer New York, 13. Why Not

Notes: This volume is subtitled *Alternate Toronto Mix and More*.

733. THE LOST LENNON TAPES – VOL. 23

Bag Records 5095

Format: CD

Time: 70.27

Source: various

Sound quality: very good to excellent

1. I Don't Wanna Face It (acoustic demo (1.78), 2. Beautiful Boy/Howling at the Moon/Dakota Rap/Across the River (5.08), 3. Real Love (take 5) (2.45), 4. Beautiful Boy (take 2), 5. Clean-up Time (7.56), 6. Stepping Out (take 2), 7. Beautiful Boy (3.56), 8. Watching the Wheels (3.31)/Dear Yoko (2.27), 9. Clean-up Time (alternate mix) (4.24), 10. You Saved My Soul (take 2) (2.37), 11. Illusions (2.43

Bonus Tracks (Off The Walls – Part One)
12. Bless You (5.20), 13. Move Over Ms L (2.45), 14. Scared (4.47), 15. Surprise Surprise (3.06), 16. Whatever Gets You Through the Night (3.11), 17. Going Down on Love (3.51)

Notes: This was the first release by Bag Records on compact disc of *The Lost Lennon Tapes* series. For details of the tracks listings for the vinyl releases (volumes 1–23) see entries in Part One. See also entry in Part One for details of the tracks on this release.

734. THE LOST LENNON TAPES – VOL. 24

Bag Records 5096

Format: CD

Time: 49.05

Source: various

Sound quality: very good to excellent

1. He Said He Said (2.01), 2. She Said She Said (0.55), 3. Yer Blues (4.31), 4. Oh, My Love (1.24), 5. Oh, My Love (1.19), 6. Because (0.37), 7. Happiness Is a Warm Gun (0.41), 8. Give Peace a Chance (0.38), 9. Give Peace a Chance (2.12), 10. Give Peace a Chance (1.28), 11. Give Peace a Chance (5.22), 12. Give Peace a Chance (0.25), 13. God (3.41), 14. My Mummy's Dead (0.46), 15. It's So Hard (4.24), 16. Come Together (3.52), 17. Honky Tonk Blues (2.49), 18. I Know (3.14), 19. Rock 'n' Roll People (2.50), 20. Only People (2.44)

Notes: This was the second release by Bag Records on compact disc of *The Lost Lennon Tapes* series. See also entry in Part One for details of the tracks on this release.

735. THE LOST LENNON TAPES – VOL. 25

Bag Records 5097

Format: CD

Time: 42.16

Source: various

Sound quality: very good to excellent

1. Whatever Gets You Through the Night (2.52), 2. Steel and Glass (5.11), 3. Beef Jerky (3.18), 4. You Saved My Soul (1.29), 5. Serve Yourself (8.25), 6. Memories (3.30), 7. Real Life (3.18), 8. Watching the Wheels (3.15), 9. Don't Be Crazy (3.07), 10. Woman (2.43), 11. (Just Like) Starting Over (4.14), 12. I Don't Want to Face It (0.43)

736. THE LOST LENNON TAPES – VOL. 26

Bag Records 5098

Format: CD

Time: 44.32

Source: various

Sound quality: very good to excellent

1. Nobody Told Me (3.13), 2. Real Love (3.09), 3. I'm Losing You (4.20), 4. Beautiful Boy (7.23), 5. Nobody Told Me (3.59), 6. Clean-up Time (4.35), 7. Starting Over (3.58), 8. Lennon's Lost Diary Tape (13. 36)

Notes: Re-issue of original vinyl release. See also entry in Part One for details of the tracks on this release.

737. THE LOST LENNON TAPES – VOL. 27

Bag Records 5099

Format: CD

Source: various

Sound quality: very good to excellent

1. If I Fell (3.59), 2. I Sat Belonely (0.43), 3. Foyle's Speech (0.04), 4. National Health Cow (0.30), 5. Strawberry Fields Forever (2.38), 6. Get It Together (1.57), 7. Happy Xmas (War Is Over) (2.20), 8. Power to the People (1.23), 9. Don't Be Cruel/Hound Dog (4.17), 10. I'm the Greatest (3.11), 11. I Know (3.16), 12. Rock 'n' Roll People (3.26), 13. Meat City (2.34), 14. Meat City (3.28), 15. Meat City (2.29), 16. One Day at a Time (3.17), 17. Only People (2.54)

Notes: Track 6: acoustic guitar rendition probably from Montreal Bed-In.

738. THE LOST LENNON TAPES – VOL. 28

Bag Records 5100

Format: CD

Source: various

Sound quality: very good to excellent

1. Tight A$ (4.16), 2. You Are Here (4.37), 3. Going Down on Love (4.06), 4. No. 9 Dream (4.40), 5. Whatever Gets You Through the Night (3.20), 6. Surprise Surprise (Sweet Bird of Paradox) (2.35), 7. John on KHJ-AM, Los

Angeles (1.06), 8. Do You Want to Dance (3.05), 9. You Can't Catch Me (3.33), 10. Free as a Bird (2.42), 11. Serve Yourself (5.15), 12. She'll Be Coming Round the Mountain (1.01), 13. She Run Them Round in Circles/Beautiful Boy (5.38)

Notes: Track 3, acoustic demo. Tracks 4 and 8 are monitor mixes. Track 9, alternate take. Track 10, take 3.

739. THE LOST LENNON TAPES – VOL. 29
Bag Records 5101

Format: CD

Source: various

Sound quality: very good to excellent

1. Memories/Watching the Wheels (4.16), 2. Stranger's Room (3.51), 3. Woman (0.30), 4. Woman (3.53), 5. I'm Stepping Out (1.42), 6. I'm Stepping Out (6.14), 7. (Just Like) Starting Over (3.43), 8. Dream Lover/Stay (3.41), 9. Clean-up Time (0.55), 10. Beautiful Boy (2.03), 11. Watching the Wheels (4.41), 12. I'm Stepping Out (5.01), 13. Woman (3.08)

740. THE LOST LENNON TAPES – VOLS 30/31/32
Bag Records 5102/3/4

Format: CD (double)

Source: various

Sound quality: very good to excellent

CD 1

1. It's Not Too Bad (3.29), 2. She Can Talk to Me (0.46), 3. Cry Baby Cry (3.23), 4. *Two Virgins* outtake (1.47) 5. Plastic Ono Band Jam (1.39), 6. Look at Me (2.52), 7. I'm the Greatest (0.37), 8. How?/Child of Nature/Oh, Yoko (4.25), 9. Oh, Yoko (3.23), 10. Sally and Billy (2.03), 11. Come Together (1.47), 12. Happy Girl (1.10), 13. I'll Make You Happy (3.56), 14. How Do You Sleep? (3.45), 15. It's So Hard (4.44), 16. I Don't Want to Be a Soldier, Mama (I Don't Want To Die) (4.34), 17. Intuition (3.04), 18. I Know (3.00), 19. I Know (3.43), 20. Aisumasen (I'm Sorry)

(3.43), 21. Steel and Glass (1.44), 22. *Walls and Bridges* Rundown (1.56), 23. Mirror Mirror (On the Wall) (4.34)

CD 2

1. Tennessee (2.26), 2. Memories (6.03), 3. Sally and Billy (3.28), 4. She is a Friend of Dorothy (3.55), 5. The Boat Song (2.08), 6. Pedro the Fisherman (1.04), 7. Many Rivers to Cross Pt. 2/My Girl (2.24), 8. Instrumental 1979 (1.02), 9. I'm Stepping Out (1.29), 10. Dear Yoko (5.04), 11. Woman (4.26), 12. Woman (1.54), 13. Woman (2.13), 14. Clean-up Time (6.01), 15. Nobody Told Me (3.51), 16. I Am the Walrus/Watching the Wheels (4.01), 17. Woman (2.26), 18. Woman (3.39), 19. Living on Borrowed Time (4.20), 20. I'm Losing You (3.54)

Notes: This double-disc set comprises the three volumes numbered 30, 31 and 32 which were originally released on vinyl. The set starts with three demo tracks recorded in Spain in late 1966. 'It's Not Too Bad' became 'Strawberry Fields Forever'. This early piano demo of 'She Can Talk to Me' became 'Hey Bulldog'. 'Cry Baby Cry' is comprised of early piano and electric demo fragments. The *Two Virgins* outtake is John and Yoko playing around in his home studio. 'Plastic Ono Band Jam' is a send up of Fifties rockabilly. 'Look at Me' is an outtake from *Plastic Ono Band* with alternate vocals. 'I'm the Greatest' and the medley of 'How?'/'Child of Nature'/'Oh, Yoko', 'Oh, Yoko' and 'Sally and Billy' are all piano demos recorded in December 1970. 'Come Together' is from the One-to-One rehearsals in August 1972. From just prior to the *Mind Games* era we have Yoko's 'Happy Girl' and John's 'I'll Make You Happy' (which includes some lyrics from 'Cold Turkey').

This set continues with some music from the *Imagine* session. Firstly, rehearsals of 'How Do You Sleep?' followed by more run-throughs from the King Curtis sax overdub sessions in New York for 'It's So Hard 'and 'I Don't Want to Be a Soldier'. 'Intuition' is take 4 of a series of piano demos. 'I Know' is take 2 of a series of guitar demos. 'Aisumasen' is a near final mix. 'Steel and Glass' is a dark piano version featuring extra lyrics. To promote the *Walls and Bridges* album John called a Canadian radio station and gave a run down of the album's contents. 'Mirror Mirror (On the Wall)' is take 2 of the piano demos.

The second disc starts with 'Tennessee', 'Memories' and 'Sally and Billy' which are home demos from 1976. 'She is a Friend of Dorothy' is from 1977. Lennon explores a nautical theme in the piano demos 'The Boat Song' and 'Pedro the Fisherman'. 'Many Rivers to Cross' is part of a demo and has John doodling on the old Motown song 'My Girl'. The focus on the remaining tracks is the *Double Fantasy* sessions which began on 6 August 1980. 'I'm Stepping Out' is an incomplete take. 'Dear Yoko' is interrupted when John breaks a string on his guitar. 'Woman' is presented in three stages. 'Clean-up Time' is a rehearsal. 'Nobody Told Me' is a run through of a song which would be released on the *Milk and Honey* album. 'Watching the Wheels' is preceded by a brief parody of 'I Am the Walrus'. The first version of 'Woman' is an instrumental which is followed by an alternate take. 'Borrowed Time', also destined for *Milk and Honey*, is an early take. 'I'm Losing You' is an alternate take followed by some studio chat.

741. THE LOST LENNON TAPES – VOLS 33, 34 AND 35

Bag Records 5105/6/7

Format: CD (double)

Released: 1997

Time: Disc One 70.02, Disc Two 65.32

Source: various

Sound quality: very good to excellent

Disc One

1. Imagine (2.57), 2. How Do You Sleep? (2.53), 3. J.J. (1.11), 4. Rock Island Line/Maybe Baby/Peggy Sue (3.50), 5. Out the Blue (3.15), 6. Old Dirt Road (4.52), 7. Steel and Glass (4.15), 8. Whatever Gets You Through the Night (3.30), 9. *Rock 'n' Roll* radio spot (1.02), 10. Stand By Me (4.09), 11. Serve Yourself (3.17), 12. Everybody (2.48), 13. Everybody/Nobody Told Me (3.11), 14. Nobody Told Me (3.49), 15. Falling In Love Again (1.24), 16. Cathy's Clown (1.12), 17. You Send Me (2.08), 18. Real Love (4.20), 19. My Life (1.35), 20. My Life (2.44), 21. Dear Yoko (5.16), 22. I'm Stepping Out (4.50)

Disc Two

1. I'm Stepping Out (20.50), 2. I'm Stepping Out (6.26), 3. Borrowed Time (15.51), 4. I Don't Wanna Face It (2.33), 5. Watching the Wheels (6.08), 6. Beautiful Boy (3.58), 7. (Just Like) Starting Over (4.15), 8. (Just Like) Starting Over (3.37).

742. THE LOST SLEEPY BLIND LEMON LENNON TAPES

Library Products 2341

Format: CD

Released: 1990

Source: various – see notes

Sound quality: excellent stereo and mono

1. Serve Yourself (8.24), 2. You Saved My Soul (1.29), 3. The Worst is Over (2.16), 4. When a Boy Meets a Girl (2.06), 5. She is a Friend of Dorothy (4.06), 6. One of the Boys (3.04), 7. He Got the Blues (3.04), 8. Sleepy Blind Lemon Live: John Henry/I Ain't Got The Time (5.27), 9. Cooking (in the Kitchen of Love) (2.40), 10. Free as a Bird (3.25), 11. People (1.52), 12. Down in the Caribbean (3.01), 13. Well (Baby Please Don't Go) (5.59), 14. Only the Lonely (2.58), 15. Gone from This Place (3.19), 16. Howling at the Moon (1.57), 17. Memories (2.33), 18. Mucho Mungo (2.57).

Notes: Track 1, piano version. Track 2, take 2, Dakota, late 1980. Track 3, acoustic with rhythm box, Dakota. Track 4, acoustic take 1, 1970. Track 5, piano, take 7 with chat, Dakota. Track 6, acoustic take 1, Dakota. Track 7, acoustic late 1971/early 1972. Track 8, unknown. Track 9, piano, take 1, Dakota. Track 10, piano, take 1, Dakota. Track 11, acoustic. Track 12, exact title unclear – recorded during New York City sessions. Track 13, Tittenhurst, June 1971. Track 14, with chat, riffs and brief instrumental versions of '(Just Like) Starting Over' and 'Gone from This Place'. Track 15, acoustic, Dakota. Track 16, electric with rhythm box, Dakota. Track 17, piano, take 2, Dakota. Track 18, acoustic 1974. All tracks from *The Lost Lennon Tapes* radio series.

The front cover has a colour picture of John and Yoko.

743. LOST WEEKEND

Unknown

Format: CD

Source: unknown

Sound quality: unknown

Notes: We have been unable to trace any details of this release.

744. THE MAN, THE MEMORY – VOLS ONE AND TWO

Black Cat BC 015/016

Format: CD (double)

Source: WXLO FM, New York City, broadcast 14 December 1980

Sound quality: unknown

Volume One

1. Introduction, 2. Starting over in the 80s, 3. Watching the Wheels, 4. A diarrhea of creativity, 5. Starting Over, 6. Just another rocker, 7. Clean-up Time, 8. Almost like twins, 9. Narration, 10. Don't touch don't feel, 11. Narration, 12. Just a daddy, 13. Beautiful Boy, 14. Narration, 15. Expectation, 16. Narration, 17. I'm not running for office, 18. Narration, 19. Back to roots, 20. Rock 'n' Roll Music, 21. Choosing partners, 22. Narration, 23. Meeting Yoko, 24. Out the Blue, 25. Longer than the Beatles, 26. Narration, 27. Macho women, 28. Narration, 29. Whatever Gets You Through The Night, 29. I needed her so much, 30. Dear Yoko

Volume Two

1. No. 9 Dream, 2. Yoko kicked me out, 3. Narration, 4. A blank cheque, 5. Narration, 6. Freaky music and Two Virgins, 7. Narration, 8. What are they doing?, 9. The Ballad of John and Yoko, 10. We're in enough trouble as it is, 11. Woman Is the Nigger of the World, 12. Our intentions were good, 13. Give Peace a Chance, 14. We're human again, 15. Love, 16. Love is the answer, 17. Narration, 18. This time they're ready for us, 19. Narration, 20. *Double fantasy*, 21. Narration, 22. We all survived, 23. Narration, 24. One whole piece of works, 25. Starting Over,

26. Now I know both sides, 27. Narration, 28. It's kids stuff, 29. Mind Games, 30. There was no time to reflect, 31. Oh, Yoko, 32. Everyone knows what love is, 33. Narration, 34. A reflection on us all, 25. Woman

745. THE MAN, THE MEMORY – VOL. THREE
Black Cat BC. 017
Format: CD
Source: WXLO FM, New York City, broadcast 14 December 1980
Sound quality: unknown

1. It's Only Love, 2. Narration. 3. Just imagine it, 4. Imagine, 5. Projecting the futures, 6. Narration, 7. We all created this together, 8. Only People, 9. Crying for it wasn't enough, 10. I Want To Kick Your Pants, 11. Remember, 12. It's an insecurity, 13. Narration, 14. In My Life, 15. Narration 16. Be-Bop-A-Lula, 17. Fresh as ever, 18. Narration, 19. The Beatles never stuck to one style, 20. Narration, 21. An evening out, 22. I'm Your Angel, 23. Let's take it on the road, 24. Narration, 25. Starting Over, 26. Closing, 27. An Ultima Entrevista de John Lennon

Notes: These two sets have colour fronts with full track listing on the back.

746. THE MAN, THE MEMORY
Air-Check WMJQ
Format: CD (triple)
Source: broadcast 14 December 1980
Sound quality: excellent

Notes: see *John Lennon: The Man, The Memory* (WMJQ)

747. MAXIMUM LENNON
Chrome Dreams ABCD 070
Format: CD
Released: 2000
Source: various interviews
Sound quality: unknown

1. I only learnt to play to back myself, 2. Who am I to regard as mother, 3. The beatnik horror, 4. Beatles spelt like in beat music, 5. Aggressive restraint, a Brando type, 6. Which way are we going boys, 7. Kids everywhere go for the same stuff, 8. Controlled weirdness, 9. An escape valve from The Beatles, 10. You should have been there, 11. Other plans, 12. John who

Notes: A collection of interviews – whether this release can be considered a bootleg in the strict use of the term is debatable but we have included this in the listings as this is now difficult to find.

748. MEGAMIX (JOHN LENNON AND PAUL MCCARTNEY)
Unknown BMB 007
Format: CD
Source: various, Tracks 1–21 John Lennon. Tracks 22–46 Paul McCartney
Sound quality: unknown

1. (Just Like) Starting Over, 2. Mind Games, 3. Instant Karma, 4. Give Peace a Chance, 5. Watching the Wheels, 6. No. 9 Dream, 7. Beautiful Boy, 8. Imagine, 9. Woman, 10. Cold Turkey, 11. Woman Is the Nigger of the World/Give Peace a Chance (reprise), 12. Dear Yoko, 13. Clean-up Time, 14. I'm Losing You, 15. Power to the People, 16. Whatever Gets You Through the Night, 17. Nobody Told Me, 18. Happy Xmas (War Is Over), 19. Love, 20. Jealous Guy, 21. (Just Like) Starting Over (reprise)

Notes: Tracks 22–46 by Paul McCartney

749. MEMORIES
Strapple Records
Format: CD (double)
Released: 2000
Source: various
Sound quality: unknown

Disc One

1. Memories, 2. Howling at the Moon, 3. Pill, 4. Peggy Sue, 5. Clean-up Time, 6. Many Rivers to Cross, 7. God, 8. I'm Losing You (trial version),

9. My Life, 10. She is a Friend of Dorothy, 11. Cold Turkey, 12. Watching the Wheels, 13. Be-Bop-A-Lula, 14. Mucho Mungo, 15. Girls and Boys, 16. Real Life, 17. Woman, 18. God (acoustic demo), 19. Well, Well, Well (early demo), 20. My Mummy's Dead (early demo), 21. Instant Karma, 22. How Do You Sleep? 23. Rock Island Line, 24. Child of Nature, 25. Surprise Surprise (acoustic demo), 26. Help (home demo), 27. You Know My Name, 28. Meat City

Disc Two
1. Free as a Bird, 2. Whatever Happened To, 3. As Time Goes By, 4. Subterranean Homesick Blues, 5. He Said She Said, 6. Every Man Has a Woman, 7. Give Me Some Truth, 8. Luck of the Irish, 9. Now and Then, 10. India, 11. Lennon/McCartney feud, 12. Comments to Bob Dylan, 13. One of the Boys, 14. You Saved My Soul, 15. Help Me to Help Myself, 16. John Henry, 17. Tennessee Oh Tennessee, 18. Sea Ditty Melody, 19. How Do You Sleep? (obscene lyrics version), 20. Out the Blue, 21. How? 22. Crippled Inside, 23. That's the Way the World It, 24. Rave On/Not Fade Away, 25. Illusions, 26. Sean's With a Little Help from My Friends, 27. I'm Losing You

Notes: Disc Two, track 12 is from the film *Eat the Document*.

750. MIND GAMES ACETATE
Unknown
Format: CD
Source: *Mind Games* album acetate
Sound quality: very good

1. Mind Games, 2. Tight A$, 3. Aisumasen (I'm Sorry), 4. One Day (at a Time), 5. Bring on the Lucie (Freeda People), 6. Nutopian International Anthem, 7. Intuition, 8. Out the Blue, 9. Only People, 10. I Know (I Know), 11. You Are Here, 12. Meat City

751. MIND GAMES (ALTERNATES AND DEMOS)
Howdy Records CD-555-03
Format: CD

Released: 1991

Source: *Mind Games* rough mixes and outtakes

Sound quality: excellent stereo/mono

1. Mind Games, 2. Tight A$, 3. Aisumasen (I'm Sorry), 4. One Day at a Time, 5. Bring on the Lucie (Freeda People), 6. Intuition, 7. Out the Blue, 8. Only People, 9. I Know (I Know), 10. Meat City, 11. Make Love Not War, 12. Tight A$, 13. Call My Name, 14. Call My Name, 15. Bring on the Lucie (Freeda People), 16, Intuition, 17. I Know (I Know), 18. Just Gotta Give Me Some Rock and Roll/Shoeshine, 19. Meat City

Notes: Tracks 1–10 are early rough mixes. Tracks 11–12 are piano demos. 'Call My Name' is a prototype of 'Aisumasen' – track 13 is an electric guitar demo and track 14 is an acoustic guitar demo. 'Bring on the Lucie' is a slide guitar demo. 'I Know (I Know)' is acoustic guitar demo, take 3. 'Just Gotta Give Me Some Rock and Roll' is an acoustic guitar demo prototype of 'Meat City'. 'Meat City' is an electric guitar demo.

752. MIND GAMES SESSIONS

Unknown

Format: CD

Source: *Mind Games* album outtakes

Sound quality: unknown

Disc One

1. Mind Games, 2. Tight A$, 3. Tight A$, 4. Tight A$, 5. Aisumasen (I'm Sorry), 6. Aisumasen (I'm Sorry), 7. One Day at a Time, 8. One Day at a Time, 9. One Day at a Time, 10. Bring on the Lucie (Freda People), 11. Bring on the Lucie (Freda People), 12. Intuition, 13. Out the Blue, 14. Out the Blue, 15. Out the Blue, 16. Only People, 17. Only People

Disc Two

1. I Know (I Know), 2. I Know (I Know), 3. I Know (I Know), 4. I Know (I Know), 5. I Know (I Know), 6. You Are Here, 7. You Are Here, 8. Meat City, 9. Rock 'n' Roll People, 10. Rock 'n' Roll People, 11. Rock 'n' Roll People, 12. Rock 'n' Roll People, 13. Rock 'n' Roll People

Bonus Tracks

14. Mind Games, 15. Meat City, 16. radio spot No. 1, 17. radio spot No. 2

Notes: All tracks recorded at the Record Plant East, New York, July–August 1973. Disc Two: Tracks 9 and 10 – 1 August 1973. Tracks 11, 12 and 13 – 4 August 1973. Track 14 – US promo 45. Track 15 – 45 mix. Tracks 16 and 17 – 24 October 1973.

753. MISCELLANEOUS TRACKS

Yellow Dog/Orange YD-Orange YD 018
Format: CD
Released: 1995
Time: 53.53
Source: various
Sound quality: excellent stereo

Jerry Lewis on Telethon, 6 September 1972
1. Imagine, 2. Now Or Never, 3. Give Peace a Chance

Salute To Sir Lew Grade, 13 June 1975
4. Slippin' and Slidin', 5. Stand By Me, 6. Imagine

Studio outtakes with Cheap Trick, 1980
7. I'm Losing You, 8. Beautiful Boy, 9. I'm Moving On

The Old Grey Whistle Test
10. Stand By Me, 11. Slippin' and Slidin'

Home demos
12. Mucho Mungo (version 1), 13. Mucho Mungo (version 2), 14. Mucho Mungo (version 3), 15. Goodnight, Vienna

Notes: Tracks 12–14 are demos for Harry Nilsson. Track 15 is a demo for Ringo Starr. Most of the material had been previously released on vinyl but the sound quality is probably the best available. This disc was re-issued by Cool Orangecicle in 1997.

Full colour front cover.

754. MISCELLANEOUS TRACKS

Cool Orangecicle

Format: CD

Released: 1997

Time: 53.53

Source: various

Sound quality: very good stereo

Notes: This is a re-issue of the Yellow Dog/Orange release.

755. MOVE OVER MS L (THE (NOT SO) LOST WEEKEND)

KTKK DIY GB No. 5069

Format: CD

Released: 2001

Source: various

Sound quality: unknown

1. Intro, 2. It Wasn't So Lost, 3. Tight A$, 4. Rock 'n' Roll People, 5. Only People, 6. You Can't Catch Me, 7. Here We Go Again, 8. My Baby Left Me, 9. Just Because, 10. Too Many Cooks (Spoil The Soup), 11. Waiting for My Green Card with Thee, 12. Lucille, 13. Cupid/Chain Gang/Take this Hammer, 14. Stand By Me Reggae, 15. Stand By Me, 16. Mucho Mungo/Mt. Elga, 17. Whatever Gets You Through the Night, 18. Goodnight, Vienna, 19. Only You, 20. That'll Be the Day, 21. C'mon Everybody, 22. Blue Danube Waltz/I Saw Her Standing There, 23. Funny Shoes and Glasses, 24. Fame, 25. Move Over Ms L (45 rpm version)

Bonus Tracks

26. Sleepwalk, 27. I'm Walking

Notes: Full colour front inserts with pictures of John from 1974. The insert also includes a collection of pictures of John with Keith Moon, Paul and Linda, George Harrison, May Pang, his son Julian, Elton John, David Bowie, Ringo, Phil Spector and Mick Jagger.

756. MORE MIND GAMES

JL 4
Format: CD
Released: 2000
Source: *Mind Games* outtakes
Sound quality: excellent

1. Tower Records promo spot

Rough Mixes, August 1973, Record Plant, New York

2. Mind Games, 3. Tight A$, 4. Aisumasen, 5. One Day at a Time, 6. Bring on the Lucie, 7. Intuition, 8. Out the Blue, 9. Only People, 10. I Know (I Know), 11. You Are Here, 12. Meat City

Demos

13. Make Love Not War (early version of 'Mind Games'), 14. Tight A$, 15. Intuition, 16. I Know (I Know), 17. Rock 'n' Roll People, 18. Here We Go Again, 19. Just Give Me Some Rock 'n' Roll, 20. Meat City, 21. Call My Name (early version of Aisumasen), 22. Free The People

Alternates

23. Out the Blue, 24. Rock 'n' Roll People (rehearsal), 25. *Mind Games* promo spot (Keith Moon)

757. MR. AND MRS. LENNON'S HONEYMOON

Banana Inc MMRSLHM2
Format: CD
Time: 40.40
Source: documentary film *Mr. and Mrs. Lennon's Honeymoon*
Sound quality: very good

Notes: This disc is the soundtrack of the documentary film *Mr. and Mrs. Lennon's Honeymoon* (A Film by Peter Goessens) and features the Montreal Bed-In.

The disc does not include any booklet or packaging.

758. MSG Back in '72/They Say It's Your Birthday

Unknown JNY 0072

Format: CD

Source: One-to-One concert (evening show)

Sound quality: very good

MSG BACK IN '72

1. Mother, 2. Imagine, 3. Come Together, 4. Give Peace a Chance

THEY SAY IT'S YOUR BIRTHDAY

5. Happy Birthday John (Ringo Starr, Stephen Stils, Billy Preston), In My Life (Rod Stewart), It's Johnny's Birthday (George Harrison), Lucy in the Sky with Diamonds (Elton John), Isolation (John Lennon), Jealous Guy (Bryan Ferry), Across the Universe (David Bowie), With a Little Help from My Friends (The Beatles), Woman (John Lennon), Here Today (Paul McCartney), Empty Garden (Elton John), Imagine (John Lennon)

759. Mucho Macho

Walrus Records CD 909

Format: CD

Released: 1999

Source: various – see below

Sound quality: unknown

1. Whatever Gets You Through the Night/Lucy in the Sky with Diamonds/I Saw Her Standing There (live with Elton John, Madison Square Garden, New York), 2. Incantation (Dog Soldier with Patrick Jude, producers John Lennon and Roy Cicala), 3. Let's Spend the Night Together (Lori Burton and Patrick Jude, produced and arranged John Lennon), 4. Answer Me My Love (Lori Burton, producers John Lennon and Roy Cicala), 5. Yer Blues (*Rock and Roll Circus*), 6. Now Or Never (Spirit Choir, produced by John and Yoko), 7. Fame (David Bowie), 8. Move Over Ms L (Keith Moon), 9. Lucy in the Sky with Diamonds (Elton John with John Lennon), 10. Mucho Mungo/Mt. Elga (Harry Nilsson, producer John Lennon), 11. Love (single remix), 12. Every Man Has a Woman Who Loves Him,

13. Save the Last Dance for Me (Harry Nilsson, producer John Lennon), 14. Many Rivers to Cross (Harry Nilsson, producer John Lennon), 15. Walking on Thin Ice (Yoko Ono, producer John Lennon)

Notes: Back-and-white inserts with a collage of pictures of John on the front from his solo years.

760. MY LOVE WILL TURN YOU ON

Vigotone VT-CD-09

Format: CD

Released: 1996

Source: various

Sound quality: very good to excellent

1. Watching the Wheels (piano version), 2. Meat City (alternate mix), 3. Woman (take 9 – acoustic demo), 4. Oh, My Love (take 1 – acoustic demo with Yoko), 5. Come Together (One-to-One rehearsal), 6. Nobody Told Me (double-tracked acoustic demo), 7. Rock 'n' Roll People (piano demo), 8. Oh, Yoko/I Want You (take 1 – acoustic guitar demo with Yoko), 9. (Just Like) Starting Over (early rough mix), 10. Move Over Ms L (early guitar demo with May Pang), 11. People Get Ready/How? (piano demo), 12. One Day at a Time (early rough mix), 13. Serve Yourself (modified piano demo), 14. You Can't Catch Me (alternate mix), 15. Watching the Wheels (alternate mix), 16. God (take 2 – acoustic demo), 17. Rock 'n' Roll People (take 7 – alternate version), 18. Borrowed Time (double-tracked acoustic demo), 19. Oh, Yoko (alternate take), 20. He Said He Said, 21. He Said He Said (composing fragments), 22. She Said She Said (acoustic demo)

Notes: Tracks taken from *The Lost Lennon Tapes* radio show. Most of the tracks were previously available but appear here in the best quality and the longest versions. The rendition of I Want You is not the same song as I Want You (She's So Heavy) from the Abbey Road album.

Colour picture of John from 1974 on front cover. See also *The 1968 Demos*.

761. My Love Will Turn You On

Howdy CD 555-02

Format: CD

Source: various

Sound quality:

Notes: Re-release of Vigotone VT-CD-09

762. News of the Day

Vigotone VT-CD-02

Format: CD

Source: various – see notes

Sound quality: very good–excellent

1. How Do You Sleep? (8.06), 2. Everybody's Talking Nobody's Talking (2.19), 3. Nobody Told Me (3.15), 4. Woman Is the Nigger of the World (2.09), 5. Sally and Billy (3.22), 6. Whatever Happened To (4.38), 7. I'm Stepping Out (4.30), 8. Oh, Yoko (5.45), 9. New York City (2.09), 10. Woman (3.27), 11. Out the Blue (4.10), 12. Mother (4.38), 13. Beautiful Boy (Darling Boy) (3.59), 14. Make Love Not War (3.26), 15. I Found Out (3.58), 16. The News of the Day (from Reuters) (4.18), 17. Well (Baby Please Don't Go) (5.50)

Notes: Track 1, alternate take, Tittenhurst, June 1971. Track 2, piano with rhythm box. Track 3, rough mix. Track 4, acoustic late 1971. Track 5, piano, take 3 with rhythm box, Dakota mid–late 1970s. Track 6, acoustic Dakota, 1980. Track 7, acoustic with rhythm box, double-tracked. Bermuda mid-1980. Track 8, rough mix with count-in and reference vocal, Tittenhurst, June 1971. Track 9, acoustic. Track 10, acoustic with rhythm box, Bermuda mid-1980. Track 11, rough mix with reference vocal. Track 12, early alternate take, October 1970. Track 13, acoustic with rhythm box, double-tracked, Bermuda mid-1980, with message to Sean. Track 14, piano version, Tittenhurst, late 1970. Track 16, acoustic Dakota. Track 17, Tittenhurst, June 1971.

Colour front cover with track listing on back.

763. THE NEWSWEEK INTERVIEW

See *The Real John Lennon: The Newsweek Interview* (Black Cat BC 011)

764. NEW YORK, NEW YORK (ELTON JOHN)

T-Jay 1999

Format: CD – CDR

Time: 71.35

Source: Elton John Concert, Madison Square Garden, New York, 28 November 1974

Sound quality: unknown

1. Funeral for a Friend/Love Lies Bleeding (11.53), 2. Rocket Man (5.03), 3. Take Me to the Pilot (6.00), 4. Bennie and the Jets (5.59), 5. Grey Seal (5.27), 6. Daniel (4.06), 7. You're So Static (4.32), 8. Whatever Gets You Through the Night (4.40), 9. Lucy in the Sky with Diamonds (6.15), 10. I Saw Her Standing There (3.17), 11. Don't Let the Sun Go Down On Me (5.57), 12. Your Song (3.58), 13. The Bitch is Back (4.23)

Notes: This is an Elton John concert. John Lennon appeared as a guest on tracks 8–10.

765. *NIGHT RIDE* (JOHN LENNON AND YOKO ONO)

Flo FLO 005

Format: CD

Source: BBC Radio, *Night Ride*, 12 December 1968 with John and Yoko

Sound quality: very good

1. Intro, 2. Different from the Book (John Martyn/Harold McNair), 3. Chat, 4. You've Got to Hold On (The Deviants), 5. Chat, 6. Watch the Stars (Jacqui Mchee/John Renbourn), 7. Chat, 8. *Two Virgins* (excerpt) (John and Yoko), 9. Chat, 10. Poem – Christopher Logue, 11. Jellyroll Baker Blues (John Martyn/Harold McNair), 12. Alchemical Wedding Plug, 13. Dvorak: Slavonec Dances Op. 46 No 1 In C: Presto (Czech Philharmonic Orchestra), 14. Chat, 15. John, My Love (a cappella demo) (Yoko Ono), 16. Crying Sometime (Jacqui McShee/John Renbourn), 17. Chat, 18. Azerbaijani Music, 19. Chat, 20. Wine Women and Whiskey (Papa

George Lightfoot), 21. Chat, 22. Why? (Christopher Logue), 23. Dusty (John Martyn/Harold McNair), 24. Wabash Cannonball (Lonnie Donegan), 25. Chat, 26. Every Night When the Sun Gone In (Jacqui McShee/John Renbourn), 27. Chat, 28. Here We Go Round the Mulberry Bush (Traffic), 29. Chat, 30. Jock and Yoko (John Lennon), 31. Once Upon a Pool Table (John Lennon), 32. Hello Train (John Martyn/Harold McNair), 33. Chat, 34. Sheik of Araby (Spike Jones and His City Slickers)

Bonus Track

35. Song for John, Let's Go Flying/Snow Is Falling all the Time/Mummy's Only Looking for Her Hand in the Snow

Notes: Following the recording of *Rock and Roll Circus*, John and Yoko went to Broadcasting House in London to take part in the BBC Radio show *Night Ride* which was transmitted live from 12.05 to 2 a.m. They discussed their new album *Two Virgins* with the host John Peel. The bonus track features 'Song for John' from Queen Charlotte Hospital. First released on Aspen 7 flexi disc.

Full track listing on back.

766. NOW AND THEN

Lazy Bones Inc
Format: CD (single)
Released: 1999
Source: probably Dakota demo
Sound quality: unknown

Now and Then (5.02)

Notes: A strange release. This disc only has one track and runs for 5 minutes and 2 seconds. We have a copy of the sleeve in our files but have not seen this item. Rumours still circulate that Paul and Ringo are working on John's tapes of this song for release as a Beatles single.

The front cover has a colour picture of John wearing his New York City t-shirt.

767. OFF THE WALLS

Birthday Records BR 003

Format: CD

Released: 1998

Source: *Walls and Bridges* outtakes

Sound quality: excellent

1. Bless You (5.20), 2. Move Over Ms L (2.45), 3. Scared (4.47), 4. Surprise Surprise (Sweet Bird of Paradox) (3.00), 5. Whatever Gets You Through the Night (3.11), 6. Going Down on Love (3.51), 7. Nobody Loves You (When You're Down and Out) (5.00), 8. What You Got (7.31), 9. Old Dirt Road (5.00), 10. Steel and Glass (5.56), 11. I Saw Her Standing There (rehearsal with Elton John), 12. I Saw Her Standing There (rehearsal with Elton John), 11. I'm the Greatest (complete session with George Harrison, Ringo Starr and Klaus Voorman)

Notes: This is a reissue of the vinyl album of the same title with the addition of extra tracks.

The front and back covers are similar to the vinyl release.

768. OFF THE WALLS

Hawg Leg HL 151

Format: CD

Released: 1997

Source: *Walls and Bridges* sessions, 1974

Sound quality: unknown

1. Bless You, 2. Move Over Ms L, 3. Scared, 4. Surprise Surprise, 5. Whatever Gets You Through the Night, 6. Going Down on Love, 7. Nobody Loves You (When You're Down and Out), 8. What You Got, 9. Old Dirt Road, 10. Beef Jerky, 11. Surprise Surprise, 12. Going Down on Love, 13. Whatever Gets You Through the Night, 14. Whatever Gets You Through the Night, 15. Steel and Glass, 16. Old Dirt Road, 17. No. 9 Dream

Notes: Tracks 1–9, 15 and 16: monitor mix. Tracks 10–13: rehearsal session. Tracks 14 and 17: rough mixes.

Front cover is blue with a cartoon sketch drawing of John. The back is also blue with full track listing.

769. OH, MY LOVE

JLD 001

Format: CD

Source: see below

Sound quality: unknown

1. Don't Let Me Down (demo, 1969), 2. Oh, My Love No. 1, 3. Oh, My Love No. 2, 4. Oh, My Love No. 3, 5. Mind Games, 6. Oh, My Love No. 4, 7. I'm Stepping Out No. 1, 8. I'm Stepping Out No. 2, 9. I'm Stepping Out No. 3, 10. I'm Stepping Out No. 4, 11. I'm Stepping Out No. 1, 12. Stepping Out No. 2

Notes: Tracks 2–6: *Imagine* session. Tracks 7–10: Studio sessions. Tracks 11 and 12: acoustic demos.

The front cover has a colour picture of John holding a copy of his birth certificate. The back has a colour picture of John in front of a mixing desk plus full track listing.

770. OLDIES BUT MOULDIES

Adam V III Ltd

Format: CD (double)

Released: 1996

Source: *Rock 'n' Roll* album sessions

Sound quality: good

Disc One

1. Be-Bop-A-Lula, 2. Ain't That a Shame, 3. Stand By Me, 4. Rip It Up, 5. Angel Baby, 6. Do You Want to Dance, 7. Bring It on Home to Me, 8. Slippin' and Slidin', 9. Be My Baby, 10. Ya Ya, 11. Just Because,

12. That'll Be the Day, 13. Ain't That a Shame, 14. Bring It on Home to Me, 15. Ya Ya, 16. That'll Be the Day, 17. Do You Want to Dance, 18. Stand By Me, 19. Peggy Sue, 20. Be-Bop-A-Lula, 21. Slippin' and Slidin', 22. Guitar Jam – Whole Lotta Love, 23. Thirty Days, 24. Bo Diddley Jam – C'mon Everybody, 25. Ain't That a Shame

Disc Two

1. Be My Baby, 2. Be My Baby, 3. Be My Baby, 4. Only You, 5. Here We Go Again, 6. Ain't That a Shame, 7. Sweet Little Sixteen, 8. Bony Moronie, 9. You Can't Catch Me, 10. You Can't Catch Me, 11. Stand By Me, 12. Do You Want to Dance, 13. Rock 'n' Roll People, 14. Slippin' and Slidin', 15. Just Because, 16. Send Me Some Loving, 17. Move Over Ms L, 18. Move Over Ms L, 19. Move Over Ms L, 20. Angel Baby

Notes: The front cover has a similar picture to the *Rock 'n' Roll* album.

771. ONCE UPON A TIME/LEGEND COLLECTION

Sweet Zapple SZ-201

Format: CD

Source: various

Sound quality: unknown

1. Imagine (take 1), 2. Instant Karma (from BBC TV Top of the Pops), 3. Mother (acetate), 4. Jealous Guy (take 1), 5. Power to the People (alternate mix), 6. Cold Turkey (acetate with alternate vocal, early mix), 7. Love (tremolo guitar), 8. Love (remix), 9. Woman Is the Nigger of the World (rough mix, no strings), 10. Mind Games (early rough mix), 11. Whatever Gets You Through the Night (rough mix), 12. No. 9 Dream (monitor mix), 13. Stand By Me (monitor mix, rehearsal), 14. (Just Like) Starting Over (rough mix), 15. Woman (rough mix), 16. Beautiful Boy (rough mix), 17. Oh, My Love (alternate mix), 18. Working Class Hero (Australian mix), 19. Happy Xmas (War Is Over) (early rough mix, no strings), 20. Give Peace a Chance (rehearsal)

Notes: The front cover has a colour picture of John with a car in the background.

772. ONE AND ONE AND ONE IS THREE

(The Emotions of Our First Day Without John Lennon, Recorded 8/9 December 1980)

Phantom PH 1001 CD

Format: CD

Source: see below

Sound quality: unknown

Includes: Walking on Thin Ice (disco mix), (Just Like) Starting Over (extended version), Twist and Shout (Royal Command Performance), A Day in the Life (countdown intro), John and Yoko's 1980 Christmas Message

Interviews With: Emergency room personnel, Richard Lester, Eye witnesses on 8 December, Fan reaction

Notes: The front cover is black with a small colour picture of John and Yoko. The back has brief details of the contents. An insert shows a collage of pictures of fans following John's death.

773. ONE DAY AT A TIME

Vigotone VT-1971

Format: CD

Source: various

Sound quality: unknown

1. Imagine, 2. Yer Blues, 3. Cold Turkey No. 1, 4. Cold Turkey No. 2, 5. Love, 6. When a Boy Meets a Girl, 7. Honey Don't/Matchbox, 8. How?, 9. I'm the Greatest, 10. Oh, My Love, 11. I Don't Want to Be a Soldier Mama (I Don't Want to Die), 12. Happy Xmas (War Is Over), 13. Woman Is the Nigger of the World, 14. It's So Hard (live), 15. Mother (live), 16. Come Together (live), 17. Out the Blue, 18. You Are Here, 19. Aisumasen (I'm Sorry), 20. One Day at a Time

774. ONE-TO-ONE CONCERT

Zeus Z904001/2/3

Format: CD (triple)

Released: 2000

Source: One-to-One concert, Madison Square Garden, New York, 30 August 1972

Sound quality: poor audience tape

Disc One – Afternoon Show

Intro, Power to the People, New York City, It's So Hard, Move On Fast, Woman Is the Nigger of the World, Sisters Oh Sisters, Well, Well, Well, Born in a Prison, Instant Karma, Mother, We're All Water, Come Together, Imagine, Open Your Box, Cold Turkey, Don't Worry Kyoko, Hound Dog

Disc Two – Evening Show (Part One)

Intro, Power to the People, New York City, It's So Hard, Sisters Oh Sisters, Woman Is the Nigger of the World, Move On Fast, Well, Well, Well, Instant Karma, Mother, We're All Water

Disc Three – Evening Show (Part Two)

Born in a Prison, Come Together, Imagine, Open Your Box, Cold Turkey, Hound Dog, Give Peace a Chance, We're All Water (FM Radio broadcast)

Notes: Parts of both shows were officially released on the *Live in New York* album and video. This set presents both shows in their entirety for the first time but the downside is that the quality is poor apart from the last track which was taken from a radio broadcast.

The three discs are housed in a box with a twelve-page booklet with extensive notes and photographs from the concert.

775. ONE-TO-ONE CONCERT REHEARSALS

Chapter One CO 25124

Format: CD

Released: 1990

Source: rehearsals for the One-to-One concert, 22 August 1972

Sound quality: unknown

1. One-to-One concert – radio spot (0.39), 2. New York City (3.57), 3. It's So Hard (2.53), 4. Woman Is the Nigger of the World (5.45), 5. Instrumental (2.40), 6. Well, Well, Well (4.05), 7. Instant Karma (3.25), 8. Mother (4.24), 9. Come Together (4.04), 10. Cold Turkey (4.30), 11. Medley: Don't Be Cruel/Hound Dog (4.21), 12. Send Me Some Loving (2.32), 13. Roll Over Beethoven (2.28), 14. Medley: Whole Lotta Shakin' Goin' On/It'll Be Me (5.29), 15. On The Caribbean (3.03), 16. Well (Baby Please Don't Go) (6.00)

Notes: The front cover has a picture of John from an appearance on the BBC TV show *Top of the Pops* performing 'Instant Karma'. The back shows a picture of John from the One-to-One concert with full track listing.

776. ONE-TO-ONE REHEARSALS VOL. 1

Orange Sixteen

Format: CD

Released: 1995

Source: rehearsal with Elephant's Memory Band for the One-to-One concert

Sound quality: very good to excellent

1. Come Together (2.18), 2. Tequila (mostly instrumental) (2.36), 3. New York City (excerpt) (4.51), 4. It's So Hard (4.29), 5. Move On Fast/Back off Boogaloo (4.18), 6. Woman Is the Nigger of the World (false start) (6.15), 7. Sisters Oh Sisters (3.55), 8. Give Peace a Chance (10.25), 9. Instrumental Jam (9.07), 10. Unchained Melody/It's Only Make Believe/Whispering Bells (6.28), 11. Well, Well, Well (6.40), 12. Born in a Prison (6.19), 13. Instant Karma (4.06)

Notes: These rehearsals were held at Butterfly Studios, New York in late August 1972. Tracks 1–9 were previously released on Volume One of the triple vinyl release One and One and One is Three. Tracks 10–13 were released on Volume Two of the same set. Other tracks also available on CD releases *The Lost Lennon Rehearsal* (John Records) and *The One-to-One Concert Rehearsals* (Chapter One). The only new item on this disc is 'Whispering Bells' (part of track 10).

The sleeve shows a close up colour photo of John singing at the One-to-One concert at Madison Square Garden.

777. ONE-TO-ONE REHEARSALS VOL. 2

Orange Seventeen

Format: CD

Released: 1995

Source: rehearsal with Elephant's Memory Band for the One-to-One concert

Sound quality: very good to excellent

1. Mother/Mother (reprise) (5.12), 2. We're All Water (6.37), 3. Come Together/Come Together (reprise) (5.42), 4. Open Your Box (3.30), 5. Cold Turkey (10.44), 6. Instrumental Jam (5.48), 7. Instrumental Jam (9.12), 8. We're All Water (6.25), 9. Roll Over Beethoven (3.22), 10. Give Peace a Chance (7.42), 11. Tequila (3.52), 12. Jam (Bunny Bop) (5.13)

Notes: Rehearsals with Elephant's Memory Band at Butterfly Studios, New York in late August 1972 for the One-to-One concert. Tracks 1–4 previously available on Volume Two of the vinyl three-disc set *One and One and One is Three*. Tracks 5–10 on Volume Three of the same set. Tracks 11 and 12 also available on the vinyl release *Goodnight, Vienna*. Various tracks also available on CDs including *The Lost Lennon Rehearsal* (John Records) and the *One-to-One Rehearsals* (Chapter One).

Sleeve features colour photo of John and Yoko at the One-to-One concert at Madison Square Garden.

778. ON THE CANNES

Black Cat BC 085

Format: CD

Source: various – see below

Sound quality: unknown

'God Save Us' Sessions, April–June 1971

1. Acoustic demo, 2. Reference vocal No. 1, 3. Reference vocal No. 2, 4. Promotional Ad, 5. Commercial version

Radio Monte Carlo With Kenny Everett, 25 April 1971

6. Home studios, 7. The man who broke the bank, 8. A jolly LP, 9. On 'Mother', 10. On 'Hold On John', 11. Favourite tracks, 13. More on home studios, 14. A startling fact, 15. Being liked, 16. Tittenhurst Park, 17. Ringo and George, 18. Violence, 19. Pain and agony, 20. Plugging Plastic Ono Band, 21. On love and Paul, 22. Preferring his own work, 23. Childhood memories, 24. Yoko's singing

Cannes France Interview, 15 May 1971

25. Introduction, 26. Foreign press, 27. Answering the same questions, 28. Norwegian Wood, 29. The media, 30. Help, 31. Making money, 32. Happiness is a Warm Gun, 33. Being isolated, 34. Give Peace a Chance, 35. Politics, 36. Working class hero, 37. In my life, 38. Being yourself, 39. Primal therapy, 40. Imagine, 41. Closing

779. OUT OF THE BLUE

Toasted Condor 1968

Format: CD

Released: 1989

Source: various

Sound quality: excellent

1. Julia, 2. Out the Blue, 3. Watching the Wheels, 4. Jealous Guy, 5. Rock Island Line, 6. Here We Go Again, 7. Only You, 8. Cold Turkey, 9. Maybe Baby, 10. Rave On, 11. Move Over Ms L, 12. Send Me Some Loving, 13. It's So Hard, 14. Happy Xmas (War Is Over), 15. Nobody Told Me, 16. I Found Out, 17. Surprise Surprise (Sweet Bird of Paradox), 18. Imagine, 19. Sexy Sadie, 20. Mind Games, 21. Woman, 22. God Save Us, 23. Strawberry Fields Forever

Notes: 'Julia', 'Watching the Wheels', 'Here We Go Again', 'Cold Turkey', 'Send Me Some Loving', 'Happy Xmas', 'Surprise Surprise' and 'God Save Us' are acoustic demos. 'Out the Blue' is an early take. 'Jealous Guy', 'It's So Hard', 'Nobody Told Me', 'Imagine', 'Mind Games' and 'Woman' are alternate takes. 'Rock Island Line' is an electric version. 'Only You' is John's version without spoken interlude. 'Maybe Baby' and 'Rave On' are from *Clock*. 'Move Over Ms L' is an early run through. 'I Found Out' is a basic take. 'Sexy Sadie' is a Kinfauns demo.

Front cover has colour picture of John on a bed with a guitar. The back shows a colour picture of John on *Top of the Pops* performing 'Instant Karma' (this is a different picture to the one on *One-to-One Concert Rehearsals*).

780. OVER WALLS UNDER BRIDGES

No Manufacturer Listed

Format: CD

Released: 1996

Time: 72.38

Source: *Walls and Bridges* home demos and studio recordings

Sound quality: very good to excellent

1. *Walls and Bridges* radio spot (1.02), 2. Whatever Gets You Through the Night (3.29), 3. Steel and Glass (4.14), 4. Going Down on Love (3.58), 5. Beef Jerky (3.15), 6. Only You (3.13), 7. Surprise Surprise (2.34), 8. No. 9 Dream (4.40), 9. Old Dirt Road (4.52), 10. Bless You (5.20), 11. Goodnight, Vienna (2.57), 12. Move Over Ms L (1.50), 13. What You Got (3.17), 14. Going Down on Love (4.07), 15. Surprise Surprise (3.12), 16. Whatever Gets You Through the Night (2.52), 17. No. 9 Dream (2.08), 18. Steel and Glass (1.45), 19. Mucho Mungo (3.28), 20. Bless You (3.44), 21. Whatever Gets You Through the Night (3.48), 22. *Walls and Bridges* track rundown

Notes: A nice collection of *Walls and Bridges* home demos and studio recordings. Track 1 is Ringo Starr promoting the album – 'Hope you do the same for me when mine comes out'. Tracks 2–11 are rehearsals, rough mixes and outtakes. Tracks 6 and 11, demos for Ringo Starr. Track 10 is take 1. Tracks 12–19, various demos. Track 19, a demo for Harry Nilsson. Track 20, take 3. Track 22, Lennon running through the track list of his new album – 'On "Ya Ya" it's my five-year-old, Julian, playing the drums'. Tracks are taken from *The Lost Lennon Tapes* radio series.

Sleeve features a full colour alternate photo from the *Listen To This...* promo pack for *Walls and Bridges*. The front cover has a colour picture of John from 1974.

781. PEACE OFF

Vigorous VR-06

Format: CD

Source: various

Sound quality: unknown

1. She Said She Said (1.58), 2. Hair Peace (0.20), 3. Give Peace a Chance (6.08), 4. Laugh/Whisper (EMI session) (2.27), 5. Instant Karma No. 1 (longer) (3.37), 6. Instant Karma No. 2 (knitting take) (2.06), 7. Working Class Hero (6.39), 8. This Fly (1.45), 9. Oh, My Love (rehearsal) (7.13), 10. Mind Games/Oh, My Love (rehearsal) (4.56), 11. He's Got the Whole World/Tandoori Chicken/Attica State (3.26), 12. David Frost Intro/New York City (4.47), 13. Bring on the Lucie (Freeda People) (0.15), 14. Imagine (live) (3.14), 15. Too Many People/Back Seat of My Car (ad lib) (0.24), 16. Woman Is the Nigger of the World (demo) (2.13), 17. Interview with Dick Cavett (3.18), 18. Woman Is the Nigger of the World (live) (6.19), 19. Woman Is the Nigger of the World (ad lib/interview) (1.05), 20. Interview with Geraldo/Magic Mirror (ad lib) (3.19), 21. Flipside interview (0.51), 22. Mind Games (promo outtake) (1.01), 23. Interview/Lady Marmalade (1.40), 24. We'll Meet Again (ad lib) (0.20), 25. Dear Yoko No. 1 (demo) (2.42), 26. Dear Yoko No. 2 (demo) (2.58), 27. John and Sean (dialogue) (0.52), 28. The Beatles – The End (bonus track) (1.58)

Notes: The front cover has a brown tinged picture of John playing a guitar with the track listing on the back. Included in the inserts is a rare photograph of John taken in the late 1940s which sold at auction for £2,200. We had not seen this picture until it appeared with this set.

782. PHASING PHUN WITH YOUR CLOTHES ON

Two Boys Limited TBL-007

Format: CD

Source: various

Sound quality: unknown

1. Instant Karma (1970) ((3.23), 2. I Found Out (1970) (3.37), 3. Working Class Hero (1970) (3.50), 4. Power to the People (1971) (3.22), 5. Imagine (1971) (3.04), 6. Give Me Some Truth (1971) (3.16), 7. Jealous Guy (1971) (4.14), 8. How? (1971) (3.45), 9. John Sinclair (1972) (3.28), 10. Mind Games (1973) (4.14), 11. Whatever Gets You Through the Night (1974) (3.28), 12. No. 9 Dream (1974) (4.47), 13. (Just Like) Starting Over (1980) (3.56), 14. Beautiful Boy (Darling Boy) (1980) (4.04), 15. Watching the Wheels (1980) (3.59), 16. Woman (1980) (3.31), 17. I'm Stepping Out (1983) (4.06), 18. I Don't Wanna Face It (1983) (3.21), 19. Nobody Told Me (1983) (3.34), 20. Grow Old with Me (1983) (3.09), 21. Happy Xmas (War Is Over) (1971) (3.34)

Notes: The front and back covers are a colourful mauve with a colour picture of John inset on the front with the track listing on the back.

783. PILL

Missing In Action MIA Act 12

Format: CD

Source: various outtakes

Sound quality: very good

1. Imagine (acoustic) (2.47), 2. Child of Nature (2.33), 3. Let's Twist Again (with David Bowie 1975) (3.03), 4. One of the Boys (unreleased) (3,05), 5. Mind Games (3.44), 6. Yer Blues (instrumental) (1.20), 7. Out the Blue (no choir), (3.12), 8. She Was A Friend of Dorothy (unreleased) (2.36), 9. Girls and Boys (2.19), 10. Mucho Mungo (solo) (2.04), 11. Cold Turkey (4.46), 12. I Found Out (uncensored solo version) (3.19), 13. No. 9 Dream (1.21), 14. Instant Karma (3.06), 15. Dear Yoko (3,31), 16. I'm Stepping Out (4.23), 17. Pill (1.39), 18. Real Love (3.50)

Notes: The front insert is claret with a black-and-white picture of John on the front with a colour picture on the back. The front insert has the full track listing with details on the inside.

784. PILL
Missing In Action Never End
Format: CD
Source: various outtakes
Sound quality: very good

Notes: Same track listing as disc above, *Pill* (Missing In Action MIA Act 12).

785. PLASTIC ONO BAND – HOME AND STUDIO
Green Grape
Format: CD (double)
Source: various outtakes
Sound quality: very good

Notes: see *1970 Plastic Ono Band – Home and Studio*

786. PLASTIC ONO BAND – LIVE
DV More Record Productions CDDV 5516
Format: CD
Released: 1991
Source: live performances
Sound quality: unknown

1. Imagine (live in New York, November 1971), 2. Give Peace a Chance (live in Toronto, September 1969), 3. Cold Turkey (live in Toronto), 4. John Sinclair (live in Ann Arbor), 5. Yer Blues (live in Toronto), 6. Dizzy Miss Lizzie (live in Toronto), 7. Blue Suede Shoes (live in Toronto), 8. The Luck of the Irish (live in Ann Arbor), 9. Attica State (live in Ann Arbor), 10. Money (That's What I Want) (live in Toronto)

Notes: Sleeve says, Made In Italy

787. PLEASE HANG UP AND TRY AGAIN: THE ROCK 'N' ROLL CONFERENCE CALL
Black Cat BC 110
Format: CD

Source: The Rock 'n' Roll Conference Call, 21 February 1975, WRRM FM Cincinnati, Oh and
KSHE FM Crestwood, MO
Sound quality: unknown

Roll Call, The First Question, The *Rock 'n' Roll* LP, Roots, Déjà Vu, The LP Cover, Beatle Reunions, Immigration, Wiretapping, Living In The USA, Touring and More Reunion Questions, The Next LP, Plastic Ono Band, Trends In Music, The Stand By Me Single, The Mellotron, Sgt. Pepper Live, Producing Other Artists, The Rock 'n' Roll Musicians, Paul In New Orleans, Musical Direction, Back With Yoko, Vocal Insecurities, Unreleased Beatles Material, Disco, Movie Roles, Write To Your Congressmen, The Bust, Red Tape, A Promo Spot, More Unreleased Beatles Tracks, Charity Work and TV, Your Call Didn't Go Through, Thank You and Goodbyes

788. PLOP PLOP FIZZ FIZZ
Unknown
Format: CD
Source: various
Sound quality: unknown

1. Mother, 2. Imagine, 3. Come Together, 4. Cold Turkey, 5. Hound Dog, 6, Slippin' and Slidin', 7. Imagine, 8, Whatever Gets You Through the Night, 9. Move Over Ms L

Notes: Tracks 1–5 are probably from the One-to-One concert. The front cover has one of John's cartoons showing him sitting at a piano.

789. PRECIOUS AND RARE (VOL. 1)
Banana BAN-020-A
Format: CD
Source: various outtakes
Sound quality: good to very good (some tracks excellent)

1. Watching the Wheels (acoustic) (3.01), 2. Corrina Corrina (electric) (1.44), 3. Beautiful Boy (acoustic and congas), 4. Dear Yoko (No. 1

acoustic) (1.00), 5. Dear Yoko (No. 2 acoustic) (4.23), 6. Borrowed Time (acoustic) (5.01), 7. Move Over Ms L (No. 1 acoustic) (1.34), 8. Move Over Ms L (No. 2 acoustic) (1.54), 9. Here We Go Again (acoustic) (3.01), 10. Maybe Baby (acoustic) (1.55), 11. Rave On (acoustic) (1.16), 12. Whatever Gets You Through the Night (5.30), 13. Woman (acoustic and rhythm box), 14. God Save Us (acoustic and congas) (1.58), 15. I Know (I Know) (acoustic) (3.16), 16. (Just Like) Starting Over (acoustic and rhythm box) (4.18)

Notes: Australian release.

790. PRECIOUS AND RARE (VOL. 2)
Banana BAN-020-B

Format: CD

Source: various outtakes

Sound quality: very good to excellent

1. Meat City, 2. Send Me Some Loving, 3. Give Peace a Chance, 4. God, 5. Real Love, 6. I'm Losing You, 7. I Found Out, 8. Rock Island Line, 9. (Just Like) Starting Over, 10. Cold Turkey, 11. Tight A$, 12. Julia, 13. Happy Xmas (War Is Over), 14. Watching the Wheels, 15. Many Rivers to Cross

791. PRECIOUS AND RARE (VOL. 3)
Banana BAN-020-C

Format: CD

Source: various outtakes

Sound quality: very good to excellent

1. Cooking (in the Kitchen of Love) (piano) (2.29), 2. Nobody Told Me (piano) (2.19), 3. Woman Is the Nigger of the World (acoustic) (2.14), 4. I'm Stepping Out (acoustic with rhythm box) (4.33), 5. New York City (acoustic) (2.13), 6. Woman (acoustic with rhythm box) (3.31), 7. Beautiful Boy (acoustic) (4.05), 8. Mind Games (piano) (3.32), 9. I Found Out (acoustic) (4.06), 10. Watching the Wheels (piano) (3.21), 11. Woman (take 9 acoustic) (3.58), 12. Nobody Told Me (3.19),

13. Rock 'n' Roll People (piano) (3.32), 14. Oh, Yoko (acoustic with Yoko) (4.40)

792. PRECIOUS AND RARE (VOL. 4)
Banana BAN-020-D
Format: CD
Source: various outtakes
Sound quality: very good. Some excellent. Some poor

1. People Get Ready (piano)/How? (3.02), 2. God (take 2 acoustic) (3.45), 3. Borrowed Time (acoustic) (3.54), 4. She Said She Said (excerpts) (1.06), 5. She Said She Said (acoustic) (0.59), 6. She Said She Said (acoustic) (1.00), 7. (Just Like) Starting Over (acoustic and rhythm box) (2.18), 8. Cooking (in the Kitchen of Love) (piano) (2.42), 9. Only the Lonely (acoustic) (1.02), 10. Mucho Mungo (take 2 acoustic) (3.03), 11. No. 9 Dream (take 2 acoustic) (3.11), 12. I'm Stepping Out (piano) (3.30), 13. Well, Well, Well (acoustic) (1.15), 14. Watching the Wheels (3.02), 15. San Francisco Bay Blues (acoustic) (0.45), 16. Look at Me (acoustic 1968), 17. Cold Turkey (acoustic) (3.44), 18. Maggie Mae (acoustic) (0.28), 19. Julia (acoustic instrumental)

793. PRIMAL SCREAM – THE STUDIO SESSIONS
JL. 70
Format: CD (digipack)
Released: 2008
Time: 79.59
Source: *Plastic Ono Band* album sessions
Sound quality: excellent

1. Mother (early take – guitar based arrangement), 2. Mother (alternate mix of the released version – with additional rhythm guitar and different primal screams at the end), 3. Hold On John (early run through), 4. Hold On John (early take), 5. Hold On John (instrumental take), 6. I Found Out ((alternate mix with additional bongo player), 7. Working Class Hero (folky guitar picking style), 8. Isolation (early take), 9. Remember (John leads Klaus Voorman and Ringo through a lengthy rehearsal at a faster pace),

10. Remember (almost the finished article. John did not know how to finish the song – he solved the problem by adding a line about Guy Fawkes and added an explosion. A further noise can be heard on this track which is believed to be Yoko playing a mouth organ in order to enhance the rhythm track. This idea was later abandoned), 11. Love (John singing and strumming the guitar), 12. Love (John using folksy picking guitar style), 13. Love (with added guitar piano playing by Phil Spector), 14. Love (piano intro), 15. Love (loose rehearsal with whole band), 16. Well, Well, Well (rough mix), 17. Look at Me (early take), 18. God (early take with John playing guitar with bass and drums), 19. My Mummy's Dead (complete version), 20. Rock 'n' Roll Jam: That's Alright Mama/Glad All Over/Honey Don't/Don't Be Cruel/Hound Dog/Matchbox/You're So Square

Notes: Black-and-white sleeve.

794. RARE DEMOS AND OUTTAKES – ULTRA RARE DEMOS AND LOST TRACKS: VOL. 1

Unknown

Format: CD

Source: various

Sound quality: unknown

1. Child of Nature (demo), 2. Real Life (demo), 3. India (demo), 4. It's Not Too Bad, 5. I'm In Love, 6. Free as a Bird (demo), 7. She Can Talk to Me, 8. I Am the Walrus, 9. House of The Rising Sun, 10. Revolution (demo), 11. Bad To Me, 12. Hide Your Love Away (outtake)

Notes: Track 1, this song evolved into 'Jealous Guy' and was written during The Beatles' visit to Rishikesh, India. Track 2 is the original acoustic demo. Track 3 was also written during John's stay with the Maharishi. Track 4 is the original demo for 'Strawberry Fields Forever' with John on acoustic guitar. Track 5, early demo of a song John wrote for *The Fourmost*. Track 6 is the original piano demo. Track 7 is the original demo for 'Hey Bulldog'. Track 8 is a Beatles studio outtake with John on keyboards and no orchestra. Track 9 is a Beatles outtake. Track 10 is an acoustic demo. Track 11 is an early Beatles demo. Track 12 is a studio outtake.

795. RARE DEMOS AND OUTTAKES – ULTRA RARE DEMOS AND LOST TRACKS: VOL. 2

Unknown

Format: CD

Source: various

Sound quality: unknown

1. Come Together (The Beatles), 2. Let's Twist Again (with David Bowie), 3. Dig It (long version), 4. Lady Marmalade, 5. Norwegian Wood (The Beatles), 6. Mucho Mungo, 7. Lucy from Littletown (poem), 8. Mellotron Music, 9. I Lost My Little Girl (The Beatles), 10. Tennessee, 11. I Saw Her Standing There, 12. The Luck of the Irish, 13. Cry Baby Cry, 14. God (demo), 15. Julia, 16. Everyone Had a Hard Year, 17. Matchbox (The Beatles), 18. Too Many Cooks, 19. It's Only Love

Notes: Track 1, alternate take. Track 2 is with David Bowie in 1974. Track 4 is from a French television interview. Track 5, outtake with false starts. Track 7 is from *A Spaniard in the Works*. Track 9 is a studio demo. Track 11 is live with Elton John. Track 13, original acoustic demo. Track 14 is an original acoustic demo, take 3. Track 15 is a home demo. Track 16 is the original demo version. Track 17 is The Beatles live in Hamburg. Track 18 is Mick Jagger with John on the mixing desk and back vocals. Track 19 is take 2.

796. RAVE ON

Toasted Record Works TRW 1941

Format: CD

Source: various

Sound quality: very good to excellent

1. Cold Turkey (demo), 2. Cold Turkey (alternate take), 3. I'm the Greatest (demo), 4. Make Love Not War (demo), 5. I Promise (demo), 6. Help (piano run through), 7. Love (alternate take), 8. God (demo fragment), 9. Sally and Billy (demo), 10. Power to the People (outtake), 11. Power to the People (alternate take), 12. God Save Us (demo), 13. God Save Us (studio demo from acetates), 14. I'm the Greatest

(studio demo), 15. Imagine (take 1), 16. Crippled Inside (alternate take), 17. Jealous Guy (alternate take), 18. It's So Hard (raw version), 19. How Do You Sleep? (extended alternate take), 20. Send Me Some Loving, 21. Maybe Baby, 22. Rave On, 23 Not Fade Away, 24. Heartbeat/Peggy Sue Got Married, 25. Peggy Sue, 26. New York City, 27. The Luck of the Irish (demo), 28. Attica State, 29. The Luck of the Irish, 30. John Sinclair

Notes: Tracks 20–26 were recorded at St. Regis Hotel, New York. Tracks 27–30 are the John Sinclair Benefit Concert. This set was previously released as a double vinyl album.

Black-and-white front and back covers with picture of John on the front and picture of John and Yoko on the back with track listing.

797. REAL LOVE

Real Pig RP 01

Format: CD

Source: various

Sound quality: good to very good

1. Girls and Boys (early version of 'Real Love') (2.48), 2. Julia (very early acoustic demo) (3.02), 3. Real Life (piano demo, take 1, Dakota, 1977) (4.53), 4. Real Life (piano demo, take 2 1977) (3.19), 5. Real Love (take 1, Dakota piano demo) (4.10). 6. Girls and Boys (early 'Real Love' demo) (2.22), 7. Real Love (take 5 acoustic demo) (2.47), 8. Real Love (take 6 acoustic demo) (1.33), 9. Free as a Bird (piano demo, take 1) (3.29), 10. Free as a Bird (piano demo, take 3) (2.42), 11. Now and Then (alternate take) (5.06), 12. Grow Old with Me (alternate mix with double-tracked vocals) (3.06), 13. Dear Yoko (alternate mix), 14. Oh, Yoko (outtake take 9) (5.47), 15. Gone from This Place (from 1980) (3.26), 16. You Saved My Soul (With Your True Love) (1.36), 17. Real Love (take 4 acoustic demo) (4.04), 18. Julia (take 1 acoustic demo) (3.23), 19. Mother (outtake) (3.23), 20. My Mummy's Dead (long solo verse) (1.15), 21. Grow Old with Me (3.41), 22. Dear John (from 1980) (4.33), 23. Real Love (acoustic demo) (1.11)

798. REAL LOVE

Real Pig RP 001
Format: CD
Source: rare *Anthology* related tracks and 1970s rarities
Sound quality: unknown

Rare Anthology Related Tracks

1. Free as a Bird (extended video version), 2. Free as a Bird (piano demo, take 1), 3. Free as a Bird (piano demo, take 3), 4. Real Love (1995 Beatles session outtake), 5. Real Love (aka Baby Make Love to You), 6. Real Love (aka That's the Way the World It), 7. Real Love (aka Real Life/I'm Stepping Out), 8. Real Love (aka Boys and Girls), 9. Real Love (piano demo, take 1), 10. Grow Old with Me (unused piano and rhythm ace demo), 11. Now and Then (elusive abandoned piano demo), 12. Blue Moon of Kentucky (1996 sessions)

1970s Rarities

13–23. I'm the Greatest (takes 1–11), 24. It Don't Come Easy (Harrison vocal), 25. Six O'clock (1973 session with Paul and Linda), 26. Only You (Lennon guide vocal demo), 27. Thanks and Bless You John

Notes: Sleeve says, Limited Edition of 500. Same title and catalogue number as entry above.

THE REAL COMPLETE LOST LENNON TAPES (ANGRY DOG)

Notes: Highlights from the radio series *The Lost Lennon Tapes* were released on sets released by Bag Records (vinyl and compact disc), Walrus Records and Living Legend. We understand that Angry Dog intended to release a set of CDs comprising the complete shows, less the advertisement breaks. We know for certain that ten volumes were released but there are almost certainly more. We have traced the track listings for the first four volumes (including the *Premiere Show*) and catalogue numbers for a further six volumes. This information is shown below. As far as subsequent releases are concerned, we presume that the track listings are, in essence, the same as the two sets detailed in

Part Three. The sound quality on the Angry Dog set is excellent. The artwork on the discs we know exist are identical with a pink cover and John's cartoon showing him at a piano. The back has full track listing. See also *Lost Lennon Tapes* and *The Lost Lennon Tapes* Story in Part Three.

799. THE REAL COMPLETE LOST LENNON TAPES (PREMIERE SHOW)

Angry Dog AD 2005/6

Format: CD (double)

Source: Westwood One Radio, 18 January 1988

Sound quality: excellent

Disc One

1. Introduction, 2. Elliot Mintz/Yoko Ono/Quarrymen, 3. Early 1962 interview/Love Me Do, 4. About 'Twist and Shout'/Twist and Shout, 5. Sweet Little Sixteen (BBC Radio), 6. Lost Lennon promo Westwood One, 7. Beatlemania/A Hard Day's Night/touring, 8. Tomorrow Never Knows, 9. More popular than Jesus Christ, 10. Nowhere Man, 11. Approaching song writing/Lucy in the Sky with Diamonds, 12. Drugs and LSD, 13. Basement Dakota storage tapes, 14. Acoustic demo – Strawberry Fields Forever, 15. Strawberry Fields Forever, 16. Help, 17. The day John met Yoko, 18. Soulmates/bed-in/Give Peace a Chance, 19. Elliot Mintz first interview with John 1971, 20. Instant Karma, 21. Power to the People, 22. Imagine, 23. Los Angeles April 1973/interview, 24. How Do You Sleep?/Paulie, 25. Mind Games/Relationship with Yoko

Disc Two

1. Woman Is the Nigger of the World, 2. The lost weekend, 3. Whatever Gets You Through the Night/And about being famous, 4. Stand By Me/Beatles reunion, 5. Beatles reunion/About *Double Fantasy*, 6. Watching the Wheels – piano demo/acoustic demo, 7. Watching the Wheels, 8. Jamming Be-Bop-a-Lula, 9. About Starting Over/Starting Over, 10. I'm Losing You – guitar demo – rehearsing, 11. I'm Losing You, 12. Take 1, Beautiful Boy/Playing tape to the band, 13. Beautiful Boy, 14. About woman, 15. Woman, 16. Clean-up Time – rehearsing,

17. Clean-up Time, 18. Lennon on Lennon – Frost BBC interview, 19. Five years with Andy Peebles – highlights, 20. What will come in our journey through *The Lost Lennon Tapes*/credits

800. THE REAL COMPLETE LOST LENNON TAPES (PART 1)
Angry Dog AD 2007
Format: CD
Source: Westwood One Radio, 25 January 1988
Sound quality: excellent

1. Introduction, 2. Yoko Ono, 3. About 'Instant Karma', 4. Instant Karma rehearsal August 1972, 5. Instant Karma (One-to-One concert), 6. About 'Instant Karma', 7. About the lost weekend, 8. John about Troubadour nightclub incident, 9. Mucho Mungo (Harry Nilsson), 10. Mucho Mungo (demo, late 1975), 11. Lost Lennon promo Westwood One, 12. Lennon remembers/*Rolling Stone* mag. 13. Jan Werner interview highlights, 14. Working Class Hero, 15. Ballad of John and Yoko, 16. Lost Lennon promo Westwood One, 17. About rooftop concert, January 30 1969, 18. Don't Let Me Down, 19. About 'One After 909', 20. One After 909, 1960 version, 21. One After 909, 22. About the Beatles breaking up, 23. Get Back, 24. Lost Lennon promo Westwood One, 25. I Found Out, 26. About the *Mother* album, 27. I found out how to cry, 28. Well, Well, Well, 29. John about his father, 30. Isolation (partly)/My Mummy's Dead, 31. God (demo version flowing into final verses), 32. Outro/Credits

801. THE REAL COMPLETE LOST LENNON TAPES (PART 2)
Angry Dog AD 2008
Format: CD
Source: Westwood One Radio, 1 February 1988
Sound quality: excellent

1. Introduction, 2. British invasion, 3. I Want to Hold Your Hand, 4. Sean's birth, 5. Sean about the Beatles and John, 6. Life Begins at Forty (demo version), 7. Intro Jan Werner interview, about *Plastic Ono Band* LP, 8. Mother, 9. John's side of the story, 10. I Am the Walrus, 11. About Yoko's divorce/Allan Klein/cutting hair for peace/Live Peace in Toronto,

12. Blue Suede Shoes (partially)/John about Live Peace in Toronto, 13. Cold Turkey (Live Peace in Toronto), 14. Give Peace a Chance (Live Peace in Toronto), 15. About 'Power to the People', 16. Power to the People (rough mix), 17. Lost Lennon promo Westwood One, 18. About the Dakota building and raising cows, 19. Clean-up Time (piano home demo), 20. About the *Two Virgins* LP and *Grapefruit*, 21. Imagine (live at the Apollo Theatre), 22. About Inspiration Image/Outro, 23. Credits

802. THE REAL COMPLETE LOST LENNON TAPES (PART 3)
Angry Dog AD 2009
Format: CD
Source: Westwood One Radio, 8 February 1988
Sound quality: excellent

1. Intro/about first album sessions, 2. Please Please Me (BBC), 3. About Ed Sullivan/All My Loving (*Ed Sullivan Show*), 4. She Loves You (*Ed Sullivan Show*), 5. About the Beatles and Tony Sheridan, 6. John about Hamburg, 7. Twist and Shout (live, Hamburg), 8. Lost Lennon promo Westwood One, 9. John interviews Sean Ono Lennon, 10. Sean about John being a house husband, 11. Beautiful Boy (acoustic demo), 12. Sean about Beautiful Boy, 13. Girls and Boys (acoustic guitar demo), 14. About Rock 'n' Roll, 15. Be-Bop-A-Lula, 16. John about Phil Spector/May Pang about *Rock 'n' Roll* session, 17. John about sessions collapsing into crazy mania, 18. Sean about trip to Japan/favourite Beatles song, 19. With a Little Help from My Friends, 20. Sean about 'Woman', 21. Woman (acoustic demo version), 22. Sean about relationship with Julian Lennon, 23. Valotte (Julian Lennon), 24. Outro/Credits

803. THE REAL COMPLETE LOST LENNON TAPES (PART 4)
Angry Dog AD 2010
Format: CD
Source: Westwood One Radio, 15 February 1988
Sound quality: excellent

Notes: Track details unknown but see details of this show in Part Three.

804. THE REAL COMPLETE LOST LENNON TAPES (PART 5)
Angry Dog AD 2011

Format: CD

Source: Westwood One Radio, 22 February 1988

Sound quality: excellent

Notes: Track details unknown but see details of this show in Part Three.

805. THE REAL COMPLETE LOST LENNON TAPES (PART 6)
Angry Dog AD 2012

Format: CD

Source: Westwood One Radio, 29 February 1988

Sound quality: excellent

Notes: Track details unknown but see details of this show in Part Three.

806. THE REAL COMPLETE LOST LENNON TAPES (PART 7)
Angry Dog AD 2013

Format: CD

Source: Westwood One Radio, 7 March 1988

Sound quality: excellent

Notes: Track details unknown but see details of this show in Part Three.

807. THE REAL COMPLETE LOST LENNON TAPES (PART 8)
Angry Dog AD 2014

Format: CD

Source: Westwood One Radio, 14 March 1988

Sound quality: excellent

Notes: Track details unknown but see details of this show in Part Three.

808. THE REAL COMPLETE LOST LENNON TAPES (PART 9)
Angry Dog AD 2016

Format: CD

Source: Westwood One Radio, 21 March 1988
Sound quality: excellent

Notes: Track details unknown but see details of this show in Part Three.

809. THE REAL JOHN LENNON: THE NEWSWEEK INTERVIEW
Black Cat BC 011
Format: CD
Source: WNEW FM, New York City, 25 September 1980; Dennis Elsas with Barbara Granstark
Sound quality: unknown

1. To what do I owe this honour?, 2. It's me, 3. Oh, Yoko, 4. What was he doing?, 5. Picasso didn't go to museums, 6. Whatever Gets You Through the Night, 7. A funny comment, 8. Picasso didn't go to museums, 9. Clearing out the channel, 10. Quack quack quack, 11. Good Morning, Good Morning, 12. The Ballad of John and Yoko, 13. Letting it all hang out, 14. A lot of things worked, 15. All You Need Is Love, 16. Love, 17. Scenes from a marriage, 18. Elvis Beatle, 19. Remember, 20. There's an edge to it, 21. Do you mind ringing first?, 22. Instant Karma, 23. Does he need the magic?, 24. I've chosen to go with Yoko Ono, 25. The end, 26. Starting Over premiere, WNEW FM, October 17, 1980: Starting Over

Notes: Black-and-white picture of John and Yoko on the front with full track listing on the back.

810. REMEMBER LENNON
Yellow Cat Records YC 2004
Format: CD
Source: various – see below
Sound quality: unknown

Outtakes – John Lennon/Plastic Ono Band, September/October 1970
1. Love (acoustic guitar/piano, take 31) (6.22), 2. Love (acoustic guitar/piano, take 32) (3.04), 3. Remember (take unknown) (9.46), 4. Remember (take unknown) (5.43)

Outtakes – *Sometime in New York City*, February/March 1972

5. New York City (take unknown) (5.32), 6. New York City (take unknown) (5.15)

Outtakes – March 1973

7. I'm the Greatest (take unknown) (5.12), 8. I'm the Greatest (take unknown) (5.50), 9. I'm the Greatest (take unknown) (3.05), 10. I'm the Greatest (take unknown) (3.57)

Yoko Ono, B-Side of 'Cold Turkey', October 1969

11. Don't Worry Kyoko (extended studio version) (9.08)

811. REMEMBER NEW YORK (JOHN LENNON/YOKO ONO)

His Masters Choice HMC 003
Format: CD (double) with book
Released: 2007
Source: 'New York City' outtakes and 'Remember' outtake
Sound quality: excellent

Disc One

1. New York City (take unknown) (8.39), 2. New York City (take unknown) (3.58), 3. New York City (take unknown) (1.13), 4. New York City (take unknown) (2.30), 5. New York City (take unknown) (1.06), 6. New York City (take unknown) (4.15), 7. New York City (take unknown) (4.48), 8. New York City (take unknown) (1.55), 9. New York City (take unknown) (4.43), 10. New York City (take unknown) (3.52), 11. New York City (take unknown) (4.29), 12. New York City (take unknown) (2.36), 13. New York City (take unknown) (3.28), 14. New York City (take unknown) (0.46), 15. New York City (take unknown) (3.04), 16. 'Let's Ride' (improvisation) (0.43)

Disc Two

1. Remember (takes unknown) (4.00), 2. Remember (takes unknown) (9.03), 3. Remember (takes unknown) (9.28), 4. Remember (takes unknown) (3.30), 5. Remember (takes unknown) (4.33), 6. Remember (takes unknown) (8.49), 7. Remember (takes unknown) (2.15),

8. Remember (takes unknown) (5.15), 9. Remember (take unknown) (3.20)

Notes: This was the third release by a new label, His Masters Choice – the first being *The Beatles and The Great Concert At Shea!* (details will be shown in *The Beatles Bootleg Discography*). This set features outtakes of the 'New York City' track from the *Sometime in New York City* album and outtakes of 'Remember' from the *Plastic Ono Band* album. It comes packaged as a hardback book with twenty pages of text and photographs and includes reproduction of the lyrics of 'New York City' and 'Remember'. Copies of the set have since become available in a slimline DVD case but without the book. Owning the book is not essential but it is a nice item to have. Two further John Lennon releases in a similar format are available: *Come On Listen To Me* (HMC 004) and *It's Gonna Be Alright* (HMC 002).

812. REMINISCING

Black Cat BC 098

Format: CD

Source: *The Scott Muni Show*, WNEW FM 102.7, New York, 13 February 1975

Sound quality: unknown

1. Oldies but mouldies, 2. Be-Bop-A-Lula, 3. Meeting Paul, Gene, Richard and Roy; Variations of the originals, 4. Stand By Me, 5. Rip It Up/Ready Teddy, 6. Korvettes ad, Woman under the influence ad, 7. You Can't Catch Me, 8. Chuck and Fats, 9. Ain't That a Shame, 10. The LP cover, Capital theatre ad No. 1, a reggae feel, 11. Do You Want to Dance, 12. Sweet Little Sixteen, 13. More on Chuck and Richard, 14. Slippin' and Slidin', 15. A cosmic joke, 16. Peggy Sue, 17. One of the tragedies, 18. Bring It on Home to Me/Send Me Some Loving, 19. Doing it for real/black roots/the Spector sessions/Capital theatre ad No. 2, 20. Bony Moronie, 21. Disguises/rock dreams/snow/picking songs/Lee Dorsey, 22. Ya Ya, 23. A weird version on TV/the separation was a failure/a dedication, 24. Just Because, 25. One last plug/good wishes and thank yous

Notes: Sleeve says:

> 'There were so many great artists and songs I would have loved to have included, I could go on forever. Elvis Presley, Eddie Cochrane, Carl Perkins, Jerry Lee Lewis, Bo Diddley... The behind the scenes story on this long unwinding album will be revealed by a congressional committee to investigate phsychodrama [sic] in the music business, but only after a period of graceful silence: hail hail rock and roll you should'a been there. J.L. RIP to the ones who have gone.'

813. REVOLUTION

Vigotone VT-117

Format: CD

Released: 1994

Time: 71.27

Source: 1968 Weybridge Mellotron experiments plus alternate mix of 'Revolution 9'

Sound quality: very good

1. Mellotron Music No. 1 (Mellotron experiment, Weybridge, 1968), 2. Girl (mono mix), 3. We Can Work It Out, Lucy From The Little Town (Paul's acoustic home demo, 1965 with John's spoken word), 4. Michelle (acoustic home demo, 1965), 5. We Can Work It Out (rough mono mix), 6. It's Not Too Bad (three composing demos for 'Strawberry Fields Forever', Spain, 1966), 7. Good Morning, Good Morning (home demo, 1967), 8. Mellotron Music No. 2 (Mellotron experiment, Weybridge, 1968), 9. Revolution (alternate mix, 1968), 10. Across the Universe (alternate mix February 1968), 11. Revolution 9 (alternate mono mix, June 1968), 12. Mellotron Music No. 3 (Mellotron experiment, Weybridge, 1968), 13. Julia (acoustic demo Weybridge May 1968), 14. Stranger in My Arms (unfinished, Weybridge, May 1968), 15. Revolution 1 (Yoko's observations), 16. Hey Jude (promo film soundtrack), 17. Revolution (promo film soundtrack)

Notes: Disc suffers from some hiss and surface noise.

814. ROCK 'N' ROLL IS HERE TO STAY (JOHN LENNON AND FRIENDS)

Pony JEL 001
Format: CD
Source: see notes
Sound quality: excellent

1. Roll Over Beethoven, 2. Honey Don't, 3. Ain't That a Shame, 4. Maybe Baby/Not Fade Away, 5. Send Me Some Loving, 6. Instrumental, 7. Whole Lotta Shakin' Goin' On, 8. Looking For You, 9. Don't Be Cruel/Hound Dog, 10. Instrumental, 11. Honey Don't, 12. Glad All Over, 13. Lend Me Your Comb, 14. Instrumental, 15. Wake Up Little Suzie, 16. Baby, I Don't Care, 17. Vacation Has Just Began, 18. Heartbeat, 19. Peggy Sue Got Married, 20. Peggy Sue, 21. Maybe Baby, 22. Mailman Bring Me No More Blues, 23. Rave On, 24. Peggy Sue, 25. Be-Bop-A-Lula, 26. Slippin' and Slidin', 27. Whole Lotta Love, 28. Thirty Days, 29. Jam, 30. Ain't That a Shame

Notes: Tracks 1–7, 1972 with Elephant's Memory. Tracks 11–23, 1971 with Yoko. Tracks 23–30, 1973 with Phil Spector.

815. ROCK 'N' ROLL SESSIONS (FEATURING THE JESSE ED DAVIS TAPES)

VOXX Records Voxx 0002/01/02/03
Format: CD (triple)
Released: 2000
Time: Disc One 74.23, Disc Two 67.58
Disc Three 73.35
Source: *Rock 'n' Roll* album sessions
Sound quality: excellent

Disc One

A and M Rehearsals

1. *Rock 'n' Roll* radio spot (1.05), 2. Be My Baby (long version – first tape to CD transfer) (6.21), 3. Just Because (long A and M rehearsal, take – first tape to CD transfer) (6.01)

The Jesse Ed Davis Rehearsal Tapes – transfer from the source tapes 10/74

4. Ain't That a Shame (false start) (1.44), 5. warm up (0.37), 6. Be-Bop-A-Lula (2.36), 7. Ya Ya (2.25), 8. Do You Want to Dance (false start) (3.48), 9. Stand By Me (3.49), 10. Slippin' and Slidin' (3.49), 11. Rip It Up/Ready Teddy (2.21), 12. Bring It on Home to Me/Send Me Some Loving (2.03), 13. Bring It on Home to Me/Send Me Some Loving (3.34), 14. Peggy Sue (2.05), 15. Ain't That a Shame (2.45), 16. Stand By Me (excerpt) (0.47), 17. Bring It on Home to Me/Send Me Some Loving (3.43), 18. Ya Ya (false start) (2.42), 19. That'll Be the Day (false start) (2.30), 20. Do You Want to Dance (3.26), 21. Stand By Me (3.39), 22. Peggy Sue (2.15), 23. Be-Bop-A-Lula (excerpt) (1.56), 24. Slippin' and Slidin' (excerpt) (1.56), 25. Guitar jam/Rumble (1.49), 26. Whole Lotta Love (0.13), 27. Thirty Days (1.30), 28. C'mon Everybody (2.15), 29. Ain't That a Shame (excerpts) (1.44), 30. Ain't That a Shame (excerpts) (0.54)

Notes: Sleeve notes state: 'Disc One features what will now be known as The Jesse Ed Davis Tapes. First off we get the first ever tape to CD transfer of the earliest known rehearsals done at A and M studios in October of 1973 with a very drunken John. Then we have the first ever tape to CD transfer of the famous October 1974 rehearsals. These rehearsals have long thought to have been recorded at The Record Plant but were actually taped at Morris Levy's Barn in up state New York with John and the same set of musicians that played on *Walls and Bridges*. These rehearsals were taken from the original cassettes and are many generations above any previous issue.'

Disc Two

Rock 'n' Roll sessions (The outtakes) 73–74

1. You Can't Catch Me (alternate mix) (3.36), 2. Bony Moronie (rough mix) (4.01), 3. Angel Baby No. 1 (original *Roots* version) (3.09), 4. Be My Baby No. 1 (original *Roots* version) (4.34), 5. Here We Go Again No. 1 (demo version) (3.00), 6. Here We Go Again No. 2 (studio outtake) (4.53), 7. Since My Baby Left Me (studio outtake) (3.49), 8. To Know Her Is to Love Her (studio outtake) (4.39), 9. Angel Baby No. 2 (extended version) (3.44), 10. Be My Baby No. 2 (alternate mix/vocal) (5.53), 11. Sweet Little Sixteen (alternate mix) (4.22), 12. Peggy Sue (alternate mix) (2.09)

Bonus Tracks

13. Stand By Me (raw stereo take for *The Old Grey Whistle Test*) (2.16), 14. Stand By Me (*The Old Grey Whistle Test* broadcast) (4.11), 15. Slippin' and Slidin' (*The Old Grey Whistle Test* broadcast) (3.50), 16. Slippin' and Slidin' (*Salute To Sir Lew Grade*) (2.30), 17. Stand By Me (*Salute To Sir Lew Grade*) (2.23), 18. Imagine (*Salute To Sir Lew Grade*) (2.37)

Notes: The sleeve notes state: 'Disc Two features various outtakes, demos and rough mixes from the 73/74 sessions. Bonus tracks include The Raw Stereo take of 'Stand By Me' recorded for The *Old Grey Whistle Test* along with the finished take. We have also included the complete three songs recorded for the *Salute To Sir Lew Grade* TV special, John's last ever live performance.'

Disc Three

Dr Winston O'Boogie Plays The Roots of Rock 'n' Roll

1. Introductions/LP concept/intro to (2.46), 2. Be-Bop-A-Lula (2.37), 3. Meeting Paul/Meeting the classic rock stars/intro to (4.05), 4. Stand By Me (3.26), 5. Rip It Up/Ready Teddy (1.36), 6. Commercial/LP plug/intro to (1.53), 7. You Can't Catch Me (4.06), 8. On Chuck Berry/Fats Domino/Mother/Intro to (3.36), 9. Ain't That a Shame (2.35), 10. LP cover story/the only song messed with/Intro to (1.33), 11. Do You Want to Dance (2.56), 12. Sweet Little Sixteen (3.00), 13. On Chuck Berry/More songs for your money/Intro to (2.07), 14. Slippin' and Slidin' (2.22), 15. LP out next week/Paul owning Buddy Holly songs/Intro to (1.16), 16. Peggy Sue (2.06), 17. The tragedy of Sam Cooke/John's fav song/Intro to (4.42), 18. Bring It on Home to Me/Send Me Some Loving (5.59), 19. On Rock 'n' Roll/Inspirations/Song writing/Larry Williams/Intro to (3.43), 20. Bony Moronie (3.48), 21. Rock 'n' Roll 2/About Lee Dorsey/Intro to (2.46), 22. Ya Ya (2.14), 23. About Roots LP/Back with Yoko/Intro to (2.21), 24. Just Because (4.19), 25. Thank you/Goodbyes/I'll Be Back (1.27)

Notes: The notes on this release state: 'Disc Three incorporates a new way to listen to the *Roots* album. The songs are intertwined by an early (stereo) 1975 interview with John talking and introducing each of the *Rock 'n' Roll* tracks, only we swapped these for the more obscure *Roots* versions. The *Roots* tracks have now been taken from a rare and restored 8 track tape. With the listener in mind, we have made it possible to programme your CD player to play only the *Roots* tracks or just the John interview.'

Digipack which holds the three CDs in this set. Sleeve notes include the story behind the making and release of the *Rock 'n' Roll* album. The front cover has nine black-and-white pictures taken during the photographic session for the official album cover.

816. THE ROCK 'N' ROLL SESSIONS (PART 1)
Ghost Records CD 53-41
Format: CD
Released: 1991
Source: rehearsals for the *Rock 'n' Roll* album
Sound quality: good to excellent

1. Ain't That a Shame, 2. Jam, 3. Be-Bop-A-Lula, 4. Ya Ya, 5. Do You Want to Dance? 6. Stand By Me, 7. Slippin' and Slidin', 8. Rip It Up/Ready Teddy, 9. Bring It on Home to Me/Send Me Some Loving, 10. Peggy Sue, 11. Ain't That a Shame, 12. Stand By Me, 13. Bring It on Home to Me/Send Me Some Loving, 14. Ya Ya, 15. That'll Be the Day, 16. Do You Want to Dance, 17, Stand By Me, 18. Peggy Sue, 19. Be Bop A Lula, 20. Slippin' and Slidin', 21. Jam, 22. Whole Lotta Love, 23. Thirty Days, 24. C'mon Everybody, 25. Ain't That a Shame, 26. Ain't That a Shame

Notes: This is basically a CD release of the double vinyl set *You Should-a Been There* with a different sleeve and the tracks in a different order.

Sleeve features the famous Jurgen Vollmer black-and-white photo of John standing in a Hamburg doorway – as used on the official album.

817. THE ROCK 'N' ROLL SESSIONS (PART 2)
Ghost Records CD 53-42
Format: CD
Released: 1991

Source: rehearsals for the *Rock 'n' Roll album*

Sound quality: good to excellent

1. Just Because (obscene version), 2. Be My Baby (late night session version), 3. Slippin' and Slidin', 4. You Can't Catch Me, 5. Be My Baby (original *Roots* version), 6. Be My Baby (remix extra intro vocals), 7. Starting Over, 8. I'm Losing You, 9. Studio Talk, 10. Dream Lover, 11. Stay, 12. Mystery Train, 13. She's a Woman, 14. Rip It Up, 15. I'm a Man, 16. Be-Bop-A-Lula, 17. She's a Woman, 18. C'mon Everybody, 19. She's a Woman, 20. Instant Karma (US different single mix), 21. I Found Out, 22. Working Class Hero (censored Australian LP version)

Notes: All tracks were previously available on bootlegs.

818. ROCK SPEAK '74

See *Walls and Bridges Rockspeak '74* (Unicorn Records)

819. ROOTS JOHN LENNON SINGS THE GREAT ROCK AND ROLL HITS

Walrus Records WR 42

Format: CD

Source: tracks 1–15 from the original *Roots* album which was distributed by Adam VIII

Tracks 16–22 bonus

Sound quality: Tracks 1–20 excellent. Tracks 21 and 22 poor/good

1. Be-Bop-A-Lula (2.35), 2. Ain't That a Shame (2.31), 3. Stand By Me (3.23), 4. Sweet Little Sixteen (2.58), 5. Rip It Up (1.32), 6. Angel Baby (3.04), 7. Do You Want to Dance (2.52), 8. You Can't Catch Me (4.04), 9. Bony Moronie (3.47), 10. Peggy Sue (2.02), 11. Bring It on Home to Me (3.39), 12. Slippin' and Slidin' (2.18), 13. Be My Baby (4.29), 14. Ya Ya (2.13), 15. Just Because (4.18), 16. Here We Go Again (4.46), 17. Since My Baby Left Me (3.46), 18. To Know Her Is to Love Her (4.35), 19. Do You Want to Dance (3.04), 20. Be My Baby (5.48), 21. Just Because (5.53), 22. Be My Baby (1.24)

Notes: Most of the tracks appear on *Rock 'n' Roll Sessions* (Voxx Records). Sleeve shows John and Yoko playing Instant Karma on *Top of the Pops*.

820. ROOTS JOHN LENNON SINGS THE GREAT ROCK AND ROLL HITS

CD 49-028

Format: CD

Released: 1991

Source: tracks 1–15 from the original *Roots* album which was distributed by Adam VIII

Tracks 16–24 bonus

Sound quality: unknown

1. Be-Bop-A-Lula (2.35), 2. Ain't That a Shame (2.31), 3. Stand By Me (3.23), 4. Sweet Little Sixteen (2.58), 5. Rip It Up (1.32), 6. Angel Baby (3.04), 7. Do You Want to Dance (2.52), 8. You Can't Catch Me (4.04), 9. Bony Moronie (3.47), 10. Peggy Sue (2.02), 11. Bring It on Home to Me (3.39), 12. Slippin' and Slidin' (2.18), 13. Be My Baby (4.29), 14. Ya Ya (2.13), 15. Just Because (4.18)

Bonus Tracks

16. Only You, 17. Move Over Ms L, 18. Rock 'n' Roll People, 19. Well Baby Please Don't Go, 20. Honey Don't (with Ringo Starr and Klaus Voorman), 21. Don't Be Cruel (with Ringo Starr and Klaus Voorman), 22. Matchbox (with Ringo Starr and Klaus Voorman), 23. Send Me Some Loving, 24. Move Over Ms L (false start)

821. SAN FRANCISCO BAY BLUES

Oil Well RSC CD 084

Format: CD

Source: outtakes from the *Imagine* album sessions

Sound quality: unknown

1. Imagine, 2. Crippled Inside, 3. Jealous Guy, 4. It's So Hard, 5. How Do You Sleep? No. 1, 6. Give Me Some Truth, 7. Oh, My Love, 8. How Do You Sleep? No. 2, 9. How? 10. Oh, Yoko, 11. San Francisco Bay Blues

Notes: Sleeve says, 'Live San Francisco, CA, August 2 1969' but disc contains recordings from the *Imagine* session. Front of sleeve has a colour picture of John with a yellow border.

822. SERVE YOURSELF

Vigotone VT-CD-04

Format: CD

Source: various – see notes

Sound quality: very good

1. Shoeshine (3.38), 2. It's So Hard (2.21), 3. Tight A$ (3.18), 4. I'm the Greatest (3.54), 5. Woman (3.18), 6. Julia (2.53), 7. I Found Out (3.55), 8. How Do You Sleep? (6.02), 9. Beautiful Boy (Darling Boy) (3.16), 10. Corrina Corrina (1.13), 11. Happy Xmas (War Is Over) (3.12), 12. J.J. (1.06), 13. Watching the Wheels (2.49), 14. Imagine (3.06), 15. Steel and Glass (5.10), 16. Many Rivers to Cross (2.59), 17. Cooking (in the Kitchen of Love) (2.31), 18. Serve Yourself (6.08), 19. Dear Yoko (2.26), 20. Give Me Some Truth (3.42)

Notes: Track 1, acoustic. Track 2, alternate take, Tittenhurst, June 1971. Track 3, electric. Track 4, studio. Track 5, rough mix with reference vocal. Track 6, acoustic, Kenwood 1968. Track 7, alternate mix with chat and extended ending. Track 8, rough mix. Track 9, rough mix. Track 10, electric, probably Dakota early 1973. Track 11, acoustic. Track 12, acoustic, St Regis Hotel, New York. Track 13, electric blues version, Dakota. Track 14, take 1. Track 15, rehearsal. Track 16, electric with rhythm box, Dakota. Track 17, piano, Dakota, 1976. Track 18, piano, Dakota. Track 19, rough mix with reference vocal. Track 20, rough mix with count-in.

Front of sleeve has a colour picture of John.

823. SHOT DEAD

Unknown

Format: CD

Time: 30.00

Source: WBCN Radio, Boston, 1982

Sound quality: excellent

Notes: This radio show is a montage of interviews and songs.

824. SHOT OF SALVATION (ROLLING STONES)

Scorpio OM 90-64-17

Format: CD

Source: recorded at Record Plant, New York, 28 April 1974

Sound quality: excellent

Notes: This Rolling Stones bootleg included the unreleased track 'Too Many Cooks' with John on the mixing desk.

825. ...SINCE I LEFT THE ROLLING STONES

Yellow Panda YP 004/5

Format: CD (double)

Source: One-to-One concert (Evening Show)

Sound quality: very Good

Disc One

1. Superstition (Stevie Wonder), 2. Reverend Lee (Roberta Flack), 3. Somewhere (Roberta Flack), 4. Power to the People/New York City, 5. It's So Hard, 6. Sisters Oh Sisters, 7. Woman Is the Nigger of the World, 8. Move On Fast, 9. Well, Well, Well, 10. Instant Karma, 11. Mother

Disc Two

1. We're All Water, 2. Born in a Prison, 3. Come Together, 4. Imagine, 5. Open Your Box, 6. Cold Turkey, 7. Hound Dog, 8. Give Peace a Chance, 9. Bonus Track: Sisters Oh Sisters (double-tracked)

826. S.I.R. JOHN WINSTON ONO LENNON

Moonlight Records ML 9506

Format: CD

Released: 1995

Source: various – see notes
Sound quality: very good

1. Roll Over Beethoven (2.30), 2. Honey Don't (3.05), 3. Ain't That a Shame (2.34), 4. My Babe/Not Fade Away (2.30), 5. Send Me Some Loving (2.49), 6. Yoko Jam (2.21), 7. Whole Lotta Shakin' Going On/It'll Be Me (5.29), 8. Ooh My Soul/Honey Hush (2.13), 9. Don't Be Cruel/Hound Dog (4.27), 10. Studio chat/Caribbean (3.09), 11. Honky Tonk (3.11), 12. Mind Train (8.07), 13. Come Together (7.00), 14. We're All Water (11.04)

Notes: Tracks 1–10, John and Yoko plus Elephant's Memory Band rehearsing for the *Sometime in New York City* album at Record Plant Studios, New York in March 1972. Tracks 2, 3, 6, 8 and 10 were released on bootleg for the first time. Other tracks had been released on various discs including *The Lost Lennon Tapes* and *One-to-One Concert Rehearsals*. Tracks 11–14 are a previously unbootlegged tape of John and Yoko plus Elephant's Memory Band at Butterfly Studios, New York on 18, 21 and 22 August 1972 rehearsing for the One-to-One concert.

The sleeve features a colour photo of John with a detailed track listing on the back along with a colour photo of Elephant's Memory Band.

827. THE SMITH COLLECTION: JOHN AND YOKO – DECEMBER 1969

Black Cat BC 089/090
Format: CD (double)
Source: interviews with Howard Smith – see below
Sound quality: unknown

Disc One – WABC 95.5 FM New York, Taped 17 December 1969

1. Introduction, 2. The Men From The Press, 3. Hanratty, 4. Selecting Causes, 5. Having An Effect, 6. A Poster Event, 7. The Toronto Peace Festival, 8. The Get Back LP, 9. Recording Sessions, 10. Break Up Rumours, 11. Allen Klein, 12. A Peace Committee, 13. Fasting For Peace, 14. Returning The MBE, 15. US Visas, 16. Beatles Tours, 17. How About Ringo, 18. Changing In Public

Disc Two – WABC 95.5 FM New York, Taped 17 December 1969

1. Do Things Change, 2. The Black Panthers, 3. Moog Synthesizer, 4. Going As Far As You Can, 5. A Dialog, 6. A Successful Marriage, 7. Show Your Colours Locally, 8. At Home Listening, 9. Socializing With Others, 10. Animal Rights, 11. Skinheads, 12. Selling Peace

13. The National (17/12/69), 14. Japanese Message (18/12/69), 15. CBC TV Interview (18/12/69), 16. CBS TV Interview (20/12/69)

828. THE SMITH COLLECTION: JOHN AND YOKO – DECEMBER 1970

Black Cat BC 091/092

Format: CD (double)

Source: interviews with Howard Smith

Sound quality: unknown

Disc One – WABC 95.5 New York, Broadcast 6 December 1970

1. Two Quick Films, 2. Selecting Films, 3. Plastic Ono Sessions, 4. Phil Spector, 5. Psychoanalysis Set To Music, 6. Primal Therapy, 7. One Year Later, 8. Howard Smith Narration, 9. Expressing Myself, 10. A Writer Who Sings, 11. Feeling The Freedom, 12. Listening To Records, 13. The Rock Beat, 14. Ringo Again, 15. Movies and Music, 16. Gaining Weight

Disc Two – WABC 95.5 FM New York, Broadcast 6 December 1970

1. Events For Peace and Charities, 2. Being Recognised, 3. Mick Jagger, 4. Howard Smith Narration, 5. Constant Togetherness, 6. Promiscuity. 7. 365 Naked Bodies, 8. More On Plastic Ono Band, 9. Forcing Joy, 10. I Don't Believe In, 11. Which Paul? 12. Follow The Fly, 13. On The Set of Fly (12/70), 14. Up Your Legs Forever (12/70)

829. THE SMITH COLLECTION: JOHN AND YOKO – JUNE 1971

Black Cat BC 093

Format: CD

Source: live event with Howard Smith, WPLJ 95.5 FM New York, Broadcast 6 June 1971

Sound quality: unknown

1. Are You Expecting To Be Entertained? 2. Who Wants To Know? 3. Who Do They Think They Are? 4. Good God, This Is Rubbish! 5. Ah-Ee-Mon-Da, 6. Huh? 7. What's Going On Here? 8. More Intelligent Questions, 9. Commies On The Radio, 10, *Grapefruit* Readings (12 August 1971)

830. THE SMITH COLLECTION: JOHN AND YOKO – SEPTEMBER 1971

Black Cat BC 094

Format: CD

Source: interview with Howard Smith, WPLJ 95.5 New York, Broadcast 26 September 1971

Sound quality: unknown

1. Another Flurry of Activity, 2. Fly, 3. Beatles Product, 4. Rock and Ballads, 5. Picking A Single, 6. Recording Tone Deaf Jam, 7. Being More Relaxed, 8. Lawyers, 9. Citizens of The World, 10. Too Much Togetherness, 11. Collaboration Isn't Easy, 12. A Letter To The Voice, 13. Correcting George Martin, 14. No Sense of Humour, 15. Touring With George, 16. Utopia, 17. Future Plans, 18. You Are Here, 19. Moving To The US, 20. The Zappa Tapes, 21. Going Out Ir Public, 22. Visiting China and Russia, 23. The Radio Happening, 24. The New Films, 25. Closing

St Regis Hotel Demos 1971

26. Happy Christmas, 27. J.J., 28. J.J.

831. THE SMITH COLLECTION: JOHN AND YOKO – JANUARY 1972

Black Cat BC 095/096

Format: CD (double)

Source: interviews with Howard Smith

Sound quality: unknown

Disc One – WPLJ FM 95.5 New York, Broadcast 23 January 1972

1. Listening To The Beatles, 2. Howard Smith Narration, 3. 14 Tracks A Side, 4. Missing Having A Group, 5. The Decca Audition, 6. Rain, 7. Relations With Paul, 8. It Wouldn't Work, 9. It Had To Break, 10. Not A

Second Time, 11. On Your Own, 12. Elephant's Memory, 13. Happiness Is a Warm Gun, 14. Bits and Pieces, 15. Strawberry Fields Forever, 16. Indian Influences, 17. The Wind Meets The Mountain, 18. Describing The Apartment, 19. New York and England, 20. Sugar Coating, 21. Arthur Janov

Disc Two – WPLJ FM 95.5 New York, Broadcast 23 January 1972

1. Analysis, 2. Television, 3. *The Mike Douglas Show*, 4. Channel 13, 5. Back To Janov, 6. Going On Stage, 7. I'll Cry Instead, 8. A New Album, 9. The *Imagine* Film, 10. Music and Commercials, 11. New York Rumours, 12. Jerry Rubin and Bobby Seale, 13. The San Diego Convention, 14. The Mail, 15. Ripped off From Start To Finish, 16. Eric Wonderdog, 17. Happy Christmas, 18. What Time Is It On? 19. Interview With Dave Morrel, 20. The Role of Artists (NYC Interview, mid-1972), 21. David Peel (NYC Interview, mid-1972), 22. Attica State (take 2 – Bank Street Demos, 1971), 23. Attica State (take 3 – Bank Street Demos, 1971)

832. SNAP SHOTS – A MUSICAL TAPESTRY

Gnat Records/Paper Plane Music

Format: CD

Source: various

Sound quality: excellent

1. Some Other Guy, 2. Keep Your Hands off My Baby, 3. Honey Don't, 4. Twist and Shout, 5. Be My Baby, 6. Angel Baby, 7. All I Want Is You, 8. Blue Suede Shoes, 9. Bad Boy, 10. Almost Grown, 11. Child of Nature, 12. Ob-La-Di Ob-La-Da, 13. Mad Man Is Coming, 14. Mother, 15. Cold Turkey, 16. Slippin' and Slidin', 17. Stand By Me, 18. Imagine, 19. Whatever Gets You Through the Night, 20. I'm the Greatest

Notes: Front cover consists of strips of photos of John and Yoko which look like rolls of film. Back has colour picture of John with full track listing.

833. SOMETHING PRECIOUS AND RARE

Vigotone VT-CD-07

Format: CD

Source: 'I'm the Greatest' rehearsals and *Walls and Bridges* outtakes

Sound quality: excellent

1. I'm the Greatest: false start (0.48), false start (0.31), false start (0.22), complete take 1 (3.37), false start (0.50), false start (0.18), complete take 2 (4.26), false start (0.44), complete take 3 (2.19), complete take 4 (3.53), 2. Steel and Glass (5.16), 3. Going Down on Love (4.00), 4. Move Over Ms L (with false start) (2.55), 5. Surprise Surprise (Sweet Bird of Paradox) (with count-in) (3.36), 6. Beef Jerky (with count-in) (3.17), 7. Scared (4.52), 8. Old Dirt Road (4.41), 9. Bless You (with two false starts, count-in, chat and riffs) (6.32), 10. Whatever Gets You Through the Night (1.44), 11. Nobody Loves You (When You're Down and Out) (5.15)

Notes: Track 1, rehearsals for the song given to Ringo, John on vocals. Tracks 2–11, *Walls and Bridges* rehearsals 13 July 1974. Surprise Surprise is not listed on the cover.

Front cover is the same as the vinyl release. See also *I'm the Greatest/Something Precious and Rare*.

834. SOMEWHERE IN NEW YORK CITY (THE UN-TELECAST PERFORMANCES)

VOXX Records Voxx 0006-01

Format: CD

Released: 2000

Source: outtakes from *Sometime In New York City* album

Sound quality: fair to excellent

1. The Luck of the Irish (rehearsal)/New York City/Guitar riffs (1.25), 2. The Luck of the Irish (rehearsal) (1.41), 3. The Luck of the Irish (rehearsal – fast version) (0.33), 4. The Luck of the Irish (rehearsal – slow version) (0.33), 5. The Luck of the Irish (rehearsal – ending) (0.27), 6. Studio talk, lyric discussion, set up (3.09), 7. The Luck of the Irish (practice take – false start) (0.11), 8. The Luck of the Irish (take 1 complete) (2.36), 9. The Luck of the Irish (take 2 – breakdown) (2.20), 10. The Luck of the Irish (final take complete) (2.47), 11. Well (Baby Please Don't Go) (9.13), 12. Jamrag

(5.26), 13. Scumbag (6.01), 14. Au (3.23), 15. Attica State (3.14), 16. Woman Is the Nigger of the World (2.54), 17. Fools Like Me (1.36), 18. The Calypso Song (2.50)

Notes: Tracks 1–10 are rehearsals and demos for The Luck of the Irish. Tracks 11–14, John and Yoko live with Frank Zappa's Mother of Invention and the New York Filmore East on 6 June 1971. The same set of songs appeared on the official album. Track 15, John and Yoko filmed for *Aquarius*, a television show broadcast by London Weekend. This song was recorded on 28 February 1972. Tracks 16–18, an electric set of songs filmed for *Eyewitness News* on 5 August 1972, an ABC programme, hosted by Geraldo Rivera.

The front cover consists of a four-page booklet containing black-and-white photographs.

835. SONGS FROM LATE IN THE AFTERNOON
Barrier Records BAR 012/013
Format: CD (double)
Released: 2001
Source: *Double Fantasy* and *Milk and Honey* sessions
Sound quality: very good

Disc One

Tracks 1–5: I'm Losing You (demos), Tracks 6–11: I'm Losing You (studio), Tracks 12 and 13: I'm Moving On, Tracks 14 and 15: Clean-up Time (demos), Tracks 16–23: Clean-up Time (studio), Track 24: Yes I'm Your Angel

Disc Two

Tracks 1–3: I Don't Wanna Face It (demos), Track 4: I Don't Wanna Face It, Tracks 5 and 6: Borrowed Time (demos), Tracks 7–19: Borrowed Time (studio), Track 20: Happy, Track 21: John's Diary Tape

Notes: The colour front cover picture has a picture of John and Yoko sitting on the grass outside their house, Tittenhurst Park. The front insert consists of an eight page booklet with extensive notes and photographs.

836. SOUL OF JOHN LENNON
MIDO Enterprises ZS-9110

Format: CD

Source: various

Sound quality: unknown

1. Mother, 2. Hold On, 3. I Found Out, 4. Working Class Hero, 5. Isolation, 6. Remember, 7. Love, 8. Well, Well, Well, 9. Look at Me, 10. God, 11. My Mummy's Dead, 12. Mother, 13. I Found Out, 14. How Do You Sleep? 15. God, 16. Well, Well, Well, 17. It's So Hard

837. SPANIARD IN THE WORKS/LET'S HAVE A DREAM
Spaced Records SR. 001

Format: CD

Source: various

Sound quality: unknown

Spaniard In The Works

1. John sings 'My Life'. Recorded at the Dakota in late 1979, later combined with 'Don't Be Crazy' and reworked into 'Starting Over' (2.30), 2. John talks about how he met Yoko and their relationship (1.44), 3. John sings 'Dear John'. Home recording from the Dakota in November 1980 (4.10), 4. John talks about the Cosmic Joke Number 9; the paradox of responsibility and the idea of leadership as a false God (1.30), 5. John sings his Bob Dylan parody 'Lord Take This Make-up Off Me' (2.18), 6. John talks about how important it is for everyone to produce their own dreams and go their own ways. Don't follow headers (1.13), 7. John sings 'Make Love Not War'. Recorded at Tittenhurst Park in late 1970. This song later developed into 'Mind Games' (3.13) 8. John talks about the rock star life. He is not interested in all that any longer, he is now interested in the family and in making music (1.45), 9. John sings 'Here We Go Again'. Demo recording made before the *Rock 'n' Roll* sessions in October 1973. The finished version was released on the *Menlove Avenue* album (2.57), 10. John talks about the pacifists that got shot, Ghandi, Martin Luther King. Yoko talks about the beauty

of life (0.57), 11. Yoko talks about her feeling that John's spirit is still here (0.46)

Let's Have A Dream

12. Jock and Yono: Once Upon a Pool Table, 13. I Sat Belonely, 14. Radio Peace, 15. Bed Peace/Stay In Bed/Grow Your Hair, 16. *Wedding Album* ad, 17. *Grapefruit* readings

Notes: The spoken word tracks derive from the interview which John and Yoko gave to the reporter David Sheff in the autumn of 1980, except for track 11 which derives from an interview that Yoko gave to Elliot Mintz in 1981. The sleeve cover shows the front of John's book, *A Spaniard in the Works*. See also Bakhall Bonus CDs.

838. SPECIAL INTERVIEW 1971 (JOHN LENNON AND YOKO ONO)

Red Apple
Format: CD (double)
Source: interviews from 1971
Sound quality: unknown

Disc One
January 25, 1971 at Imperial Hotel. Interview for *Plastic Ono Band* LP

Disc Two
September 2, 1971 in New York. Interview for *Imagine* LP.

Notes: Japanese release.

839. STAND BY ME

Oil Well RSC 054 CD
Format: CD
Source: unknown
Sound quality: unknown

Notes: Track details unknown.

840. St. Regis Hotel and Hotel Syracuse, NY

Green Grape

Format: CD (double)

Source: recorded at St Regis Hotel and Hotel Syracuse in New York, 1971

Sound quality: good

Notes: see 1971 St. Regis Hotel and Hotel Syracuse, NY

841. Studio Rehearsal – 13 July 1974

Unknown

Format: CD

Source: rehearsals for *Walls and Bridges* album

Sound quality: very good

1. Steel and Glass, 2. Going Down on Love, 3. Move Over Ms L, 4. Surprise Surprise (Sweet Bird of Paradox), 5. Beef Jerky, 6. Scared, 7, Old Dirt Road, 8. Bless You, 9. Whatever Gets You Through the Night, 10. Nobody Loves You (When You're Down and Out)

842. Studio Sessions One

Silent Sea Productions SS 111-12

Format: CD

Source: outtakes and outmixes from the Plastic Ono Band era

Sound quality: excellent

Disc One

1. Working Class Hero (alternate take) (4.20), 2. Well, Well, Well (take 4, early remix) (5.52), 3. Love (breakdown, partial) (0.13), 4. Love (alternate take) (2.30), 5. Love (1982 remix) (3.08), 6. Mother (alternate take) (3.48), 7. Mother (alternate take) (3.28), 8. Mother (early remix, acetate) (5.00), 9. I Found Out (early remix) (3.55), 10. That's Alright Mama (1.51), 11. Glad All Over (1.05), 12. Honey Don't (1.35), 13. Don't Be Cruel (0.51), 14. Hound Dog (0.38), 15. Mock Elvis pastiche (1.39), 16. Matchbox (2.24), 17. Instrumental Jam (0.40), 18. Hold On (jam, partial) (0.43), 19. Instrumental fragment (0.06), 20. Remember (breakdown, partial)

(0.12), 21. Remember (alternate take) (2.32), 22. Remember (early remix, acetate) (8.15), 23. Look at Me (alternate take) (2.49), 24. Look at Me (early remix) (2.52), 25. Long Lost John (Railroad Bill) (2.15), 26. Isolation (breakdown, partial) (0.42), 27. Isolation (alternate take) (3.07), 28. God (alternate take) (3.31)

Disc Two

Room 1743, Queen Elizabeth Hotel, Montreal, 1 June 1969

1. Give Peace a Chance (rehearsal) (2.17), 2. Give Peace a Chance (rehearsal, partial) (0.54), 3. Give Peace a Chance (rehearsal, partial) (0.57), 4. Give Peace a Chance (early remix, partial (1.23), 5. Cold Turkey (alternate take, acetate – Abbey Road Studios, 25 September 1969) (4.48), 6. Cold Turkey (early remix, acetate – Abbey Road Studios, 28 September 1969) (4.53), 7. Don't Worry Kyoko (Mummy's Only Looking for Her Hand in the Snow) (early remix, acetate, 3 October 1969) (4.45), 8. Item One (outtake, acetate) (4.06), 9. Instant Karma (video take, partial) (1.58), 10. Instant Karma (video take, partial) (3.23), 11. I Found Out (early remix) (3.58), 12. Look at Me (early remix) (2.49), 13. Power to the People (rehearsal) (1.19), 14. Power to the People (alternate take) (2.46), 15. Power to the People (alternate take (3.41), 16. Power to the People (early remix) (3.57)

Notes: Front cover has a picture of John and Yoko from the 'Bed-In' period.

843. STUDIO TRACKS VOL. 1

Chapter One 25115

Format: CD

Released: 1990

Source: studio outtakes 1969–1974

Sound quality: excellent stereo except tracks 5 and 17 – excellent mono

1. I'm the Greatest (4.00), 2. Going Down on Love (4.00), 3. Honey Don't (1.35), 4. Matchbox (1.50), 5. How Do You Sleep? (8.07), 6. Out the Blue (4.15), 7. Goodnight, Vienna (2.52), 8. God (3.38), 9. Mucho Mungo

(3.25), 10. Woman Is the Nigger of the World (2.10), 11. I Found Out (2.55), 12. Cold Turkey (3.25), 13. Cold Turkey (take 1) (3.35), 14. Do the Oz (3.06), 15. Beef Jerky (3.18), 16. Power to the People (3.45), 17. God Save Us (3.08), 18. Only You (3.12), 19. Be My Baby (4.34), 20. I'm the Greatest (version 2) (3.00)

844. STUDIO TRACKS VOL. 2

Chapter One CO 25116

Format: CD

Released: 1990

Source: studio outtakes 1975–1976

Sound quality: excellent stereo except track 5 – excellent mono

1. Imagine (3.10), 2. Crippled Inside (3.48), 3. Jealous Guy (4.06), 4. It's So Hard (3.48), 5. How Do You Sleep? (version 2) (2.54), 6. How? (3.41), 7. Oh, Yoko (5.48), 8. San Francisco Bay Blues (0.46)

845. STUDIO TRACKS VOL. 3

Chapter One 251181

Format: CD

Released: 1990

Source: studio outtakes 1971–1980

Sound quality: good to excellent

1. Maggie Mae (0.24), 2. I Don't Want to Be a Soldier (5.35), 3. People (1.38), 4. Watching the Wheels (3.06), 5. Corrina Corrina (1.16), 6. Whatever Happened To (4.42), 7. Move Over Ms L (2.35), 8. Bless You (3.44), 9. Real Love (3.53), 10. I'm Stepping Out (4.36), 11. Dear Yoko (4.10), 12. (Just Like) Starting Over (4.52), 13. Dear John (3.53), 14. Imagine (2.47), 15. A Nice Noise (1.50)

846. STUDIO TRACKS VOL. 4

Chapter One CO 25131

Format: CD

Released: 1990

Source: home demos recorded in the Bermudas and in New York, 1979/1980

Sound quality: good to excellent

1. Woman (3.02), 2. She is a Friend of Dorothy (4.10), 3. I Don't Wanna Face It (2.02), 4. Free as a Bird (3.25), 5. Howling at the Moon (1.58), 6. Memories (2.35), 7. Beautiful Boy (2.47), 8. Everybody's Talking (Nobody Told Me) (2.20), 9. Borrowed Time (4.40), 10. I'm Losing You (piano version) (1.30), 11. I'm Losing You (guitar version) (3.10), 12. Clean-up Time (3.06), 13. One of the Boys (2.52), 14. Rock Island Line (2.48), 15. Forgive Me (My Little Flower Princess) (2.44), 15. Real Life (4.51), 16. Boys and Girls (Real Love) (2.20)

847. STUDIO TRACKS VOL. 5

Chapter One CO 25163

Format: CD

Released: 1991

Source: alternate versions and rough mixes from the *Double Fantasy/Milk and Honey* sessions; recorded live at Record Plant Studios, New York, summer 1980

Sound quality: good to excellent

1. Watching the Wheels (3.23), 2. I'm Stepping Out (5.03), 3. Woman (3.56), 4. Dear Yoko (3.16), 5. I'm Losing You (3.54), 6. Clean-up Time (rehearsal) (1.58), 7. Clean-up Time (3.27), 8. Beautiful Boy (1.27), 9. In The Studio (1.48), 10. (Just Like) Starting Over (4.22), 11. Forgive Me (My Little Flower Princess) (3.40), 12. Nobody Told Me (3.20), 13. Living on Borrowed Time (3.30), 14. Life Begins at Forty (2.03)

848. STUDIO TRACKS VOL. 6

Chapter One CO 25164

Format: CD

Released: 1991

Source: home demos and studio outtakes from *Plastic Ono Band/Imagine* albums sessions; recorded 1969–1971

Sound quality: good to excellent

1. Mother (3.55), 2. Love (2.29), 3. Well, Well, Well (1.13), 4. Look at Me (2.44), 5. I Found Out (4.00), 6. Medley: Honey Don't/Don't Be Cruel/Matchbox (4.52), 7. I Don't Want to Be a Soldier (5.46), 8. Well (Baby Please Don't Go) (5.51), 9. How Do You Sleep? (3.27), 10. Cold Turkey (3.27), 11. Mother (4.42), 12. God (2.44), 13. My Mummy's Dead (1.17), 14. Oh, My Love (2.41)

849. STUDIO TRACKS VOL. 7

Chapter One CO 25186

Format: CD

Released: 1992

Source: demos and alternate studio outtakes for the *Mind Games* album

Sound quality: good to excellent

1. Mind Games radio spot (1.00), 2. Make Love Not War (demo) (1.52), 3. Mind Games (studio) (4.02), 4. Tight A$ (demo) (3.20), 5. Tight A$ (studio) (4.14), 6. Meat City (demo) (2.35), 7. Meat City (studio) (2.35), 8. Intuition (demo) (2.23), 9. Intuition (studio) (2.55), 10. One Day at a Time (studio) (3.21), 11. I Know (I Know) (demo) (3.16), 12. I Know (I Know) (3.49), 13. Freeda People (demo) (1.00), 14. Freeda People (studio) (4.03), 15. Call My Name (demo) (3.46), 16. Aisumasen (I'm Sorry) (studio) (4.43), 17. Only People (studio) (2.37), 18. Here We Go Again (demo) (2.33), 19. Out the Blue (studio) (4.11), 20. Nutopian International Anthem (extended 12" version) (0.19)

850. STUDIO TRACKS VOL. 8

Chapter One CO 25187

Format: CD

Released: 1992

Source: various – see notes

Sound quality: very good to excellent

1. *Walls and Bridges* (radio spot) (1.06), 2. Move Over Ms L (2.47), 3. Beef Jerky (3.19), 4. Going Down on Love (4.05), 5. Surprise Surprise (3.14), 6. Only You (3.14), 7. Steel and Glass (4.06), 8. Scared ((4.13), 9. Bless

You (3.54), 10. Nobody Loves You (When You're Down and Out (4.21), 11. Old Dirt Road (1.57), 12. Whatever Gets You Through the Night (1.37), 13. Rock 'n' Roll People (studio) (2.42), 14. Rock 'n' Roll People (demo) (2.15), 15. Move Over Ms L (1.52), 16. What You Got (3.20), 17. Surprise Surprise (3.13), 18. Mucho Mungo (2.19), 19. No. 9 Dream (version 1) (2.11), 20. No. 9 Dream (version 2) (3.08)

Notes: Tracks 2–12 Recorded at Record Plant, 13/14 July 1974. Tracks 13 and 14 Recorded 1973. Tracks 15–20 Home demos.

851. STUDIO TRACKS VOL. 9

Chapter One CO 25200

Format: CD

Released: 1992

Source: various outtakes

Sound quality: very good

1. Hello Little Girl, 2. Bad To Me, 3. I'm In Love, 4. If I Fell, 5. *A Spaniard in the Works*, 6. He Said He Said, 7. Strawberry Fields Forever, 8. Strawberry Fields Forever (organ), 9. You Know My Name, 10. Good Morning, Good Morning, 11. She Can Talk to Me, 12. Cry Baby Cry (piano), 13. Cry Baby Cry (guitar), 14. Dear Prudence, 15. Sexy Sadie, 16. Everybody's Got Something to Hide, 17. Child of Nature, 18. What a Shame Mary Jane, 19. Bungalow Bill, 20. I'm So Tired, 21. Yer Blues, 22. Revolution, 23. Julia, 24. Maharishi Song, 25. Oh, My Love, 26. Everyone Had a Hard Year, 27. A Case of the Blues, 28. Don't Let Me Down, 29. Because, 30. Happiness Is A Warm A Gun, 31. Give Peace a Chance, 32. Give Peace a Chance (final version)

Notes: The sleeves on this series include colour and black-and-white photographs, and some of John's colour cartoons. All the discs have full track listings on the back. The tracks are all taken from *The Lost Lennon Tapes* radio series.

852. TEA FOR TWO

Stamp Out The Beatles STAB 01

Format: CD

Time: 70.24

Source: a collection of Duet Recordings with John, Paul, George and Ringo from 1970

Sound quality: excellent

This disc includes contributions from all four ex-Beatles. Lennon's tracks are as follows:

5. Mildred Mildred (Yoko Ono with John Lennon), 9. I Saw Her Standing There (Elton John and John Lennon), 14. Memphis Tennessee (John Lennon and Chuck Berry), 19. Give Peace a Chance (John and Yoko/Elephant's Memory with Stevie Wonder and Melanie Safka)

853. TELECASTS

Contra Band 3711

Format: CD

Released: 1995

Source: *The Mike Douglas Show*, 31 January 1972 to 7 February 1972

Sound quality: very good

1. It's So Hard (Show 1), 2. Midsummer New York (Yoko) (Show 2), 3. Sisters Oh Sisters (Yoko) (Show 3), 4. Memphis Tennessee (John and Chuck Berry) (Show 3), 5. Johnny B. Goode (John and Chuck Berry) (Show 3), 6. Imagine (Show 4), 7. The Luck of the Irish (Show 5), 8. Sakura (Yoko) (Show 5)

Notes: John and Yoko made five appearances on *The Mike Douglas Show*. These were first issued on the vinyl bootlegs *Telecasts*.

854. TELECASTS

Unknown

Format: CD

Source: various television performances – see notes

Sound quality: unknown

1. John Sinclair, 2. It's So Hard, 3. The Luck of the Irish, 4. Sisters Oh Sisters, 5. We're All Water, 6. Woman Is the Nigger of the World, 7. Attica State,

8. Midsummer New York, 9. Sakura Sakura, 10. Memphis, 11. Johnny B. Goode, 12. Imagine, 13. Imagine, 14. Now Or Never, 15. Give Peace a Chance

Notes: Tracks 1 and 7, *David Frost Show* 13 January 1971. Tracks 5 and 6, *David Cavett Show*, 11 May 1972. Tracks 2, 4, 8 and 12, *The Mike Douglas Show*, 14/18 September 1972. Tracks 13 and 15, *The Jerry Lewis Telethon* 6 September 1972.

The front cover has a colour picture of John from the BBC TV show *Top of the Pops* performing 'Instant Karma'.

855. TESTIMONY THE LIFE AND TIMES OF JOHN LENNON IN HIS OWN WORDS

Magnum Music Group CDTB 095

Format: CD

Time: 75 mins approx

Source: interview, 8 December 1980 conducted by RKO Radio

Sound quality: unknown

1. *Double Fantasy*, 2. John – Man and Daddy, 3. Retrospective, 4. John Meets Yoko, 5. *Two Virgins*, 6. Give Peace a Chance, 7. Artists Objectivity, 8. Starting Over, 9. Househusband, 10. Dreams, 11. Mellowing of Attitude, 12. Musical Philosophy, 13. Using Sound, 14. Unfinished Music

Notes: Sleeve notes: 'This album features one of the last interviews given by John Lennon and Yoko Ono. It was recorded at the offices of Geffen Records in New York City as part of the promotion for the *Double Fantasy* album. The interviewer is Bob Miles and the interview was originally intended for US radio broadcast.'

The front insert consists of a four-page booklet with a colour picture of John and Yoko on the front and extensive notes on the inside.

856. THIS IS NOT HERE (JOHN LENNON FEATURING THE BEATLES)

TMOQ Records

Format: CD

Source: various outtakes and demos

Sound quality: unknown

1. Oh, My Love, 2. Cooking (In The Kitchen of Love), 3. I'm the Greatest, 4. Free as a Bird No. 1, 5. Free as a Bird No. 2, 6. You Saved My Soul, 7. Now and Then, 8. Across the River, 9. Gone from This Place, 10. One of the Boys, 11. Free as a Bird No. 3, 12. Free as a Bird No. 4, 13. The Beatles Early Mix 1996, 14. Free as a Bird No. 5, 15. Full Extended Version 1996, 16. Dear John

857. THIS IS NOT HERE

Black Cat BC 054

Format: CD

Source: various – see below

Sound quality: unknown

1. A Conversation With Scott Muni For WNEW, FM. NYC.

Taped Late September/Early October 1971

Recording Mind Train, Favourite Lennon Works, Understanding Art, Rock Poetry, Yoko Learns About Rock, Contemporary Musicians, Keeping It Simple, Shakin', Companion Quotes, Word Association, Groups, Woman's Liberation, Drugs and Communication, Finding Yourself, Ignoring Yoko, Bagism, Cake and Ginger Ale

2. The Hotel Syracuse Press Conference, 5 October 1971

3. Everson Museum Press Conference, 8 October 1971

858. THIS IS THE TRUTH

Beatle Boots BB-CD 01

Format: CD

Source: *Gimme Some Truth* DVD

Sound quality: excellent

1–3. Crippled Inside, 4–6. Oh, Yoko, 7–9. Jealous Guy, 10–12. It's So Hard, 13–15. I Don't Want to Be a Soldier Mama (I Don't Want to Die),

16–18. Give Me Some Truth, 19–21. Oh, My Love, 22–24. How?, 25–27. Imagine, 28–30. Look at Me

Notes: Sleeve says, Dolby 5.1 Surround Sound Mixes. All tracks from *Gimme Some Truth* DVD presented as centre channel followed by front and rear stereo channels. Japanese release. The back insert has John's handwritten lyrics of 'I Don't Want to Be a Soldier, Mama'.

859. A Toot and a Snore in '74 (John Lennon and Paul McCartney)

Mistral MM 9225

Format: CD

Released: 1992

Time: 29.20

Source: live in Los Angels in 1974

Sound quality: excellent stereo

1. A Toot and A Snore, 2. Blues Jam Session, 3. Studio Talk, 4. Lucille, 5. Nightmares, 6. Stand By Me, 7. Stand By Me, 8. Stand By Me, 9. Cupid/Take This Hammer

Notes: John Lennon, vocals and guitar. Paul McCartney, vocals and drums. Jesse Ed Davis, guitar. Harry Nilsson, vocals. Stevie Wonder, electric piano. Bobby Keys, sax. 'Malcolm Evans, tea. May Pang, sympathy.'

The front sleeve has drawings of John and Paul either side (similar to the drawings on the front of The Beatles' *Revolver* album) with small drawings at the bottom of the other personalities involved in this event.

860. The Toy Boy

Penny Lane Records

Format: CD

Source: various – see below

Sound quality: unknown

1. As Time Goes By (Earth News Radio), 2. I Saw Her Standing There (rehearsal with Elton John), 3. Whatever Gets You Through the Night (demo), 4. Move Over Ms L (released version), 5. Angel Baby (released version), 6. I Found Out (slightly longer version), 7. Happy Xmas (War Is Over) (released version), 8. Nutopian National Anthem (long version), 9. Give Peace a Chance (released version), 10. I'm the Greatest (released version), 11. Be My Baby (released version), 12. Yer Blues (*Rock and Roll Circus*), 13. Do the Oz (Apple single), 14. What a Shame Mary Jane Had a Pain at the Party, 15. As Time Goes By (during interview), 16. Starting Over (post script) (unreleased ending), 17. Good Night (from *Wedding Album*)

861. THE TROPICAL LENNON TRAX

Bell Edge Records BE-001

Format: CD

Released: 2001

Source: various

Sound quality: unknown

Notes: See Lost Lennon Archives – Vol. 1

862. TWO VERSIONS

Sapcor 43

Format: CD (see notes)

Released: 1988

Source: various

Sound quality: unknown

1. Imagine, 2. Attica State, 3. The Luck of the Irish, 4. John Sinclair, 5. Give Peace a Chance, 6. Money Money (Howard Cosell), 7. Chuck Berry/Macca, 8. Johnny DJ (on WNEW)

Notes: We have included this in the compact disc section although we are not certain if this is a vinyl release.

We do have a copy of part of the sleeve in our files. The front cover shows a naked John and Yoko holding a copy of *The Times Business News*. Part of the sleeve we have shows a reproduction of a vinyl label which lists the above tracks and states 'Side D' so the tracks listed above may be part of a double vinyl album. The back of the sleeve says this is a New Zealand release.

863. TWO VIRGINS

Goblin Records CD 3008

Format: CD

Source: copy of official release

Sound quality: unknown

Notes: A copy of the official release of *Two Virgins*.

864. UNBOOTLEGGED 08 – GET THAT FLY

No Label Records NLR 0402

Format: CD

Released: 2004

Time: 63.13

Source: various

Sound quality: good to very good

1. What'd I Say (jam, 9 October 1971) (3.38), 2. Yellow Submarine (jam, 9 October 1971) (2.49), 3. On Top of Old Smokey (2.03), 4. Good Night Irene (3.01), 5. Jesse James Was a Man (0.04), 6. Take This Hammer (0.06), 7. He's Got the Whole World in His Hands (2.44), 8. He's Got the Whole World in His Hands (1.24), 9. He's Got the Whole World in His Hands (1.41), 10. Tandoori Chicken – Attica State (5.47), 11. Like a Rolling Stone (2.06), 12. Twist and Shout (1.12), 13. Louie Louie (0.23), 14. La Bamba (0.55), 15. Bring It on Home to Me (2.46), 16. Yesterday (1.45), 17. Tandoori Chicken (2.14), 18. Power to the People (0.59), 19. Maybe Baby (2,51), 20. Peggy Sue (2.30), 21. Bring out the Joints (0.25), 22. My Baby Left Me (2.05), 23. Blue Suede Shoes (3.04), 24. God Save the Queen (0.08), 25. Crippled Inside (0.56), 26. Give Peace a Chance (3.18), 27. Crippled Inside (0.32), 28. Uncle Albert/Admiral Halsey (1.54),

29. Happy Birthday (1.02), 30.Uncle Albert/Admiral Halsey (0.18), 31. My Sweet Lord (0.17), 32. Imagine (0.36), 33. Oh, Yoko (1.22), 34. Nurse's Song (4.07), 35. Angel Baby (1.51)

865. UNBOOTLEGGED 09 – LOST LENNON TROUSERS

No Tapo Records

Format: CD

Source: various

Sound quality: good to very good

1. John Sinclair, 2. Pill, 3. Instrumental (unknown), 4. New York City, 5. Be My Baby, 6. Tennessee, 7. Tennessee, 8. Mirror Mirror (On the Wall), 9. Mirror Mirror (On the Wall), 10. Whatever Happened To, 11. Electric guitar/drum machine blues, 12. Electric guitar/drum machine improvisation, 13. Electric guitar/drum machine improvisation, 14. Real Life, 15. Real Life, 16. Beautiful Boy (Darling Boy), 17. Borrowed Time, 18. Dear Yoko, 19. Real Love (Waiting For You), 20. The Worst is Over Now, 21. You Saved My Soul (With Your True Love), 22. Borrowed Time, 23. Gone from This Place, 24. Forgive Me (My Little Flower Princess), 25. I'm Losing You, 26. (Just Like) Starting Over, 27. (Just Like) Starting Over, 28. Woman, 29. Only the Lonely (Know How I Feel)/(Just Like) Starting Over/Crying/Gone from This Place

Notes: All tracks taken from *Lost Lennon Tapes* radio series. There are seven volumes numbered 01–07 in this series which contain Beatles tracks. Track 21 is the same as You Saved My Soul.

866. UNEDITED RKO INTERVIEW

Darthouse DD 014-015

Format: CD (double)

Released: 2002

Time: Disc One 63.50, Disc Two 77.22

Source: interview, Yoko Ono's office, the Dakota, for RKO Radio Network, 8 December 1980

Sound quality: very good

Disc One

Yoko Ono

1. Opening/Relationship aspects of the new album (3.13), 2. (Just Like) Starting Over (1.14), 3. Marriage/Commitment (3.20), 4. The dialogue concept of *Double Fantasy* (1.54), 5. Hard Times Are Over (1.20), 6. How The Songs Came About (0.55), 7. Hearing John's songs for the first time (2.04), 8. Finding the time to write (0.51), 9. Her reaction to hearing 'Starting Over' for the first time (2.13), 10. Watching the Wheels (0.24), 11. Being credited with saving John's life (1.11) 12. Stand offs with John in the early days (1.11), 13. Her background (2.51), 14. Her creativity being furthered by her relationship with John (1.00), 15. Her music being more direct on *Double Fantasy* (0.38), 16. I'm Your Angel (1.40), 17. Switching roles (3.13), 18. The impression that she still controls John (0.51), 19. Being role models (2.11)

John Lennon and Yoko Ono

20. Greetings/Sesame Street (1.48), 21. A day in the life of John and Yoko (3.55) 22. John and Sean's relationship (1.47), 23. Television commercials (1.48), 24. Being able to spend time with Sean (2.03), 25. Teenagers (0.47), 26. Children in today's society (2.04), 27. Making the decision to devote time to Sean (2.35), 28. Feeling guilty for not spending time with your children (2.08), 29. Schools (1.19), 30. Discipline (2.20), 31. The urge to make music again (3.03), 32. Hearing Yoko's songs for the first time (1.19), 33. Public acceptance of *Double Fantasy* (1.30), 34. Personal songs (1.47)

Disc Two

John Lennon and Yoko Ono (continued)

1. Creativity (3.47), 2. Meeting Yoko (5.42), 3. John's music reflecting Yoko's influence (2.00), 4. Public reaction to *Two Virgins* (0.25), 5. Commercial success (1.59), 6. Yoko getting interested in pop music/being banned (4.49), 7. Communication/Politics (1.40), 8. What are they doing?/Being ahead of their time (6.17), 9. Working with Yoko (0.47), 10. *Double Fantasy* (3.48), 11. Surviving the 70s (1.15), 12. The evolution to 'Starting Over' (0.34), 13. *Walls and Bridges* (1.00), 14. No. 9

Dream (0.38), 15. Being a bachelor (1.32), 16. Destroying the macho image (0.43), 17. Being image orientated (1.45), 18. Defining love (0.53), 19. Hold On (2.30), 20. Woman (2.53), 21 Imagine (2.20), 22. The concept of Imagine (4.34), 23. Politics (5.17), 24. Illusion/The sixties (4.46), 25. Holistic potential (2.30), 26. Their generation (3.30), 27. Radio/Oldies (3.10), 28. New projects/Touring (1.59), 29. Farewells (3.43)

Notes: This interview was held in Yoko Ono's office at the Dakota from 2.30 p.m. on Monday, 8 December 1980. This was conducted for RKO Radio Network by Dave Sholin, Ron Hummel and Lawrie Kaye. Until the release of this set, only portions of the interview were available from the RKO broadcast which was first transmitted cn 14 December 1980. Colour front cover with track listing on the back.

The set includes two pages of notes about the interview.

867. UNFINISHED MUSIC NO. 2 – LIFE WITH THE LIONS

Goblin Records

Format: CD

Released: 1990

Source: various – see below

Sound quality: unknown

Unfinished Music No. 2 – Life with the Lions
1. Cambridge, 2. No Bed for Beatle John, 3. Baby's Heartbeat, 4. Two Minutes Silence, 5. Radio Play

Bonus Tracks

6. Song for John (from Queen Charlotte Hospital), 7. Snow Is Falling all the Time (from Queen Charlotte Hospital), 8. Don't Worry Kyoko (from Queen Charlotte Hospital), 9. AOS (rehearsal for Albert Hall show with Ornette Coleman), 10. A Quick One While He's Away (John, Yoko, George and Ringo jamming 1969), 11. Yer Blues (bizarre mix salvaged, allegedly, from rubbish bin, Toronto 1970), 12. John Peace (interviews 1969)

Notes: The front cover has a colour picture of Yoko in her hospital bed following her miscarriage in 1969 with John on his bed which he made up on the floor next to Yoko. The back has a black-and-white picture of John and Yoko with two London policemen following their drugs arrest plus the full track listing.

868. THE UNHEARD LENNON 1969 INTERVIEWS

SNE CD 001

Format: CD

Source: interviews 1969

Sound quality: unknown

1. Montreal Bed-In Highlights, 26 May to 2 June 1969; 2. A Visit To Canada, Press Conferences 17 December 1969.

Notes: This set comes with an eight page booklet.

869. UNPLUGGED

Unknown

Format: CD

Released: 1997

Source: home recordings

Sound quality: very good

1. Imagine, 2. Watching the Wheels, 3. Woman Is the Nigger of the World, 4. Girls and Boys, 5. The Luck of the Irish, 6. Maggie Mae, 7. Corrina Corrina, 8. Look at Me, 9. J.J./People, 10. Beautiful Boy, 11. God, 12. Maybe Baby, 13. Love, 14. The Happy Rishikesh Song, 15. I Know (I Know), 16. Woman, 17. What You Got, 18. I'm a Man, 19. Dear Yoko, 20. (Just Like) Starting Over, 21. Mucho Mungo, 22. Howling at the Moon, 23. I'm Losing You, 24. Mother, 25. My Mummy's Dead

Notes: This is a collection of home recordings plus one live track, Imagine from the Apollo Theatre, New York in 1975. Included are alternate versions of 'Watching the Wheels', 'Woman', and '(Just Like) Starting Over' plus acoustic versions of 'Woman Is the Nigger of the

World', 'What You Got' and a 1968 demo of 'Look at Me'. Also included are unreleased songs 'Howling at the Moon', 'The Happy Rishikesh Song', 'Mucho Mungo' and 'J.J./People' (which was later released as 'Angela').

The booklet supplied is informative although the back cover contains a glaring error when it states that the songs were recorded between 1968 and 1990. Colour front sleeve with track listing on the back. Reissued as Acoustic Masterpieces.

870. UNSURPASSED MASTERS – VOL. 1

Egg Records EGG 005

Format: CD

Released: 1998

Time: 72.30

Source: various

Sound quality: very good to excellent

1. I'm Stepping Out (5.35), 2. Going Down on Love (4.22), 3. Dear Yoko (2.43), 4. Borrowed Time (3.03), 5. I'm the Greatest (2.36), 6. Well (Baby Please Don't Go) (5.51), 7. Clean-up Time (3.18), 8. Beef Jerky (3.21), 9. How Do You Sleep? (8.02), 10. Nobody Told Me (3.15), 11. Oh, Yoko (5.50), 12. Out the Blue (4.10), 13. I Don't Want to Be a Soldier Mama (I Don't Want to Die) (5.47), 14. Power to the People (3.46), 15. Jealous Guy (4.06), 16. Forgive Me (My Little Flower Princess) (3.43), 17. Look at Me (2.56)

Notes: All tracks taken from *The Lost Lennon Tapes* radio series.

871. UNSURPASSED MASTERS – VOL. 2

Egg Records EGG 006

Format: CD

Released: 1998

Time: 73.40

Source: various

Sound quality: very good to excellent

1. Aisumasen (I'm Sorry) (4.38), 2. Rock 'n' Roll People (5.58), 3. How Do You Sleep? (4.31), 4. Mind Games (4.00), 5. Be My Baby (5.53), 6. It's So Hard (2.23), 7. I'm the Greatest (3.56), 8. Woman (3.20), 9. I Found Out (3.55), 10. How Do You Sleep? (6.05), 11. Beautiful Boy (3.15), 12. Imagine (3.08), 13. Steel and Glass (5.17), 14. Dear Yoko (2.28), 15. Give Me Some Truth (3.40), 16. Only People (2.41), 17. Bring on the Lucie (4.02), 18. Out the Blue (4.12)

Notes: All tracks taken from *The Lost Lennon Tapes* radio series.

872. UNSURPASSED MASTERS – VOL. 3
Egg Records EGG 007
Format: CD
Released: 1998
Time: 74.14
Source: various
Sound quality: very good to excellent

1. Rock 'n' Roll People (2.41), 2. I'm Losing You (3.54), 3. Bony Moronie (3.57), 4. How Do You Sleep? (5.56), 5. Look at Me (2.51), 6. I'm the Greatest (2.55), 7. Clean-up Time (3.57), 8. I Found Out (3.43), 9. Watching the Wheels (3.27), 10. I'm Stepping Out (5.01), 11. Well, Well, Well (3.36), 12. Power to the People (2.50), 13. I'm the Greatest (3.26), 14. Move Over Ms L (3.00), 15. Surprise Surprise (Sweet Bird of Paradox) (3.38), 16. Scared (4.56), 17. Whatever Gets You Through the Night (1.46), 18. Old Dirt Road (4.44), 19. Bless You (6.06)

Notes: All tracks taken from *The Lost Lennon Tapes* radio series. Some of the tracks on these first three volumes in this series are included twice, e.g. 'Look at Me', 'Out the Blue', 'How Do You Sleep?'

873. UNSURPASSED MASTERS – VOL. 4
Egg Records EGG 008
Format: CD
Released: 1998
Time: 73.18

Source: various

Sound quality: very good to excellent

1. Nobody Loves You (When You're Down and Out) (5.17), 2. I'm the Greatest (2.14), 3. Oh, My Love (2.55), 4. How? (3.46), 5. Crippled Inside (3.49), 6. Clean-up Time (4.37), 7. Tight A$ (4.15), 8. Move Over Ms L (2.42), 9. Only People (2.47), 10. Imagine (3.09), 11. Peggy Sue (2.08), 12. Happy Xmas (War Is Over) (3.21), 13. Meat City (2.31), 14. Come Together (3.55), 15. (Just Like) Starting Over (4.02), 16. One Day at a Time (3.18), 17. You Can't Catch Me (3.36), 18. Watching the Wheels (3.35), 19. Rock 'n' Roll People (2.53), 20. Oh, Yoko (4.07), 21. Jealous Guy (4.27)

Notes: All tracks taken from *The Lost Lennon Tapes* radio series.

874. UNSURPASSED MASTERS – VOL. 5

Egg Records EGG 009

Format: CD

Released: 1998

Time: 71.52

Source: various

Sound quality: very good to excellent

1. Imagine (2.55), 2. I Know (I Know) (3.47), 3. Jealous Guy (4.12), 4. Clean-up Time (6.04), 5. I'm Losing You (3.59), 6. Oh, My Love (2.42), 7. Woman (3.43), 8. Nobody Told Me (3.56), 9. How? (3.46), 10. Aisumasen (I'm Sorry) (4.44), 11. Borrowed Time (4.25), 12. I Am the Walrus/Watching the Wheels (4.05), 13. Woman Is the Nigger of the World (5.38), 14. Intuition (2.51), 15. Woman (3.14), 16. I Don't Want to Be a Soldier Mama (I Don't Want to Die) (5.40), 17. How Do You Sleep? (1.56), 18. Whatever Gets You Through the Night (3.54)

Notes: All tracks taken from *The Lost Lennon Tapes* radio series.

875. UNSURPASSED MASTERS – VOL. 6

Egg Records EGG 010

Format: CD

Released: 1998
Time: 71.58
Source: various
Sound quality: very good to excellent

1. Steel and Glass (4.16), 2. Old Dirt Road (4.54), 3. How Do You Sleep? (2.56), 4. Bless You (3.46), 5. Whatever Gets You Through the Night (3.20), 6. Out the Blue (3.19), 7. Stand By Me (4.10), 8. Imagine (2.58), 9. I'm Stepping Out (5.51), 10. I Don't Want to Face It (2.36), 11. (Just Like) Starting Over (3.40), 12. Surprise Surprise (Sweet Bird of Paradox) (2.37), 13. Whatever Gets You Through the Night (3.31), 14. Borrowed Time (5.32), 15. Power to the People (2.31), 16. No. 9 Dream (4.35), 17. That's All Right/Glad All Over/Honey Don't/Don't Be Cruel/Hound Dog/Matchbox/Jam (10.46)

Notes: All tracks taken from *The Lost Lennon Tapes* radio series.

876. UNSURPASSED MASTERS – VOL. 7
Egg Records EGG 011
Format: CD
Released: 1998
Time: 72.40
Source: various
Sound quality: very good to excellent

1. Tight A$ (4.25), 2. Beautiful Boy (4.02), 3. Hound Dog/Long Tall Sally (5.17), 4. You Are Here (4.38), 5. Dream Lover/Stay (3.42), 6. Steel and Glass (5.07), 7. I Know (I Know) (3.41), 8. One Day at a Time (3.10), 9. Meat City (2.53), 10. Love (3.09), 11. Do the Oz (3.11), 12. Power to the People (1.22), 13. God Save Us (3.14), 14. Tight A$ (4.28), 15. Only People (3.07), 16. Nobody Told Me (3.56), 17. I Know (I Know) (3.56), 18. I'm Stepping Out (4.42), 19. Rock 'n' Roll People (4.22)

Notes: All Tracks taken from *The Lost Lennon Tapes* radio series.

877. UNSURPASSED MASTERS – VOL. 8
Egg Records EGG 020
Format: CD
Released: 1998
Source: various
Sound quality: very good to excellent

1. I Know (I Know), 2. Only You, 3. I'm Stepping Out, 4. How? 5. Imagine, 6. Rock 'n' Roll Music, 7. Beef Jerky, 8. Crippled Inside, 9. Clean-up Time, 10. Borrowed Time, 11. Jealous Guy, 12. I Know (I Know), 13. Oh, My Love, 14. I'm Stepping Out, 15. How? 16. I'm Losing You, 17. Imagine, 18. How Do You Sleep?

Notes: All tracks taken from *The Lost Lennon Tapes* radio series.

878. UNSURPASSED MASTERS – VOL. 9
Egg Records EGG 021
Format: CD
Released: 1998
Source: various
Sound quality: very good to excellent

1. Well, Well, Well, 2. Woman, 3. How Do You Sleep? 4. I'm the Greatest, 5. Rip It Up/Ready Teddy, 6. Beautiful Boy, 7. Send Me Some Loving, 8. How? 9. I Don't Want to Be a Soldier Mama (I Don't Want to Die), 10. I'm Stepping Out, 11. Don't Be Cruel/Hound Dog, 12. Woman, 13. Mother, 14. How Do You Sleep? 15. Dear Yoko, 16. Whole Lotta Shakin' Goin' On/It'll Be Me, 17. Cold Turkey, 18. Every Man Has a Woman Who Loves Him

Notes: All tracks taken from *The Lost Lennon Tapes* radio series.

879. UNSURPASSED MASTERS – VOL. 10
Egg Records EGG 025
Format: CD

Released: 1998

Source: various

Sound quality: very good to excellent

1. Whatever Gets You Through the Night, 2. Roll Over Beethoven, 3. Blues Jam, 4. It's So Hard, 5. What You Got, 6. Come Together, 7. Scared, 8. Ain't That a Shame, 9. Surprise Surprise (Sweet Bird of Paradox), 10. I Don't Want to Be a Soldier, 11. Steel and Glass, 12. Woman Is the Nigger of the World, 13. Nobody Loves You (When You're Down and Out), 14. Honey Don't, 15. Old Dirt Road, 16. San Francisco Bay Blues, 17. Going Down on Love, 18. Instant Karma, 19. Move Over Ms L, 20. I Saw Her Standing There, 21. What You Got

Notes: All tracks taken from *The Lost Lennon Tapes* radio series. All the volumes in this series have colour front covers with the track listing on the back.

880. THE VILLAGE TAPES LAST SESSIONS

PR Records IMM 40.95015

Format: CD

Source: various

Sound quality: unknown

1. Well Baby (5.50), 2. I Found Out (3.19), 3. When a Boy Meets a Girl (2.09), 4. Be My Baby (5.48), 5. Dear Yoko (2.09), 6. (Just Like) Starting Over (4.53), 7. No. 9 Dream (2.09), 8. The Luck of the Irish (1.16), 9. Move Over Ms L (1.50), 10. Real Love (2.25), 11. Out the Blue (4.08), 12. What You Got (3.18), 13. Love (3.57), 14. Imagine (3.05)

Bonus Tracks

15. Well, Well, Well (Part 1) (1.10), 16. Well, Well, Well (Part 2) (3.41)

Notes: The front cover has the same picture of John as the compact disc release *Kaleidoscope Eyes*.

881. WALKING ON THIN ICE

Dolphin Productions CDP 700102

Format: CD

Released: 1997

Source: various

Sound quality: unknown

1. How I Won the War (3.06), 2. Day Tripper (3.07), 3. Real Life (4.18), 4. Rock 'n' Roll People (5.55), 5. Dear John (4.58), 6. I'm the Greatest (3.35), 7. Amazing Walk (2.33), 8. Every Man Has a Woman Who Loves Him (3.34), 9. God Save Us (3.12), 10. Do the Oz (3.11), 11. Move Over Ms L (2.58), 12. Only You (4.41), 13. Goodnight, Vienna (2.54), 14. Imagine (3.05), 15. As Time Goes By (1.04), 16. I Saw Her Standing There (3.16), 17. Whatever Gets You Through the Night (1.25), 18. Walking on Thin Ice (vocal, Yoko Ono), 19. Be My Baby (4.33), 20. Goodnight, Vienna (vocal, Ringo Starr) (2.47)

Notes: The front insert is a four-page booklet with colour pictures on the front and back with notes in the centre printed inside two halves of apples.

882. *WALLS AND BRIDGES* (QUAD)

Quadrapple 003

Format: CD

Released: 1999

Source: 2 channel stereo mix from the direct discrete 4 channel tape

Sound quality: excellent

1. Going Down on Love, 2. Whatever Gets You Through the Night, 3. Old Dirt Road, 4. What You Got, 5. Bless You, 6. Scared, 7. No. 9 Dream, 8. Surprise Surprise (Sweet Bird of Paradox), 9. Steel and Glass, 10. Beef Jerky, 11. Nobody Loves You (When You're Down and Out), 12. Ya Ya

Notes: Front cover is a colour reproduction of the *Walls and Bridges* vinyl release. The back has a colour picture of John from 1974 wearing five pairs of glasses!

883. *WALLS AND BRIDGES* REVISITED

Featuring The Jesse Ed Davis Tapes
Voxx Records VOXX 0013
Format: CD (double)
Released: 2001
Time: Disc One 73.55, Disc Two 72.05
Source: *Walls and Bridges* album sessions
Sound quality: excellent

Disc One

1. *Walls and Bridges* rundown by John (2.01), 2. Steel and Glass (5.17), 3. Going Down on Love (4.04), 4. Move Over Ms L (2.58), 5. Surprise Surprise (Sweet Bird of Paradox) (3.42), 6. Beef Jerky (3.22), 7. Scared (4.55), 8. Old Dirt Road (4.44), 9. Bless You (false start) (6.33), 10. Whatever Gets You Through the Night (1.50), 11. Nobody Loves You (When You're Down and Out) (5.17), 12. Bless You (5.25), 13. Move Over Ms L (2.51), 14. Scared (4.51), 15.Surprise Surprise (Sweet Bird of Paradox) (3.09), 16. Whatever Gets You Through the Night (3.13), 17.Going Down on Love (4.00), 18. Nobody Loves You (When You're Down and Out) (5.04), 19. Whatever Gets You Through the Night (excerpt) (0.20)

Disc Two

1. What You Got (three segments) (7.49), 2. Deejay Winston O'Boogie takes over KHJ Radio 'Super Star Week' introduction (0.20), 3. Good morning from Winston (0.16), 4. Comment on 'Come Together', intro for Harry (0.29), 5. Callers and requests, time check (0.38), 6. Callers and requests: will they reform? (1.27), 7. Weather check, Tobias commercial No. 1, intro for Stevie Wonder (2.16), 8. Callers and requests (2.21), 9. Listen to this radio spot No. 1, intro for Bob Marley (1.33), 10. Winston does Vons commercial, intro into... (0.38), 11. Surprise Surprise (Sweet Bird of Paradox) (8-track mix) (2.40), 12. Tobias commercial No. 2 (1.39), 13. Callers, Tobias commercial No. 3, intro into... (1.50), 14. No. 9 Dream (8-track mix) (4.35), 15. Tower Records commercial No. 1 (1.15), 16. Callers, intro into... (3.25), 17. Beef Jerky (8-track mix) (3.25), 18. Comments on Beef Jerky, time check, Thrifty drug commercials

(2.04), 19. Taking request (0.48), 20. Intro for Elton, Tobias commercial No. 4, news break, callers 'Have you heard the word?', intro into… (4.14), 21. Nobody Loves You (When You're Down and Out) (8-track mix) (5.06), 22. Time check, callers and requests, Tower Records commercial No. 2 (2.32), 23. Commercial for 'Funny Car Show' (1.35), 24. Deejay Winston plays 'Jet' and comments on Paul, Tobias commercial No. 5 (1.38), 25. Deejay Winston plays 'My Sweet Lord' and comments on George, intro into… (0.18), 26. Going Down on Love (8-track mix) (3.53), 27. Callers and request (2.28), 28. Introduction for 'Scared' (0.10), 29. Scared (8-track mix) (4.27), 30. *Walls and Bridges* plug, Listen to this radio spot No. 2, Tobias commercial No. 6, intro into… (1.23), 31. Steel and Glass (8-track mix) (5.16), 32. Deejay Winston O'Boogie says goodbye, plays request for Capital Records doorman (0.35)

Notes: Disc One: track 1, John goes through the tracks of his recently released *Walls and Bridges* album. Tracks 2–11, rehearsals for *Walls and Bridges* recorded at Record Plant East Studios, New York on 13 July 1974. Tracks 12–19 and Disc Two track 1, further recording session on 21 July 1974. Disc Two, tracks 2–32, deejay Winston O'Boogie takes over at KHJ-AM Radio plugging his new album on 27 September 1974. John plays records and receives requests from callers between 6 a.m. and 9 a.m.

Sleeve is full colour with eight pictures of John pulling faces! The back has another eight faces, this time in black and white.

884. *WALLS AND BRIDGES* ROCKSPEAK '74

Unicorn Records UK-086
Format: CD
Released: 2001
Source: radio 2, 4 October 1974. *Rock Speak*, hosted by Michael Wale
Sound quality: unknown

1. Interview on new album, 2. Going Down on Love, 3. Whatever Gets You Through the Night, 4. Old Dirt Road, 5. What You Get, 6. Bless You, 7. Scared, 8. John says a few words about Side 2, 9. No. 9 Dream,

10. Surprise Surprise, 11. Steel and Glass, 12. Beef Jerky, 13. Nobody Loves You (When You're Down and Out), 14. Ya Ya, 15. Outro

Notes: The front cover has a colour picture of John and Yoko with the track listing on the back with some brief but informative notes.

885. *WALLS AND BRIDGES* SESSIONS
Green Grape
Format: CD (double)
Source: *Walls and Bridges* album outtakes, demos and rehearsals
Sound quality: very good

Notes: see 1974 *Walls and Bridges* Sessions

886. WARSHIP THE LORD YOUR GOD AND SERVE HIM ONLY
Master of Orange MOO-10006
Format: CD
Released: 1997
Source: various
Sound quality: excellent

1. Stand By Me, 2. Slippin' and Slidin', 3. Stand By Me, 4. Slippin' and Slidin', 5. Stand By Me, 6. Slippin' and Slidin', 7. Imagine, 8. Slippin' and Slidin', 9. Imagine, 10. Slippin' and Slidin', 11. Stand By Me, 12. Imagine

Notes: Tracks 1 and 2, *The Old Grey Whistle Test*, 18 April 1976, direct master. Tracks 3 and 4, *The Old Grey Whistle Test*, rehearsal version No. 1, stereo mix with different vocal. Tracks 5 and 6, *The Old Grey Whistle Test*, rehearsal version No. 2, unedited. Track 7, salute to Sir Lew Grade, stereo. Tracks 8 and 9, *Salute To Sir Lew Grade* 13 January 1975. Tracks 10–12, *Salute To Sir Lew Grade*, complete audience recording.

Front has spare design of ten drawings from John of facial features. The back has a colour picture of John stretched out on a sofa with the track listing printed on top (this makes the picture hard to see).

887. WATCHING THE WHEELS

Vigotone VT-CD-03

Format: CD

Released: 1990

Source: various – see notes

Sound quality: very good to excellent

1. I Don't Want to Be a Soldier Mama (I Don't Want to Die) (5.45), 2. Free as a Bird (3.23), 3. Watching the Wheels (2.57), 4. Power to the People (3.43), 5. Honey Don't/Don't Be Cruel/Matchbox (4.55), 6. Borrowed Time (4.56), 7. Aisumasen (4.35), 8. Jealous Guy (4.04), 9. Surprise Surprise (Sweet Bird of Paradox) (2.55), 10. Forgive Me (My Little Flower Princess) (3.37), 11. Rock 'n' Roll People (5.56), 12. Gone from This Place (3.17), 13. How Do You Sleep? (4.30), 14. The Rishikesh Song (1.49), 15. Mind Games (3.58), 16. Be My Baby (5.49), 17. San Francisco Bay Blues (0.46)

Notes: Track 1, take 1, Tittenhurst Park. Track 2, piano, take, Dakota. Track 3, acoustic Bermuda June/July 1980. Track 4, alternate with count-in and false start. Track 5, jam, *Plastic Ono Band* album sessions. Track 6, acoustic. Track 7, rough mix *Mind Games* album sessions. Track 8, alternate take. Track 9, early electric version. Track 10, *Double Fantasy* sessions. Track 11, alternate, take 5 with count-in, *Mind Games* album sessions, 4 August 1973. Track 12, acoustic, take 4. Track 13, rehearsal with chat and riffs, edited to remove a broadcast voice over. Track 14, acoustic. Track 15, rough mix with reference vocal. Track 16, rough mix with reference vocal. Track 17, vocal version, Tittenhurst, June 1971. All tracks taken from *The Lost Lennon Tapes* radio series.

Colour front cover with another colour picture of John on the back with the track listing.

888. WE ARE ALL TOGETHER – THE INTERVIEWS

Delta Music 47 034

Format: CD

Released: 2000

Time: 73.50

Source: various interviews – compiled and narrated by Geoffrey Giuliano
Sound quality: very good

1. Introduction (1.22), 2. Love, We Do (1.13), 3. To Know Her Is Loving Her (1.00), 4. Every Man Has a Woman (5.55), 5. Me and Paul and George and Ringo (1.50), 6. Fame and Friends (5.13), 7. Eppy (10.35), 8. Apple – The Forbidden Fruit (1.53), 9. The Beatles (0.43), 10. Montreal Bed-In (1.14), 11. Toronto Rock 'n' Roll (2.19), 12. Amsterdam Bed-In (21.41), 13. Why Am I Here? (3.45), 14. Turkey (1.51), 15. Taking It To The States (3.17), 16. Our Mission (1.51), 17. What Now (1.02), 18. On The Bed (3.21), 19. Making The Ballad (1.18), 20. Let It Be (0.48), 21. The Sergeant's Song (1.29)

Notes: Sleeve says: 'This CD offers the listener the opportunity to hear John Lennon's own words on just what he hoped to achieve with the Bed-Ins, on Apple, Brian Epstein, Allen Klein, his relationship with Yoko Ono and, of course, on The Beatles'. Track details are as follows (taken from the sleeve notes):

1. Introduction by Geoffrey Giuliano. 2. John explains his relationship with Yoko. 3. John expands on the beneficial effects of their relationship. 4. An overview on how their relationship must have appeared from the outside. 5. John talks about The Beatles and their future. 6. John talks about fame, friends and hangers on. Yoko and Derek Taylor contribute. 7. On Brian Epstein. 8. On Apple, accountants and difficulties of getting money out of the firm. 9. Plans for The Beatles for 1969. 10. John's Telephone Press Conference for the second Bed-In, Montreal on 26 May 1969. 11. A rare recording of a Press Conference held after the Rock 'n' Roll revival in Toronto. 12. Press Conference. 13. More from the Bed-In at The Hilton. 14. John discusses 'Cold Turkey'. 15. Press Conference for the Bed-In that never was! 16. John and Derek Taylor explain their mission in the Bahamas. 17. What would John do if he got into the USA? 18. John explains the impact of Bed-Ins. 19. John talks about the making of 'The Ballad of John and Yoko', 20. On the making of *Let It Be*. 21. John discusses the impact of *Sgt. Pepper* and what it meant to him.

Front insert is in the form of a four-page booklet with a colour picture on the front with three pages of notes about the tracks. The track listing is on the back.

889. WEDDING ALBUM

Goblin Records CD 3007

Format: CD

Released: 1990

Source: official album plus Yoko B-sides

Sound quality: unknown

1. John and Yoko Amsterdam, 2. John John (Let's Hope For Peace), 3. Peace Talk, 4. Stay In Bed, 5. Reading about Ringo, 6. Ordering Breakfast, 7. A Brief Gift, 8. Reading Headlines, 9. Interviews and Photos, 10. Goodbye Amsterdam, 11. Grow Your Hair, 12. Goodnight, 13. Grow Your Hair, Hair Peace, Bed Peace

John and Yoko B Sides

14. Remember Love, 15. Who Has Seen the Wind? 16. Listen The Snow Is Falling, 17. Why, 18. Don't Worry Kyoko, 19.Open Your Box

Notes: This is a reissue of the commercial album with some B-sides by Yoko (tracks 14–19). This is an Australian release.

890. WE'D LIKE TO CHANGE THE TEMPO NOW

Barrier BAR 014/015

Format: CD (double)

Source: *Double Fantasy* and *Milk and Honey* demos and outtakes

Sound quality: excellent

Disc One

1. Help Me to Help Myself (piano demo), 2. Memories (Howling at the Moon) (piano demo, take 1), 3. Memories (piano demo, take 2), 4. Memories (piano demo with overdubbed acoustic guitar and vocal – unknown take), 5. Tennessee (piano demo, take 1), 6. Tennessee (piano demo with rhythm box, unknown take), 7. Tennessee (piano demo with

rhythm box, take 4), 8. Watching the Wheels (Howling at the Moon) (piano demo – unknown take), 9. Watching the Wheels (piano demo – take 6), 10. Watching the Wheels (I'm Crazy) (piano demo – take 1), 11. Watching the Wheels (piano demo – unknown take), 12. Watching the Wheels (piano demo – alternate 1), 13. Watching the Wheels (piano demo – unknown take), 14. Watching the Wheels (electric guitar demo, unknown take), 15. Watching the Wheels (acoustic guitar – unknown take), 16. Watching the Wheels (studio rehearsal/run through, vocal booth take 3), 17. Audio verite (control room discussion), 18. Audio verite (studio rehearsal discussion), 19. Watching the Wheels (rough mix with reference vocal), 20. Audio verite (studio rehearsal discussion), 21. Watching the Wheels (alternate mix no. 1 – multi-track take 6), 22. Watching the Wheels (alternate mix no. 2 – multi-track take 8), 23. Sea Ditties (piano demo), 24. Pedro the Fisherman (acoustic guitar with overdub demo), 25. Whatever Happened To (electric guitar demo, take 1)

Disc Two

1. Dear Yoko (acoustic guitar demo 'Coldspring Harbour' video take 1), 2. Dear Yoko (acoustic guitar demo 'Coldspring Harbour' video take 2), 3. Dear Yoko (acoustic guitar demo, take 1), 4. Dear Yoko (acoustic guitar, take 2), 5. Dear Yoko (acoustic guitar demo with overdubs, unknown take), 6. Dear Yoko (studio rehearsal run through, vocal booth), 7. Audio verite (studio rehearsal discussion), 8. Dear Yoko (alternate mix no. 1 – multi-take no. 5), 9. Dear Yoko (alternate mix no. 2 with harmonica – multi-take no. 6), 10. Forgive Me (My Little Flower Princess) (acoustic guitar demo, take 2), 11. Forgive Me (My Little Flower Princess) (studio – multi-track take 2), 12. Gone from This Place (acoustic guitar demo, take 1), 13. Gone from This Place (acoustic guitar demo, take 2), 14. Gone from This Place (acoustic guitar demo, take 4), 15. Audio Verite (studio rehearsal discussion), 16. Sally and Billy (piano demo with drum machine, take 2), 17. Sally and Billy (piano demo with drum machine take 3), 18. Mirror Mirror (On the Wall), piano demo, takes 1 and 5), 19. One of the Boys (acoustic guitar demo, take 1), 20. One of the Boys (acoustic guitar demo, take 2), 21. Maurice DuPont Agent Provocateur Du Jour (22 March 1978), 22. Tape letter from Aunt Mimi.

Notes: Front insert is a four-page booklet with colour pictures on the front and back and notes about the tracks in the centre. The notes are extremely difficult to read being white printing on a black background with very small sized font.

891. THE WEEKEND STARTS HERE

Black Cat BC 117/118
Format: CD (double)
Source: various – see below
Sound quality: unknown

Disc One

1. Flipside US TV 16 February 1973

Introduction, Producing Records, Ticket to Ride, Ignoring Yoko, Jose Joi Banzale, The Death of Your Soul, Death of Samantha, The Rosies, Catman (The Rosies are Coming), Don't Do It When I'm Around, Winter Song, Living Together, Death of Samantha

2. INS Press Conference 23 March 1973

3. Nutopia Press Conference 2 April 1973

4. Beverley Hills Hotel Interview, Elliot Mintz 16 April 1973

Beatle Reunions, Allen Klein, Apple Business, Immigration, Hollywood Parties, Paul, The Lennons Are in Trouble, Drugs, Exchanging Energy

Disc Two

1. International Women's Conference, Danny Schechter, 3 June 1973

The Conference, Immigration and Nutopia, Current Projects, Reunion Rumours

2. *Mind Games* Commercials, 24 October 1973

Commercial No. 1, Commercial No. 2, outtakes

3. *Eyewitness News* KABC TV, Los Angeles, Elliot Mintz, Taped 10 November 1973

5 p.m. News Broadcast, 6 p.m. News Broadcast, 11 p.m. News Broadcast, outtakes

4. *The Mike Douglas Show*, 23 November 1973
Angry Young Woman/Interview

5. Capital Rap, Capital Radio, UK, 23 November 1973
The Band, Out the Blue, The Ringo Sessions, Communication, Meat City, Impressions of the LP, Favourite Beatles Songs, Capital Radio

6. Mimi Remembers

892. THE WFIL-AM HELPING HAND MARATHON
Black Cat BC 020/021
Format: CD (double)
Source: WFIL-AM Helping Hand Marathon, 16 May to 18 May 1975 (see notes)
Sound quality: unknown

Disc One

1. March of Dimes Walk-a-thon, Central Park, NYC, 28 April 1974, 2. Larry Kane remembers the WFIL-AM Helping Hand Marathon (December 1980)

The WFIL-AM Helping Hand Marathon
3. Friday, 16 May 1975, 4–6. Saturday, 17 May 1975

Disc Two

The WFIL-AM Helping Hand Marathon
1–6. Sunday, 18 May 1975

Notes: John went to Philadelphia and for three days and nights he helped out for the second successive year on the WFIL-AM Helping Hand Marathon. This event involved raising money for Multiple Sclerosis. John spoke on the telephone and helped to read the weather. He was invited to do the shows by Larry Kane who John first met during The

Beatles first tour of America in 1964. There is some confusion on the dates on this CD (see Part 4 – Sources – for explanation).

Front insert shows a reproduction of the poster for the event against a brick wall with a black-and-white picture of John on the other side. The track listing is shown on the back.

893. WHEN I GET OLDER (BEATLES IN THE '90S)
Fab 4

Format: CD

Time: 71.51

Source: various outtakes from ex-Beatles

Sound quality: excellent

1. Hi Hi Hi (Paul – short intro), 2. Grow Old with Me (John – home demo), 3. Now and Then (demo), 4. Real Love, 5. I'm the Greatest (rehearsal), 6. Let It Be (from *Get Back* sessions), 7. Cooking (in the Kitchen of Love) (John, demo), 8. Honey Don't (*Sometime in New York City* sessions), 9. Don't Be Cruel (*Sometime in New York City* sessions), 10. Matchbox (*Sometime in New York City* sessions), 11. I Need Your Loving (Beatles – Ready Steady Go 1965), 12. Six O'clock (Ringo), 13. India (John – demo), 14. Illusions (John – demo), 15. Life Begins at 40 (John – demo for Ringo Starr), 16. You Saved My Soul (John – demo), 17. Help Me to Help Myself (John – demo), 18. One of the Boys (John – home demo), 19. Whatever Happened To (John – home demo), 20. Baby Make Love To You (John – home demo), 21. That's the Way the World It (John – home demo), 22. Across the River (John – home demo), 23. Dear John (John – home demo), 24. Free as a Bird (complete)

Notes: Many of the tracks were new to bootleg. Most of the items on this disc are John rehearsals and demos although the front cover shows George, Ringo and Paul with a picture of Yoko on the back. See also *Free as a Bird: the Dakota Beatle Demos*. This release was a follow up to *Come Together (Beatles In The '90s)* (Fab 3).

894. WHEN WAS THE LAST TIME YOU KISSED MICKEY MOUSE?

Unknown

Format: CD

Time: 77.23

Source: WPLJ FM Radio, New York, 6 June 1971

Sound quality: fair to good

Notes: John and Yoko as guest DJs. Black-and-white cover of sleeve stating 'Andy Warhol Wants To Know: When Was The Last Time You Kissed Mickey Mouse?'

895. WHY AND WHY NOT?

Black Cat BC 064

Format: CD

Source: various radio broadcasts

Sound quality: unknown

An Hour With John and Yoko

WIBG 990 AM Philadelphia, PA, Interview with Long John Wade, Taped 27 January 1972, Broadcast 10 February 1972

Memories of The Beatles, Planning The Next Album, Not Having A Band, Why Can't We See Them? Jerry Rubin and Bobby Seale, Going On The Road, Taping *The Mike Douglas Show*, Yoko The Manager, Press Conferences, Selling Peace, Getting Old, Closing

Aquarius

London Weekend TV, Taped 28 February 1972, Broadcast 11 March 1972

ABC NEWS

Deportation Hearing 18 April 1972, National Peace Action Coalition Rally 22 April 1972

896. WILLOWBROOK REHEARSALS

Unknown

Format: CD (double)

Source: One-to-One concert rehearsals, Butterfly Studios and Filmore East, 22–26 August 1972

Sound quality: unknown

Disc One

1. New York City, 2. Unchained Melody, 3. Instrumental, 4. New York City, 5. It's So Hard, 6. Woman Is the Nigger of the World, 7. Give Peace a Chance, 8. Instrumental

Disc Two

1. Unchained Melody, 2. Well, Well, Well, 3. Instant Karma, 4. Mother, 5. Come Together, 6. Cold Turkey, 7. Instrumental, 8. Instrumental, 9. Roll Over Beethoven

Notes: Rehearsals featuring John – guitar and vocals, Stan Bronstein – sax, Gary Van Bevox – bass, Adam Ippolito – keyboards, Rick Frank – drums, Wayne 'Tex' Gabriel – guitar.

Front cover has black-and-white picture of John and Yoko with members of Elephant's Memory Band. The back has more black-and-white pictures plus the track listing.

897. WINSTON O'BOOGIE

Bag Records 5072

Format: CD

Time: 69.02

Source: various

Sound quality: excellent

1. Move Over Ms L No. 1, 2. Move Over Ms L No. 2, 3. Move Over Ms L No. 3, 4. Surprise Surprise (Sweet Bird of Paradox) No. 1, 5. Whatever Gets You Through the Night No. 1, 6. Whatever Gets You Through the Night No. 2, 7. Move Over Miss L No. 4, 8. Surprise Surprise (Sweet Bird of

Paradox No. 2, 9. Going Down on Love, 10. Beef Jerky, 11. Whatever Get You Through The Night No. 3, 12. Steel and Glass, 13. Scared, 14. Old Dirt Road, 15. Nobody Loves You (When You're Down and Out), 16. Bless You, 17. What You Got, 18. No. 9 Dream No. 1, 19. No. 9 Dream No. 2

Notes: Studio recordings. Although this release from Bag Records contains the same catalogue number as the vinyl release, it has a different track listing.

The sleeve cover is virtually the same as the vinyl release.

898. WINSTON O'BOOGIE
Bag Records CD 5072 A/B
Format: CD (double)
Source: various
Sound quality: excellent

Disc One
1. Just Because, 2. Be My Baby, 3. Be My Baby, 4. Starting Over, 5. I'm Losing You, 6. Dream Lover, 7. Stay, 8. Mystery Train, 9. She's a Woman, 10. Rip It Up, 11. I'm a Man, 12. Be-Bop-A-Lula, 13. She's a Woman, 14. C'mon Everybody/She's a Woman, 15. I'm the Greatest Recording Session

Disc Two
1. Move Over Ms L, 2. Move Over Ms L, 3. Move Over Ms L, 4. Surprise Surprise (Sweet Bird of Paradox), 5. Whatever Gets You Through the Night, 6. Whatever Gets You Through the Night, 7. Move Over Ms L, 8. Going Down on Love, 9. Beef Jerky, 10. Whatever Gets You Through the Night, 11. Steel and Glass, 12. Scared, 13. Old Dirt Road, 14. Nobody Loves You (When You're Down and Out), 15. Bless You, 16. What You Got, 17. No. 9 Dream, 18. No. 9 Dream

Notes: This double CD set features virtually the same cover as the original vinyl release and the CD release above. It also has the same catalogue number.

899. WORKING CLASS HERO

Chet Mar Records CMR 75

Format: CD

Source: various

Sound quality: unknown

1. Be My Baby (4.33), 2. Angel Baby (4.32), 3. Yer Blues (8.31) 4. Imagine (3.22), 5. Mother (5.15), 6. Come Together (4.35), 7. Give Peace a Chance (7.47) 8. Slippin' and Slidin' (2.20), 9. Stand By Me (3.50), 10. Whatever Gets You Through the Night/Lucy in the Sky with Diamonds, I Saw Her Standing There (14.30) 11. Lady Marmalade (1.22), 12. Memphis, Johnny B. Goode (7.45), 13. Oh, My Love (2.47), 14. Working Class Hero (2.20), 15. Day Tripper (3.10), 16. Do the Oz (3.09)

Notes: 'Be My Baby' and 'Angel Baby' are *Rock 'n' Roll outtakes*. 'Yer Blues' is from Rolling Stones *Rock and Roll Circus*. 'Imagine' is from *Mike Douglas Show* 1972. 'Mother', 'Come Together' and 'Give Peace a Chance' are from the One-to-One concert. 'Slippin' and Slidin'' and 'Stand By Me' are *The Old Grey Whistle Test* outtakes. 'Whatever Gets You Through the Night', 'Lucy in the Sky with Diamonds' and 'I Saw Her Standing There' are with Elton John at Madison Square Garden in 1974. 'Lady Marmalade' is a Dakota recording. 'Memphis' and 'Johnny B. Goode' are from *Mike Douglas Show* in 1972. 'Oh, My Love' is an outtake. 'Working Class Hero' is from John's thirty-first birthday party. 'Day Tripper' is from *Top Gear* in 1967 with Jimi Hendrix. 'Do the Oz' is an Elastic Oz Band single from 1974.

This set was previously available as a vinyl two-disc set. Black-and-white picture of John on the front cover with track listing on the back.

900. WPLJ-FM, NEW YORK CITY, 6 JUNE 1971

YelloSub Records YSR 002

Format: CD

Released: 1990

Source: interviews, 1971 and 1975 (see notes)

Sound quality: unknown

1. Segment 1, live (16.22), 2. Segment 2, live (8.05), 3. Segment 3, live (7.57), 4. Segment 4, Live (8.01)

Bonus Track

5. Question-and-Answer Session, live, John Lennon (14.43)

Notes: Tracks 1–4, John and Yoko on WPLJ-FM, NYC, 6 June 1971. Track 5, John on NYC radio station reading questions and answering them. Live, 1975, taken from an unaired programme 'Cheer Up New York'.

Front cover has small picture of John and Yoko holding War Is Over cards. Back cover features the *Two Virgins* nude photo of John and Yoko.

901. WRITTEN THE DAY BEFORE YESTERDAY

Unknown JLYOWDBY

Format: CD

Time: 66.07

Source: various

Sound quality: varies

1. Oh, My Love outtakes/Woman's Hour Interview (12.29), 2. Free John Now Rally, Ann Arbor, 10 December 1971 (47.12), 3. One-to-One Benefit Concert Ad (studio outtakes, Butterfly studios, August 1972 (1.27), 4. John Lennon on Ronnie Hawkins (short rap) (0.08), 5. John Lennon on Ronnie Hawkins (long rap) (1.27), 6. Down in the Alley (3.32)

Notes: Track 1, 'Oh, My Love' is outtakes from the *Imagine* session in 1971. *Woman's Hour* interview (edited version) recorded in August 1971 and extracts broadcast on BBC Radio 2 on 9 November 1971. Tracks 4–6, taken from radio promo 1969. The following notes are taken from the *Bootleg Zone*:

> In 1969, John Lennon and Yoko Ono stayed with Ronnie on his farm in Mississauga for a couple of weeks during their peace crusade and took the Hawkins on their train ride to see Canada's Prime Minister, Pierre Trudeau. Afterwards (remember the Bed-In!), Ronnie and music journalist

Ritchie Yorke were recruited by Lennon as peace emissaries and visited China. When Ronnie went to Muscle Shoals, Alabama, and recorded Down in the Alley with Duane Allman in 1970, Lennon helped boost the single and recorded a promotional spot for it.

902. YER BLUES

Library 2329

Format: CD

Source: various – see notes

Sound quality: excellent

1. Jam (3.44), 2. Yer Blues (3.58), 3. Yer Blues (3.58), 4. Watching the Wheels (3.00), 5. Corrina Corrina (1.15), 6. Beautiful Boy (Darling Boy) (2.44), 7. Whatever Gets You Through the Night (3.48), 8. Only You (3.13), 9. Mother (3.15), 10. Give Peace a Chance (7.37), 11. Send Me Some Loving (2.32), 12. Bless You (3.51), 13. Dear Yoko (5.17), 14. Borrowed Time (4.58), 15. Move Over Ms L (1.31), 16. Move Over Ms L (1.51), 17. Move Over Ms L (2.38)

Notes: Track 1, *Rock and Roll Circus* rehearsal. Tracks 2 and 3, *Rock and Roll Circus*. Track 4, acoustic. Track 5, electric. Track 6, acoustic, Bermuda, summer 1980. Track 7, early rehearsal. Track 8, John's vocal, no spoken verse, summer 1974. Track 9, alternate. Track 10, One-to-One concert. Track 11, jam. Track 12, rehearsal. Track 13, acoustic take 2, Bermuda. Track 14, acoustic. Track 15, early acoustic with chat. Track 16, electric. Track 17, rehearsal. Cover picture shows John on stage at the *Rock and Roll Circus*.

903. YER BLUES

Vigotone VT-CD-05

Format: CD

Source: various – see notes

Sound quality: excellent

1. Only People (2.38), 2. Move Over Ms L (1.50), 3. Forgive Me (My Little Flower Princess) (3.20), 4. Rock 'n' Roll People (2.36), 5. The Luck of the

Irish (1.16), 6. No. 9 Dream (2.07), 7. Mother (4.34), 8. Stranger's Room (6.03), 9. Bring on the Lucie (Freeda People) (3.59), 10. Clean-up Time (3.28), 11. Yer Blues (3.58), 12. Jam (3.42), 13. Yer Blues (3.58), 14. John Henry (2.13), 15. I'm Losing You (3.51), 16. Love (2.23), 17. Out the Blue (4.08), 18. What You Got (3.18), 19. Real Love (3.59), 20. Bony Moronie (3.55)

Notes: Track 1, rough mix. Tracks 2 and 3, acoustic. Track 4, alternate take. Tracks 5 and 6, acoustic. Track 7, electric with tremolo. Track 8, piano with intro, Dakota. Track 9, rough mix with count-in. Track 10, piano, Dakota. Tracks 11 and 12, *Rock and Roll Circus* rehearsal, 11 December 1968. Track 13, *Rock and Roll Circus* 11 December 1968. Track 14, live. Track 15, rough mix with reference vocal. Track 16, electric with tremolo. Track 17, rough mix with final vocal. Track 18, acoustic. Track 19, acoustic with whistled chorus, Dakota. Track 20, rough mix with count-in.

Front cover has colour picture of John with track listing on the back.

904. YOUR DADDY'S HERE

Geritol DPRO-79972

Format: CD

Released: 2001

Time: 69.32

Source: outtakes and Dakota demos

Sound quality: excellent

1. Borrowed Time (4.54), 2. Watching the Wheels (3.01), 3. Real Love (2.41), 4. Beautiful Boy (4.10), 5. Serve Yourself (3.52), 6. I Don't Wanna Face It (2.05), 7. I Don't Wanna Face It (2.54), 8. I'm Losing You (2.58), 9. I'm Stepping Out (4.58), 10. Watching the Wheels (7.33), 11. Watching the Wheels (4.21), 12. Watching the Wheels (4.40), 13. Watching the Wheels (7.33), 14. Watching the Wheels (2.43), 15. Watching the Wheels (1.04), 16. Watching the Wheels (2.22), 17. Watching the Wheels (0.29), 18. Watching the Wheels (4.15), 19. Watching the Wheels (3.13), 20. Don't Be Afraid (2.44), 21. Woman (4.05), 22. This One's Probably for Mr Richard Starkey

Notes: Tracks 1 and 2, guitar demos. Tracks 3, 6 and 8, double vocal tracks. Track 4, handclap version. Track 5 is the cursing version. Track 7, rhythm box version. Track 9, alternate lyrics. Tracks 10–19, rehearsals and outtakes. Track 20, piano version. Track 21, acoustic version with rhythm box. Track 22, a few mumbled words.

Cover has a brown border with a picture of John in the centre with the track listing on the back.

905. YOU SHOULD'A BEEN THERE

See *The Rock 'n' Roll Sessions, Parts 1 and 2* (Ghost Records)

906. A SIXTIETH BIRTHDAY CELEBRATION FROM MJI RADIO

Unknown

Format: CD

Source: see below

Sound quality: unknown

Sleeve notes state: 'The programme features an exclusive interview with Yoko, as well as comments from John, Paul McCartney, George Harrison, Ringo Starr, Eric Clapton, Steven Tyler, Mick Jagger, George Martin, Elton John, Ozzie Osbourne, David Crosby, Brian Wilson, Alice Cooper and many others. The world premiere of the previously unreleased John song "Help Me to Help Myself" is played during the special broadcast. Plus, you'll hear dozens of Lennon songs from his Beatle days and solo, as well as rare tracks and interviews.'

907. THE 1968 DEMOS

Howdy 555-04

Format: CD

Source: *White Album* demos, plus various John Lennon demos

Sound quality: good

1. Back in the USSR, 2. Dear Prudence, 3. The Continuing Story of Bungalow Bill, 4. I'm So Tired, 5. Piggies, 6. Julia, 7. Yer Blues, 8. Mother Nature's Son, 9. Everybody's Got Something to Hide Except Me and My Monkey,

10. Sexy Sadie, 11. Not Guilty, 12. Revolution, 13. Cry Baby Cry, 14. What's the New Mary Jane, 15. Child of Nature, 16. Julia (version 1), 17. Julia (version 2), 18. Don't Let Me Down (version 1), 19. Don't Let Me Down (version 2), 20. Everyone Had a Hard Year (version 2), 21. A Case of the Blues, 22. Oh, My Love (version 1), 23. Oh, My Love (version 2), 24. The Maharishi Song, 25. I Want You

Notes: Tracks 1–15, demo sessions at George's house, late May 1968. Tracks 16–25. Various John Lennon demos, May–December 1968. Reissued as *1968 Demos* (Vigotone). Comes with booklet. Track 25: 'I Want You'. This is not the same song 'I Want You' (She's So Heavy) which was on The Beatles album *Abbey Road*. It features John and Yoko on slide guitar with an improvised vocal. This recording is taken from *The Lost Lennon Tapes* radio series programme broadcast on 21 January 1991. See also *My Love Will Turn You On*.

908. 1968 DEMOS

Vigotone Vigo 100

Format: CD

Source: *White Album* demos, plus various John Lennon demos

Sound quality: very good

Notes: Reissue of The 1968 Demos (Howdy) with better sound quality.

909. 1970 NOVEMBER HOME RECORDINGS

Green Grape

Format: CD

Source: home recordings, Tittenhurst Park, Ascot, November 1970

Sound quality: excellent

1. Make Love Not War (4.14), 2. I'm the Greatest (1.39), 3. I'm the Greatest (0.43), 4. How? (1.52), 5. Child of Nature (0.59), 6. Child of Nature (1.18), 7. Oh, Yoko (0.53), 8. Oh, Yoko (1.19), 9. Sally and Billy (1.19), 10. Sally and Billy (4.24), 11. Oh, Yoko (2.53), 12. Oh, Yoko (0.50), 13. Help (2.27), 14. I'm Having a Baby by My Love (1.38), 15. Instrumental (4.08), 16. Christmas Message (3.20), 17. Christmas Message (2.18), 18. Somewhere in My Sky

(1.51), 19. People Get Ready/How? (5.28), 20. How? (5.08), 21. How? (4.53), 22. Can't Believe You Wanna Leave (1.30), 23. Mailman Bring Me No More Blues (2.08), 24. I Promise (2.50), 25. I'm Not as Strong as You Think (2.13), 26. You Know How Hard It Is (2.01), 27. Happy Gi1 (1.11), 28. I'll Make You Happy (1.58), 29. I'll Make You Happy (3.46)

910. 1970 PLASTIC ONO BAND – HOME AND STUDIO
Green Grape

Format: CD (double)

Source: various outtakes

Sound quality: very good

Disc One

California. Home Recordings, Summer 1970

1. Love, 2. Mother, 3. My Mummy's Dead, 4. My Mummy's Dead, 5. I Found Out, 6. I Found Out, 7. God, 8. God, 9. God, 10. God, 11. Yoko Ono Poem Game, 12. When a Boy Meets a Girl, 13. When a Boy Meets a Girl, 14. Well, Well, Well

EMI Studios, London, Studio Sessions, September–October 1970

15. Mother, 16. Mother, 17. Mother, 18. Hold On, 19. I Found Out, 20. I Found Out, 21. Working Class Hero

Disc Two

EMI Studios, London, Studio Sessions, September–October 1970

1. Isolation, 2. Remember, 3. Remember, 4. Love, 5. Well, Well, Well, 6. Look at Me, 7. Look at Me, 8. Look at Me, 9. God, 10. Studio Medley: That's All Right Mama/Glad All Over/Honey Don't/Don't Be Cruel/Hound Dog/Unknown/Matchbox, 11. Long Lost John, 12. Something More Abstract, 13. Between the Takes, 14. Slow Blues Jam, 15. Fast Rocker, 16. Greenfield Morning I Pushed a Baby Carriage all Over The City

Bonus Track

17. Love (1982 stereo remix)

911. 1971 Home Recordings

Green Grape

Format: CD

Source: home recordings

Sound quality: unknown

1. God Save Oz, 2. *Grapefruit* readings, 3. Happy Xmas (War Is Over), 4. J.J. 5. J.J. 6. Call My Name, 7. Attica State, 8. Attica State, 9. Woman Is the Nigger of the World, 10. Call My Name, 11. Just Gotta Give Me Some Rock 'n' Roll, 12. New York City, 13. People, 14. Send Me Some Lovin', 15. He Got the Blues, 16. Pill, 17. I Ain't Got Time, 18. She'll Be Coming Round the Mountain, 19. The Luck of the Irish, 20. The Luck of the Irish, 21. Free The People, 22. John Sinclair

912. 1971 St Regis Hotel and Hotel Syracuse, NY

Green Grape

Format: CD (double)

Source: recorded at St Regis Hotel and Hotel Syracuse in New York, 1971

Sound quality: good

Disc One

St. Regis Hotel, September 1971

1. Shazam!, 2. Honey Don't, 3. Glad All Over, 4. Lend Me Your Comb, 5. New York City, 6. Wake Up Little Suzie, 7. Vacation Time, 8. Peggy Sue, 9. Not Fade Away, 10. (You're So Square) Baby I Don't Care, 11. Heartbeat, 12. Peggy Sue Got Married, 13. Peggy Sue, 14. Maybe Baby, 15. Mailman Bring Me No More Blues, 16. Rave On, 17. Exit Peace, 18. Call My Name

Disc Two

Hotel Syracuse, 9 October 1971

1. What'd I Say, 2. Yellow Submarine, 3. On Top of Old Smokey, 4. Goodnight Irene, 5. 'Jesse James Was a Man', 6. Take This Hammer, 7. He's Got the Whole World in His Hands, 8. He's Got the Whole World in

His Hands, 9. He's Got the Whole World in His Hands, 10. Tandoori Chicken/Attica State, 11. Like a Rolling Stone, 12. Twist and Shout, 13. Louie Louie, 14. La Bamba, 15. Bring It on Home to Me, 16. Yesterday, 17. Tandoori Chicken, 18. Power to the People, 19. Maybe Baby, 20. Peggy Sue, 21. 'Bring out the joints', 22. My Baby Left Me, 23. Blue Suede Shoes, 24. God Save the Queen, 25. Crippled Inside, 26. Give Peace a Chance, 27. Crippled Inside, 28. Uncle Albert/Admiral Halsey, 29. Happy Birthday, 30. Uncle Albert/Admiral Halsey, 31. My Sweet Lord, 32. Imagine, 33. Oh, Yoko, 34. Nurse's Song, 35. Angel Baby

Notes: see also *St. Regis Hotel and Hotel Syracuse, NY*

913. 1974 HOME RECORDINGS

Unknown

Format: CD

Source: various outtakes

Sound quality: unknown

1. Steel and Glass (piano), 2. Going Down on Love (piano), 3. Going Down on Love (acoustic guitar, take 1), 4. Going Down on Love (acoustic guitar, take 2), 5. Going Down on Love (acoustic guitar, take 3), 6. Move Over Ms L (electric guitar), 7. Move Over Ms L (acoustic guitar), 8. No. 9 Dream (acoustic guitar), 9. No. 9 Dream (acoustic guitar), 10. No. 9 Dream (acoustic guitar), 11. Surprise Surprise (Sweet Bird of Paradox) (electric guitar), 12. Surprise Surprise (Sweet Bird of Paradox) (acoustic guitar), 13. What You Got (unplugged electric guitar), 14. What You Got (electric guitar), 15. Whatever Gets You Through the Night (electric guitar), 16. Whatever Gets You Through the Night (electric guitar), 17. Whatever Gets You Through the Night (electric guitar)

914. 1974 *WALLS AND BRIDGES* SESSIONS

Green Grape

Format: CD

Source: *Walls and Bridges* album sessions

Sound quality: very good

Disc One

July–August 1974, The Record Plant East, New York

1. Going Down on Love, 2. Whatever Gets You Through the Night, 3. Whatever Gets You Through the Night, 4. Whatever Gets You Through the Night, 5. Whatever Gets You Through the Night, 6. Whatever Gets You Through the Night, 7. Old Dirt Road, 8. What You Got, 9. Bless You, 10. Bless You, 11. Scared, 12. No. 9 Dream, 13. Surprise Surprise (Sweet Bird of Paradox), 14. Steel and Glass, 15. Beef Jerky, 16. Nobody Loves You (When You're Down and Out), 17. Move Over Ms L, 18. Move Over Ms L, 19. Move Over Ms L, 20. Ain't She Sweet

July–August 1974, offline monitor mixes

21. Old Dirt Road, 22. No. 9 Dream, 23. Steel and Glass

Disc Two

21 July 1974, offline monitor mixes

1. Bless You, 2. Move Over Ms L, 3. Scared, 4. Surprise Surprise (Sweet Bird of Paradox), 5. Whatever Gets You Through the Night, 6. Going Down on Love, 7. Nobody Loves You (When You're Down and Out), 8. What You Got, 9. What You Got, 10. What You Got, 11. Old Dirt Road, 12. Steel and Glass

Bonus Tracks

13. Whatever Gets You Through the Night (US promo 45 mono), 14. What You Got (US promo 45 mono), 15. No. 9 Dream (US promo 45 mono), 16. No. 9 Dream (US promo 45 stereo), 17. TV Spot, 18. radio spot No. 1, 19. radio spot No. 2

3. The Lost Lennon Tapes

Although the solo career of John Lennon only lasted just over ten years and considering he decided to 'retire' and take on the role of a house husband for five years in 1975 an amazing amount of unissued material was stored in the basement at the Dakota in New York. When Yoko Ono employed a researcher to catalogue the tapes he discovered more than 300 hours of recordings. Some of these tapes were the various interviews John had given over the years but there was a huge amount of music tapes containing outtakes, home demos, rehearsals, live concerts, television performances and so on. There were basically two reasons why there was so much material. Firstly John recorded everything from his initial efforts when writing a new song, in order to have a reference guide for future use, right up to the final recordings. During the recording sessions for the *Imagine* and *Double Fantasy* albums, the tapes were running throughout the sessions and even the control room discussions were taped. Every live performance was taped including the rehearsals. Secondly John was a hoarder and never disposed of anything. Yoko had already agreed at that time to the issue of four albums containing new recordings, although many of the tracks had been bootlegged – *Heart Play* (which was an interview record), *Milk and Honey*, *Live in New York City* and *Menlove Avenue*.

The dilemma for Yoko was what to do with the wealth of material contained in her basement archives, most of which was unfinished. Following discussions with the radio station Westwood One, who confirmed their commitment to the project, she gave them access to the Dakota archives to enable them to prepare for *The Lost Lennon Tapes* radio series. Westwood One called on the services of Elliot Mintz who was a long standing friend of the Lennons who narrated the shows and also provided excerpts from his own collection of Lennon interviews.

The broadcasting system in America is somewhat different to the UK It is a much larger country and therefore is not served by a national radio station. Each city or state has its own station and networks such as Westwood One syndicate their programmes around the country in the form of discs. These include the music and talk plus several adverts. There are also gaps for local stations to insert their own advertisement breaks. These discs are made in sufficient quality to supply the stations who are taking the series. Each programme in the series runs for an hour including adverts and accordingly there were two discs for each show. The covers stated *The Lost Lennon Tapes* with Westwood One Radio Networks printed underneath one of John's drawings from his book *Skywriting by Word of Mouth*.

The first show in *The Lost Lennon Tapes* series was broadcast in America on 18 January 1988 with the *Premiere Show*. The first few shows were a disappointment for fans expecting to hear rare and unreleased tracks as these programmes consisted mainly of familiar Beatles and Lennon tracks plus lots of talk. These only contained a few minutes of rare material. As the series progressed more rare material was included and although this was supposed to be taken from the Dakota archives, it does seem that the show's producers used material from Beatles bootlegs which were in circulation. Some of these tracks include surface noise which indicates that these are taken from vinyl discs rather than archive tapes. It also seems that the series at times strayed from the original intentions. The shows included a great number of official releases both from The Beatles and Lennon's solo career. One show (as can be seen from the programme details on the following pages) even concentrated on the music of Paul McCartney. The series ran for five years and 218 shows.

As the programmes progressed during the first year of the broadcasts, the amount of unreleased material increased. Some shows were dominated by interviews including extracts from the *Rolling Stone* magazine interview from 1970. Obviously Westwood One did not have access to the EMI archives but they did discover in the Lennon vaults a number of Beatles recording which were not owned by EMI including the demos recorded in May 1968 at George Harrison's home studio in Esher. These demos were recorded in preparation for The Beatles next album which was released in November of that year and became known as the *White Album*. Lennon had kept a full set of the recordings but only his songs were broadcast in the series. The demos were acoustic and recorded on home equipment but are fascinating to listen to.

At the start of the series Elliot Mintz said in an interview with *Musician* magazine: 'Let's just play it on the radio and let everybody enjoy it. And let those who want to tape it off the air, tape it off the air. One of the things this series should do is put an end to the John and Yoko bootleg market.' He could not have been more wrong! This series opened the floodgates of Lennon bootlegs.

Unfortunately the shows were not broadcast in the UK However the first bootlegs of tracks taken from the shows appeared in 1988. These were the vinyl releases by Bag Records with thirty-five volumes in the series. These vinyl discs are very difficult to obtain now. Occasionally a second hand one appears at a record fair. Details of all these albums can be found in Part One (see entry numbers 069 tc 103 – *The Lost Lennon Tapes*). These vinyl releases were well presented with colour sleeves, detailed track listings and informative notes. Although the first twenty-three albums from Bag Records were only available on vinyl, volumes twenty-four to thirty-five were also released on compact disc with some consisting of two discs containing three of the original vinyl albums. It was following the compact disc releases that we entered into the minefield of what is available. Further compact disc releases followed on different labels such as Living Legend Records who issued their own series, also titled *The Lost Lennon Tapes*, with a different track listing. Walrus Records also released a series of double CDs titled *The Complete Lost Lennon Tapes*. To add to the confusion Angry Dog Records issued a series titled *The Real Complete Lost Lennon Tapes*. If they were not enough to keep collectors busy, two sets of CDs are available (not including the series from Angry Dog) containing the complete show, minus the advert breaks, starting with the *Premiere Show*. Full track listings from these two sets are listed below. The sound quality of these discs is excellent. As far as the Angry Dog series is concerned (*The Real Complete Lost Lennon Tapes*), we have traced details of the first four volumes and these are shown in Part Two – Compact Discs. We know that there are further releases in this series but we have been unable to trace details. Apart from the sets titled *The Lost Lennon Tapes*, the bootleg labels issued a number of other releases including tracks taken from the radio series such as *It's Hard to Be Butterflies* and *We'd Like to Change the Tempo Now*, both of which comprised outtakes and demos from the *Double Fantasy* and *Milk and Honey* sessions.

The Lost Lennon Tapes – *Westwood One Radio Series*

Notes: Listed below are details of all the discs released in this series of the radio shows which started with the *Premiere Show* on 18 January 1988. Most of the releases in Set One were double-disc sets. The two sets listed below basically cover the same pattern with each disc being tracks taken from a complete show. The details shown provide a record of all the 218 programmes in the series.

The sleeve for each disc contained one of John's sketches. A more detailed description of the contents of these programmes can be found in the various volumes of the books *Unfinished Music – An Unauthorized Companion to The Lost Lennon Tapes* by L R E King. Comparing the details in these books to compact disc track listings, it does appear that some items from the original broadcasts have been omitted. As the second set is to all intents and purposes identical to the first set, we have not repeated all the tracks. We have shown for each disc which programme is included on that disc. The major difference is that the second set is single discs whereas the first set is mainly double-disc sets.

Each of the shows was called an episode and each episode contained five segments of varying length. At the end of each segment there is usually an interview snippet and a comment on what is coming up in the next part of the programme. The reason there are five segments in each show is because they contained four commercial breaks. They have been edited out of these releases.

We have shown the track listings exactly as printed on the compact discs' inlays, which means there are some small anomalies in the song titles.

Set One

Westwood One

Format: Compact Discs

Source: complete original broadcasts

Sound quality: excellent

389. PREMIERE SHOW (CDs 1 AND 2)

Disc One – 18 January 1988. Premiere Show

1. Segment 1, 2. Love Me Do (The Beatles), Twist and Shout (The Beatles), 3. Segment 3: A Hard Day's Night (The Beatles), Tomorrow Never Knows (The Beatles), Nowhere Man (The Beatles), Lucy in the Sky (The Beatles), Segment 4: Strawberry Fields Forever (The Beatles), Help! (The Beatles), Give Peace a Chance

Disc Two – 18 January 1988 (continued). Premiere Show

1. Segment 4: Instant Karma, Power to the People, Imagine, 2. Segment 5: How Do You Sleep? Mind Games, Woman Is the Nigger of the World, 3. Segment 6: Whatever Gets You Through the Night, Stand By Me, No. 9 Dream

390. PREMIERE SHOW (CD 3)

18 January 1988 (continued). *Premiere Show*

1. Segment 7: Watching the Wheels, Starting Over, Losing You, 2. Segment 8: Beautiful Boy, Woman, Clean-up Time, 3. Segment 9: Lennon Montage, 4. Preview, 5. Commercial 3 hour preview

391. SHOWS 1 AND 2 (WO 001/002)

Disc One – 25 January 1988. Program No. 88–05

1. Segment 1: Elliot Mintz introduction, 2. Instant Karma, 3. Segment 2, 4. Mucho Mungo (Harry Nilsson), 5. Segment 3, 6. Working Class Hero, Ballad of John and Yoko (The Beatles), 7. Segment 4, 8. Don't Let Me Down (The Beatles), 9. One After 909 (The Beatles), 10. Get Back (The Beatles), 11. Segment 5: I Found Out, 12. Well, Well, Well, 13. My Mummy's Dead, 14. God

Disc Two – 1 February 1988. Program No. 88–06

1. Segment 1: America, 2. I Want to Hold Your Hand (The Beatles), 3. Segment 2: Sean interview, 4. Life Begins at Forty, 5. Segment 3: First solo LP, 6. Mother, 7. I Am the Walrus (The Beatles), 8. Segment 4: Managers, 9. Blue Suede Shoes (partial), 10. Cold Turkey, 11. Give Peace a Chance, 12. Power to the People, 13. Segment 5: Properties, 14. Clean-up Time, 15. *Two Virgins* (excerpt), 16. Imagine (live)

392. SHOWS 3 AND 4 (WO 003/004)

Disc One – 8 February 1988. Program No. 88–07

1. Segment 1: February 11 1963, 2. Please Please Me (The Beatles), 3. All My Loving (The Beatles), 4. She Loves You (The Beatles), 5. Segment 2: Invade East Coast, 6. Cry for a Shadow (partial) (The Beatles), 7. Twist and Shout (The Beatles), 8. Segment 3: Sean interview, 9. Beautiful Boy, 10. Girls and Boys, 11. Segment 4: *Rock 'n' Roll* session, 12. Be Bop A Lula, 13. Be My Baby (partial), 14. Segment 5: Sean interview, 15. With a Little Help from My Friends (The Beatles), 16. Woman, 17. Valotte (Julian Lennon)

Disc Two – 15 February 1988. Program No. 88–08

1. Segment 1: Media Playboy, 2. Norwegian Wood (The Beatles), 3. Girl (The Beatles), 4. Segment 2: Maharishi, 5. Yer Blues (The Beatles), 6. I'm So Tired (The Beatles), 7. Sexy Sadie (The Beatles), 8. The Rishikesh Song, 9. Segment 3: Writing style, 10. Lennon reads, 11. Segment 4: Playboy interviews. 12. I Want You (She's So Heavy) (The Beatles), 13. Segment 5: Sgt Pepper, 14. Strawberry Fields Forever (demo)

393. SHOWS 5 AND 6 (WO 005/006)

Disc One – 22 February 1988. Program No. 88–09

1. Segment 1: *Walls and Bridges*, 2. Whatever Gets You Through the Night (John with Elton John), 3. Lucy in the Sky with Diamonds (John with Elton John), 4. Segment 2: Bed in, 5. Ballad of John and Yoko (partial) (The Beatles), 6. Give Peace a Chance, 7. Segment 3: Mid 1950s, 8. Rock Island Line (Lonnie Donegan), 9. Rock Island Line, 10. John Henry, 11. Segment 4: Surprise Surprise (demo, partial), 12. I Saw Her Standing There (The Beatles), 13. Segment 5: Work tapes, 14. Tennessee

Disc Two – 29 February 1988. Program No. 88–10

1. Segment 1: DJ on WNEW, 2. Revolution (demo), 3. Segment 2: airwaves – Dennis Elsas, 4. Whatever Gets You Through the Night, 5. No. 9 Dream, 6. Segment 3: India return, 7. Child of Nature, 8. Jealous Guy, 9. Segment 4: More Elsas, 10. Some Other Guy (Ritchie Barrett), 11. What'd I Say (Ray Charles), 12. Segment 5: More Elsas, 13. I Wanna Be Your Man (The Rolling Stones), 14. I Wanna Be Your Man (The Beatles), 15. Daddy Rolling Stone (Derek Martin)

394. SHOWS 7 AND 8 (WO 007/008)

Disc One – 7 March 1988. Program No. 88–11

1. Segment 1: Power to the People (partial), 2. The Luck of the Irish (demo), 3. Segment 2: Jesus controversy, 4. August 1966 Chicago Press Conference, 5. Segment 3: Yoko attraction, 6. *Every Man* album, 7. Every Man Has a Woman Who Loves Him (John and Yoko), 8. I'm Moving On (Eddie Money), 9. Segment 4: Birth of 'She Said She Said', 10. She Said She Said (demo), 11. She Said She Said (The Beatles), 12. Segment 5: *Every Man* album, 13. Dream Love (Harry Nilsson), 14. It's Alright (Sean Lennon)

Disc Two – 14 March 1988. Program No. 88–12

1. Segment 1: Ringo's Lennon songs, 2. I'm the Greatest (demo), 3. Goodnight, Vienna, 4. Segment 2: Abbey Road, 5. Mean Mr Mustard (demo), 6. Polythene Pam (partial) (The Beatles), 7. Carry That Weight/The End (partial) (The Beatles), 8. Segment 3: Evolution of 'Mind Games', 9. Make Love Not War (demo), 10. I Promise (demo), 11. Mind Games, 12. Segment 4: Composing 'In My Life', 13. In My Life (The Beatles), 14. Segment 5: Abbey Road, 15. Come Together (The Beatles), 16. You Can't Catch Me (partial) (Chuck Berry), 17. You Can't Catch Me

395. SHOWS 9 AND 10 (WO 009/010)

Disc One – 21 March 1988. Program No. 88–13

1. Segment 1: Second movie, 2. Help! (demo), 3. Help! (The Beatles), 4. Segment 2: Feud. 5. Too Many People (Paul and Linda McCartney), 6. How Do You Sleep? 7. Segment 7: Lennon reads, 8. You Know My

Name (Look Up the Number) (demo)/You Know My Name (Look Up the Number) (The Beatles), 9. Segment 4: Mal Evans and Keith Moon, 10. Move Over Ms L (Keith Moon), 11. In My Life (Keith Moon), 12. Segment 5: John live, 13. Memphis Tennessee (Chuck Berry and John Lennon), 14. Johnny B. Goode (Chuck Berry and John Lennon)

Disc Two – 28 March 1988. Program No. 88–14

1. Segment 1: Beatles live in Stockholm, 2. Money (The Beatles), 3. She Loves You (The Beatles), 4. Twist and Shout (The Beatles), 5. Segment 2: Pete Shotton and Cynthia Lennon – John's school days, 6. Segment 3: first single, 7. Starting Over, 8. Segment 4: John sailing, 9. Sea ditties, 10. Segment 5: ambitious recordings, 11. I Am the Walrus (The Beatles)

396. SHOWS 11 AND 12 (WO 011/012)

Disc One – 4 April 1988. Program No. 88–15

1. Segment 1: *Menlove Avenue*, 2. Whatever Happened To (demo), 3. Segment 2: Early childhood, 4. Strawberry Fields Forever (The Beatles), 5. Segment 3: Birth of The Quarrymen, 6. One After 909 (The Beatles), 7. Segment 4: Strawberry Fields Forever (demo), 8. Segment 5: John's mother Julia, 9. Julia (demo), 10.My Mummy's Dead, 11. Mother

Disc Two – 11 April 1988. Program No. 88–16

1. Segment 1: Composing tapes, 2. Whatever Gets You Through the Night, 3. Segment 2: First trip to Hamburg, 4. Interview bits, 5. Segment 3: extra tracks, 6. Dear John (demo), 7. Segment 4: Second trip to Hamburg, 8. My Bonnie (Tony Sheridan and The Beatles), 9. The Saints (Tony Sheridan and The Beatles), 10. Segment 5: Tony Sheridan, 11. Toilet seat incident

397. SHOWS 13 AND 14 (WO 013/014)

Disc One – 18 April 1988. Program No. 88–17

1. Segment 1: Early 1969, 2. Across the Universe (The Beatles), 3. Segment 2: Immigration battle, 4. Scared, 5. Segment 3: Beatles at The Cavern, 6. Interviews, 7, Some Other Guy (The Beatles), 8. Segment 4: Unpublished songs, 9. What's the New Mary Jane (demo),

10. Segment 5: Ringo's *Rotogravure* sessions, 11. Cooking (in the Kitchen of Love) (demo)

Disc Two – 25 April 1988. Program No. 88-18

1. Segment 1: Bob Dylan, 2. Blowing in the Wind (Bob Dylan), 3. Corrina Corrina (partial) (Bob Dylan), 4. A Hard Rain's A-Gonna Fall (Bob Dylan), 5. You've Got to Hide Your Love Away (The Beatles), 6. Cold Turkey (partial), 7. Segment 2: Dylan myth, 8. God (partial), 9. Segment 3: parodies, 10. Knocking on Heaven's Door (Bob Dylan), 11. Lord Take This Make-up Off Me, 12. News of the Day (from Reuters), 13. Segment 4: Dylan's conversion, 14. Subterranean Homesick Blues (partial) (Bob Dylan), 15. Segment 5: more Dylan, 16. Gotta Serve Somebody (Bob Dylan), 17. Serve Yourself

398. SHOWS 15 AND 16 (WO 015/016)

Disc One – 2 May 1988. Program No. 88-19

1. Segment 1: Sgt Pepper, 2. Good Morning, Good Morning (demo), 3. Good Morning, Good Morning (The Beatles), 4. Segment 2: 1968 marijuana bust, 5. Dr. Robert (The Beatles), 6. I've Got a Feeling (demo), 7. Everybody's Got Something to Hide Except Me and My Monkey (demo), 8. Clean-up Time (outtake), 9. Segment 3: Blues, 10. I'm a Man, 11. Brown Eyed Handsome Man, 12. Segment 4: John's father, 13. Mother/That's My Life (Freddie Lennon), 14. Segment 5: more sea ditties and songs, 15. 'Twas A Night Like Ethel Merman, 16. Beyond the Sea/Blue Moon/Young Love

Disc Two – 9 May 1988. Program No. 88-20

1. Segment 1: move to New York City, 2. Power to the People (alternate), 3. Segment 2: Free John Sinclair, 4. Rally to free John Sinclair, 5. Attica State, 6. The Luck of the Irish, 7. John Sinclair, 8. Segment 3: John Sinclair freed, 9. Lennon post-release phone call, 10. Pope Smokes Dope (David Peel and The Lower East Side), 11. Segment 4: aborted Rock and Radical tour, 12. Going To San Diego (Allen Ginsburg with Bob Dylan), 13. Revolution (alternate) (The Beatles), 14. Segment 4: Nixon showdown, 15. Give Me Some Truth (partial)

399. SHOWS 17 AND 18 (WO 017/018)

Disc One – 16 May 1988. Program No. 88–21

1. Segment 1: *Mind Games* album, 2. Rock 'n' Roll People (composing), 3. Rock 'n' People (take 5), 4. Segment 2: Brian Epstein affair, 5. Bad To Me (demo), 6. Segment 3: evolution of 'Stepping Out', 7. Real Life/Stepping Out (composing), 8. Stepping Out (demo), 9. Segment 4: John on KSAN-FM, San Francisco, with Tom Donahue, 10. River Deep Mountain High (Ike and Tina Turner), 11. Blue Suede Shoes (Carl Perkins), 12. Segment 5: Evolution of 'Tight A$' and 'Beef Jerky', 13. Tight A$ (composing)

Disc Two – 23 May 1988. Program No. 88–22

1. Segment 1, 2. Rock Island Line, 3. Segment 2: Liverpool College of Art, 4. Bad Boy (partial) (The Beatles), 5. Look at Me (partial), 6. Segment 3: return to poetry corner, 7. Neville Club, 8. Clinic (Cynthia Lennon), 9. Once Upon A Pool Table, 10. Segment 4: Sean Ono Lennon, 11. EXP (partial) (Jimi Hendrix Experience), 12. A Little Story (Sean Lennon), 13. It's Alright (partial) (Sean Lennon), 14. It's Alright (chat), 15. Starpeace (partial) (Yoko Ono), 16. One Chord Bit (John and Sean), 17. Segment 5: Live in '65, 18. I Feel Fine/Ticket to Ride/Help! (*Ed Sullivan Show*)

400. SHOWS 19 AND 20 (WO 019/020)

Disc One – 30 May 1988. Program No. 88–23

1. Segment 1: Oz Controversy, 2. God Save Us (studio), 3. God Save Us (demo), 4. Segment 2: Live in New York City, 5. Instant Karma (rehearsal), 6. New York City (rehearsal), 7. Segment 3: One-to-One rehearsals, 8. Give Peace a Chance (rehearsal, partial), 9. Segment 4: How I Won the War, 10. Help (The Beatles), 11. How I Won the War (Ken Thorne), 12. Segment 5: On the Set in Spain, 13. Strawberry Fields Forever (The Beatles) (version 1, take 1)

Disc Two – 6 June 1988. Program No. 88–24

1. Segment 1: Trip to Japan 1977, 2. Jealous Guy (alternate), 3. Mirror Mirror (take 1), 4. Mirror Mirror (take 5), 5. Segment 2: Dakota Mind Movie Mystery Theatre, 6. Maurice Dupont Agent Provocateur Du Jour,

7. Segment 3: Dear Prudence (The Beatles) (partial), 8. Dear Prudence (demo), 9. Dear Prudence (The Beatles) (alternate), 10. Segment 4: One-to-One rehearsals, 11. Cold Turkey (rehearsal), 12. Segment 5: One-to-One concert, 13. New York City (live), 14. Imagine (live)

401. SHOWS 21 AND 22 (WO 021/022)

Disc One – 13 June 1988, Program No. 88–25

1. Segment 1: Return To Studio 1980, 2. Watching the Wheels ('That's My Style' take), 3. Life Begins at Forty (partial), 4. Segment 2: New Songs, 5. Stepping Out (*Milk and Honey* version), 6. Dear Yoko (Bermuda demo), 7. Segment 3: Evolution of 'Starting Over', 8. My Life (version 1), 9. My Life (version 2), 10. Don't Be Crazy, 11. The Worst is Over, 12. Segment 4: Hit Factory, 13. Starting Over (Bermuda demo, partial), 14. Studio Jamming, 15. Starting Over (studio), 16. Segment 5, 17. Starting Over (early rough mix)

Disc Two – 20 June 1988, Program No. 88–26

1. Segment 1: Buddy Holly, 2. Words of Love (The Beatles), 3. Hello Little Girl (The Fourmost), 4. Maybe Baby/Rave On/Not Fade Away (St Regis Hotel), 5. Not Fade Away (One-to-One rehearsal), 6. That'll Be the Day, 7. Segment 2: Development of Woman, 8. Woman (composing), 9. Woman (Bermuda demo, partial), 10. Segment 3: Recording 'Woman', 11. Woman (studio), 12. Woman (rough mix), 13. Segment 4: Dakota Mind Movie Mystery Theatre, 14. Return of Maurice DuPont Agent Provocateur, 15. Segment 5: Rockabilly Rave Up, 16. Blue Suede Shoes (Carl Perkins), 17. Honey Don't/Don't Be Cruel/Matchbox (Plastic Ono Band jam)

402. SHOWS 23 AND 24 (WO 023/024)

Disc One – 27 June 1988, Program No. 88–27

1. Segment 1: *Rock 'n' Roll* session, 2. Here We Go Again (demo), 3. Here We Go Again (*Menlove Avenue* version), 4. Segment 2: Cold Turkey (live, partial), 5. Heroin experiment, part 1, 6, Cold Turkey (demo), 7. Cold Turkey (studio alternate), 8. Segment 3: Heroin experiment, part 2, 9. Clean-up Time (composing), 10. Segment 4: Dakota Mind Movie

Comedy Theatre, 11. Podgy and Jasper, 12. Being for the Benefit of Mr Kite (The Beatles), 13. Nowhere Man (Tiny Tim), 14. Segment 4: *Rock 'n' Roll* session, 15. Sweet Little Sixteen (alternate take), 16. You Can't Catch Me (alternate take)

Disc Two – 4 July 1988. Program No. 88–28

1. Segment 1: Unreleased songs, 2. One of the Boys (take 2), 3. Segment 2: Decca Records audition, 1 January 1962, 4. Money (partial) (The Beatles), 5. To Know Her Is to Love Her (The Beatles), 6. Memphis Tennessee (The Beatles), 7. Segment 3: Mind Games, 9. Make Love Not War (partial), 10. Segment 4: Sign with Parlophone, 11. One After 909 (1962 rehearsal), 12. Besame Mucho (studio, 6 June 1962) (The Beatles), 13. How Do You Do It (studio, 4 September 1962), 14. Love Me Do (version 1, 4 September 1962) (The Beatles), 15. Segment 5, 16. Sign with Geffen Records, 17. I Don't Want to Face It (Bermuda demo), 18. Hard Times Are Over (partial) (Yoko Ono)

403. SHOWS 25 AND 26 (WO 025/026)

Disc One – 11 July 1988. Program No. 88–29

1. Segment 1: Dr Winston O'Boogie, 2. Tom Donahue, KSAN-FM, 3. Girl (The Beatles), 4. Segment 2: WNEW-FM Dennis Elsas, 5. Watch Your Step (Bobby Parker), 6. Day Tripper (The Beatles), 7. I Call Your Name (The Beatles), 8. Segment 3: More WNEW-FM, 9. Surprise Surprise, 10. Bless You, 11. Segment 4: more Dennis Elsas, 12. I Am the Walrus (The Beatles), 13. More Tom Donahue, 14. A Day in the Life (The Beatles)

Disc Two – 18 July 1988. Program No. 88–30

1. Segment 1: Live at the Star Club, 31 December 1962, 2. Mr Moonlight (The Beatles), 3. Ask Me Why (The Beatles), 4. Matchbox (The Beatles), 5. Segment 2: Creative dyslexia, part 1, 6. Rain (The Beatles), 7. I'm Only Sleeping (The Beatles), 8. Segment 3: Buddy Holly encore, 9. Heartbeat/Peggy Sue Got Married/Peggy Sue. 10. Segment 4: creative dyslexia, part 2, 11. Tomorrow Never Knows (reference mix) (The Beatles), 12. Strawberry Fields Forever (early mix) (The Beatles), 13. Segment 5: Rock 'n' Roll meltdown, 14. Steel and Glass (studio rehearsal), 15. Move Over Ms L (studio rehearsal)

404. SHOWS 27 AND 28 (WO 027/028)

Disc One – 25 July 1988, Program No. 88–31

1. Segment 1: Spring '72 studio jams, 2. Roll Over Beethoven, 3. Whole Lotta Shakin' Goin' On/I'll Be Looking For You, 4. Segment 2: Dylan Revisited, 5. Corrina Corrina, 6. Serve Yourself (Mother version), 7. The Best Things In Life Are Free, 8. Segment 3: *Rock and Roll Circus*, 9. Untitled warm up, 10. Yer Blues, 11. Her Blues (Yoko Ono), 12. Segment 4: Jesse Ed Davis tribute, part 1, 13. Further On Down The Road (Jesse Ed Davis), 14. Mucho Mungo (demo), 15. Segment 5: Jesse Ed Davis tribute, part 2, 16. Mucho Mungo (Jesse Ed Davis), 17. Beef Jerky

Disc Two – 1ST August 1988, Program No. 88–32

1. Segment 1: Song writing team, 2. P.S. I Love You (The Beatles), 3. Segment 2: John on Paul, 4. Please Please Me (version 2) (The Beatles), 5. From Me to You (The Beatles), 6. From Me to You (Del Shannon), 7. Segment 3: Lennon on McCartney, 8. Do You Want to Know a Secret (early mix) (The Beatles), 9. Twist and Shout (partial) (The Beatles), 10. There's a Place (The Beatles), 11. Segment 4: Collaborations, 12. I Saw Her Standing There (The Beatles), 13. Baby It's You (The Beatles), 14. She Loves You (The Beatles), 15. Segment 5: More Lennon on McCartney, 16. I Wanna Be Your Man (partial) (The Beatles), 17. I Wanna Be Your Man (partial) (Rolling Stones), 18. I'm in Love (The Fourmost), 19. It Won't Be Long (The Beatles), 20. I Want to Hold Your Hand (The Beatles)

405. SHOWS 29 AND 30 (WO 029/030)

Disc One – 8 August 1988, Program No. 88–33

1. Segment: Psychedelic summer 1967, 2. Our World: 25 June 1967, 3. All You Need Is Love (The Beatles), 4. Segment 2: Bermuda demos, 5. Watching the Wheels (demo), 6. Segment 3: Dakota Mind Movie Theatre, 7. Opening Act: Juanito Lennon at Chi Chi's Cafe, 8. Headliner: Return of the Return of Maurice DuPont Agent Provocateur, 9. Segment 4: The *Ed Sullivan Show*, 10. Twist and Shout (The Beatles)/Please Please Me (The Beatles), 11. I Want to Hold Your Hand (The Beatles),

12. Segment 5: *Imagine* session with Alan White, 13. How Do You Sleep? (partial), 14. Crippled Inside (early take), 15. Oh, Yoko (partial), 16. Imagine (early take)

Disc Two – 15 August 1988. Program No. 88–34
1. Segment 1, 2. Sally and Billy (demo, partial), 3. Sally and Billy (demo), 4. Segment 2: Frolicking in the myth, 5. I Can't Get No Nookie (partial) (The Masked Marauders), 6. Have You Heard The Word (Fut), 7. Lullaby For A Lazy Day (partial) (*Grapefruit*), 8. Lullaby (*Grapefruit*), 9. Segment 3: Sleepy Blind Lemon Lennon, 10. I'm a Man (partial), 11. A Case of the Blues, 12. It's So Hard (outtake), 13. Send Me Some Loving (outtake), 14. Nobody Loves You (*Menlove Avenue*), 15. Segment 4: story behind 'I'm Losing You', 16. Stranger's Room (partial), 17. I'm Losing You (Bermuda demo), 18. I'm Losing You, 19. Segment 5: *Some Time in New York City* album, 20. New York City (demo), 21. New York City (demo)

406. SHOWS 31 AND 32 (WO 031/032)

Disc One – 22 August 1988. Program No. 88–35
1. Segment 1: Live in Stockholm 24 October 1963, 2. I Saw Her Standing There (The Beatles), 3. From Me to You (The Beatles), 4. Roll Over Beethoven (The Beatles), 5. You Really Got a Hold on Me (The Beatles), 6. Segment 2: The story behind Woman Is the Nigger of the World, 7. Woman Is the Nigger of the World (demo), 8. Woman Is the Nigger of the World (demo), 9. Segment 3: Dakota Mind Movie Theatre, 10. Peter Sellers, 11. A Hard Day's Night (Peter Sellers), 12. She Loves You (Peter Sellers), 13. Segment 4: O'Reggae with Tom Donahue KSAN-FM, September 1974, 14. What You Got, 15. Get Up Stand Up (The Wailers), 16. Segment 5: Reggae Fascination – Rastafars, 17. Borrowed Time (Bermuda demo)

Disc Two – 29 August 1988. Program No. 88–36
1. Segment 1: Apple Corps Ltd, 2. Taxman (The Beatles), 3. Segment 2: *Magical Mystery Tour*, 4. Magical Mystery Tour (The Beatles), 5. Segment 3: Magical Mystery Tour, 6. Aerial Tour Instrumental (The Beatles), 7. Hello Goodbye (partial) (The Beatles), 8. I Am the Walrus (The Beatles), 9. Segment 4: Apple Goes into Business, 10. With a Little Help from My

Friends (The Beatles), 11. Segment 5: Nutty at Apple, 12. Ob-La-Di Ob-La-Da (The Beatles)

407. SHOWS 33 AND 34 (WO 033/034)

Disc One – 5 September 1988. Program No. 88-37

Lennon at Large in Hollywood. Part 1, Spector Sessions

1. Segment 1: Hollywood, 2. Do You Wanna Dance (alternate take), 3. Be My Baby (alternate take), 4. Segment 2 Jim Keltner Interview, 5. Just Because (alternate take), 6. Stand By Me (alternate take), 7. Segment 3: Jim Keltner Interview, 8. Bring It on Home to Me/Send Me Some Loving (alternate take), 9. Segment 4: Jim Keltner, 10. Rip It Up (alternate take), 11. Segment 5: You Can't Catch Me (partial), 12. Slippin' and Slidin' (alternate take)

Disc Two – 12th September 1988. Program No. 83-38

Lennon at Large in Hollywood, Part 2, Nilsson Phase

1. Segment 1: Hollywood, part 2, 2. Ya Ya (alternate take), 3. Ain't That a Shame (alternate take), 4. Segment 2: Lennon and Nilsson, 5. Rock 'n' Roll People (*Menlove Avenue*), 6. Troubadour incident with Harry Nilsson and The Smothers Brothers, 7. Segment 3: Pussy Cats sessions, 8. Loop De Loop (Harry Nilsson), 9. Rock Around the Clock (Harry Nilsson), 10. Segment 4: Pussy Cats, 11. Mucho Mungo/Mt. Elga (rehearsal) (John Lennon and Harry Nilsson), 12. Mucho Mungo/Mt. Elga (Harry Nilsson), 13. Segment 5: Returns to New York, 14. Many Rivers to Cross (rough mix) (Harry Nilsson)

408. SHOWS 35 AND 36 (WO 035/036)

Disc One – 19 September 1988. Program No. 88-39

Lennon at Large: Coast-to-Coast

1. Segment 1: Coast-to-Coast, 2. Subterranean Homesick Blues (Harry Nilsson), 3. Segment 2: *Walls and Bridges*, 4. Surprise Surprise (demo), 5. Whatever Gets You Through the Night (rehearsal), 6. Surprise Surprise (studio with Elton John), 7. Move Over Ms L, 8. Segment 3: It's All Da-Da-Down, 9. Only You, 10. Segment 4: Immigraticn 1974, 11. Give Me

Some Truth, 12. Segment 5: At Caribou, 13. Lucy in the Sky with Diamonds (Elton John and John Lennon)

Disc Two – 26 September 1988. Program No. 88–40

Dr Winston O'Boogie On the Air, Part 2

1. Segment 1: O'Boogie with Dennis Elsas, WNEW-FM, 28 September 1974, 2. Discussion of Pussy Cats, 3. Save the Last Dance for Me (Harry Nilsson), 4. O'Boogie weatherman, 5. Segment 2: O'Boogie with Tom Donahue on KSAN-FM, September 1974, 6. Angel Baby (Rosey and The Originals), 7. Brontosaurus Stomp (Roy Wood), 8. Segment 3: Elsas continued, 9. Showdown (Electric Light Orchestra), 10. I Heard It Through the Grapevine (Marvin Gaye), 11. Segment 4: Elsas continued, 12. Gravy Train (Splinter), 13. I'm the Greatest (Ringo Starr), 14. What You Got, 15. Segment 5: Dr O'Boogie West, 16. Old Dirt Road

409. SHOWS 37 AND 38 (WO 037/038)

Disc One – 3 October 1988. Program No. 88–41

Sean and John Birthday Show

1. Segment 1: Birthdays – Sean, 2. Beautiful Boy (rough mix), 3. Segment 2: Childbirth, 4. Hold On, 5. Beautiful Boy (rough mix), 6. Segment 3: John interview Sean, 1 January 1976, 7. John and Sean talk about birthdays, late 1979, 8. Segment 4: Birthdays – John, 9. Here Come the Threes (Donovan), 10. Happy Trails (Janis Joplin and The Full Tilt Boogie Band), 11. Happy Birthday John (Ringo Starr), 12. What'd I Say/Yellow Submarine (partial), 13. Real Love, 14. Imagine (piano demo)

Disc Two – 10 October 1988. Program No. 88–42

Imagine: John Lennon Spotlight, Part 2, Julian Lennon, Part 1

1. Segment 1: *Imagine* – John Lennon film, 2. A Day in the Life (The Beatles), 3. Segment 2: More *Imagine*, 4. How? (partial), 5. Jealous Guy, 6. Segment 3: Julian Part 1 (with Cynthia Lennon), 7. Please Please Me (The Beatles), 8. Julian's first interview, mid-1963, 9. Segment 4: Julian continued, 10. Lucy in the Sky with Diamonds (The Beatles), 11. Segment 5: Julian continued, 12.Hey Jude (The Beatles)

410. SHOWS 39 AND 40 (WO 039/040)

Disc One – 17 October 1988. Program No. 88–43

Imagine: John Lennon Spotlight, Part 3, Julian Lennon, Part 2

1. Segment 1: Imagine John Lennon, Part 3, 2. Twist and Shout (partial) (The Beatles), 3. Ballad of John and Yoko (The Beatles), 4. Segment 2: Julian, Part 2 circa 1968–71, 5. I Want You (She's So Heavy) (partial) (The Beatles), 6. How? (alternate take), 7. Segment 3: Julian, circa 1971–74, 8. Isolation, 9. Julian's 11 birthday thank you tape, 10. Segment 4: Dakota Mind Movie Comedy Theatre, 11. She Loves You (Peter Sellers), 12. Help (Peter Sellers), 13. Segment 5: Julian continued, 14. Bony Moronie, 15. Ya Ya (John Lennon with Julian Lennon), 16. Stand By Me (*The Old Grey Whistle Test*)

Disc Two – 24 October 1988. Program No. 88–44

Lennon's Star on the Hollywood Walk of Fame Special

1. Segment 1: Yoko Ono press conference, 30 September 1988, 2. Segment 2: Walk of Fame induction, 3. Jim Ladd interview Jeff Pollack, 4. Mike Reynolds interviews Joe Smith, 5. Imagine (solo rehearsal), 6. Segment 3: Walk of Fame induction, continued, 7. Mike Reynolds interviews Davis Wolper, 8. Jim Ladd interviews Andrew Solt, 9. Segment 4: Walk of Fame induction continued, 10. Jim Ladd interviews Yoko Ono and Elliot Mintz, 11. Segment 5: Walk of Fame induction continued, 12. Star unveiling ceremony

411. SHOWS 41 AND 42 (WO 041/042)

Disc One – 31 October 1988. Program No. 88–45

Rock 'n' Roll, Part 2

1. Segment 1: Phil Spector sessions, 2. Sweet Little Sixteen (partial), 3. Angel Baby, 4. Since My Baby Left Me, 5. Segment 2: Song publishing, 6. To Know Her Is to Love Her, 7. Segment 3: In the Can, 8. Be Bop A Lula, 9. Rumble/Whole Lotta Love (rehearsal jam), 10. Rip It Up/Ready Teddy, 11. Peggy Sue, 12. Segment 4: Farewell message, 13. Just

Because, 14. Ain't That a Shame (partial), 15. Segment 5: Everybody's Talking Nobody's Talking (demo), 16. Nobody Told Me (rough mix)

Disc Two – 7 November 1988. Program No. 88–46
1. Segment 1: On the BBC, 16 July 1963, 2. Carol (The Beatles), 3. Soldier of Love (The Beatles), 4. Lend Me Your Comb (The Beatles), 5. Segment 2: Mark Lewisohn, Part 1, 6. How Do You Do It (The Beatles), 7. Kansas City/Hey Hey Hey (The Beatles), 8. Rock 'n' Roll Music (The Beatles), 9. Segment 3: Breakfast Jam, March 1972, 10. Send Me Some Loving, 11. Don't Be Cruel, 12. Segment 4: Mark Lewisohn, Part 2, 13. Revolution 1 (partial) (The Beatles), 14. Happiness Is a Warm Gun (The Beatles), 15. Leave My Kitten Alone (The Beatles), 16. Segment 5: Lennon For President, 17. Nomination (David Peel), 18. John Lennon for President (David Peel)

412. SHOWS 43 AND 44 (WO 043/044)

Disc One – 14 November 1988. Program No. 88–47
1. Segment 1: Abbey Road Studio 2, 2. Continuing Story of Bungalow Bill (demo), 3. Segment 2: Double tracking, 4. Not a Second Time (The Beatles), 5. Tomorrow Never Knows (The Beatles), 6. Segment 3: Plastic Ono Band, 7. I Found Out (alternate mix), 8. Love, 9. Segment 4: In studio work habits, 10. Yer Blues (The Beatles), 11. Mean Mr Mustard/Polythene Pam/She Came in Through the Bathroom Window (The Beatles), 12. Segment 5: Live At Palais Des Sports, Paris, 20 June 1965, 13. I'm a Loser (The Beatles), 14. A Hard Day's Night (The Beatles)

Disc Two – 21 November 1988. Program No. 88–48
1. Segment 1: Julia Baird Interview, 2. Julia (demo), 3. There's a Place (The Beatles), 4. Segment 2: Julia Baird Interview continued, 5. Bad Boy (partial) (The Beatles), 6. Ain't That a Shame, 7. Help (The Beatles), 8. Segment 3: Dakota Mind Movie Comedy Theatre, 9. Julio Juanito Lenono and Billy Shears, 10. Sailor Come Back to Me (Ringo Starr), 11. El Tango Terrible, 12. Coochie from Brazil/Down on the Sea (John and Ringo), 13. Segment 4: Julia Baird interview continued, 14. Mother (alternate take), 15. Any Time at All (partial) (The Beatles), 16. Be Bop A Lula, 17. Segment 5: studio zone, 18. Rain (basic track with backing vocals) (The Beatles)

413. SHOWS 45 AND 46 (WO 045/046)

Disc One – 28 November 1988. Program No. 88–49

1. Segment 1: *David Frost Show*, 13 January 1972, 2. John Sinclair, 3. It's So Hard, 4. Luck of the Irish, 5. Segment 2: French Connection, 6. My Bonnie (Tony Sheridan and The Beatles), 7. Money (Decca audition) (The Beatles), 8. Segment 3: Live Paris Encore, 9. Can't Buy Me Love (The Beatles), 10. Rock 'n' Roll Music (The Beatles), 11. Segment 4, 12. Demo Us Interruptus, 13. We Can Work It Out (demo, partial) (The Beatles), 14. We Can Work It Out (rough mix) (The Beatles), 15. Day Tripper (takes 1 and 3) (The Beatles), 16. Segment 5: Lost Lennon Tapes – Tennessee, 17. Howling at the Moon, 18. Memories (take 2)

Disc Two – 5 December 1988. Program No. 88–50

Lennon's Spiritual Development, Part 1

1. Segment 1: John's life, 2. There's a Place (take 4) (The Beatles), 3. Misery (The Beatles), 4. I'll Cry Instead (The Beatles), 5. Segment 2: A Hard Day's Night (partial) (The Beatles), 6. Help (The Beatles), 7. You've Got to Hide Your Love Away (The Beatles), 8. Segment 2: psychedelic era, 9. The Word (The Beatles), 10. She Said She Said (The Beatles), 11. Segment 4: psychedelic imagery, 12. Strawberry Fields Forever (The Beatles), 13. All You Need Is Love (partial) (The Beatles), 14. Segment 5: Brian's death, 15. Sexy Sadie (demo) (The Beatles)

414. SHOWS 47 AND 48 (WO 047/048)

Disc One – 12th December 1988. Program No. 88–51

Lennon's Spiritual Development, Part 2

1. Segment 1: New Apple adventure, 2. Revolution (*David Frost Show* version) (The Beatles), 3. Segment 2: late 1968, 4. Give Peace a Chance, 5. Segment 3: December 1969, 6. Cold Turkey (live), 7. Instant Karma, 8. Power to the People (partial), 9. Segment 4, 10. I Found Out, 11. Segment 5, 12. God (demo)

Disc Two – 19 December 1988. Program No. 88–52

Lennon's Spiritual Development, Part 3

1. Segment 1: End of 1980, 2. Mother (partial), 3. Imagine (alternate take), 4. Segment 3: Christmas Rhyme, 5. Happy Xmas (studio, partial), 6. Happy Xmas (demo), 7. Happy Xmas (alternate take), 8. Segment 3: Yoko equal time, 9. Woman Is the Nigger of the World, 10. Segment 4: Fall 1973, 11. Mind Games, 12. Out the Blue (rough mix), 13. Nobody Loves You (When You're Down and Out), 14. Segment 5: reunited 1975, 15. Serve Yourself (demo), 16. Living on Borrowed Time (rough mix), 17. Gone from This Place

415. SHOW 49 (WO 049)

26 December 1988. Program No. 89–01

Best of *The Lost Lennon Tapes* – Year One

1. Segment 1, 2. Twist and Shout (Sweden, 24 October 1963) (The Beatles), 3. Whatever Gets You Through the Night (live – John Lennon and Elton John), 4. Segment 2: studio jamming, 5. Honey Don't/Don't Be Cruel/Matchbox (Rockabilly Rave Up), 6. Segment 3: Spoken word, 7. John on art school, 8. Aunt Mimi throwing out his poems, 9. On critics who don't have a clue, 10. Poems: The Neville Club/Jock and Yono, 11. Julian and Sean's first interview, 12. With a Little Help from My Friends (Sean Lennon), 13. Segment 4: favourite unreleased songs. 14. Strawberry Fields Forever, 15. News of the Day (from Reuters), 16. Whatever Happened To (take 2), 17. Segment 5: favourite unreleased studio takes, 18. Across the Universe (alternate mix), 19. How Do You Sleep (alternate take)

416. SHOWS 050 AND 051 (WO 050/051)

Disc One – 2 January 1989. Program No. 89–02

The Year Two Preview

1. Segment 1: Good News, 2. Great Wok's 1979 New Year Resolution, 3. Jams and rehearsals, 4. Instrument 42 (The Beatles), 5. San Francisco Bay Blues, 6. Tequila Jam, 7. Whatever Gets You Through the Night,

8. Rip It Up (*Double Fantasy* sessions), 9. Segment 2: Lennon and The Beatles live, 10. A Hard Night Day's Night (The Beatles), 11. I Saw Her Standing There (Star Club) (The Beatles), 12. Too Much Monkey Business (BBC Radio 1963) (The Beatles), 13. Yer Blues [*Rock and Roll Circus*], 14. You Can't Do That (Melbourne, 15 June 1964), 15. Come Together (One-to-One concert), 16. Segment 3: Spoken word, 17. Segment 4: alternate studio takes and mixes, 18. Norwegian Wood (The Beatles), 19. A Day in the Life (The Beatles), 20. Dig It (The Beatles), 21. Rock 'n' Roll People, 22. Dear Yoko (a cappella), 23. Dear Yoko (basic track), 24. Segment 5: Unreleased songs and home demos), 25. No. 9 Dream, 26. Mirror Mirror (take 4), 27. John Henry, 28. She is a Friend of Dorothy's

Disc Two – 9 January 1989. Program No. 89–03

1. Segment 1: On the air in Hollywood, Part 1, 2. Come Together (The Beatles), 3. Subterranean Homesick Blues (Harry Nilsson), 4. Mind Games, 5. Segment 2: *Rubber Soul* spotlight, 6. Drive My Car (The Beatles), 7. Norwegian Wood (take 1, partial) (The Beatles), 8. Norwegian Wood (take 4, early mix) (The Beatles), 9. Segment 3: On the air in Hollywood, continued, 10. Cold Turkey, 11. Hold On, 12. Segment 4: On the air in Hollywood, continued, 13, Get Up Stand Up (partial) (The Wailers), 14. I'm the Greatest (Ringo Starr), 15. Segment: One-tc-One jams, 21 August 1972, 16. Hound Dog/Long Tall Sally

417. SHOWS 52 AND 53 (WO 052/053)

Disc One – 16 January 1989. Program No. 89–04

1. Segment 1: One-to-One encore, 2. It's So Hard, 3. Segment 3: Middle of a shave, 4. Oh, Yoko (demo), 5. Oh, Yoko (partial), 6. Oh, Yoko (rough mix), 7. Segment 3: On the air in Hollywood, Part 2, 8.KHJ Los Angeles, 27 September 1974, 9. No 9 dream, 10. Tobias Spot No. 5, 11. I Am the Walrus (The Beatles), 12. Segment 4: Beatles In Philadelphia, 2 September 1964, 13. If I Fell (The Beatles), 14. I Want to Hold Your Hand (The Beatles), 15. A Hard Day's Night (The Beatles), 16. Segment 5, 17. Give Me Some Truth (partial), 18. Give Me Some Truth (*Get Back* sessions) (The Beatles), 19. Give Me Some Truth (alternate take)

Disc Two – 23 January 1989. Program No. 89–05

1. Segment 1: Return to Tittenhurst, part 1, 2. People Get Ready/How (demo), 3. How (alternate take), 4. Segment 2: Elliot's first interview highlights, 5. I Don't Want to Be a Soldier (partial), 6. Luck of the Irish, 7. Segment 3: Return to Tittenhurst, part 2, 8. Oh, My Love (alternate take), 9. San Francisco Bay Blues, 10. How Do You Sleep (alternate), 11. Segment 4: Dr John – The Day Tripper, 12. Dr Robert (partial) (The Beatles), 13. Pill (demo), 14. Segment 5: One-to-One rehearsals, 15. Woman Is the Nigger of the World (One-to-One rehearsal)

418. SHOWS 54 AND 55 (WO 054/055)

Disc One – 30 January 1989. Program No. 89–06

Grapefruit Can You Dig It

1. Segment 1: Beatles In Philadelphia, 2 September 1964, 2. You Can't Do That (The Beatles), 3. She Loves You (The Beatles), 4. Things We Said Today (The Beatles), 5. Long Tall Sally (The Beatles), 6. Segment 2: *Grapefruit* readings, Part 2, 7. John and Yoko read excerpts, 8. Segment 3: I/You/He/She/They/We Can Dig It, 9. Dig It (The Beatles), 10. Dig It (alternate take) (The Beatles), 11. Segment 4: More of the Elliot first interview, 10 October 1971, 12. Money/New York City/Dreams, 13. Money (Live Peace in Toronto, 13 September 1969), 14. Segment 5: *Grapefruit* readings, Part 2, 15. Imagine (alternate take)

Disc Two – 6 February 1989. Program No. 89–07

The Beatles: Coming to America, Part 1

1. Segment 1: American Music, 2. Baby It's You (partial) (The Beatles), 3. Love Me Do (version 1) (The Beatles), 4. From Me to You (alternate take) (The Beatles), 5. Segment 2: Black Music Experience, 6. All I've Got to Do (The Beatles), 7. Baby Let's Play House (partial) (Elvis Presley), 8. I Saw Her Standing There (take 2) (The Beatles), 9. Segment 3: Imagine, 10. Money (partial) (The Beatles), 11. You Really Got a Hold on Me (The Beatles), 12. Segment 4, 13. Please Please Me (The Beatles), 14. From Me to You (partial) (Del Shannon), 15. She Loves You (The Beatles), 16. Segment 5: *The Ed Sullivan Show*, 17. Twist and Shout (Stockholm, partial) (The Beatles), 18. I Want to Hold Your Hand (The Beatles)

419. SHOWS 56 AND 57 (WO 056/057)

Disc One – 13 February 1989. Program No. 89-08

The Beatles: Coming to America, Part 2

1. Segment 1: Capital capitulates, 2. Misery (take 1) (The Beatles), 3. Twist and Shout (Royal Variety, 4 November 1963) (The Beatles), 4. Segment 2: American Mood, November – December 1963, 5. She Loves You (pop '63, 24 October 1963) (The Beatles), 6. Not a Second Time (stereo mix) (The Beatles), 7. Segment 3: Capital attacks 'Hand' hits yanks, 8. Money (stereo mix), 9. Good King Wenceslaus (1963 Christmas disc) (The Beatles), 10. I'll Get You (The Beatles), 11. Segment 4: The Fabs finish off the French, 12. From Me to You (Paris June 1964, partial) (The Beatles), 13. I Want to Hold Your Hand (Paris June 1964) (The Beatles), 14. Segment 5: …and give it to the Germans, 15. Komm Gib Mir Deine Hand (partial) (The Beatles), 16. Sie Liebt Dich (The Beatles), 17. My Bonnie (Tony Sheridan and The Beatles)

Disc Two – 20 February 1989. Program No. 89-09

The Beatles: Coming to America, Part 3

1. Segment 1: The Beatles arrive in New York, 7 February 1964. 2. There's a Place (alternate take) (The Beatles), 3. Segment 2: Motorcade from JFK to the Plaza Hotel, 4. Twist and Shout (stereo mix) (The Beatles), 5. This Boy (Paris, June 1964) (The Beatles), 6. Segment 3: Beatles debut on *Ed Sullivan Show*, 9 February 1964, 7. All My Loving (Ed Sullivan) (The Beatles), 8. Till There Was You (Ed Sullivan) (The Beatles), 9. She Loves You (Ed Sullivan) (The Beatles), 10. Segment 4: The thrill of victory, the agony of first impressions, 11. I Saw Her Standing There (stereo mix, partial) (The Beatles), 12. Little Child (stereo) (The Beatles), 13. Segment 5: The Beatles second *Ed Sullivan Show*), 14. I Saw Her Standing There (Ed Sullivan) (The Beatles), 15. I Want to Hold Your Hand (Ed Sullivan) (The Beatles)

420. SHOWS 58 AND 59 (WO 058/059)

Disc One – 27 February 1989. Program No. 89-10

Toronto Rock 'n' Roll Revival Spotlight, Part 1

1. Segment 1: But first, 2. Real Love (piano demo, take 1), 3. Segment 2: Toronto 1969 – context and genius) with John Brower), 4. Come Together

(The Beatles), 5. I Want You (She's So Heavy) (The Beatles), 6. Segment 3: Sceptics, Alan White, Toronto media, 7. Mean Mr Mustard (The Beatles), 8. Segment 4: Because, we like you, 9. Because (partial) (The Beatles), 10. Because (rough mix) (The Beatles), 11. Because (a cappella mix) (The Beatles), 12. Segment 5: the plane from London to Toronto, 13. Sun King (The Beatles)

Disc Two – 6 March 1989. Program No. 89–11

Toronto Rock 'n' Roll Revival Spotlight, Part 2

1. Segment 1: John Brower interview, 2. Blue Suede Shows (*Get Back* sessions) (The Beatles), 3. Segment 2: John Brower (continued) and Alan White, 4. Rip It Up/Ready Teddy (partial), 5. Blue Suede Shoes (Live Peace in Toronto), 6. Segment 3: John Brower continued, 7. Dizzy Miss Lizzie (Live Peace in Toronto), 8. Cold Turkey (Live Peace in Toronto), 9. Segment 4: John Brower continued, 10. Give Peace a Chance (Live Peace in Toronto), 11. Segment 5: the record, the movie, the legend, 12. I Found Out (demo, take 2)

421. SHOWS 60 AND 61 (WO 060/061)

Disc One – 13 March 1989. Program No. 89–12

(Almost) Nothing But Beatles and Elvis

1. Segment 1: Lennon and McCartney discover Elvis, 2. Heartbreak Hotel (partial) (Elvis Presley), 3. That's All Right (Mama) (BBC Radio, 16 July 1963) (The Beatles), 4. Segment 2: The influence of Elvis on The Beatles, 5. I Got A Woman (BBC Radio, 13 August 1963) (The Beatles), 6. Blue Suede Shoes (live), 7. Segment 3: Lennon on the air in Hollywood/Help, 8. The Night Before (partial) (The Beatles), 9. You're Gonna Lose That Girl (The Beatles), 10. Segment 4: The Beatles audience with Elvis 27 August 1965, 11. You've Got to Hide Your Love Away (The Beatles), 12. Such a Night (Elvis Presley), 13. Hound Dog (One-to-One concert), 14. Segment 5: It was like meeting Engelbert Humperdinck, 15. That's All Right Mama (Plastic Ono Band jam), 16. Mystery Train (*Double Fantasy* jam)

Disc Two – 20 March 1989. Program No. 89–13

Lennon and The Beatles in the Studio and on the Set

1. Segment 1: Ascot Sounds Studio 1971, 2. I'm the Greatest (studio demo 2), 3. Segment 2: Piccadilly Studios and Abbey Road 1965, 4. Ticket to Ride (BBC Radio 7 June 1965) (The Beatles), 5. Yes It Is (partial) (The Beatles), 6. Segment 3: The Hit Factory, 1980, 7. I'm Stepping Out (partial, MCRT take), 8. I'm Stepping Out (rough mix), 9. Segment 4: Twickenham Film Studios and Abbey Road 1965, 10. Walter Shenson interview, 11. Act Naturally (The Beatles), 12. Help (takes 1 and 5 basic track) (The Beatles), 13. Segment 5: Abbey Road, one more time 1965, 14. Strawberry Fields Forever (take 4) (The Beatles)

422. SHOWS 62 AND 63 (WO 062/063)

Disc One – 27 March 1989. Program No. 89–14

1. Segment 1: Beatles on the Beeb doing Berry, 2. Rock 'n' Roll Music (*Saturday Club*, 26 December 1964) (The Beatles), 3. Memphis Tennessee (Teenager's Turn, 8 March 1962) (The Beatles), 4. Too Much Monkey Business (*Pop Go The Beatles*, 23 July 1963) (The Beatles), 5. Sweet Little Sixteen (*Pop Go The Beatles*, 23 July 1963) (The Beatles), 6. Segment 2: I'm Still the Greatest – In the studio with John and Ringo plus the 1973 Beatles reunion, 7. I'm the Greatest (first studio take), 8. Segment 3: Bring on the Lucie, 9. Bring on the Lucie (jam fragment), 10. Bring on the Lucie (rough mix), 11. Segment 4: John and Yoko way out west, Part 1, no reunion, no way, 12. God, 13. Segment 5: The Beatles down under, Part 1, 14. A Hard Day's Night (partial) (The Beatles), 15. I Saw Her Standing There (Adelaide, 12 June 1964) (The Beatles)

Disc Two – 3 April 1989. Program No. 89–15

1. Segment 1: The Beatles down under, Part 2, 2. A Hard Day's Night (partial) (The Beatles), 3. All My Loving (Adelaide, 12 June 1964) (The Beatles), 4. Interview and Adelaide balcony scene, 5. Twist and Shout (The Beatles), 6. Segment 2: Julian Lennon *Mr Jordan* album, 7. Now You're in Heaven (Julian Lennon), 8. Segment 3: *Some Time in New York City* demos, 9. Luck of the Irish (demo 1), 10. Luck of the Irish (demo 2), 11. Luck of the Irish (LP version), 12. Segment 4: Mr Jordan, Part 2,

13. Mother Mary (Julian Lennon), 14. Segment 5: Trip to dreamland, 15. No. 9 Dream (demo), 16. No. 9 Dream (LP version)

423. SHOWS 64 AND 65 (WO 064/065)

Disc One – 10 April 1989. Program No. 89–16

1. Segment 1: Beatles on the Beeb doing Berry encore, 2. Roll Over Beethoven (From Us to You, 30 March 1964) (The Beatles), 3. Johnny B. Goode (*Saturday Club*, 15 February 1964) (The Beatles), 4. I've Got To Find My Baby (*Pop Go The Beatles*, 29 June 1963) (The Beatles), 5. Segment 2: Julian's *Mr Jordan* album, Part 3, 6. Second Time (Julian Lennon), 7. Segment 3: Beatles down under, Part 3, 8. Interviews, 9. I Want to Hold Your Hand (Adelaide, 12 June 1964) (The Beatles), 10. Interviews, 11. Segment 4: *Mr Jordan*, Part 4, 12. You're the One (Julian Lennon), 13. Segment 5, 14. Move Over Ms L (demos and rehearsals 2), 15. Move Over Ms L (demo 1), 16. Move Over Ms L (demo 2), 17. Move Over Ms L (studio rehearsal 2)

Disc Two – 17 April 1989. Program No. 89–17

1. Segment 1: Around The Beatles Medley, 19 April 1964, 2. Love Me Do/Please Please Me/From Me to You/She Loves You/I Want to Hold Your Hand (The Beatles), 3. Can't Buy Me Love (The Beatles), 4. Segment 4: *Mr Jordan*, Part 5, 5. I Get Up (Julian Lennon), 6. Segment 3: Beatles down under, Part 4, 7. Interviews: Jimmy Nichol, Ringo, Melbourne balcony scene, 8. You Can't Do That (Melbourne, 15 June 1964) (The Beatles), 9. Segment 4: *Mr Jordan*, Part 6, 10. Open Your Eyes (Julian Lennon), 11. Johnny B. Goode (Julian Lennon), 12. Segment 5, 13. John Sinclair (partial), 14. People (demo), 15. Angela

424. SHOWS 66 AND 67 (WO 066/067)

Disc One – 24 April 1989. Program No. 89–18

1. Segment 1: A Mid Summer's Night Scream, 2. Beatles Shakespeare (Around The Beatles, 6 May 1964), 3. Roll Over Beethoven (The Beatles), 4. Shout (The Beatles), 5. Segment 2: John and Yoko way out west, Part 2, 6. Interview with Elliot, April 1973, 7. Only People (rough mix), 8. Segment 4: John and Yoko way out west, Part 3, 9. I'm the Greatest

(studio outtake), 10. Segment 5: John and Yoko way out west, Part 4, 11. Oh My My (partial) (Ringo Starr), 12. Rock 'n' Roll People (alternate take), 13. One Day at a Time (*Mind Games* promo), 14. Mind Games (partial), 15. Segment 6: Beatles down under, Part 5, 16. She Loves You (Melbourne, 15 June 1964) (The Beatles), 17. Twist and Shout (The Beatles), 18. Long Tall Sally (The Beatles)

Disc Two – 1 May 1989. Program No. 89-19

1. Segment 1: encore breakfast jam with Elephant's Memory, March 1972, 2. Ain't That a Shame, 3. On The Caribbean, 4. Segment 2: (Forgive Me) My Little Flower Princess, Part 1, 5. (Forgive Me) My Little Flower Princess (partial), 6. (Forgive Me) My Little Flower Princess (demo), 7. Segment 3: Lennon on the air in Hollywood revisited (KHJ, Los Angeles, 27 September 1974), 8. Instant Karma/Tower Spot, 9. Scared/*Walls and Bridges* Spot, 10. Intuition/Surprise Surprise/Tobias Spot No. 4/Long Tall Sally (Little Richard), 11. Nobody Loves You, 12. Segment 4: Rock 'n' Roll hero spotlight – Larry Williams, 13. Dizzy Miss Lizzie (partial), 14. Dizzy Miss Lizzie (BBC Radio, 7 June 1965) (The Beatles), 15. Segment 5: (Forgive Me) My Little Flower Princess, Part 2, 16. (Forgive Me) My Little Flower Princess (rough mix)

425. SHOWS 68 AND 69 (WO 068/069)

Disc One – 8 May 1989. Program No. 89-20

1. Segment 1: With a Little Help from Ringo, 2. Get Back (The Beatles), 3. Across the Universe/Rock 'n' Roll Music (*Get Back* sessions) (The Beatles), 4. Segment 2: *Get Back* sessions, 5. Across the Universe (rough mix, partial) (The Beatles), 6. Across the Universe (*Get Back* sessions) The Beatles), 7. Get Back (alternate take) (The Beatles), 8. Shakin' In The Sixties (*Get Back* sessions) The Beatles), 9. Shakin' In The Sixties (continued) (The Beatles), 10. Segment 3: John and pacifist views; would he fight? 11. I Don't Want to Be a Soldier, 12. I Don't Want to Be a Soldier (alternate take), 13. Segment 4: *Get Back* sessions begin, 14. Magic Alex test the Apple Studios, 15. Rip It Up/Shake Rattle and Roll/Kansas City/Miss Ann/Lawdy Miss Claudy (*Get Back* sessions), 16. Segment 5: *Get Back* sessions, 17. One After 909 (alternate take) (The Beatles)

Disc Two – 15 May 1989. Program No. 89-21

1. Segment: another tall tale from the Land of Oz, 2. John and Yoko's Radio Free London *Oz* Magazine Message, 3. Keep Right on to the End of the Road (John and Yoko), 4. God Save Us (Bill Elliot and the Elastic Oz Band), 5. Segment 2: another run through Strawberry Fields, 6. Strawberry Fields Forever (takes 5 and 6) (The Beatles), 7. Segment 3: Rock 'n' Roll hero spotlight – Little Richard, 8. Long Tall Sally (partial) (Little Richard), 9. Long Tall Sally (BBC Radio, 16 July 1964) (The Beatles), 10. Rip It Up/Ready Teddy (rough mix), 11. Segment 4: two Tittenhurst takes, summer 1971, 12. How Do You Sleep? (rehearsal), 13. Well Baby Please Don't Go (outtake), 14. Segment 5: *Double Fantasy* demos, 15. I'm Crazy (take 1, 2 batch), 16. Beautiful Boy (demo), 17. Clean-up Time (demo)

426. SHOWS 70 AND 71 (WO 070/071)

Disc One – 22 May 1989. Program No. 89-22

1. Segment 1, 2. Mother (demo), 3. Segment 2: Jonathan Cott/Rolling Stone interviews, 5 December 1980, Part 1, 4. (Just Like) Starting Over (partial), 5. I'm Stepping Out (demo), 6. Segment 3: Rock 'n' Roll hero spotlight – Roy Orbison, 7. Only the Lonely (*Double Fantasy* sessions), 8. Please Please Me (stereo mix) (The Beatles), 9. Dream Baby (BBC Radio, 8 March 1962) (The Beatles), 10. Segment 4: Elton John encore 1974), 11. One Day at a Time (Elton John), 12. I Saw Her Standing There (rehearsal, John Lennon and Elton John), 13. Segment 5: Rolling Stone interview, Part 2, 14. Woman (demo)

Disc Two – 29 May 1989. Program No. 89-23

1. Segment 1: Rock 'n' Roll hero spotlight – Buddy Holly, Part 1, 2. That'll Be the Day (partial) (Buddy Holly), 3. That'll Be the Day (1958 partial) (The Quarrymen), 4. Hello Little Girl (1960 rehearsal, partial) (The Quarrymen), 5. Hello Little Girl (Decca audition) (The Beatles), 6. Maybe Baby/Crying Waiting Hoping/Mailman Bring Me No More Blues (*Get Back* sessions) (The Beatles), 7. Segment 2: Welcome to the inner sanctum, 8. Rolling Stone interview, 5 December 1980, continued, 9. Stranger's Room (demo), 10. Segment 3: original 'Dig It', 11. Dig It (outtake), 12. Segment 4: 'Stranger's Room' becomes 'I'm Losing You', 13. I'm Losing You

(Bermuda demo), 14. I'm Losing You (rough mix), 15. Segment 5: Buddy Holly, Part 2, 16. Mailman Bring Me No More Blues ((partial) (Buddy Holly), 17. Mailman Bring Me No More Blues (*Clock*, demo), 18. Peggy Sue

427. SHOWS 72 AND 73 (WO 072/073)

Disc One – 5 June 1989. Program No. 89-24

1. Segment 1: Beatles on the Beeb – *Top Gear*, 26 November 1964. 2. I'm a Loser (The Beatles), 3. Interview, 4. She's a Woman (The Beatles), 5. I Feel Fine (The Beatles), 6. Segment 2: Another shot of cold turkey, 7. Cold Turkey (demo, take 1), 8. Segment 3: Eschew obfuscation: Lennon on Zen, 9. Simplicity of *Double Fantasy* songs, 10. Dear Yoko (demo, takes 2 and 3), 11. Segment 4: More neat stuff from 1974, 12. Bless You (rehearsal 14 July 1974), 13. Move Over Ms L (rough mix, take 3), 14. Stand By Me (single mix, partial), 15. Segment 5: Zen reggae from *Double Fantasy* sessions, 16. Living on Borrowed Time (demo 1)

Disc Two – 12 June 1989. Program No. 89-25

Lost Lennon Songs, Part 1

1. Segment 1, 2. This Boy (BBC Radio, 21 December 1963) (The Beatles), 3. She Loves You (Paris, January 1964) (The Beatles), 4. The Honeymoon Song (BBC Radio, 6 August 1964) (The Beatles), 5. If I Fell (Hollywood Bowl, 23 August 1964) (The Beatles), 6. Segment 2, 7. I Want to Hold Your Hand (Hollywood Bowl, 23 August 1964) (The Beatles), 8. I Feel Fine (single mix) (The Beatles), 9. Norwegian Wood (take 2) (The Beatles), 10. Girl (The Beatles), 11. Segment 3, 12. The Word (The Beatles), 13. All You Need Is Love (The Beatles), 14. Segment 4, 15. When I'm 64 (The Beatles), 16. Julia (demo), 17. Don't Let Me Down (demo), 18. Segment 5, 19. Hold On, 20. Oh, My Love (rough mix), 21. Jealous Guy (rough mix)

428. SHOWS 74 AND 75 (WO 074/075)

Disc One – 19 June 1989. Program No. 89-26

1. Segment 1, 2. Surprise Surprise, 3. Surprise Surprise (Sweet Bird of Paradox) (demo), 4. Surprise Surprise (rehearsal), 5. Segment 2: Son of Return to the Part 13 of the *Get Back* sessions (see notes), 6. Dig It (take

2) (The Beatles), 7. Mintz busted by time police and music militia, 8. Segment 3: Return of John Rasta-far-eye, 9. Living on Borrowed Time (take 3, vocal booth), 10. Segment 4: Beatles at the Palais Des Sports, Paris, 20 June 1965, afternoon show, 11. I'm a Loser/Can't Buy Me Love/I Wanna Be Your Man (The Beatles), 12. A Hard Day's Night/Rock 'n' Roll Music (The Beatles), 13. Segment 5: Real Gone quotes, 1980, 14. Gone from This Place

Disc Two – 26 June 1989. Program No. 89–27
1. Segment 1: back under the *Rock and Roll Circus* big top, 2. Yer Blues (a cappella) (John Lennon and Mick Jagger), 3. Yer Blues (rehearsal), 4. Segment 2, 5. Don't Let Me Down (demo 2), 6. Don't Let Me Down (rehearsal) (The Beatles), 7. Segment 3: Way out west with John and Yoko, continued, 8. Elliot's 16 April 1974 interview, 9. I Know (I Know) (demo), 10. I Know (I Know) (rough mix), 11. Just Gotta Give Me Some Rock 'n' Roll/Shoeshine (demo), 12. Segment 4: Way out west with John and Yoko, continued, 13. I'm the Greatest (rehearsal), 14. Segment 5: Lennon on McCartney and How Do You Sleep?, 15. How Do You Sleep? (rough mix)

Notes: Disc One, Track 5: This track is almost certainly 'Dig It' from the *Get Back* Sessions on 26 January 1969.

429. SHOWS 76 AND 77 (WO 076/077)

Disc One – 3 July 1989. Program No. 89–28
1. Segment 1: ...but first 'Power to the People', 2. Power to the People (alternate take), 3. Segment 2: John and Yoko with Jerry Rubin on *The Mike Douglas Show*, 15 February 1972, 4. Oh, My Love (*Imagine* film mix), 5. Imagine (*Mike Douglas Show*), 6. Segment 3: John and Yoko and Jerry Rubin on *Mike Douglas*, continued – The Vote, 7. Crippled Inside (partial), 8. I Don't Want to Be a Soldier (partial), 9. Segment 4: John and Yoko and Jerry Rubin on *Mike Douglas*, continued, 10. Jerry goes off the deep end, 11. Give Me Some Truth (alternate mix), 12. Power to the People (alternate take), 13. John and Yoko and Jerry Rubin on Mike Douglas, continued, 14. Mike goes for the jugular, 15. John Sinclair (live, 12 December 1971)

Disc Two – 10 July 1989. Program No. 89–29

Lost Lennon Love Songs, Part 2

1. Segment 1, 2. Love (demo), 3. Oh, Yoko (rough mix), 4. Segment 2, 5. Out the Blue (rough mix), 6. Segment 3, 7. Bony Moronie (rough mix), 8. Be My Baby (rough mix), 9. Segment 4, 10. What You Got (demo), 11. Going Down on Love (rehearsal), 12. Segment 5, 13. Woman (rough mix), 14. Grow Old with Me, 15. Real Love (demo, take 4)

430. SHOWS 78 AND 79 (WO 078/079)

Disc One – 17 July 1989. Program No. 89–30

1. Segment 1: another pass at the *Please Please Me* sessions, 11 February 1963, 2. Misery (take 1) (The Beatles), 3. Misery (takes 2–6) (The Beatles), 4. Segment 2: more One-to-One fun, 5. Well, Well, Well (rehearsal 22 August 1972), 6. One-to-One promo (John and Yoko and Geraldo), 7. Segment 2: evening *Please Please Me* sessions, 8. Baby It's You (stereo mix) (The Beatles), 9. Twist and Shout (stereo mix) (The Beatles), 10. Segment 4: clever John's token One-to-One Beatles tune, 11. Come Together (One-to-One concert, partial), 12. Come Together (rehearsal, 18 August 1972), 13. Come Together (rehearsal), 14. Segment 5: refried 'Cooking', 15. Cooking in the Kitchen of Love (partial) (Ringo Starr), 16. Cooking in the Kitchen of Love (demo, take 1), 17. Free as a Bird (demo, take 1)

Disc Two – 24 July 1989. Program No. 89–31

1. Segment 1: Strawberry Fields Forever (two sessions), 2. Strawberry Fields Forever (version 1, take 7), 3. Strawberry Fields Forever (version 2, take 25), 4. Segment 2: How's your Intuition, 5. Intuition (partial), 6. Intuition (demo), 7. Intuition (rough mix), 8. Segment 3: I Want You, Part 1, 9. I Want You (She's So Heavy) (*Get Back* sessions), 10. I Want You (She's So Heavy) (alternate take), 11. I Want You (She's So Heavy) (Israeli Radio take), 12. Segment 4: Sleepy Blind Lemon Lennon live at the 99 Annual Dakota Mind Movie Delta Blues Festival, 13. John Henry (electric guitar, take), 14. I Ain't Got Time (acoustic guitar, take), 15. Old Dirt Road (*Menlove Avenue*, partial), 16. Segment 5: I Want You, Part 2, 17. I Want You (She's So Heavy) (partial) (The Beatles)

431. SHOWS 80 AND 81 (WO 080/081)

Disc One – 31 July 1989. Program No. 89–32

MBE Spotlight, Part 1

1. Segment 1: On Her Majesty's Service, 2. I Feel Fine (take 6, basic track) (The Beatles), 3. I Don't Want to Spoil the Party (stereo mix) (The Beatles), 4. Segment 2: MBE Interview, 12 June 1965. 5. BBC Interviews, 6. Act Naturally (The Beatles), 7. Segment 3: MBE Interviews, continued, 8. Ticket to Ride (partial) (The Beatles), 9. British Newsreel Interview, 10. Segment 4: Evolution of Aisumasen, 11. Aisumasen (partial), 12. Call My Name (demo), 13. Call My Name (demo), 14. Aisumasen (rough mix), 15. Segment 5: MBEs react to The Beatles induction, 16. Rock 'n' Roll Music (stereo) (The Beatles)

Disc Two – 7 August 1989. Program No. 89–33

1. Segment 1: Rock around the *Clock* takes, September 1971, 2. Duane Eddy Jam, 3. Honey Don't/Glad All Over/Lend Me Your Comb, 4. Segment 2: Mucho Mas Mungo, 5. Mucho Mungo (demo, takes 1 and 2), 6. No. 9 Dream (demo 2), 7. Segment 3, 8. She is a Friend of Dorothy's (demo, take 7), 9. One of the Boys (demo, take 7), 10. Segment 4: Clyde Mc Slyde Presents Sleepy's Greatest sessions on BLZ, 11. A Shot of Rhythm and Blues (BBC Radio 1963) (The Beatles), 12. 12 Bar Original (The Beatles), 13. He Got the Blues, 14. Segment 5: Tom Donahue, KSAN, 15. No. 9 Dream (rough mix), 16. No. 9 Dream (partial)

432. SHOWS 82 AND 83 (WO 082/083)

Disc One – 14 August 1989. Program No. 89–34

MBE Part 2/Plastic Ono Band

1. Segment 1: MBE chat in Madrid with John and George, 2 July 1965, 2. You're Gonna Lose That Girl (take 2) (The Beatles), 3. McCartney on investiture, 26 October 1965, 4. Bad Boy (The Beatles), 5. Segment 2: Lennon remembers – more on Plastic Ono Band, 6. Look at Me (demo), 7. My Mummy's Dead (take 2), 8. Segment 3: John's views on MBE,

December 1968, 9. Revolution, 10. Segment 4: Plastic Ono Band, primal and sparse, 11. Well, Well, Well (demo), 12. Well, Well, Well (take 4), 13. Segment 5: John returns MBE, 25 November 1969, 14. Give Peace a Chance (partial), 15. Cold Turkey (demo, take 3)

Disc Two – 21 August 1989. Program No. 89-35

1. Segment 1: Sex, race and rock and soul way out west, Part 1, 2. Woman Is the Nigger of the World (demo), 3. Segment 2: Another Dakota kitchen encounter with the Lennons, Thanksgiving 1979, Part 1, 4. Real Life (piano demo 2), 5. I'm Stepping Out (take 1), 6. Segment 3: Getting faced, 7. I Don't Wanna Face It (demo), 8. I Watch Your Face (demo), 9. My Life (demo, take 1), 10. Segment 4: Sex, race and rock and soul way out west, Part 2, 11. Woman Is the Nigger of the World (alternate take), 12. Segment 5: Dakota kitchen encounter, Part 2, 13. Beautiful Boy (rough mix)

433. SHOWS 84 AND 85 (WO 084/085)

Disc One – 28 August 1989. Program No. 89-36

Mike Douglas No. 4, Pt 1/More Plastic Ono Band and *Double Fantasy*

1. Segment 1: John and Yoko on *Mike Douglas Show*, 17 February 1972, 2. Imagine (rough mix), 3. Segment 2: F**k you all! You don't get me twice. 4. I Found Out (rough mix), 5. Segment 3: Connection between *Plastic Ono Band* and *Double Fantasy*, 6. Watching the Wheels (electric guitar demo), 7. Segment 4: Bobby Seal on Mike Douglas, Part 1, 8. Attica State (demo, takes 1 and 2), 9. J.J. (demo), 10. Segment 5, 11. Watching the Wheels (rough mix), 12. I'm Your Angel (partial) (Yoko Ono)

Disc Two – 4 September 1989. Program No. 89-37

Lennon's Spiritual Development Revisited, Part 1

1. Segment 1: Return to Rishikesh, spring 1968, with Mike Love, 2. I'm So Tired (demo), 3. Segment 2: Return to Rishikesh, continued, 4. Sexy Sadie (demo), 5. The Maharishi Song, 6. Segment 3: Apple and 'Revolution', mid-1968, 7. Baby You're a Rich Man (The Beatles), 8. Revolution

(demo), 9. Segment 4: Late 1968 and late 1970, 10. It's All Too Much (partial) (The Beatles), 11. God (demo, take 1), 12. Segment 5: late 70–early 71, 13.How (demo)

434. SHOWS 86 AND 87 (WO 086/087)

Disc One – 11 September 1989. Program No. 89–38

Lennon's Spiritual Development Revisited, Part 2

1. Segment 1: The early house husband phase, 2. Many Rivers to Cross (demo), 3. Segment 2: Role reversal, 4. Cooking in the Kitchen of Love (demo), 5. Segment 3: D.S.D. 6. Serve Yourself (demo), 7. Segment 4: Later house husband phase, 8. Clean-up Time (partial), 9. Clean-up Time (rehearsal), 10. Clean-up Time (rehearsal), 11. Segment 5: late 1980, 12. Dear Yoko (rough mix), 12. You Saved My Soul (demo)

Disc Two – 18 September 1989. Program No. 89–39

1. Segment 1: Lennon live at the Dakota, late 70s, 2. J-9 Medley: Beautiful Boy/Memories (Howling at the Moon)/the Dakota Rap/Across the River, 3. Segment 2: Nicky Hopkins on the *Imagine* session, Part 1, 4. We Love You (partial) (The Rolling Stones), 5. Crippled Inside, 6. Segment 3: The 23 March 1973 deportation order and press conference and Nutopia press conference/way out west again, 7. Bring on the Lucie (Freeda People), 8. I'm the Greatest (alternate take), 9. Segment 4: Hopkins on *Imagine*, Part 2, 10. How Do You Sleep (rehearsal), 11. Oh, My Love (rough mix), 12. Segment 5: Hopkins on *Imagine*, Part 3, 13. Untitled Jam, 14. Imagine (solo piano rehearsal)

435. SHOWS 88 AND 89 (WO 088/089)

Disc One – 25 September 1989. Program No. 89–40

The John and Yoko Argument Interview, 1971

1. Segment 1: The John and Yoko argument interview, Part 1, 2. Look at Me (rough mix), 3. Segment 2: The next-to-last phase in the evolution of 'Strawberry Fields Forever', 4. Strawberry Fields Forever (The Beatles), 5. Segment 3: The John and Yoko argument interview, Part 2, 6. Sweet Little Sixteen (Star Club, 31 December 1962) (The Beatles), 7. Twist and

Shout (Star Club, 31 December 1962) (The Beatles), 8. Segment 4: Beatlefest, the Lennon connection with Mark Lapidos, 9. From Us To You (BBC Radio 1963) (The Beatles), 10. So How Come (No One Loves Me) (BBC Radio, 23 July 1963) (The Beatles), 11. Glass Onion (The Beatles), 12. Segment 5: The John and Yoko argument interview, Part 3, 13. Long Tall Sally (Star Club, 31 December 1962) (The Beatles)

Disc Two – 2 October 1989. Program No. 89–41

The John and Sean Birthday Show, Part 2

1. Segment 1: John's birthday 1957–1959, 2. Julia (demo, take 2), 3. Segment 2: Sean's birth 1975, 4. Elliot's 1 January 1976 baby interview, 5. Clean-up Time (rough mix), 6. Segment 3: John's birthdays 1960–1964, 7. Why (partial) (Tony Sheridan and The Beatles), 8. Please Please Me (partial) (The Beatles), 9. Happy Birthday *Saturday Club* (BBC Radio 1963) (The Beatles), 10. She Loves You (Stockholm 24 October 1963) (The Beatles), 11. Twist and Shout (Hollywood Bowl, 23 August 1964) (The Beatles), 12. Segment 4: Sean's birth, continued, 13. Baby interview, continued, 14. Beautiful Boy (demo), 15. Segment 5: John's birthday 1965, 16. Run for Your Life (take 5, rough mix partial) (The Beatles), 17. Run for Your Life (The Beatles), 18. Goodnight Irene (partial)

436. SHOWS 90 AND 91 (WO 090/091)

Disc One – 9 October 1989. Program No. 89–42

The John and Sean Birthday Show, Part 3

1. Segment 1: John's birthday 1965–67, 2. In My Life (The Beatles), 3. How I Won the War (Muskateer Gripweed and the Third Troop), 4. Segment 2: John's 75 birthday present from INS, 5. Baby interview, continued, 6. The Worst is Over (demo, take 1), 7. Segment 3: John's birthday 1968, 8. The Continuing Story of Bungalow Bill (The Beatles), 9. Birthday (The Beatles), 10. Segment 4: Sean's first interview by John, 1 January 1976, 11. Beautiful Boy (composing sequence), 12. Segment 5: John's birthdays 1969–70, 13. Hold On John (partial), 14. When a Boy Meets a Girl (demo, take 1)

Disc Two – 16 October 1989. Program No. 89–43

The John and Sean Birthday Show, Part 4

1. Segment 1: John's 30 birthday greetings, 2. Here Come The Threes (Donovan), 3. It's Johnny's Birthday (rough mix) (George Harrison), 4. Happy Trails (Janis Joplin), 5. Happy Birthday John (Ringo Starr), 6. Hey John (Blossom Dearie), 7. Segment 2: John's birthday 1971, 8. Blue Suede Shoes, 9. Happy Birthday, 10. It's So Hard (rough mix), 11. Segment 3: John's birthday 1972–73, tale of the tape, 12. Sweet Little Sixteen (rough mix), 13. Whatever Gets You Through the Night (partial), 14. Bless You (rehearsal), 15. Segment 4: John and Sean's birthday 1978–79, 16. Sean's third birthday party, 17. Beautiful Boys (partial) (Yoko Ono), 18. John and Sean Autumn 1979 interview, 19. Real Love (guitar demo)

437. SHOWS 92 AND 93 (WO 092/093)

Disc One – 22 October 1989. Program No. 89–44

The John and Sean Birthday Show, PT 5

1. Segment 1: Elliot's thirty-first birthday interview, 10 October 1971, 2. My Mummy's Dead (take 1 rough mix), 3. I Am the Walrus (basic track) (The Beatles), 4. Segment 2: John and Sean's birthday 1980, Part 1, 5. Beautiful Boy (rehearsal), 6. Segment 3: John's birthday 1971, 'This Is Not Here Show' 7. The Everson Press Conference 8 October 1971, 8. Oh, Yoko (guitar demo), 9. Crippled Inside (thirty-first birthday party), 10. Segment 4: We're All Water (partial) Yoko Ono), 11. Imagine/Oh, Yoko (thirty-first birthday party), 12. Segment 5: John and Sean's birthday 1980, Part 2, 13. Serve Yourself (Sean Lennon), 14. Be Bop A Lula (Sean Lennon), 15. Beautiful Boy (partial)

Disc Two – 29 October 1989. Program No. 89–45

Montreal Revisited, Pt 1 With Roger Scott

1. Segment 1, 2. Ballad of John and Yoko (partial) (The Beatles), 3. Highlights and bites from *Bed Peace* the film, 4. Come Together (The Beatles), 5. Segment 2: The scene in Suite 1742 – Bedlam, 6. Helter

Skelter (The Beatles), 7. Segment 3: John and Yoko rap the revolutionaries, 8. Revolution 1 (The Beatles), 9. Segment 4: People's Park phones, 10. Make Love Not War (piano demo), 11. Segment 5: Showdown at People's Park, 12. Give Peace a Chance (acoustic rehearsal)

438. SHOWS 94 AND 95 (WO 094/095)

Disc One – 6 November 1989. Program No. 89–46

Montreal Revisited, Pt 2 With Roger Scott

1. Segment 1: meanwhile, on the Fab Four front, 2. Let It Be (*Get Back* version) (The Beatles), 3. Segment 2: The Mt Royal Peace March, 4. Across the Universe (original mix) (The Beatles), 5. Segment 3: The KYA Peace Talk, 6. Give Peace a Chance (rehearsal), 7. Getting Better (partial) (The Beatles), 8. Get Back (alternate take) (The Beatles), 9. Get Back (reprise, alternate take) (The Beatles), 10. Segment 4: The Al Capp confrontation, Part 1, 11. Nowhere Man (The Beatles), 12. Segment 5: Hippie hustles at the Queen Elizabeth, 13. You Never Give Me Your Money (alternate take) (The Beatles), 14. Good Night (partial) (The Beatles)

Disc Two – 13 November 1989. Program No. 89–47

Montreal Revisited, Pt 3 With Roger Scott

1. Segment 1: Al Capp confrontation continued, 2. Mean Mr Mustard (*Get Back* sessions) (The Beatles), 3. Segment 2: You can syndicate any boat you row, 4. Dig a Pony (*Get Back* sessions) The Beatles), 5. Segment 3: Capp confrontation climax, 6. I've Got a Feeling (*Get Back* sessions) (The Beatles), 7. Segment 4: KYA peace talk wrap up, 8. Remember Love (rough mix) (Yoko Ono), 9. Segment 5: Tom, Dick and Leary, 10. Revolution (Twickenham version) (The Beatles)

439. SHOWS 96 AND 97 (WO 096/097)

Disc One – 20 November 1989. Program No. 89–48

Montreal Revisited, Pt 4 With Roger Scott

1. Segment 1: 'Give Peace a Chance' session, 2. Give Peace a Chance (acoustic version), 3. Give Peace a Chance (film mix), 4. Segment 2:

Fred Peabody interview highlights, 5. You Win Again (*Get Back* sessions) (The Beatles), 6. Segment 3: Gettin' Back with Billy Preston, 7. Get Back (alternate take) (The Beatles), 8. One After 909 (alternate mix) (The Beatles), 9. Segment 4: Fred Peabody interview continued, 10. Hey Bulldog (The Beatles), 11. Segment 5: Bed-In wrap up and aftermath, 12. Give Peace a Chance (last chance take), 13. Tomorrow Never Knows (partial) (The Beatles)

Disc Two – 27 November 1989. Program No. 89–49

Coleman On Epstein, John and The Fabs, PT 1

1. Segment 1: Kick out the *Double Fantasy* jams, 2. Ants In My Pants (*Double Fantasy* sessions), 3. I'm Stepping Out (take 2), 4. Segment 2: Ray Coleman on Brian Epstein biography, 5. Bad Boy (The Beatles), 6. Segment 3: Coleman on Brian and John, 7. Bad To Me (Billy J. Kramer and the Dakotas), 8. Do You Want to Know a Secret? (alternate mix) (The Beatles), 9. Segment 4: Get Back To Abbey Road, 10, Save the Last Dance for Me/Don't Let Me Down (*Get Back* sessions) (The Beatles), 11. Sun King (*Get Back* sessions) (The Beatles), 12. Sun King/Mean Mr Mustard (The Beatles), 13. Segment 5: Coleman on Epstein's business acumen, 14. Taxman (The Beatles)

440. SHOWS 98 AND 99 (WO 098/099)

Disc One – 4 December 1989. Program No. 89–50

Lennon's Spiritual Development, PT 2

1. Segment 1: Macho School of Pretence Class of 1960, 2. There's a Place (alternate take) (The Beatles), 3. Segment 2: Lennon remembers Liverpool, 4. Rock 'n' Roll Music (BBC Radio, 20 December 1964), 5. A Hard Day's Night (alternate take) (The Beatles), 6. Segment 3: Lennon on making and breaking The Beatles, 7. I Feel Fine (rough mix) (The Beatles), 8. I Should Have Known Better (partial) (The Beatles), 9. Can't Buy Me Love (alternate take) (The Beatles), 10. Segment 4: Beatles at the Palais de Sports, 20 June 1965, afternoon show, 11. I Feel Fine (Paris) (The Beatles), 12, Ticket to Ride (Paris) (The Beatles), 13. Long Tall Sally (Paris) (The Beatles), 14. Segment 5: Lennon on Leary on LSD, 15. She Said She Said (The Beatles)

Disc Two – 11 December 1989. Program No. 89-51

Lennon's Spiritual Development, PT 4

1. Segment 1: Readings on LSD 1969–70, 2. Instant Karma, 3. Hold On (partial), 4. Segment 2: Lennon remembers 1970, 5. God (demo, take 2), 6. I Found Out (rough mix), 7. Segment 3: A little pagan worship, 8. Serve Yourself (p-worshipper take), 9. Segment 4: Everything is real, 10.Watching the Wheels ($ 50 M demo), 11. Segment 5: Songs of love for Yoko), 12. Woman (acoustic guitar demo, take 1), 13. You Saved My Soul (demo, take 1)

441. SHOWS 100 AND 101 (WO 100/101)

Disc One – 18 December 1989. Program No. 89-52

Christmas with John and Yoko and The Beatles, Part 1

1. Segment 1: Flashback on Christmas past, 2. I Saw Her Standing There (Stockholm 1963) (The Beatles), 3. Segment 2: Beatles 1963 Christmas Fan Club disc with Tony Barrow, 4. I Want to Hold Your Hand (Empire Theatre 7 December 1963) (The Beatles), 5. Segment 3: Beatles 1963 Christmas Fan Club disc continued, 6. This Boy (BBC Radio) 31 December 1963) (The Beatles), 7. Segment 4: Beatles 1964 Fan Club disc with Jimmy Saville, 8. When I Get Home (The Beatles), 9. Segment 5: Beatles 1965 Fan Club disc, 10. In My Life (The Beatles)

Disc Two – 25 December 1989. Program No. 89-53

Christmas with John and Yoko and The Beatles, Part 2

1. Segment 1: Everywhere It's Christmas with Tony Barrow, 2. Beatles 1966 Christmas Fan Club disc, 3. Christmastime Is Here Again, 4. Beatles 1967 Christmas Fan Club disc, 5. Segment 3: '67 disc continued, 6. Christmastime Is Here Again (The Beatles), 7. Segment 4: Christmas 1968, 8. Beatles 1968 Christmas Fan Club disc with Kenny Everett and Tiny Tim, 9. Segment 5: Christmas 1969, 10. Beatles 1969 Christmas Fan Club disc

442. Shows 102 and 103 (WO 102/103)

Disc One – 1 January 1990. Program No. 90–01

Best of Year 2, Part 1

1. Segment 1: Stepping Out, 2. I'm Stepping Out (alternate take), 3. I'm Stepping Out (rough mix), 4. Segment 2: Fave demos, 5. People Get Ready/How (demo), 6. Pill (demo), 7. Gone from This Place (take 1), 8. Segment 3: More fave studio takes, 9. Help (take 1) (The Beatles), 10. Help (take 5) (The Beatles), 11. How Do You Sleep (alternate take), 12. Segment 4: Live and on the air, 13. I'm a Loser (Paris 20 June 1965) (The Beatles), 14. A Hard Day's Night (Paris 20 June 1965) (The Beatles), 15. Too Much Monkey Business (BBC Radio 10 September 1965) (The Beatles), 16. Segment 5: Just give me some truth, 17. Give Me Some Truth (rehearsal) (The Beatles), 18. Give Me Some Truth (rough mix)

Disc Two – 8 January 1990. Program No. 90–02

Best of Year 2, Part 2

1. Segment 1: He's the greatest, 2. I'm the Greatest (alternate take), 3. Segment 2: More fave studio takes, 4. Get Back (alternate take) (The Beatles), 5. Rip It Up/Shake Rattle and Roll/Kansas City/Miss Ann/Lawdy Miss Claudy (*Get Back* sessions) (The Beatles), 6. Segment 3: On stage and on the air, 7. Johnny B. Goode (BBC Radio, 15 February 1964) (The Beatles), 8. You Can't Do That (Melbourne 15 June 1964) (The Beatles), 9. Segment 4: The important part, 10. Watching the Wheels (alternate take), 11. Serve Yourself (a cappella) (Sean Lennon), 12. Be Bop A Lula (Sean Lennon), 13. Segment 5: Radical rehearsals, 14. Move Over Ms L (demo 1), 15. Move Over Ms L (demo 2), 16. Move Over Ms L (rehearsal 2), 17. Imagine (piano solo demo)

443. Shows 104 and 105 (WO 104/105)

Disc One – 15 January 1990. Program No. 90–03

Year 3 Premiere

1. Segment 1: More One-to-One fun, 2. Come Together (rehearsal), 3. Segment 2: A tale of two demos 1973–74, 4. I Know (demo, take 3),

5. Whatever Gets You Through the Night (demo), 6. Segment 3: Reading into the glass onion, etc. (see notes), 7. Glass Onion (The Beatles), 8, Helter Skelter (partial) (The Beatles), 9. Piggies (demo) (The Beatles), 10. Segment 4: Yoko cleans up 'Clean-up Time', 11. Clean-up Time (take 2 basic track), 12. Clean-up Time (partial), 13. Segment 5: Two versions: 'The Strawberry Fields Forever' edit, 14. Strawberry Fields Forever (version 1 partial) (The Beatles), 15. Strawberry Fields Forever (version 2 partial) (The Beatles), 16. Strawberry Fields Forever (The Beatles)

Disc Two – 22 January 1990. Program No. 90–04

1. Segment 1, 2. Ticket to Ride (rough mix) (The Beatles), 3. Yes It Is (take 1 partial) (The Beatles), 4. Yes It Is (take 2) (The Beatles), 5. Yes It Is (take 14 rough mix) (The Beatles), 6. Segment 2: Pete Shotton on John's Jesus complex and first night with Yoko, 7. I Am the Walrus (take 9 basic track) (The Beatles), 8. Julia (demo), 9. Segment 3: I Don't Want to Face It (guitar, take 2), 10. Nobody Told Me (double-tracked demo, take 1), 11. Segment 4: John and Yoko's first morning after, 12. Cry Baby Cry (demo), 13. Segment 5: From Russia with love, 14. Back in the USSR (demo) (The Beatles), 15. Kansas City (Paul McCartney)

Notes: Disc One, Track 6 is a discussion about The Beatles track from *The White Album*.

444. SHOWS 106 AND 107 (WO 106/107)

Disc One – 29 January 1990. Program No. 90–05

The Man Who Gave The Beatles Away

1. Segment 1: Inside the Hit Factory, 1980, 2. Nobody Told Me (basic track take 1), 3. Segment 2: Alan Williams, 4. I Saw Her Standing There (Star Club) (The Beatles), 5. Mr Moonlight (Star Club) (The Beatles), 6. Segment 3: Alistair Taylor, 7. Money (The Beatles), 8. Segment 4: Dick Rowe, 9. Memphis Tennessee (Decca audition) (The Beatles), 10. Searching (Decca audition) (The Beatles), 11. Segment 5: Bert Kaempfert, 12. Crying Waiting Hoping (Decca audition) (The Beatles)

Disc Two – 5 February 1990. Program No. 90–06

The Fab Four In D.C.

1. Segment 1: Mystery Train to Washington DC 2. I Want To Hold Your Hold (*Ed Sullivan*, 9 February 1964) (The Beatles), 3. From Me to You (Washington DC, 11 February 1964) (The Beatles), 4. Segment 2: Carroll James/WWDC interview, Part 1, 5. She Loves You (Washington DC, 11 February 1964) (The Beatles), 6. Segment 3, 7. A sax session with King Curtis, 8. It's So Hard (rehearsal), 9. It's So Hard (overdub session), 10. I Don't Want to Be a Soldier (overdub session), 11. Segment 4: Carroll James/WWDC interview, Part 2, 12. This Boy (Washington DC, 11 February 1964) (The Beatles), 13. Segment 5: British Embassy incident John Lennon and Fred Martin), 14. Please Please Me (Washington DC, 11 February 1964) (The Beatles)

445. SHOWS 108 AND 109 (WO 108/109)

Disc One – 12th February 1990. Program No. 90–07

1. Segment 1: Another great memory, 2. Memories (take 2), 3. Segment 2: Decca audition encore, 4. To Know Her Is to Love Her (Decca audition) (The Beatles), 5. Three Cool Cats (Decca audition) (The Beatles), 6. Like Dreamers Do (Decca audition) (The Beatles), 7. Segment 3: John and Yoko on *The Mike Douglas Show*, 14 February 1972, 8. It's So Hard (One-to-One concert), 9. Segment 4: John, Paul and Julian on 'Hey Jude', 10. Hey Jude (rehearsal, take 9) (The Beatles), 11. Segment 5: evolution of 'Revolution' single with John Lennon, Phil McDonald and Nicky Hopkins, 12. Revolution (The Beatles)

Disc Two – 19 February 1990. Program No. 90–08

Epstein on Epstein, Part 1

1. Segment 1, 2. A Taste of Honey (alternate take, 11 February 1963) (The Beatles), 3. Segment 2: Epstein's Empire 1964, 4. Montage of Epstein's artists, 5. I Call Your Name (The Beatles), 6. Roll Over Beethoven (BBC Radio, 30 March 1964) (The Beatles), 7. Segment 3: Raymond Jones and meeting The Beatles, 8. Till There Was You (Decca audition) (The Beatles), 9. Segment 4: Billy Grundy BBC interview, 10. Do You Want

to Know a Secret (The Beatles), 11. Segment 5: The kick inside, 12. I Want to Hold Your Hand (Paris, January 1964) (The Beatles)

446. SHOWS 110 AND 111 (WO 110/111)

Disc One – 26 February 1990. Program No. 90–09

Epstein on Epstein, Part 2

1. Segment 1: One After 909 (1962 rehearsal) (The Beatles), 2. Catswalk (The Beatles), 3. Segment 2: Epstein's strategy for the States, 4. I'll Get You (The Beatles), 5. I Saw Her Standing There (Ed Sullivan, 9 February 1964) (The Beatles), 6. Segment 3: Bi-continental Beatles, 7. She Loves You (Paris June 1964) (The Beatles), 8. Can't Buy Me Love (The Beatles), 9. Segment 4, 10. Brian's favourite new Fab Four covers, 11. Love of the Loved (Cilla Black), 12. A World Without Love (Peter and Gordon), 13. Segment 5: Epstein takes NEMS to London, 14. I'll Be On My Way (BBC Radio) (The Beatles), 15. Slow Down (The Beatles)

Disc Two – 5 March 1990. Program No. 90–10

Epstein on Epstein, Part 3

1. Segment 1: Epstein with Murray the K. WOR-FM, March 1967, 2. Getting Better (The Beatles), 3. Segment 2: Epstein/Murray the K. 1967, break-up rumours, 4. I Want to Tell You (The Beatles), 5. Yesterday (Tokyo 30 June 1966) (The Beatles), 6. Segment 3: Epstein on NEMS clients, The Who and Cream on Hendrix, 7. Lawdy Mama (BBC Radio, December 1966) (Cream), 8. Segment 4: Epstein/Murray the K. Insulation of The Beatles from problems, 9. Day Tripper (Tokyo, 30 June 1966) (The Beatles), 10. Tomorrow Never Knows (rough mix) (The Beatles), 11. Segment 5: Brian takes Murray down to Penny Lane, 12. Penny Lane (promo mix) (The Beatles), 13. A Day in the Life (partial) (The Beatles)

447. SHOWS 112 AND 113 (WO 112/113)

Disc One – 12th March 1990. Program No. 90–11

Epstein on Epstein, Part 4

1. Segment 1: Epstein and Murray the K, WOR-FM March 1967, continued, 2. Think For Yourself (The Beatles), 3. Segment 2: Epstein/Murray:

Beatles tour in 1967? 4. Paperback Writer (Tokyo 30 June 1966) (The Beatles), 5. I'm Down (Tokyo 30 June 1966) (The Beatles), 6. Segment 3: Epstein *Pepper* update, 7. Lucy in the Sky with Diamonds (The Beatles), 8. Segment 4: Through Strawberry Fields down Penny Lane to Abbey Road, 9. Strawberry Fields Forever (take 1) (The Beatles), 10. Penny Lane (brass overdub session) (The Beatles), 11. Penny Lane (rough mix) (The Beatles), 12. Segment 5: Epstein on post *Pepper* plans, 13. She's Leaving Home (The Beatles)

Disc Two – 19 March 1990. Program No. 90–12

John and Yoko Anniversary Show: Courtship

1. Segment 1: John's pre-Yoko state of mind, Fall 1966, 2. Nowhere Man (Munich, 24 June 1966) (The Beatles)/Strawberry Fields Forever (demo), 3. Segment 2: The Indica encounter (Peebles BBC interview), 4, Drive Your Car (partial) (The Beatles), 5. I've Just Seen A Face (partial) (The Beatles), 6. Girl (partial) (The Beatles)/Segment 3: Private 1967, Public 1968, 7. Julia (demo, takes 1 and 2), 8. Mother Nature's Son (demo) (The Beatles), 9. Not Guilty (demo partial) (The Beatles), 10. Segment 4: Paul, Ringo and John on Yoko in the studio, 11. Revolution 9 (partial) (The Beatles), 12. Happiness Is a Warm Gun (The Beatles), 13. Segment 5: Yoko in the studio continued, 14. What's the New Mary Jane (demo) (The Beatles), 15. Oh, My Love (demo, take 1), 16. Oh, My Love (demo, take 2), 17. Oh, My Love (demo partial) (Yoko Ono)

448. SHOWS 114 AND 115 (WO 114/115)

Disc One – 26 March 1990. Program No. 90–13

John and Yoko Anniversary Show: Wedding and Honeymoon

1. Segment 1: Get Back To The *Rock and Roll Circus*, 2. Yer Blues (*Rock and Roll Circus*), 3. I've Got a Feeling (acoustic demo), 4. Untitled Jam (The Beatles and Yoko Ono), 5. Segment 2: Ballad of Paul and Linda and George and Patti, 6. The Honeymoon Song (partial) (Mary Hopkins), 7. It's All Too Much (The Beatles), 8. Segment 3: John and Yoko marry in Gibraltar, 9. On Our Way Home/Two of Us (The Beatles), 10. Segment 4: Bedlam at the Amsterdam Bed-In, 11. Hey Bulldog (The Beatles),

12. Segment 5: John and Yoko got a brand new bag, 13. Come Together (partial) (The Beatles), 14. Get Back (*Get Back* sessions, German version) (The Beatles), 15. The Ballad of John and Yoko (rough mix) (The Beatles)

Disc Two – 2 April 1990. Program No. 90–14

April 1964 and More

1. Segment 1, 2. Real Life (piano demo 2), 3. Real Love (early piano demo), 4. Segment 2: March 1964 USA/UK, 5. All My Loving (BBC Radio, 30 March 1964) (The Beatles), 6. Can't Buy Me Love (BBC Radio, 30 March 1964) (The Beatles), 7. Segment 3: April 1964, USA, 8. Scott Muni on Billboard Top 5, 5 April 1964, 9. Twist and Shout (The Beatles), 10. Segment 4: April 1964, UK, 11. A Hard Day's Night (The Beatles), 12. I Wanna Be Your Man (Around The Beatles) (The Beatles), 13. Long Tall Sally (Around The Beatles) (The Beatles), 14. Segment 5: Loving the Beatles, NME, 26 April 1964, 15. She Loves You (The Beatles), 16. You Can't Do That (partial) (The Beatles)

449. SHOWS 116 AND 117 (WO 116/117)

Disc One – 9 April 1990. Program No. 90–15

1. Segment 1, 2. Twist and Shout (6 May 1964) (The Beatles), 3. Can't Buy Me Love (6 May 1964) (The Beatles), 4. Segment 2: Just like starting over again, 5. Don't Be Crazy (demo, take 1), 6. (Just Like) Starting Over (demo, take 1), 7. Segment 3: Europe, 1966, 8. Rain (The Beatles), 9. Rock 'n' Roll Music (Munich, 24 June 1966) (The Beatles), 10. I Feel Fine (Munich 24 June 1966) (The Beatles), 11. Segment 4: Nothing but The Beatles and Elvis, revisited, 12. That's All Right Mama (BBC Radio, 16 July 1963) (The Beatles), 13. Blue Suede Shoes (*Get Back* sessions) (The Beatles), 14. You're So Square (*Get Back* sessions) (The Beatles), 15. Don't Be Cruel (*Get Back* sessions) (The Beatles), 16. That's All Right Mama (*Plastic Ono Band* sessions), 17. Segment 5: Elvis Orbison, 18. (Just Like) Starting Over (rough mix)

Disc Two – 16 April 1990. Program No. 90–16

The Fab Four's Far East Fiasco 1966

1. Segment 1: Terror in Tokyo, Part 1, 2. Yesterday (The Beatles), 3. Rock 'n' Roll Music (The Beatles), 4. Segment 2: Terror in Tokyo, Part 2, 5. She's a Woman (The Beatles), 6. Segment 3: Thrilla in Manila, Part 1, 7. If I Needed Someone (The Beatles), 8. Baby's in Black (The Beatles), 9. Segment 4: Thrilla in Manila, Part 2, 10. I Wanna Be Your Man (The Beatles), 11. Nowhere Man (The Beatles), 12. Segment 5: Thrilla in Manila, Part 3, 13. I Feel Fine (The Beatles), 14. I'm Down (The Beatles)

450. SHOWS 118 AND 119 (WO 118/119)

Disc One – 23 April 1990. Program No. 90–17

1. Segment 1: Beatles at the Beeb covering Perkins, 2. Everybody's Trying to Be My Baby (BBC Radio, 26 December 1964) (The Beatles), 3. Honey Don't (BBC Radio, 7 June 1965) (The Beatles), 4. Segment 2: John and Tom Snyder on *Tomorrow*, 28 April 1975, 5. Ob-La-Di-Ob-La-Da (mono mix) (The Beatles), 6. She's a Woman (The Beatles), 7. Segment 3: More *Tomorrow*, 8. Rock 'n' Roll People (take 7 alternate mix), 9. Segment 4: John Rastafar-Eye returns, 10. Power to the People (rehearsal), 11. How Do You Sleep? (rehearsal), 12. Love Is Strange (partial) (Wings), 13. Segment 5: April 1970: Behind The Beatles break-up, 13. Across the Universe (alternate mix) (The Beatles)

Disc Two – 30 April 1990. Program 90–18

Live in '65/Rastafar-Eye and P McSplivney

1. Segment 1: Beatles in 1965: Hollywood Bowl, 2. Twist and Shout (Hollywood Bowl, 30 August 1965) (The Beatles), 3. She's a Woman (Hollywood Bowl, 30 August 1965) (The Beatles), 4. Dizzy Miss Lizzy (Hollywood Bowl, 30 August 1965) (The Beatles), 5. Segment 2: John Rastafar-Eye and P. McSplivney, 6. Sisters Oh Sisters (partial) (Yoko Ono), 7. Live and Let Die (partial) (Wings), 8. Mind Games (rough mix), 9. Segment 3: Steel and Glass – Dr Winston O'Reggae, 10. Lucy in the Sky with Diamonds (partial) (Elton John and John Lennon), 11. Do You Want to Dance?, 12. Seaside Woman (partial) (Suzie and the Red Stripes),

13. Segment 4: Famous Groupies (Wings), 14. Living on Borrowed Time (double track demo, take 1), 15. Segment 5, 16. Living on Borrowed Time (rough mix)

451. SHOWS 120 AND 121 (WO 120/121)

Disc One – 7 May 1990. Program No. 90-19

So, Who Did Break Up The Beatles?

1. Segment 1: I'm Stepping Out – First Steps, 2. I'm Stepping Out (demo, take 1), 3. I'm Stepping Out (demo, take 3), 4. Segment 2: Wasn't me, it was John, 5. You Always Hurt the One You Love (partial) (The Beatles), 6. I've Got a Feeling (The Beatles), 7. You Never Give Me Your Money (partial) (The Beatles), 8. Segment 3, 9. Cold Turkey (Toronto 13 September 1969), 10. Cold Turkey (demo 1, partial), 11. Segment 4: Move On Fast (Yoko Ono), 12. I'm Stepping Out (take 8), 13. Segment 5: Cold Turkey (partial), 14. Come Together (partial) (The Beatles), 15. Something (The Beatles)

Disc Two – 14 May 1990. Program No. 90-20

Ringo Bails from The Beatles

1. Segment 1, 2. Tight A$ (take 4), 3. Segment 2: Hey Jude (partial) (The Beatles), 4. Tensions mount during *White Album* sessions – 1968, 5. Don't Pass Me By (The Beatles), 6. Segment 3: Woman Is the Nigger of the World (partial), 7. John and Yoko with Danny Schecter, 8. Only People (alternate mix), 9. Segment 4: John and Yoko with Schecter (continued), 10. I Know (I Know) (demo, take 4), 11. Nutopian National Anthem, 12. Imagine (alternate mix), 13. Segment 5: Ringo bails during the *White Album* sessions, 14. Back in the USSR (The Beatles), 15. Dear Prudence (partial) (The Beatles), 16. Revolution (The Beatles)

452. SHOWS 122 AND 123 (WO 122/123)

Disc One – 21 May 1990. Program No. 90-21

1. Segment 1: Beatles on the Beeb covering Carl, encore, 2. Matchbox (BBC, 30 July 1963) (The Beatles), 3. Honey Don't (BBC, 1 May 1964) (The Beatles), 4. Segment 2: Further development of 'Woman', 5. Woman

(acoustic guitar, demo, take 4), 6. Woman, acoustic guitar demo, take 7), 7. Every Man Has a Woman Who Loves Him (alternate mix) (John and Yoko), 8. Segment 3: McCartney sights Elvis, 9. Just Because (Paul McCartney), 10. That's All Right Mama (BBC) (The Beatles), 11. It's Now Or Never (Paul McCartney), 12. Segment 4: I'm Losing You (the next step), 13. Stranger's Room (demo), 14. Segment 5: John reacts to Paul's 10 April 1970 press release, 15. Let It Be (single mix) (The Beatles)

Disc Two – 28 May 1990. Program No. 90–22

1. Segment 1: Ringo's first session after rejoining The Beatles, 2. While My Guitar Gently Weeps (mono mix) (The Beatles), 3. Segment 2: John and Yoko with Schecter, Cambridge 3 June 1973, 4. Meat City (electric guitar demo 1), 5. One Day at a Time (alternate mix), 6. Segment 3: Hamburg stage smashing incident, 7. Matchbox (Star Club) (The Beatles), 8. Roll Over Beethoven (Star Club) (The Beatles), 9. Segment 4: John and Yoko with Schecter, continued, 10. Rock 'n' Roll People (piano demo), 11. Intuition (demo, take 3), 12. Segment 5: *Ringo* sessions 1973, 13. Six O'clock (Ringo Starr), 14. I'm the Greatest (rough mix) (Ringo Starr), 15. God (partial)

453. SHOWS 124 AND 125 (WO 124/125)

Disc One – 4 June 1990. Program No. 90–23

Coast-to-Coast with O'Boogie and The Beatles

1. Segment 1: O'Boogie with Dennis Elsas WNEW-FM, New York, 28 September 1974, 2. I Wanna Be Your Man (The Rolling Stones), 3. I Wanna Be Your Man (The Beatles), 4. Daddy Rolling Stone (Derek Martin), 5. Segment 2: O'Boogie with Tom Donahue, KSAN-FM, San Francisco, September 1974, 6. Girl (The Beatles), 7. River Deep Mountain High (partial) (Ike and Tina Turner), 8. Blue Suede Shoes (partial) (Carl Perkins), 9. Segment 3:O'Boogie as guest DJ, KHJ, Los Angeles, 27 September 1974, 10. You're Going to Lose That Girl (The Beatles), 11. Segment 4: O'Boogie w/Elsas, continued, 12. Watch Your Step (Bobby Parker), 13. Day Tripper (The Beatles), 14. I Call Your Name (The Beatles), 15. Segment 5: O'Boogie with Donahue, continued, 16. A Day in the Life (The Beatles), 17. Preview

Disc Two – 11 June 1990. Program No. 90–24

From 'Get Back' to 'Let It Be'

1. Segment 1: Get Back/Let It Be, 2. Don't Let Me Down (The Beatles), 3. Segment 2: Meat City Revisited, 4. Just Gimme Some Rock 'n' Roll (demo, partial), 5. Meat City (guitar demo 2), 6. Meat City (alternate mix), 7. Segment 3: Get Back/Let It Be (continued), 8. Carry That Weight (The Beatles), 9. Because (The Beatles), 10. Segment 4: Evolution of 'I'm Losing You' (continued), 11. Stranger's Room (demo), 12. Segment 5: Get Back/Let It Be (Continued), 13. You Know My Name (Look Up the Number) (The Beatles), 14. Instant Karma (partial), 15. I Me Mine (The Beatles)

454. SHOWS 126 AND 127 (WO 126/127)

Disc One – 18 June 1990. Program No. 90–25

The Spectorization of *Let It Be*

1. Segment 1: I Me Mine (partial) (The Beatles), 2. Dig a Pony (The Beatles), 3. Segment 2, 4. Get Back (album version) (The Beatles), 5. Maggie Mae (The Beatles), 6. Dig It (The Beatles), 7. Segment 3, 8. For You Blue (partial) (The Beatles), 9. Let It Be (album version) (The Beatles), 10. Segment 4, 11. Two of Us (The Beatles), 12. Segment 5, 13. Long and Winding Road (The Beatles), 14. All Things Must Pass (George Harrison), 15. I Found Out (demo)

Disc Two – 25 June 1990. Program No. 90–26

Liberation Celebration Part 1

1. Segment 1, 2. Misery (stereo mix) (The Beatles), 3. There's a Place (stereo mix) (The Beatles), 4. Segment 2, 5. Bad Boy (The Beatles), 6. Segment 3, 7. Help (Hollywood Bowl, 30 August 1965) (The Beatles), 8. He Said He Said (demo fragments), 9. She Said She Said (demo), 10. She Said She Said (The Beatles), 11. Segment 4, 12. Yer Blues (*Rock and Roll Circus*), 13. Segment 5, 14. Look at Me (rough mix), 15. God (partial)

455. SHOWS 128 AND 129 (WO 128/129)

Disc One – 2 July 1990. Program No. 90–27

Freedom Liberation Celebration Part 1

1. Segment 1, 2. Happy Xmas (War Is Over) (alternate mix), 3. Imagine (rehearsal, partial), 4. Segment 2, 5. You Can't Catch Me (alternate mix), 6. Segment 3, 7. Give Me Some Truth (alternate mix), 8. Stand By Me (partial), 9. Segment 4, 10. No. 9 Dream (alternate mix), 11. Free as a Bird (demo, take 1), 12. Segment 5, 13. Serve Yourself (demo)

Disc Two – 9 July 1990. Program No. 90–28

The Beatles on Film, Part 1

1. Segment 1, 2. I Want to Hold Your Hand (*Ed Sullivan Show*) (The Beatles), 3. I Should Have Known Better (The Beatles), 4. Segment 2, 5. Things We Said Today (The Beatles), 6. Any Time at All (The Beatles), 7. Segment 3, 8. A Hard Day's Night (The Beatles), 9. If I Fell (The Beatles), 10. Segment 4, 11. Can't Buy Me Love (The Beatles), 12. I'm Happy Just to Dance With You (The Beatles), 13. Segment 5, 14. Tell Me Why (The Beatles), 15. I'll Cry Instead (The Beatles)

456. SHOWS 130 AND 131 (WO 130/131)

Disc One – 16 July 1990. Program No. 90–29

Help!

1. Segment 1, 2. Yes It Is (The Beatles), 3. You're Going to Lose That Girl (The Beatles), 4. Segment 2, 5. Another Girl (The Beatles), 6. The Night Before (The Beatles), 7. Segment 3, 8. I Need You (The Beatles), 9. Ticket to Ride (The Beatles), 10. I've Just Seen a Face (The Beatles), 11. Segment 4, 12. Act Naturally (The Beatles), 13. You've Got to Hide Your Love Away (The Beatles), 14. Segment 5, 15. Help (The Beatles), 16. Yesterday (The Beatles)

Disc Two – 23 July 1990. Program No. 90–30

Magical Mystery Tour

1. Segment 1, 2. Magical Mystery Tour (The Beatles), 3. The Fool On The Hill (The Beatles), 4. Segment 2, 5. Blue Jay Way (The Beatles),

6. Segment 3, 7. Baby You're a Rich Man (The Beatles), 8. Penny Lane (The Beatles), 9. Strawberry Fields Forever (demo), 10. Strawberry Fields Forever (The Beatles), 11. Strawberry Fields Forever (ending) (The Beatles), 12. Segment 4, 13. I Am the Walrus (The Beatles), 14. Segment 5, 15. Your Mother Should Know (The Beatles)

457. SHOWS 132 AND 133 (WO 132/133)

Disc One – 30 July 1990. Program No. 90-31

Revolver

1. Segment 1, 2. Eleanor Rigby (The Beatles), 3. Good Day Sunshine (The Beatles), 4. She Said She Said (demo), 5. Segment 2, 6. Tomorrow Never Knows (The Beatles), 7. Segment 3, 8. Love You To (The Beatles), 9. Got to Get You into My Life (The Beatles), 10. Segment 4, 11. The Word (The Beatles), 12. Think for Yourself (The Beatles), 13. Taxman (The Beatles), 14. What Goes On (The Beatles), 15. Segment 5, 16. Here, There and Everywhere (The Beatles)

Disc Two – 6 August 1990. Program No. 90-32

Brian Epstein

1. Segment 1, 2. My Bonnie (Tony Sheridan and The Beatles), 3. Please Please Me (The Beatles), 4. Segment 2, 5. I Want to Hold Your Hand (The Beatles), 6. All My Loving (live) (The Beatles), 7. Segment 3, 8. She Loves You (live) (The Beatles), 9. Chains (The Beatles), 10. Segment 4, 11. It Won't Be Long (The Beatles), 12. Misery (The Beatles), 13. Segment 5, 14. We Can Work It Out (The Beatles), 15. All You Need Is Love (The Beatles)

458. SHOWS 134 AND 135 (WO 134/135)

Disc One – 13 August 1990. Program No. 90-33

Double Fantasy – Part 1

1. Segment 1, 2. Kansas City (BBC) (The Beatles), 3. Everybody's Trying To Be My Baby (BBC) (The Beatles), 4. Segment 2, 5. Watching the Wheels (rough mix), 6. Segment 3, 7. (Just Like) Starting Over, 8. Segment 4, 9. Hey Jude (The Beatles), 10. Segment 5, 11. Real Love, 12. Dear Yoko

Disc Two – 20 August 1990. Program No. 90–34

Double Fantasy – Part 2

1. Segment 1, 2. Roll Over Beethoven (BBC) (The Beatles), 3. Till There Was You (BBC) (The Beatles), 4. Segment 2, 5. Woman (rough mix), 6. Kiss Kiss Kiss, 7. Segment 3, 8. Beautiful Boy, 9. Segment 4, 10. Revolution 1 (The Beatles), 11. Revolution 9 (The Beatles), 12. Segment 5, 13. Serve Yourself (demo), 14. I'm Losing You

459. SHOWS 136 AND 137 (WO 136/137)

Disc One – 27 August 1990. Program No. 90–35

Double Fantasy – Part 3

1. Segment 1, 2. I Wanna Be Your Man (BBC) (The Beatles), 3. Can't Buy Me Love (BBC) (The Beatles), 4. Segment 2, 5. (Just Like) Starting Over, 6. Beautiful Boys (Yoko Ono), 7. Segment 3, 8. Clean-up Time, 9. Every Man Has a Woman Who Loves Him (Yoko Ono), 10. I'm Moving On (Yoko Ono), 11. Segment 4, 12. Carol (BBC) (The Beatles), 13. Soldier of Love (BBC) (The Beatles), 14. Segment 5, 15. Yes I'm Your Angel (Yoko Ono), 16. Hard Times Are Over (Yoko Ono)

Disc Two – 3 September 1990. Program No. 90–36

Live Peace in Toronto

1. Segment 1, 2. Blue Suede Shoes, 3. Money, 4. Segment 2, 5. Dizzy Miss Lizzy, 6. Cold Turkey, 7. Segment 3, 8. Fame (David Bowie), 9. Segment 4, 10. Don't Worry Kyoko (Yoko Ono), 11. Give Peace a Chance, 12. Segment 5, 13. Love Me Do (The Beatles), 14. How Do You Do It? (The Beatles), 15. Please Please Me (The Beatles)

460. SHOWS 138 AND 139 (WO 138 AND 139)

Disc One – 10 September 1990. Program No. 90–37

Walls and Bridges

1. Segment 1, 2. Nobody Loves You, 3. Old Dirt Road, 4. Segment 2, 5. Going Down on Love (demo), 6. No. 9 Dream, 7. Segment 3,

8. Surprise Surprise (Sweet Bird of Paradox), 9. Bless You, 10. Segment 4, 11. Ya Ya, 12. What You Got, 13. Segment 5, 14. Whatever Gets You Through the Night, 15. I Saw Her Standing There (live) (Elton John and John Lennon)

Disc One – 17 September 1990. Program No. 90–38

Abbey Road

1. Segment 1, 2. Don't Let Me Down (demo), 3. Come Together (The Beatles), 4. Segment 2, 5. Maxwell's Silver Hammer (The Beatles), 6. Something (The Beatles), 7. Segment 3, 8. Sun King (The Beatles), 9. Segment 4, 10. Octopus Garden (The Beatles), 11. I Want You (She's So Heavy) (The Beatles), 12. Segment 5, 13. Her Majesty (The Beatles)

461. SHOWS 140 AND 141 (WO 140/141)

Disc One – 24 September 1990. Program No. 90–39

Abbey Road – Part 2

1. Segment 1, 2. What's the New Mary Jane, 3. Segment 2, 4. Because (The Beatles), 5. Oh Darling (The Beatles), 6. Segment 3, 7. You Never Give Me Your Money (The Beatles), 8. Here Comes the Sun (The Beatles), 9. Segment 4, 10. Mean Mr Mustard (demo, partial and outtake), 11. Polythene Pam (The Beatles), 12. She Came in Through the Bathroom Window (The Beatles), 13. Golden Slumbers (The Beatles), 14. Segment 5, 15. I Want You (She's So Heavy) (The Beatles), 16. Carry That Weight (The Beatles), 17. The End (The Beatles)

Disc Two – 1 October 1990. Program No. 90–40

Milestones – Part 1

1. Segment 1, 2. Lennon montage, 3. Mother, 4. Julia (demo), 5. Segment 2, 6. Beatles montage, 7. One After 909 (The Beatles), 8. Segment 3, 9. Hello Little Girl (The Beatles), 10. Love, 11. Segment 4, 12. Oh, Yoko, 13. Ballad of John and Yoko (The Beatles), 14. Give Peace a Chance, 15. Segment 5, 16. Imagine

462. SHOWS 142 AND 143 (WO 142/143)

Disc One – 8 October 1990. Program No. 90–41
1. Segment 1, 2. God (demo), 3. Don't Let Me Down (The Beatles), 4. Segment 2, 5. Give Me Some Truth, 6. Let It Be (The Beatles), 7. Segment 3, 8. Give Me Some Truth, 9. Stand By Me, 10. Segment 4, 11. Isolation, 12. Segment 5, 13. Watching the Wheels

Disc Two – 15 October 1990. Program No. 90–42

White Album – Part 1
1. Segment 1, 2. It's So Hard, 3. Segment 2, 4. Back in the USSR (The Beatles), 5. Dear Prudence (The Beatles), 6. Segment 3, 7. Birthday (The Beatles), 8. Don't Pass Me By (The Beatles), 9. Segment 4, 10. Why Don't We Do It In The Road (The Beatles), 11. Savoy Truffle (The Beatles), 12. Everybody's Got Something to Hide Except Me and My Monkey (The Beatles), 13. Segment 5, 14. Happiness Is a Warm Gun (The Beatles), 15. Glass Onion (The Beatles)

463. SHOWS 144 AND 145 (WO 144/145)

Disc One – 22 October 1990. Program No. 90–43

White Album – Part 2
1. Segment 1, 2. Rocky Raccoon (The Beatles), 3. Yer Blues (The Beatles), 4. Segment 2, 5. Sexy Sadie (The Beatles), 6. Continuing Story of Bungalow Bill (The Beatles), 7. While My Guitar Gently Weeps (The Beatles), 8. Segment 3, 9. Ob-La-Di-Ob-La-Da (The Beatles), 10. I'm So Tired (The Beatles), 11. Segment 4, 12. Revolution (The Beatles), 13. Segment 5, 14. Blackbird (The Beatles), 15. Piggies (The Beatles), 16. Helter Skelter (The Beatles), 17. Good Night (The Beatles)

Disc Two – 29 October 1990. Program No. 90–44

Stu Sutcliffe – The Forgotten Beatle
1. Segment 1, 2. She Loves You (The Beatles), 3. Twist and Shout (The Beatles), 4. Till There Was You (The Beatles), 5. I Want to Hold Your Hand

(The Beatles), 6. Segment 2, 7. Three Cool Cats (The Beatles), 8. Money (The Beatles), 9. Segment 2, 10. Thank You Girl (The Beatles), 11. I Saw Her Standing There (The Beatles), 12. Segment 4, 13. Norwegian Wood (The Beatles), 14. Segment 5, 15. Cathy's Clown (acoustic demo), 16. You Send Me (acoustic and demo), 17. Stand By Me

464. SHOWS 146 AND 147 (WO 146/147)

Disc One – 5 November 1990. Program No. 90–45

1. Segment 1, 2. She's a Woman (BBC) (The Beatles), 3. I Feel Fine (BBC) (The Beatles), 4. Segment 2, 5. A Day in the Life (The Beatles), 6. I Am the Walrus (The Beatles), 7. Segment 3, 8. The Ballad of John and Yoko (The Beatles), 9. Give Ireland Back to the Irish (Wings), 10. Give Peace a Chance, 11. Woman Is the Nigger of the World (from One-to-One concert), 12. Segment 4, 13. Two Virgins (excerpt) (John and Yoko), 14. Segment 4, 15. Hi Hi Hi (Wings), 16. Cold Turkey (demo)

Disc Two – 12th November 1990. Program No. 90–46

The Beatles in Hamburg

1. Segment 1, 2. It's So Hard, 3. Segment 2, 4. Hippy Hippy Shake (Star Club) (The Beatles), 5. Roll Over Beethoven (Star Club) (The Beatles), 6. Segment 2, 7. Sweet Little Sixteen (Star Club) (The Beatles), 8. Twist and Shout (Star Club) (The Beatles), 9. Segment 4, 10. Little Queenie (Star Club) (The Beatles), 11. My Bonnie (Tony Sheridan and The Beatles), 12. Segment 5, 13. Long Tall Sally (The Beatles), 14. Lucille (Little Richard), 15. Kansas City/Hey Hey Hey Hey (The Beatles)

465. SHOWS 148 AND 149 (WO 148/149)

Disc One – 19 November 1990. Program No. 90–47

Influences

1. Segment 1, 2. Too Much Monkey Business (demo), 3. Memphis Tennessee (Chuck Berry), 4. Brown Eyed Handsome Man (demo), 5. Segment 2, 6. Rock Island Line (demo), 7. Baby Let's Play House (Elvis Presley), 8. Heartbreak Hotel (Elvis Presley), 9. Segment 3, 10. That'll Be the Day, 11. House of the Rising Sun (Animals), 12. Segment 4, 13. I

Should Have Known Better (The Beatles), 14. Chords of Fame (demo) (Phil Ochs and John Lennon), 15. Segment 5, 16. Matchbox (The Beatles), 17. Lovely Rita (The Beatles)

Disc Two – 26 November 1990. Program No. 90–48

The Fans

1. Segment 1, 2. You Really Got a Hold on Me (The Beatles), 3. Do You Want to Know a Secret? (The Beatles), 4. Segment 2, 5. It Won't Be Long (The Beatles), 6. From Me to You (The Beatles), 7. Segment 3, 8. Can't Buy Me Love (The Beatles), 9. You Won't See Me (The Beatles), 10. Segment 4, 11. P.S. I Love You (The Beatles), 12. No Reply (The Beatles), 13. Segment 5, 14. What Goes On (The Beatles), 15. Thank You Girl (The Beatles)

466. SHOWS 150 AND 151 (WO 150/151)

Disc One – 3 December 1990. Program No. 90–49

Collector's Edition

1. Segment 1, 2. French Medley (demo), 3. Segment 2, 4. The Boat Show (demo), 5. Help Me to Help Myself (demo), 6. Segment 3, 7. I Promise (demo), 8. Make Love Not War (demo), 9. Mind Games, 10. Segment 4, 11. Sgt Pepper's Lonely Hearts Club Band (live) (Paul McCartney), 12. Love Me Do (The Beatles), 13. Segment 5, 14. Things We Said Today (The Beatles), 15. Hey Jude (live) (Paul McCartney)

Disc Two – 10 December 1990. Program No. 90–50

Rubber Soul

1. Segment 1, 2. Yesterday (The Beatles), 3. Run for Your Life (The Beatles), 4. Drive My Car (The Beatles), 5. Segment 2, 6. Day Tripper (The Beatles), 7. Fourth Time Around (partial) (Bob Dylan), 8. Norwegian Wood (The Beatles), 9. Nowhere Man (The Beatles), 10. Segment 3, 11. In My Life (The Beatles), 12. Michelle (The Beatles), 13. Segment 3, 14. What Goes On (The Beatles), 15. Think For Yourself (The Beatles), 16. Segment 5, 17. Wait (The Beatles), 18. Girl (The Beatles), 19. The Word (The Beatles)

467. SHOWS 152 AND 153 (WO 152/153)

Disc One – 17 December 1990 Program No. 90–51

Christmas Show

1. Segment 1, 2. Wonderful Christmastime (Paul McCartney), 3. Be Bop A Lu La (Star Club) (The Beatles), 4. Segment 2, 5. I Want to Hold Your Hand (The Beatles), 6. I Feel Fine (The Beatles), 7. Segment 3, 8. And Your Bird Can Sing (The Beatles), 9. Segment 4, 10. I Am the Walrus (The Beatles), 11. Revolution (The Beatles), 12. Segment 5, 13. Happy Xmas (War Is Over) (demo)

Disc Two – 24 December 1990 Program No. 90–52

The Break-up of The Beatles

1. Segment 1, 2. Ob-La-Di-Ob-La-Da (The Beatles), 3. Real Love (demo), 4. Segment 2, 5. There's a Place (The Beatles), 6. She Came in Through the Bathroom Window (The Beatles), 7. Segment 3, 8. Sexy Sadie (The Beatles), 9. You Never Give Me Your Money (The Beatles), 10. Segment 4, 11. We Can Work It Out (The Beatles), 12. Get Back (The Beatles), 13. It's All Too Much (The Beatles), 14. Segment 5, 15. Hello Goodbye (The Beatles)

468. SHOW 154 (WO 154)

31 December 1990 Program No. 91–01

New Beginnings

1. Segment 1, 2. Maybe I'm Amazed (Paul McCartney), 3. Segment 2, 4. Awaiting On You All (George Harrison), 5. My Sweet Lord (George Harrison), 6. Segment 3, 7. Mother (alternate take), 8. God, 9. Segment 4, 10. Working Class Hero (radio edit), 11. Love (alternate mix), 12. Segment 5, 13. Instant Karma

469. SHOWS 155 AND 156 (WO 155/156)

Disc One – 7 January 1991 Program No. 91–02

The Disintegration of Lennon and McCartney

1. Segment 1, 2. Oh, My Love (alternate take), 3. I Saw Her Standing There (The Beatles), 4. Please Please Me (The Beatles), 5. Segment 2, 6. She Loves You (The Beatles), 7. Anytime at All (The Beatles), 8. Segment 3, 9. Eleanor Rigby (The Beatles), 10. Getting Better (The Beatles), 11. Segment 4, 12. Misery (The Beatles), 13. How Do You Sleep? 14. Too Many People (Paul and Linda McCartney), 15. Segment 5, 16. Twist and Shout (The Beatles)

Disc Two – 14 January 1991 Program No. 91–03

Beatles vs. The Rolling Stones

1. Segment 1, 2. I Wanna Be Your Man (The Rolling Stones), 3. I Wanna Be Your Man (The Beatles), 4. Dizzy Miss Lizzie (The Beatles), 5. Segment 2, 6. (I Can't Get No) Satisfaction (Rolling Stones), 7. Sgt Pepper's Lonely Hearts Club Band (The Beatles), 8. With a Little Help from My Friends (The Beatles), 9. Honky Tonk Woman (The Rolling Stones), 10. Segment 3, 11. Too Many Cooks (Mick Jagger), 12. We Love You (The Rolling Stones), 13. Segment 4, 14. Yer Blues (*Rock and Roll Circus*), 15. Segment 5, 16. Memories (demo)

470. SHOWS 157 AND 158 (WO 157/158)

Disc One – 21 January 1991 Program No. 91–04

1. Segment 1, 2. I Want You (demo) (John and Yoko), 3. Segment 2, 4. Here, There and Everywhere (The Beatles), 5. Fixing A Hole (The Beatles), 6. No Matter What (Badfinger), 7. Segment 3, 8. Three Cool Cats (BBC) (The Beatles), 9. Let It Be (The Beatles), 10. Segment 4, 11. Dig a Pony (The Beatles), 12. Segment 5, 13. Remember

Disc Two – 28 January 1991 Program No. 91–05

Rock 'n' Roll

1. Segment 1, 2. Rock 'n' Roll Music (The Beatles), 3. Roll Over Beethoven (The Beatles), 4. Twenty Flight Rock (live) (Paul McCartney), 5. Segment 2, 6. You Can't Catch Me (alternate take), 7. Be Bop A Lula, 8. Segment 3, 9. Be My Baby, 10. Segment 4, 11. Ain't That a Shame, 12. Slippin' and Slidin', 13. Just Because, 14. Segment 5, 15. I'm Losing You (alternate take)

Notes: Disc One, track 8 – Although the sleeve states that this recording of 'Three Cool Cats' is from the BBC sessions it is more likely from The Decca Audition. The Beatles recorded this song twice for the BBC but neither was broadcast and they have never been bootlegged. John referred to this song in the Andy Peebles interview as being a BBC recording which is probably where the confusion originated. The tapes have most likely been lost forever.

471. SHOWS 159 AND 160 (WO 159/160)

Disc One – 4 February 1991 Program No. 91–06

Beatles Conquer the Colonies – Part 1

1. Segment 1, 2. It Won't Be Long (The Beatles), 3. I Want to Hold Your Hand (The Beatles), 4. Ask Me Why (The Beatles), 5. Segment 2, 6. Baby It's You (The Beatles), 7. Boys (The Beatles), 8. Love Me Do (The Beatles), 9. Segment 3, 10. A Taste of Honey (The Beatles), 11. All My Loving (Ed Sullivan) (The Beatles), 12. Segment 4, 13. She Loves You (Ed Sullivan) (The Beatles), 14. I Saw Her Standing There (Ed Sullivan) (The Beatles), 15. Segment 5, 16. Please Please Me (The Beatles), 17. P.S. I Love You (The Beatles)

Disc Two – 11 February 1991 Program No. 91–07

1. Segment 1, 2. Roll Over Beethoven (BBC) (The Beatles), 3. Till There Was You (The Beatles), 4. Segment 2, 5. Hold Me Tight (The Beatles), 6. Little Child (The Beatles), 7. Do You Want to Know a Secret (The Beatles), 8. Devil In Her Heart (The Beatles), 9. Segment 3, 10. This Boy (Ed Sullivan) (The

Beatles), 11. There's a Place (The Beatles), 12. Segment 4, 13. She Loves You (The Beatles), 14. All My Loving (The Beatles), 15. A Hard Day's Night (The Beatles), 16. Segment 5, 17. Woman (alternate take)

472. SHOWS 161 AND 162 (WO 161/162)

Disc One – 18 February 1991 Program No. 91–08

The Beatles at the Beeb

1. Segment 1, 2. Dream Baby (BBC) (The Beatles), 3. Too Much Monkey Business (BBC) (The Beatles), 4. Thank You Girl (BBC) (The Beatles), 5. From Me to You (BBC) (The Beatles), 6. Segment 2, 7. I'll Be on My Way (BBC) (The Beatles), 8. I Saw Her Standing There (BBC) (The Beatles), 9. Some Other Guy (BBC) (The Beatles), 10. A Taste of Honey (BBC) (The Beatles), 11. Segment 3, 12. A Shot of Rhythm and Blues (BBC) (The Beatles), 13. Gonna Find My Baby (BBC) (The Beatles), 14. I'll Get You (BBC) (The Beatles), 15. Segment 5, 16. Youngblood (BBC) (The Beatles), 17. Sure to Fall (BBC) (The Beatles), 18. Anna (BBC) (The Beatles), 19. Twist and Shout (BBC) (The Beatles), 20. Segment 5, 21. Dear Yoko (alternate take), 22. Dear Yoko (studio chat), 23. Dear Yoko (rough mix)

Disc Two – 25 February 1991 Program No. 91–09

Birthday Salute to George Harrison

1. Segment 1, 2. Crackerbox Palace (George Harrison), 3. Sie Liebt Dich (The Beatles), 4. Segment 2, 5. Got My Mind Set on You (George Harrison), 6. Segment 3, 7. What Is Life (George Harrison), 8. Bangla Desh (George Harrison), 9. Segment 4, 10. Everybody's Trying to Be My Baby (The Beatles), 11. Something (The Beatles), 12. Segment 5, 13. When We Was Fab (George Harrison), 14. Blow Away (George Harrison)

Notes: Disc Two, track 13 – Sleeve describes this as a Beatles track

473. SHOWS 163 AND 164 (WO 163/164)

Disc One – 4 March 1991 Program No. 91–10

1. Segment 1, 2. Watching the Wheels (demo), 3. Watching the Wheels, 4. Segment 2, 5. Dr Robert (The Beatles), 6. And Your Bird Can Sing (The

Beatles), 7. Yesterday (montage), 8. Yesterday (The Beatles), 9. Segment 3, 10. Can't Buy Me Love (The Beatles), 11. What Goes On (The Beatles), 12. Segment 4, 13. The Word (The Beatles), 14. Love, 15. Love, 16. Segment 5, 17. Across the Universe (alternate mix) (The Beatles), 18. Clean-up Time

Disc Two – 11 March 1991 Program No. 91–11

Advertising for Peace

1. Segment 1, 2. Give Peace a Chance (Peace Choir), 3. Ballad of John and Yoko (The Beatles), 4. No. 9 Dream, 5. Segment 2, 6. Get It Together (John and Yoko), 7. Give Peace a Chance, 8 I Don't Want to Be a Soldier, 9. Segment 3, 10. Imagine (solo piano version), 11. Bless You, 12. Segment 4, 13. Power to the People (alternate mix), 14. Only People (alternate mix), 15. Segment 5, 16. Mind Games (alternate take)

474. SHOWS 165 AND 166 (WO 165/166)

Disc One – 18 March 1991 Program No. 91–12

John's Enlightenment

1. Segment 1, 2. Whatever Gets You Through the Night (composing demo), 3. Segment 2, 4. She Said She Said (The Beatles), 5. Give Me Some Truth, 6. Segment 3: The Rishikesh Song, Magical Mystery Tour (The Beatles), 7. Sexy Sadie (partial) (The Beatles), 8. The Maharishi Song, 9. Yer Blues (The Beatles), 10. Segment 4, 11. Hold On, 12. Look at Me, 13. Mother, 14. Dear John (demo), 15. Segment 5, 16. She Runs Them Round In Circles (demo), 17. Beautiful Boy

Disc One – 25 March 1991 Program No. 91–13

The Beatles at the Beeb – Part 2

1. Segment 1, 2. Nothin' Shakin' (But the Leaves on the Trees) (The Beatles), 3. So How Come (No One Loves Me) (The Beatles), 4. The Hippy Hippy Shake (The Beatles), 5. To Know Her Is to Love Her (The Beatles), 6. Segment 2, 7. Matchbox (The Beatles), 8. Please Mr Postman (The Beatles), 9. Do You Want to Know a Secret (The Beatles), 10. Segment 3,

11. The Honeymoon Song (The Beatles), 12. Please Please Me (The Beatles), 13. I've Got a Woman (The Beatles), 14. Chains (The Beatles), 15. Segment 4, 16. You Really Got a Hold on Me (The Beatles), 17. Honey Don't (The Beatles), 18. I Forgot to Remember to Forget (The Beatles), 19. Segment 5, 20. You Can't Do That (The Beatles), 21. I'm Sure to Fall (The Beatles), 22. Long Tall Sally (The Beatles)

475. SHOWS 167 AND 168 (WO 167/168)

Disc One – 1 April 1991 Program No. 91–14

Beatle Rumours

1. Segment 1, 2. Do You Want to Know a Secret (The Beatles), 3. Bad To Me (Billy J Kramer), 4. Act Naturally (The Beatles), 5. Segment 2, 6. Another Girl (The Beatles), 7. I Feel Fine (The Beatles), 8. God, 9. Segment 3, 10. Golden Slumbers/Carry That Weight/The End (The Beatles), 11. A Day in the Life (The Beatles), 12. Segment 4, 13. Strawberry Fields Forever (The Beatles), 14. Strawberry Fields Forever (The Beatles), 15. Glass Onion (The Beatles), 16. Segment 5, 17. She'll Be Coming Round the Mountain

Disc Two – 8 April 1991 Program No. 91–15

John's Political Awakening

1. Segment 1, 2. Revolution (The Beatles), 3. Only People, 4. Segment 2, 5. Attica State (rehearsal), 6. New York City, 7. John Sinclair, 8. Segment 3, 9. Woman Is the Nigger of the World, 10. Sisters Oh Sisters (Yoko Ono), 11. Segment 4, 12. Sunday Bloody Sunday, 13. Segment 5, 14. Revolution (The Beatles)

476. SHOWS 169 AND 170 (WO 169/170)

Disc One – 15 April 1991 Program No. 91–16

The Beatles Backwards in Time

1. Segment 1, 2. The Luck of the Irish (alternate take), 3. Penny Lane, 4. Julia (demo), 5. Segment 2, 6. In My Life (The Beatles), 7. That's My Life (partial) (Freddie Lennon), 8. Real Love (demo), 9. Segment 3, 10. Good

Night (The Beatles), 11. Beautiful Boy, 12. Segment 4, 13. Rain (The Beatles), 14. Segment 5, 15. I Saw Her Standing There (The Beatles), 16. Can't Buy Me Love (The Beatles), 17. Twist and Shout (The Beatles), 18. She Loves You (The Beatles), 19. I Want to Hold Your Hand (The Beatles)

Disc Two – 22 April 1991 Program No. 91–17

1. Segment 1, 2. New York City (demo), 3. Talkin' New York (Bob Dylan), 4. Segment 2, 5. Blowing in the Wind (Bob Dylan), 6. Corrina Corrina (Bob Dylan), 7. Rainy Day Women (Bob Dylan), 8. Help! (The Beatles), 9. Segment 3, 10. I'm a Loser (The Beatles), 11. Subterranean Homesick Blues (Bob Dylan), 12. Segment 4, 13. Positively Fourth Street (Bob Dylan), 14. Like a Rolling Stone (Bob Dylan), 15. Segment 5, 16. Gotta Serve Somebody (Bob Dylan), 17. Serve Yourself (demo)

Notes: Disc Two, track 17 – sleeve incorrectly says this track is by Bob Dylan.

477. SHOWS 171 AND 172 (WO 171/172)

Disc One – 29 April 1991 Program No. 91–18

The Beatles at the Beeb – Part 3

1. Segment 1, 2. I Saw Her Standing There (*Easy Beat*) (The Beatles), 3. Love Me Do (*Easy Beat*) (The Beatles), 4. She Loves You (*Easy Beat*) (The Beatles), 5. Segment 2, 6. This Boy (*Saturday Club*) (The Beatles), 7. Roll Over Beethoven (*Saturday Club*) (The Beatles), 8. Tie Me Kangaroo Down Sport (*From Us To You*) (The Beatles with Rolf Harris), 9. Segment 3, 10. I Want to Hold Your Hand (*Saturday Club*) (The Beatles), 11. Johnny B Goode (*Saturday Club*) (The Beatles), 12. Segment 4, 13. Till There Was You (*From Us To You*) (The Beatles), 14. She's a Woman (*Saturday Club*) (The Beatles), 15. Segment 5, 16. Kansas City (*Ticket to Ride*) (The Beatles), 17. Ticket to Ride (*Ticket to Ride*) (The Beatles), 18. Dizzy Miss Lizzie (*Ticket to Ride*) (The Beatles)

Disc Two – 6 May 1991 Program No. 91–19

Beatles Parodies

1. Segment 1, 2. Knocking On Heaven's Door (demo), 3. Segment 2, 4. A Hard Day's Night (The Beatles), 5. Within You Without You (The

Beatles), 6. L.S. Bumblebee (Peter Cook and Dudley Moore), 7. Segment 3, 8. Magical Misery Tour (National Lampoon), 9. Give Booze a Chance (Bonzo Dog Band), 10. He's So Fine/My Sweet Lord (Jonathan King), 11. Segment 4, 12. Hold My Hand (The Rutles), 13. Girl Like You (The Rutles), 14. Ouch (The Rutles), 15. Love Life (The Rutles), 16. Segment 5, 17. Piggy in the Middle (The Rutles), 18. Get Up and Go (The Rutles)

478. SHOWS 173 AND 174 (WO 173/174)

Disc One – 13 May 1991 Program No. 91–20

Milk and Honey outtakes/*Pussy Cats* sessions

1. Segment 1, 2. Too Many Cooks (Mick Jagger), 3. Segment 2, 4. Whatever Gets You Through the Night (partial) (John Lennon and Elton John), 5. Old Dirt Road, 6. Mucho Mungo (composing demo), 7. Segment 3, 8. Subterranean Homesick Blues (Harry Nilsson), 9. Many Rivers to Cross (Harry Nilsson), 10. Segment 4, 11. I'm Stepping Out (rough mix), 12. I Don't Want to Face It (rough mix), 13. Segment 5, 14. Borrowed Time (demo), 15. Borrowed Time (rough mix)

Disc Two – 20 May 1991 Program No. 91–21

Sgt Pepper – Part 1

1. Segment 1, 2. Sloop John B (The Beach Boys), 3. Penny Lane (The Beatles), 4. Segment 2, 5. Sgt Pepper's Lonely Hearts Club Band (The Beatles), 6. With a Little Help from My Friends (The Beatles), 7. Lucy in the Sky with Diamonds (The Beatles), 8. Segment 3, 9. Getting Better (The Beatles), 10. Fixing A Hole (The Beatles), 11. She's Leaving Home (The Beatles), 12. Segment 4, 13. Being for the Benefit of Mr Kite (The Beatles), 14. Segment 5, 15. Nobody Told Me (demo), 16. Nobody Told Me (rough mix)

479. SHOWS 175 AND 176 (WO 175/176)

Disc One – 27 May 1991 Program No. 91–22

Sgt Pepper – Part 2

1. Segment 1, 2. Sgt Pepper Medley (The Beatles), 3. Within You Without You (The Beatles), 4. Segment 2, 5. When I'm 64 (The Beatles), 6. Lovely

Rita (The Beatles), 7. Good Morning, Good Morning (composing demo), 8. Good Morning, Good Morning (The Beatles), 9. Segment 3, 10. Sgt Pepper Reprise (The Beatles), 11. Segment 4, 12. A Day in the Life (The Beatles), 13. Run-off Groove, 14. Segment 5, 15. Stranger's Room (demo), 16. I'm Losing You

Disc Two – 3 June 1991 Program No. 91–23

Paul and George Speak

1. Segment 1, 2. Twenty Flight Rock (Paul McCartney), 3. Yesterday (The Beatles), 4. Segment 2, 5. Here, There and Everywhere (The Beatles), 6. Norwegian Wood (The Beatles), 7. All You Need Is Love (The Beatles), 8. Two of Us (The Beatles), 9. Segment 2, 10. I Need You (The Beatles), 11. I Want to Tell You (The Beatles), 12. Segment 4, 13. It's All Too Much (The Beatles), 14. No. 9 Dream, 15. Segment 5, 16. I'm the Greatest (Ringo Starr)

480. SHOWS 177 AND 178 (WO 177/178)

Disc One – 10 June 1991 Program No. 91–24

Paul's Birthday – Part 1

1. Segment 1, 2. I Lost My Little Girl (Paul McCartney), 3. Be Bop A Lula (Paul McCartney), 4. Baby You're a Rich Man (The Beatles), 5. Segment 2, 6. Listen to What the Man Said (Wings), 7. Segment 3, 8. Give Ireland Back to the Irish (Wings), 9. Band on the Run (Wings), 10. Segment 4, 11. Get It (Paul McCartney and Carl Perkins), 12. Ebony and Ivory (Paul McCartney and Stevie Wonder), 13. Live and Let Die (Wings), 14. Segment 5, 15. Put It There (Paul McCartney), 16. My Brave Face (Paul McCartney)

Disc Two – 17 June 1991 Program No. 91–25

Paul's Birthday – Part 2

1. Segment 1, 2. Ain't That a Shame (live) (Paul McCartney), 3. Figure of Eight (partial) (Paul McCartney), 4. Roll Over Beethoven (Star Club) (The Beatles), 5. Segment 2, 6. Here, There and Everywhere (live) (Paul McCartney), 7. We Can Work It Out (live) (Paul McCartney), 8. Segment

3, 9. Sgt Pepper's Lonely Hearts Club Band (live) (Paul McCartney), 10. Hey Jude (live) (Paul McCartney), 11. Segment 4, 12. I Saw Her Standing There (live) (Paul McCartney), 13. Yesterday (Paul McCartney), 14. Segment 5, 15. She's a Woman (single version) (The Beatles), 16. She's a Woman (live) (Paul McCartney)

481. SHOWS 179 AND 180 (WO 179/180)

Disc One – 24 June 1991 Program No. 91–26

John's Songwriting Process – Part 1

1. Segment 1, 2. I Am the Walrus (The Beatles), 3. Segment 2, 4. Glass Onion (The Beatles), 5. Cry Baby Cry (early demo), 6. Cry Baby Cry (demo), 7. Segment 3, 8. Clean-up Time (demo), 9. Clean-up Time (outtake), 10. Clean-up Time, 11. Segment 4, 12. Across the Universe (The Beatles), 13. Segment 5, 14. She Can Talk to Me (demo), 15. Hey Bulldog (The Beatles)

Disc Two – 1 July 1991 Program No. 91–27

John's Songwriting Process – Part 2

1. Segment 1, 2. Help Me to Help Myself (piano demo), 3. Help Me to Help Myself (guitar demo), 4. Segment 2, 5. Strawberry Fields Forever (demo), 6. Strawberry Fields Forever (demos), 7. Strawberry Fields Forever (The Beatles), 8. Strawberry Fields Forever (endings) (The Beatles), 9. Segment 3, 10. Baby Make Love To You (demo), 11. That's the Way the World It (demo), 12. Girls and Boys (demo), 13. Segment 4, 14. My Life (demo), 15. My Life (demo), 16. Don't Be Crazy (demo), 17. The Worst is Over (demo), 18. Segment 5, 19. (Just Like) Starting Over (demo), 20. (Just Like) Starting Over

482. SHOWS 181 AND 182 (WO 181/182)

Disc One – 8 July 1991 Program No. 91–28

Ringo's Birthday

1. Segment 1, 2. Ringo (partial) (Lorne Greene), 3. It Don't Come Easy (Ringo Starr), 4. I'm the Greatest (Ringo Starr), 5. Segment 2, 6. Ringo I Love You (Bonnie Jo Mason), 7. Love Me Do (The Beatles), 8. Please

Please Me (The Beatles), 9. Segment 3, 10. With a Little Help from My Friends (The Beatles), 11. Segment 3, 12. Act Naturally (The Beatles), 13. Yellow Submarine (The Beatles), 14. Segment 5, 15. Photograph (Ringo Starr), 16. You're Sixteen (Ringo Starr)

Disc Two – 15 July 1991 Program No. 91–29

John and Yoko – Part 1

1. Segment 1, 2. When a Boy Meets a Girl (demo), 3. Readings from *Grapefruit* (Yoko's book), 4. Because (The Beatles), 5. Segment 2, 6. Oh, My Love (demo) (Yoko Ono), 7. Oh, My Love (demo), 8. Segment 3, 9. Ballad of John and Yoko, 10. Oh, Yoko, 11. Oh, Yoko, 12. Oh, Yoko, 13. Segment 4, 14. Happy Girl (demo) (Yoko Ono), 15. I'll Make You Happy (demo), 16. No One Sees You Like I Do (demo) (Yoko Ono), 17. Bless You, 18. Segment 5, 19. Somewhere in the Sky (demo) (Yoko Ono), 20. Isolation

483. SHOWS 183 AND 184 (WO 183/184)

Disc One – 22 July 1991 Program No. 91–30

John and Yoko – Part 2

1. Segment 1, 2. Love, 3. I Saw Her Standing There (live) (Elton John and John Lennon), 4. Segment 2, 5. I'm Having a Baby by My Love (demo) (Yoko Ono), 6. Beautiful Boy, 7. I'm Moving On (partial) (Yoko Ono), 8. I'm Losing You, 9. Segment 3, 10. Dear Yoko (demo), 11. I'm Not as Strong as You Think (demo) (Yoko Ono), 12. Segment 4, 13. Woman (overdubs), 14. Woman, 15. Segment 5, 16. You Saved My Soul (demo), 17. I'm Your Angel (horn overdubs) (Yoko Ono)

Disc Two – 29 July 1991 Program No. 91–31

John and Yoko – Part 3

1. Segment 1, 2. Imagine, 3. Segment 2, 4. Every Man Has a Woman (outtakes) (Yoko Ono), 5. Every Man Has a Woman (rough mix) (Yoko Ono), 6. Segment 3, 7. Hard Times Are Over (outtakes) (Yoko Ono), 8. Hard Times Are Over (Yoko Ono), 9. Segment 4, 10. Walking on Thin

Ice (outtckes) (Yoko Ono), 11. Walking on Thin Ice (Yoko Ono), 12. Segment 5, 13. Grow Old with Me (demo), 14. Remember Love (Yoko Ono), 15. Out the Blue

484. SHOWS 185 AND 186 (WO 185/186)

Disc One – 5 August 1991 Program No. 91–32

John's Alter Egos

1. Segment 1, 2. Life Begins at Forty (demo), 3. Sea Ditty (demo), 4. Pedro the Fisherman (demo), 5. Boat Song (demo), 6. Segment 2, 7. The Great Wok (home recording), 8. Untitled instrumental (home recording), 9. Beautiful Boys (Yoko Ono), 10. Segment 3, 11. Goodnight, Vienna (Ringo Starr), 12. Mind Games, 13. Segment 4, 14. Cold Turkey, 15. Hold On, 16. Segment 5, 17. Surprise Surprise (Sweet Bird of Paradox), 18. No. 9 Dream

Disc Two – 12th August 1991 Program No. 91–33

One-to-One

1. Segment 1, 2. Give Me Some Truth, 3. Segment 2, 4. J.J. (demo), 5. People (demo), 6. Angela, 7. Segment 3, 8. God Save Us (demo), 9. God Save Us, 10. Segment 4, 11. It's So Hard (rehearsal), 12. New York City (rehearsal), 13. Segment 3, 14. Instant Karma (rehearsal), 15. Mother (rehearsal), 16. Imagine

485. SHOWS 187 AND 188 (WO 187/188)

Disc One – 19 August 1991 Program No. 91–34

On the Air

1. Segment 1, 2. Honey Don't/Don't Be Cruel/Matchbox (Plastic Ono Band sessions), 3. I Found Out (alternate take), 4. Segment 2, 5. My Mummy's Dead (take 2), 6. Look at Me (demo), 7. Look at Me, 8. Segment 3, 9. Beef Jerky, 10. It's Only Love (The Beatles), 11. Tight A$, 12. Segment 4, 13. The Night Before (The Beatles), 14. You're Gonna Lose That Girl (The Beatles), 15. Segment 5, 16. God, 17. Get Up Stand Up (The Wailers), 18. Whatever Gets You Through the Night

Disc Two – 26 August 1991 Program No. 91–35

The Other Side of the Glass – Part 1

1. Segment 1, 2. I'm Stepping Out (rehearsal), 3. Nobody Sees Me Like You Do (rehearsal) (Yoko Ono), 4. Segment 2, 5. Watching the Wheels (rehearsal), 6. Nobody Told Me (rehearsal), 7. Segment 3, 8. Woman (rehearsal), 9. Segment 4, 10. I Want to Hold Your Hand (The Beatles), 11. Maxwell's Silver Hammer (The Beatles), 12. Segment 5, 13. Woman (acoustic), 14. Clean-up Time (rehearsal)

486. SHOWS 189 AND 190 (WO 189/190)

Disc One – 2 September 1991 Program No. 91–36

The Other Side of the Glass – Part 2

1. Segment 1, 2. Watching the Wheels, 3. Segment 2, 4. All You Need Is Love (The Beatles), 5. I'm Losing You (alternate take), 6. Segment 3, 7. (Just Like) Starting Over, 8. Segment 4, 9. Dear Yoko (alternate take), 10. Dear Yoko, 11. Segment 5, 12. Rain (The Beatles), 13. Woman (double-tracked vocals), 14. Woman (alternate take), 15. Woman

Disc Two – 9 September 1991 Program No. 91–37

The Other Side of the Glass – Part 3

1. Segment 1, 2. Living on Borrowed Time (rehearsal), 3. I've Just Seen A Face (The Beatles), 4. I'm Your Angel (Yoko Ono), 5. Segment 2, 6. I'm Stepping Out, 7. Segment 3, 8. Every Man Has a Woman Who Loves Him (Yoko Ono), 9. Beautiful Boy, 10. Segment 4, 11. (Just Like) Starting Over (alternate take), 12. Watching the Wheels

487. SHOWS 191 AND 192 (WO 191/192)

Disc One – 16 September 1991 Program No. 91–38

Playboy Interview – Part 1

1. Segment 1, 2. She Loves You (The Beatles), 3. Misery (The Beatles), 4. I Call Your Name (The Beatles), 5. It Won't Be Long (The Beatles), 6. Segment 2, 7. All My Loving (The Beatles), 8. I'll Be Back (The Beatles),

9. Things We Said Today (The Beatles), 10. Segment 3, 11. This Boy (The Beatles), 12. In My Life (The Beatles), 13. Hey Jude (The Beatles), 14. Segment 4, 15. Within You Without You (The Beatles), 16. Segment 5, 17. I Want to Hold Your Hand (The Beatles), 18. Nowhere Man (The Beatles)

Disc Two – 23 September 1991 Program No. 91–39

Playboy Interview – Part 2

1. Segment 1, 2. One After 909 (The Beatles), 3. Here, There and Everywhere (The Beatles), 4. Dr Robert (The Beatles), 5. Segment 2, 6. For No One (The Beatles), 7. Got to Get You into My Life (The Beatles), 8. There's a Place (The Beatles), 9. I Saw Her Standing There (The Beatles), 10. Segment 3, 11. You Can't Do That (The Beatles), 12. If I Fell (The Beatles), 13. Tell Me Why (The Beatles), 14. Segment 4, 15. Ticket to Ride (The Beatles), 16. I Want You (She's So Heavy) (The Beatles), 17. Segment 4, 18. Let It Be (The Beatles), 19. Strawberry Fields Forever (The Beatles)

488. SHOWS 193 AND 194 (WO 193/194)

Disc One – 30 September 1991 Program No. 91–40

Joe Butler/David Peel

1. Segment 1, 2. Eight Days A Week (The Beatles), 3. Help (The Beatles), 4. Segment 2, 5. I Found Out, 6. Oh, Yoko, 7. Segment 3, 8. The Pope Smokes Dope (David Peel). 9. Segment 4, 10. The Luck of the Irish (live), 11. Power to the People, 12. Segment 5, 13. I'm Losing You

Disc Two – 7 October 1991 Program No. 91–41

1. Segment 1, 2. My Life (demo), 3. Living on Borrowed Time (early version), 4. Segment 2, 5. Penny Lane (The Beatles), 6. Julia (The Beatles), 7. Segment 3, 8. I Don't Want to Face It, 9. Segment 4, 10. Give Me Some Truth, 11. Beautiful Boy, 12. Segment 5, 13. Love Me Do (The Beatles)

489. SHOWS 195 AND 196 (WO 195/196)

Disc One – 14 October 1991 Program No. 91–42

The FBI Files

1. Segment 1, 2. Power to the People, 3. Surprise Surprise (Sweet Bird of Paradox), 4. John Sinclair, 5. Segment 2, 6. Memphis Tennessee (The Beatles), 7. What Goes On (The Beatles), 8. Revolution (The Beatles), 9. Segment 3, 10. Misery (The Beatles), 11. Street Fighting Man (Rolling Stones), 12. Segment 4, 13. Attica State, 14. Segment 5, 15. Revolution (The Beatles)

Disc Two – 21 October 1991 Program No. 91–43

The *Playboy* Interviews – Part 3

1. Segment 1, 2. P.S. I Love You (The Beatles), 3. Please Please Me (The Beatles), 4. From Me to You (The Beatles), 5. Segment 2, 6. It's Only Love (The Beatles), 7. Do You Want to Know a Secret (The Beatles), 8. Drive My Car (The Beatles), 9. The Word (The Beatles), 10. Segment 3, 11. Day Tripper (The Beatles), 12. Hey Bulldog (The Beatles), 13. Segment 4, 14. Maxwell's Silver Hammer (The Beatles), 15. Dig a Pony (The Beatles), 16. I've Got a Feeling (The Beatles), 17. Segment 5, 18. Don't Let Me Down (The Beatles), 19. The Long and Winding Road (The Beatles)

490. SHOWS 197 AND 198 (WO 197/198)

Disc One – 28 October 1991 Program No. 91–44

Fillmore East/Donovan

1. Segment 1, 2. Well (Baby Please Don't Go) (live) (John and Yoko with the Mothers of Invention), 3. Segment 2, 4. Scumbag (live) (John and Yoko with the Mothers of Invention), 5. King Kong (live) (John and Yoko with the Mothers of Invention), 6. Remember, 7. Segment 3, 8. How Do You Sleep? (rehearsal), 9. How Do You Sleep?, 10. Segment 4, 11. Steel and Glass (demo), 12. Steel and Glass (rough mix), 13. Segment 5, 14. Hurdy Gurdy Man (live) Donovan

Disc Two – 4 November 1991 Program No. 91–45

The Beatles in Hollywood

1. Segment 1, 2. Twist and Shout (Hollywood Bowl) (The Beatles), 3. Ticket to Ride (Hollywood Bowl) (The Beatles), 4. Long Tall Sally (Hollywood Bowl) (The Beatles), 5. Segment 2, 6. A Hard Day's Night (Hollywood Bowl) (The Beatles), 7. Things We Said Today (Hollywood Bowl) (The Beatles), 8. Help (Hollywood Bowl) (The Beatles), 9. Segment 3, 10. All Shook Up (Elvis Presley), 11. Crippled Inside, 12. Segment 4, 13. She's a Woman (Hollywood Bowl) (The Beatles), 14. She Loves You (Hollywood Bowl) (The Beatles), 15. Segment 5, 16. Nobody Told Me (partial), 17. Look at Me

491. SHOWS 199 AND 200 (WO 199/200)

Disc One – 11 November 1991 Program No. 91–46

George Martin

1. Segment 1, 2. Baby It's You (The Beatles), 3. Two of Us (The Beatles), 4. Segment 2, 5. Can't Buy Me Love (The Beatles), 6. Because (The Beatles), 7. Yellow Submarine (The Beatles), 8. Segment 3, 9. All Together Now (The Beatles), 10. Being for the Benefit of Mr Kite (The Beatles), 11. Come Together (The Beatles), 12. Segment 4, 13. Ob-La-Di-Ob-La-Da (The Beatles), 14. While My Guitar Gently Weeps (The Beatles), 15. Segment 5, 16. Live and Let Die (Wings), 17. Ebony and Ivory (Paul McCartney with Stevie Wonder)

Disc Two – 18 November 1991 Program No. 91–47

1980

1. Segment 1, 2. Kiss Kiss Kiss (Yoko Ono), 3. I Call Your Name (The Beatles), 4. Segment 2, 5. Sisters Oh Sisters (Yoko Ono), 6. Mind Games, 7. Do You Want to Dance?, 8. Segment 3, 9. Clean-up Time (rehearsals), 10. (Just Like) Starting Over, 11. Segment 4, 12. Everybody (demo), 13. Nobody Told Me (demo), 14. Nobody Told Me, 15. Segment 5, 16. Dear Prudence (The Beatles)

492. SHOWS 201 AND 202 (WO 201/202)

Disc One – 25 November 1991 Program No. 91-48

Unfinished Work

1. Segment 1, 2. Stand By Me, 3. Here We Go Again, 4. Segment 2, 5. I'm the Greatest (demos), 6. I'm the Greatest (Ringo Starr), 7. Segment 3, 8. Many Rivers to Cross (demos), 9. Goodnight, Vienna (demo), 10. Goodnight, Vienna (Ringo Starr), 11. Segment 4, 12. Sally and Billy (demos), 13. Segment 5, 14. She is a Friend of Dorothy's, 15. Tennessee (demo), 16. Memories (demo)

Disc Two – 2 December 1991 Program No. 91-49

Fantasy Concert

1. Segment 1, 2. Cold Turkey, 3. (Just Like) Starting Over, 4. Segment 2, 5. Whatever Gets You Through the Night, 6. I Don't Want to Be a Soldier, 7. Segment 3, 8. Imagine, 9. Watching the Wheels, 10. I'm Your Angel (Yoko Ono), 11. Segment 4, 12. It's So Hard, 13. Jealous Guy, 14. Woman, 15. Kiss Kiss Kiss (Yoko Ono), 16. Segment 5, 17. Power to the People, 18. Happy Xmas (War Is Over)

493. SHOWS 203 AND 204 (WO 203/204)

Disc One – 9 December 1991 Program No. 91-50

A Critic's View – Part 1

1. Segment 1, 2. She Loves You (The Beatles), 3. Every Little Thing (The Beatles), 4. Bad Boy (The Beatles), 5. Segment 2, 6. Nowhere Man (The Beatles), 7. Twist and Shout (The Beatles), 8. Rock 'n' Roll Music (The Beatles), 9. Segment 2, 10. Please Mr Postman (The Beatles), 11. Getting Better (The Beatles), 12. Penny Lane (The Beatles), 13. Segment 4, 14. No. 9 Dream (composing demo), 15. No. 9 Dream (rough mix), 16. Segment 5, 17. Norwegian Wood (The Beatles), 18. Lucy in the Sky with Diamonds (The Beatles)

Disc Two – 16 December 1991 Program No. 91–51

A Critic's View – Part 2

1. Segment 1, 2. Bangla Desh (George Harrison), 3. Isolation, 4. With a Little Help from My Friends (The Beatles), 5. Segment 2, 6. Mother, 7. I'm Losing You, 8. Segment 3, 9. A Case of the Blues (demo), 10. Life Begins at Forty (demo), 11. Segment 4, 12. Goodbye Sadness (Yoko Ono), 13. Dear Yoko), 14. Watching the Wheels, 15. Segment 5, 16. Look at Me (rehearsal), 17. Look at Me (double-tracked vocal)

494. SHOWS 205 AND 206 (WO 205/206)

Disc One – 23 December 1991 Program No. 91–52

Christmas Show

1. Segment 1, 2. Rudolph the Red Nosed Reggae (Paul McCartney), 3. Wonderful Christmastime (Paul McCartney), 4. Be Bop A Lula (Star Club) (The Beatles), 5. Segment 2, 6. I Want to Hold Your Hand (The Beatles), 7. I Feel Fine (The Beatles), 8. Segment 3, 9. And Your Bird Can Sing (The Beatles), 10. Segment 4, 11. I Am the Walrus (The Beatles), 12. Revolution (The Beatles), 13. Segment 5, 14. Happy Xmas (War Is Over)

Disc Two – 30 December 1991 Program No. 92–01

Ray Coleman

1. Segment 1, 2. Love Me Do (The Beatles), 3. I'll Follow The Sun (The Beatles), 4. Martha My Dear (The Beatles), 5. Segment 2, 6. Here Comes the Sun (The Beatles), 7. Act Naturally (The Beatles), 8. Segment 3, 9. The Long and Winding Road (The Beatles), 10. Segment 4, 11. The Hippy Hippy Shake (The Beatles), 12. Yesterday (The Beatles), 13. Segment 5, 14. Out the Blue (rough mix), 15. Whatever Gets You Through the Night

495. SHOWS 207 AND 208 (WO 207/208)

Disc One – 6 January 1992 Program No. 92–02

Memories of Mimi/King Curtis

1. Segment 1, 2. Julia (The Beatles), 3. Segment 2, 4. God, 5. Love, 6. And I Love Her, 7. Segment 3, 8. Yackety Yak (The Coasters), 9. It's So

Hard (overdub session), 10. It's So Hard, 11. Segment 4, 12. I Don't Want to Be a Soldier (overdub session), 13. I Don't Want to Be a Soldier, 14. Segment 5, 15. How? (demo), 16. Child of Nature (demo), 17. Oh, Yoko (demo)

Disc Two – 13 January 1992 Program No. 92-03

Kenny Everett's Interviews

1. Segment 1, 2. Ticket to Ride (Hollywood Bowl) (The Beatles), 3. Things We Said Today (The Beatles), 4. Segment 2, 5. Girl (The Beatles), 6. Good Morning, Good Morning) (The Beatles), 7. I Am the Walrus (The Beatles), 8. Segment 3, 9. Mother, 10. Segment 4, 11. Isolation, 12. Segment 5, 13. All Together Now (The Beatles), 14. Hold On, 15. Well, Well, Well

496. SHOWS 209 AND 210 (WO 209/210)

Disc One – 20 January 1992 Program No. 92-04

Mind Games Sessions

1. Segment 1, 2. Make Love Not War (demo), 3. I Promise (demo), 4. Mind Games, 5. Segment 2, 6. One Day at a Time (rough mix), 7. Intuition (demo), 8. Intuition (rough mix), 9. Segment 3, 10. Tight A$ (demo), 11. Aisumasen (rough mix), 12. Segment 4, 13. Only People, 14. You Are Here (rough mix), 15. Segment 5, 16. I Know (demo), 17. Meat City (demo), 18. Meat City (rough Mix)

Disc Two – 27 January 1992 Program No. 92-05

Beatles B-Sides/American Singles

1. Segment 1, 2. Ask Me Why (The Beatles), 3. Thank You Girl (The Beatles), 4. I'll Get You (The Beatles, 5. Please Mr Postman (The Beatles), 6. Segment 2, 7. I Saw Her Standing There (The Beatles), 8. This Boy (The Beatles), 9. There's a Place (The Beatles), 10. You Can't Do That (The Beatles), 11. Segment 2, 12. I Should Have Known Better (The Beatles), 13. I'm Happy Just to Dance with You (The Beatles), 14. If I Fell (The Beatles), 15. Segment 4, 16. She's a Woman (The Beatles), 17. I Don't Want to Spoil the Party (The Beatles), 18. Yes It Is (The Beatles), 19. Segment 5, 20. Borrowed Time (demo)

497. SHOWS 211 AND 212 (WO 211/212)

Disc One – 3 February 1992 Program No. 92–06

Beatles B-Sides – Part 2

1. Segment 1, 2. Help (The Beatles), 3. I'm Down (The Beatles), 4. Act Naturally (The Beatles), 5. Day Tripper (The Beatles), 6. Segment 2, 7. What Goes On (The Beatles), 8. Rain (The Beatles), 9. Eleanor Rigby (The Beatles), 10. Segment 3, 11. Strawberry Fields Forever (The Beatles), 12. Baby You're a Rich Man (The Beatles), 13. Segment 4, 14. I Am the Walrus (The Beatles), 15. The Inner Light (The Beatles), 16. Segment 5, 17. One of the Boys (demo)

Disc Two – 10 February 1992 Program No. 92–07

Beatles B-Sides – Part 3

1. Segment 1, 2. Hey Jude (The Beatles), 3. Revolution (The Beatles), 4. Don't Let Me Down (The Beatles), 5. Segment 2, 6. Old Brown Shoe (The Beatles), 7. Come Together (The Beatles), 8. Segment 3, 9. You Know My Name (Look Up the Number) (The Beatles), 10. Segment 4, 11. For You Blue (The Beatles), 12. The Long and Winding Road (The Beatles), 13. Segment 5, 14. Mirror Mirror (On the Wall) (demo)

498. SHOWS 213 AND 214 (WO 213/214)

Disc One – 17 February 1992 Program No. 92–08

1980 Demos

1. Segment 1, 2. New York City (rehearsal), 3. Whatever Happened To (demo), 4. Segment 2, 5. Memories (demo partial), 6. Free as a Bird (demo), 7. Grow Old with Me (demo), 8. Segment 3, 9. I Don't Want to Face It (alternate take), 10. Segment 4, 11. You Saved My Soul (demo), 12. Segment 5, 13. Gone from This Place (demo), 14. Life Begins at 40 (demo), 15. Dear John (demo)

Disc Two – 24 February 1992 Program No. 92-09

Stepping Out at the Hit Factory

1. Segment 1, 2. I'm Stepping Out (take 1), 3. I'm Stepping Out (take 2), 4. Segment 2, 5. Working Class Hero (radio edit), 6. Dear Yoko, 7. Segment 3, 8. I'm Stepping Out (take 3), 9. Segment 4, 10. Beautiful Boy, 11. Segment 5, 12. I'm Stepping Out (take 4)

499. SHOWS 215 AND 216 (WO 215/216)

Disc One – 2 March 1992 Program No. 92-10

Stepping Out at the Hit Factory – Part 2

1. Segment 1, 2. I'm Stepping Out (partial), 3. Borrowed Time (alternate take), 4. Segment 2, 5. If I Fell (The Beatles), 6. When I Get Home (The Beatles), 7. New York City, 8. Segment 3, 9. Borrowed Time (alternate take), 10. Segment 4, 11. Real Life (take 2), 12. Real Life (take 3), 13. I'm Stepping Out, 14. Segment 5, 15. Real Life (demo, take 5), 16. Real Love (demo)

Disc Two – 9 March 1992 Program No. 92-11

Spector and Lennon

1. Segment 1, 2. Rock 'n' Roll People (alternate take), 3. Instant Karma, 4. Segment 2, 5. Imagine (alternate take), 6. Ain't That a Shame (rough mix), 7. Segment 3, 8. Be My Baby, 9. Segment 4, 10. Stand By Me (alternate take), 11. Move Over Ms L, (rehearsal), 12. Segment 5, 13. Whatever Gets You Through the Night (composing demo), 14. Whatever Gets You Through the Night (alternate take), 15. I Saw Her Standing There (rehearsal) (John Lennon and Elton John)

500. SHOWS 217 AND 218 (WO 217/218)

Disc One – 16 March 1992 Program No. 92-12

Best of *The Lost Lennon Tapes* – Part 1

1. Segment 1, 2. My Life/Don't Be Crazy/The Worst is Over/Starting Over (demos), 3. Segment 2, 4. The Great Wok (home recording), 5. Serve

Yourself (demo), 6. God (alternate take), 7. Help Me to Help Myself (demo), 8. You Saved My Soul (demo), 9. Segment 3, 10. Cold Turkey (demo), 11. Beautiful Boy (demo), 12. Segment 4, 13. I Promise/Make Love Not War/Mind Games (demos), 14. How Do You Sleep (alternate take), 15. Segment 5, 16. Jock and Yono (from The Beatles 1968 Christmas flexidisc), 17. Out the Blue (alternate take)

Disc Two – 23 March 1992 Program No. 92–13

Best of *The Lost Lennon Tapes* – Part 2

1. Segment 1, 2. Watching the Wheels (rehearsals), 3. Woman (rehearsal), 4. Segment 2, 5. Child of Nature/Jealous Guy (demos), 6. Dakota Mind Movie Mystery Theatre (home recording), 7. I'm In Love (demo), 8. Segment 3, 9. Stranger's Room (demo), 10. I'm the Greatest (demo), 11. Segment 4, 12. (Just Like) Starting Over (alternate take), 13. Segment 5, 14. 'The Beatles Years' preview

SET TWO

Westwood One

Format: CD

Source: complete original broadcasts

Sound quality: excellent

Notes: This set comprises all the broadcasts from *The Lost Lennon Tapes* as broadcast by Westwood One Radio Network. The main difference between Set One as detailed above and Set Two is all the releases in Set Two were issued in single discs. Details of the track listings for the discs listed below can be found by referring to the Program Number shown in the information for Set One as listed above.

Entry No.	Catalogue No.	Programme No.	Broadcast Date
501	n/a	*Premiere Show*	18 January 1988 – Disc One
502	n/a	*Premiere Show*	18 January 1988 – Disc Two
503	n/a	*Premiere Show*	18 January 1988 – Disc Three
504	WO.001	Program No. 88–05	25 January 1988
505	WO.002	Program No. 88–06	1 February 1988
506	WO.003	Program No. 88–07	8 February 1988
507	WO.004	Program No. 88–08	15 February 1988
508	WO.005	Program No. 88–09	22 February 1988
509	WO.006	Program No. 88–10	29 February 1988
510	WO.007	Program No. 88–11	7 March 1988
511	WO.008	Program No. 88–12	14 March 1988
512	WO.009	Program No. 88–13	21 March 1988
513	WO.010	Program No. 88–14	28 March 1988
514	WO.011	Program No. 88–15	4 April 1988
515	WO.012	Program No. 88–16	11 April 1988
516	WO.013	Program No. 88–17	18 April 1988
517	WO.014	Program No. 88–18	25 April 1988
518	WO.015	Program No. 88–19	2 May 1988
519	WO.016	Program No. 88–20	9 May 1988
520	WO.017	Program No. 88–21	16 May 1988
521	WO.018	Program No. 88–22	23 May 1988
522	WO.019	Program No. 88–23	30 May 1988
523	WO.020	Program No. 88–24	6 June 1988
524	WO.021	Program No. 88–25	13 June 1988
525	WO.022	Program No. 88–26	20 June 1988
526	WO.023	Program No. 88–27	27 June 1988
527	WO.024	Program No. 88–28	4 July 1988
528	WO.025	Program No. 88–29	11 July 1988

Entry No.	Catalogue No.	Programme No.	Broadcast Date
529	WO.026	Program No. 88–30	18 July 1988
530	WO.027	Program No. 88–31	25 July 1988
531	WO.028	Program No. 88–32	1 August 1988
532	WO.029	Program No. 88–33	8 August 1988
533	WO.030	Program No. 88–34	15 August 1988
534	WO.031	Program No. 88–35	22 August 1988
535	WO.032	Program No. 88–36	29 August 1988
536	WO.033	Program No. 88–37	5 September 1988
537	WO.034	Program No. 88–38	12 September 1988
538	WO.035	Program No. 88–39	19 September 1988
539	WO.036	Program No. 88–40	26 September 1988
540	WO.037	Program No. 88–41	3 October 1988
541	WO.038	Program No. 88–42	10 October 1988
542	WO.039	Program No. 88–43	17 October 1988
543	WO.040	Program No. 88–44	24 October 1988
544	WO.041	Program No. 88–45	31 October 1988
545	WO.042	Program No. 88–46	7 November 1988
546	WO.043	Program No. 88–47	14 November 1988
547	WO.044	Program No. 88–48	21 November 1988
548	WO.045	Program No. 88–49	28 November 1988
549	WO.046	Program No. 88–50	5 December 1988
550	WO.047	Program No. 88–51	12 December 1988
551	WO.048	Program No. 88–52	19 December 1988
552	WO.049	Program No. 89–01	26 December 1988
553	WO.050	Program No. 89–02	2 January 1989
554	WO.051	Program No. 89–03	9 January 1989
555	WO.052	Program No. 89–04	16 January 1989
556	WO.053	Program No. 89–05	23 January 1989
557	WO.054	Program No. 89–06	30 January 1989

Entry No.	Catalogue No.	Programme No.	Broadcast Date
558	WO.055	Program No. 89–07	6 February 1989
559	WO.056	Program No. 89–08	13 February 1989
560	WO.057	Program No. 89–09	20 February 1989
561	WO.058	Program No. 89–10	27 February 1989
562	WO.059	Program No. 89–11	6 March 1989
563	WO.060	Program No. 89–12	13 March 1989
564	WO.061	Program No. 89–13	20 March 1989
565	WO.062	Program No. 89–14	27 March 1989
566	WO.063	Program No. 89–15	3 April 1989
567	WO.064	Program No. 89–16	10 April 1989
568	WO.065	Program No. 89–17	17 April 1989
569	WO.066	Program No. 89–18	24 April 1989
570	WO.067	Program No. 89–19	1 May 1989
571	WO.068	Program No. 89–20	8 May 1989
572	WO.069	Program No. 89–21	15 May 1989
573	WO.070	Program No. 89–22	22 May 1989
574	WO.071	Program No. 89–23	29 May 1989
575	WO.072	Program No. 89–24	5 June 1989
576	WO.073	Program No. 89–25	12 June 1989
577	WO.074	Program No. 89–26	19 June 1989
578	WO.075	Program No. 89–27	26 June 1989
579	WO.076	Program No. 89–28	3 July 1989
580	WO.077	Program No. 89–29	10 July 1989
581	WO.078	Program No. 89–30	17 July 1989
582	WO.079	Program No. 89–31	24 July 1989
583	WO.080	Program No. 89–32	31 July 1989
584	WO.081	Program No. 89–33	7 August 1989
585	WO.082	Program No. 89–34	14 August 1989
586	WO.083	Program No. 89–35	21 August 1989

Entry No.	Catalogue No.	Programme No.	Broadcast Date
587	WO.084	Program No. 89–36	28 August 1989
588	WO.085	Program No. 89–37	4 September 1989
589	WO.086	Program No. 89–38	11 September 1989
590	WO.087	Program No. 89–39	18 September 1989
591	WO.088	Program No. 89–40	25 September 1989
592	WO.089	Program No. 89–41	2 October 1989
593	WO.090	Program No. 89–42	9 October 1989
594	WO.091	Program No. 89–43	16 October 1989
595	WO.092	Program No. 89–44	23 October 1989
596	WO.093	Program No. 89–45	30 October 1989
597	WO.094	Program No. 89–46	6 November 1989
598	WO.095	Program No. 89–47	13 November 1989
599	WO.096	Program No. 89–48	20 November 1989
600	WO.097	Program No. 89–49	27 November 1989
601	WO.098	Program No. 89–50	4 December 1989
602	WO.099	Program No. 89–51	11 December 1989
603	WO.100	Program No. 89–52	18 December 1989
604	WO.101	Program No. 89–53	25 December 1989
605	WO.102	Program No. 90–01	1 January 1990
606	WO.103	Program No. 90–02	8 January 1990
607	WO.104	Program No. 90–03	15 January 1990
608	WO.105	Program No. 90–04	22 January 1990
609	WO.106	Program No. 90–05	29 January 1990
610	WO.107	Program No. 90–06	5 February 1990
611	WO.108	Program No. 90–07	12 February 1990
612	WO.109	Program No. 90–08	19 February 1990
613	WO.110	Program No. 90–09	26 February 1990
614	WO.111	Program No. 90–10	5 March 1990
615	WO.112	Program No. 90–11	12 March 1990

Entry No.	Catalogue No.	Programme No.	Broadcast Date
616	WO.113	Program No. 90-12	19 March 1990
617	WO.114	Program No. 90-13	26 March 1990
618	WO.115	Program No. 90-14	2 April 1990
619	WO.116	Program No. 90-15	9 April 1990
620	WO.117	Program No. 90-16	16 April 1990
621	WO.118	Program No. 90-17	23 April 1990
622	WO.119	Program No. 90-18	30 April 1990
623	WO.120	Program No. 90-19	7 May 1990
624	WO.121	Program No. 90-20	14 May 1990
625	WO.122	Program No. 90-21	21 May 1990
626	WO.123	Program No. 90-22	28 May 1990
627	WO.124	Program No. 90-23	4 June 1990
628	WO.125	Program No. 90-24	11 June 1990
629	WO.126	Program No. 90-25	18 June 1990
630	WO.127	Program No. 90-26	25 June 1990
631	WO.128	Program No. 90-27	2 July 1990
632	WO.129	Program No. 90-28	9 July 1990
633	WO.130	Program No. 90-29	16 July 1990
634	WO.131	Program No. 90-30	23 July 1990
635	WO.132	Program No. 90-31	30 July 1990
636	WO.133	Program No. 90-32	6 August 1990
637	WO.134	Program No. 90-33	13 August 1990
638	WO.135	Program No. 90-34	20 August 1990
639	WO.136	Program No. 90-35	27 August 1990
640	WO.137	Program No. 90-36	3 September 1990
641	WO.138	Program No. 90-37	10 September 1990
642	WO.139	Program No. 90-38	17 September 1990
643	WO.140	Program No. 90-39	24 September 1990
644	WO.141	Program No. 90-40	1 October 1990

Entry No.	Catalogue No.	Programme No.	Broadcast Date
645	WO.142	Program No. 90–41	8 October 1990
646	WO.143	Program No. 90–42	15 October 1990
647	WO.144	Program No. 90–43	22 October 1990
648	WO.145	Program No. 90–44	29 October 1990
649	WO.146	Program No. 90–45	5 November 1990
650	WO.147	Program No. 90–46	12 November 1990
651	WO.148	Program No. 90–47	19 November 1990
652	WO.149	Program No. 90–48	26 November 1990
653	WO.150	Program No. 90–49	3 December 1990
654	WO.151	Program No. 90–50	10 December 1990
655	WO.152	Program No. 90–51	17 December 1990
656	WO.153	Program No. 90–52	24 December 1990
657	WO.154	Program No. 91–01	7 January 1991
658	WO.155	Program No. 91–02	14 January 1991
659	WO.156	Program No. 91–03	21 January 1991
660	WO.157	Program No. 91–04	28 January 1991
661	WO.158	Program No. 91–05	4 February 1991
662	WO.159	Program No. 91–06	11 February 1991
663	WO.160	Program No. 91–07	18 February 1991
664	WO.161	Program No. 91–08	25 February 1991
665	WO.162	Program No. 91–09	4 March 1991
666	WO.163	Program No. 91–10	11 March 1991
667	WO.164	Program No. 91–11	18 March 1991
668	WO.165	Program No. 91–12	25 March 1991
669	WO.166	Program No. 91–13	1 April 1991
670	WO.167	Program No. 91–14	8 April 1991
671	WO.168	Program No. 91–15	15 April 1991
672	WO.169	Program No. 91–16	22 April 1991
673	WO.170	Program No. 91–17	29 April 1991

Entry No.	Catalogue No.	Programme No.	Broadcast Date
674	WO.171	Program No. 91–18	6 May 1991
675	WO.172	Program No. 91–19	13 May 1991
676	WO.173	Program No. 91–20	20 May 1991
677	WO.174	Program No. 91–21	27 May 1991
678	WO.175	Program No. 91–22	3 June 1991
679	WO.176	Program No. 91–23	10 June 1991
680	WO.177	Program No. 91–24	17 June 1991
681	WO.178	Program No. 91–25	24 June 1991
682	WO.179	Program No. 91–26	1 July 1991
683	WO.180	Program No. 91–27	8 July 1991
684	WO.181	Program No. 91–28	15 July 1991
685	WO.182	Program No. 91–29	22 July 1991
686	WO.183	Program No. 91–30	29 July 1991
687	WO.184	Program No. 91–31	5 August 1991
688	WO.185	Program No. 91–32	12 August 1991
689	WO.186	Program No. 91–33	19 August 1991
690	WO.187	Program No. 91–34	26 August 1991
691	WO.188	Program No. 91–35	2 September 1991
692	WO.189	Program No. 91–36	9 September 1991
693	WO.190	Program No. 91–37	16 September 1991
694	WO.191	Program No. 91–38	23 September 1991
695	WO.192	Program No. 91–39	30 September 1991
696	WO.193	Program No. 91–40	7 October 1991
697	WO.194	Program No. 91–41	14 October 1991
698	WO.195	Program No. 91–42	21 October 1991
699	WO.196	Program No. 91–43	28 October 1991
700	WO.197	Program No. 91–44	4 November 1991
701	WO.198	Program No. 91–45	11 November 1991
702	WO.199	Program No. 91–46	18 November 1991

Entry No.	Catalogue No.	Programme No.	Broadcast Date
703	WO.200	Program No. 91–47	25 November 1991
704	WO.201	Program No. 91–48	2 December 1991
705	WO.202	Program No. 91–49	9 December 1991
706	WO.203	Program No. 91–50	16 December 1991
707	WO.204	Program No. 91–51	23 December 1991
708	WO.205	Program No. 91–52	30 December 1991
709	WO.206	Program No. 92–01	6 January 1992
710	WO.207	Program No. 92–02	13 January 1992
711	WO.208	Program No. 92–03	20 January 1992
712	WO.209	Program No. 92–04	27 January 1992
713	WO.210	Program No. 92–05	3 February 1992
714	WO.211	Program No. 92–06	10 February 1992
715	WO.212	Program No. 92–07	17 February 1992
716	WO.213	Program No. 92–08	24 February 1992
717	WO.214	Program No. 92–09	2 March 1992
718	WO.215	Program No. 92–10	9 March 1992
719	WO.216	Program No. 92–11	16 March 1992
720	WO.217	Program No. 92–12	23 March 1992
721	WO.218	Program No. 92–13	30 March 1992

4. Sources

The bootlegs listed in Parts One, Two and Three include tracks from many sources. The recording sessions, live performances and interviews listed below are more or less in chronological order. We have listed the tracks which appear on the official albums and also the main vinyl or compact disc bootleg albums where the outtakes, demos and rehearsals appear. These do not include every appearance as many of the albums are basically compilations and many of the performances are spread across these albums. We have not included, with a couple of exceptions, any of the releases in the *Lost Lennon Tapes* series of discs in the listings below as most of the albums are more or less compilations. Some of the radio shows were 'themed' – see Part Three for details of each broadcast. This catalogue of the recording sessions, live performances, television shows and interviews is a guide to where they appear on the various bootleg albums.

STRAWBERRY FIELDS FOREVER SESSIONS

The first recordings for 'Strawberry Fields Forever' took place during the filming of *How I Won the War* while John was in Santa Isabel, Spain in the autumn of 1966. Several takes were made in Spain. The song at that time was titled 'It's Not Too Bad'. John then recorded several demos at his home studio in Kenwood. The track was then recorded at Abbey Road studios with the sessions starting on 24 November 1966 together with the rest of The Beatles. The track was originally planned for the *Sgt Pepper* album but was released as a Beatles single in February 1967. The compact disc *It's Not Too Bad* (Pegboy PB 1008) gathers these sessions together in the best sound quality. Whether this disc can be considered a Lennon or a Beatles bootleg is debatable but as many of the takes are Lennon solos it is worthy of inclusion in this discography.

Compact Disc: *It's Not Too Bad*

Day Tripper – *Top Gear*, BBC Radio, 15 December 1967

It was rumoured that John Lennon appeared on this Jimi Hendrix performance on BBC Radio but it has since been established with reasonable certainty that the backing vocals were provided by Noel Redding. This recording has been heavily bootlegged and appears on several releases. It is available in the best quality on the official CD released in 1998 – *Jimi Hendrix BBC Sessions*.

Compact Disc: *Day Tripper Jam* (Instant Analysis/King Kong)

White Album Sessions

While The Beatles were in India in 1968 visiting the Maharishi they wrote several new songs. When they returned to England they did not initially go straight to Abbey Road to record them but met on 30 May 1968 at George's house called Kinfauns in Esher. George owned a four-track Ampex tape recorder and the group decided to record the songs on it. Most of these songs had been written in India. Little was known about this session until songs were broadcast during *The Lost Lennon Tapes* radio series. A large proportion of the songs recorded during this session were Lennon's – eleven out of the twenty-three. Four of the songs from the session were officially released on *Anthology 3* – 'Glass Onion', 'Junk', 'Piggies' and 'Honey Pie'. The sleeve notes claim that 'Mean Mr Mustard' and 'Polythene Pam' are from the session on 30 May but these two tracks probably come from a different session. All the tracks have been bootlegged with the best sound quality on The Beatles bootleg *From Kinfauns To Chaos* (Vigotone). The Lennon tracks are as follows which appears on several bootlegs including the *Lost Lennon Tapes*: 'Cry Baby Cry', 'Child of Nature', 'The Continuing Story of Bungalow Bill', 'I'm So Tired', 'Yer Blues', 'Everybody's Got Something to Hide Except Me and My Monkey', 'What's the New Mary Jane', 'Revolution', 'Julia', 'Dear Prudence' and 'Sexy Sadie'.

Compact Disc: *Studio Tracks, Vol. 9*
The 1968 Demos
1968 Demos

Home Demos, Weybridge, 1968

While in his home studio in Weybridge during 1968 John made some experimental music including some improvisation tracks on the Mellotron.

Compact Disc: *John Lennon Anthology, Weybridge*
Lost in Weybridge
Revolution

Rolling Stones Rock and Roll Circus, 11 December 1968

John appeared with his band called The Dirty Mac in The Rolling Stones film called *Rock and Roll Circus*. His band comprised John and Yoko, Keith Richards, Eric Clapton and Mitch Mitchell. Two songs were recorded, 'Yer Blues' and 'Whole Lotta Yoko'. The recordings were eventually officially released on 14 October 1996 on CD, video and DVD. 'Yer Blues', both the film version and the rehearsals, has appeared on many bootlegs. The discs listed below are a sample of where the recordings can be found.

Vinyl: *British Blues Jam*
Dirty Mac Sessions
Gulp
John Lennon and Friends Live: 1968–1971
Working Class Hero
Yer Blues

Interview, *Night Ride*, BBC Radio, 12 December 1968

Following the recording of *Rock and Roll Circus*, John and Yoko travelled into central London to take part in the BBC Radio programme *Night Ride*. This was transmitted live from 12.05 a.m. to 2 a.m. They discussed the new album *Two Virgins* with John Peel, the host of the programme to 1 a.m. The BBC played a 3 minute 20 second extract from the album.

Compact Disc: *Night Ride*

MIDDAY SPIN, BBC RADIO ONE, 15 FEBRUARY 1969
Interview with Emperor Rosko. John and Yoko discuss several topics.

Compact Disc: *Interviews, 1969–1970 Vol. 1*

AMSTERDAM BED-IN, 25–31 MARCH 1969
For seven days John and Yoko were the centre of attraction in Room 902 at the Amsterdam Hilton where they gave endless interviews.

Compact Disc: Mr. and Mrs. Lennon's Honeymoon

UNFINISHED MUSIC NO. 2 – LIFE WITH THE LIONS

Zapple Zapple 01

Released: 9 May 1969

This was John and Yoko's second album of avant-garde performances. The tracks were recorded at a live concert in Cambridge and in a London hospital.

Vinyl: *Aspen 7 – The British Box – Spring and Summer (Section 11 Aspen No. 7)*
Life with the Lennons (Tobe Milo)
Unfinished Music No 2 – Life with the Lions

MONTREAL BED-IN, 26 MAY–2 JUNE 1969
John and Yoko hold another seven-day Bed-In in Room 1742 of the Queen Elizabeth Hotel, Montreal. On 1 June they record 'Give Peace a Chance' assisted by a roomful of people including the Smothers Brothers, Timothy Leary, Derek Taylor, Murray the K and the Canadian Radha Temple.

Compact Disc: *Bedism*
In His Life
The Jerry Levitan Interview
KYA-FM 1969 and Man of the Decade
The Unheard Lennon 1969 Interview

LIVE IN TORONTO, 12 SEPTEMBER 1969

It was while John and Yoko were in Toronto for their Bed-In they were invited to appear in the Rock 'n' Roll Revival Concert. At short notice they contacted Eric Clapton (guitar), Alan White (drums) and Klaus Voorman (bass guitar). Together with Anthony Fawcett (John and Yoko's personal assistant), Terry Doran (George Harrison's assistant) and Jill and Dan Richter (who were filming John and Yoko) they boarded a Boeing 707 to Toronto. During the flight the band rehearsed several songs in the rear of the plane. The following day, the band appeared in front of an audience of 26,000 in the Varsity Stadium performing eight numbers. The concert also featured legends such as Little Richard, Gene Vincent, Chuck Berry and Bo Diddley. The album *Live Peace in Toronto 1969* was released on 12 December 1969 (Apple CORE 2001) with the following songs:

> John: Blue Suede Shoes, Money, Dizzy Miss Lizzie, Yer Blues, Cold Turkey, Give Peace a Chance

> Yoko: Don't Worry Kyoko (Mummy's Only Looking For A Hand In The Snow), John John (Let's Hope For Peace)

Compact Disc: *Give Peace a Chance (The Easy Rider Years)*

Interviews: 1969–1970 (Vol. 1)

John Lennon and Friends Live: 1968–1971

John Lennon Live

Journals

Live Peace in Toronto 1969 Audience

The Plastic Ono Band – Live (DV More Record Production)

RADIO LUXEMBOURG, 27 SEPTEMBER 1969

During this interview John also plays tracks from the just released new Beatles album *Abbey Road*.

Compact Disc: *John Lennon Presents... Abbey Road on Radio Luxembourg*

Interview, Kenny Everett, 8 November 1969

Compact Disc: *Interviews: Nov–Dec 1969*

Radio South Africa, 12 December 1969

Interview promoting Live Peace in Toronto album

Compact Disc: *Interviews, 1969–1970 Vol. 1*

Concert for Unicef, Lyceum Ballroom, London, 15 December 1969

John, backed by a group including Yoko, George Harrison, Eric Clapton, Billy Preston, Keith Moon and several others, plays at a Peace For Christmas concert in aid of Unicef.

Compact Disc: *The Lost Lennon Tapes* (Radio Series – Entries 414 and 550)

Toronto Press Conference, 17 December 1969

Compact Disc: Interviews, 1969–1979 Vol. 1

Interview, WABC FM, New York, 17 December 1969

An interview conducted by Howard Smith

Compact Disc: *The Smith Collection – John and Yoko, December 1969*

Everett Is Here, 1969

John is interviewed by DJ Kenny Everett for BBC Radio One and talks about several topics.

Compact Disc: *Interviews, Nov–Dec 1969*

Ken Zelig Interview, 1969

This interview concerns the return of John's MBE award.

Compact Disc: *Interviews, Nov–Dec 1969*

RADIO LUXEMBOURG INTERVIEW, 1969

This interview is a promo for the *Live Peace in Toronto* album. He talks about the concert, the Plastic Ono Band and the album. During the original broadcast tracks were played from the album.

Compact Disc: *Interviews, Nov–Dec 1969*

HOME RECORDINGS, NOVEMBER 1970

A large amount of recordings were made in John's home studio, Tittenhurst Park, Ascot. Some of these were later recorded for the Imagine album.

Compact Disc: *Compositions*
1970 November Home Recordings (Green Grape)

INTERVIEW, WABC, NEW YORK, BROADCAST 6 DECEMBER 1970

An interview conducted by Howard Smith

Compact Disc: *The Smith Collection – John and Yoko, December 1970*

ROLLING STONE INTERVIEW, 8 DECEMBER 1970

This interview was conducted by Jann Wenner of Rolling Stone magazine at John's rented apartment in New York. The long interview was featured in two parts in *Rolling Stone* magazine on 21 January and 4 February 1971 and was reprinted in the book *Lennon Remembers*. John was not happy about the publication of the book and criticised Wenner for publishing without his permission. The complete interview appears on the two-volume CD release *Lennon Remembers*.

Compact Disc: *Lennon Remembers – Part One*
Lennon Remembers – Part Two

PLASTIC ONO BAND ALBUM SESSIONS

Apple PCS 7124
Released: 11 December 1970

'Mother', 'Hold On', 'I Found Out', 'Working Class Hero', 'Isolation', 'Remember', 'Love', 'Well, Well, Well', 'Look at Me', 'God', 'My Mummy's Dead'

The sessions for what was John's first proper solo album began on 26 September 1970 at Abbey Road Studios in London. John, together with Ringo and Klaus Voorman, started recording the demos which John had made in Los Angeles. These sessions were produced by John and Yoko and Phil Spector. Also appearing on the album were Billy Preston (piano on 'God') and Phil Spector (piano on 'Love'). In between the takes of the songs which would appear on the album several other songs were performed, including 'That's All Right Mama', 'Glad All Over', 'Honey Don't', 'Don't Be Cruel', 'Hound Dog', 'Matchbox' and 'When a Boy Meets a Girl'.

Compact Disc: *The Alternate Plastic Ono Band* (Pear Records)
The Alternate John Lennon/Plastic Ono Band (Ghost)
The Dream Is Over (Pegboy)
Hushed Bell Overs
It's Gonna Be Alright
Journals
Plastic Ono Band – Home and Studio
Primal Scream – The Studio Sessions
Remember Lennon
Remember New York
Studio Sessions One
Studio Tracks, Vol. 6
1970 Plastic Ono Band – Home and Studio (Green Grape)

JAN WENNER INTERVIEW, KFRC AM, JANUARY 1971

This interview was for a radio show called *Focus 71*.

Compact Disc: *KFRC AM: Focus '71 (The Jan Wenner Interview)* (Air-Check)

INTERVIEW, KENNY EVERETT, 27 MARCH 1971

This interview was held at John's house in Ascot and broadcast on Radio Monte Carlo. During the interview tracks from the *Plastic Ono Band* album were played.

Compact Disc: *Kenny Everett Talks to John Lennon*

GOD SAVE US SESSIONS, APRIL–JUNE 1971

Compact Disc: *On the Cannes*

INTERVIEW, KENNY EVERETT, RADIO MONTE CARLO, 25 APRIL 1971

Compact Disc: *On the Cannes*

INTERVIEW, CANNES, FRANCE, 15 MAY 1971

John and Yoko attended the annual Cannes Film Festival where two of their films, *Apotheosis* (Balloon) and *Fly* were being shown.

Compact Disc: *On the Cannes*

JOHN AND YOKO WITH FRANK ZAPPA AND THE MOTHERS, 6 JUNE 1971

'Well (Baby Please Don't Go)'. An edited version of this recording appeared on the *Sometime in New York City* album. The full-length version can be found on the following releases:

Vinyl Album: *John Lennon and Friends Live: 1968–1971*
Mystery Box (Frank Zappa) (Nifty Tuff and Bitchen 8611)

Compact Disc: *Lennon Remembers*
Somewhere in New York City

INTERVIEW, WPLJ NEW YORK, BROADCAST 6 JUNE 1971

An interview conducted by Howard Smith.

Compact Disc: *The Smith Collection – John and Yoko, June 1971*
When Was The Last Time You Kissed Mickey Mouse
WPLJ FM, New York City, 6 June 1971

Interview with Alex Bennett, WPLJ FM 95.5, New York City, 8 June 1971

This interview with a freelance American journalist was recorded on 6 June 1971.

Compact Disc: *Alex Bennett Show* (unknown)
Have You Had Your Breakfast Yet? (Black Cat)

Clock Soundtrack Recordings, 10 September 1971

Recordings commenced at the St. Regis Hotel in New York. The soundtrack of the unreleased film includes versions of 'Glad All Over', 'Heartbeat', 'Honey Don't', 'J.J.' (which evolved into 'Angela'), 'Lend Me Your Comb', 'Mailman Bring Me No More Blues', 'Maybe Baby', 'New York City', 'Not Fade Away', 'Peggy Sue', 'Peggy Sue Got Married', 'Send Me Some Lovin'' and 'Shazam!'. The film was premiered at Yoko's art exhibition in Syracuse on 9 October.

Compact Disc: *Clock*
Rave On
1971 St. Regis Hotel and Hotel Syracuse, NY (Green Grape)

Interview, WPLJ, New York, 26 September 1971

An interview conducted by Howard Smith.

Compact Disc: *The Smith Collection – John and Yoko, September 1971*

Everson Museum of Art, Syracuse, N.Y. – Press Conference, 8 October 1971

John and Yoko held a press conference to announce Yoko's art exhibition.

Vinyl: *Serve Yourself* (Karan Records)

Compact Disc: *This Is Not Here*

John's Thirty-first Birthday Party, 9 October 1971

At a hotel in Syracuse John and Yoko held his thirty-first birthday. They were joined by Klaus Voorman, Allan Ginsberg, Jim Keltner, Mal Evans,

Neil Aspinall and Eric Clapton. A tape is made of the party with the group performing several numbers.

Compact Disc: *The Birthday Tape*
John Lennon's 31 Birthday Party
Let's Have A Party
Live in L.A. and 31 Birthday Party
Unbootlegged 08 – Get That Fly
1971 St. Regis Hotel and Hotel Syracuse, NY (Green Grape)

THE DON SINGLETON INTERVIEW, NOVEMBER 1971

John and Yoko were interviewed by Don Singleton of the *New York Daily News*. In the interview John speaks frankly about a wide range of matters.

Compact Disc: *Interviews: 1971 – The Don Singleton Interview*

THE FREE JOHN SINCLAIR RALLY, 10–11 DECEMBER 1971

John Sinclair was a leading radical in America during the 1960s. He became Minister of Information for the White Panthers in 1968 and was also manager of the group MC5. He was arrested after an undercover policewoman enticed him to give her two joints of marijuana and he was sentenced to ten years in prison. Two years later John and Yoko heard about his case and Jerry Ruben talked them into appearing at a Free John Sinclair Rally – the concert was officially called Ten For Two. It was held over a seven hour period at Chrysler Stadium, Ann Arbor on 10–11 December 1971. Among the other artists were Phil Ochs, Alan Ginsberg, Bob Seeger, David Peel and Stevie Wonder. John was scheduled to appear at 2 a.m. but eventually come on after 3 a.m. and announced: 'We came here tonight to say apathy isn't it, and that we can all do something. So Flower Power didn't work. So what! We start again!' John then performed these songs – 'Attica State' and 'The Luck of the Irish'. Yoko sang 'Sisters Oh Sisters' and then John performed a song which was specially written for the occasion – 'John Sinclair'. After such a long wait to see John the audience were disappointed that he only performed four unfamiliar songs. However fifty-five hours after John and Yoko's performance, John Sinclair was freed. John and Yoko's part of the concert has been bootlegged many times and 'Attica State' and 'John Sinclair' appeared on the official 2007 compact disc and DVD release *The U.S. vs. John Lennon*

Vinyl: *Angel Baby*
Ann Arbor – Now Hear This (CBM WEC R1 3665)
John and Paul in Michigan
One + One Concert + More
One/One
One-to-One concert
Rave On

Compact Disc: *Dedicated to John Lennon (Part 4) (unknown)*
Give Peace a Chance
John's Lost Home Demos, Vol. 1
John Lennon Live
Live Lennon Tapes
The Plastic Ono Band – Live (DV More Record Production)
Rave On
Two Versions

CHORDS OF FAME, JOHN WITH PHIL OCHS, MICHIGAN HOTEL, 10 DECEMBER 1971

In the morning of the John Sinclair Rally John and Phil Ochs record 'Chords of Fame' in John's hotel room.

Compact Disc: *Christmas Present*
Come Together
Lennon Renumbers
Lost Lennon Archives, Vol. 1
The Tropical Lennon Trax

CONCERT, APOLLO THEATRE, NEW YORK, 17 DECEMBER 1971

Another appearance by John at a benefit concert. This one was for the families of the victims of the riot at New York's Attica State Prison. John performed acoustic versions of 'Imagine' and 'Attica State' – Yoko sang 'Sisters Oh Sisters'.

Compact Disc: *Acoustic Masterpieces*

IMAGINE ALBUM SESSIONS

Apple PAS 10004

Released: 8 October 1971

'Imagine', 'Crippled Inside', 'Jealous Guy', 'It's So Hard', 'I Don't Want to Be a Soldier', 'Mama I Don't Want To Die', 'Give Me Some Truth', 'Oh, My Love', 'How Do You Sleep?', 'How?', 'Oh, Yoko'

The sessions for this album took place in July 1971 at John's recording studio (which he called Ascot Sound Studios) in his house at Tittenhurst Park. The album was produced by John and Yoko and Phil Spector. The strings (credited on the album as The Flux Fiddlers) were overdubbed at The Record Plant, New York. The sessions have been heavily bootlegged. During the sessions John performed the impromptu 'San Francisco Bay Blues' which appears on several bootlegs including *The Lost Lennon Tapes*. Other songs recorded at the sessions which appear on several bootlegs include 'People Get Ready', 'Deep Water', 'Corrina Corrina', 'Sally and Billy', 'Mailman Bring Me No More Blues' and 'I'll Make You Happy'.

Vinyl: *Imagine – The Alternate Album* – (Apple Records SW A 3379)

Imagine – The Alternate (unknown)

Imagine World (unknown)

The Alternate Imagine (Pear Records)

The Lost Lennon Tapes (various) (Bag Records)

Compact Disc: *The Alternate Imagine*

Apple 2 x 1 Sided Rough Acetate

Ascot Sound Studios (Stoneage Music SAM 011)

Imagine Complete Sessions

Imagine – Apple 2 x 1 Sided Rough Acetate (Unicorn Records)

Imagine Acetate

Imagine… All the Outtakes, Vols 1–3

Imagine – The Alternate

Imagine – The Alternate Album

Imagine: Apple 2 x 1 Sided Rough Acetate

Imagine Collectors Edition

Imagine Complete Sessions

Imagine 5.1

Imagine… More Session Tapes

The Imagine Outtakes, Vols 1–3

The Imagine Outtakes, Vol. 4

The Imagine Outtakes, Vol. 5

The Imagine Outtakes, Vol. 6

The Imagine Outtakes, Vol. 7

The Imagine Outtakes, Vol. 8

The Imagine Outtakes, Vol. 9

Imagine Quadrosonics

Imagine – The Sessions

Imagine World

Jealous Guy – The Imagine Sessions

Journals

Oh, My Love

San Francisco Bay Blues

Studio Tracks, Vol. 6

This Is The Truth (Beatle Boots BB-CD 01)

Japan Interview, 1971

John and Yoko talk in Japanese about the *Imagine* album.

Compact Disc: *Japan Interview*

'I'm the Greatest' Rehearsals

The first demos for this song were recorded at John's home studio in Ascot on 28 and 29 December 1970. During this session he also recorded a demo for 'Make Love Not War' which was later recorded as 'Mind Games'. On the 13 March 1973 at the Sunset Sounds Recorders Studios during the sessions for the *Ringo* album, John on vocals together with George, Ringo, George and Klaus Voorman record ten takes of 'I'm the Greatest' (including breakdowns) in a session which lasts for eighteen minutes. The song eventually was included on the *Ringo* album with Ringo on vocals.

Vinyl: *Journals*
Serve Yourself (Love and Peace)

Compact Disc: *Remember Lennon*
Something Precious and Rare

The David Frost Show, Transmitted 13 January 1972

This show was recorded on 16 December 1971. John and Yoko were guests together with David Peel and The Lower East Side Band on this American television show.

Vinyl: *Telecasts*

Interview, WPLJ FM, New York, Broadcast 23 January 1972

An interview conducted by Howard Smith.

Compact Disc: *The Smith Collection – John and Yoko, January 1972*

The Mike Douglas Show, 31 January–7 February 1972

The recordings for these programmes began on 31 January and continued until 7 February 1972. The shows were broadcast between 14 and 18 February 1972. John and Yoko were co-hosts on this WBC (Westinghouse Broadcasting Corporation) afternoon talk show – *The Mike Douglas Show*. All the five shows were released on video in America on 19 May 1998.

Vinyl: *Joshua Tree Tapes*
Stand By Me
Telecasts
Working Class Hero

INTERVIEW, WIBG 990 AM, PHILADELPHIA, TAPED 27 JANUARY 1972, BROADCAST 10 FEBRUARY 1972

Interview conducted by Long John Wade

Compact Disc: *Why and Why Not*

AQUARIUS, LWT, RECORDED 28 FEBRUARY 1972

John and Yoko were visited by a crew from London Weekend Television who were filming the Lennons for a documentary on the theme 'The Pursuit of Happiness In Modern Day America'. Their three-minute thirteen second performance was to form part of documentary for their programme *Aquarius*. Apart from the interview, John was seen performing 'Attica State' which broke down after just over a minute. The programme, directed by Tony Palmer, was transmitted on Saturday 11 March 1972.

Compact Disc: *Somewhere in New York City*
Why and Why Not

INTERVIEW, ABC NEWS, 18 APRIL 1972

John and Yoko are interviewed by Geraldo Rivera following a hearing with the Immigration and Naturalisation Service in New York regarding the deportation proceedings against John. They are asked about the case for ABC Television *Eyewitness News*.

Compact Disc: *Why and Why Not*

DICK CAVETT SHOW, 5 MAY 1972

This was John and Yoko's second and final appearance on the show which was transmitted on 11 May 1972. Backed by Elephant's Memory Band they performed 'Woman Is the Nigger of the World' and 'We're All Water'. The couple were also interviewed about a number of topics. Before the show was transmitted the top brass at ABC wanted to delete 'Woman Is the Nigger of the World' as they were concerned it might upset some viewers. Cavett insisted that the song should remain.

Vinyl: *Telecasts*

ABC, *EYEWITNESS NEWS*, FILMED 5 AUGUST 1972

John and Yoko are interviewed by Geraldo Rivera. Later that evening back at the hotel John (acoustic guitar) and Yoko perform, for the *Eyewitness News* cameras, a medley of which include 'Rock Island Line', 'Maybe Baby', 'Peggy Sue', 'Woman Is the Nigger of the World', 'A Fool Like Me', 'Well (Baby Please Don't Go)' and 'The Calypso Song'.

Compact Disc: *Somewhere in New York City*

ONE-TO-ONE CONCERT, 30 AUGUST 1972

John and Yoko staged two benefit concerts (afternoon and evening) at Madison Square Garden, New York backed by The Plastic Ono Elephant's Memory Band. The concerts were arranged for the benefit of Willowbrook School For Children. The following songs were performed by John and Yoko:

Afternoon: 'Power to the People', 'New York City', 'It's So Hard', 'Move On Fast', 'Woman Is the Nigger of the World', 'Sisters Oh Sisters', 'Well, Well, Well', 'Born in a Prison', 'Instant Karma', 'Mother', 'We're All Water', 'Come Together', 'Imagine', 'Open Your Box', 'Cold Turkey', 'Don't Worry Kyoko', 'Hound Dog'

Evening: 'Power to the People', 'New York City', 'It's So Hard', 'Woman Is the Nigger of the World', 'Sisters Oh Sisters', 'Well, Well, Well', 'Instant Karma', 'Mother', 'We're All Water', 'Come Together', 'Imagine', 'Cold Turkey', 'Hound Dog', 'Give Peace a Chance' (with other stars of the shows).

Also appearing in the shows were Stevie Wonder, Roberta Flack and Sha Na Na. Prior to the shows John purchased $60,000 worth of tickets which he gave to the volunteer fund raisers. The event raised more than $1,500,000 for the Willowbrook School. On entering the arena the audience were given a tambourine and requested to shake it during the concert. Tracks from the shows were released officially on the album *John Lennon: Live in New York City* and the video of the same title (both released 1986). Rehearsals for the show started on 18 August at the Butterfly Studios, New York and continued on 20–22 August at Fillmore East Theatre. The final rehearsals were held on 29 August.

Vinyl: *Come Back Johnny*
Hound Dog
Joshua Tree Tapes
Live From The Live
One + One Concert + More
One/One
One-to-One concert
Plop Plop… Fizz Fizz
Compact Disc: *Come Back Johnny*
COME Together
Give Peace a Chance
Live and Rare
Live Lennon Tapes
MSG Back in '72/They Say It's Your Birthday
Since I Left The Rolling Stones
Willowbrook Rehearsals
Working Class Hero

ONE-TO-ONE CONCERT REHEARSALS

Vinyl: *One and One and One is Three – Part One*
One and One and One is Three – Part Two
One and One and One is Three – Part Three

One and One and One is Three
Willowbrook Rehearsals

Compact Disc: *Come Together*
Lennon Renumbers
The Lost Lennon Rehearsal
One-to-One concert Rehearsals
One-to-One Rehearsals, Vol. 1
One-to-One Rehearsals, Vol. 2
Rock 'n' Roll Is Here To Stay
S.I.R. John Winston Ono Lennon

JERRY LEWIS TELETHON, 6 SEPTEMBER 1972

John and Yoko appeared live in New York with Elephant's Memory Band towards the end of the annual all day television special *Jerry Lewis Labor Day Telethon*. This event raised money for the illness muscular dystrophy. They performed live versions of 'Imagine', 'Now or Never' and 'Give Peace a Chance' (reggae version).

Compact Disc: *Miscellaneous Tracks*
Telecasts

MIKE DOUGLAS SHOW, 14–18 SEPTEMBER 1972

Compact Disc: *Telecasts*

SOMETIME IN NEW YORK CITY

CITY ALBUM SESSIONS

Apple PCSP 716

Released: 15 September 1972

Disc One: 'Woman Is the Nigger of the World', 'Sisters Oh Sisters', 'Attica State', 'Born in a Prison', 'New York City', 'Sunday Bloody Sunday', 'The Luck of the Irish', 'John Sinclair', 'Angela', 'We're All Water'.

Disc Two: Live, Lyceum Ballroom in London, 15 December 1969 (in aid of UNICEF) – 'Cold Turkey', 'Don't Worry Kyoko'

Live, Fillmore East auditorium, New York, 6 June 1971 – 'Well (Baby Please Don't Go)', 'Jamrag', 'Scumbag'.

This album was released in America on 12 June 1972. Due to copyright problems the release in the UK would be delayed for three months. The album was supposed to be sold as a single LP disc with a free bonus disc of the live tracks but retailed at a slightly higher price than a normal album. The first two sides of the vinyl release were recorded in New York between 1 and 20 March 1972 – produced by John and Yoko and Phil Spector. The bonus disc (sides three and four of the vinyl release) titled *Live Jam* included two live sessions. Side three comprising 'Cold Turkey' and 'Don't Worry Kyoko' was recorded on 15 December 1969 at a concert for UNICEF in the Lyceum Ballroom, London. Due to contractual problems the record sleeve lists the stars who appeared on these tracks as pseudonyms. The line up for the Plastic Ono Band supergroup was: John – vocals and guitar, George Harrison, Eric Clapton, Delaney Bramlett – guitars, Klaus Voorman – bass, Jim Gordon, Keith Moon, Alan White – drums, Billy Preston – organ, Bonnie Bramlett – percussion, Bobby Keyes – saxophone, Jim Price – trumpet plus Bobby Whitlock, Carl Radle, 'Legs' Larry Smith and Dino Danelli. Interestingly, Billy Preston's organ missed the original recording and was replaced on this release by Nicky Hopkins electric piano, which was overdubbed in New York. Side four containing the rest of the tracks was recorded at Filmore East in New York on 6 June 1971 when John and Yoko appeared unannounced at a performance with Frank Zappa's Mothers of Invention. These live recordings were mixed at the Record Plant in New York.

Compact Disc: *The Alternate Sometime in New York City* (John Records)
The Alternate Sometime in N.Y. (Pear Records)
The Fillmore Tapes
Remember Lennon
Remember New York
S.I.R. John Winston Ono Lennon
Somewhere in New York City

Interview, Flipside US TV, 16 February 1973

Compact Disc: *The Weekend Starts Here*

Beverley Hills Hotel Interview, Elliot Mintz, 26 April 1973

Excerpts from this interview appear through *The Lost Lennon Tapes* radio series.

Compact Disc: *The Weekend Starts Here*

Mind Games Album Sessions

Apple PCS 7165

Released: 16 November 1973

'Mind Games', 'Tight A$', 'Aisumasen (I'm Sorry)', 'One Day (at a Time)', 'Bring on the Lucie' (Freeda People), 'Nutopian National Anthem', 'Intuition', 'Out the Blue', 'Only People', 'I Know (I Know)', 'You Are Here', 'Meat City'

The album was recorded in September 1973 at the New York Record Plant. The album was produced by John and the following musicians were used: Ken Ascher – piano, organ and Mellotron, David Spinozza – guitar, Gordon Edwards – bass, Jim Keltner – drums, Michael Brecker – saxophone, 'Sneaky' Pete Kleinow – pedal steel guitar plus John – percussion, guitar and clavinet. Other songs recorded at the sessions include 'I Promise', 'Make Love Not War', 'Call My Name', 'Shoeshine', 'Just Gotta Give Me Some Rock 'n' Roll' which were developed and included on the album with different titles. One outtake was the song 'Rock 'n' Roll People' which was to be released on the *Menlove Avenue* album.

Compact Disc: *Absolute Elsewhere*
The Alternate Mind Games (Pear Records)
The Alternate Mind Games and Shaved Fish (Ghost Records)
Bring on the Lucie
Mind Games Acetate

Mind Games (Alternates and Demos)
Mind Games Sessions 1973 (Green Grape)
More Mind Games
Studio Tracks, Vol. 7

TOMORROW SHOW, 8 APRIL 1974

Compact Disc: *Interviews: 1974/1975*

EMI PROMO TAPE, SEPTEMBER 1974

In this promo tape for the *Walls and Bridges* album, Lennon answers questions and encourages record outlets to support the new album.

Compact Disc: *Interviews 1974* (Disc 1)

INTERVIEW, 18 SEPTEMBER 1974

Compact Disc: *In His Life*

RKO RADIO INTERVIEW, 25 SEPTEMBER 1974

John's interview with RKO Radio lasted 70 minutes.

Compact Disc: *Interviews 1974* (Disc 1)

INTERVIEWS 1974 (DISC 2)

Chum FM Radio Interview, 26 September 1974

Notes: The album *Walls and Bridges* was released on this day in America. In this interview, John talks about the album and other subjects.

Compact Disc: *Interviews 1974* (Disc 1)

WAXB FM RADIO INTERVIEW, 27 SEPTEMBER 1974

An interview by Mark Parenteau from the Detroit radio station. John plugs the *Walls and Bridges* album and talks about several other topics.

Compact Disc: *Interviews 1974 (Disc 1)*

Radio WNEW-FM 102.7, New York, 28 September 1974

John was interviewed by Denis Elsas. He talks about several subjects including The Beatles original recordings. During his appearance, he acted as a DJ, read the weather forecast and advertisements.

Compact Disc: *DJ Winston O'Boogie* (Unicorn Records)
Listen to This Radio Show (WNEW NYC 9/28/74) (Mad Scot Records)

Radio WRKO Interview, 29 September 1974

Compact Disc: *Interviews: 1974 (Disc 3)*

Interview by Jim Ladd, October 1974

Another interview to promote the *Walls and Bridges* album. This was probably recorded after 9 October as John says during the interview: '...had my thirty-fourth birthday yesterday...'

Compact Disc: *Jim Ladd Interview 1974 – Upgraded*

Walls and Bridges Album Sessions

Apple PCTC 253

Released: 4 October 1974

'Going Down on Love', 'Whatever Gets You Through the Night', 'Old Dirt Road', 'What You Got', 'Bless You', 'Scared', 'No. 9 Dream', 'Surprise Surprise (Sweet Bird of Paradox)', 'Steel and Glass', 'Beef Jerky', 'Nobody Loves You (When You're Down and Out)', 'Ya Ya'

The album was recorded between June and August 1974 at New York's Record Plant with one track, 'Nobody Loves You (When You're Down and Out)' recorded in Los Angeles. The backing musicians include Jim Keltner – drums, Jesse Ed Davis – guitar, Eddie Mottau – acoustic guitar and Klaus Voorman – bass. Also recorded at the sessions was a version of 'Ain't She Sweet'.

Vinyl: *Body Stripping Off the Walls*
Off the Walls (TMOQ)

Something Precious and Rare (TMOQ)
Winston O' Boogie

Compact Disc: *The Alternate Walls and Bridges* (Pear Records PDP 035)
Bring On the Lucie
Come On Listen to Me (His Masters Choice)
Journals
KSAN Tom Donahue Interview (unknown)
Listen to This
Off the Walls
Over Walls Under Bridges
Rockspeak '74
Studio Rehearsal – 13 July 1974 (Green Grape)
Walls and Bridges (Quad)
Walls and Bridges Revisited
Walls and Bridges Rockspeak '74
Walls and Bridges Sessions
Winston O'Boogie
1974 Home Recordings (Green Grape)
1974 Walls and Bridges Sessions (Green Grape)

2SM 1269 AM SYDNEY, AUSTRALIA, OCTOBER 1974

John answers questions about himself and the *Walls and Bridges* album. Edited tracks from the album are played.

Compact Disc: *Interviews, 1974* (Disc 2)

LIVE WITH ELTON JOHN, 28 NOVEMBER 1974

John joined Elton John on stage at Madison Square Garden, New York, and they performed three numbers: 'Whatever Gets You Through the Night', 'Lucy in the Sky with Diamonds' and 'I Saw Her Standing There'. John's appearance was unannounced.

Vinyl: *A Guitar's All Right John But You'll Never Earn Your Living By It*
Live From The Live

Working Class Hero

Compact Disc: *A Guitar's All Right John But You'll Never Earn Your Living By It*
Mucho Mungo
New York New York

WORKING CLASS HERO TODAY, 16 DECEMBER 1974

John and his lawyer appeared on this programme during his fight against deportation.

Compact Disc: *Interviews 1974/1975*

INTERVIEW, CAPITAL RADIO, 1975

This interview from the archives of Capital Radio was recorded in 1975 when John returned to New York following his so called 'Lost Weekend'.

Compact Disc: *The Hall of Fame (Capital Radio Interview 1975)*

INTERVIEW, THE SCOTT MUNI SHOW, WNEW FM, NEW YORK, 13 FEBRUARY 1975

John gave this radio interview to Scott Muni – he was uninvited and arrived with an early copy of the *Rock 'n' Roll* album.

Compact Disc: *Reminiscing*

INTERVIEW, WRRM FM, CINCINNATI, OH, 21 FEBRUARY 1975

Compact Disc: *Please Hang Up and Try Again*

INTERVIEW, KSHE FM, CRESTWOOD, 21 FEBRUARY 1975

Compact Disc: *Please Hang Up and Try Again*

Rock 'n' Roll Album Sessions

Apple PCS 7169

Released: 21 February 1975

'Be-Bop-A-Lula', 'Stand By Me', 'Rip It Up/Ready Teddy', 'You Can't Catch Me', 'Ain't That a Shame', 'Do You Wanna Dance', 'Sweet Little Sixteen', 'Slippin' and Slidin'', 'Peggy Sue', 'Bring It on Home to Me/Send Me Some Lovin'', 'Bony Moronie', 'Ya Ya', 'Just Because'

The recording sessions for this album started between October and December 1973 with Phil Spector producing in Los Angeles. Disagreements between John and Phil Spector meant that the sessions were halted. Spector then disappeared with the tapes and it was then rumoured that he had been involved in a motor accident and accordingly Lennon was unable to recover the tapes. Eventually he managed to retrieve the tapes but discovered that only four tracks were suitable – 'You Can't Catch Me', 'Sweet Little Sixteen', 'Bony Moronie' and 'Just Because'. John then commenced recording at New York's Record Plant between 21 and 25 January 1974 and another ten tracks were taped. As the album *Walls and Bridges* had only recently been released, it was decided to delay this album until April 1975. At the beginning of February 1975 an album called *Roots – John Lennon Sings The Great Rock and Roll Hits* was issued in America by the mail order firm Adam VIII Ltd. The album claimed that it was authorised by John Lennon and Apple and featured recordings from the Phil Spector sessions including 'Angel Baby' and 'Be My Baby' which were not included on the subsequent official release. The story behind the release of tracks from the sessions had further twists and turns. Morris Levy, the publisher of Chuck Berry's song catalogue, had sued John for allegedly infringing the copyright of the Berry song 'You Can't Catch Me' from which Lennon had plagiarised 'Come Together'. An out of court settlement was agreed when Lennon agreed to record several Chuck Berry numbers for inclusion on his next album. Lennon gave Levy the tapes from the Spector sessions. Levy used those to produce the *Roots* album claiming that Lennon had given a verbal agreement to produce the album. This situation was denied by Lennon and Apple who then brought forward the release of the *Rock 'n' Roll album* and then sued Levy. The *Roots* album was taken off the market and John was awarded $45,000 compensation. 'Lady Marmalade' was recorded during the sessions which appears on several bootlegs. 'Angel Baby' together with 'To Know Her Is to Love Her', 'Since My Baby Left Me' and 'Just Because' (reprise) subsequently appeared as bonus tracks on the reissued *Rock 'n' Roll* CD. 'Be My Baby' was issued on the official release *John Lennon Anthology*.

Vinyl: *A Collection of Rock 'n' Roll Rehearsals*
Lennon Roots
The May Pang Tapes
Roots – John Lennon Sings The Great Rock and Roll Hits
Roots
You Should'a Been There

Compact Disc: *The Alternate Rock 'n' Roll* (Pear Records)
Brandy Alexanders and the Wall of Sound – Volumes 1–3
The Complete May Pang Tapes
Journals
Oldies but Mouldies (Adam VIII Ltd)
Rock 'n' Roll Is Here To Stay
Rock 'n' Roll Sessions
The Rock 'n' Roll Sessions, Part 1
The Rock 'n' Roll Sessions, Part 2
Roots
You Should'a Been There

THE OLD GREY WHISTLE TEST

In addition to performing 'Stand By Me' and 'Slippin' and Slidin'' for this BBC2 television series, John was also interviewed by Bob Harris.

Compact Disc: *Ascot Sound Studios*
A Guitar's All Right John But You'll Never Earn Your Living By It

INTERVIEWS 1974/1975

Miscellaneous Tracks
Warship the Lord Your God and Serve Him Only

JEAN-FRANCOIS VALLEE INTERVIEW, 7 APRIL 1975

John was interviewed at the Dakota by journalist Jean-Francois Vallee for inclusion in the French television programme *Un Jour Futur*. John sings and plays Labelle's 'Lady Marmalade' with the famous question 'Voulez Vous Coucher Avec Moi Ce Soir?'

Compact Disc: Interviews 1974/1975

THE TOMORROW SHOW, 28 APRIL 1975

Hosted by Tom Snyder. The entire fifty-minute television show was devoted to John who is joined by his lawyer Leon Wildes. The show was released on video in 1983.

Vinyl: *All You Need Is John* (CX 297)
Doctor Winston O'Boogie on the Tomorrow Show (CX 297)

Compact Disc: *John Lennon with Tom Snyder*

WFIL AM HELPING HAND MARATHON, 16–18 MAY 1975 (SEE NOTES BELOW)

This was an event to raise money for multiple sclerosis. For three days and nights he helped out by talking on the phone and reading the weather. He was invited to participate by DJ Larry Kane, who John met during The Beatles first American tour in 1964. There is some confusion as to the dates on the Compact Disc available (see entry 892 in Part 2 – Compact Discs). According to the sleeve, the release features John's participation between 16 and 18 May 1975. The sleeve features what appears to be a poster advertising the event. Have they made an error on this poster? According to both Keith Badman's book, *The Beatles – After The Break-Up 1970–2000* and Mark Lewisohn's book, *The Beatles – 25 Years in the Life* these dates are incorrect. According to Badman, John appeared at a two day event in 1974 on 17 and 18 May and he made a further appearance the following year and the dates were 9–11 May 1975. If the poster on the front of the sleeve is correct, then the dates in both Badman's and Lewisohn's books are wrong. If anyone can throw any light on this anomaly it would be appreciated.

Compact Disc: *The WFIL AM Helping Hand Marathon*

SALUTE TO SIR LEW GRADE, 13 JUNE 1975

This show was recorded on 18 April 1975 at the Grand Ballroom of the Hilton Hotel, New York. This ATV/ITC television special *Salute To Sir Lew – The Master Showman* was a star-studded event to celebrate the career of Sir Lew Grade, head of Associated Television (ATV). John appeared wearing dark glasses and a red boiler suit with his hair tied in a ponytail. Playing an acoustic guitar, John performed 'Slippin' and Slidin'', 'Stand By Me' and 'Imagine'. He was backed by a group called Etcetra who wore face masks attached to back of their heads. When asked about these masks, John said, 'It was a sardonic reference to my feelings on Lew Grade's personality.' His feelings are probably due to Lew Grade's ATV gaining control of The Beatles Northern Songs in 1969. The 52 minute show was first transmitted in America on 13 June and was shown a week later in the UK on 20 June. Both shows omitted 'Stand By Me' from their broadcasts.

Vinyl: *Plop Plop... Fizz Fizz*

Compact Disc: *Ascot Sound Studios*
Interviews 1974/1975
Miscellaneous Tracks
Warship the Lord Your God and Serve Him Only

INTERVIEW, CAPITAL RADIO, 1975

Compact Disc: John Lennon, The Hall of Fame (Capital Radio Interview 1975)

DOUBLE FANTASY ALBUM SESSIONS

Geffen Records K99131
Released: 17 November 1980

'(Just Like) Starting Over', 'Kiss Kiss Kiss' (Yoko), 'Clean-up Time', 'Give Me Something' (Yoko), 'I'm Losing You', 'I'm Moving On' (Yoko), 'Beautiful Boy', 'Watching the Wheels', 'I'm Your Angel' (Yoko), 'Woman', 'Beautiful Boys' (Yoko), 'Dear Yoko', 'Every Man Has a Woman Who Loves Him' (Yoko), 'Hard Times Are Over' (Yoko)

After a period of five years a new John Lennon album was released. Despite announcing in 1975 that he was retiring for five years after the birth of his son Sean, he continued to write and work on songs. In 1976 he revived 'Sally and Billy' and from the same period wrote [I Don't Want to Face It' which would appear on *Milk and Honey*. He also wrote 'Mirror Mirror' and many of the songs which would form the basis of the *Double Fantasy* and *Milk and Honey* albums. Early in 1980 he began to work on some of the songs he had written. During a period of recording home demos in February 1980 he developed the song 'My Life' which is now called 'Don't Be Crazy' and then 'The Worst is Over'. The song eventually became 'Starting Over'. While in Bermuda John recorded several demos and wrote 'I'm Losing You' after being frustrated that he could not reach Yoko on the telephone. On 31 July Yoko gave record producer Jack Douglas a cassette of John's songs and on 2 August rehearsals started at the Dakota with the backing musicians. Songs at this session included 'Beautiful Boy,' Borrowed Time', plus Yoko's 'I'm Your Angel'. On 4 August the recording sessions started at the Hit Factory and continued until 10 September. Some of the songs being developed were intended to be included on John's follow up album provisionally titled *Milk and Honey* (see entry below). After John's death this album was shelved but was released in 1984. During the sessions a number of other songs were recorded which appear on several bootlegs. These include 'Maggie Mae', 'I Am the Walrus', 'It's Now or Never', 'I Watch Your Face', 'My Life', 'Don't Be Crazy', 'The Worst is Over', 'Emotional Wreck', 'Howling at the Moon', 'Illusion', 'You Saved My Soul', 'Help Me to Help Myself', 'Memories', 'Sally and Billy', 'Mirror Mirror' and 'One of the Boys'.

Vinyl: *Another Fantasy*
Before Play – August 1980
Fulfilling the Fantasies

Lost Lennon Tapes (Various volumes)
Winston O'Boogie

Compact Disc: *The Alternate Double Fantasy* (Pear Records)
Before Play – August 1980
Bermuda Shorts
Double Fantasy/Milk and Honey
Double Fantasy Working Version
Filming The Fantasies
For the Other Half of the Sky
Fulfilling The Fantasies
A Heart Play
It's Hard to Be Butterflies
Journals
Life Is What Happens (Barrier Records)
Miscellaneous Tracks
Songs from Late in the Afternoon
Studio Tracks, Vol. 4
Studio Tracks, Vol. 5
We'd Like to Change the Tempo Now
Your Daddy's Here

MILK AND HONEY ALBUM

Polydor POLH 5

Released: 23 January 1984

'I'm Stepping Out', 'Sleepless Night' (Yoko), 'I Don't Want to Face It', 'Don't Be Scared' (Yoko), 'Nobody Told Me', 'O'Sanity' (Yoko), 'Borrowed Time', 'Your Hands' (Yoko), 'Forgive Me (My Little Flower Princess)', 'Let Me Count The Ways' (Yoko), 'Grow Old with Me', 'You're the One' (Yoko).

This album was the follow up to *Double Fantasy*. The Lennon tracks had been recorded during the sessions for the *Double Fantasy* album and he intended to return to them in the early part of 1981 for inclusion on his next album. Following his death the idea was shelved and Yoko released her own album *Season of Glass*. It would be some three years before this album was released with the Lennon songs virtually how he left them which gave the slight feel of an official bootleg.

Vinyl: *Fulfilling The Fantasies*
Lost Lennon Tapes (Various volumes)

Compact Disc: *The Alternate Double Fantasy*
Bermuda Shorts
Between the Lines – Vol. 8
The Dakota and Bermuda Demos 1977–1980 (Vol. 1)
Double Fantasy/Milk and Honey
Double Fantasy – Demos and Outtakes
Double Fantasy – Working Versions
Fulfilling The Fantasies
Heart Play
It's Hard to Be Butterflies
Journals
Lost Lennon Tapes (Various volumes)
Phasing Phun with Your Clothes ON
Songs from Late in The Afternoon
Studio Tracks – Vol. 4
Studio Tracks – Vol. 5
Your Daddy's Here

INTERVIEW, LISA ROBINSON, 24 SEPTEMBER 1980

The mixing of the *Double Fantasy* album on this day moved from the Hit Factory to Record Plant East in New York. John was in attendance and was interviewed during the session by Lisa Robinson from the 97-FM Buffalo radio station.

Compact Disc: *The Inside Track: John Lennon*

The Newsweek Interview, WNEW FM, New York City, 25 September 1980

Interview with Dennis Elsas with Barbara Granstock.

Compact Disc: *The Real John Lennon: The Newsweek Interview* (Black Cat)

BBC Radio Interview with Andy Peebles, 6 December 1980

This interview with BBC Radio One DJ Andy Peebles was held at the Hit Factory. The interview was broadcast in a five part series called *The Lennon Tapes* starting on Sunday 18 January 1981 on BBC Radio One. The series included Beatles and Lennon tracks. A book accompanying the series, also called *The Lennon Tapes*, was published by the BBC on 6 February 1981. This contained a transcript of the interview.

Compact Disc: *BBC Tribute to John Lennon* (Long Version) – Vol. 1

BBC Tribute to John Lennon (Long Version) – Vol.2

BBC Tribute to John Lennon (Short Version)

I'm Just Sitting Here Reminiscing

The John Lennon Story – Volumes One and Two

The John Lennon Story – Volumes Three and Four

The John Lennon Story – Volume Five

Interview, RKO Radio, 8 December 1980

John was interviewed by Dave Sholin, Laurie Kaye, Ron Hummel and Bert Keane for an RKO Radio special. The started at around 10 a.m. and lasted about ninety minutes.

Compact Disc: *Testimony*

Unedited RKO Interview

Menlove Avenue

Capital SJ-12533

Released: 3 November 1986

'Here We Go Again', 'Rock 'n' Roll People', 'Angel Baby', 'Since My Baby Left Me', 'To Know Her Is to Love Her', 'Steel and Glass', 'Scared', 'Old Dirt Road', 'Nobody Loves You (When You're Down and Out)', 'Bless You'

This release featured mainly outtakes from two albums – *Rock 'n' Roll* and *Walls and Bridges*. It was not a commercial success. The takes on this album have all appeared on bootleg albums.

ANTHOLOGY

Capital 830 6042

Released: 2 November 1998

Disc One (Ascot): 'Working Class Hero', 'God', 'I Found Out', 'Hold On', 'Isolation', 'Love', 'Mother', 'Remember', 'Imagine' (take 1), 'Fortunately', 'Well (Baby Please Don't Go)', 'Oh, My Love', 'Jealous Guy', 'Maggie Mae', 'How Do You Sleep?', 'God Save Oz', 'Do the Oz', 'I Don't Want to Be a Soldier', 'Give Peace a Chance', 'Look at Me', 'Long Lost John'

Disc Two (New York City): 'Attica State' (live), 'Imagine' (live), 'Bring on the Lucie', 'Woman Is the Nigger of the World', 'Geraldo Rivera – One-to-One concert', 'Woman Is the Nigger of the World' (live), 'It's So Hard' (live), 'Come Together' (live), 'Happy Xmas (War Is Over)', 'Luck of the Irish' (live), 'John Sinclair' (live), 'The *David Frost Show*', 'Mind Games (I Promise)', 'Mind Games (Make Love Not War)', 'One Day at a Time', 'I Know', 'I'm the Greatest', 'Goodnight, Vienna', '*Jerry Lewis Telethon*', 'A Kiss Is Just a Kiss', 'Real Love', 'You Are Here'

Disc Three (The Lost Weekend): 'What You Got', 'Nobody Loves You (When You're Down and Out)', 'Whatever Gets You Through the Night' (home), 'Whatever Gets You Through the Night' (studio), 'Yesterday' (parody), 'Be-Bop-A-Lula', 'Rip It Up', 'Ready Teddy', 'Scared', 'Steel and Glass', 'Surprise Surprise (Sweet Bird of Paradox)', 'Bless You', 'Going Down on Love', 'Move Over Ms L', 'Ain't She Sweet', 'Slippin' and Slidin'', 'Peggy Sue', 'Bring It on Home to Me', 'Send Me Some Loving', 'Phil and John 1', 'Phil and John 2', 'Phil and John 3', 'When in Doubt F**k It', 'Be My Baby', 'Stranger's Room'.

Disc Four (Dakota): 'I'm Losing You', 'Sean's Little Help', 'Serve Yourself', 'My Life', 'Nobody Told Me', 'Life Begins at 40', 'I Don't Want to Face It', 'Woman', 'Dear Yoko', 'Watching the Wheels', 'I'm Stepping Out', 'Borrowed Time', 'The Rishikesh Song', 'Sean's Loud', 'Beautiful Boy', 'Mr Hyde's Gone (Don't Be Afraid)', 'Only You', 'Grow Old with Me', 'Dear John', 'The Great Wok', 'Mucho Mungo', 'Satire 1', 'Satire 2', 'Satire 3', 'Sean's in the Sky', 'It's Real'

Although this box set was released in 1998 the seed for the idea of issuing a set of Lennon outtakes, demos and the like dated back some ten years. In the late 1980s a number of reels of Lennon outtakes were sent to Abbey Road Studios in London. It was during this period that Yoko agreed to the radio show *The Lost Lennon Tapes* (see Part Three). Realising that the radio shows would be bootlegged, EMI and Yoko agreed to issue a box set that would use the best of the tracks from *The Lost Lennon Tapes* and these recently acquired studio outtakes. EMI asked Mark Lewisohn, the renowned Beatles authority, to listen to the tapes received from the USA and compile a track listing for the proposed CD box set. He worked on this task between 1991 and 1993 but in 1994 the project seemed to have been shelved. However, the task was then passed to Rob Stevens who had worked on several projects with Yoko. After he had listened to all the tapes he selected about fifty hours of recordings which he offered to Yoko so she could make the final selection. The set selected by Stevens/Ono differed from the original Lewisohn compilation. A 'Best of' single CD was released on 2 November 1998 which was obviously aimed at the casual fan rather than the committed collector. The four-disc set included a number of previously unreleased tracks, although most of these had appeared on bootlegs. These include:

'Maggie Mae' – Dakota recording.

'Long Lost John' – recorded at Abbey Road during the *Plastic Ono Band* album sessions.

'I'm the Greatest' – John (piano and vocals), George Harrison (guitar), Klaus Voorman (bass), Ringo Starr (drums). Recorded at Sunset Sound, Los Angeles.

'Goodnight, Vienna' – John on vocals.

'Yesterday' – John, vocals and guitar.

'Ain't She Sweet' – recorded at Record Plant East, New York

'Be My Baby' – from *Rock 'n' Roll* session

'Serve Yourself' – John, vocals and guitar.

'Life Begins at 40' – Dakota recording.

'The Rishi Kesh Song' – Dakota recording.

'Sean's Loud' – Dakota recording.

'Mr Hyde's Gone (Don't Be Afraid)' – Dakota recording.

'Only You' – recorded at Sunset Sound, Los Angeles.

'Dear John' – Dakota recording.

'Mucho Mungo' – Dakota recording.

'Satires 1, 2 and 3' – Dakota recordings.

'Sean's in the Sky' – Dakota recording.

'It's Real' – Dakota recording.

ACOUSTIC

Capitol 7243 8 74428 2 5

Released: 1 November 2004

'Working Class Hero', 'Love', 'Well, Well, Well', 'Look at Me', 'God', 'My Mummy's Dead', 'Cold Turkey', 'The Luck of the Irish', 'John Sinclair', 'Woman Is the Nigger of the World', 'What You Got', 'Watching the Wheels', 'Dear Yoko', 'Real Love', 'Imagine', 'It's Real'

This album, released in time for Christmas 2004, includes seven previously officially unreleased tracks and has the feel of a sort of official bootleg. Collectors had all these tracks in their collections already. 'The Luck of the Irish' and 'John Sinclair' are from The Free John Sinclair Rally. 'Imagine' is from *Salute To Sir Lew Grade*. The rest of the tracks are various demos and outtakes.

5. Songs Index

All the songs which appear in this discography, in Parts One, Two and Three are listed below together with interviews and radio documentaries. Although the object of this work is to concentrcte on the solo bootleg releases of John Lennon, a number of the discs include Beatles bootleg recordings. We have decided to include some of these Beatles outtakes in the following listings as many of these although planned for Beatles sessions are solo Lennon demos. These are shown in the second section of the songs listings, entitled simply Beatles Bootlegs. The last column shows the entry number of the disc or discs listed in Parts One, Two and Three. We have tried to identify the different takes, rehearsals, demos or live performances of each song but in many cases it is impossible to ascertain the exact context of a particular take Where we own the disc we have usually been able to identify the source of the track by comparing it to other releases where we are certain of the source. As many of the discs listed in Parts One to Three are virtually impossible to obtain (although we do have copies of the sleeves) we can only be guided by whatever information is available from the sleeves, bootleg reviews in fanzines or other sources. We prefer not to make a guess, whether it be inspired, wild or otherwise, and we have listed these tracks as 'unknown take'. However, in many cases we have made an arbitrary decision where to place a particular track. We have been unable to identify some titles as shown on the sleeves and it is likely that the bootleggers have made up a title as they did not know which song was being performed. We have shown these in the listings, cross referenced where applicable. One example is 'The Sadness of My Soul' which is actually 'You Saved My Soul' (see entry 387). Several other titles are incorrect. For example, 'Out the Blue' is constantly shown on the sleeves as 'Out of the Blue'. Many of the discs include extracts from some of the interviews but we have not included these in the listings below unless a substantial portion is featured. We have, however, itemised the discs which include the complete interviews. We did have problems in identifying the tracks on *The Lost Lennon Tapes* radio series (see Part Three). Although we own some of the discs and copies of the sleeves for the rest, where we do not own the disc we were uncertain whether the track listed is an outtake, live performance or the commercial version. There are bound to be anomalies in the listings below but this index will provide a useful guide as to what John Lennon unreleased tracks are available and where they can be found.

SECTION ONE – SOLO BOOTLEGS

Title	Source	Entry No.
AAAK	Fillmore East, New York, alternate mix	269, 353
AAAK	Fillmore East, New York, Frank Zappa mix	269, 328
About the Awful	unknown	330
A Case of the Blues	Weybridge, demo	015, 078, 191, 236, 329, 386, 405, 493, 533, 707, 723, 851, 907, 908
Across the River	*Double Fantasy* sessions, medley with drum machine	091, 222, 240, 249, 273, 274, 384, 387, 434, 590, 733, 856, 861, 893
Admiral Halsey	live, Hotel Syracuse, 9 October 1971, John's thirty-first birthday	840, 912
Ain't She Sweet	*Walls and Bridges* sessions, improvisation	225, 885, 914
Ain't That a Shame	*Some Time in New York City* sessions	424, 570
Ain't That a Shame	*Rock 'n' Roll* album rehearsals	023, 060, 108, 109, 110, 157, 174, 219, 222, 250, 353, 378, 407, 470, 537, 661, 770, 814, 815, 816, 819, 879

Title	Source	Entry No.
Ain't That a Shame	*Rock 'n' Roll* rehearsals, Morris Levy's Farm, New York	245, 815
Ain't That a Shame	*Rock 'n' Roll* rehearsals (false start), Morris Levy's Farm, New York	815
Ain't That a Shame	official released version	C61
Ain't That a Shame	from *Roots*	132, 133, 217, 820
Ain't That a Shame	rough mix, longer fade	171, 218, 499, 719
Ain't That a Shame	One-to-One concert rehearsals	814, 826
Aisumasen	*Mind Games* album, unknown take	087, 099, 159, 169, 179, 220, 239, 353, 377, 740, 752, 773, 849, 874
Aisumasen	*Mind Games* sessions, early rough mix	431, 583, 496, 712, 751, 756, 871, 887
Aisumasen	*Mind Games* sessions, rough mix with steel guitar overdub	168
Aisumasen	*Mind Games* album, near final mix	242
Aisumasen	*Mind Games* album, from acetate	750
Aisumasen	*Clock* rehearsals, St Regis Hotel, New York, September 1971	223, 244
Alec Speaking	John reading from *In His Own Write*	330
Amazing Talking Guitar	7" Apple Acetate	160
Amazing Walk	unknown	387, 861, 881
Angela J.J.	early prototype	173
Angela People	early prototype	173
Angel Baby	from *Roots*	002, 003, 004, 005, 050, 060, 063, 066, 132, 133, 136, 149, 150, 154, 157, 171, 217, 231, 815, 820
Angel Baby	unknown take	373, 770, 815, 819, 832, 864, 899

Title	Source	Entry No.
Angel Baby	live, Hotel Syracuse, 9 October 1971, John's thirty-first birthday	840, 912
Angel Baby	official release.	365, 860
Answer Me My Love Lori Burton	John Lennon co-producer	201, 759
Ants In My Pants,	see I Got Ants In My Pants	439, 600
AOS	rehearsal with Ornette Coleman	867
As Time Goes By	Dakota 1976, interview with Elliot Mintz	030, 066, 149, 150, 192, 231, 233, 373, 731, 749, 860, 881
As Time Goes By	Earth News Radio	860
As Time Goes By	take 1	377
As Time Goes By	take 2	377
Attica State	acoustic version, take 1	182
Attica State	acoustic demos	089, 240, 285, 433, 587, 911
Attica State	unknown take	174, 178, 251, 285, 352, 781
Attica State	live, Hotel Syracuse, 9 October 1971, John's thirty-first birthday	840, 912, 864
Attica State	live, Free John Sinclair Rally, 10 December 1971	002, 003, 005, 006, 011, 026, 027, 046, 048, 057, 058, 065, 072, 113, 121, 122, 123, 128, 173, 174, 187, 192, 228, 232, 235, 255, 276, 334, 349, 379, 382, 398, 519, 726, 786, 796, 862, 901
Attica State	Apollo Theatre, 17 December 1971	285, 379

Title	Source	Entry No.
Attica State	live, *The Mike Douglas Show*, 14–18 February 1972	144, 145, 146, 147
Attica State	Radio Hilversum, March 1972	235
Attica State	rehearsal with Elephant's Memory	285, 475, 671
Attica State	*David Frost Show*, 1972	173, 231 731, 854
Attica State	*Aquarius*, London Weekend Television	382, 834
AU	Filmore East, New York, original Lennon mix	269, 368, 834
Automatic Pier	unknown	330
Baby I Don't Care	*Plastic Ono Band* sessions, improvisation	321, 793
Baby I Don't Care	*Clock* rehearsals, St Regis Hotel, New York, September 1971	223, 244, 814, 840, 912
Baby Make Love To You	unknown take	249, 273, 274, 285, 481, 683, 893
Baby Please Don't Go	from medley during TV interview	024, 142, 143
Baby's Heartbeat	from *Life with the Lions*	867
Back off Boogaloo	One-to-One rehearsals, 18 August 1972	152, 353, 388, 776
Back Seat of My Car	ad lib	781
Beautiful Boy	*Double Fantasy* sessions, outtakes, Bermuda, June 1980	211
Beautiful Boy	*Double Fantasy* sessions, outtake, Bermuda, July 1980	069, 071, 165, 902
Beautiful Boy	*Double Fantasy* sessions, Record Plant, unknown outtake	007, 079, 091, 096, 097, 103, 184, 234, 371, 782
Beautiful Boy	*Double Fantasy* sessions, with Sean's goodnight	260, 261

Title	Source	Entry No.
Beautiful Boy	*Double Fantasy* sessions, Hit Factory, vocal booth, take 1	241, 371
Beautiful Boy	*Double Fantasy* sessions, Hit Factory, New York	283
Beautiful Boy	*Double Fantasy*, electric guitar demo, rhythm box, take 1	371
Beautiful Boy	*Double Fantasy*, electric guitar demo, rhythm box, take 2	371, 733
Beautiful Boy	*Double Fantasy*, electric guitar demo with hand claps	371, 904
Beautiful Boy	*Double Fantasy*, acoustic, take 1	390, 392, 503, 506
Beautiful Boy	*Double Fantasy* sessions, take 2 acoustic, drum machine	165, 240
Beautiful Boy	*Double Fantasy* sessions, acoustic with rhythm box	762
Beautiful Boy	*Double Fantasy* sessions, acoustic with bongo	435, 592, 789
Beautiful Boy	*Double Fantasy* sessions, electric guitar demo, rhythm box	371
Beautiful Boy	*Double Fantasy* sessions, vocal overdubs	242
Beautiful Boy	*Double Fantasy*, John teaching the session musicians	094
Beautiful Boy	*Double Fantasy* album, Bermuda, 1979	008, 111
Beautiful Boy	*Double Fantasy* album, unedited rough mix	032, 371, 409, 434, 540, 586, 771, 822
Beautiful Boy	*Double Fantasy* album, double-tracked guitar demo	084, 238
Beautiful Boy	*Double Fantasy* sessions, extended composing tape	090, 222, 240, 436, 593

Title	Source	Entry No.
Beautiful Boy	*Double Fantasy* sessions, with Cheap Trick	753, 754
Beautiful Boy	*Double Fantasy* sessions, medley with drum machine	091, 240, 384, 434, 590, 733
Beautiful Boy	*Double Fantasy* sessions, early acoustic, take	165, 264, 265, 791, 802
Beautiful Boy	*Double Fantasy* sessions, unknown takes and rehearsals	161, 165, 179, 192, 204, 233, 234, 237, 240, 242, 243, 252, 275, 279, 283, 335, 337, 348, 353, 371, 425, 437, 458, 474, 476, 500, 572, 595, 638, 668, 672, 720, 733, 736, 738, 739, 741, 799, 846, 847, 865, 869, 871, 876, 878
Beautiful Boy	5.1 centre channel mixes from *Lennon Legend* DVD	221, 363, 364
Beautiful Boy	*Double Fantasy* album, official release version	259, 365, 748
Beautiful Boys	*Double Fantasy* album, official release version	259
Be-Bop-A-Lula	*Rock 'n' Roll* album rehearsals	023, 060, 108, 109, 110, 157, 171, 219, 371, 470, 660, 770, 770, 814, 815, 816, 817, 819
Be-Bop-A-Lula	*Rock 'n' Roll* rehearsals, Morris Levy's farm, New York	245, 815
Be-Bop-A-Lula	from *Roots*	132, 133, 171, 217, 820
Be-Bop-A-Lula	official released version	061
Be-Bop-A-Lula	rehearsals, Hit Factory, New York August 1980	008, 017, 111, 153, 390, 503

Title	Source	Entry No.
Be-Bop-A-Lula	from promotional video, August 1980	203, 270
Be-Bop-A-Lula	offline rough mix – Lennon sessions	218
Be-Bop-A-Lula	unknown take	184, 250, 348, 353, 749, 898
Be-Bop-A-Lula	official release	365
Because	King Edward Hotel, Toronto, 25 May 1969	092
Beef Jerky	*Walls and Bridges* rehearsal, 13 July 1974	018, 137, 153, 309, 374, 833, 850, 883
Beef Jerky	*Walls and Bridges*, Record Plant East, July/August 1974	885, 914
Beef Jerky	from *Walls and Bridges* 8-track	093, 241, 883
Beef Jerky	*Walls and Bridges*, from quad mix	882
Beef Jerky	*Walls and Bridges* sessions, alternate takes and rehearsals	140, 176, 225, 277, 353, 735, 768, 780, 841, 843, 870, 877, 897, 898
Beef Jerky	*Walls and Bridges* album, official release version	818, 884
Be My Baby	from *Roots*	002, 003, 004, 005, 050, 060, 063, 066, 132, 133, 136, 149, 150, 153, 157, 217, 353, 817, 820
Be My Baby	*Rock 'n' Roll* outtake (long version)	157, 815
Be My Baby	*Rock 'n' Roll* album sessions, rough mix	086, 171, 218, 239, 429, 580, 887
Be My Baby	unknown take	373, 385, 407, 470, 536, 661, 770, 815, 817, 819, 843, 865, 871, 880, 881, 898, 899
Be My Baby	official release	365, 860

Title	Source	Entry No.
The Best Things in Life Are Free	Dakota recording, outtake	076, 236, 283, 350, 404, 530, 727
Beyond the Sea, medley	Dakota cassette recording	010, 186, 206, 235, 349, 398, 518
Billy and Sally	See Sally and Billy	
Bless You	*Walls and Bridges* rehearsal, 13 July 1974	018, 137, 374, 427, 575, 850, 883
Bless You	*Walls and Bridges* rehearsal, 21 July 1974	114, 309, 374, 833, 883
Bless You	*Walls and Bridges*, Record Plant East, July/August 1974	385, 914
Bless You	*Walls and Bridges* sessions, early rehearsal	240
Bless You	*Walls and Bridges* sessions, take 1	780
Bless You	*Walls and Bridges* sessions, take 3	780
Bless You	*Walls and Bridges* sessions, rehearsal – false start	225
Bless You	*Walls and Bridges*, monitor mix	768, 885, 914
Bless You	*Walls and Bridges*, from quad mix	882
Bless You	*Walls and Bridges*, unknown takes and rehearsals	085, 090, 176, 179, 225, 238, 353, 374, 436, 460, 473, 482, 594, 641, 667, 685, 733, 767, 841, 845, 872, 875, 897, 898, 902
Bless You	*Walls and Bridges* album, official release version	818, 884
Blue Danube Waltz	unknown	755
Blue Moon medley	Dakota cassette recording	010, 186, 206, 235, 285, 349, 398, 518

Title	Source	Entry No.
Blues Improvisation	from promotional video, August 1980	017, 203, 210
Blues in the Night	from promotional video, August 1980	017, 203
Bluesy Jam Session	Los Angeles, California, 1974	380, 859
Blue Suede Shoes	live, Toronto, 1969	175, 228, 276, 328, 334, 353, 383, 391, 420, 421, 459, 505, 562, 563, 640, 732, 786
Blue Suede Shoes	live, New York Hotel, 9 October 1971, John's thirty-first birthday	215, 244, 346, 370, 380, 727, 840, 864, 912
The Boat Song	piano demo	099, 243, 374, 387, 466, 653, 740, 861
Bony Moronie	from *Roots*	132, 133, 217, 820
Bony Moronie	*Rock 'n' Roll* album rehearsals	060, 063, 086, 218, 239, 353, 770, 815, 819, 872
Bony Moronie	rough mix, longer fade	171, 429, 579, 815, 903
Boogaloo at Thirty-Two	See I'm the Greatest	
Born in a Prison	One-to-One concert rehearsals	118, 120, 173, 776
Born in a Prison	One-to-One concert, afternoon show	774
Born in a Prison	One-to-One concert, evening show	774, 825
Borrowed Time	*Double Fantasy* album outtake, Bermuda, 1979	009, 085, 111, 238, 406, 534
Borrowed Time	*Double Fantasy* album, demo	022, 025, 165, 236, 427, 478, 496, 499, 575, 676, 713, 718, 789
Borrowed Time Long	long acoustic guitar version, Bermuda, 1980	015, 078, 191, 211, 902

Title	Source	Entry No.
Borrowed Time	*Double Fantasy* album, acoustic guitar overdub	032, 165
Borrowed Time	*Double Fantasy* album, alternate studio take	080, 237
Borrowed Time	*Double Fantasy* sessions, double-tracked acoustic demo	450, 622, 760, 761
Borrowed Time	*Double Fantasy* album, talk version	238
Borrowed Time	*Double Fantasy* sessions, Hit Factory, New York, rough mix	283
Borrowed Time	*Double Fantasy* sessions, discussion and riffs	285
Borrowed Time	*Double Fantasy* album, unknown takes and rehearsals	086, 097, 100, 185, 204, 216, 220, 243, 244, 249, 260, 261, 275, 279, 283, 335, 338, 353, 486, 488, 693, 697, 740, 741, 792, 835, 846, 847, 865, 870, 874, 875, 877, 887, 904
Borrowed Time	*Double Fantasy*, session tape	103
Borrowed Time	*Double Fantasy*, alternate mix	160
Borrowed Time	*Double Fantasy*, rough mix	165, 242, 277, 414, 450, 478, 622, 676
Borrowed Time	*Double Fantasy*, take 3, vocal booth	428, 577
Borrowed Time	5.1 centre channel mixes from *Lennon Legend* DVD	221, 363, 364
Borrowed Time	*Milk and Honey* album, official release version	259, 365
Boys and Girls	piano demo	285, 846

Title	Source	Entry No.
Bring It on Home to Me	live, New York Hotel, 9 October 1971, John's thirty-first birthday	215, 244, 346, 370, 380, 840, 864, 912
Bring It on Home to Me	from *Roots*	132, 133, 217, 820
Bring It on Home to Me	*Rock 'n' Roll* album rehearsals	023, 060, 108, 109, 110, 157, 171, 219, 250, 407, 536, 770, 815, 816, 819
Bring It on Home to Me	*Rock 'n' Roll* rehearsals, Morris Levy's Farm, New York	245, 815
Bring It on Home to Me	offline rough mix – Lennon sessions	218
Bring It on Home to Me	official released version	061
Bring on the Lucie	*Mind Games* album (Freeda People), unknown take	159, 162, 169, 220, 353, 377, 752, 756, 781, 849, 871, 911
Bring on the Lucie	*Mind Games* sessions (Freeda People), early rough mix	422, 565, 751, 756
Bring on the Lucie	*Mind Games* album (Freeda People), riff outtake	083, 238
Bring on the Lucie	*Mind Games* album (Freeda People), complete rough mix	083, 168, 238, 903
Bring on the Lucie	*Mind Games* sessions (Freeda People), acoustic guitar demo	168
Bring on the Lucie	*Mind Games* sessions (Freeda People), slide guitar	751
Bring on the Lucie	*Mind Games* album (Freeda People), from acetate	750
Bring out the Joints	live, New York Hotel, 9 October 1971, John's thirty-first birthday	215, 840, 864, 912
Brown Eyed Handsome Man medley	Dakota cassette recording	010, 072, 186, 206, 222, 226, 235, 285, 349, 368, 377, 398, 465, 518, 651
Bunny Hop	One-to-One concert, rehearsals	034

Title	Source	Entry No.
Call My Name	demos, outtakes (song evolved into 'Aisumasen')	087, 159, 168, 220, 239, 431, 583, 751, 756, 849, 911
The Calypso Song	*Eyewitness*, ABC TV, 5 August 1972	387, 834, 861
Cambridge	from *Life with the Lions*	867
Can't Believe You Wanna	home recording, Tittenhurst	909
Caribbean	unknown take	174, 826
Cathy's Clown	*Double Fantasy* sessions, early outtake	102, 210, 243, 387, 463, 648, 741
Chain Gang,	unknown	755
Chi-Chi's Café,	unknown take	237, 249, 329, 350, 387, 727, 861
Child of Nature	rehearsal (song evolved into 'Jealous Guy')	008, 019, 021, 111, 184, 242, 246, 290, 298, 303, 393, 495, 500, 509, 710, 721, 740, 749, 783, 784, 794, 832, 909
Chinese Laundry Blues	from 'Sea Ditty' medley, Dakota recording	395, 513
Chords of Fame	John with Phil Ochs, hotel room after John Sinclair rally	222, 226, 368, 387, 861
Christmas Message	1970	040, 909
Christmas Message	1980	772
Christmas Song	press conference, John and Yoko, Denmark, 1970	019
Circus Jam	*Rock and Roll Circus* rehearsal	014, 190
Clean-up Time	*Double Fantasy* sessions, piano demo, Dakota, 1979	013, 084, 165, 189, 238, 391, 505, 801, 903
Clean-up Time	*Double Fantasy* sessions, Record Plant outtcke	007, 008, 069, 071, 111, 234

Title	Source	Entry No.
Clean-up Time	*Double Fantasy* sessions, Hit Factory, New York	283
Clean-up Time	*Double Fantasy* sessions, rough mix of backing track	094, 264, 265
Clean-up Time	*Double Fantasy*, different mix	072, 091, 240, 733
Clean-up Time	*Double Fantasy* sessions, take 2, basic track	443, 607
Clean-up Time	*Double Fantasy* sessions, take 7	032, 241
Clean-up Time	*Double Fantasy* sessions, vocal overdubs	242, 285
Clean-up Time	*Double Fantasy* sessions, rough mix, reference vocal	384, 435, 592
Clean-up Time	*Double Fantasy* sessions, John directs studio musicians	240
Clean-up Time	*Double Fantasy*, unknown takes and rehearsals	075, 091, 097, 100, 184, 213, 234, 235, 236, 243, 252, 260, 261, 275, 277, 283, 348, 350, 353, 376, 377, 390, 398, 402, 425, 459, 473, 481, 485, 491, 503, 518, 526, 572, 639, 666, 682, 691, 703, 733, 736, 739, 740, 749, 799, 835, 846, 847, 870, 872, 873, 874, 877
Clean-up Time	*Double Fantasy* rehearsal, no backing vocal	165, 434, 589
Clean-up Time	*Double Fantasy*, unedited mix	165
Clean-up Time	*Double Fantasy* album, official release version	259, 748
C'mon Everybody	*Rock 'n' Roll* session	034, 157, 171, 219, 278, 348, 353, 770, 816, 817

Title	Source	Entry No.
C'mon Everybody	*Rock 'n' Roll* rehearsals, Morris Levy's Farm, New York	815
C'mon Everybody	from promotional video, August 1980	017, 153, 203, 270, 278
C'mon Everybody	unknown take	732, 755, 898
Cold Turkey	home demo	013, 074, 128, 189, 192, 796
Cold Turkey	Abbey Road Studios, 25 and 28 September 1969	842
Cold Turkey	acoustic demo, take 1	085, 222, 238, 427, 451, 575, 623, 843
Cold Turkey	acoustic demo, take 3	088, 239, 432, 585
Cold Turkey	acoustic guitar demo, unknown take	172, 232, 277, 464, 649, 779, 792
Cold Turkey	from acetate	075, 160, 162, 235, 771
Cold Turkey	electric rehearsal	222
Cold Turkey	rough mix	172
Cold Turkey	alternate vocals, early mix for acetate	169
Cold Turkey	alternate take	128, 796
Cold Turkey	US single version	182
Cold Turkey	unknown takes, demos and rehearsals	179, 182, 226, 235, 279, 336, 338, 351, 353, 402, 500, 526, 720, 727, 730, 749, 773, 783, 784, 788, 790, 832, 843, 848, 878
Cold Turkey	live, Toronto, 1969	175, 228, 276, 328, 334, 353, 383, 391, 420, 451, 459, 505, 562, 623, 640, 732, 786, 801
Cold Turkey	UNICEF concert	414, 550

Title	Source	Entry No.
Cold Turkey	One-to-One concert, 30 August 1972 (afternoon show)	774
Cold Turkey	One-to-One concert, 30 August 1972 (evening show)	005, 024, 041, 049, 068, 121, 124, 126, 136, 142, 143, 224, 402, 526, 774, 825
Cold Turkey	One-to-One concert rehearsals	119, 120, 152, 172, 173, 775, 777, 896
Cold Turkey	5.1 centre channel mixes from *Lennon Legend* DVD	221, 363, 364
Cold Turkey	official release	365, 748
Come Together	One-to-One concert rehearsals	092, 098, 118, 120, 152, 222, 227, 240, 242, 382, 388, 400, 430, 523, 581, 740, 760, 761, 775, 776, 777, 826, 896
Come Together (Instr.)	One-to-One rehearsals, 18 August 1972	152
Come Together	One-to-One concert, 30 August 1972 (afternoon show)	126, 167, 774
Come Together	One-to-One concert, 30 August 1972 (evening show)	005, 024, 040, 041, 049, 050, 054, 068, 121, 122, 123, 124, 142, 143, 154, 224, 227, 228, 276, 353, 416, 430, 553, 581, 725, 731, 758, 773, 774, 825, 899
Come Together	unknown take	179, 222, 226, 279, 353, 378, 734, 788, 873, 879
Cookin' (in the Kitchen of Love)	demo – piano, take 1	247, 430, 581, 742

Title	Source	Entry No.
Cookin' (in the Kitchen of Love)	demo – piano, take 8	247
Cookin' (in the Kitchen of Love)	demo – piano, unknown take	010, 071, 087, 089, 186, 205, 234, 239, 240, 247, 349, 397, 434, 516, 589, 791, 792, 822
Cookin' (in the Kitchen of Love)	unknown take	337, 338, 377, 856, 893
Corrina Corrina	home demo, Dakota, 1979	014, 076, 161, 179, 190, 210, 216, 236, 283, 325, 335, 404, 530, 723, 727, 789, 822, 845, 869, 902
Crippled Inside	*Imagine* album sessions, Tittenhurst	405, 532
Crippled Inside	*Imagine* album sessions, unknown outtake	015, 043, 078, 128, 162, 191, 216, 236, 288, 292, 302, 307, 325, 351, 429, 579, 749, 796, 821, 844, 858, 864, 873, 877
Crippled Inside	*Imagine* album sessions, take 2	166, 290, 294, 295, 298, 353
Crippled Inside	*Imagine* album sessions, take 17	166, 290, 295, 298, 353
Crippled Inside	*Imagine* album sessions, rough mix	291
Crippled Inside	*Imagine* album sessions, rough mix	291
Crippled Inside	*Imagine* album sessions, from acetate	288, 293
Crippled Inside	*Imagine* album, quad mix	294, 296, 302, 304
Crippled Inside	Imagine 5.1 surround mixes, centre channel	304

Title	Source	Entry No.
Crippled Inside	Imagine 5.1 surround mixes, front channels	304
Crippled Inside	Imagine 5.1 surround mixes, rear channels	304
Crippled Inside	from *Imagine – The Film*	301
Crippled Inside	live, New York hotel, 9 October 1971, John's thirty-first birthday	215, 244, 346, 370, 380, 437, 595, 840, 912
Crying	unknown take	865
Cupid	Los Angeles, California 1974	380, 755, 859
Dakota Mind	Movie Mystery Theatre home recording	500, 721
Dakota Rap	*Double Fantasy* sessions, Medley with drum machine	091, 222, 240, 249, 384, 434, 590, 733
Dance for the Chicken	live, New York Hotel, 9 October 1971, John's thirty-first birthday	244, 380
Day Tripper	*Top Gear*, October 1967, with Jimi Hendrix (unconfirmed)	026, 027, 037, 038, 049, 141, 154, 251, 280, 881, 899
Dear John	demo, 1980	010, 071, 179, 186, 192, 196, 213, 216, 233, 234, 249, 273, 274, 474, 498, 668, 716, 797, 845, 856, 881
Dear John	*Double Fantasy*, acoustic with rhythm box	371, 396, 515, 837
Dear John	unknown take	893
Dear Yoko	*Double Fantasy* sessions, unknown takes and demos,	007, 075, 081, 091, 100, 165, 210, 222, 226, 235, 237, 240, 243, 260, 261, 275, 283, 285, 335, 350, 353, 376, 385, 416, 458, 472, 483, 486, 553, 637, 664, 686, 692, 727, 733, 740, 741, 781, 783, 784, 797, 845, 847, 865, 870, 871, 878, 880, 890

Title	Source	Entry No.
Dear Yoko	*Double Fantasy* sessions, demo, take 1	313
Dear Yoko	*Double Fantasy* sessions, demo, take 2	313, 902
Dear Yoko	*Double Fantasy* sessions, early rough mix	264, 265, 472, 664
Dear Yoko	*Double Fantasy* album, official release version	259, 748
Dear Yoko	*Double Fantasy* sessions, Bermuda, 1979	012, 161, 188, 869
Dear Yoko	*Double Fantasy* sessions, Bermuda, 1979	012, 161, 188, 869
Dear Yoko	*Double Fantasy* sessions, Bermuda June 1980	211, 401, 524
Dear Yoko	*Double Fantasy* rehearsal, mono	032
Dear Yoko	*Double Fantasy* sessions, acoustic, take 1, breakdown	155, 281, 285, 789, 890
Dear Yoko	*Double Fantasy* sessions, take 2	035, 238, 281, 285, 472, 575, 789, 890
Dear Yoko	*Double Fantasy*, acoustic guitar demo with overdubs	890
Dear Yoko	*Double Fantasy* sessions, take 3	085, 238, 281, 472, 575
Dear Yoko	*Double Fantasy*, composing run through	102
Dear Yoko	*Double Fantasy*, rough mix with studio chat and riffs	277, 434, 589, 822
Dear Yoko	*Double Fantasy*, vocal booth	165, 348
Dear Yoko	Coldspring Harbour video, acoustic guitar demo, take 1	890
Dear Yoko	Coldspring Harbour video, acoustic guitar demo, take 2	890

Title	Source	Entry No.
Dear Yoko	*Double Fantasy* sessions, Hit Factory, additional overdubs	283
Dear Yoko	*Double Fantasy*, incomplete take, John breaks guitar string	243
Dear Yoko	*Double Fantasy* sessions, unfinished rough take	256
Deep Water	*Imagine* album sessions	325
Dirty Mac Jam	*Rock and Roll Circus* rehearsal	076, 236, 328, 722
Dizzy Miss Lizzie	live, Toronto, 1969	175, 228, 276, 328, 334, 353, 383, 420, 459, 640, 562, 732, 786
John's 'Bigger Than Jesus' remark	Documentary	214
Documentary	BBC Radio 2, December 1999	360, 361, 362
Dog Town	guitar version	107
Dog Town	piano version	107
Dog Town	unknown take	231
Don't Be Afraid	demo, Bermuda, 1980	204, 212, 249, 904
Don't Be Crazy	home demo, unreleased song, Dakota, 1979	012, 073, 093, 165, 188, 235, 241, 249, 253, 271, 273, 274, 283, 350, 401, 449, 481, 500, 524, 619, 683, 720, 735
Don't Be Cruel	recorded during *Plastic Ono Band* sessions	074, 235, 262, 286, 287, 401, 415, 485, 525, 552, 690, 785, 793, 820, 848, 875, 887, 910
Don't Be Cruel	recorded during *Some Time in New York City* rehearsals	232, 411, 544, 893
Don't Be Cruel	*Clock* rehearsals, St Regis Hotel, New York, September 1971	814

Title	Source	Entry No.
Don't Be Cruel	One-to-One concert rehearsals, with Elephant's Memory	080, 167, 192, 237, 241, 775, 826
Don't Be Cruel	unknown take	095, 174, 351, 353, 737, 842, 878
Don't Be Scared	*Double Fantasy*, unknown take	260, 261
Don't Be Scared	*Milk and Honey* album, official release version	259
Don't Worry Kyoko	live, Toronto, 1969	175, 328, 383, 732
Don't Worry Kyoko	Queen Charlotte Hospital	867
Don't Worry Kyoko	One-to-One concert rehearsals	119, 120, 173
Don't Worry Kyoko	One-to-One concert, 30 August 1972 (afternoon show)	774
Don't Worry Kyoko	extended version	810
Don't Worry Kyoko	official release	016, 064, 889
Don't Worry Kyoko	7" Apple Acetate	160
Don't Worry Kyoko	unknown take	842
Do the Oz	from Apple 1835, June 1971	051, 066, 107, 149, 150, 154, 231, 291, 352, 353, 373, 843, 860, 876, 881, 899
Down in Cuba with Julio Juanita,	tongue in cheek calypso send up	015, 078, 191, 236, 329, 350, 387, 727
Down in The Caribbean	unknown	742
Do You Want to Dance	from *Roots*	132, 133, 171, 217, 820
Do You Want to Dance	*Rock 'n' Roll* album rehearsals	023, 060, 096, 108, 109, 110, 157, 219, 250, 407, 536, 738, 770, 815, 816, 819
Do You Want to Dance	*Rock 'n' Roll* rehearsals, Morris Levy's Farm, New York	245, 815

Title	Source	Entry No.
Do You Want to Dance	*Rock 'n' Roll* rehearsals (false start), Morris Levy's Farm, New York	815
Do You Want to Dance	monitor mix	241
Do You Want to Dance	offline rough mix – Lennon sessions	218
Do You Want to Dance	official released version	061
Dream Lover	from promotional film, August 1980	017, 030, 097, 153, 179, 203, 242, 270, 283, 348, 353, 739, 817, 876, 898
Duane Eddy Jam	*Clock* rehearsals, St Regis Hotel, New York, September 1971	088, 239, 431, 584, 729
Earth News Radio	January 1976	247
Eat the Document	from the film, with Bob Dylan	024, 065, 076, 142, 143, 224, 236, 350, 722, 749
Emotional Wreck	early version of *Watching the Wheels*, piano	165, 204, 387, 861
Everglade Woman Elephant's Memory Band,	10" Metformedia Acetate	160
Everybody	piano and drum machine, 1975–6	101, 205, 243, 247, 387, 491, 703, 741, 861
Everybody's Talking Nobody's Talking	*Double Fantasy* sessions, demo, take 1	271
Everybody's Talking Nobody's Talking	*Double Fantasy* sessions, demo with overdubs	272
Everybody's Talking Nobody's Talking	*Double Fantasy* sessions, piano with rhythm box	411, 544, 762
Everybody's Talking Nobody's Talking	*Double Fantasy* sessions, unknown take	079, 179, 237, 283, 846
Every Man Has a Woman Who Loves Him	*Double Fantasy* sessions, vocal booth	322

Title	Source	Entry No.
Every Man Has a Woman Who Loves Him	*Double Fantasy* sessions, multi-track mix down	322
Every Man Has a Woman Who Loves Him	Hit Factory, 1980, duet with Yoko	009, 070, 111, 185, 234, 250, 261
Every Man Has a Woman Who Loves Him	John solo version	231
Every Man Has a Woman Who Loves Him	Yoko vocal	281, 459, 639
Every Man Has a Woman Who Loves Him	unknown take	373, 394, 452, 483, 510, 625, 687, 749, 759, 878, 881
Every Man Has a Woman Who Loves Him	*Double Fantasy* album, official release version	259, 281, 365
Everson Museum	press conference	167
Face It	unknown take (probably 'I Don't Want to Face It')	387, 861
Falling in Love Again	*Double Fantasy* sessions, acoustic demo	102, 206, 243, 387, 741, 861
Fame,	with David Bowie	755, 759
The Fat Budgie,	John reading from *A Spaniard in the Works*	330
Feeling,	unknown take	107
A Fool Was I,	probably not John Lennon,	023, 278
Fools Like Me	*Eyewitness*, ABC TV, 5 August 1972	834
Forgive Me (My Little Flower Princess),	early take	165
Forgive Me (My Little Flower Princess)	acoustic guitar demo, take 2	890, 903
Forgive Me (My Little Flower Princess)	multi-track, take 2	890

Title	Source	Entry No.
Forgive Me (My Little Flower Princess)	Dakota demo, take 3	083, 238, 281, 424, 569
Forgive Me (My Little Flower Princess)	*Double Fantasy* sessions, Hit Factory, New York	283, 887
Forgive Me (My Little Flower Princess)	alternate take	084, 238, 260, 261, 353, 376, 424, 570, 846, 847, 865, 870
Forgive Me (My Little Flower Princess)	Bermuda, July 1980	212
Forgive Me (My Little Flower Princess)	*Milk and Honey* album, official release version	259
Frank Cummings	poem	051, 352
Free as a Bird	piano demo	087, 096, 233, 239, 794, 887
Free as a Bird	take 1	177, 272, 273, 274, 430, 455, 581, 631, 742, 797, 798
Free as a Bird	take 2	177
Free as a Bird	take 3	241, 272, 273, 274, 797, 798
Free as a Bird	unknown takes and demos	179, 205, 230, 249, 498, 716, 738, 749, 798, 846, 856, 893
Free The People, see *Bring on the Lucie (Freeda People)*		
French Medley	demo	466, 653
The General Erection, see *We Must Not Forget The General Erection*		
Get Back	unknown take	206, 285

Title	Source	Entry No.
Get It Together Peace Message,	acoustic guitar rendition, Montreal, 1969	095, 241, 387, 737, 861
Girls and Boys	home demo, Dakota	008, 069, 111, 161, 204, 481, 683, 797, 802, 869
Girls and Boys	Bermuda, June 1980	211
Girls and Boys	unknown take	234, 252, 728, 749, 783, 784, 797
Give Me Something	*Double Fantasy* album, official release version	259
Give Me Some Truth	outtake, Tittenhurst	237, 306
Give Me Some Truth	*Imagine* album sessions, take 1	353
Give Me Some Truth	*Imagine* album sessions, rough mix	291, 294, 442, 605
Give Me Some Truth	rough mix with count-in	429, 579, 822
Give Me Some Truth	*Imagine* album sessions, unknown outtake	043, 082, 162, 166, 184, 222, 288, 290, 292, 295, 298, 303, 307, 325, 417, 455, 462, 474, 555, 631, 645, 668, 749, 782, 821, 858, 871
Give Me Some Truth	*Imagine* album sessions, from acetate	289, 293
Give Me Some Truth	*Imagine* album, quad mix	294, 296, 302, 305
Give Me Some Truth	Imagine 5.1 surround mix, centre channel	304
Give Me Some Truth	Imagine 5.1 surround mix, front channels	304
Give Me Some Truth	Imagine 5.1 surround mix, rear channels	304
Give Me Some Truth	from *Imagine – The Film*	301
Give Peace a Chance	rehearsal, Montreal, 1969	065, 172, 231, 240

Title	Source	Entry No.
Give Peace a Chance	King Edward Hotel, Toronto, 25 May 1969, rehearsals	092, 240
Give Peace a Chance	Queen Elizabeth Hotel, Montreal, 1 June 1969	842
Give Peace a Chance	live, Toronto, 1969	175, 228, 276, 328, 334, 383, 420, 562, 732, 786, 801
Give Peace a Chance	Apple 1809, Montreal, 1 June 1969	066, 149, 150
Give Peace a Chance	documentary soundtrack	240
Give Peace a Chance	Peace Choir version	473, 666
Give Peace a Chance	live, New York hotel, 9 October 1971, John's thirty-first birthday	215, 244, 346, 370, 380, 727, 840, 864, 912
Give Peace a Chance	One-to-One concert, 30 August 1972 (afternoon show)	126
Give Peace a Chance	One-to-One concert, 30 August 1972 (evening show)	002, 003, 005, 026, 027, 040, 041, 054, 068, 121, 122, 123, 124, 154, 169, 227, 353, 726, 758, 774, 825, 899, 902
Give Peace a Chance	One-to-One concert, 30 August 1972 (finale)	852
Give Peace a Chance	One-to-One concert rehearsals	117, 119, 120, 156, 382, 388, 400, 522, 727, 776, 777, 896
Give Peace a Chance	One-to-One rehearsals, 18 August 1972	152
Give Peace a Chance	*Jerry Lewis Telethon*	753, 754, 854
Give Peace a Chance	Holland	026, 027, 251
Give Peace a Chance	acoustic, John and Yoko, unknown take	029, 169, 172, 173, 192, 222, 264, 265, 439, 599

Title	Source	Entry No.
Give Peace a Chance	unknown take	226, 232, 240, 251, 279, 336, 353, 373, 377, 378, 437, 438, 596, 597, 734, 771, 781, 790, 862
Give Peace a Chance	official release	106, 365, 748, 851, 860
Give Peace a Chance	5.1 centre channel mixes from *Lennon Legend* DVD	221, 363, 364
Glad All Over	*Plastic Ono Band* album sessions	262, 286, 785, 793, 910, 842, 875
Glad All Over	*Clock* rehearsals, St Regis Hotel, New York, September 1971	088, 223, 239, 244, 384, 431, 584, 729, 814, 840, 912
God	*Plastic Ono Band* album sessions, California, summer 1970	785, 910
God	*Plastic Ono Band* album, demo, acoustic version	069, 092, 167, 192, 237, 240, 277, 286, 321, 391, 462, 590, 645, 749, 795, 796, 800
God	*Plastic Ono Band* album sessions, demo, take 1	433, 588
God	*Plastic Ono Band* album sessions, acoustic demo, take 2	414, 440, 550, 602, 760, 761, 792
God	*Plastic Ono Band* album, acoustic with false start	170
God	*Plastic Ono Band* album, demo (take unknown)	008, 080, 089, 111, 170, 179, 184, 222, 232, 234, 239, 252, 262, 287
God	*Plastic Ono Band* album sessions, unknown take	336, 338, 377, 387, 468, 475, 500, 657, 670, 720, 725, 728, 734, 749, 785, 790, 793, 836, 842, 843, 843, 861, 910

Title	Source	Entry No.
God	home demo, Tittenhurst Park	161, 321, 869
God	demo fragment	128
God	*Plastic Ono Band*, official version	340, 365
God	*Plastic Ono Band*, 5.1 mix	341
God Save the Queen	live, Hotel Syracuse, 9 October 1971, John's thirty-first birthday	840, 864, 912
God Save Us	home demo, June 1971	005, 112, 026, 027, 030, 033, 051, 069, 073, 076, 128, 182, 188, 192, 232, 234, 235, 236, 251, 252, 253, 264, 265, 277, 291, 335, 351, 352, 353, 400, 484, 522, 689, 726, 778, 779, 796, 843, 876, 881, 911
God Save Us	acoustic with congas	789
God Save Us	studio demo from acetate	128, 162, 400, 522, 796
God Save Us	Morgan Studios	012, 188
God Save Us	reference vocals 1 and 2	778
God Save Us	promo ad.	778
God Save Us	official release	121, 778
Going Down on Love	*Walls and Bridges* rehearsal, 13 July 1974	018, 137, 153, 309, 374, 429, 580, 833, 850, 883
Going Down on Love	*Walls and Bridges* rehearsal, 21 July 1974	114, 374, 883
Going Down on Love	*Walls and Bridges* sessions, piano	913
Going Down on Love	*Walls and Bridges* sessions, acoustic, take 1	913
Going Down on Love	*Walls and Bridges* sessions, acoustic, take 2	913

Title	Source	Entry No.
Going Down on Love	*Walls and Bridges* sessions, acoustic, take 3	913
Going Down on Love	*Walls and Bridges*, Record Plant East, July/August 1974	885, 914
Going Down on Love	*Walls and Bridges* sessions, monitor mix	758, 885, 914
Going Down on Love	*Walls and Bridges*, from quad mix	882
Going Down on Love	*Walls and Bridges*, 8-track mix	883
Going Down on Love	*Walls and Bridges* sessions, unknown takes and rehearsals	096, 140, 225, 241, 277, 285, 353, 374, 460, 641, 733, 738, 767, 768, 780, 841, 843, 870, 879, 897, 898
Going Down on Love	*Walls and Bridges*, official release version	818, 884
Gone from This Place	Dakota recording, unknown take	080, 176, 213, 237, 249, 273, 274, 277, 353, 414, 498, 515, 716, 730, 742, 797, 856, 865
Gone from This Place	acoustic guitar demo, take 1	442, 605, 890
Gone from This Place	acoustic guitar demo, take 2	890
Gone from This Place	acoustic guitar demo, take 4	428, 577, 890
Gone from This Place	Dakota recording, take 4	085, 238, 887
Good Dog Nigel	John reading from *In His Own Write*	330
Good Night	from *Wedding Album*	860
Goodnight Irene	live, New York hotel, 9 October 1971, John's thirty-first birthday	215, 244, 346, 370, 380, 387, 435, 592, 840, 861, 864, 912
Goodnight, Vienna	demo for *Ringo*, Record Plant West, June 1974	009, 030, 034, 051, 069, 111, 140, 780
Goodnight, Vienna	studio outtake	162, 179

Title	Source	Entry No.
Goodnight, Vienna	rough mix	176
Goodnight, Vienna	radio spot	024, 030, 142, 143, 224
Goodnight, Vienna	unknown take	185, 234, 252, 278, 352, 353, 374, 492, 704, 753, 754, 755, 843, 881
Grapefruit Excerpts	John and Yoko read from Yoko's book	. 082, 237, 350, 418, 582, 557, 685, 837, 911
The Great WOK	Dakota, 1979, spoken word	081, 206, 237, 256, 283, 285, 350, 484, 500, 688, 720
Greenfield Morning Yoko Ono,	unknown take	175, 272, 785, 910
Grow Old with Me	demo, piano and drum machine, Dakota,	009, 070, 111, 165, 185, 234, 249, 273, 274, 349, 371, 394, 483, 498, 510, 687, 716, 782, 797, 798, 893
Grow Old with Me	double-tracked vocal	797
Grow Old with Me	Bermuda, July 1980	212
Grow Old with Me	*Milk and Honey* album, official release version	259, 365
Guitar Jam	*Rock 'n' Roll* album sessions	023, 770, 815
Happiness Is a Warm Gun	King Edward Hotel, Toronto, 25 May 1969	092
Happy Birthday To John	live, New York hotel, 9 October 1971, John's thirty-first birthday	079, 192, 215, 236, 244, 346, 840, 864, 912
Happy Christmas	unknown take	095, 116
Happy Girl	*Mind Games* sessions, Yoko outtake	098, 242, 482, 685, 740, 909

Title	Source	Entry No.
The Happy Rishikesh Song	home acoustic demo, Dakota, 1980	008, 069, 111, 161, 184, 212, 216, 234, 249, 252, 392, 474, 507, 668, 728, 869, 887, 911
Happy Xmas (War Is Over)	original demo	080, 237, 414, 551, 779
Happy Xmas (War Is Over)	studio outtake	162, 169, 179, 182, 192, 229, 232, 250, 279, 336, 353, 373, 414, 455, 467, 550, 631, 655, 730, 737, 773, 782, 790, 873
Happy Xmas (War Is Over)	*Imagine* album rehearsal, Tittenhurst Park, 1970	246
Happy Xmas (War Is Over)	acoustic guitar demo, John – solo vocal	172, 822
Happy Xmas (War Is Over)	early rough mix, no strings	771
Happy Xmas (War Is Over)	different mix	241
Happy Xmas (War Is Over)	rough mix	172, 264, 265
Happy Xmas (War Is Over)	Apple 1842	066, 149, 150
Happy Xmas (War Is Over)	5.1 centre channel mix from *Lennon Legend* DVD	221, 363, 364
Happy Xmas (War Is Over)	official release version	365, 748, 860
Hard Times Are Over	*Double Fantasy*, unknown take	260, 261, 281, 459, 483, 639, 687
Hard Times Are Over	*Double Fantasy* sessions, backing vocals	281

Title	Source	Entry No.
Hard Times Are Over	*Double Fantasy*, choir overdub, multi-track mix down	322
Hard Times Are Over	*Double Fantasy* album, official release version	259
Hava Nagila	Amsterdam Hilton, March 1969	034, 051, 368
Heartbeat	*Clock* rehearsals, St Regis Hotel, New York, September 1971	014, 076, 128, 190, 223, 236, 244, 403, 529, 722, 796, 814, 840, 912
Help!	home recording, Dakota, John piano	009, 071, 111, 128, 185, 234, 246, 349, 395, 512, 723, 749, 796, 909
Help Me to Help Myself	piano demo, take 2	285
Help Me to Help Myself	piano demo, take 3	285
Help Me to Help Myself	piano demo, unknown take	466, 481, 500, 653, 683, 720, 890
Help Me to Help Myself	guitar demo	285, 481, 683
Help Me to Help Myself	unknown take	213, 249, 273, 274, 749, 893
Here We Go Again	studio demo, 1973	013, 069, 140, 189, 196, 402, 526
Here We Go Again	acoustic guitar demo	168, 171, 264, 265, 756, 779, 789
Here We Go Again	demo, take 2	074, 088, 235
Here We Go Again	*Mind Games* sessions, unknown take	159, 234, 252, 770, 815, 819
Here We Go Again	from *Menlove Avenue* album	402, 526
Here We Go Again	unknown take	335, 755, 837, 849
He Got the Blues	Lennon original, late 1970s	239, 431, 584, 742, 911
He's Got the Whole World in His Hands	live, New York Hotel, 9 October 1971, John's thirty-first birthday	215, 244, 346, 370, 380, 781, 840, 812, 864

Title	Source	Entry No.
Hold On	*Plastic Ono Band* album sessions, take 1	321
Hold On	*Plastic Ono Band* album sessions, take 2	321
Hold On	*Plastic Ono Band* album sessions, take 3	321
Hold On	*Plastic Ono Band* album sessions, take 4	321
Hold On	*Plastic Ono Band* album sessions, take 5	321
Hold On	*Plastic Ono Band* album sessions, take 5	321
Hold On	*Plastic Ono Band* album sessions, take 30	321
Hold On	*Plastic Ono Band* album sessions, up tempo version	321
Hold On	*Plastic Ono Band* album sessions, instrumental take	321, 793
Hold On	*Plastic Ono Band* album sessions, unknown take	321, 474, 668, 785, 793, 836, 842, 910
Hold On	*Plastic Ono Band*, official version	340
Hold On	*Plastic Ono Band*, 5.1 mix	341
Hold On	ad lib during interview, broadcast 27 March 1971	355
Honey Don't	recorded during *Plastic Ono Band* sessions	074, 167, 235, 286, 401, 415, 485, 525, 552, 690, 773, 785, 793, 820, 842, 843, 848, 875, 887, 910
Honey Don't	*Sometime in New York City* sessions	893

Title	Source	Entry No.
Honey Don't	*Clock* rehearsals, St Regis Hotel, New York, September 1971	088, 223, 239, 244, 384, 431, 584, 729, 814, 840, 912
Honey Don't	rehearsal with Elephant's Memory	826
Honey Don't	unknown take	174, 179, 287, 351, 353, 879
Honey Hush	unknown take	174, 826
Honky Tonk Blues	One-to-One rehearsals with Elephant's Memory	092, 174, 227, 240, 734, 814, 826
Hound Dog	One-to-One rehearsals with Elephant's Memory	080, 192, 237, 241, 368, 416, 554, 775, 826
Hound Dog	rehearsal, 22 August 1972	222
Hound Dog	One-to-One concert, 30 August 1972 (afternoon show)	774
Hound Dog	One-to-One concert, 30 August 1972 (evening show)	024, 041, 042, 049, 068, 124, 126, 142, 143, 224, 421, 563, 774, 825
Hound Dog	*Plastic Ono Band* album sessions	262, 286, 785, 793, 842, 875, 910
Hound Dog	*Clock* rehearsals, St Regis Hotel, New York, September 1971	814
Hound Dog	recorded during *Some Time in New York City* rehearsals	233
Hound Dog	unknown take	095, 353, 737, 788, 876, 878
House of the Rising Sun	unknown	794
How?	*Imagine* album, demo, unknown take	081, 495, 710
How?	*Imagine* album rehearsal, Tittenhurst Park, 1970	246, 417, 556, 909

Title	Source	Entry No.
How?	*Imagine* album, piano demo	089, 239, 290, 294, 298, 433, 588, 760, 761
How?	*Imagine* album sessions, rough mix with acoustic guitar	291
How?	*Imagine* album sessions, vocal overdub	294, 295
How?	*Imagine* album sessions, from acetate	289, 293
How?	*Imagine* album, quad mix	294, 296, 302, 305
How?	Imagine 5.1 surround mix, centre channel	304
How?	Imagine 5.1 surround mix, front channels	304
How?	Imagine 5.1 surround mix, rear channels	304
How?	*Imagine* album, unknown outtake	043, 079, 082, 216, 222, 236, 237, 256, 288, 290, 292, 295, 297, 298, 300, 303, 307, 325, 353, 409, 410, 442, 540, 542, 605, 749, 773, 782, 792, 821, 844, 858, 873, 874, 877, 878
How?	*Imagine* album sessions, take 2	295
How?	*Imagine* album sessions, take 12, no overdubs	166, 290, 295, 298
How?	*Imagine* album sessions, alternate take 1	295
How?	*Imagine* album sessions, alternate take 2	295, 417, 556
How?	from *Imagine – The Film*	301

Title	Source	Entry No.
How?	from medley	242, 290, 740
How?	*Imagine* album, official release version	365
How Do You Sleep?	home studio outtake, Ascot, 1971	009, 111, 185, 306, 395, 425, 512, 572, 762
How Do You Sleep?	*Imagine* album sessions, rehearsal, take 1	295
How Do You Sleep?	*Imagine* album sessions, rehearsal, take 2	295
How Do You Sleep?	*Imagine* album sessions, rehearsal, take 3	295
How Do You Sleep?	*Imagine* album sessions, rehearsal, take 4	295
How Do You Sleep?	*Imagine* album sessions, unknown rehearsal	290, 291, 294, 434, 450, 490, 590, 621, 700
How Do You Sleep	*Imagine* album sessions, vocal overdub	294, 295
How Do You Sleep?	*Imagine* album, unknown outtake	043, 070, 082, 083, 086, 098, 101, 128, 182, 192, 216, 222, 232, 234, 237, 238, 239, 242, 243, 288, 290, 291, 292, 295, 297, 298, 299, 303, 307, 325, 351, 353, 415, 417, 442, 469, 500, 552, 556, 605, 658, 720, 728, 740, 741, 749, 796, 799, 821, 836, 843, 844, 848, 870, 871, 872, 874, 875, 877, 878, 887
How Do You Sleep?	*Imagine* album sessions, take 2	166, 295, 384
How Do You Sleep?	*Imagine* album sessions, version 2	295

Title	Source	Entry No.
How Do You Sleep?	*Imagine* album sessions, version 3	295
How Do You Sleep?	*Imagine* album, 'low octave' version	089, 239, 297, 299
How Do You Sleep?	*Imagine* album, obscene lyrics version	749
How Do You Sleep?	*Imagine* album sessions, instrumental jam	295
How Do You Sleep?	*Imagine* album sessions, rough mix	428, 578, 822
How Do You Sleep?	*Imagine* album, from acetate	162, 289, 293, 295
How Do You Sleep?	*Imagine* album, quad mix	294, 296, 302, 305
How Do You Sleep	from *Imagine – The Film*	301
How I Won the War	from 45 rpm single	167, 881
Howling at the Moon	*Double Fantasy* sessions, unknown take	079, 165, 237, 240, 387, 742, 749, 861
Howling at the Moon	home demo, Dakota, 1980	161, 283, 413, 548, 846, 869, 890
Howling at the Moon	*Double Fantasy* sessions, medley with drum machine	091, 384, 434, 590, 733
I Ain't Got The Time	unknown, probably home recording	430, 582, 742, 911
I Am the Walrus	*Double Fantasy* sessions, brief parody	100, 165, 243, 283, 353, 740, 794, 874
I Do Like To Be Beside The Seaside from Sea Ditty	medley, Dakota recording	349, 395, 513
I Don't Want to Be a Soldier, Mama (I Don't Want To Die)	*Imagine* session, Tittenhurst	306, 887

Title	Source	Entry No.
I Don't Want to Be a Soldier, Mama (I Don't Want To Die)	*Imagine* album sessions, take 1	166, 290, 294, 295, 298, 353, 425, 571
I Don't Want to Be a Soldier, Mama (I Don't Want To Die)	*Imagine* album sessions, take 2	290, 295, 298, 353
I Don't Want to Be a Soldier, Mama (I Don't Want To Die)	*Imagine* album, King Curtis sax overdub sessions	242, 290, 295, 297, 298, 300
I Don't Want to Be a Soldier, Mama (I Don't Want To Die)	*Imagine* album sessions, from acetate	289, 293
I Don't Want to Be a Soldier, Mama (I Don't Want To Die)	*Imagine* album, overdub sessions	444, 495, 610, 710
I Don't Want to Be a Soldier, Mama (I Don't Want To Die)	*Imagine* album, quad mix	294, 296, 302
I Don't Want to Be a Soldier, Mama (I Don't Want To Die)	Imagine 5.1 surround mix, centre channel	304
I Don't Want to Be a Soldier, Mama (I Don't Want To Die)	Imagine 5.1 surround mix, front channels	304
I Don't Want to Be a Soldier, Mama (I Don't Want To Die)	Imagine 5,1 surround mix, rear channels	304
I Don't Want to Be a Soldier, Mama (I Don't Want To Die)	*Imagine* album, unknown take	083, 098, 162, 179, 192, 232, 238, 290, 291, 295, 298, 303, 307, 325, 473, 667, 740, 773, 845, 848, 858, 870, 874, 878, 879

Title	Source	Entry No.
I Don't Want to Be a Soldier, Mama (I Don't Want To Die)	from *Imagine – The Film*	301
I Don't Want to Be a Soldier, Mama (I Don't Want To Die)	two-sided Bell Acetate	160
I Don't Want to Face It	*Double Fantasy* sessions, acoustic demo, take 1	091, 432, 586
I Don't Want to Face It	*Double Fantasy* sessions, acoustic demo, take 2	165
I Don't Want to Face It	*Double Fantasy* sessions, early guitar demo	241
I Don't Want to Face It	*Double Fantasy* sessions, double-tracked demo, take 1	443, 608
I Don't Want to Face It	*Double Fantasy*, demo, rhythm box	285, 904
I Don't Want to Face It	acoustic demo, unknown take	093, 165, 185, 222, 240, 243
I Don't Want to Face It	demo, Bermuda, 1980	014, 190, 204, 211, 212, 402, 527
I Don't Want to Face It	outtake, Hit Factory, 1980	009, 022, 111, 283
I Don't Want to Face It	outtake, unknown	025, 075, 206, 235, 249, 260, 261, 275, 279, 283, 325, 376, 498, 716, 733, 735, 741, 782, 835, 846, 875, 904
I Don't Want to Face It	rough mix, mono	032, 103, 165, 478, 676
I Don't Want to Face It	*Milk and Honey* album, official release version	259
I Don't Want To Lose You	unknown take	205

Title	Source	Entry No.
I Found Out	*Plastic Ono Band* album, album version with longer fade	066, 079, 115, 116, 149, 150, 822, 860
I Found Out	*Plastic Ono Band* sessions, California, summer 1970	785, 910
I Found Out	*Plastic Ono Band* album, 5.1 mix	340
I Found Out	*Plastic Ono Band* album, 5.1 mix	341
I Found Out	*Imagine* album, original demo on acoustic guitar	080, 167, 222, 237, 277, 791
I Found Out	demo, take 1	286, 414, 550
I Found Out	guitar demo, take 2	167, 237, 256, 286, 420, 562
I Found Out	*Imagine* album, demo	081, 454, 629
I Found Out	*Imagine* album, studio outtake	162, 167, 170, 216, 264, 265
I Found Out	rough mix	286, 321, 337, 384, 433, 440, 587, 602
I Found Out	*Plastic Ono Band* album sessions, alternate with bongos	793
I Found Out	unknown take	287, 325, 336, 353, 373, 385, 412, 485, 546, 690, 723, 762, 779, 782, 783, 784, 785, 790, 800, 817, 836, 842, 843, 848, 871, 872, 880, 910
I Found Out	Australian version, censored and longer	170
I Found Out	long uncensored version	182
I Found Out	alternate mix	237
I Got Ants In My Pants	*Double Fantasy* sessions, ad lib, 6 August 1980	439, 600
I Know	*Mind Games* album, rough version	086, 168, 239, 751

Title	Source	Entry No.
I Know	*Mind Games* album, rough mix	428, 578, 756
I Know	*Mind Games* album, acoustic demo, take 3	092, 240, 264, 265, 443, 607, 751
I Know	*Mind Games* album, acoustic demo, unknown take	241, 789
I Know	*Mind Games* album, guitar demo, take 2	099, 242, 428, 578
I Know	*Mind Games* album, demo, take 4	451, 624
I Know	*Mind Games* album, unknown takes and demos	095, 099, 159, 161, 168, 220, 242, 335, 353, 496, 712, 734, 737, 740, 752, 756, 849, 869, 874, 876, 877
I Know	*Mind Games* album, from acetate	750
I Know (I Know)	see I Know	various
(I Know) I'm Losing You	see I'm Losing You	various
I Love You My Love	demo, Weybridge	386
I'll Be Looking For You	rehearsal, One-to-One concert	014, 140, 404, 530
I'll Make You Happy	*Imagine* album rehearsal, Tittenhurst Park, 1970	246, 387, 473, 482, 667, 685, 740, 861, 909
I'll Make You Happy	outtake, circa 1973	098, 242
Illusions	unreleased song	091, 240, 249, 273, 274, 371, 387, 733, 749, 861, 893
Imagine	*Imagine* album sessions, Tittenhurst	306, 405, 410, 414, 434, 532, 543, 551, 590
Imagine	original demo	295, 409, 442, 540, 606
Imagine	*Imagine* album sessions, take 1	128, 172, 290, 295, 298, 771, 796, 822

Title	Source	Entry No.
Imagine	*Imagine* album sessions, take 2	290, 294, 295, 298
Imagine	*Imagine* album sessions, take 3	290, 295, 298
Imagine	*Imagine* album sessions, alternate take 1	295
Imagine	*Imagine* album sessions, alternate take 2	295
Imagine	version 2, take 1	290, 295, 298
Imagine	take 7, alternate vocal	166
Imagine	*Imagine* album sessions, from acetate	289, 293
Imagine	Imagine 5.1 surround mix, centre channel	304
Imagine	Imagine 5.1 surround mix, front channels	304
Imagine	Imagine 5.1 surround mix, rear channels	204
Imagine	*Imagine* album, quad mix	294, 296, 302, 305
Imagine	*Imagine* album, unknown outtakes and rehearsals	043, 078, 080, 082, 089, 101, 107, 162, 166, 179, 182, 192, 222, 224, 226, 229, 232, 236, 237, 239, 240, 243, 250, 264, 265, 278, 279, 288, 290, 291, 292, 294, 297, 298, 300, 303, 307, 325, 348, 352, 353, 378, 418, 451, 455, 499, 557, 624, 631, 725, 719, 730, 741, 773, 779, 782, 783, 784, 788, 799, 821, 832, 844, 845, 858, 862, 871, 873, 874, 875, 877, 880, 881

Title	Source	Entry No.
Imagine	*Imagine* album sessions, rough mix	291, 433, 587
Imagine	King Biscuit mix	301
Imagine	*Imagine* outtake, with Ringo and Klaus Voorman	015, 191
Imagine	from *Imagine – The Film* (slower version)	294, 301
Imagine	live, New York hotel, 9 October 1971, John's thirty-first birthday	215, 346, 437, 595, 840, 364, 912
Imagine	live, Apollo Theatre, New York, 17 December 1971	161, 228, 231, 276, 334, 379, 382, 391, 505, 731, 786, 801, 869
Imagine	One-to-One concert rehearsals	400, 523
Imagine	One-to-One concert, 30 August 1972 (afternoon show)	126, 169, 774
Imagine	One-to-One concert, 30 August 1972 (evening show)	002, 003, 005, 024, 026, 027, 040, 054, 121, 122, 123, 124, 166, 227, 228, 276, 301, 353, 758, 774, 825
Imagine	live, *Mike Douglas Show*, 14–18 February 1972	049, 142, 143, 144, 145, 146, 147, 154, 222, 301, 428, 579, 853, 854, 899
Imagine	*Jerry Lewis TV Show*	172, 251, 301, 753, 754, 854
Imagine	live, unknown TV show	382, 781
Imagine	live, *Salute To Sir Lew Grade*, 13 June 1975	034, 051, 065, 126, 136, 140, 156, 194, 219, 231, 301, 320, 731, 753, 754, 815, 886
Imagine	live, *Salute To Sir Lew Grade*, 13 June 1975 (audience)	219, 886

Title	Source	Entry No.
Imagine	acoustic, take unknown	030
Imagine	Imagine 5.1 centre channel mix from *Lennon Legend* DVD	221, 363, 364
Imagine	*Imagine* album, official release version	365, 748
I'm a Man	rehearsals, Dakota cassette August 1980	010, 017, 072, 153, 161, 186, 206, 235, 283, 348, 349, 353, 377, 817, 869
I'm a Man	from promotional film, August 1980	203, 270, 898
I'm Crazy	outtake, song evolved into 'Watching the Wheels'	084, 165, 238, 425, 572
I'm Having a Baby My Love	Yoko Ono, vocals and piano 1975	281, 483, 686, 909
I'm in Love	demo for The Fourmost	500, 721, 794
I'm Losing You	*Double Fantasy*, acoustic guitar version, Bermuda, 1980	015, 078, 161, 165, 191, 204, 212, 390, 405, 426, 503, 533, 574, 846, 869
I'm Losing You	*Double Fantasy* rehearsals, Dakota, August 1980	007, 008, 017, 111, 153, 203, 283
I'm Losing You	from promotional video, August 1980	203, 270
I'm Losing You	*Double Fantasy* sessions, Record Plant outtake	071, 079, 100
I'm Losing You	*Double Fantasy* sessions, rough mix	085, 238, 426, 573, 903
I'm Losing You	alternate take, with Cheap Trick	032, 094, 165, 233, 241, 260, 261, 283, 753, 754
I'm Losing You	*Double Fantasy* rehearsal, no backing vocal	165

Title	Source	Entry No.
I'm Losing You	*Double Fantasy*, alternate take with studio chat	243
I'm Losing You	*Double Fantasy* sessions, horn section overdub	285
I'm Losing You	*Double Fantasy*, acoustic with rhythm box, Bermuda	277, 349
I'm Losing You	unknown takes and rehearsals	179, 184, 192, 222, 234, 236, 249, 275, 279, 285, 336, 348, 353, 376, 377, 390, 458, 470, 479, 486, 503, 638, 661, 678, 692, 736, 740, 749, 790, 799, 817, 835, 846, 847, 865, 872, 874, 877, 898, 904
I'm Losing You	*Double Fantasy* album, official release version	259, 365, 748
I'm Moving On	alternate take, with Cheap Trick	032, 260, 261, 753, 754
I'm Moving On	unknown take	459, 639, 835
I'm Moving On	*Double Fantasy* album, official release version	259
I'm Not as Strong as You Think	Yoko Ono on vocals	281, 483, 686, 909
I'm Ready to Sing for the World	unknown take	243, 387, 861
I'm So Tired	unknown take – with Mike Love	222
I'm Stepping Out	*Double Fantasy*, first day, breakdowns and complete take	244
I'm Stepping Out	*Double Fantasy* sessions, take 1, acoustic demo	083, 165, 222, 238, 239, 242, 283, 384, 432, 498, 586, 717
I'm Stepping Out	*Double Fantasy* sessions, take 1 overdub	102

Title	Source	Entry No.
I'm Stepping Out	*Double Fantasy* sessions, take 2	165, 242, 439, 498, 600, 717, 733
I'm Stepping Out	*Double Fantasy* sessions, take 3, acoustic demo	165, 498, 717
I'm Stepping Out	*Double Fantasy* sessions, take 4	498, 717
I'm Stepping Out	*Double Fantasy* sessions, take 8	242
I'm Stepping Out	*Double Fantasy* sessions, acoustic with rhythm box	399, 520, 762, 791
I'm Stepping Out	*Double Fantasy* sessions, complete take	243
I'm Stepping Out	*Double Fantasy* sessions, rehearsal, August 1980	032, 083, 485, 691
I'm Stepping Out	*Double Fantasy*, control room tape sessions, 6 August 1980	102
I'm Stepping Out	demo, Bermuda, 1979	011, 255
I'm Stepping Out	demo, Bermuda, 1980	204, 211, 212, 426, 573
I'm Stepping Out	*Double Fantasy* sessions, Hit Factory, New York	283
I'm Stepping Out	*Double Fantasy* sessions, unknown take	075, 091, 097, 100, 103, 179, 187, 236, 240, 243, 260, 261, 275, 279, 283, 322, 337, 338, 353, 376, 401, 421, 442, 524, 564, 605, 739, 740, 741, 782, 783, 784, 792, 845, 847, 870, 872, 875, 876, 877, 878, 904
I'm Stepping Out	*Double Fantasy* sessions, double-tracked guitar demo	084, 238
I'm Stepping Out	*Double Fantasy* sessions, vocal booth, unknown take	275

Title	Source	Entry No.
I'm Stepping Out	*Double Fantasy* sessions, vocal booth, take 1	322, 451, 623
I'm Stepping Out	*Double Fantasy* sessions, vocal booth, take 2	322
I'm Stepping Out	*Double Fantasy* sessions, vocal booth, take 3	322, 451, 623
I'm Stepping Out	*Double Fantasy* sessions, vocal booth, take 4	322
I'm Stepping Out	*Double Fantasy* sessions, vocal booth, take 5	322
I'm Stepping Out	*Double Fantasy* sessions, vocal booth, take 6	322
I'm Stepping Out	*Double Fantasy* sessions, vocal booth, take 7	322
I'm Stepping Out	*Double Fantasy* sessions, vocal booth, take 8	322, 451, 623
I'm Stepping Out	*Double Fantasy* sessions, multi-track mix down, take 1	322
I'm Stepping Out	*Double Fantasy* sessions, multi-track mix down, take 2	322
I'm Stepping Out	*Double Fantasy* sessions, multi-track mix down, take 9	322
I'm Stepping Out	*Double Fantasy*, discussions and rehearsal, vocal booth	322
I'm Stepping Out	*Double Fantasy* sessions, rough mix	277, 421, 442, 478, 564, 605, 676
I'm Stepping Out	*Milk and Honey* album, official release version	259
I'm the Greatest	early home demo, Ascot, 1971, John piano	009, 070, 083, 111, 185, 232, 234, 242, 246, 277, 285, 290, 298, 349, 394, 421, 511, 564, 909

Title	Source	Entry No.
I'm the Greatest	demo, unknown	030, 040, 052, 066, 095, 098, 115, 116, 128, 136, 149, 150, 162, 166, 179, 192, 222, 234, 238, 241, 291, 294, 295, 297, 300, 306, 325, 353, 373, 377, 384, 428, 434, 442, 492, 500, 578, 590, 606, 704, 721, 725, 728, 737, 740, 773, 796, 798, 810, 822, 832, 833, 843, 860, 870, 871, 872, 873, 878, 881, 893
I'm the Greatest	demo, Regent's Park, 1971	009, 111, 185
I'm the Greatest	complete rehearsal, 1973	070, 134, 138, 309, 353, 422, 565, 767, 833
I'm Walking	unknown	755
I'm Your Angel	*Double Fantasy* sessions, rough mix	032, 260, 261, 281
I'm Your Angel	*Double Fantasy* sessions, horn overdubs	483, 686
Incantation Dog Soldier	with Patrick Jude, co-producer John Lennon	201, 759
India demo,	unknown take	249, 273, 274, 749, 794, 893
Instant Karma	studio demo	030, 353
Instant Karma	*Top of the Pops*	029, 169, 192, 232, 328, 771, 842
Instant Karma	One-to-One concert, 30 August 1972 (afternoon show)	774
Instant Karma	One-to-One concert, 30 August 1972 (evening show)	005, 024, 041, 049, 121, 124, 142, 143, 224, 228, 276, 391, 504, 727, 731, 774, 800, 825, 856

Title	Source	Entry No.
Instant Karma	One-to-One concert rehearsals	118, 120, 152, 388, 391, 400, 484, 504, 522, 689, 775, 776, 800, 896
Instant Karma	US single mix	172, 817
Instant Karma	different mix	172
Instant Karma	5.1 centre channel mix from *Lennon Legend* DVD	221, 363, 364
Instant Karma	official release version	365, 748
Instant Karma	unknown takes and rehearsals	222, 250, 378, 468, 657, 749, 781, 782, 783, 784, 799, 879
Instrumental	*Imagine* album rehearsal, Tittenhurst Park, 1970	246
Instrumentals	*Clock* rehearsals, St Regis Hotel, New York, September 1971	223, 814
Instrumentals	One-to-One concert rehearsals	117, 119, 120, 416, 554, 775, 776, 777, 814, 896
Instrumentals	One-to-One rehearsals, 18 August 1972	152
In My Life	home demo, Dakota, 1979	012
Interview How I Won the War,	November 1966	200
Interview with Kenny Everett	BBC Radio 1968 (includes Cottonfields)	129, 139
Interview, John talks to Michael Lindsay Hogg	*Rock and Roll Circus*	086
Interview, John and Yoko	BBC Radio, *Night Ride*, 12 December 1968	765
Interview with Jerry Leviton	Toronto Bed-In, May 1969	326

Title	Source	Entry No.
Interview, re: Abbey Road	Radio Luxembourg, 27 September 1969	342
Interview with Kenny Everett,	8 November 1969	314
Interview with Ken Zelig		314
Interview	Radio South Africa, 12 December 1969	315
Interview	Toronto Press Conference, 17 December 1969	315
Interview with Tom Campbell and Bill Holley	KYA-FM, Montreal Bed-In, 29 May 1969	358
Interview, Bed-In		106, 202
Interview with Howard Smith	WABC 95.5 FM, New York, 17 December 1969	827
Interview, Pop Goes The Bulldog	December 1969	200
Interview	Unknown, 1969	354
Interview John talks about David Peel		046
Interview, re: *Live Peace in Toronto* album	Radio Luxembourg	314
Interview Midday Spin	BBC Radio One, 15 February 1970	315
Interview	*Rolling Stone* magazine	366, 367
Interview with Howard Smith	WABC 95.5 FM, New York, 6 December 1970	828
Interview for Plastic Ono Band	Imperial Hotel, 25 January 1971	838

Title	Source	Entry No.
Interview with Kenny Everett	broadcast 27 March 1971	355
Interview	Cannes, France, 15 April 1971	778
Interview with Kenny Everett	Radio Monte Carlo, 25 April 1971	778
Interview with Howard Smith	WPLJ 95.5 FM, New York, 6 June 1971	829, 894, 900
Interview with Alex Bennet	WPLJ FM 95.5, New York City, 8 June 1971	282
Interview for Imagine album	New York, 2 September 1971	838
Interview	WNEW FM, New York City, September/October 1971	857
Interview	Hotel Syracuse, 5 October 1971	857
Interview, John and Yoko	Everson Museum, 8 October 1971	135, 437, 595, 857
Interview with Howard Smith	WPLJ 95.5 FM, New York, 26 September 1971	830
Interview with Don Singleton	*New York Daily News*, November 1971	316
Interview with Jan Wenner	KRFC AM, Focus '71	356
Interview with John and Yoko	Japan 1971	324
Interview Howard Smith	unknown, 1971	83⁻
Interview with Howard Smith	WPLJ 95.5 FM, New York, 23 January 1972	83⁻
Interview with John and Yoko	WIBG 990 AM, *Philadelphia, An Hour*, taped 27 January 1972, Broadcast 10 February 1972	895

555

Title	Source	Entry No.
Interview on *Aquarius*	*London Weekend TV*, broadcast 11 March 1972	895
Interviews	One-to-One concert	227
Interview with Howard Smith	New York City, mid-1972	831
Interview	*Flipside US TV*, 16 February 1973	891
Interview ABC News	ABC News, 18 April 1972	895
Interview	ABC News, 22 April 1972	895
Interview	INS Press Conference, 23 March 1973	891
Interview	Nutopia Press Conference, 2 April 1973	891
Interview with Elliot Mintz	Beverley Hills Hotel, 16 April 1973	891
Interview with Danny Scheckle	International Women's Conference, 3 June 1973	891
Interview with Elliot Mintz	*Eyewitness News*, KABC TV, Los Angeles, taped 10 November 1973	891
Interview	*Mike Douglas Show*, 23 November 1973	891
Interview	Capital Radio, 23 November 1973	
Interview	unknown, September 1974	002, 003, 005
Interview	WFIL AM Helping Hand Marathon, 9–11 May 1974	892
Interview	KHJ-AM L.A.	096, 738
Interview	EMI promo tape for *Walls and Bridges*, September 1974	317
Interview, Lisa Robinson,	24 September 1974	312
Interview	RKO Radio, 25 September 1974	317, 318

Title	Source	Entry No.
Interview	CHUM FM Radio, 26 September 1974	317
Interview	WAXB FM Radio, 27 September 1974	317
Interview	KHJ AM Radio, 27 September 1974	417, 555, 883
Interview	WNEW, 28 September 1974	065, 067, 129, 258, 375, 408, 453, 538, 627
Interview	WRKO Radio, 29 September 1974	319
Interview	2SM 1269, Sydney, Australia, October 1974	318
Interview	KQRS Radio, *Walls and Bridges*, 1 October 1974	313
Interview, hosted by Michael Wale,	BBC Radio 2, *Walls and Bridges* album, 4 October 1974	813, 884
Interview with Tom Donahue, re *Walls and Bridges* album	KSAN	357, 408, 453, 538, 627
Interview, Jim Ladd	*Walls and Bridges* promo, October 1974	327
Interview with Howard Cosel	*Monday Night Football*, 9 December 1974	024, 065, 142, 143, 375
Interview	Today Show, 16 December 1974	320
Interview, Dick Cavett		781
Interview, Bob Harris	*The Old Grey Whistle Test*	313, 320
Interview	WNEW FM 102.7, New York, 13 February 1975	812
Interview	WRRM FM Cincinnati and KSHE FM Crestwood, 787, 21 February	1975
Interview with Jean-Francois Vallee	Dakota, 7 April 1975	320

Title	Source	Entry No.
Interview hosted by Tom Snyder	*Tomorrow Show*, 28 April 1975	001, 028, 320, 347
Interview	Capital Radio, 1975	333
Interview	Cheer Up New York, 1975	900
Interview with Tom Campbell and Bill Holley		056
Interview with Robert Hilburn		270
Interview, Dennis Elsa and Barbara Granstock	WNEW FM, New York City, 25 September 1980	763, 809
Interview David Sheff	Autumn 1980	837
Interview BBC, Andy Peebles	6 December 1980	040, 197, 198, 199, 308, 343, 344, 345
Interview	RKO General Radio, New York, 8 December 1980	196, 248, 339, 359, 746, 855, 866
Interview	WXLO FM, New York City, broadcast, 14 December 1980	744, 745
Interview	*Woman's Hour*, BBC Radio 2, broadcast, 9 November '91	901
Interview	MJI Radio, December 2000, sixtieth birthday celebration	906
Intuition	*Mind Games* album, composing demo	087, 239, 430, 582
Intuition	*Mind Games* album, rough mix	087, 168, 239, 430, 496, 582, 712, 751, 756
Intuition	*Mind Games* album demo, take 3	452, 626
Intuition	*Mind Games* album, piano demo, take 4	099, 242
Intuition	*Mind Games* album, unknown takes and demos	159, 162, 220, 222, 353, 377, 496, 712, 751, 752, 756, 874

Title	Source	Entry No.
Intuition	*Mind Games* album, from acetate	750
I Promise	home demo, Ascot, 1970, John piano	009, 070, 111, 128, 185, 234, 246, 394, 511, 740, 796, 849, 909
I Promise	*Mind Games* album, unknown take	159, 168, 220, 466, 496, 500, 653, 712, 720, 728
I Sat Belonely	John reading a poem	051, 095, 115, 116, 241, 330, 352, 737, 837
I Saw Her Standing There	rehearsal with Elton John	030, 066, 115, 116, 140, 149, 150, 192, 217, 231, 233, 353, 426, 499, 573, 719, 767, 860
I Saw Her Standing There	live, with Elton John	037, 038, 068, 154, 217, 222, 250, 280, 353, 460, 483, 641, 686, 759, 764, 795, 852, 881, 899
I Saw Her Standing There	unknown take (probably with Elton John)	229, 373, 731, 755, 879
I Saw Her Standing There	Elton John, official release	217
I Saw Her Standing There	official release	365
Isolation	*Plastic Ono Band* album, unknown take	462, 482, 645, 685, 785, 793, 836, 842, 910
Isolation	*Plastic Ono Band* album, official release	340
Isolation	*Plastic Ono Band* album, 5.1 mix	341
It Happened	outtake – Yoko Ono	148, 373
It'll Be Me	*Plastic Ono Band* album sessions, improvisation	321, 353, 878

It'll Be Me	One-to-One rehearsals with Elephant's Memory	076, 174, 190, 236, 722, 775, 826
It's Now or Never	*Double Fantasy* sessions	165
It's Now or Never	*Jerry Lewis Telethon*	753, 754
It's Only Make Believe	One-to-One rehearsals, 18 August 1972	152, 388, 776
It's Real	unknown take	206
It's So Hard	*Imagine*, outtake, Ascot, summer 1971	015, 191, 306, 436, 594, 822
It's So Hard	*Imagine* album, unknown outtakes and rehearsals	043, 078, 128, 162, 179, 236, 288, 292, 303, 307, 325, 351, 352, 353, 405, 444, 464, 533, 610, 649, 734, 740, 779, 796, 821, 836, 844, 858, 871, 879
It's So Hard	*Imagine* album sessions, take 2	166, 290, 294, 295, 298
It's So Hard	*Imagine* album, King Curtis sax overdub	092, 098, 240, 242, 290, 295, 297, 298, 300
It's So Hard	*Imagine* album sessions, minus sax overdub	291, 353
It's So Hard	*Imagine* album sessions, overdub sessions	444, 495, 610, 710
It's So Hard	*Imagine* album sessions, from acetate	289, 293
It's So Hard	*Imagine* album, quad mix	294, 296, 302, 305
It's So Hard	Imagine 5.1 surround mix, centre channel	304
It's So Hard	Imagine 5.1 surround mix, front channels	304
It's So Hard	Imagine 5.1 surround mix, rear channels	304
It's So Hard	from *Imagine – The Film*	301

It's So Hard	One-to-One concert, 30 August 1972 (afternoon show)	774
It's So Hard	One-to-One concert, 30 August 1972 (evening show)	024, 041, 054, 124, 142, 143, 224, 301, 445, 611, 773, 774, 825
It's So Hard	One-to-One concert rehearsals	117, 120, 417, 484, 555, 689, 775, 776, 896
It's So Hard	One-to-One rehearsals, 18 August 1972	152
It's So Hard	live, *Mike Douglas Show*	049, 166, 244, 301, 853, 854
It's So Hard	live, *David Frost Show*, 13 January 1972	144, 145, 146, 147, 413, 548
It's So Hard	live, unknown TV show	382
It's So Hard	official release	365
I Want You	Amsterdam Hilton, March 1969	034, 278, 368
I Want You	home recording, 1969	470, 660
I Watch Your Face	*Double Fantasy*, demo (evolved into 'Starting Over')	090, 165, 206, 222, 240, 271, 283, 387, 432, 586, 861
Jam	Plastic Ono Band album sessions	262, 816, 842, 875
Jam	Imagine album sessions	089, 239, 306
Jam	One-to-One concert rehearsals	388, 777, 826
Jamrag	Fillmore East, New York, original Lennon mix	269, 328, 368, 834
Jealous Guy	*Imagine* album, studio outtake, 1971	012, 073, 188
Jealous Guy	*Imagine* album sessions, Tittenhurst	306
Jealous Guy	*Imagine* album sessions, take 1, no overdubs or strings	166, 290, 285, 298, 353, 77˙
Jealous Guy	*Imagine* album sessions, take 2	290, 295, 298, 353

Jealous Guy	*Imagine* album sessions, take 3	290, 295
Jealous Guy	*Imagine* album sessions, take 7	298
Jealous Guy	*Imagine* album sessions, take 17	353
Jealous Guy	*Imagine* album sessions, vocal, take 20	290, 295, 298
Jealous Guy	*Imagine* album sessions, vocal overdub	294, 295
Jealous Guy	*Imagine* album, unknown outtake	043, 128, 222, 226, 235, 253, 288, 291, 292, 302, 307, 325, 351, 400, 500, 523, 721, 779, 782, 796, 821, 844, 858, 870, 873, 874, 877, 887
Jealous Guy	*Imagine* album rough mix	085, 238, 291, 427, 576
Jealous Guy	*Imagine* album sessions, from acetate	289, 293
Jealous Guy	*Imagine* album sessions, final backing tracks	353
Jealous Guy	from *Imagine – The Film*	301
Jealous Guy	*Imagine* album, quad mix	294, 296, 302, 305
Jealous Guy	Imagine 5.1 surround mix, centre channel	304, 363
Jealous Guy	Imagine 5.1 surround mix, front channels	304, 363
Jealous Guy	Imagine 5.1 surround mix, rear channels	304, 364
Jealous Guy	5.1 centre channel mix from *Lennon Legend* DVD	221, 363, 364
Jealous Guy	*Imagine* album, official release version	365, 748
Jerusalaim	Amsterdam Hilton, March 1969	034, 051, 278, 368

Jesse James Was a Man	live, New York hotel, 9 October 1971, John's thirty-first birthday	215, 840, 864, 912
J.J.	St Regis Hotel, 1972 (early version of Angela)	089, 240, 822
J.J.	demo – prototype for Angela	101, 161, 173, 174, 243, 285, 325, 433, 484, 587, 689, 741, 869, 911
Jock and Yono	outtake	500, 720
John and Yoko's Happy home recording Xmas Ditty,		030, 237
John Henry	piano demo, Dakota, 1970s	C08, 069, 081, 111, 184, 210, 216, 234, 237, 252, 256, 349, 350, 416, 553, 728, 730, 742, 749, 903
John Henry	electric guitar, take	430, 582
John John (Let's Hope For Peace)	live, Toronto, 1969	328, 383, 732
John John (Let's Hope For Peace)	Yoko Ono, unknown take	175
John Sinclair	live, Free John Sinclair Rally, 10 December 1971	005, 006, 011, 046, 048, 054, 057, 058, 065, 072, 113, 121, 122, 128, 173, 174, 187, 228, 235, 255, 276, 334, 349, 382, 398, 429, 519, 579, 726, 786, 796, 862, 901
John Sinclair	unknown take	107, 174, 222, 352, 378, 782, 865, 911
John Sinclair	live, *David Frost Show*, 13 January 1972	144, 145, 146, 147, 173, 244, 382, 413, 548, 854
Johnny B. Goode	*Mike Douglas Show*, with Chuck Berry	024, 049, 054, 140, 142, 143, 144, 145, 146, 147, 154, 192, 224, 232, 352, 382, 395, 512, 726, 853, 854, 899
Josejoi Banzai	outtake – Yoko Ono	148

Just A Little Story	unknown take	295
Just Because	from *Roots*	132, 133, 171, 217, 820
Just Because	*Rock 'n' Roll* rehearsals, Morris Levy's Farm, New York	815
Just Because	*Rock 'n' Roll* session, outtake	060, 153, 157, 353, 407, 470, 536, 661, 755, 770, 815, 819, 898
Just Because	*Rock 'n' Roll* session, obscene version	817
Just Because	rough mix – Spector sessions	218
Just Because	official released version	061
Just Because	*Mind Games* sessions, unknown take	159, 168, 250
Just Gotta Give Me Some Rock 'n' Roll/Shoeshine	medley: evolved into 'Meat City'	086, 220, 239, 428, 453, 578, 628, 751, 756, 911
(Just Like) Starting Over, see *Starting Over*		
Keep Right on to the End of the Road	improvisation, summer 1971	069, 234, 252, 349, 387, 425, 572, 861
King Kong	see Jamrag	
Kiss Kiss Kiss	*Double Fantasy* album, official release version	259
Knocking on Dylan's Door	acoustic satire, 1979	010, 186, 371
La Bamba	live, New York hotel, 9 October 1971, John's thirty-first birthday	215, 244, 346, 370, 380, 840, 864, 912
Lady Marmalade	ad-lib during interview	037, 038, 115, 154, 171, 219, 231, 377, 781, 795, 899
Laugh	acetate, December, 1969	162, 182, 781

The Laughing Policeman	ad lib during interview, broadcast, 27 March 1971	355
Leaning on a Lamp Post from Sea Ditty	medley, Dakota recording	070, 234, 349, 395, 513
Lend Me Your Comb	*Clock* rehearsals, St Regis Hotel, New York, September 1971	088, 223, 239, 244, 384, 431, 584, 729, 814, 840, 912
Lennon's Lost Diary Tape	John's personal diary tape from September 1979	094, 242, 270, 736, 835
Let Me Count The Ways	*Milk and Honey* album, official release version	259
Let's Get Peculiar	*Double Fantasy* sessions	243
Let's Go Flying	from *Life with the Lions*	016
Let's Ride	*Some Time in New York City* sessions, improvisation	811
Let's Spend the Night Together	Lori Burton and Patrick Jude, co-producer John Lennon	201, 759
Let's Twist Again	outtake, Lennon and David Bowie	030, 033, 231, 731, 783, 784, 795
Life Begins at Forty	demo, Dakota, 1980	008, 069, 111, 184, 234, 249, 252, 273, 274, 349, 371, 391, 401, 484, 493, 498, 505, 524, 688, 707, 716, 801, 847, 893
Life is Something	unknown	387, 861
Like a Rolling Stone	live, New York hotel, 9 October 1971, John's thirty-first birthday	215, 244, 346, 370, 380, 840, 864, 912
Listen the Snow is Falling	outtake	148
Listen the Snow is Falling	official release	064, 889
Little Bitty Pretty One	unknown take	353

Living on Borrowed Time, see *Borrowed Time*		
Long Lost John	*Plastic Ono Band* album sessions, unknown	875, 842, 910
Long Tall Sally	One-to-One concert rehearsal, 22 August 1972	222, 353, 416, 554, 876
Look at Me	*Plastic Ono Band* album, unknown outtakes and demos	088, 089, 098, 162, 167, 170, 239, 242, 262, 264, 265, 286, 287, 303, 321, 338, 353, 384, 399, 474, 485, 493, 521, 668, 690, 707, 729, 740, 785, 793, 836, 842, 848, 858, 869, 872, 910
Look at Me	*Plastic Ono Band*, double-tracked vocal	493, 707
Look at Me	*Plastic Ono Band*, rough mix	435, 454, 591, 630
Look at Me	*Plastic Ono Band* album, official release	340
Look at Me	Plastic Ono Band, 5.1 mix	341
Look at Me	5.1 surround mix, centre channel	303
Look at Me	5.1 surround mix, front channels	303
Look at Me	5.1 surround mix, rear channels	303
Look at Me	electrified acoustic guitar demo	170, 432, 585
Look at Me	*Plastic Ono Band* album sessions, rough mix	321
Look at Me	7" Apple Acetate, different mix)	160
Look at Me	Weybridge, 1968	161, 239, 384
Looking For You	*Clock* rehearsals, St Regis Hotel, New York, September 1971	814
Lord Take This Make-up Off Me	John's Bob Dylan parody	072, 196, 235, 264, 265, 397, 517, 722, 837

Lost Diary Tape, see *Lennon's Lost Diary Tape*		
Louie Louie	live, New York hotel, 9 October 1971, John's thirty-first birthday	215, 244, 346, 370, 380, 840, 864, 912
Love	1882 remix of UK 45 rpm	011, 115, 116, 128, 156, 170, 187, 239, 262, 759, 771, 785, 842, 910
Love	*Plastic Ono Band* album sessions, guitar demo	086, 167, 239, 286, 321
Love	*Plastic Ono Band* sessions, acoustic guitar piano demo	321
Love	*Plastic Ono Band* album sessions, acoustic guitar rehearsal	321, 793
Love	*Plastic Ono Band* album sessions, piano rehearsal	321, 793
Love	*Plastic Ono Band* album sessions, tremolo guitar	429, 580, 730, 771, 903
Love	*Plastic Ono Band* album sessions, folky guitar version	793
Love	*Plastic Ono Band* album sessions, take 2	321
Love	*Plastic Ono Band* album sessions, take 14	321
Love	*Plastic Ono Band* album sessions, take 15	321
Love	*Plastic Ono Band* album sessions, take 16	321
Love	*Plastic Ono Band* album sessions, take 17	321
Love	*Plastic Ono Band* album sessions, take 18	321

Love	*Plastic Ono Band* album sessions, take 19	321
Love	*Plastic Ono Band* album sessions, take 20	321
Love	*Plastic Ono Band* album sessions, take 21	321
Love	*Plastic Ono Band* album sessions, take 22	321
Love	*Plastic Ono Band* album sessions, take 23	321
Love	*Plastic Ono Band* sessions, acoustic guitar, piano, take 31	810
Love	*Plastic Ono Band* sessions, acoustic guitar, piano, take 32	810
Love	*Plastic Ono Band* album sessions, unknown take	107, 170, 179, 262, 279, 287, 377, 468, 473, 657, 666, 725, 773, 785, 793, 796, 836, 842, 848, 876, 880, 910
Love	Home demo, Tittenhurst Park	161, 255, 869
Love	*Plastic Ono Band* album, official release version	365, 748
Love	(backing track) 5.1 centre channel mix from *Lennon Legend* DVD	221, 363, 364
Lucille	John and Paul, Los Angeles, 1974	233, 380, 859
Lucille	unknown take	353, 755
The Luck of the Irish	acoustic guitar demo	070, 083, 174, 182, 192, 234, 725, 903, 911
The Luck of the Irish	studio demo, 1971	009, 083, 111, 128, 161, 796, 869
The Luck of the Irish	false start, take 1	178, 348, 394, 510
The Luck of the Irish	acoustic, take 1	174, 178, 351, 353, 422, 565

The Luck of the Irish	studio outtake, take 2	173, 178, 348, 351, 353, 394, 422, 510, 565
The Luck of the Irish	unknown take	174, 185, 238, 251, 352, 476, 672, 749, 795, 834, 880
The Luck of the Irish	live, Free John Sinclair Rally, 10 December 1971	002, 003, 005, 006, 011, 026, 027, 046, 048, 057, 058, 065, 072, 113, 121, 122, 123, 128, 173, 174, 137, 228, 232, 235, 255, 276, 334, 349, 379, 382, 398, 488, 519, 696, 726, 786, 796, 862, 901
The Luck of the Irish	live, *The Mike Douglas Show*, 1972	C19, 049, 054, 244, 853, 854
The Luck of the Irish	live, The *David Frost Show*, 13 January 1972	144, 145, 146, 147, 173, 413, 548
The Luck of the Irish	live, unknown TV show	382
The Luck of the Irish	Radio Hilversum, March 1972	285
Lucy from Littletown	poem, from *A Spaniard in the Works*	795, 813
Lucy in the Sky with Diamonds	live, with Elton John	037, 038, 068, 154, 217, 280, 393, 508, 759, 764, 899
Lucy in the Sky with Diamonds	Elton John with John Lennon, official release	759
Maggie Mae	Record Plant, New York 1973	013, 189, 792
Maggie Mae	Hit Factory, 1980	074, 161, 165, 206, 235, 283, 338, 350, 351, 371, 845, 869
The Maharishi Song	home recording, 1968	089, 222, 239, 329, 386, 433, 474, 588, 668, 756, 851, 907, 908

Title	Source	Entry No.
Mailman Bring Me No More Blues	*Imagine* album rehearsal, Tittenhurst Park, 1970	246, 909
Mailman Bring Me No More Blues	*Clock* rehearsals, St Regis Hotel, New York, September 1971	085, 223, 238, 244, 426, 574, 814, 840, 912
Make Love Not War	home demo, Ascot, 1970, John piano	009, 052, 070, 111, 128, 185, 196, 234, 246, 394, 402, 437, 511, 527, 596, 751, 762, 796, 837, 909
Make Love Not War	*Mind Games* sessions, unknown take	159, 168, 169, 192, 216, 220, 233, 466, 496, 500, 653, 712, 720, 728, 849
Make Love to the End	Bed-In outtake	030, 104, 105, 231, 731
Mama You're So Beautiful This Morning	Unknown	387, 861
Many Rivers to Cross	home demo	090, 099, 240, 243, 285, 336, 387, 434, 492, 589, 704, 740, 749, 790, 822, 861
Many Rivers to Cross	Harry Nilsson, producer John Lennon	759
The Man Who Broke The Bank at Monte Carlo	ad lib during interview, broadcast 27 March 1971	355
Matchbox	recorded during *Plastic Ono Band* sessions	074, 167, 179, 235, 262, 286, 287, 351, 353, 401, 415, 485, 525, 552, 690, 773, 785, 793, 820, 842, 843, 848, 875, 887, 893, 910
Maurice Dupont Agent	Dakota, 1973	012, 013, 015, 076, 188, 189, 191, 206, 236, 237, 249, 349, 350, 400, 401, 405, 523, 525, 532, 890

Title	Source	Entry No.
Maybe Baby	One-to-One concert rehearsals	814, 826
Maybe Baby	*Clock* rehearsals, St Regis Hotel, New York, September 1971	013, 076, 128, 161, 223, 236, 244, 401, 525, 722, 779, 796, 814, 840, 869, 912
Maybe Baby	live, New York hotel, 9 October 1071, John's thirty-first birthday	189, 215, 244, 346, 370, 380, 840, 864, 912
Maybe Baby	medley, during TV interview	024, 065, 101, 142, 143, 224, 243, 741
Maybe Baby	home tape, take unknown	264, 265, 335, 789
Meat City	*Mind Games* sessions, early rough mix	496, 712, 751, 756
Meat City	Mind Games sessions, take 1, electric guitar demo	241, 264, 265, 452, 626, 751
Meat City	*Mind Games* sessions, take 2, electric guitar demo	453, 628
Meat City	*Mind Games* album, unknown takes and demos	095, 159, 162, 168, 220, 496, 712, 749, 756
Meat City	acoustic guitar demo	168
Meat City	unknown take	336, 353, 453, 628, 737, 752, 760, 761, 790, 849, 873, 876
Meat City	*Mind Games* album, from acetate	750
Medley: Baby Please Don't Go/Rock Island Line/Maybe Baby/Peggy Sue	*Eyewitness News*, during TV interview, Summer 1972	024, 065, 101, 142, 143, 224
Medley: Beyond the Sea/Blue Moon/Young Love	Dakota recording	010, 072, 206, 235, 349

Title	Source	Entry No.
Medley: Heartbeat/Peggy Sue Got Married/Peggy Sue	*Clock* rehearsals, St Regis Hotel, New York, September 1971	014, 190, 244
Medley: That's All Right Mama/Glad All Over/Honey Don't/Don't Be Cruel/Hound Dog/Matchbox	Recorded during *Plastic Ono Band* album sessions	785, 793, 842, 848, 875, 887, 910
Medley: Beautiful Boy/Howling at the Moon/Dakota Rap/Across the River	*Double Fantasy* sessions with drum machine	091, 222, 240, 384, 434, 589, 733
Medley: How?/Child of Nature/Oh, Yoko	*Imagine* session, piano demos	098, 166, 242, 290, 298, 740
Medley: Intuition/How?/God	piano demo	168
Medley: Rit It Up/Ready Teddy	rough mix	171
Medley; Bring It on Home to Me/Send Me Some Loving	from *Roots*	217
Medley: Bring It On Home to Me/Send Me Some Loving	rehearsal	171
Mellotron Music	Improvisation, Weybridge	329, 386, 795, 813
Memories	*Double Fantasy* sessions, piano demo, take 1	093, 241, 277, 890
Memories	*Double Fantasy* sessions, piano demo, take 2	413, 445, 548, 611, 742, 890
Memories	piano demo with overdubbed acoustic guitar	469, 659, 890

Title	Source	Entry No.
Memories	home demo, 1976	059, 242, 285, 492, 498, 704, 716
Memories	Bermuda, June 1980	211
Memories	*Double Fantasy* sessions, from medley	079, 097, 210, 237, 242, 387, 434, 590, 739, 740, 749, 846, 861
Memphis	live, *Mike Douglas Show*	049, 140, 144, 145, 146, 147, 154, 382, 726, 852, 853, 854, 899
Memphis	unknown take	352, 735
Midsummer	New York, Yoko Ono, outtake	148, 175, 732
Midsummer	New York, live, *Mike Douglas Show*	049, 144, 145, 146, 147, 382, 853, 854
Mildred Mildred	Yoko Ono, unreleased track	267, 852
Mind Games	unreleased version	014, 190, 748
Mind Games	*Mind Games* album, alternate take with rough vocal	075, 140, 169, 887
Mind Games	*Mind Games* sessions, early rough mix	450, 622, 751, 756, 771
Mind Games	promo	083, 238, 756, 791
Mind Games	*Mind Games* album, unknown take	159, 162, 168, 172, 220, 222, 235, 250, 279, 337, 351, 353, 466, 473, 500, 653, 667, 720, 752, 769, 779, 781, 782, 783, 784, 799, 849, 871
Mind Games	radio spots	159, 752, 849, 891
Mind Games	5.1 centre channel mix from *Lennon Legend* DVD	221, 363, 364
Mind Games	*Mind Games* album, from acetate	750

Title	Source	Entry No.
Mind Games	*Mind Games* album, official release version	365
Mind Train	One-to-One concert rehearsals	227, 826
Mind Train	Yoko Ono, unknown take	175
Mirror Mirror	outtake, Dakota, 1977	012, 188, 206, 249, 497, 715, 865
Mirror Mirror	piano demo, take 2	099, 242, 740
Mirror Mirror	take 1	074, 222, 235, 273, 274, 350, 400, 523
Mirror Mirror	take 4	416, 553
Mirror Mirror	take 5	074, 222, 235, 350, 400, 523, 890
Mirror Mirror	ad lib	781
Mirror Mirror (On The Wall)	see Mirror Mirror	various
Money	live, Toronto, 1969	175, 228, 276, 328, 334, 353, 383, 418, 459, 557, 640, 732, 786
Montreal Bed-In	1 June 1969	310
Mother	*Plastic Ono Band* album, unknown outtake	079, 161, 167, 170, 172, 179, 182, 192, 216, 222, 226, 237, 262, 279, 286, 287, 353, 376, 378, 412, 461, 468, 474, 484, 546, 644, 657, 668, 689, 726, 762, 785, 788, 793, 797, 801, 832, 836, 842, 848, 869, 878, 902, 910
Mother	*Plastic Ono Band* album, official release	340, 365
Mother	*Plastic Ono Band*, 5.1 mix	341, 363, 364
Mother	acetate version	286, 771

Title	Source	Entry No.
Mother	*Plastic Ono Band* album, electric guitar demo	084
Mother	electric guitar, heavy tremolo	238, 426, 573, 729, 903
Mother	*Plastic Ono Band* sessions, alternate with longer fade	321
Mother	One-to-One concert, 30 August 1972 (afternoon show)	126, 169, 774
Mother	One-to-One concert, 30 August 1972 (evening show)	005, 024, 040, 053, 054, 058, 121, 122, 123, 124, 136, 142, 143, 154, 170, 224, 227, 228, 276, 353, 731, 758, 773, 774, 825, 899
Mother	One-to-One concert rehearsals	118, 120, 152, 170, 233, 388, 775, 777, 896
Mother	chimes only	115, 116
Mother	7" Apple Acetate	160
Move On Fast	One-to-One concert, 30 August 1972 (afternoon show)	774
Move On Fast	One-to-One concert, 30 August 1972 (evening show)	041, 774, 825
Move On Fast	One-to-One concert rehearsals	117, 120, 388, 776
Move Over Ms L	*Walls and Bridges* rehearsal, 13 July 1974	018, 137, 153, 309, 374, 423, 567, 833, 850, 883
Move Over Ms L	*Walls and Bridges* rehearsal, 21 July 1974	114, 374, 883
Move Over Ms L	*Walls and Bridges*, Record Plant East, July/August 1974	885, 914
Move Over Ms L	early guitar demo with May Pang	760, 761
Move Over Ms L	take 3 with piano intro	176, 427, 525
Move Over Ms L	acoustic guitar demo	176, 789, 913

Title	Source	Entry No.
Move Over Ms L	electric guitar demo	913
Move Over Ms L	piano demo	264, 265
Move Over Ms L	*Walls and Bridges* sessions, monitor mix	768, 885, 914
Move Over Ms L	Apple 1881	066, 149, 150, 755
Move Over Ms L	*Walls and Bridges* sessions, unknown takes and rehearsals	050, 083, 084, 085, 126, 140, 176, 192, 220, 225, 233, 238, 335, 353, 373, 374, 403, 442, 499, 529, 606, 719, 733, 767, 770, 779, 780, 788, 820, 841, 845, 850, 872, 873, 879, 880, 881, 897, 898, 902, 903
Move Over Ms L	*Walls and Bridges*, rehearsal – false start	225, 820, 902
Move Over Ms L	Keith Moon	759
Move Over Ms L	official release	365, 860
Mr and Mrs Lennon's Honeymoon F	film soundtrack	757

Mr. Hyde's Gone, see *Don't Be Afraid*

Title	Source	Entry No.
Mt Elga	*Pussycats* sessions with Harry Nilsson	080, 237, 350, 377, 387, 407, 537, 755, 759, 861
Mucho Mungo	*Pussycats* sessions with Harry Nilsson	051, 080, 115, 116, 350, 407, 537, 759, 800
Mucho Mungo	demo, Dakota, probably late 1975	008, 030, 069, 111, 140, 161, 404, 530, 869
Mucho Mungo	acoustic guitar demo	176, 247, 800
Mucho Mungo	composing demo	478, 676

Title	Source	Entry No.
Mucho Mungo	take 1	107, 156, 231, 377, 431, 584, 753, 754
Mucho Mungo	take 2	107, 156, 231, 431, 584, 753, 754, 792
Mucho Mungo	take 3	107, 156, 231, 377, 753, 754
Mucho Mungo	unknown take	184, 192, 205, 233, 234, 237, 249, 252, 287, 338, 349, 352, 384, 742, 749, 755, 780, 783, 784, 795, 843, 850
Mummy's Only Looking For Her Hand in the Snow	from *Life with the Lions* (see *Don't Worry Kyoko*)	016
My Babe, see *Maybe Baby*		
My Baby Left Me	live, New York hotel, 9 October 1971, John's thirty-first birthday	215, 244, 380, 840, 864, 912
My Girl	outtake	099, 243, 285, 740
My Heart Is In Your Hands	*Imagine* album rehearsal, Tittenhurst Park, 1970	246, 387, 861
My Life	demo, take 1, unreleased song, Dakota	073, 222, 235, 253, 432, 586
My Life	demo, take 3, unreleased song, Dakota	073, 235, 253, 350
My Life	piano version	102
My Life	guitar version	102
My Life	demo, unknown take	090, 165, 188, 196, 210, 213, 216, 226, 233, 240, 243, 249, 271, 283, 387, 401, 481, 488, 500, 524, 683, 697, 720, 741, 749, 837, 861

Title	Source	Entry No.
My Mummy's Dead	*Plastic Ono Band* album, unknown outtake	088, 092, 170, 192, 262, 287, 353, 729, 734, 749, 785, 797, 836, 848, 910
My Mummy's Dead	take 1, rough mix	437, 595
My Mummy's Dead	take 2	432, 485, 585, 690
My Mummy's Dead	*Plastic Ono Band* album, official release	340
My Mummy's Dead	Plastic Ono Band, 5.1 mix	341
My Mummy's Dead	*Plastic Ono Band* album sessions, take 2	167, 239, 384
My Mummy's Dead	home demo, Tittenhurst Park	161, 232, 869
My Mummy's Dead	*Plastic Ono Band* sessions, complete acoustic guitar demo	321, 793
My Mummy's Dead	rough mix	240
My Mummy's Dead	complete version	286
My Old Man's A Dustman	from 'Sea Ditty' medley, Dakota recording	349, 395, 513
Mystery Train	from promotional video, August 1980	007, 017, 153, 203, 270, 348, 353, 421, 563
Mystery Train	unknown take	817, 898
My Sweet Lord	live, New York hotel, 9 October 1971, John's thirty-first birthday	215, 244, 346, 840, 864, 912
The National Health Foyle's speech		095, 241, 330, 737
The Neville Club	John reading from his book *In His Own Write*	074, 235, 330, 350, 399, 415, 521, 552
The News of the Day	(from Reuters) John's Bob Dylan parody	072, 192, 233, 235, 371, 397, 415, 517, 552, 722, 729, 762
New York City	*Clock* rehearsals, St Regis Hotel, New York, September 1971	015, 128, 191, 223, 796, 840, 912

Title	Source	Entry No.
New York City	One-to-One concert, 30 August 1972 (afternoon show)	774
New York City	One-to-One concert, 30 August 1972 (evening show)	024, 124, 142, 143, 222, 224, 400, 523, 774, 825
New York City	One-to-One concert rehearsals	117, 120, 152, 174, 236, 388, 400, 484, 498, 522, 639, 716, 775, 896
New York City	*Some Time in New York City* album, demo, take unknown	076, 078, 079, 080, 174, 237, 405, 476, 533, 673, 776
New York City	*David Frost Show*	781
New York City	acoustic, take unknown	173, 174, 226, 791, 911
New York City	acoustic demo as 'Que Pasa'	173, 236, 350
New York City	final demo	140
New York City	unknown take	337, 353, 378, 729, 762, 810, 811, 834, 865
New York City	official release	365
A Nice Noise	John with Sean	076, 236, 727, 845
Nightmares	Los Angeles, California, 1974	380, 859
No Bed for Beatle John	from *Life with the Lions*	016, 064, 867
Nobody Loves You (When You're Down and Out)	acoustic demo, 1974	015, 191
Nobody Loves You (When You're Down and Out)	*Walls and Bridges* rehearsal, 13 July 1974	018, 137, 309, 374, 833, 850
Nobody Loves You (When You're Down and Out)	*Walls and Bridges* rehearsal, 21 July 1974	114, 374, 883

Title	Source	Entry No.
Nobody Loves You (When You're Down and Out)	*Walls and Bridges*, Record Plant East, July/August 1974	885, 914
Nobody Loves You (When You're Down and Out)	rehearsal – no strings	176
Nobody Loves You (When You're Down and Out)	*Walls and Bridges* sessions, unknown take	225, 353, 374, 460, 641, 767, 841, 879, 897, 898
Nobody Loves You (When You're Down and Out)	*Walls and Bridges* sessions, monitor mix	768, 885, 914
Nobody Loves You (When You're Down and Out)	*Walls and Bridges*, from quad mix	882
Nobody Loves You (When You're Down and Out)	*Walls and Bridges*, 8-track mix	883
Nobody Loves You (When You're Down and Out)	from *Menlove Avenue* album	405, 533
Nobody Loves You (When You're Down and Out)	*Walls and Bridges* album, official release	365, 818, 884
Nobody Sees Me Like You	*Double Fantasy* sessions, unknown take	260, 261, 281, 285, 482, 485, 685, 691
Nobody Told Me	*Double Fantasy* sessions, take 1, mono	032, 271, 444, 609
Nobody Told Me	*Double Fantasy* sessions, take	2101, 271
Nobody Told Me	*Double Fantasy* sessions, rough mix	411, 544, 478, 677, 762

Title	Source	Entry No.
Nobody Told Me	double-tracked demo	241, 443, 478, 608, 677, 760, 761
Nobody Told Me	Bermuda, June 1980	211
Nobody Told Me	Bermuda, July 1980	212
Nobody Told Me	*Double Fantasy* sessions, unknown takes and rehearsals	079, 094, 100, 165, 179, 229, 237, 241, 243, 260, 261, 271, 275, 279, 283, 337, 353, 485, 490, 491, 691, 701, 703, 736, 740, 741, 779, 782, 791, 847, 870, 873, 874, 876
Nobody Told Me	5.1 centre channel mix from *Lennon Legend* DVD	221, 363, 364
Nobody Told Me	*Milk and Honey* album, official release version	259, 365, 748
No. 9 Dream	early demo	238, 422, 565, 913
No. 9 Dream	take 2	792
No. 9 Dream	composing demo	493, 706
No. 9 Dream	*Walls and Bridges*, Record Plant East, July/August 1974	885, 914
No. 9 Dream	*Walls and Bridges*, from quad mix	882
No. 9 Dream	*Walls and Bridges*, 8-track mix	883
No. 9 Dream	demos and outtakes, unknown takes	081, 083, 088, 096, 169, 172, 176, 237, 239, 241, 250, 256, 279, 287, 373, 374, 376, 455, 460, 631, 641, 738, 780, 782, 783, 784, 850, 875, 880, 897, 898, 903
No. 9 Dream	rough mix	431, 493, 584, 706, 768
No. 9 Dream	monitor mix	771, 885, 914

Title	Source	Entry No.
No. 9 Dream	promo edit	225, 338, 885, 914
No. 9 Dream	5.1 centre channel mix from *Lennon Legend* DVD	221, 363, 364
No. 9 Dream	*Walls and Bridges* album, official release version	365, 748, 818, 884
Not Fade Away	*Clock* rehearsals, St Regis hotel, New York, September 1971	013, 128, 189, 232, 236, 401, 525, 722, 796, 840, 912
Not Fade Away	with Elephant's Memory Band	074, 076, 174, 235, 348, 401, 525, 749, 814, 826
Not Only... But Also Skits	from John's book, 29 November 1964	200
Now and Then	take 1	273
Now and Then	unknown take	249, 749, 766, 797, 798, 856, 893
Now Or Never Spirit Choir	producer John Lennon	759
Now Or Never	*Jerry Lewis Telethon*	753, 754, 854
Nutopian International Anthem	silent track	159, 168, 750, 860
Nutopian International Anthem	long version (silent track)	066, 149, 150, 168, 849
Oh, My Love	*Imagine* album, unknown take	037, 038, 043, 082, 089, 092, 115, 116, 141, 154, 166, 179, 222, 231, 240, 272, 280, 288, 292, 303, 307, 325, 417, 429, 469, 556, 579, 658, 769, 771, 773, 781, 821, 848, 858, 873, 874, 877, 899, 901

Title	Source	Entry No.
Oh, My Love	outtake, Tittenhurst	237, 239, 306
Oh, My Love	early home demos	240, 291, 386, 447, 616
Oh, My Love	acoustic home demo	166, 194, 239, 290, 298, 482, 685
Oh, My Love	*Imagine* album sessions, rehearsal, take 1	295, 760, 761
Oh, My Love	*Imagine* album sessions, rehearsal, take 2	295, 298
Oh, My Love	*Imagine* album sessions, rehearsal, take 3	295
Oh, My Love	*Imagine* album sessions, rehearsal, take 4	295
Oh, My Love	*Imagine* album sessions, rehearsal, take 5	295
Oh, My Love	*Imagine* album sessions, rehearsal, take 6	295
Oh, My Love	*Imagine* album sessions, rehearsal, take 7	295
Oh, My Love	*Imagine* album sessions, rehearsal, take 8	295
Oh, My Love	*Imagine* album sessions, rehearsal, take 9	295
Oh, My Love	*Imagine* album sessions, rehearsal, take 10	295
Oh, My Love	Imagine album sessions, rehearsal, take 11	295
Oh, My Love	*Imagine* album sessions, rehearsal, take 12	295
Oh, My Love	*Imagine* album sessions, rehearsal, take 13	295
Oh, My Love	*Imagine* album sessions, take 1, mix A	295, 298

Oh, My Love	*Imagine* album sessions, take 1, mix B	295
Oh, My Love	*Imagine* album sessions, take 1, unknown mix	353
Oh, My Love	*Imagine* album sessions, take 2	290, 295, 353
Oh, My Love	*Imagine* album sessions, take 11	290, 353
Oh, My Love	*Imagine* album sessions, take 16	290
Oh, My Love	*Imagine* album sessions, rehearsals, outtakes, etc.	302
Oh, My Love	*Imagine* album, rough mix	085, 238, 427, 434, 576, 590
Oh, My Love	Yoko vocal, John on backing guitar	281
Oh, My Love	*Imagine* album sessions, from acetate	289, 293
Oh, My Love	*Imagine* album, quad mix	294, 296, 302, 304
Oh, My Love	Imagine 5.1 surround mix, centre channel;	304
Oh, My Love	Imagine 5.1 surround mix, front channels	304
Oh, My Love	Imagine 5.1 surround mix, rear channels	304
Oh, My Love	from *Imagine – The Film*	301
Oh, My Love	two-sided Bell Acetate	160
Oh, My Love	*Mind Games* sessions, rehearsal	295
Oh, My Love	official release	365
Oh, Yoko	*Imagine* album, unknown takes and demos	043, 086, 089, 098, 162, 222, 237, 256, 279, 288, 291, 292, 298, 303, 307, 325, 337, 353, 417, 495, 555, 710, 740, 760, 761, 791, 821, 844, 856, 858, 864, 870, 873

Oh, Yoko	*Imagine* album sessions, demo, take 1	313, 760, 761
Oh, Yoko	*Imagine* album sessions, demo, take 2	313
Oh, Yoko	*Imagine* album sessions, demo, take 3	313
Oh, Yoko	*Imagine* album sessions, acoustic and piano demo	290, 350
Oh, Yoko	*Imagine* album sessions, take 7	290, 295, 298
Oh, Yoko	*Imagine* album sessions, take 9, longer	166, 290, 294, 295, 298, 797
Oh, Yoko	*Imagine* album sessions, vocal overdubs	294, 295
Oh, Yoko	*Imagine* album, demo	081, 166, 237, 242, 298, 437, 595
Oh, Yoko	*Imagine* album, outtake, Ascot, extended ending	082, 239, 246, 306, 909
Oh, Yoko	*Imagine* album, Ascot, rough mix with count-in	417, 429, 555, 580, 762
Oh, Yoko	*Imagine* album sessions, from acetate	289, 293
Oh, Yoko	*Imagine* album, quad mix	294, 296, 302
Oh, Yoko	Imagine 5.1 surround mix, centre channel	303
Oh, Yoko	Imagine 5.1 surround mix, front channels	303
Oh, Yoko	Imagine 5.1 surround mix, rear channels	303
Oh, Yoko	from *Imagine – The Film*	301
Oh, Yoko	live, New York hotel, 9 October 1971, John's thirty-first birthday	215, 346, 437, 595, 840, 912
Oh, Yoko	from Medley	242, 290, 740

Old Dirt Road	*Walls and Bridges* rehearsal, 13 July 1974	018, 137, 309, 374, 833, 850, 883
Old Dirt Rocd	*Walls and Bridges* rehearsal, 21 July 1974	114, 374
Old Dirt Road	*Walls and Bridges*, Record Plant East, July/August 1974	885, 914
Old Dirt Road	*Walls and Bridges*, demo	030
Old Dirt Road	*Walls and Bridges*, rehearsal – no strings	176
Old Dirt Road	*Walls and Bridges* sessions, off line monitor mix	101, 768, 885, 914
Old Dirt Road	*Walls and Bridges*, from quad mix	882
Old Dirt Road	*Walls and Bridges* sessions, rehearsal, unknown take	225, 243, 353, 460, 641, 741, 767, 780, 841, 872, 875, 879, 897, 898
Old Dirt Road	from *Menlove Avenue* album	430, 582
Old Dirt Road	*Walls and Bridges* album, official release version	818, 884
Old Smokey Mountain, see *On Top of Old Smokey*		
Once Upon a Pool Table	John reading poetry	399, 521, 837
One Day at a Time	*Mind Games* album, unknown take	095, 159, 220, 241, 353, 424, 452, 626, 569, 737, 752, 773, 849, 873, 876
One Day at a Time	rough mix with overdubs	168, 751
One Day at a Time	*Mind Games* sessions, early rough mix	496, 712, 751, 756, 760, 761
One Day at a Time	*Mind Games* album, from acetate	750
One of the Boys	home demo, Dakota, 1977	014, 075, 087, 190, 206, 235, 239, 249, 273, 274, 742, 749, 783, 784, 846, 856, 893

One of the Boys	acoustic guitar demo, take 1	890
One of the Boys	acoustic guitar demo, take 2	402, 527, 890
One of the Boys	demo, take 7	431, 584
One-to-One radio spot outtakes	outtakes One-to-One radio spot	071, 076, 152, 167, 234, 236, 430, 581, 775, 901
Only People	rough mix	083, 168, 169, 238, 264, 265, 424, 475, 569, 670, 751, 756, 903
Only People	alternate mix	092, 240, 241
Only People	*Mind Games* album, from acetate	750
Only People	*Mind Games* album, unknown take	095, 159, 162, 220, 353, 451, 473, 624, 667, 737, 752, 755, 849, 871, 873, 876
Only the Lonely	unknown take – probably *Double Fantasy* sessions	353, 373, 426, 573, 734, 742, 792, 865
Only You	John's completed studio version	078, 233, 236, 408, 538, 779, 780, 798
Only You	*Roots* outtake	125, 353, 755, 770, 820, 843
Only You	Record Plant, New York, 13 July 1974	850
Only You	unknown take	877, 881
On The Caribbean	*Sometime in New York City* sessions	424, 570
On The Caribbean	One-to-One rehearsals	775
On The Caribbean	unknown take	222, 353, 378
On the Road To Marrakesh	evolved into Jealous Guy, outtakes	303
On Top of Old Smokey	live, New York hotel, 9 October 1971, John's thirty-first birthday	215, 244, 346, 370, 380, 387, 725, 840, 861, 864, 912

Only the Lonely	*Double Fantasy* sessions	007, 084, 238, 338
Ooh My Soul	rehearsal with Elephant's Memory	826
Open Your Box	One-to-One concert rehearsals	118, 120, 388, 777
Open Your Box	One-to-One concert (afternoon show)	774
Open Your Box	One-to-One concert (evening show)	774, 825
Open Your Box	acetate	272
Open Your Box	single version	182, 889
O' Sanity	*Milk and Honey* album, official release version	259
Out the Blue	*Mind Games* outtake, basic track with rough vocals	081, 086, 237, 256, 762
Out the Blue	*Mind Games* sessions, rough mix	101, 168, 169, 239, 414, 429, 494, 551, 580, 709, 756, 903
Out the Blue	*Mind Games* album, from acetate	750
Out the Blue	*Mind Games* sessions, no choir	783, 784
Out the Blue	*Mind Games* album, unknown take	159, 162, 179, 220, 243, 353, 500, 720, 741, 749, 752, 756, 773, 779, 843, 849, 870, 871, 875, 880
Paper Shoes	Yoko Ono, unknown take	175
Pedro the Fisherman	piano demo, Weybridge	099, 243, 329, 387, 484, 688, 740, 861, 890
Peggy Sue	from *Roots*	132, 133, 217, 820
Peggy Sue	*Rock 'n' Roll* album rehearsals	023, 060, 108, 109, 110, 157, 218, 814, 815, 816
Peggy Sue	*Rock 'n' Roll* rehearsals, Morris Levy's Farm, New York	245, 815
Peggy Sue	official released version	061

Peggy Sue	rough mix – Lennon sessions	218, 238
Peggy Sue	offline rough mix – Lennon sessions	218
Peggy Sue	*Clock* rehearsals, St Regis Hotel, New York, September 1971	014, 076, 128, 190, 223, 236, 244, 390, 403, 503, 529, 722, 796, 814, 840, 912
Peggy Sue	unknown take	008, 085, 111, 171, 184, 250, 264, 265, 353, 749, 770, 815, 819, 873
Peggy Sue	live, New York hotel, 9 October 1971, John's thirty-first birthday	215, 244, 246, 370, 380, 726, 840, 864, 912
Peggy Sue	from medley during TV interview	024, 065, 101, 142, 143, 224, 243, 741
Peggy Sue	home recording, John guitar	071, 234
Peggy Sue Got Married	*Clock* rehearsals, St Regis Hotel, New York, September 1971	014, 076, 128, 190, 236, 244, 403, 529, 722, 796, 814, 840, 912
Peggy Sue Got Married	unknown outtake	076
People	demo, tune evolved into 'Angela'	083, 173, 174, 238, 423, 484, 568, 689, 742, 845, 911
People Get Ready	unknown take	237, 298, 338, 387, 442, 605, 792, 861
People Get Ready	*Imagine* album rehearsal, Tittenhurst Park, 1970	246, 290, 294, 417, 442, 556, 605, 760, 761, 909
Pill	*Sometime in New York City*, unreleased song	081, 237, 256, 277, 287, 417, 556, 730, 749, 783, 784, 865, 911
Plastic Ono Band Jam	outtake	098, 242, 740
Power to the People	live, New York hotel, 9 October 1971, John's thirty-first birthday	215, 244, 346, 370, 380, 840, 912

Power to the People	rough mix of unreleased version	069, 172, 384, 391, 505, 801
Power to the People	early alternate take	008, 011, 072, 111, 128, 169, 291
Power to the People	alternate takes and rehearsals	087, 095, 128, 162, 172, 187, 239, 255, 348, 351, 353, 398, 429, 519, 450, 579, 621, 771, 782, 796, 875, 876
Power to the People	One-to-One concert (afternoon show)	774
Power to the People	One-to-One concert (evening show)	774, 825
Power to the People	ragged take, John attempts reggae vocal	086, 239, 241
Power to the People	official release	005, 121, 182, 365, 748
Power to the People	5.1 centre channel mix from *Lennon Legend* DVD (bass and drums)	221, 363, 364
Power to the People	unknown take	184, 222, 234, 235, 252, 473, 667, 737, 796, 799, 842, 843, 864, 870, 872, 887
Pushed An Empty (Carriage All Over Town)	Yoko Ono, unknown take	175
A Quick One While He's Away	John, Yoko, George and Ringo	867
Radio Free London	*Oz* magazine message	084
Radio Peace Jingle	1970	030, 156, 231, 267, 731, 837
Radio Play	from *Life with the Lions*	016, 064, 867
Radio Special	John acting as a DJ	310

Radio Special	broadcast 9 October 1975	265
Radio Special Documentary	NBC Radio, 8 December 1981	331
Radio Special	Interviews and songs, WBCN Radio, Boston 1982.	823
Radio Special Documentary	BBC Radio 2, December 1999	360, 361, 362
Rave On	*Clock* rehearsals, St Regis Hotel, New York, September 1971	013, 076, 189, 223, 232, 236, 244, 401, 525, 722, 779, 796, 840, 912
Rave On	*Rock 'n' Roll* album rehearsals	814
Rave On	home tape, unknown take	264, 265, 335, 749, 789
Ready Teddy	*Rock 'n' Roll* album rehearsals	023, 060, 108, 109, 110, 157, 171, 420, 562, 815, 816, 878
Ready Teddy	*Rock 'n' Roll* rehearsals, Morris Levy's Farm, New York	245, 815
Ready Teddy	from *Roots*	217
Ready Teddy	official released version	062
Ready Teddy	rough mix – Lennon sessions	218, 238
Ready Teddy	offline rough mix – Lennon sessions	218
Real Life	piano demo, Dakota recording	073, 081, 088, 093, 094, 187, 222, 235, 237, 239, 241, 243, 249, 253, 255, 350, 384, 392, 506, 735, 794, 846, 865, 881
Real Life	piano demo, take 1	797, 798
Real Life	piano demo, take 2	432, 448, 499, 586, 617, 718, 797
Real Life	take 3	499, 718
Real Life	take 5	499, 718

Real Love	take 1	420, 561, 177, 272, 273, 274, 797
Real Love	acoustic demo, take 4	087, 239, 272, 273, 274, 429, 580, 797
Real Love	acoustic demo, take 5	091, 177, 240, 272, 733, 797
Real Love	acoustic demo, take 6	272, 797
Real Love	piano demo	285, 448, 618
Real Love	guitar demo	436, 594
Real Love	Bermuda, July 1980	215
Real Love	unknown take	102, 177 179, 230, 241, 249, 256, 272, 277, 336, 376, 458, 467, 476, 499, 637, 655, 673, 718, 736, 741, 749, 783, 784, 790, 797, 798, 845, 865, 880, 893, 903, 904
Real Love	official release	365
Remember	*Plastic Ono Band* album sessions, unknown outtake	162, 170, 182, 321, 785, 793, 910, 810, 811, 836, 842
Remember	7" Apple Acetate	160, 286
Remember A Fly Is Just A Fly	from *The Making of Fly* film	178
Remember Love	official release	889
Remember Love	outtake	148, 438, 483, 598, 687
The Return of Maurice Dupont		081, 256
Rip It Up	from Roots	132, 133, 217, 820
Rip It Up	*Rock 'n' Roll* album rehearsals	023, 060, 108, 109, 110, 157, 171, 353, 420, 562, 770, 815, 816, 817, 819, 878, 898

Rip It Up	*Rock 'n' Roll* rehearsals, Morris Levy's Farm, New York	245, 407, 536, 815
Rip It Up	rough mix – Lennon sessions	213, 238
Rip It Up	offline rough mix – Lennon sessions	213
Rip It Up	official released version	062
Rip It Up	from promotional video, August 1980	017, 153, 203, 270, 416, 553
Rip It Up/Ready Teddy	*Rock 'n' Roll* session, rough mix	084
Rock 'n' Roll People	original acoustic demo	011, 073, 253
Rock 'n' Roll People	composing demo	140, 399, 520
Rock 'n' Roll People	*Imagine* album rehearsal, Tittenhurst Park, 1970	246, 756
Rock 'n' Roll People	demo, Sunset Sound, 15 May 1973	255
Rock 'n' Roll People	demo, Sunset Sound, 4 August 1973	255
Rock 'n' Roll People	piano demo	011, 168, 241, 452, 626, 760, 761, 791
Rock 'n' Roll People	take 5	140, 187, 399, 520, 887
Rock 'n' Roll People	take 7	450, 621, 760, 761
Rock 'n' Roll People	rough mix of take 7	092, 168, 240
Rock 'n' Roll People	alternate take	074, 083, 095, 238, 424, 569, 903
Rock 'n' Roll People	from *Menlove Avenue* album	407, 537
Rock 'n' Roll People	*Mind Games* sessions, unknown take	159, 162, 187, 216, 222, 235, 337, 353, 376, 499, 719, 734, 737, 752, 755, 756, 770, 820, 850, 871, 872, 873, 876, 877, 881
Rock 'n' Roll radio spot	advertisement for album	101, 243, 741, 815
Rockabilly Rave Up	unknown take	216

Rock Island Line	acoustic, Dakota, 1970s	011, 069, 222, 277
Rock Island Line	electric guitar, Dakota	073, 222, 253, 255, 399, 521, 779
Rock Island Line	unknown take, Dakota	008, 111, 184, 187, 206, 234, 235, 252, 336, 376, 393, 465, 651, 508, 728, 749, 790, 846
Rock Island Line Medley	during TV interview	024, 065, 101, 142, 143, 224, 226, 243, 741
Roll Over Beethoven	One-to-One concert rehearsal with Elephant's Memory	014, 076, 119, 120, 152, 190, 353, 388, 404, 530, 722, 775, 777, 814, 826, 896
Roll Over Beethoven	live, *Mike Douglas Show* with Chuck Berry	140
Roll Over Beethoven	unknown take	174, 236, 879
Rule Britannia	ad lib during interview, broadcast 27 March 1971	355
Rumble	*Rock 'n' Roll* album rehearsals	023, 108, 109, 110, 157
Rumble	*Rock 'n' Roll* rehearsals, Morris Levy's Farm, New York	245, 411, 544, 815
The Sadness of Your Soul, see *You Saved My Soul*		
Sakura	live, *The Mike Douglas Show*, 14–18 February 1972	144, 145, 146, 147, 382, 853, 854
Sakura	outtake	148, 352
Sally and Billy	demo, Ascot, 1970	015, 242, 243, 246, 909
Sally and Billy	home demo, 1976	099, 128, 492, 704
Sally and Billy	unknown outtake	078, 098, 191, 205, 236, 249, 273, 274, 405, 532, 728, 740, 796

Sally and Billy	take 1	350
Sally and Billy	piano/drum machine, take 2	247, 285, 890
Sally and Billy	piano/drum machine, take 3	078, 236, 247, 762, 890
San Francisco Bay Blues	*Imagine* album sessions, outtake	043, 082, 166, 237, 288, 290, 292, 294, 295, 298, 306, 325, 338, 348, 353, 416, 417, 553, 556, 730, 792, 821, 844, 879, 887
Saturday Morning Song, see *We Come Along On Saturday Morning*		
Save The Last Dance For Harry Nilsson	producer John Lennon	759
Say Please	Fillmore East, New York, alternate mix (see also *Jamrag*)	269, 353
Say Please	Fillmore East, New York, Frank Zappa mix	269, 328
Scared	*Walls and Bridges* rehearsal, 13 July 1974	018, 137, 309, 374, 833, 850, 883
Scared	*Walls and Bridges* rehearsal, 21 July 1974	114, 374, 883
Scared	*Walls and Bridges*, Record Plant East, July/August 1974	885, 914
Scared	*Walls and Bridges* sessions, monitor mix	768, 885, 914
Scared	*Walls and Bridges*, from quad mix	882
Scared	*Walls and Bridges*, 8-track mix	883
Scared	*Walls and Bridges* rehearsal, unknown takes and rehearsals	176, 179, 225, 353, 733, 767, 841, 872, 879, 897, 898
Scared	*Walls and Bridges* album, official release version	818, 884

Screaming Lord McNasty	unknown take	249
Scumbag	Fillmore East, New York, alternate mix	269, 353, 368
Scumbag	Fillmore East, New York, Frank Zappa mix	269
Scumbag	Fillmore East, New York, original Lennon mix	269, 328, 834
Sea Ditty Medley	demo, Dakota, 1979, John piano	009, 070, 111, 185, 206, 234, 285, 349, 395, 484, 513, 688, 749, 890
Send Me Some Loving	St Regis Hotel, New York, probably 1972	015, 128, 191, 796
Send Me Some Loving	jamming in the studio with Elephant's Memory	080
Send Me Some Loving	*Sometime in New York City* sessions	411, 545
Send Me Some Loving	*Rock 'n' Roll* album rehearsals	023, 060, 108, 109, 110, 125, 157, 171, 174, 219, 236, 237, 336, 353, 407, 536, 790, 815, 816, 820, 878, 902
Send Me Some Loving	home demo, take unknown	264, 265, 405, 533, 727, 770, 911
Send Me Some Loving	*Rock 'n' Roll* rehearsals, Morris Levy's Farm, New York	245, 815
Send Me Some Loving	from *Roots*	217
Send Me Some Loving	offline rough mix – Lennon sessions	218
Send Me Some Loving	with acoustic guitar accompaniment	078, 779
Send Me Some Loving	One-to-One rehearsals	775, 814, 826
Send Me Some Loving	official released version	062

Serve Yourself	acoustic version 1980	134, 167, 231, 904
Serve Yourself	piano version 1980	010, 014, 072, 076, 080, 090, 093, 101, 186, 190, 240, 241, 277, 349, 350, 371, 730, 742, 760, 761, 822
Serve Yourself	slow bluesy version	237, 397, 404, 517, 530
Serve Yourself	Bermuda, June 1980	211
Serve Yourself	Bermuda, July 1980	051, 156, 204
Serve Yourself	unknown take	096, 135, 192, 210, 213, 233, 235, 236, 242, 243, 249, 352, 414, 434, 440, 455, 458, 476, 500, 551, 589, 601, 631, 638, 673, 720, 727, 735, 738, 741
Shake Hands With Your Uncle Dick	ad lib during interview, broadcast 27 March 1971	355
Shazam	*Clock* rehearsals, St Regis Hotel, New York, September 1971	223, 384, 840, 912
She'll Be Coming Round the Mountain	unknown take	096, 242, 387, 475, 670, 738, 861, 911
She is a Friend of Dorothy	outtake from 1977	081, 099, 205, 237, 243, 249, 256, 350, 416, 492, 553, 704, 740, 742, 749, 783, 784, 846
She is a Friend of Dorothy	piano demo, take 1	371
She is a Friend of Dorothy	piano demo, take 2	247, 285, 371
She is a Friend of Dorothy	piano demo, take 7	247, 273, 274, 371, 384, 431, 584
She Runs Them Round in Circles	unknown take	096, 242, 387, 474, 668, 738, 861

Title	Source	Entry No.
She's a Woman	from promotional film, August 1980	017, 153, 203, 270, 353, 817, 898
She's Not a Girl Who Misses Much, see *Beatles Bootlegs*		
She's Walking Past My Door	Weybridge demo	329, 386
Shoeshine	*Mind Games* sessions, unknown take	159, 168, 220, 239, 428, 578, 751, 822
Since My Baby Left Me	live, New York hotel, 9 October 1971, John's thirty-first birthday	246, 370
Since My Baby Left Me	unknown take	755, 815, 819
Sisters Oh Sisters	outtake, acoustic	148
Sisters Oh Sisters	outtake, electric	148
Sisters Oh Sisters	One-to-One concert rehearsals	117, 120, 173, 775
Sisters Oh Sisters	One-to-One concert (afternoon show)	774
Sisters Oh Sisters	One-to-One concert (evening show)	774, 825
Sisters Oh Sisters	live, Free John Sinclair Rally	006, 046, 048, 057, 058, 113, 122, 123, 901
Sisters Oh Sisters	live, *David Frost Show*, 13 January 1972	144, 145, 146, 147, 173
Sisters Oh Sisters	*Mike Douglas Show*	244, 853, 854
Sisters Oh Sisters	live, unknown TV show	382
Sisters Oh Sisters	unknown take	352
Sleepless Night	*Milk and Honey* album, official release version	259
Sleepwalk	unknown	755
Slippin' and Slidin'	from *Roots*	132, 133, 171, 217, 820

Title	Source	Entry No.
Slippin' and Slidin'	*Rock 'n' Roll* album rehearsals	023, 060, 108, 109, 110, 157, 219, 407, 470, 536, 661, 814, 816, 817, 819
Slippin' and Slidin'	*Rock 'n' Roll* rehearsals, Morris Levy's Farm, New York	245, 815
Slippin' and Slidin'	offline rough mix – Lennon sessions	218
Slippin' and Slidin'	official released version	062
Slippin' and Slidin'	*The Old Grey Whistle Test*	037, 038, 140, 154, 156, 171, 194, 219, 280, 313, 320, 753, 754, 815, 886
Slippin' and Slidin'	*The Old Grey Whistle Test* rehearsal	886, 899
Slippin' and Slidin'	*The Old Grey Whistle Test* (instrumental backing)	219
Slippin' and Slidin'	*The Old Grey Whistle Test* (raw version with count-in)	219
Slippin' and Slidin'	live, *Salute To Sir Lew Grade*, 13 June 1975	034, 126, 136, 194, 219, 231, 731, 753, 754, 815, 886
Slippin' and Slidin'	live, *Salute To Sir Lew Grade*, 13 June 1975 (audience)	219
Slippin' and Slidin'	unknown take	107, 250, 278, 353, 770, 788, 815, 832
A Small Eternity	Fillmore East, New York, alternate mix (with Yoko Ono)	269, 353
A Small Eternity	Fillmore East, New York, Frank Zappa mix (with Yoko Ono)	269, 328
Snow Is Falling all the Time	from *Life with the Lions*	016, 867
Somewhere in the Sky	Yoko on vocal	281, 482, 684, 909
Song for John	Queen Charlotte Hospital	867
So Long	unknown take	384

Title	Source	Entry No.
Stand By Me	from *Roots*	132, 133, 217, 820
Stand By Me	Los Angeles, California, 1974	380, 859
Stand By Me	*Rock 'n' Roll* album rehearsals	023, 060, 108, 109, 110, 157, 171, 219, 237, 243, 353, 499, 719, 741, 770, 816, 819
Stand By Me	*Rock 'n' Roll* rehearsals, Morris Levy's Farm, New York	245, 815
Stand By Me	reggae version	755
Stand By Me	offline rough mix – Lennon sessions	218
Stand By Me	monitor mix	771
Stand By Me	official released version	062, 182, 365
Stand By Me	*The Old Grey Whistle Test*	037, 038, 101, 154, 156, 171, 194, 219, 280, 313, 320, 410, 542, 753, 754, 815, 886
Stand By Me	*The Old Grey Whistle Test* rehearsal	886, 899
Stand By Me	*The Old Grey Whistle Test*, take 2	219
Stand By Me	*The Old Grey Whistle Test*, stereo	219
Stand By Me	live, *Salute To Sir Lew Grade*, 13 June 1975	034, 136, 194, 753, 754, 815, 886
Stand By Me	live, *Salute To Sir Lew Grade*, 13 June 1975 (audience)	219
Stand By Me	5.1 centre channel mix from *Lennon Legend* DVD	221, 363, 364
Stand By Me	unknown take	107, 222, 250, 278, 279, 353, 407, 462, 481, 536, 645, 683, 755, 799, 816, 832, 875
Starting Over	*Double Fantasy*, studio warm up, 1980	012, 188

Title	Source	Entry No.
Starting Over	*Double Fantasy* sessions, early outtake	073, 165, 253, 401, 524, 760, 761
Starting Over	*Double Fantasy* sessions, demo, take 1	449, 619
Starting Over	*Double Fantasy*, take 3, Dakota, 1980	009, 111, 185, 271, 277, 395, 513
Starting Over	*Double Fantasy*, home demo, Dakota, 1980	161, 179, 283
Starting Over	*Double Fantasy*, acoustic demo	241, 242, 264, 265, 271
Starting Over	*Double Fantasy*, studio demo, 1980	030, 179, 283
Starting Over	from promotional video, August 1980	007, 017, 153, 203, 270
Starting Over	*Double Fantasy*, guitar and drum machine	052, 070, 234, 789, 792
Starting Over	*Double Fantasy*, rough take, vocal booth	073, 235, 244, 253, 348
Starting Over	*Double Fantasy* sessions, rough mix	449, 619, 771
Starting Over	*Double Fantasy*, monitor mix	103, 244
Starting Over	playback tape	285
Starting Over	*Double Fantasy*, studio unknown take	081, 093, 094, 097, 103, 165, 213, 216, 222, 226, 231, 235, 241, 260, 261, 271, 335, 336, 338, 348, 351, 353, 373, 377, 401, 426, 458, 486, 500, 524, 573, 637, 693, 720, 721, 735, 736, 739, 782, 790, 799, 817, 845, 847, 860, 865, 869, 873, 875, 880, 898

Title	Source	Entry No.
Starting Over	chimes only	115, 250
Starting Over	*Double Fantasy*, longer fade version, withdrawn	030, 066, 149, 150, 237, 256, 772
Starting Over	12" promo, long version	160, 272
Starting Over	*Double Fantasy*, complete home demo	165
Starting Over	*Lennon Legend* DVD 5.1 mixes	363, 364
Starting Over	*Double Fantasy* album, official release version	259, 365, 748
Stay	from promotional video, August 1980	017, 030, 097, 153, 203, 242, 270v
Stay	*Double Fantasy* sessions, Hit Factory, New York	283, 348, 353, 739, 817, 876, 898
Stay In Bed (Grow Your Hair)	from *Wedding Album*	082, 237, 387, 861
Steel and Glass	*Walls and Bridges* rehearsal, 13 July 1974	018, 137, 309, 374, 833, 850, 883
Steel and Glass	*Walls and Bridges* rehearsal, 21 July 1974	114, 374
Steel and Glass	*Walls and Bridges*, Record Plant East, July/August 1974	885, 914
Steel and Glass	from *Walls and Bridges* 8-track	093, 241, 883
Steel and Glass	*Walls and Bridges*, from quad mix	882
Steel and Glass	*Walls and Bridges*, piano version with extra lyrics	099, 242, 740, 913
Steel and Glass	*Walls and Bridges*, off line monitor mix	101, 768, 885, 914
Steel and Glass	*Mind Games* sessions, unknown takes and rehearsals	159, 176, 179, 216, 225, 243, 353, 374, 403, 490, 529, 700, 735, 741, 767, 780, 822, 841, 871, 875, 876, 879, 897, 898

Steel and Glass	Mind Games album, official release version	818, 884
Stepping Out, see *I'm Stepping Out*		
Stranger in My Arms	Weybridge demo	329, 386, 387, 813, 861
Stranger's Room	*Double Fantasy* sessions, Dakota, early piano demo, late 1979, song evolved into 'I'm Losing You'	015, 084, 097, 165, 191, 210, 237, 238, 242, 249, 283, 285, 405, 426, 452, 453, 479, 500, 533, 574, 625, 628, 678, 721, 739, 903
Strawberry Field's Forever	home demo, 1979	008, 111
Subterranean Homesick Blues	*Double Fantasy* sessions, Dakota recording	206, 283, 368, 749
Surprise Surprise (Sweet Bird of Paradox)	*Walls and Bridges* rehearsal, 13 July 1974	018, 137, 153, 309, 374, 833, 850, 883
Surprise Surprise (Sweet Bird of Paradox)	*Walls and Bridges* rehearsal, 21 July 1974	114, 374, 883
Surprise Surprise (Sweet Bird of Paradox)	*Walls and Bridges*, Record Plant East, July/August 1974	428, 577, 885, 914
Surprise Surprise (Sweet Bird of Paradox)	*Walls and Bridges*, demo	008, 069, 111, 140, 184, 393, 408, 428, 508, 538, 577, 779
Surprise Surprise (Sweet Bird of Paradox)	guitar based demo	078, 085, 350, 913
Surprise Surprise (Sweet Bird of Paradox)	*Walls and Bridges* sessions, monitor mix	768, 885, 914
Surprise Surprise (Sweet Bird of Paradox)	*Walls and Bridges*, from quad mix	882
Surprise Surprise (Sweet Bird of Paradox)	*Walls and Bridges*, 8-track mix	883

Surprise Surprise (Sweet Bird of Paradox)	studio with Elton John	408, 538
Surprise Surprise (Sweet Bird of Paradox)	unknown take	096, 140, 176, 220, 225, 234, 236, 238, 252, 349, 374, 377, 460, 641, 738, 749, 767, 768, 780, 841, 850, 872, 879, 887, 897, 898
Surprise Surprise (Sweet Bird of Paradox)	*Walls and Bridges* album, official release version	818, 884
Sweet Little Sixteen	from *Roots*	132, 133, 217, 820
Sweet Little Sixteen	*Rock 'n' Roll* album rehearsals, unknown take	060, 063, 074, 089, 140, 162, 171, 189, 235, 240, 250, 281, 348, 353, 402, 526, 733, 770, 815, 819, 875
Sweet Little Sixteen	rough mix – Lennon sessions	218, 436, 594
Sweet Little Sixteen	*Rock 'n' Roll*, alternate extended version	013
Sweet Little Sixteen	official release	365
Take This Hammer	live, New York hotel, 9 October 1971, John's thirty-first birthday	215, 840, 864, 912
Take This Hammer	Los Angeles, California, 1974	380, 755, 859
Talkin' Roget's Thesaurus Headline Blues	acoustic satire	010
Tandoori Chicken	live, New York hotel, 9 October 1971, John's thirty-first birthday	215, 346, 370, 781, 840, 864, 912
Tell Me What I Say, see *What I Say*		

Tennessee Oh Tennessee	demo, Dakota, early 1975	003, 069, 099, 111, 184, 205, 234, 243, 247, 413, 548, 740, 865
Tennessee Oh Tennessee	piano demo, take 1	247, 252, 349, 890
Tennessee Oh Tennessee	piano demo, take 4	247, 252, 728, 890
Tennessee Oh Tennessee	piano demo with rhythm box	890
Tennessee Oh Tennessee	piano demo, unknown take	264, 265, 492, 704, 749, 795
Tequila	One-to-One concert rehearsals	034, 278, 365, 416, 553, 776, 777
Tequila	One-to-One rehearsals, 18 August 1972	152
That's All Right Mama	*Plastic Ono Band* album sessions	262, 286, 421, 449, 563, 619, 785, 793, 842, 875, 876, 910
That'll Be the Day	*Rock 'n' Roll* session, Record Plant, New York 1973	013, 023, 051, 076, 108, 109, 110, 157, 171, 179, 189, 401, 465, 525, 651, 755, 770, 816
That'll Be the Day	*Rock 'n' Roll* (false start) rehearsals, Morris Levy's Farm, New York	815
That'll Be the Day	rehearsal, Gwent, New York, October 1974	219
That'll Be the Day	*Rock 'n' Roll* rehearsals, Morris Levy's Farm, New York	245
That's the Way the World It	unknown take	249, 273, 274, 481, 683, 749, 893
Theme	from the film *Rape*	051
Thirty Days	*Rock 'n' Roll* album rehearsals	023, 034, 108, 109, 110, 157, 171, 278, 770, 816

Thirty Days	*Rock 'n' Roll* rehearsals, Morris Levy's Farm, New York	245, 814, 815
Thirty Days	rehearsal, Gwent, New York, October 1974	219
This Fly	unknown	781
Tight A$	demo	011, 075, 140, 187, 235, 399, 496, 520, 712, 756
Tight A$	early rough mix	264, 265, 751, 756
Tight A$	rough mix with guitar overdub	168
Tight A$	electric guitar demo	168, 169, 822
Tight A$	demo, Sunset Sound, May 1973	255
Tight A$	take 4	451, 624
Tight A$	*Mind Games* album, from acetate	750
Tight A$	*Mind Games* sessions, unknown take	096, 159, 162, 216, 220, 241, 336, 353, 738, 752, 755, 790, 849, 873, 876
Tobias Casuals	advertisements	078, 080, 081, 082, 236, 237, 238, 256, 349, 883
To Know Her Is to Love Her	*Rock 'n' Roll* rehearsals, Morris Levy's Farm, New York	815
To Know Her Is to Love Her	official release	365, 819
Too Many Cooks	Mick Jagger, John on mixing desk	019, 036, 469, 478, 658, 676, 755, 795, 824
Too Many People	ad lib	781
Too Much Monkey Business	acoustic demo, Dakota recording	206, 222, 226, 283, 365
Touch Me Yoko Ono	unknown take	175, 732
Tower Records Spot	advertisement	083, 238, 756

'Twas a Night like Ethel Merman	Dakota, cassette recording, recitation	010, 072, 186, 206, 235, 349, 398, 518
Twist and Shout	live, New York hotel, 9 October 1971, John's thirty-first birthday	215, 244, 380, 840, 864, 912
Two Face Man	unknown	192
Two Minutes Silence	from *Life with the Lions*	867
Two Virgins	official album	863
Two Virgins	outtake home studio recording, John and Yoko	098, 242, 386, 740
Unchained Melody	One-to-One concert rehearsals	118, 120, 388, 776, 896
Unchained Melody	One-to-One rehearsals, 18 August 1972	152
Uncle Albert	live, New York hotel, 9 October 1971, John's thirty-first birthday	215, 244, 346, 370, 380, 840, 864, 912
Under the Influence	unknown take	374
Vacation Has Just Began	*Clock* rehearsals, St Regis hotel, New York, September 1971	223, 244, 814, 840, 912
Voulez Vous Coucher Avec Moi	recorded 18 March 1975	116, 136, 141, 280
Wake Up Little Susie	*Clock* rehearsals, St Regis hotel, New York, September 1971	223, 244, 814, 840, 912
Walking on Thin Ice	rough mix, mono	032
Walking on Thin Ice	vocal booth	271, 281
Walking on Thin Ice	remix	373
Walking on Thin Ice	unknown take	148, 156, 260, 261, 271, 353, 483, 687
Walking on Thin Ice	from US 45 release (stereo)	115, 116
Walking on Thin Ice	Yoko Ono, producer John Lennon, official version	759, 881

Walls and Bridges	radio spots, promos	024, 030, 052, 099, 142, 143, 176, 224, 231, 238, 241, 242, 780, 850, 883
Watching the Wheels	*Double Fantasy*, acoustic demo, Bermuda, 1980	015, 071, 191, 204, 211, 390, 405, 503, 532, 779, 789, 902
Watching the Wheels	*Double Fantasy* sessions, rehearsal, vocal booth, take 3	890
Watching the Wheels	*Double Fantasy* sessions, Hit Factory, New York	283
Watching the Wheels	*Double Fantasy*, acoustic demo, blues style	165, 239, 240, 822
Watching the Wheels	*Double Fantasy*, acoustic version, folk version	165
Watching the Wheels	*Double Fantasy* sessions, acoustic guitar	890, 904
Watching the Wheels	*Double Fantasy* sessions, piano demo, take 1	890
Watching the Wheels	*Double Fantasy* sessions, piano demo, take 6	890
Watching the Wheels	*Double Fantasy*, piano demo, unknown take	071, 093, 234, 241, 349, 760, 761, 791, 799
Watching the Wheels	*Double Fantasy* sessions, electric guitar demo	433, 587, 890
Watching the Wheels	*Double Fantasy*, guitar-based demo	078, 234, 236, 887
Watching the Wheels	*Double Fantasy*, session tape	103
Watching the Wheels	*Double Fantasy* session, take 3	165
Watching the Wheels	*Double Fantasy* sessions, take 6	890
Watching the Wheels	*Double Fantasy* sessions, take 8	890
Watching the Wheel	vocal overdubs	242
Watching the Wheels	*Double Fantasy* sessions, rough mix, count-in	384, 433, 458, 587, 637, 890

Watching the Wheels	*Double Fantasy*, unknown outtakes and rehearsals	007, 008, 075, 088, 089, 091, 097, 100, 111, 165, 179, 184, 192, 210, 220, 222, 226, 233, 236, 240, 242, 243, 249, 260, 261, 279, 335, 336, 337, 338, 350, 353, 376, 377, 401, 440, 442, 462, 473, 485, 500, 524, 602, 606, 645, 666, 691, 721, 733, 735, 739, 740, 741, 749, 760, 761, 782, 790, 792, 845, 847, 872, 873, 874, 904
Watching the Wheels	Home demo, Dakota, 1980	161, 188, 283, 869
Watching the Wheels	5.1 centre channel mix from *Lennon Legend* DVD	221, 363, 364
Watching the Wheels	*Double Fantasy* album, official release version	259, 365, 748
We Come Along On Saturday Morning	from Andy Peebles BBC interview, 6 December 1980	308, 349, 387, 861
Wedding Album	official release	889
Wedding Album	commercial	082, 237
Welcome to Cold Spring Harbour	unknown take	210
Well (Baby Please Don't Go)	*Imagine* album sessions, studio outtake	162, 166, 238, 294, 298, 306, 425, 572, 880
Well (Baby Please Don't Go)	Fillmore East, New York, 6 June 1971, with Frank Zappa	328, 353, 834
Well, Well, Well	One-to-One concert, 30 August 1972 (afternoon show)	774
Well, Well, Well	One-to-One concert, 30 August 1972 (evening show)	124, 224, 774, 825
Well, Well, Well	One-to-One concert rehearsal, 22 August 1972	222, 430, 581, 775

Well, Well, Well	One-to-One concert rehearsals	118, 120, 152, 776, 896
Well, Well, Well	*Plastic Ono Band* album sessions, take 4	239, 384, 432, 585, 842
Well, Well, Well	*Plastic Ono Band* album sessions, rough mix	321, 793
Well, Well, Well	unknown take	024, 088, 162, 167, 170, 182, 192, 232, 262, 286, 287, 325, 338, 353, 365, 384, 749, 785, 792, 800, 836, 848, 872, 878, 880, 910
Well, Well, Well	*Plastic Ono Band* album, official release	340, 365
Well, Well, Well	Plastic Ono Band, 5.1	341
Well, Well, Well	acoustic demo	167, 170, 239, 286, 432, 585
Well, Well, Well	from WNEW Radio, with John as guest DJ	024, 142, 143
Well Baby Please Don't Go	official released version	062
Well Baby Please Don't Go	rehearsal for the Frank Zappa gig	173, 269
Well Baby Please Don't Go	full length version, John and Yoko with Frank Zappa and GO the Mothers, 6 June 1971	112, 127, 365
Well Baby Please Don't Go	*Imagine* session, outtake	083, 277, 290, 291, 295, 325, 353, 742, 820, 848, 870
Well Baby Please Don't Go	*Eyewitness News*, TV interview, Summer 1972	224
Well Baby Please Don't Go	One-to-One rehearsals	775

We Must Not Forget The General Erection	John reading from *A Spaniard in the Works*	071, 234, 330, 349, 386, 723
We'll Meet Again	ad lib	781
We're All Water	One-to-One concert, 30 August 1972 (afternoon show)	774
We're All Water	One-to-One concert, 30 August 1972 (evening show)	122, 123, 774, 825
We're All Water	One-to-One concert rehearsals	118, 119, 120, 173, 227, 388, 777, 826
We're All Water	live, *The Dick Cavett Show*, 11 May 1972	144, 145, 146, 147, 173, 244, 382, 854
Whatever Gets You Through the Night	*Walls and Bridges* rehearsal, 13 July 1974	018, 066, 115, 116, 137, 149, 150, 153, 309, 374, 833, 850, 883
Whatever Gets You Through the Night	*Walls and Bridges* rehearsals, 21 July 1974	114, 374, 883
Whatever Gets You Through the Night	*Walls and Bridges*, Record Plant East, July/August 1974	885, 914
Whatever Gets You Through the Night	guitar based demo, take unknown	071, 078, 093, 172, 234, 240, 264, 265, 279, 374, 396, 515
Whatever Gets You Through the Night	composing demo	474, 499, 668, 719
Whatever Gets You Through the Night	*Walls and Bridges* sessions, take 10	225
Whatever Gets You Through the Night	*Walls and Bridges* sessions, take 11	225
Whatever Gets You Through the Night	*Walls and Bridges* sessions, take 12	225
Whatever Gets You Through the Night	*Walls and Bridges* sessions, take 13	225

Whatever Gets You Through the Night	*Walls and Bridges* sessions, take 14	225
Whatever Gets You Through the Night	*Walls and Bridges* sessions, take 15	225
Whatever Gets You Through the Night	*Walls and Bridges* sessions, take 16	225
Whatever Gets You Through the Night	*Walls and Bridges* sessions, take 17	225
Whatever Gets You Through the Night	*Walls and Bridges* sessions, take 18	225
Whatever Gets You Through the Night	overdub on take 7	225
Whatever Gets You Through the Night	*Walls and Bridges* sessions, monitor mix	768, 885, 914
Whatever Gets You Through the Night	*Walls and Bridges*, home demo, 1974	010, 443, 607
Whatever Gets You Through the Night	quad 8-track mix	241, 882
Whatever Gets You Through the Night	rough mix, without Elton John	101, 225, 771
Whatever Gets You Through the Night	radio spot	055
Whatever Gets You Through the Night	live, with Elton John	037, 038, 126, 154, 172, 217, 280, 393, 415, 508, 552, 759, 764, 899
Whatever Gets You Through the Night	unknown take (probably with Elton John)	229
Whatever Gets You Through the Night	5.1 centre channel mix from *Lennon Legend* DVD	221, 363, 364
Whatever Gets You Through the Night	unknown takes and rehearsals	096, 136, 140, 169, 172, 176, 186, 225, 236, 243, 250, 335, 353, 373, 374, 408, 460, 478, 538, 641, 676, 733, 735, 738, 741, 755, 767, 768, 780, 782, 788, 789, 799, 832, 841, 860, 872, 874, 875, 879, 881, 897, 898, 902, 913

Title	Source	Entry No.
Whatever Gets You Through the Night	*Walls and Bridges* album, official release version	365, 748, 818, 884, 885, 914
Whatever Happened to	The Ballad of John and Yoko (proposed play), outtakes	071, 179, 205, 216, 234, 249, 267, 273, 274, 396, 415, 498, 514, 552, 716, 729, 749, 762, 845, 865, 890, 893
What I Say	live, New York hotel, 9 October 1971, John's thirty-first birthday	079, 215, 237, 244, 346, 370, 380, 409, 540, 725, 840, 864, 912
What You Got	*Walls and Bridges* rehearsal, 13 July 1974	850
What You Got	*Walls and Bridges* rehearsal, 21 July 1974	114, 374
What You Got	*Walls and Bridges*, Record Plant East, July/August 1974	885, 914
What You Got	*Walls and Bridges* album, acoustic demo	087, 161, 176, 239, 374, 429, 580, 869, 903
What You Got	*Walls and Bridges* album, electric demo	913
What You Got	*Walls and Bridges* album, alternate take	176, 225, 377
What You Got	*Walls and Bridges* sessions, monitor mix	768, 885, 914
What You Got	*Walls and Bridges*, from quad mix	882
What You Got	*Walls and Bridges* album, unknown take	460, 641, 767, 780, 879, 880, 897 898
What You Got	US promo 45	885, 914
When a Boy Meets a Girl	*Imagine* album sessions, demo	089, 170, 222, 239, 384, 436, 482, 593, 685, 785, 910

Title	Source	Entry No.
When a Boy Meets a Girl	*Imagine* album sessions, acoustic, take 1	742
When a Boy Meets a Girl	take 2, electrified acoustic guitar	170
When a Boy Meets a Girl	*Plastic Ono Band* album sessions	262, 286, 287, 773, 880
Whispering Bells	One-to-One rehearsals	776
Who Has Seen The Wind	Yoko Ono, official release version	889
Who Has Seen The Wind	outtake	148
Who Put the Bomp	unknown take	353
Whole Lotta Love	*Rock 'n' Roll* album rehearsals	023, 108, 109, 110, 157, 257, 770, 814, 816
Whole Lotta Love	*Rock 'n' Roll* rehearsals, Morris Levy's Farm, New York	245, 411, 544, 815
Whole Lotta Shakin' Going On	One-to-One studio rehearsal with Elephant's Memory	014, 076, 140, 174, 190, 236, 353, 404, 530, 722, 775, 814, 826
Whole Lotta Shakin' Going On	unknown take	878
Why Yoko Ono	official release version	889
Why Not Yoko Ono	unknown take	175, 732
Will You Touch Me	unknown take	107, 231
With a Little Help From Friends, Dakota	recording	069, 192, 233, 234, 252, 349, 392, 506, 724, 749
WNEW Radio guest DJ		224
Woman	first home demo	013, 189, 401, 525

Title	Source	Entry No.
Woman	*Double Fantasy* sessions, unknown outtakes	007, 013, 022, 025, 074, 075, 087, 097, 100, 165, 179, 184, 234, 235, 236, 239, 242, 243, 249, 252, 260, 261, 264, 265, 271, 279, 283, 335, 337, 351, 353, 401, 471, 483, 485, 486, 500, 525, 662, 686, 691, 692, 728, 721, 735, 739, 749, 779, 782, 799, 846, 847, 865, 871, 874, 878
Woman	demo, take 1	271, 440, 602
Woman	demo, remake, take 1	271
Woman	acoustic demo, false starts, take 4	242, 452, 625
Woman	acoustic guitar demo, take 7	452, 625
Woman	complete acoustic demo, take 9	242, 271, 760, 761, 791
Woman	acoustic guitar demo	485, 691, 802, 904
Woman	acoustic backing track	271
Woman	John recording vocals	243
Woman	John adding whispered intro	243
Woman	*Double Fantasy* sessions, instrumental	100
Woman	*Double Fantasy* sessions, vocal booth	075, 165, 235, 271, 348
Woman	Bermuda, July 1980	215, 241, 401, 525
Woman	*Double Fantasy*, double-tracked guitar demo	238, 486, 692
Woman	*Double Fantasy*, rehearsals Bermuda, takes unknown	008, 069, 093, 111, 161, 204, 869

Title	Source	Entry No.
Woman	*Double Fantasy*, acoustic demo with drum machine	165, 392, 506, 762, 789, 791
Woman	*Double Fantasy* sessions, rough mix	401, 429, 458, 525, 580, 638, 771
Woman	*Double Fantasy* sessions, rough mix with reference vocal	822
Woman	10" stereo acetate	160
Woman	*Double Fantasy* album, official release version	259, 365, 748
Woman	*Lennon Legend* DVD 5.1 mixes	363, 364
Woman	*Double Fantasy* sessions, instrumental	740
Woman	5.1 centre channel mix from *Lennon Legend* DVD (instrumental)	221
Woman Is the Nigger of the World	acoustic guitar demo	015, 088, 169, 173, 174, 191, 239, 406, 432, 534, 586, 762, 781, 791, 911
Woman Is the Nigger of the World	demo, slide guitar, 1969	368
Woman Is the Nigger of the World	no strings	368
Woman Is the Nigger of the World	*Sometime in New York City* album, outtake	089, 162
Woman Is the Nigger of the World	rough mix	771
Woman Is the Nigger of the World	Blues rendition, Greenwich Village, 1971	161, 869
Woman Is the Nigger of the World	*Mike Douglas Show*, February 1972	054, 228, 276
Woman Is the Nigger of the World	live, *Dick Cavett Show*, 11 May 1972	144, 145, 146, 147, 173, 244, 854

Title	Source	Entry No.
Woman Is the Nigger of the World	live, unknown TV show	382
Woman Is the Nigger of the World	One-to-One concert, 30 August 1972 (afternoon show)	774
Woman Is the Nigger of the World	One-to-One concert, 30 August 1972 (evening show)	024, 041, 124, 142, 143, 224, 464, 649, 774, 825
Woman Is the Nigger of the World	One-to-One concert rehearsals	117, 120, 152, 174, 388, 417, 556, 775, 776, 896
Woman Is the Nigger of the World	alternate take	172, 240
Woman Is the Nigger of the World	unknown take	174, 179, 222, 236, 337, 352, 353, 729, 773, 799, 843, 874, 879
Woman Is the Nigger of the World	ad lib	781, 834
Woman Is the Nigger of the World	official release	365, 748
Working Class Hero	*Plastic Ono Band* album, official release	340, 365
Working Class Hero	*Plastic Ono Band*, 5.1 mix	341, 363, 364
Working Class Hero	unknown, probably party in 1972	037, 038, 154, 899
Working Class Hero	*Plastic Ono Band* album sessions, folky guitar version	793
Working Class Hero	Australian album version, censored	170, 280, 321, 771, 817
Working Class Hero	radio edit version	468, 498, 657, 716
Working Class Hero	unknown take	781, 782, 785, 800, 836, 842, 910
The Worst is Over	demo, Dakota recording (evolved into 'Starting Over')	073, 090, 165, 213, 222, 235, 240, 271, 283, 285, 349, 401, 436, 481, 500, 524, 593, 683, 720, 742, 865

The Wrestling Dog	John reading from *In His Own Write*	330
The Wumberlog (The Magic Dog)	John reading from *A Spaniard in the Works*	071, 234, 330, 349, 723
Ya Ya	from *Roots*	132, 133, 217, 820
Ya Ya	*Rock 'n' Roll* album sessions	023, 051, 060, 063, 108, 109, 110, 157, 171, 352, 407, 460, 536, 641, 770, 815, 816, 819
Ya Ya	*Rock 'n' Roll* rehearsals, Morris Levy's Farm, New York	245, 815
Ya Ya	(false start), *Rock 'n' Roll* rehearsals, Morris Levy's Farm, New York	815
Ya Ya	rehearsal, Gwent, New York, October 1974	219
Ya Ya	*Walls and Bridges*, from quad mix	82
Ya Ya	offline rough mix – Lennon sessions	218
Ya Ya	*Walls and Bridges* album, official release version	365, 818, 884
Yellow Girl	unknown take	107
Yellow Submarine	live, New York hotel, 9 October 1971, John's thirty-first birthday	079, 215, 232, 237, 244, 346, 370, 380, 409, 540, 725, 840, 864, 912
Yer Blues	*Rock and Roll Circus*, 11 December 1968	002, 003, 005, 014, 020, 021, 035, 039, 051, 054, 066, 092, 115, 116, 130, 131, 134, 149, 150, 154, 155, 156, 190, 200, 222, 231, 257, 287, 328, 404, 416, 448, 454, 469, 530, 553, 617, 630, 659, 725, 730, 759, 860, 899, 902, 903

Yer Blues	*Rock and Roll Circus* rehearsal	014, 081, 086, 115, 116, 190, 200, 237, 238, 257, 287, 428, 578, 903
Yer Blues	*Rock and Roll Circus*, outtake – instrumental	348, 730, 783, 784
Yer Blues	*Rock and Roll Circus*, outtakes	014, 086, 190, 200, 238, 240, 257, 428, 578
Yer Blues	*Rock and Roll Circus*, mono acetate	257
Yer Blues	live, Toronto, 1969	175, 228, 276, 328, 334, 353, 383, 732, 786
Yer Blues	recorded in Toronto, different mix	867
Yer Blues	unknown take	107, 179, 352, 353, 378, 773
Yes I'm Your Angel	*Double Fantasy* sessions, unknown take	459, 639, 835
Yes I'm Your Angel	*Double Fantasy* album, official release version	259
Yes Sir That's My Baby	Unknown take	353
Yesterday	live, New York hotel, 9 October 1971, John's thirty-first birthday	215, 244, 346, 370, 380, 726, 840, 864, 912
You Are a Stranger in My Arms, see *Stranger in My Arms*		
You Are Here	*Mind Games* sessions, unknown take	096, 159, 179, 241, 353, 496, 712, 738, 752, 773, 876
You Are Here	rough mix with additional verse	168, 756
You Are Here	*Mind Games* album, from acetate	750
You Can't Catch Me	from *Roots*	132, 133, 217, 820

You Can't Catch Me	*Rock 'n' Roll* album rehearsals	060, 063, 074, 096, 140, 162, 171, 189, 235, 241, 353, 402, 407, 455, 470, 526, 537, 631, 660, 738, 755, 760, 761, 770, 815, 817, 819, 873
You Can't Catch Me	rough mix – Lennon sessions	218, 281
You Can't Catch Me	*Rock 'n' Roll*, alternate extended version	013
You Know How Hard It Is	*Imagine* album rehearsal, Tittenhurst Park, 1970	246, 387, 861, 909
You Saved My Soul	unknown take, evolved into 'Serve Yourself'	091, 093, 213, 240, 241, 249, 264, 265, 273, 274, 483, 498, 500, 686, 716, 720, 735, 749, 797, 856, 861, 865, 893
You Saved My Soul	take 1, evolved into 'Serve Yourself'	371, 440, 602
You Saved My Soul	take 2, evolved into 'Serve Yourself'	371, 434, 589, 733, 742
You Send Me	*Double Fantasy* sessions, early outtake	102, 210, 243, 387, 463, 648, 741, 861
Young Love	demo, Dakota	010, 186, 206, 235, 285, 349, 398, 518
(You're So Square) I Don't Care Baby, see *Baby I Don't Care*		
You're the One	*Milk and Honey* album, official release version	259
Your Hands	*Milk and Honey* album, official release version	259
Your True Love	unknown take	865

SECTION TWO – BEATLES BOOTLEGS

Most of the titles listed below appeared on official Beatles release. The takes shown are Lennon demos, some of which also included other members of The Beatles.

Title	Source	Entry No.
Across the Universe	unused different mix, 1968	010, 021, 071, 186, 234
Across the Universe	unknown take	723
Aerial Tour Instrumental, see *Flying*		
Because	vocals only, no backing track	082, 237, 240, 734
Blue Suede Shoes	*Get Back* sessions	115, 116
Chi-Chi's Café	John and Ringo – 1960s	079
Child of Nature	*White Album* demo	236, 249, 287, 724, 851, 907, 908
Child of Nature	*Get Back* sessions (evolved into Jealous Guy)	070, 076, 115, 116, 166, 234
Come On Come On, see *Everybody's Got Something to Hide Except Me and My Monkey*		
The Continuing Story of Bungalow Bill	*White Album*, demo	077, 236, 412, 546, 724, 851, 907, 908
Cry Baby Cry	Weybridge, demo	077, 236, 242, 329, 386, 443, 481, 608, 682, 724, 851, 907, 908
Cry Baby Cry	recorded Spain, 1966	098, 740, 795
Daddy's Little Sunshine Boy	John and Ringo, 1967	009, 070, 111, 185, 234, 329, 348, 724

Dear Prudence	demo from 1968	012, 021, 073, 077, 222, 226, 235, 236, 249, 253, 348, 723, 724, 725, 851, 907, 908
Dear Prudence	alternate take	021, 074, 188, 235
Don't Be Cruel	*Get Back* sessions	013, 189
Don't Let Me Down	home demo, 1968	085, 086, 222, 238, 272, 287, 329, 376, 386, 907, 908
Don't Let Me Down	demo, 1969	769
Everybody's Got Something to Hide Except Me and My Monkey	demos and rehearsals	010, 021, 072, 077, 186, 235, 236, 398, 518, 723, 851, 907, 908
Everyone Had a Hard Year	demo from 1968	010, 021, 072, 186, 235, 287, 329, 386, 723, 795, 851, 907, 908
Flying	demo	077, 236, 724
Getting Better	home demo, 1967	010, 186
Give Me Some Truth	*Get Back* sessions	115, 116, 166, 294
Give Me Some Truth	*Get Back* sessions, Paul on vocals	303
Good Morning, Good Morning	original demo from 1967, Weybridge	072, 235, 329, 349, 386, 398, 518, 723, 813
Happiness Is a Warm Gun	unknown take	240, 734
He Said He Said	acoustic guitar demo	070, 234, 724, 760, 761
He Said He Said	composing tape	092, 240
He Said She Said	home demo, Weybridge, 1966	009, 111, 185, 329, 386, 734, 749
Honey Don't	*Get Back* sessions	013, 189
If I Fell	unknown take	095, 241, 737
I'm a Loser	unknown take	250

Title	Source	Entry No.
I'm So Tired	*White Album,*	demo 077, 236, 433, 587, 724, 851, 907, 908
It's Not Too Bad	recorded Spain, 1966 (evolved into 'Strawberry Fields')	098, 242, 740, 794, 813
I Want You (She's So Heavy)	Weybridge, demo	329, 907
Jealous Guy, see *Child of Nature*		
Jock and Yono	from the 1968 Beatles Christmas record	330
Julia	*White Album,* demos	021, 071, 076, 079, 089, 234, 236, 239, 287, 329, 336, 338, 384, 386, 396, 412, 443, 447, 461, 476, 514, 546, 592, 608, 616, 643, 672, 723, 779, 790, 792, 795, 797, 813, 822, 851, 907, 908
Little Sunshine Boy, see *Daddy's Little Sunshine Boy*		
Look at Me	acoustic demo, 1968	161, 167, 792, 869
Look Up the Number, see *You Know My Name (Look Up the Number)*		
Matchbox, *Get Back*	sessions	013, 189
Oh, My Love	Weybridge, outtake	287, 329, 734, 851, 907, 908
Peace of Mind	no Beatles connection (see *Angel Baby* LP for details)	002, 003, 005

Title	Source	Entry No.
Look Up the Number, see *You Know My Name (Look Up the Number)*		
Matchbox, *Get Back*	sessions	013, 189
Oh, My Love	Weybridge, outtake	287, 329, 734, 851, 907, 908
Peace of Mind	no Beatles connection (see *Angel Baby* LP for details)	002, 003, 005
Revolution	demo, recorded Paul's house, 1968	010, 070, 077, 186, 222, 234, 236, 250, 724, 794, 813, 851, 907, 908
Revolution	remixed version, no piano and minus John's guitar	072, 235, 348, 723
Run for Your Life	from *Rubber Soul* sessions	089, 239
Sexy Sadie	demo	077, 222, 236, 413, 433, 549, 588, 724, 779, 851, 907, 908
She Can Talk to Me	recorded Spain 1966 (evolved into 'Hey Bulldog')	098, 242, 740, 794, 851
She Said She Said	demo, Weybridge	386, 734, 760, 761, 781, 792
She Said She Said	composing tape	092, 724
She Said She Said	demo with finished lyrics	240, 329, 338
She's Not a Girl Who Misses Much	demo, Weybridge (evolved into 'Happiness Is a Warm Gun')	386
Strawberry Fields Forever	Santa Isabel demos, recorded 1966	323
Strawberry Fields Forever	Kenwood demos	323
Strawberry Fields Forever	EMI sessions	323
Strawberry Fields Forever	take 1	021

Title	Source	Entry No.
Strawberry Fields Forever	demo	021, 069, 184, 241, 799
Strawberry Fields Forever	outtake – electric guitar	021, 071, 234
Strawberry Fields Forever	backwards talk test	077, 236, 350
Strawberry Fields Forever	unknown take	095, 234, 252, 351, 723, 724, 737, 779
Take This Hammer	*Get Back* sessions	115, 116
Tomorrow Never Knows	rough mix	077, 724
12 Bar Original	outtake	038, 239
What a Shame Mary Jane	Version 1 and Version 2	151
What's the New Mary Jane	*White Album*, demo and remix	002, 003, 005, 010, 021, 026, 027, 066, 071, 077, 115, 116, 139, 149, 150, 186, 234, 236, 251, 351, 373, 397, 447, 461, 516, 616, 643, 723, 724, 851, 860, 907, 908
Yer Blues	*White Album* demo	077, 236, 329, 724, 734, 851, 907, 908
You Know My Name (Look up the Number)	home demo, Weybridge, June 1967	009, 071, 111, 185, 234, 329, 349, 386, 395, 512, 723, 749
You've Got to Hide Your Love Away	unknown take	250

6. Discs Index

VL = Vinyl Release

CD = Compact Disc

Entry No.	Title	Label/Catalogue Number	Type
158	ABC Radio Today Lennon Anthology Special	Unknown	CD
159	Absolute Elsewhere	Vigotone VT-158/VT-159/VT-160	CD
160	Acetates and Alternates Mixes	Unicorn Records UC-083	CD
161	Acoustic Masterpieces	Birthday Records BR.019	CD
162	After The Remember	Masterfraction MFCD 008/009	CD
163	Afternoon Reading	Unknown	CD
164	Alex Bennett Show	Unknown	CD
001	All We Need Is John	Unknown CX 297	VL
165	The Alternate Double Fantasy	Pear Records PDP.038	CD
166	The Alternate Imagine	Pear Records PDP.032	CD
167	The Alternate John Lennon/Plastic Ono Band	Ghost Records CD 53-40	CD
168	The Alternate Mind Games	Pear Records PDP.034	CD
169	The Alternate Mind Games and Shaved Fish	Ghost Records CD 53-39	CD
170	The Alternate Plastic Ono Band	Pear Records PDP. 031	CD
171	The Alternate Rock 'n' Roll	PDP. 036	CD
172	The Alternate Shaved Fish Pear Records	Pear Records PDP. 037	CD
173	The Alternate Sometime in New York City	John Records JOHN.003	CD
174	The Alternate Some Time In N.Y.	Pear Records PDP.033	CD
175	Alternate Toronto Mix and More	Goblin Records CD.3009	CD

Entry No.	Title	Label/Catalogue Number	Type
176	The Alternate Walls and Bridges	Pear Records	CD
177	Alternates Of Free as a Bird And 14 Other Songs	Unknown	CD
002	Angel Baby	Unknown	VL
003	Angel Baby	WRMB 326	VL
004	Angel Baby	ABBY 80 L 739	VL
005	Angel Baby/One-to-One Concert and More	WRMB 326/301	VL
006	Ann Arbor: Now Hear This	CBM WEC R1 3665	VL
007	Another Fantasy Winston O'Boogie	Record Works DR 001	VL
178	Another Flaming Pie	No Label Records NLR.9714	CD
179	Anthology	Invasion Unlmited IU.9749	CD
180	Anthology Radio Special	Unknown	CD
181	Anthology Weybridge	Fire Power FP.9040	CD
182	Apple Acetate	Sweet Zapple SZ.202	CD
183	Apple 2 x 1 Sided Rough Acetate	Unicorn Records UC-081	CD
008	Archives Vol. 1	Paper Plane Music 8RCH 111	VL
009	Archives Vol. 2	Paper Plane Music 8RCH 222	VL
010	Archives Vol. 3	Paper Plane Music 8RCH 333	VL
011	Archives Vol. 4	Paper Plane Music 8RCH 444	VL
012	Archives Vol. 5	Paper Plane Music 8RCH 555	VL
013	Archives Vol. 6	Paper Plane Music 8RCH 666	VL
014	Archives Vol. 7	Paper Plane Music 8RCH 777	VL
015	Archives Vol. 8	Paper Plane Music 8RCH 888	VL
184	Archives Vol. 1	JIBUT-1301	CD
185	Archives Vol. 2	JLBUT-1302	CD
186	Archives Vol. 3	JLBUT-1303	CD
187	Archives Vol. 4	JLBUT-1304	CD
189	Archives Vol. 6	JLBUT-1306	CD

Entry No.	Title	Label/Catalogue Number	Type
190	Archives Vol. 7	JLBUT-1307	CD
191	Archives Vol. 8	JLBUT-1308	CD
192	Artifacts 111 (The Definite Collection of Beatles Big Music Rarities 1969–1974)	Big BX 009	CD
193	Artist The Beatle Years	DIY GB # 28	CD
194	Ascot Sound Studios: 21 May 1971	Stoneage Music SAM.0011	CD
016	Aspen 7 – The British Box – Spring and Summer Section 11 Aspen No. 7		VL
195	Avant Garde Happening	Unknown	CD
196	Bakhall Bonus CD's Phantom Recording	PH 1002 CD	CD
197	BBC Tribute to John Lennon (Long Version) – Vol. 1	Unknown	CD
198	BBC Tribute to John Lennon (Long Version) – Vol. 2	Unknown	CD
199	BBC Tribute to John Lennon (Short Version)	Unknown	CD
200	Beatle Lennon: Steppin' Out 1964–1969	Unknown	CD
201	Beatles Undercover	CG Publishing Inc CGPINT 8008	CD
202	Bedism	Dress To Kill 155	CD
017	Before Play – August 1980	Gnat Records, Paper Plane Music DFV 880-1	VL
203	Before Play – August 1980	Gnat Records, Paper Plane Music DFV 880-1	CD
204	Bermuda Shorts	Grand High Exalted UMKR-0003	CD
205	Between the Lines – Vol. 1	Pine Apple PNA.001	CD
206	Between the Lines – Vol. 2	Pine Apple PNA.002	CD
207	Between the Lines – Vol. 3	Pine Apple PNA.003	CD

Entry No.	Title	Label/Catalogue Number	Type
208	Between the Lines – Vol. 4	Pine Apple PNA.004	CD
209	Between the Lines – Vol. 5	Pine Apple PNA.005	CD
210	Between the Lines – Vol. 6	Pine Apple PNA.006	CD
211	Between the Lines – Vol. 7	Pine Apple PNA.007	CD
212	Between the Lines – Vol. 8	Pine Apple PNA.008	CD
213	Between the Lines – Vol. 9	Pine Apple PNA.009	CD
214	Bigger Than Jesus	Unknown	CD
215	The Birthday Tape Unknown CD	Unknown	CD
018	Body Stripping Off the Walls	JKF 71374	VL
216	Borrowed Time	Toasted Condor 1967	CD
019	Both Sides	MIW 8	VL
217	Brandy Alexanders and The Wall of Sound – Vol. 1	Vigotone VT. 235	CD
218	Brandy Alexanders and The Wall of Sound – Vol. 2	Vigotone VT. 236	CD
219	Brandy Alexanders and The Wall of Sound – Vol. 3	Vigotone VT. 237	CD
220	Bring on the Lucie	Luna Records LU.9423	CD
020	British Blues Jam	CBM 3426	VL
221	Channelling the Centre from Within	Two Boys Limited Tabs TDL.004	CD
222	Christmas Present	White Fly WF.001/3	CD
021	Chronicle, Part 1 (The Beatle Years)	Toasted Record Works TRW 1940	VL
022	Classified Document	Instant Analysis BBR 014	VL
223	Clock	Sky 101	CD
023	A Collection of 'Rock 'n' Roll' Rehearsals	Unknown WI-86	VL
024	Come Back Johnny	Melvin Records MM09	VL
224	Come Back Johnny	Melvin Records MM09	CD

Entry No.	Title	Label/Catalogue Number	Type
225	Come On Listen To Me	His Masters Choice HMC.004 CD	CD
226	Come Together	Oil Well RSC 025 CD	CD
227	Come Together	Undercover UC-006	CD
228	Come Together	Alegra CD 90004	CD
229	Come Together: A John Lennon Christmas	Black Cat BC 026	CD
230	Come Together (Beatles in the 90s)	Fab 3 FAB 3	CD
231	Completed Rarities – Vol. 1	Polyphone PH 1313	CD
232	Completed Rarities – Vol. 1	B and B Communications CDB 007	CD
233	Completed Rarities – Vol. 2	B and B Communications CDB 008	CD
234	The Complete Lost Lennon Tapes – Vols 1 and 2	Walrus Records 002/003	CD
235	The Complete Lost Lennon Tapes – Vols 3 and 4	Walrus Records 010/011	CD
236	The Complete Lost Lennon Tapes – Vols 5 and 6	Walrus Records 014/015	CD
237	The Complete Lost Lennon Tapes – Vols 7 and 8	Walrus Records 017/018	CD
238	The Complete Lost Lennon Tapes – Vols 9 and 10	Walrus Records 019/020	CD
239	The Complete Lost Lennon Tapes – Vols 11 and 12	Walrus Records 022/023	CD
240	The Complete Lost Lennon Tapes – Vols 13 and 14	Walrus Records 024/025	CD
241	The Complete Lost Lennon Tapes – Vols 15 and 16	Walrus Records 026/027	CD
242	The Complete Lost Lennon Tapes – Vols 17 and 18	Walrus Records 028/029	CD

Entry No.	Title	Label/Catalogue Number	Type
243	The Complete Lost Lennon Tapes – Vols 19 and 20	Walrus Records 030/031	CD
244	The Complete Lost Lennon Tapes – Vols 21 and 22	Walrus Records 035/036	CD
245	The Complete May Pang Tapes	Orange Fifteen	CD
246	Compositions	Vigotone VT-191	CD
025	Confidential Document	Instant Analysis BBR 014	VL
247	A Conspiracy of Silence	Black Cat BC 045/046	CD
248	A Conspiracy of Silence Speaks Louder Than Words	Darthouse DD 014-015	CD
249	the Dakota and Bermuda Demos, 1977–1980, Vol. 1	Poor Muffin Records	CD
250	A Day on the Radio	Unknown	CD
026	Day Tripper Jam	CMB 4242	VL
027	Day Tripper Jam	Instant Analysis 1056	VL
251	Day Tripper Jam	Instant Analysis/King Kong 4242	CD
252	Dedicated to John Lennon – Part 1	Unknown	CD
253	Dedicated to John Lennon – Part 2	Unknown	CD
254	Dedicated to John Lennon – Part 3	Unknown	CD
255	Dedicated to John Lennon – Part 4	Unknown	CD
256	Dedicated to John Lennon – Part 5	Unknown	CD
257	Dirty Mac Sessions	Unicorn Records UC-091	CD
258	D.J. Winston O'Boogie	Unicorn Records UC-079/80	CD
028	Doctor Winston O'Boogie On The *Tomorrow Show*	Unknown CX 297 VL	VL
029	Doll's House	Maidenhead Records MHR JET 909-1	VL
259	Double Fantasy/Milk And Honey	CDM 1199-367	CD

Entry No.	Title	Label/Catalogue Number	Type
260	Double Fantasy – Demos and Outtakes	Hen 015	CD
261	Double Fantasy Working Version	Master of Beatles Essentials MBEJ 001	CD
262	The Dream Is Over	Pegboy 1006	CD
263	Dream Is Over (Disc One)	Dill Archives JLTD 101	CD
264	Dreaming of the Past	Vigotone VT-CD-09	CD
265	Dreaming of the Past	Howdy CD-555-01	CD
266	Dreaming of the Past P	EG/Westwood One 05-41	CD
030	Dream Lover	NN-01	VL
267	Family Tree	Unknown	CD
268	FBI Files Democracy Now	DNFBI 001	CD
269	The Fillmore Tapes	Master of Orange MOO-0002	CD
270	Filming The Fantasies	VOXX Records Voxx 0009-01	CD
031	Flower	TKRWM 1803/8018/JL 517	VL
271	For the Other Half of the Sky	Barrier BAR 010/011	CD
272	Free as a Bird	No Label FAB 1	CD
273	Free as a Bird: the Dakota Beatle Demos	Pegboy 1001	CD
274	Free as a Bird: the Dakota Beatle Demos	Odeon 1001	CD
032	Fulfilling The Fantasies	TAKRL FTF 1000	VL
275	Fulfilling The Fantasies	Salamander SCD 1019	CD
276	Give Peace a Chance	The Easy Rider Years 930132	CD
033	God Save Us Demo	NW + 1	
277	Gone from This Place	Vigotone VT-CD-01	CD
034	Goodnight Vienna	Dakota Records DR 6975	VL
278	Goodnight Vienna	Dakota Records DR 6975	CD
035	The Great Rock and Roll Circus	Mushroom Records GRC 1383	VL
036	Great To Have You With Us	MHR-JET-909-3	VL
279	Greatest Hits Live	Chartbusters CHER-072-A	CD

Entry No.	Title	Label/Catalogue Number	Type
037	A Guitar's All Right John, But You'll Never Earn Your Living By It	Audifon R.6015	VL
038	A Guitar's All Right John, But You'll Never Earn Your Living By It	Ruthless Rhymes	VL
280	A Guitar's All Right John, But You'll Never Earn Your Living By It	Audifon R.6015	CD
039	Gulp	RL 007	VL
040	A Hard Road	Morriphon L05972	VL
281	Hard Times Are Over	Sweet Zapple SZ-203	CD
282	Have You Had Your Breakfast Yet?	Black Cat BC-038	CD
283	A Heart Play	Unknown	CD
284	Heart Play Dialog	Unknown	CD
285	Hidden Archives	Fire Power FP-038A/B	CD
041	Hound Dog	Instant Analysis CMB 5040	VL
042	Hound Dog/Long Tall Sally	Heavy 1C1	VL
286	Hushed Bells Over	Masterfrcction MFCD 017	CD
287	I Found Out	Luna Records LU 9424	CD
288	Imagine	Images IM 02	CD
289	Imagine Acetate	Unknown	CD
290	Imagine... All the Outtakes, Vols. 1–3	Vigotone VT 118/119/120	CD
291	Imagine – The Alternate	Unknown	CD
043	Imagine – The Alternate Album	Apple Records (bogus) SW-A-3379	VL
292	Imagine – The Alternate Album	Sidewalk Music SD 89009	CD
293	Imagine: Apple 2 x 1 Sided Rough Acetate	Unicorn Records UC-081	CD
294	Imagine Collectors Edition	Unknown	CD
295	Imagine Complete Sessions	BMI	CD
296	Imagine 5.1	Unknown CDP 7466412	CD

Entry No.	Title	Label/Catalogue Number	Type
297	Imagine … More Session Tapes	Vigotone VT 185/186	CD
298	The Imagine Outtakes, Vols. 1–3	Birthday Records BRO 015/016/017	CD
299	The Imagine Outtakes, Vol. 4	Birthday Records BR 070	CD
300	The Imagine Outtakes, Vol. 5	Birthday Records BR 071	CD
301	The Imagine Outtakes, Vol. 6	Birthday Records BR 087	CD
302	The Imagine Outtakes, Vol. 7	Birthday Records BR 088	CD
303	The Imagine Outtakes, Vol. 8	Birthday Records BR 89	CD
304	The Imagine Outtakes, Vol. 9	Birthday Records BR 90	CD
305	Imagine Quadrosonics	Quadrapple 004	CD
306	Imagine – The Sessions	Vigotone VT-CD-08	CD
307	Imagine World	Unknown	CD
308	I'm Just Sitting Here Reminiscing	Black Owl BO-CD 079/080	CD
309	I'm the Greatest/Something Precious and Rare	Vigotone VT-CD-07	CD
310	In His Life	Mastertone Multimedia 8048	CD
311	In My Life	Dressed To Kill DTKBOX 92	CD
312	The Inside Track: John Lennon	DIR Broadcasting DIR-09-1982	CD
313	In the Middle of a Cloud	Unicorn Records UC-071	CD
314	Interviews: Nov–Dec 1969	Fan Collection JLINTV1969VOL1	CD
315	Interview: 1969–1970 (Vol. 1)	Fan Collection JLGINTV196970VOL1	CD
316	Interviews: 1971 – The Don Singleton Interview	Fan Collection NYDN1971	CD
317	Interviews: 1974 (Disc 1)	Fan Collection JLINTV1974D1	CD
318	Interviews: 1974 (Disc 2)	Fan Collection JLINTV1974D2	CD
319	Interviews: 1974 (Disc 3)	Fan Collection JLINTV1974D3	CD
320	Interviews: 1974/1975	Fan Collection WRKO1974	CD

Entry No.	Title	Label/Catologue Number	Type
321	It's Gonna Be Alright	His Masters Choice HMC 002	CD
322	It's Hard to Be Butterflies	Barrier BAR 007/8	CD
323	It's Not Too Bad	Pegboy 1008	CD
324	Japan Interview	Unknown	CD
325	Jealous Guy – The Imagine Sessions	Luna Records LU 9308	CD
326	The Jerry Levitan Interview	Air-Check LEVITAN 1979	CD
044	'Je Suis Le Plus Mieux'	Jazz Series SD 6757	VL
327	Jim Ladd Interview 1974 – Upgraded	Unknown	CD
045	Joe Pope's Strawberry Fields Christmas Recordings	Strawberry Fields Forever	VL
046	John and Paul In Michigan	Unknown	VL
328	John Lennon and Friends Live: 1968–1971	KTKK Fun Boots DIY GB # 25	CD
329	John Lennon Anthology: Weybridge	Fire Power FP 9040	CD
330	John Lennon Artist The Beatle Years	DIY GB # 28	CD
331	John Lennon: A Celebration	Dill Archives JLAC 1	CD
332	John Lennon Forever	Laserlight 12 593	CD
333	John Lennon: The Hall Of Fame (Capital Radio Interview 1975)	G Cap Media 055 JLCR 11975	CD
047	John Lennon Interview/David Peel And The Apple Band	OR 70078 PD	VL
334	John Lennon Live	CDDV 5515	CD
335	John Lennon Live (SL.15)	Apple House Music BAN-020-A	CD
336	John Lennon Live (SL.16)	Apple House Music BAN-020-B	CD
337	John Lennon Live (SL.17)	Apple House Music BAN-020-C	CD
338	John Lennon Live (SL.18)	Apple House Music BAN-020-D	CD
339	John Lennon: The Man, The Memory (WMJQ)	Air-Check WMJQ	CD
048	John Lennon/Paul McCartney – Ann Arbor 'Now Hear This'	Unknown	VL

Entry No.	Title	Label/Catalogue Number	Type
340	John Lennon/Plastic Ono Band	Dr. Ebbetts SW 3372	CD
341	John Lennon/Plastic Ono Band 5.1	Unknown	CD
342	John Lennon Presents… Abbey Road on Radio Luxembourg	Blackbird Records 013	CD
343	The John Lennon Story: Volumes One and Two	Black Cat BC 001/002	CD
344	The John Lennon Story: Volumes Three And Four	Black Cat BC 003/004	CD
345	The John Lennon Story: Volume Five	Black Cat BC 005	CD
346	John Lennon's 31st Birthday Party	Rockin' Records JLBP 01	CD
049	John Lennon with Jimi Hendrix, Chuck Berry	LSD Records JCJ 37037	VL
347	John Lennon with Tom Snyder	Unknown	CD
050	John, Paul, George and Ringo in the 1970s	Melvin Records MR-12	VL
052	John's Last Songs	Shaved Fish Records SF 80001	VL
349	John's Lost Home Demos, Vol. 1	John Records John 001	CD
350	John's Lost Home Demos, Vol. 2	John Records John 002	CD
053	John Lennon	In Step Records JL 101	VL
348	John Lost in the Studio	Mongoose Records Mong CD 028	CD
351	Johnny 'L' (For Gene and Eddie And Elvis… And Buddy!)	Star Records CD 099	CD
051	Johnny Moondog	Box Top Records KOK-1-5832	VL
352	Johnny Moondog	Box Top Records	CD
054	Joshua Tree Tapes	TKBWM 1803	VL
353	Journals (Parts 1 and 3)	CEDRAM CD 121/125 and 126/130	CD
055	Just Talking	BFR 003/M-005-1	VL
354	Kaleidoscope Eyes	Delta 46076	CD
355	Kenny Everett Talks to John Lennon	Blackbird Records BBR 025	CD

Entry No.	Title	Label/Catalogue Number	Type
356	KFRC AM: Focus '71 (Jann Wenner Interview)	Air-Check KFRC 71	CD
357	KSAN Tom Donahue Interview	Unknown	CD
056	The KYA 1969 Peace Talk	KYA 1969	VL
358	KYA FM 1969 and Man of the Decade	Unknown	CD
359	The Last Word	Baktabak CBAK 4014	CD
360	Lennon Legacy – Part 1 (Beatles For Sale)	Unknown	CD
361	Lennon Legacy – Part 2 (Ballad of John and Yoko)	Unknown	CD
362	Lennon Legacy – Part 3 (Give Me Some Truth)	Unknown	CD
363	*Lennon Legend* DVD 5.1. Mixes	Unknown	CD
364	*Lennon Legend* 5.1 Channels Mixes	Unknown	CD
057	Lennon/McCartney	CBM WEC R1 3665	VL
058	Lennon/McCartney	Unknown	VL
059	Lennon/Ono Box Set	Various	VL
365	Lennon Pictures	Unknown YB 001-2	CD
366	Lennon Remembers – Part One	Darthouse DD 003/4	CD
367	Lennon Remembers – Part Two	Darthouse DD 005/6	CD
368	Lennon Renumbers	Bell Bottom 022	CD
060	Lennon Roots	RTS	VL
061	Lennon vs. The World Vol. 1	Original Rock 1009	VL
062	Lennon vs. The World Vol. 2	Original Rock 1010	VL
063	Lennon vs. The World Vol. 3	Original Rock 1011	VL
369	The Lennon Wives on 'Fresh Air'	NPR NPR0003	CD
370	Let's Have a Party	Quality Compact Prod QCP 72003	CD
371	Life Is What Happens	Barrier Records	CD
064	Life with the Lennons	TOBE MILO 4Q 13/14	VL

Entry No.	Title	Label/Catalogue Number	Type
372	Life with the Lions	Goblin Records CD 3010	CD
065	Lifting Material From The World	Apple Records SAPCOR 43	VL
066	Limited Edition	Bag Records 5069	VL
373	Limited Edition	Bag Records	CD
374	Listen to This	Vigotone VT 175/VT 176/Vt 177	CD
067	Listen to This Picture Record	Unknown	VL
375	Listen to This Radio Show	Mad Scott Records MS 01/02	CD
376	Live – Vol. 1	Joker JOK-042-A	CD
377	Live – Vol. 2	Joker JOK-042-B	CD
378	Live and Rare	Unknown	CD
068	Live from the Live	Black Disc Inc 7PP 1082	
379	Live in Ann Arbor/Apollo Theatre	Unknown	CD
380	Live in L.A. and 31st Birthday Party 1974	INP 060	CD
381	Live Jam (Live '72)	Beatles Fan For Peace BFP 004	CD
382	Live Lennon Tapes	The Early Years 02-CD-3329	CD
383	Live Peace in Toronto 1969	Audience Misterclaudel MCCD-029 C	CD
384	Look at Me	Vigotone VT-CD-06	CD
385	Lost and Found Tapes	PR Records IMM 41 95000	CD
386	Lost In Weybridge	Tea Bag One STAB 10	CD
387	Lost Lennon Archives – Vol. 1	Bell Edge Records BE-001	CD
388	The Lost Lennon Rehearsal	John Records John 004 C	CD
069	The Lost Lennon Tapes – Vol. 1	Bag Records 5073	VL
070	The Lost Lennon Tapes – Vol. 2	Bag Records 5074	VL
071	The Lost Lennon Tapes – Vol. 3	Bag Records 5075	VL
072	The Lost Lennon Tapes – Vol. 4	Bag Records 5076	VL
073	The Lost Lennon Tapes – Vol. 5	Bag Records 5077	VL

Entry No.	Title	Label/Catalogue Number	Type
074	The Lost Lennon Tapes – Vol. 6	Bag Records 5078	VL
075	The Lost Lennon Tapes – Vol. 7	Bag Records 5079	VL
076	The Lost Lennon Tapes – Vol. 8	Bag Records 5080	VL
077	The Lost Lennon Tapes – Vol. 9	Bag Records 5081	VL
078	The Lost Lennon Tapes – Vol. 10	Bag Records 5082	VL
079	The Lost Lennon Tapes – Vol. 11	Bag Records 5083	VL
080	The Lost Lennon Tapes – Vol. 12	Bag Records 5084	VL
081	The Lost Lennon Tapes – Vol. 13	Bag Records 5085	VL
082	The Lost Lennon Tapes – Vol. 14	Bag Records 5086	VL
083	The Lost Lennon Tapes – Vol. 15	Bag Records 5087	VL
084	The Lost Lennon Tapes – Vol. 16	Bag Records 5088	VL
085	The Lost Lennon Tapes – Vol. 17	Bag Records 5089	VL
086	The Lost Lennon Tapes – Vol. 18	Bag Records 5090	VL
087	The Lost Lennon Tapes – Vol. 19	Bag Records 5091	VL
088	The Lost Lennon Tapes – Vol. 20	Bag Records 5092	VL
089	The Lost Lennon Tapes – Vol. 21	Bag Records 5093	VL
090	The Lost Lennon Tapes – Vol. 22	Bag Records 5094	VL
091	The Lost Lennon Tapes – Vol. 23	Bag Records 5095	VL
092	The Lost Lennon Tapes – Vol. 24	Bag Records 5096	VL
093	The Lost Lennon Tapes – Vol. 25	Bag Records 5097	VL
094	The Lost Lennon Tapes – Vol. 26	Bag Records 5098	VL
095	The Lost Lennon Tapes – Vol. 27	Bag Records 5099	VL
096	The Lost Lennon Tapes – Vol. 28	Bag Records 5100	VL
097	The Lost Lennon Tapes – Vol. 29	Bag Records 5101	VL
098	The Lost Lennon Tapes – Vol. 30	Bag Records 5102	VL
099	The Lost Lennon Tapes – Vol. 31	Bag Records 5103	VL
100	The Lost Lennon Tapes – Vol. 32	Bag Records 5104	VL
101	The Lost Lennon Tapes – Vol. 33	Bag Records 5105	VL

Entry No.	Title	Label/Catalogue Number	Type
102	The Lost Lennon Tapes – Vol. 34	Bag Records 5106	VL
103	The Lost Lennon Tapes – Vol. 35	Bag Records 5107	VL
389–500	The Lost Lennon Tapes – *Premiere Show* to Show 218	None (set one)	CD
501–721	to The Lost Lennon Tapes – *Premiere Show* to Show 218	None (set two)	CD
722	The Lost Lennon Tapes – Vol. 1	Living Legend Records LLRCD 045	CD
723	The Lost Lennon Tapes – Vol. 2	Living Legend Records LLRCD 046	CD
724	The Lost Lennon Tapes – Vol. 3	Living Legend Records LLRCD 047	CD
725	The Lost Lennon Tapes – Vol. 4	Living Legend Records LLRCD 054	CD
726	The Lost Lennon Tapes – Vol. 5	Living Legend Records LLRCD 055	CD
727	The Lost Lennon Tapes – Vol. 6	Living Legend Records LLRCD 056	CD
728	The Lost Lennon Tapes – Vol. 7	Living Legend Records LLRCD 066	CD
729	The Lost Lennon Tapes – Vol. 8	Living Legend Records LLRCD 068	CD
730	The Lost Lennon Tapes – Vol. 9	Living Legend Records LLRCD 069	CD
731	The Lost Lennon Tapes – Vol. 10	Living Legend Records LLRCD 096	CD
732	The Lost Lennon Tapes – Vol. 11	Living Legend Records LLRCD 147	CD
733	The Lost Lennon Tapes – Vol. 23	Bag Records 5095	CD
734	The Lost Lennon Tapes – Vol. 24	Bag Records 5096	CD

735	The Lost Lennon Tapes – Vol. 25	Bag Records 5097	CD
736	The Lost Lennon Tapes – Vol. 26	Bag Records 5098	CD
737	The Lost Lennon Tapes – Vol. 27	Bag Records 5099	CD
738	The Lost Lennon Tapes – Vol. 28	Bag Records 5100	CD
739	The Lost Lennon Tapes – Vol. 29	Bag Records 5101	CD
740	The Lost Lennon Tapes – Vols. 30/31/31	Bag Records 5102/3/4	CD
741	The Lost Lennon Tapes – Vols. 32/33/34	Bag Records 5105/6/7	CD
742	The Lost Sleepy Blind Lemon Lennon Tapes	Library Products 2341	CD
743	Lost Weekend	Unknown	CD
104	Make Love to the End	SST	VL
105	Make Love to the End	SHOL 2481	VL
106	Man of the Decade	MOTD 1269	VL
744	The Man, The Memory – Volumes One and Two	Black Cat 015/016	CD
745	The Man, The Memory – Volume Three	Black Cat 017	CD
746	The Man, The Memory	Air-Check WMJQ	CD
107	The Master Showman	168 High A21250	VL
108	The May Pang Tapes	Beetle Records LEN 4080	VL
109	The May Pang Tapes	May	VL
110	The May Pang Tapes	QS 85022	VL
747	Maximum Lennon	Chrome Dreams ABCD 070	CD
748	Megamix	Unknown BMB 007	CD
111	Memories	MacLen-Hawk Records 8RCH-111-222	VL
749	Memories	Strapple Records	CD
750	Mind Games Acetate	Unknown	CD
751	Mind Games (Alternates and Demos)	Howdy Records CD-555-03	CD
752	Mind Games Sessions	Unknown	CD
753	Miscellaneous Tracks	Yellow Dog/Orange YD-Orange YD 018	CD

754	Miscellaneous Tracks	Cool Orangecicle	CD
756	More Mind Games	JL 4	CD
755	Move Over Ms L	KTKK DIY GB # 5069	CD
757	Mr and Mrs Lennon's Honeymoon	Banana Inc MMRSLHM2	CD
758	MSG Back In '72/They Say It's Your Birthday	Unknown JNY 0072	CD
759	Mucho Mungo	Walrus Records CD 909	CD
760	My Love Will Turn You On	Vigotone VT-CD-09	CD
761	My Love Will Turn You On	Howdy CD-555-02	CD
112	Mystery Box (Frank Zappa)	Nifty Tuff and Bitchen 8611	VL
762	Off the Walls	Vigotone VT-CD-02	CD
763	The Newsweek Interview	Black Cat BC 011	CD
764	New York, New York	T-Jay 1999	CD
765	*Night Ride*	Flo FLO 005	CD
766	Now and Then	Lazy Bones Inc	CD
113	Now Hear This	Unknown	VL
114	Off the Walls Trade Mark of Quality	JFK 72174-2	VL
767	Off the Walls	Birthday Records BRO 03	CD
768	Off the Walls	Hawg Leg HL 151	CD
769	Oh My Love	JLD 001	CD
770	Oldies but Mouldies	Adam III Ltd	CD
115	Once Upon a Time	Unknown JOL-40-801	VL
116	Once Upon a Time	JOL 40-80	VL
771	Once Upon a Time/*Lennon Legend*	Sweet Zapple Sz-201	CD
117	One and One and One Is Three – Part One	Benefit Records 001	VL
118	One and One and One Is Three – Part Two	Benefit Records 002	VL
119	One and One and One Is Three – Part Three	Benefit Records 003	VL
120	One and One and One Is Three	Benefit Records 001/002/003	VL
772	One and One and One Is Three	Phantom PH 1001 CD	CD
773	One Day at a Time	Vigotone VT-191	CD
121	One + One Concert + More	Wizardo Records WRMB 301	VL

122	One/One	R1-3665A/WEC 3949 AX	VL
123	One-to-One Concert	CBM 3665	VL
124	One-to-One Concert	RT 34	VL
774	One-to-One Concert	Zeus Z904001/2/3	CD
775	One-to-One Concert Rehearsals	Chapter One C025124	CD
776	One-to-One Rehearsals, Vol. 1	Orange Sixteen	CD
777	One-to-One Rehearsals, Vol. 2	Orange Seventeen	CD
778	On the Cannes	Black Cat BC 085	CD
125	Only You/Send Me Some Lovin'	Love Devotion Records LS 01	
779	Out of the Blues	Toasted Condor 1968	CD
780	Over Walls Under Bridges	Unknown	CD
781	Peace Off	Vigorous VR-06	CD
782	Phasing Phun with Your Clothes On	Two Boys Limited TBL-007	CD
783	Pill	Missing In Action MIA Act 12	CD
784	Pill	Missing In Action Never End	CD
785	Plastic Ono Band – Home and Studio	Green Grape	CD
786	Plastic Ono Band – Live	DV More Record Productions CDDV 5516	CD
787	Please Hang Up and Try Again	Black Cat BC 110	CD
126	Plop Plop… Fizz Fizz	Sean Mark HAR 170	VL
788	Plop Plop… Fizz Fizz	Unknown	CD
789	Precious and Rare, Vol. 1	Banana BAN-020-A	CD
790	Precious and Rare, Vol. 2	Banana BAN-020-B	CD
791	Precious and Rare, Vol. 3	Banana BAN-020-C	CD
792	Precious and Rare, Vol. 4	Banana BAN-020-D	CD
793	Primal Scream – The Studio Sessions	JL 70	CD
127	Randomonium (Frank Zappa)	Nifty Tuff and Bitchen 8611	VL
794	Rare Demos and Outtakes – Ultra Rare Demos and Lost Tracks, Vol. 1	Unknown	CD

795	Rare Demos and Outtakes – Ultra Rare Demos and Lost Tracks, Vol. 2	Unknown	CD
128	Rave On Toasted	Record Works TRW 1941	VL
796	Rave On Toasted	Record Works TRW 1941	CD
799	The Real Complete Lost Lennon Tapes – Premiere Show	Angry Dog AD 2005/6	CD
800	The Real Complete Lost Lennon Tapes – Part 1	Angry Dog AD 2007	CD
801	The Real Complete Lost Lennon Tapes – Part 2	Angry Dog AD 2008	CD
802	The Real Complete Lost Lennon Tapes – Part 3	Angry Dog AD 2009	CD
803	The Real Complete Lost Lennon Tapes – Part 4	Angry Dog AD 2010	CD
804	The Real Complete Lost Lennon Tapes – Part 5	Angry Dog AD 2011	CD
805	The Real Complete Lost Lennon Tapes – Part 6	Angry Dog AD 2012	CD
806	The Real Complete Lost Lennon Tapes – Part 7	Angry Dog AD 2013	CD
807	The Real Complete Lost Lennon Tapes – Part 8	Angry Dog AD 2014	CD
808	The Real Complete Lost Lennon Tapes – Part 9	Angry Dog AD 2016	CD
809	The Real John Lennon: The Newsweek Interview	Black Cat BC 011	CD
797	Real Love	Real Pig RP 01	CD
798	Real Love	Real Pig RP 01	CD
129	Recovered Tracks	Barnoby Records FF-09	
810	Remember Lennon	Yellow Cat Records YC 2004	CD
811	Remember New York	His Masters Choice HMC 003	CD
812	Reminiscing	Black Cat BC 098	CD

813	Revolution	Vigotone VT-117	CD
130	Rock and Roll Circus	RRE 101	
814	Rock and Roll Is Here to Stay	Pony JEL 001	CD
815	Rock 'n' Roll Sessions	VOXX Records Voxx 0002/01/02/03	CD
816	The Rock 'n' Roll Sessions (Part 1)	Ghost Records CD 53-41	CD
817	The Rock 'n' Roll Sessions (Part 2)	Ghost Records CD 53-42	CD
818	Rock Speak '74	Unicorn Records	CD
131	Rolling Stones Rock and Roll Circus	Unknown	VL
132	Roots	Adam V!!!	VL
133	Roots	King Kong	VL
819	Roots	Walrus Records WR 42	CD
820	Roots	CD-49-028	CD
821	San Francisco Bay Blues	Oil Well RSC CD 084	CD
134	Serve Yourself	Love And Peace Records BA 009	VL
135	Serve Yourself	Karma Records DD1 D183	VL
822	Serve Yourself	Vigotone VT-CD-04	CD
823	Shot Dead	Unknown	CD
824	Shot of Salvation (Rolling Stones)	Scorpio OM 90-64-17	CD
825	Since I Left The Rolling Stones	Yellow Panda YP 004/5	CD
826	S.I.R. John Winston Ono Lennon	Moonlight Records ML 9506	CD
827	The Smith Collection: John and Yoko – December 1969	Black Cat BC 089/90	CD
828	The Smith Collection: John and Yoko – December 1970	Black Cat BC 091/92	CD
829	The Smith Collection: John and Yoko – June 1971	Black Cat BC 093	CD
830	The Smith Collection: John and Yoko – September 1971	Black Cat BC 094	CD

831	The Smith Collection: John and Yoko – January 1972	Black Cat BC 095/096	CD
136	Snap Shots	Gnat Records/Paper Plane Music GN70083-1	CD
832	Snap Shots – A Musical Tapestry	Gnat Records/Paper Plane Music	CD
137	Something Precious and Rare	Trade Mark Of Quality JFK 72174-1	VL
833	Something Precious and Rare	Vigotone VT-CD-07	CD
834	Somewhere in New York City	VOXX Records Voxx 0006-01	CD
138	Soundcheck (The Beatles)	Rock Solid RSR 256	VL
835	Songs from Late in the Afternoon	Barrier Records BAR 012/013	CD
836	Soul of John Lennon	MIDO Enterprises Zs-9110	CD
837	Spaniard in the Works/Let's Have a Dream	Spaced Records SR.001	CD
838	Special Interview 1971	Red Apple	CD
139	Spicy Beatles Songs	MOQ 71076	VL
140	Stand By Me	Toasted Record Works TRW 1942	VL
839	Stand By Me	Oil Well RSC 054 CD	CD
840	St. Regis Hotel and Hotel Syracuse, NY	Green Grape	CD
141	Studio Outtakes	Tobe Milo TMLP 4Q 11/12	
841	Studio Rehearsals – 13 July 1974	Unknown	CD
842	Studio Sessions One	Tobe Milo TMLP 4Q 11/12	CD
843	Studio Tracks – Vol. 1	Chapter One 25115	CD
844	Studio Tracks – Vol. 2	Chapter One 25116	CD
845	Studio Tracks – Vol. 3	Chapter One 25181	CD
846	Studio Tracks – Vol. 4	Chapter One 25131	CD
847	Studio Tracks – Vol. 5	Chapter One 25163	CD
848	Studio Tracks – Vol. 6	Chapter One 25164	CD
849	Studio Tracks – Vol. 7	Chapter One 25186	CD

850	Studio Tracks – Vol. 8	Chapter One 25187	CD
851	Studio Tracks – Vol. 9	Chapter One 25200	CD
852	Tea For Two	Stamp Out The Beatles STAB 01	CD
142	Teddy Boy	Melvin Records MM 09	VL
143	Teddy Boy (picture disc)	Melvin Records MM 09	VL
144	Telecasts	TMOQ 71046	VL
145	Telecasts	Unknown JL 517	VL
853	Telecasts	Conta Band 3711	CD
854	Telecasts	Unknown	CD
146	Telecasts (picture discs)	Unknown JL 517	VL
147	Telecasts (coloured vinyl)	LXXXIV Series # 28	VL
855	Testimony	Magnum Music Group CDTB 095	CD
148	This Is Not Here (Yoko Ono)	Bag Records 5070	VL
856	This Is Not Here	TMOG Records	CD
857	This Is Not Here	Black Cat BC 054 C	CD
858	This Is The Truth	Beatle Boots BB CD 01	CD
859	A Toot and a Snore in '74	Mistral MM 9225	CD
149	Toy Boy	LXXXIV Series # 38	VL
150	The Toy Boy	Bag Records 5069	VL
860	The Toy Boy	Penny Lane Records	CD
861	The Tropical Lennon	Trax Bell Edge Records BE-001	CD
862	Two Versions	Sapcor 43	CD
863	Two Virgins	Goblin Records CD 3008	CD
864	Unbootlegged 08 – Get That Fly	No Label Records NLR 0402	CD
865	Unbootlegged 09 – Lost Lennon Trousers	No Tapo Records	CD
866	Unedited RKO Interview	Darthouse DD 014-015	CD
867	Unfinished Music No. 2 – Life with the Lions	Goblin Records	CD
868	The Unheard Lennon 1969	Interviews SNE CD 001	CD

869	Unplugged	Unknown	CD
870	Unsurpassed Masters – Vol. 1	Egg Records EGG 005	CD
871	Unsurpassed Masters – Vol. 2	Egg Records EGG 006	CD
872	Unsurpassed Masters – Vol. 3	Egg Records EGG 007	CD
873	Unsurpassed Masters – Vol. 4	Egg Records EGG 008	CD
874	Unsurpassed Masters – Vol. 5	Egg Records EGG 009	CD
875	Unsurpassed Masters – Vol. 6	Egg Records EGG 010	CD
876	Unsurpassed Masters – Vol. 7	Egg Records EGG 011	CD
877	Unsurpassed Masters – Vol. 8	Egg Records EGG 020	CD
878	Unsurpassed Masters – Vol. 9	Egg Records EGG 021	CD
879	Unsurpassed Masters – Vol. 10	Egg Records EGG 025	CD
880	The Village Tapes – Last Sessions	PR Records IMM 40.95015	CD
881	Walking on Thin Ice	Dolphin Productions CDP 700102	CD
882	Walls and Bridges	(Quad) Quadrapple 003	CD
883	Walls and Bridges Revisited	VOXX Records Voxx 0013	CD
884	Walls and Bridges Rockspeak	Unicorn Records UC-086	CD
885	Walls and Bridges Sessions	Green Grape	CD
886	Warship the Lord Your God and Serve Him Only	Master Of Orange MOO-10006	CD
887	Watching the Wheels	Vigotone VT-CD-03	CD
888	We Are All Together – The Interviews	Delta Music 47 034	CD
889	Wedding Album	Goblin Records CD 3007	CD
890	We'd Like to Change the Tempo Now	Barrier BAR 014/015	CD
891	The Weekend Starts Here	Black Cat BC 117/118	CD
892	The WFIL-AM Helping Hand Marathon	Black Cat BC 020/021	CD
151	What a Shame Mary Jane Had a Pain at the Party	R.8028	VL
893	When I Get Older (Beatles in the 90s)	Fab 4	CD

894	When Was the Last Time You Kissed Mickey Mouse?	Unknown	CD
895	Why and Why Not	Black Cat BC 064	CD
152	Willowbrook Rehearsals	Unknown L 27229	VL
896	Willowbrook Rehearsals	Unknown	CD
153	Winston O'Boogie	Bag Records 5072	VL
897	Winston O'Boogie	Bag Records 5072	CD
898	Winston O'Boogie	Bag Records CD 5072 A/B	CD
154	Working Class Hero	Chet Mar Records CMR-75	VL
899	Working Class Hero	Chet Mar Records CMR 75	CD
900	WPLJ-FM, New York City, 6 June 1971	YelloSub Records YSR 002	CD
901	Written the Day before Yesterday	Unknown JLYOWDBY	CD
155	Yer Blues	NEMS Records NR 103	VL
902	Yer Blues	Library 2329	CD
903	Yer Blues	Vigotone VT-CD-05	CD
156	Yin Yang	Bag Records 5071	VL
904	Your Daddy's Here	Geritol DPRO-79972	CD
157	You Should'a Been There	Unknown YSB 7374-1	VL
905	You Should'a Been There	Ghost Records	CD
906	A 60th Birthday Celebration from MJI Radio	Unknown	CD
907	The 1968 Demos	Howdy 555-04	CD
908	1968 Demos	Vigotone Vigo 100	CD
909	1970 November Home Recordings	Green Grape	CD
910	1970 Plastic Ono Band – Home and Studio	Green Grape	CD
911	1971 Home Recording	Green Grape	CD
912	1971 St Regis Hotel and Hotel Syracuse, NY	Green Grape	CD
913	1974 Home Recordings	Unknown	CD
914	1974 Walls and Bridges Sessions	Green Grape	CD

7. Ten Lennon Bootlegs You Must Own

So how do you pick ten discs out of almost nine hundred listed in Parts One to Three? This was almost an impossible task. Many of the discs listed, such as the *Lost Lennon Tapes* series, are mainly compilations containing tracks from various sources. We have chosen the albums below mainly on the basis of performance, content, sound quality and in particular to demonstrate a representation of John Lennon's solo bootleg recordings. Some of our final choices, particularly the vinyl albums, are controversial. There were many worthy contenders for inclusion. We are disappointed that we could not find room, for example, for *Rock 'n' Roll Sessions* (Featuring The Jesse Ed Davis Tapes) (VOXX 00002/01/02/03), *Compositions* {Vigotone VT 191) or any of the Birthday Records volumes – *The Imagine Outtakes*. The series of albums released by Pear Records in the 'Alternate Album' series were also on the short list although most of the tracks on these albums had been previously released. One of these made the Top Ten – *The Alternate Double Fantasy*. We have cheated a touch by including some sets which are double- or triple-disc sets. Is it a coincidence that five of the final ten are on the Vigotone label? One of the factors in choosing the Top Ten was to include discs featuring outtakes from arguably John's main albums, *Plastic Ono Band, Mind Games, Walls and Bridges, Rock 'n' Roll* and *Double Fantasy*. We have included two vinyl releases – *A Guitar's Alr Right John, But You'll Never Earn Your Living By It* and *Roots*. Although the tracks on these albums appeared subsequently on compact disc, we have chosen these as they were historical releases and extremely collectable although they are difficult to trace now. It can be argued that neither of these vinyl albums should have made the final list – see the explanations in the notes below. No doubt there is an album we have overlooked which deserves to be in the final list but if you own the albums below then you have a solid representation of Lennon's solo career. If you disagree with our choices why not spend an evening selecting your own Top Ten?

ABSOLUTE ELSEWHERE (VIGOTONE VT158/VT159/VT160)

This triple album of *Mind Games* outtakes comes with a thirty-two-page booklet and includes outtakes, demos and rehearsals. The sleeve states: 'the ultimate *Mind Games* anthology'.

THE ALTERNATE DOUBLE FANTASY (PEAR RECORDS PDP 038)

This double album includes outtakes and home recordings from the *Double Fantasy* album sessions including a section devoted to the evolution of 'Starting Over'.

BRANDY ALEXANDERS AND THE WALL OF SOUND (VOLS. 1–3) (VIGOTONE VT 237)

This triple disc set includes the original *Roots* album, outtakes from the *Rock 'n' Roll* session, the *Salute To Sir Lew Grade* show, the *The Old Grey Whistle Test* sessions, the concert appearance with Elton John and several other items. It comes with a thirty-two-page booklet.

FREE AS A BIRD: THE DAKOTA DEMOS (PEGBOY 1001)

An excellent set which includes the original demos used for the *Anthology* album. The album comes with good packing and sleeve notes.

A GUITAR'S ALL RIGHT JOHN BUT YOU'LL NEVER EARN YOUR LIVING BY IT (AUDIFON R.6015)

Arguably this ten-inch vinyl album should not be on this list. The case against is strong. The sound quality is variable, all the tracks appear elsewhere and the source of some of the tracks is questionable. Despite this, the album has legendary status and is extremely collectable. The album was reissued, with the cover photo reversed. It was subsequently released on compact disc but you need to own the vinyl version.

IMAGINE... ALL THE OUTTAKES (VIGOTONE RECORDS VT118/119/120)

The definitive collection of outtakes, rehearsals, alternate versions, home demos and studio overdubs from the *Imagine* album sessions. Some of the tracks had been previously released on *The Lost Lennon Tapes* but not in the superb sound quality on this three-disc CD set. The discs come in a box with a thirty-six-page booklet including an interview with John (probably from *Rolling Stone*), detailed track listing, the story of the *Imagine* album and some nice black-and-white pictures. The sources of the tracks date back to 1968 with early home demos through to the final overdub sessions.

IT'S GONNA BE ALL RIGHT (HIS MASTERS CHOICE HMC 002)

This double album comprises outtakes, demos and rehearsals from the *Plastic Ono Band* album sessions. The discs are housed in a hardback book containing photographs and notes.

IT'S NOT TOO BAD (PEGBOY 1008)

A wonderful looking box set with a slipcase and a booklet. The disc contains the complete collection of John's holiday demos from Santa Isabel which were made during the filming of *How I Won the War* and his home recordings made at Kenwood plus the EMI 'Strawberry Fields Forever' sessions. The recording quality is excellent. Some of the items had previously appeared on bootleg but this set has a far superior sound quality. Many of the photographs taken during the 'Strawberry Fields Forever' sessions are quite rare. The contents include John's first experiments to creating a masterpiece up to the last remix. The disc is very difficult to find.

LISTEN TO THIS... (VIGOTONE RECORDS VT175/176/177)

This is the ultimate *Walls and Bridges* anthology. Vigotone warns us on the back of the box 'These ought to get you through the night'.

ROOTS (ADAM VIII A 8018)

This vinyl album only just scraped into the Top Ten. The whole album was included on the CD release *Brandy Alexanders and The Wall of Sound* (see above) so in a way owning this vinyl release is superfluous. Also, whether this release can be considered a bootleg is debatable – for explanation see entry number 132 in the Vinyl Releases section. We have included this album in the Top Ten due to its rarity and historical importance – and because we like it!

8. Stop Press (Additions and Corrections)

Despite the intense research and carefully checking all the entries and after preparing the final draft for the manuscript, further information was unearthed on some of the entries. We have also located details of a further vinyl disc containing Lennon tracks (*Twice in a Lifetime*), a release titled *The Dream Is Over – Vol. II* which probably includes tracks from the *Get Back* sessions and a picture disc called *Listen to This Picture Disc*. Details of these are shown below. These discs are not included in the songs index. We have also unearthed some additional details on some of the Compact Disc entries plus details of albums released after we completed the main manuscript. There have also been further compact disc releases such as *The Esher Demos* and *The Rock 'n' Roll Sessions 1973–1975*. Complete details of these are shown below.

VINYL RELEASES

Updates and Corrections

040. A HARD ROAD

Timings of tracks are as follows:

Side A

1970 Christmas Message (0.24), Mother/Come Together (9.32), Give Peace a Chance (7.53), Imagine (3.05)

Side B

Interview 1980 (20.02), Press conference (0.32), A Day in the Life (0.31)

136. SNAP SHOTS

We have discovered some further details and corrections on the track listings plus timings of the tracks:

Disc One

Side A

1. Some Other Guy (1.57), 2. Keep Your Hands off My Baby (2.28) (*Saturday Club*, 22 January 1963), 3. Honey Don't (2.12) (*Pop Go The Beatles* 1 August 1963), 4. Twist and Shout (3.01) (*The Royal Variety Performance*, 4 November 1963), 5. Lady Marmalade (0.46) (7 April 1975), 6. Be My Baby (4.35) (from *Roots*), 7. Angel Baby (3.09) (from *Roots*), 8. John reads commercials (2.50) (KHJ-AM 27 September 1974)

Side B

1. All I Want Is You (1.07), 2. Improvisation (1.33), 3. Bad Boy (3.14), 4. Almost Grown (1.50), 5. Child of Nature (1.48), 6. Ob-La-Di Ob-La-Da (1.19), 7. Help/Please Please Me (0.52), 8. Dialogue (0.17), 9. Madman (7.15), 10. Dialogue (2.37)

Disc Two

Side C

1. Mother (4.47), 2. Cold Turkey (5.40), 3. Slippin' and Slidin'/Stand By Me/Imagine (9.19)

Side D

1. Whatever Gets You Through the Night (1.46) (studio rehearsal, 13 July 1974), 2. I'm the Greatest (17.53) (rehearsal, 13 March 1973)

Notes: Side B: are from the *Get Back* sessions. Side C – tracks 1 and 2 are from the One-to-One concert, evening show. Track 3 is an audience tape of *Salute To Sir Lew Grade*, 18 April 1975.

ADDITIONS

THE DREAM IS OVER VOL. II

Unknown

Format: 12-inch vinyl

Source: various

Sound quality: unknown

Side A

1. Two of Us, 2. Short Fat Fannie, 3. Midnight Special, 4. Someone Nice Like You, 5. Give Me Some Truth, 6. All Things Must Pass

Side B

1. Don't Let Me Down, 2. One After 909, 3. Because I Love You, 4. One After 909, 5. Tomorrow Never Comes, 6. Bring It on Home to Me, 7. Hitch Hike, 8. You Can't Do That, 9. Hippie Hippie Shake

Notes: We have a copy of the front and back of the sleeve in our files. There is no information on the sources of the tracks although it is likely these are from the *Get Back* sessions. This disc is described as Volume II although we have not been able to trace a vinyl release of Volume 1. There was a release on compact disc of the same title.

LISTEN TO THIS PICTURE DISC

Unknown

Format: 12-inch vinyl picture disc

Source: unknown but probably *Walls and Bridges* outtakes

Sound quality: unknown

Notes: This picture disc features a photograph from the *Walls and Bridges* album. We cannot trace the track listing but we presume these are outtakes and demos from the recording sessions for the album.

TWICE IN A LIFETIME

B7

Format: 12-inch vinyl

Released: 1987

Source: various tracks by Paul McCartney and John Lennon. Tracks by Lennon as listed below

Sound quality: very good/excellent

Side B

Give Peace a Chance (0.24) (rough mix, 1 June 1969), The KYA 1969 Peace Talk (9.54) (Montreal, 30 May 1969), Man of the Decade (9.06) (2 December 1969)

COMPACT DISCS

ADDITIONS

THE ESHER DEMOS (THE BEATLES)

GR. 261

Format: CD (digipack)

Released: 2008

Time: 66.49

Source: demos for forthcoming *White Album*

Sound quality: excellent

1. Cry Baby Cry, 2. Child of Nature, 3. The Continuing Story of Bungalow Bill, 4. I'm So Tired, 5. Yer Blues, 6. Everybody's Got Something to Hide Except Me and My Monkey, 7. What's the New Mary Jane, 8. Revolution, 9. While My Guitar Gently Weeps, 10. Circles, 11. Sour Milk Sea, 12. Not Guilty, 13. Piggies, 14. Julia, 15. Blackbird, 16. Honey Pie, 17. Back in the USSR, 18. Honey Pie, 19. Mother Nature's Son, 20. Ob La Di, Ob La Da, 21. Junk, 22. Dear Prudence, 23. Sexy Sadie

Notes: The Beatles recorded these tracks at George's house – Kinfauns in Esher, Surrey in the last week of May 1968. These demos were for the forthcoming album The Beatles (known as the *White Album*). They recorded on George's four track equipment and mixed in mono by George.

This session has been bootlegged previously but this set has excellent sound quality and includes excellent packaging with informative sleeve notes, colour photographs, a small poster and an insert with more colour pictures and details of the tracks. Eleven of the tracks feature Lennon compositions. See Part Four – Sources for further details regarding these sessions.

JOURNALS – VOLUME 2

Format: Eleven compact disc set with two DVDs
Released: 2008

We have seen this release but we have not heard it or obtained details of the tracks. This one comes in a CD-sized box with two DVDs (contents unknown) and a twenty-eight-page booklet. The sleeve states that this set covers the period 1969–1974. Details of the original *Journals* set can be found in Part 2 – Compact Discs including the reissue in 2008.

THE ROCK 'N' ROLL SESSIONS 1973–1975

BFB 29
Format: Three compact discs with a DVD Released: 2008
Source: *Rock 'n' Roll* album sessions plus live performances
Sound quality: excellent

Disc One – *The Original Roots Album*
1. Be-Bop-A-Lula, 2. Ain't That a Shame, 3. Stand By Me, 4. Sweet Little Sixteen, 5. Rip It Up/Ready Teddy, 6. Angel Baby, 7. Do You Want to Dance, 8. You Can't Catch Me, 9. Bony Moronie, 10. Peggy Sue, 11. Bring It on Home to Me/Send Me Some Lovin', 12. Slippin' and Slidin', 13. Be My Baby, 14. Ya Ya, 15. Just Because

Bonus Tracks – The *Old Grey Whistle Test*
16. Stand By Me (alternate stereo mix), 17. Stand By Me (take 2) 18. Slippin' and Slidin' (stereo mix), 19. Stand By Me (broadcast version)

Disc Two – *Sunnyview Rehearsals in New York 1974*
1. Be-Bop-A-Lula, 2. Ya Ya, 3. Do You Want to Dance (intro), 4. Do You Want to Dance, 5. Stand By Me, 6. Slippin' and Slidin' 7. Rip It Up/Ready

Teddy, 8. Bring It on Home to Me/Send Me Some Lovin' 9. Bring It on Home to Me/Send Me Some Lovin' (version two), 10. Peggy Sue, 11. Ain't That a Shame, 12. Bring It on Home to Me/Send Me Some Lovin' 13. Ya Ya (intro), 14. Ya Ya, 15. That'll Be the Day (take 1), 16. That'll Be the Day (take 2), 17. Do You Want to Dance, 18. Stand By Me, 19. Peggy Sue, 20. Be-Bop-A-Lula, 21. Slippin' and Slidin' 22. Guitar Jam/Whole Lotta Love, 23. Thirty Days, 24. C'mon Everybody, 25. Ain't That a Shame (take 1), 26. Ain't That a Shame (take 2), 27. Ain't That a Shame (take 3), 28. Ain't That a Shame (take 4), 29. Jam (intro), 30. Jam

Disc Three – *Session Outtakes*

1. Be My Baby, 2. In The Studio (part 1), 3. Just Because, 4. You Can't Catch Me, 5. Sweet Little Sixteen, 6. Bony Moronie, 7. Rip It Up/Ready Teddy, 8. Ain't That a Shame, 9. Peggy Sue, 10. In The Studio (part 2), 11. Angel Baby, 12. Since My Baby Left Me, 13. To Know Her Is to Love Her, 14. Bring It on Home to Me/Send Me Some Lovin' 15. When In Doubt, F**k It, 16. Be My Baby (alternate), 17. Here We Go Again (demo), 18. Here We Go Again

Bonus Tracks

19. Rock 'n' radio spot, 20. Slippin' and Slidin' (live), 21. Stand By Me (live), 22. Imagine (live), 23. Slippin' and Slidin' (instrumental), 24. Lady Marmalade

DVD

The Old Grey Whistle Test – BBC TV 1975

1. Stand By Me, 2. Slippin' and Slidin'

Salute To Sir Lew/The Master Showman – US TV 1975

3. Imagine (remastered live)

The Old Grey Whistle Test – BBC TV 1975

4. Interview

Salute To Sir Lew/The Master Showman – US TV 1975

5. Slippin' and Slidin' 6. Imagine (original TV live)

DVD Music Section

DJ Winston O'Boogie Plays the Roots of Rock 'n' Roll featuring *Rock 'n' Roll* album Elton John with John Lennon Live at the Madison Square Garden 1974.

1. I Saw Her Standing There (rehearsals), 2. I Saw Her Standing There (Elton John B-side), 3. Whatever Gets You Through the Night, 4. Lucy in the Sky with Diamonds, 5. I Saw Her Standing There (John Lennon mix + Elton John mix)

Notes: The three compact discs in this set are similar to the 2001 release *Brandy Alexanders and the Wall of Sound* (Vigotone 235/236/237). The four discs in the set are housed in a long cover with a black-and-white picture of John standing in the doorway of a grocery store. The spine says *John Lennon The Rock 'n' Roll Sessions 1973–1975* but the cover states *John Lennon Plays the Roots of Rock 'n' Roll*.

Two discs are each side of the cover with a pocket in the centre containing a sixteen-page booklet with extensive notes, details of the tracks and photographs in black-and-white and colour. A sticker on the front states that this set is a limited edition of 500 copies.

Updates

371. Life Is What Happens

The catalogue number for this release is: Barrier Records BAR–050/051 American release, 2007. Disc Two – Track 3 is listed as 'Knocking on Heaven's Door' which is incorrect. This song is a satire on Dylan titled 'Knocking on Dylan's Door'. It can also be found on *Archives (Vol. 3)* - both the vinyl and compact disc releases.

810. Remember Lennon

We have now had the opportunity to hear this disc and can confirm that the Sound quality is excellent stereo. This CD was only released in Japan and consequently was difficult to find. The versions of 'Love' 'Remember' and 'New York City' are different to those on the His Master Choice releases 'It's Gonna Be Alright' and 'Remember New York City' The running time of this disc is 63 minutes 5 seconds. The disc comes with a four-page booklet containing photographs and a drawing.

*

Just as we were going to press, we obtained a copy of a new release in the series from His Masters Choice. This release is a double disc set of piano and acoustic home demos with a hardback book.

AT HOME

His Master's Choice HMC 008

Format: CD (double) Released: 2009 Time: Disc One 67.47 Disc Two 77.15

Source: Guitar and piano home demos

Sound quality: Excellent

Disc One – Guitar Demos

1. Watching The Wheels (3.05), 2. Knocking On Dylan's Door (2.19), 3. It Sounds Like A Ballad To Me (4.33), 4. More Satire (0.47), 5. Lebenstraum (1.24), 6. French Song (1.05), 7. Serve Yourself (3.51), 8. She Is Coming Round The Mountain (1.00), 9. Dear Yoko (3.36), 10. I'm Stepping Out (2.57), 11. I Don't Wanna Face It (2.05), 12. Borrowed Time (4.48), 13. Beautiful Boy (4.08), 14. Grow Old With Me (3.05), 15. Starting Over (3.06), 16. Woman (3.27), 17. Say It Again (3 39), 18. Nobody Told Me (3.54), 19. Nobody Told Me (3.53), 20. Nobody Told Me (3.54), 21. I'm Losing You (3.05), 22 I Ain't Got Time (3.09)

Disc Two – Piano Demos

1. Grow Old With Me (3.05), 2. Help Me To Help Myself (2.19), 3. I Don't Wanna Sleep Alone (2.50), 4. Now And Then (4.59), 5. Clean-up Time (9.04), 6. Watching The Wheels (12.52), 7. Serve Yourself (3.26), 8. Memories/Cathy's Clown (5.46), 9. Real Love (4.39), 10. She's A Friend Of Dorothy (3.24), 11. Starting Over (4.21), 12. I'm Losing You (5.58), 13. I'm Stepping Out (3.12), 14. Don't Be Afraid (2.43), 15. Why Must We Be Alone (2.29), 16. Solitude (5.14)

Notes: This was the eighth release from His Master's Choice. All are double disc sets housed in a hardback book. The previous seven included three John Lennon sets (details of these can be found in the main listings), two Beatles, a Rolling Stones live concert from 1997 and a set of Beach Boys outtakes. This latest release has a twenty-page hardback book containing colour photographs, John's cartoons and some handwritten lyrics. The previous Lennon releases were It's Gonna Be Alright (HMC 002), Remember New York City (HMC 003) and Come On, Listen To Me (HMC 004).